British Government and Politics

Fifth Edition

R. M. PUNNETT
Reader in Politics at the University of Strathclyde

Dartmouth

Published by
Dartmouth Publishing Company Limited, Gower House,
Croft Road, Aldershot, Hampshire GU11 3HR, England

First published 1968 by Heinemann Educational Books
HEB paperback edition first published 1969
Reprinted with corrections 1970
Second Edition 1971, reprinted 1973, 1974
Third Edition 1976, reprinted 1977, 1978
Fourth Edition 1980, reprinted 1982, 1984, 1985
Fifth Edition 1987, reprinted 1988, 1989, 1990 (twice), 1992

British Library Cataloguing in Publication Data

Punnett, R. M.
British government and politics.—5th ed.
1. Great Britain—Politics and
government—1979–
I. Title
320.941 JN231

ISBN 1-85521-307-9 Hbk
ISBN 1-85521-107-6 Pbk

Printed and bound in Great Britain by
Biddles Ltd, Guildford and King's Lynn

To my mother and father

Contents

List of Tables

Preface to the First Edition

This book is designed to give a more detailed and all-embracing account of government and politics in Britain than is to be found in the various general works that already exist. It is presented in the hope that it will help to fill the gap that exists at present between the brief introductory guides to British government and politics, and the larger works on specific aspects of the system. My approach to the subject has been largely, but not exclusively, empirical, and I have endeavoured to include all material (sociological, institutional, constitutional or historical) that helps towards an understanding of the British political system as it operates today. In this I have tried to provide detailed information about the various aspects of the system, but at the same time I have sought to balance description with analysis.

I would like to acknowledge the considerable help that I have received from numerous sources in the preparation of the book. In particular, Professor Richard Rose of the University of Strathclyde, Mr W. Thornhill of the University of Sheffield, J. P. Mackintosh, M.P., and Professor W. A. Robson and Mr John Barnes of the London School of Economics, have commented upon large sections of the book. In addition, Dr J. A. Brand, Mr J. B. Sanderson, Mr A. L. M. Smith, Mr D. W. Urwin (all of the University of Strathclyde), Mr J. G. Bulpitt, Mr N. Johnson (both of the University of Warwick), Dr Robert J. Jackson (of Carleton University), and Dr M. Margolis (of the University of Pittsburgh) have looked at particular chapters. I am also greatly indebted to the University of Strathclyde for providing me with funds, and to both the University of Strathclyde and Carleton University, Ottawa, for giving me considerable clerical assistance. Finally, I would like to thank my wife, Marjory, for her encouragement and patience, especially during the arduous stages of revision and re-writing.

Any errors of fact or judgement remain, however, my sole responsibility.

Glasgow, 1969 R. M. Punnett

Preface to the Fifth Edition

Despite (or perhaps because of) the flood of books and articles on all aspects of British government and politics in recent years it is clear that there is still a demand for a large text that covers a wide range of topics in a single volume. This fifth edition of *British Government and Politics* has been produced in face of this continuing demand. To take account of the many political developments of the 1980s, the text has been revised more thoroughly than for any previous edition. The emergence of the SDP, and other changes in the party system and in voting behaviour, are examined in Chapters 3 and 4. The issue of electoral reform is covered in Chapter 2, and the politics of minority and coalition governments in Chapter 15. Chapters 7, 11, 12 and 13 take account of the impact of the Thatcher Government on the Cabinet system, the civil service and local government, and the Parliamentary reforms of the 1980s are incorporated in Chapter 8. The privatisation issue is examined in Chapter 12. An entirely new chapter examines the nature of the European Community and the consequences of membership for the British political system.

I am grateful to various colleagues who have made suggestions for changes in the material. I also wish to thank Grace Hunter and Jennifer Punnett for typing the revisions, under great pressure of time, and Alison Punnett and Marjory Punnett for their help with proof reading. I hope that the new edition justifies their effort and encouragement.

Glasgow, 1987 R. M. Punnett

Acknowledgements

I am grateful to the following for permission to quote from material published by them: Princeton University Press – G. A. Almond and S. Verba, *The Civic Culture*, Princeton 1963; Macmillan & Co. Ltd and Macmillan Company of Canada – D. E. Butler and J. Freeman, *British Political Facts*, London 1963, D. E. Butler, *The British General Election of 1951*, London 1951, D. E. Butler, *The British General Election of 1955*, London 1955, D. E. Butler and R. Rose, *The British General Election of 1959*, London 1960, D. E. Butler and A. King, *The British General Election of 1964*, London 1965, D. E. Butler and A. King, *The British General Election of 1966*, London 1966, *The Statesman's Year Book 1966–67*, London 1967; The Clarendon Press, Oxford – J. D. Stewart, *British Pressure Groups*, London 1958; Sir Isaac Pitman & Sons Ltd – J. A. G. Griffith and H. Street, *Principles of Administrative Law*, London 1967; Cambridge University Press – Sir Ivor Jennings, *The British Constitution*, London 1966, Sir Ivor Jennings, *Cabinet Government*, London 1959; Stevens & Sons Ltd – J. P. Mackintosh, *The British Cabinet*, London 1962; Oxford University Press – Lord Morrison, *Government and Parliament*, London 1964; Pall Mall Press Ltd – S. E. Finer, *Anonymous Empire*, London 1965; Fontana Books – Walter Bagehot, *The English Constitution*, London 1963; Benn Brothers Ltd – *Newspaper Press Directory*, London 1966; Hutchinson Publishing Group Ltd – D. E. Butler, *The Study of Political Behaviour*, London 1959; Victor Gollancz Ltd – Lord Attlee, *The Labour Party in Perspective – and Twelve Years After*, London 1949; J. Whitaker & Sons Ltd – *Whitaker's Almanack*, London 1967. I would also like to thank National Opinion Polls Ltd, Social Surveys (Gallup Poll) Ltd and The Observer Ltd for permission to quote from public opinion poll findings.

part one

Introduction

1

The Context of British Politics

FOR MUCH of the post-war period Britain was widely regarded as being characterised by homogeneity, consensus and deference. Britain was described as relatively homogeneous in its socio-economic composition, while the British people were said to exhibit a considerable degree of consensus on political issues and show a large amount of deference to political leaders and to the political system as a whole. More recently, Britain seems to have been characterised by the very absence of these features. Recent social and political conflicts have accentuated regional differences within the United Kingdom and highlighted the multi-ethnic nature of British society. Major arguments have emerged between the parties and among the electorate over the remedies to be adopted for Britain's social and economic difficulties. Far from inspiring deference, political leaders and the political system have been subjected to sustained criticism as successive governments have disappointed their supporters. Before considering whether anything remains of the traditional assessment of British society and political attitudes, it is necessary to examine the physical and cultural context of contemporary British politics.[1]

[1] S. H. Beer, *Britain Against Itself*, London 1982; H. Berrington (ed.), *Change in British Politics*, London 1984; H. Drucker (*et al.*), *Developments in British Politics*, London 1986; D. Kavanagh, *British Politics: Continuities and Change*, London 1985; R. Rose, *Politics in England: Persistence and Change*,

Geography and Insularity

From a political standpoint the most significant features of the geography of Britain are its size and insular position, and the density and distribution of the population. Consisting of a large island and numerous smaller islands, the United Kingdom of Great Britain and Northern Ireland comprises a total area of some 94,500 square miles. It is thus physically small in comparison with most major European and world powers, but more significant than the actual size of the islands of Britain is their position close to the north-west coast of Europe. Largely because of her insular position, combined with the maintenance of a powerful navy, Britain has been able to resist successfully all attempts at foreign invasion since 1066, apart from the relatively peaceful 'invasion' by William of Orange in 1688. Nevertheless, despite periods when a policy was adopted of 'splendid isolation' from European alliances, proximity to Europe has meant that British history has been bound up with that of Europe. Britain's membership of the European Community has to be seen against this background.

In the past, British political involvement in European affairs was designed primarily to prevent one power dominating the continent and thereby forming a threat to Britain. This brought England, and later the United Kingdom, into conflict with Spain in the sixteenth century, France in the eighteenth century, and Germany twice in the first half of this century. Britain's traditional insularity, however, has become less and less appropriate in modern conditions. The defensive advantage that Britain gained from her insular position has no longer applied since 1945, with the emergence of 'super' powers like the USA and the USSR, and with the development of modern forms of warfare. At the same time, in recent years Britain has been subject to a peaceful economic invasion from Europe and the USA, while the widened scope of international trade has led Britain to develop her interest in European trading communities.

London 1985; J. Blondel, *Voters, Parties and Leaders*, London 1963. See also D. Kavanagh, 'New Bottles for New Wines', *Parl. Aff.* 1977, pp. 6–21; D. Kavanagh, 'Whatever Happened to Consensus Politics?', *PS* 1985, pp. 529–46.

TABLE I

Population Density

	Area (sq. miles)	Population	Density
United Kingdom	94,499	55,776,000	590
England	50,331	46,362,000	921
Scotland	30,405	5,130,000	168
Wales	8,016	2,791,000	348
Northern Ireland	5,461	1,491,000	273
USA	3,537,000	231,107,000	65
Germany	96,000	61,333,000	639
France	213,000	54,334,000	255
Italy	131,000	56,830,000	433
Netherlands	13,500	14,394,000	1,066
Belgium	11,800	9,863,000	835
Spain	197,000	37,682,000	191

Source: Whitaker's Almanack, 1986, and Census Report 1981

With a total population of some 56 million, Britain is one of the more densely populated countries in the world, with population density being particularly high in England. There has been a remarkable rise in the population of the United Kingdom over the past century, again particularly in England (see Table II). The population of the United Kingdom more

TABLE II

Population Growth (in millions)

	1801	1841	1881	1901	1921	1951	1981
England and Wales	8.9	15.9	25.9	32.5	37.9	43.7	49.1
Scotland	1.6	2.6	3.7	4.5	4.9	5.1	5.1
Northern Ireland*	1.4	1.6	1.3	1.2	1.2	1.4	1.5
United Kingdom†	11.9	20.2	31.0	38.2	44.0	50.2	55.8

* Figures for Northern Ireland refer to the area which is now Northern Ireland
† Excluding the Isle of Man and the Channel Isles

Source: Census Report 1981

than trebled between 1801 and 1901, and in this century it has increased by almost a half, largely as a result of a fall in the death rate. Today life expectancy (70 for men and 76 for women) is about twelve years greater than in the 1930s. The consequences of this for public expenditure on pensions, health-care and other social services are considerable.

The greatest increase in population in the nineteenth century was in the new industrial areas of northern England. Since 1945, however, it has been the movement of population from the north of England and Scotland to the midlands and south-east of England that has attracted most attention. Over four-fifths of the population of the United Kingdom live in England, and about two-thirds of the population of England and Wales live in the seven main industrial conurbations. In all, about three-quarters of the population live in urban areas, though within this pattern there has been a considerable movement of population from the inner-cities to the suburbs.[1] One consequence is that the political influence of working class communities in city centres has been removed, while the decay of the inner-cities has produced a number of sociological and economic problems for national and local government.

London accounts for 15% of the total population of the United Kingdom. It is often argued that this, combined with the capital's vital role in the economic, social, cultural and political life of the country, enables London and the south-east of England to impose its character to a considerable extent on the whole of Britain. It is questionable, however, whether London 'dominates' Britain to the extent that France is dominated by Paris. Physical communications between London and the rest of Britain are not aided by the elongated shape of the country, and by the location of the capital in the extreme south-east corner of England. In Wales and Scotland mountains form a barrier to communications, while the Irish Sea, separating Northern Ireland from the rest of the United Kingdom, represents a barrier to communications that is physically as formidable as the channel that separates Britain from Europe. In England, however, the chief mountain range

[1] These and other population statistics are based on the 1981 Census Report.

runs from north to south, and thus does not hamper road or rail links between London and the north.

The Economy

Britain has long been a major industrial and trading nation. Indeed, it was the 'first industrial nation', in the sense of being first to experience an industrial revolution. Today it remains among the 'top ten' countries of the world in population and in total economic wealth (as measured by the Gross National Product). The technological advances of the eighteenth and nineteenth centuries enabled the economy to expand rapidly. The economy has continued to expand during the twentieth century, and over the past twenty years Britain, along with most other western industrial nations, has enjoyed an increase in the general level of prosperity that has been based partly on technological advances in industrial methods. Perhaps inevitably, however, Britain's economic growth rate in the twentieth

TABLE III

Distribution of Civil Employment (in thousands)

	1940	1950	1960	1970	1980
Agriculture and fishing	925	1,161	983	380	358
Mining and quarrying	886	852	761	418	344
Manufacturing industries	7,128	8,510	8,811	8,911	7,034
Building and contracting	1,064	1,434	1,567	1,367	1,254
Gas, electricity, water	213	353	370	391	336
Transport and communications	1,146	1,781	1,662	1,591	1,473
Distributive trades	2,639	2,571	3,284	2,706	2,769
Financial, professional, miscellaneous	*	3,969	4,847	5,696	7,270
Public administration	1,793	1,362	1,243	1,431	1,566

* Figures not available

Figures for different years are not completely comparable owing to changes in methods of classification.

Source: D. E. Butler and J. Freeman, *British Political Facts*, London 1968, p. 233, and *Pears Cyclopaedia*, 1982–3

century has been unable to match the expansion that came in the early years of the industrial revolution. At the same time, Britain's international trading position has declined relative to that of the countries whose initial economic expansion came later than that of Britain. Britain's dependence on imports for foodstuffs *and* raw materials for industry has meant that successive Governments have faced great difficulties in trying to ensure that exports were of sufficient quantity to balance imports. North Sea oil exports have helped to ease the problem in the last ten years, but with the fall in North Sea production from the mid-1980s onwards (in combination with the decline in manufacturing industry) balance of payments difficulties could re-emerge.

As is shown in Table III, patterns of employment have changed considerably in the post-war period. In 1950 about 10% of the workforce was employed in the primary industries of agriculture and mining, while 55% was employed in the manufacturing sector. By 1980, however, the combined figure for primary industry and manufacturing had fallen to less than half of the total. In the last fifteen years the decline in the numbers employed in manufacturing has been particularly marked, as new methods of production have been introduced and as a number of traditional manufacturing industries have declined in face of overseas competition. There has been a general increase in the numbers employed in service industries, with the biggest rise being in financial, professional and other white collar occupations. Over the post-war period as a whole there has been a movement from the private to the public sector, though this has been halted in the 1980s as a result of the Government's denationalisation policies. In common with a number of western countries, Britain experienced very high levels of inflation and unemployment in the 1970s, but the British inflation and unemployment rates were generally higher than those of the other members of the European Community. Inflation has declined since 1980, but unemployment has remained high by international and historical standards. While in the 1950s and 1960s the unemployment rate was invariably below 2% of total employees, the figure reached almost 7% in 1980, 12% in 1982 and 13% in 1984. The level of unemployment has varied considerably from one part of the country to another. It has been highest in the industrial regions of the north of England, Scotland and Wales, and lowest in the south-east of England.

The consequences of unemployment, and of other economic upheavals, have been mitigated somewhat by the existence of the elaborate system of social security that is provided by the state.[1] The welfare state emerged principally under Liberal and Labour Governments in the first half of this century. The 1905–15 Liberal Government introduced old-age pensions and a national system of health and unemployment insurance. These benefits were improved by Labour and Conservative Governments between the wars, and a system of subsidised local authority housing was introduced. The Beveridge Report in 1942 proposed that after the war a comprehensive social security system should be introduced, and the 1945–51 Labour Government sought to implement this. The National Health Service was established in 1948 and a system of family allowances and various other social security payments were introduced. During the 1950s and 1960s there were debates about the level at which the various benefits should be set, and about the extent to which charges should be made for certain services, but the basic principles on which the welfare state was based were widely accepted. More recently there has been less agreement about the principles of the system in face of the growing cost of services and their impact upon taxation.

The link between the economy and modern British politics is fundamental, economic difficulties inevitably limiting the ability of Governments to pursue adventurous social policies. In general election campaigns over the last twenty years economic issues have been particularly prominent. In 1964 the Labour Party criticised the Conservative Government's inability to break out of the recurrent 'stop-go' cycle of economic deflation and re-flation, and Labour claimed to have an alternative economic policy which would give economic expansion without uncontrollable inflation. In 1970 the Conservatives argued that Labour's strategy had failed, and had merely produced inflation without an adequate growth rate.

[1] P. Taylor-Gooby, *Public Opinion, Ideology and the Welfare State*, London 1985; D. Fraser, *The Evolution of the British Welfare State*, London 1984.

In October 1974 the Opposition's attack upon the 'three-day-week' and the Conservative Government's record on prices and overseas trade was undoubtedly a major factor in the Government's defeat. In 1979 a major feature of the Conservatives' campaign was an attack upon Labour's record of doubling prices and unemployment within five years. In 1983 Labour emphasised the continuing rise in unemployment to record post-war levels, while the Conservatives highlighted the fall in the rate of inflation. Such economic arguments are likely to re-emerge at the next and subsequent elections.

At the same time, many basic industries are publicly owned, largely as a result of the nationalisation measures of the 1945–51 Labour Government. Because of the Labour Party's continuing commitment to the 'common ownership of the means of production, distribution and exchange',[1] and the Thatcher Conservative Government's determination to return publicly owned industries to private hands, the issues of nationalisation and denationalisation have been prominent in the last ten years. Industrial questions also remain fundamental to British politics because of the links between the Labour Party and the trade unions, and the Conservative Party and the business world.

Mass Media

The press, radio, and TV are for the most part London-based and London-orientated.[2] There are over 100 daily and Sunday newspapers in Britain, which is a smaller number than in most comparable western nations. At the same time more copies of newspapers are sold in Britain than in any country in the western world. The *News of the World* has one of the largest circulations of any newspaper in the world, and *The*

[1] *Labour Party Constitution*, clause 4 (IV).

[2] C. Seymour Ure, *The Political Impact of Mass Media*, London 1973; J. Whale, *Journalism and Government*, London 1972; R. Klein, 'The Powers of the Press', *PQ* 1973, pp. 33–46; W. L. Miller (*et al.*), 'On the Power or Vulnerability of the British Press', *BJPS* 1982, pp. 357–74; J. Seaton, 'Politics, Parties and the Media in Britain', *WEP* 1985, pp. 9–26; B. Walden, 'Broadcasting and Politics', *Parl. Aff.* 1982, pp. 356–66.

TABLE IV

Newspaper Circulations 1965–85

Chief national dailies	Average daily circulation (in millions)		Proprietors
	1965	1985	
Daily Mirror	4.9	3.3	Mirror Group Newspapers
Daily Express	3.9	1.9	Express Newspapers
Daily Mail	2.4	1.8	Associated Newspapers
Daily Telegraph	1.3	1.2	Daily Telegraph
Sun	1.2	4.0	News Group Newspapers
The Guardian	0.2	0.5	Guardian Newspapers
The Times	0.2	0.5	Times Newspapers
Daily Star	—	1.4	Express Newspapers
Chief Sunday papers			
News of the World	6.1	4.8	News Group Newspapers
Sunday People	5.7	3.1	Mirror Group Newspapers
Sunday Mirror	5.0	3.2	Mirror Group Newspapers
Sunday Express	4.1	2.4	Express Newspapers
The Sunday Times	1.2	1.3	Times Newspapers
The Observer	0.8	0.7	The Observer
The Sunday Telegraph	0.6	0.7	The Sunday Telegraph
The Mail on Sunday	—	1.6	Associated Newspapers

Source: *Benn's Media Directory*, 1966 and 1986.

Sun is among the world's largest selling dailies. These large circulations result from the fact that the major newspapers in Britain are national rather than local papers (although many of the big national dailies do have separate editions for the various regions of Britain). As a result, some four-fifths of households receive a national daily paper. In addition to the national dailies most regions have their own local newspapers. The English local morning papers include the *Birmingham Post*, *Yorkshire Post*, *Western Daily Press* and *The Newcastle Journal*. In Scotland, *The Scotsman* and *Glasgow Herald* are particularly long established and widely circulating morning papers, while

Northern Ireland has its own morning newspapers printed in Belfast.

The *Morning Star* is linked with the Communist Party, but none of the large-circulation national papers has any such direct ties with a political party. All the national papers and most of the local papers exhibit some degree of political alignment, however, and the majority tend to be pro-Conservative, or at least generally right wing in outlook.[1] The *Daily Herald*, which was owned partly by the TUC, went out of circulation in 1962, and subsequent attempts to create a daily newspaper with direct links with the Labour Party have come to nothing. In the 1983 general election campaign the Mirror Group was alone in giving unambiguous support to Labour. Nevertheless, of the voters who read a 'Conservative' newspaper (about three-quarters of the electorate), only about half actually voted Conservative in 1983. Ownership of the national press tends to be concentrated in comparatively few hands, and this has caused some criticism in recent years. The *Daily Express*, *Sunday Express* and *Evening Standard* are all associated. The Mirror Group, owned by Robert Maxwell, manages the *Daily Mirror*, *Sunday People* and *Sunday Mirror*, while Rupert Murdoch's News International owns *The Times*, *The Sunday Times* and *The Sun*. A large number of the local newspapers form part of four large chains (Thomson Regional Newspapers, Northcliffe Newspapers, Westminster Press and United Provincial Newspapers).

The BBC was created a public corporation by Royal Charter in 1926. Its revenue comes primarily from the sale of radio and TV licences rather than from any form of commercial advertising. The Governors of the BBC are appointed by the Prime Minister, but once appointed they are free from direct Government control. The BBC is required to be impartial in its presentation of political items, although this ideal is difficult to attain.[2] The BBC had a legal monopoly of sound broadcasting until 1972, when the Heath Government allowed

[1] C. Seymour Ure, 'Editorial Policy Making in the Press', *G and O* 1969, pp. 426–525.

[2] M. Stanks, 'Paying For Broadcasting', *PQ* 1985, pp. 374–85; A. Wright, 'Local Broadcasting and the Local Authority', *Pub. Admin.* 1982, pp. 307–19.

the introduction of commercial radio stations. There are now about fifty local commercial radio stations, competing with the BBC's national network, and the thirty or so local BBC stations.

Until 1954 the BBC had a television monopoly, but in 1954 the Independent Television Authority (now the Independent Broadcasting Authority) was created with control over several regional programme contracting companies, the largest now including Granada, Thames, and Central TV. The Channel Four Television Company was established as a subsidiary of the IBA in 1982. The IBA and the programme contracting companies are financed from the sale of advertising time, although the programmes are not directly sponsored by the advertisers. Like the BBC, the IBA is required to be politically impartial, and political advertising is not permitted.

Since the introduction of the IBA, with its greater emphasis on regional programmes, the BBC's regional services have been extended, although national network programmes still predominate on BBC and Independent Television alike. Through the two BBC and two Independent channels, the impact of television on British politics has been considerable over the past twenty years. It has probably been most noticeable in the sphere of electioneering, and in the 1983 general election campaign all three main parties clearly attached considerable importance to the contact that could be achieved through television between the party leaders and the electorate.[1]

Nationalism, Regionalism and Religion

Within the framework of the United Kingdom there exist the separate national communities of England, Wales, Scotland, and Northern Ireland, each with its own historical, cultural, and ethnic background, and each to some extent with its own social and political characteristics. In the distant past

[1] J. Trenaman and D. McQuail, *Television and the Political Image*, London 1961; J. G. Blumler and D. McQuail, *Television in Politics*, London 1968; J. Whale, *The Politics of the Media*, London 1977; J. Curran, *Power Without Responsibility*, London 1985; M. Harrison, *TV News: Whose Bias?*, London 1985.

Britain was subjected to invasion by numerous different ethnic groups. The inhabitants of Britain today are descended either from the British or Celtic tribes who were the original inhabitants of Britain, or from the Romans, north Europeans, and Norman French who invaded Britain between 100 BC and AD 1100, or from the numerous waves of immigrants, particularly from Europe and the Commonwealth, who have peacefully invaded Britain in more recent years. The nineteenth-century Irish influx into the big cities of Great Britain created social conflicts, as has coloured immigration in the post-war period. Today, about 6% of Britain's population (and 17% of London's population) was born outside the UK. In elections over the last twenty years racial issues have been of considerable importance in some constituencies, and racial tensions have erupted in riots in parts of London, Birmingham, Liverpool and some other large cities. The social problems created by the decay of the inner-cities have been exacerbated by racial conflict. Although the party leaders have sought to keep the race issue 'above party politics', the Conservative Party in general has adopted a tougher line than Labour, the Liberals and SDP on the question of immigration, and on the racial issue in general.[1] The Macmillan Government's 1962 Commonwealth Immigration Act placed limitations on the rights of Commonwealth citizens to enter Britain, and further Acts by the Heath (1971) and Thatcher (1981) Governments extended the restrictions.

Regional factors do not play as important a part in British politics as they do, for example, in the politics of the USA, Canada, or Germany. Britain is a unitary, not a federal state, and the unification of Britain into one political unit is now of comparatively long standing.[2] The principle of strong central

[1] Z. Layton-Henry, *The Politics of Race in Britain*, London 1984; C. Hill, *Immigration and Integration*, London 1970; D. T. Studler, 'British Public Opinion, Colour Issues, and Enoch Powell', *BJPS* 1974, pp. 371–81; Z. Layton-Henry, 'Race, Electoral Strategy and the Major Parties', *Parl. Aff.* 1978, pp. 268–81; A. M. Messina, 'Race and Party Competition in Britain', *Parl. Aff.* 1985, pp. 423–36; S. Welch and D. T. Studlar, 'The Impact of Race on Political Behaviour in Britain', *BJPS* 1985, pp. 528–40.

[2] J. G. Bulpitt, 'The Making of the United Kingdom', *Parl. Aff.* 1977–8, pp. 174–89.

administration was established in England early in the middle ages. Wales was conquered (militarily) by the English in the fourteenth century. The union of the thrones of England and Scotland dates from 1603, and the Anglo-Scottish union was completed in 1707. The union of Great Britain and Ireland was achieved in 1800, though Southern Ireland gained its independence in 1922.

This is not to say, however, that regional issues have been absent from British politics in the past, or are insignificant today.[1] The question of the succession to the throne led to Anglo-Scottish conflict in 1715 and 1745. The question of Irish home rule in the last century and the early years of this century presented a major threat to the unity of the United Kingdom. The Irish question stimulated interest in Scottish and Welsh home rule, so that regionalism was a major issue in British politics from the 1880s to the 1920s. In the last fifteen years, conflict in Northern Ireland has been a central issue in British politics. There was also an upsurge of nationalist sentiment in Scotland and Wales in the 1970s, though the fortunes of the Scottish National Party and Plaid Cymru have fluctuated considerably. In the 1966–70 and 1970–4 Parliaments they achieved notable successes in by-elections, and in the October 1974 general election they won 14 seats. In the 1979 and 1983 elections, their support declined, and they won only two seats each in 1983. Nevertheless, marked regional differences in party support were a feature of these two elections. In 1983 the Conservatives won four-fifths of the seats in the south and midlands of England, but not much more than a third of the seats in the rest of Great Britain. This reflected an economic and political divide between the relatively prosperous south and the less prosperous north that has been increasingly apparent in the last twenty years.

In the United Kingdom as a whole, religion is not a major divisive force, although this is not true of all parts of the country. The religious conflicts that divided British society in the sixteenth and seventeenth centuries were largely settled in

[1] K. Morgan, 'Regional Regeneration in Britain', *PS* 1985, pp. 560–77; R. J. Johnston and P. J. Taylor, 'Political Geography: A Politics of Places Within Places', *Parl. Aff.* 1986, pp. 135–49.

TABLE V

Nominal Religious Affiliation

England and Wales	
Church of England	27,180,000
Roman Catholic	4,240,262
Methodist and Independent Methodist	492,487
Baptist	221,766
Methodist Church of Wales	85,041
Scotland	
The Church of Scotland	902,713
Roman Catholic	807,900
Episcopal Church	65,951
Northern Ireland	
Roman Catholic	414,532
Presbyterian	339,818
Church of Ireland	284,253
Methodist	58,731

Source: *The Statesman's Year Book*, 1985–6

1688 by the acknowledgement of the Protestant ascendancy, and by the gradual acceptance of the principle of religious toleration. Today, the vast majority of people in Britain are not churchgoers, but of those who are, the majority attend Protestant churches, with the Established Church of England claiming the largest number of devotees (see Table V). The proportion of *active* members of the Church of England, however, is much smaller than even the 10 million or so confirmed Anglicans, and the other churches claim that a much larger proportion of their members are regular church attenders.[1] Nevertheless, the Church of England baptises about a third of the children that are born in England and Wales, and about a third of marriages take place in Anglican Churches.

[1] G. Mayser and K. Medhurst, 'Political Participation and Attitudes in the Church of England', *G and O* 1978, pp. 81–95.

In some areas of Britain there is a clear connection between religion and political affiliation. In Northern Ireland, religion and politics are almost inseparable, with the Unionists' strength being based on Protestant opposition to the Catholic majority in the Republic, and to the large Catholic minority in Ulster. In Glasgow and Liverpool the existence of large Catholic communities with Irish origins means that some of the political attitudes of Ireland are apparent. In the nineteenth century in Great Britain as a whole there was a clear alignment between the Conservative Party and the Established Churches of England, Scotland, Ireland (disestablished in 1869) and Wales (disestablished in 1920), and between the Liberal Party and the Nonconformist Churches. In some respects this alignment remains today, with the Labour Party inheriting some of the Liberal Party's nonconformist traditions. This is reflected to some extent in voting patterns and in the religious affiliations of MPs.[1] Some religious bodies are active pressure groups, but in general the churches do not interfere directly in party politics, and apart from Northern Ireland and the other exceptions noted above, religion does not play the part in British politics that it did at times in the past.

Homogeneity and Social Class

Britain has often been presented as a relatively homogeneous nation in ethnic, linguistic, religious, economic and social terms. It has been pointed out that there is no equivalent in Britain to the racial divisions of South Africa, the linguistic divisions of Canada or Belgium, or the extremes of wealth and poverty that are to be found in Italy and Spain. To place too great an emphasis on British homogeneity, however, is to over-simplify the nature of British society.[2] As has been shown above, national, regional, religious, and ethnic variations *do* exist within the United Kingdom and are an essential part of some political questions. Further, whatever may be said about

[1] G. Alderman, *The Jewish Community in British Politics*, London 1983.

[2] See E. M. Rawstron and B. E. Coates, *Regional Variations in Britain*, London 1971.

Great Britain, the nature of Northern Irish society and the relationship between Northern Ireland and the rest of Britain, represents a major qualification to descriptions of the United Kingdom as a homogeneous unit.

More important than any of these factors, however, distinctions of social class represent a fundamental disunity in British society, in many ways as significant as the regional, ethnic, or religious factors that dominate society and politics in other countries. Comparative surveys have revealed that Britain is much more class-conscious than similar Anglo-Saxon communities like the USA, Australia, and Canada.[1] In their analysis of social and political attitudes in the 1960s, Butler and Stokes found that three-quarters of respondents readily acknowledged that they belonged to the middle class or the working class, and when prompted virtually all of the remaining quarter accepted a class label. The significance of class factors in determining voting behaviour, and in the social composition of the parties, is discussed below,[2] and here it is sufficient to emphasise the general importance of class within British society.

It is sometimes argued that class stratification in Britain is a national one, cutting across regional boundaries and thus helping to break down any tendencies towards regionalism. In so far as they do this, however, class factors merely replace one form of national division for another, and thereby place an essential limitation on any notion of British homogeneity. Thus of all the factors involved in presenting a background to British politics, considerations of social class are probably the most significant of all. The various criteria that determine class groupings are essentially vague, but family background, education, occupation, and wealth are probably the main factors.

Family Background and Social Mobility. Mobility between social classes from one generation to another has increased since the principle of free compulsory secondary education was established. A recent study of social trends showed that of

[1] R. R. Alford, *Party and Society*, London 1964. See also D. E. G. Plowman, W. E. Minchinton and M. Stacey, 'Local Social Status in England and Wales', *SR* 1962, pp. 161–202.

[2] Ch. 4.

the 46% of the population who regard themselves as 'middle class', or 'upper working class', 16% felt that their parents belonged to a lower social class.[1] Family background, however, remains fundamentally important in determining social class. Occupation and wealth to a considerable extent are determined by education, which in its turn reflects family background. Unemployment is highest among those who leave school at 16, while those who leave at 16 and do avoid unemployment tend to acquire unskilled or semi-skilled jobs. Those who stay on at school beyond the age of 16 tend to move into white collar and managerial jobs, while those with the most exclusive education generally enter the professions or the business world.

As well as any general tendency there may be for middle-class homes to produce children with a higher academic ability than children from working-class homes, the educational system contains inequalities which help to consolidate established class distinctions. In the first place, a clear distinction emerges between the state schools, which cater for the mass of the population, and the independent public schools which provide a boarding-school education for a very small and exclusive section of the population (some 5%). This is mirrored even among the public schools themselves, and there is a clear stratification ranging from the lesser public schools to the top nine 'Clarendon Schools',[2] with Eton, Harrow and Winchester generally acknowledged as the top three. As well as seeking to produce an educational elite by providing excellent teaching facilities, the best private schools encourage the self-perpetuation of a social elite through their emphasis on the importance of 'character building', leadership training, and social education.

Within the state educational system there is no formal stratification at the primary level. All children attend comprehensive infant and junior schools up to the age of 11 (or 12 in Scotland). What is more, at the secondary level over the past twenty years there has been a big increase in the number

[1] HMSO, *Social Trends*, London. See also J. Goldthorpe, *Social Mobility and Class Structure in Britain*, London, 1980.

[2] That is, Eton, Harrow, Winchester, Rugby, Westminster, Charterhouse, Merchant Taylors', St Paul's, Shrewsbury.

of comprehensive schools, which provide all types of secondary education for all levels of ability. In most areas of England and Wales comprehensive schools have now replaced the old 'tripartite' system of secondary education, whereby 25% or so of secondary pupils were allocated to grammar schools on the basis of the 'eleven plus' examination and the remainder attended secondary modern or technical schools. One of the claims advanced for comprehensive secondary schools is that they will remove some of the divisions within society which were created partly by the segregation of children at the age of 11 into strict educational categories. Despite the promptings of the 1964–70 and 1974–9 Labour Governments, however, the change to comprehensive schools has not been universal, and a number of local authorities have been able to maintain systems that are far removed from the comprehensive principle. Also, private education has enjoyed a revival in the last ten years, as an increasing proportion of parents have reacted against the comprehensive system and against perceived deficiencies in the state education system.

To some extent educational distinctions exist also at the University level, for although there are some forty Universities in Britain, Oxford and Cambridge Universities are accorded the greatest prestige and status, both in an academic and a social sense. They are theoretically open to any student with the necessary academic qualifications, but the close link that has long existed between Oxbridge and the public schools, and which is not based entirely on academic considerations, means that the upper and middle-class section of society predominates at the two senior Universities.

In an attempt to develop a more egalitarian and more modern system a number of new Universities were created in the 1960s, and a number of existing technological institutions were expanded and given University or Polytechnic status. These developments have done something to meet the increased demand for higher education that has been produced by the growth in the population, the needs of the technological age, and generally higher educational expectations. The problem remains, however, of the loss by Britain of many good graduates through the 'brain-drain' to the USA and other English-speaking countries. This factor, particularly in the technological sphere, represents something of a threat to Britain's future educational and industrial development.

Occupation and Wealth. A simple division of the community into two broad groups of middle class and working class is perhaps adequate for broad generalisation, but is too vague for a detailed examination of British society. In Census Reports seventeen socio-economic groups are distinguished, and, excluding the armed forces, these can be simplified into three main categories to distinguish the manual groups, the non-manual groups, and the professional, managerial, and proprietorial groups (see Table VI). Although recent years have seen a big increase in the number of non-manual workers, it is still the case that the manual worker category is the largest of the three broad groupings defined in Census Reports.

TABLE VI

Census 1981: Socio-Economic Groups (Great Britain)

Proprietorial, managerial, and professional			17.0
1 and 2	Employers and managers	11.9	
3 and 4	Professional	4.1	
13 and 14	Farmers	1.0	
Other non-manual			38.0
5	Intermediate non-manual	10.8	
6	Junior non-manual	21.5	
7	Personal service	5.7	
Manual			43.0
8	Foremen and supervisors	2.6	
9	Skilled manual	17.5	
10	Semi-skilled	12.1	
11	Unskilled	5.8	
12	Own-account workers	4.1	
15	Agricultural workers	0.9	
Others			2.0
16	Armed forces	1.1	
17	Indefinite	0.9	
			100.0

Source: 1981 Census Report

TABLE VII

Distribution of Wealth

	Share of Marketable Wealth (%) 1971	1976	1983
Wealthiest 1%	31	24	20
5%	52	45	40
10%	65	60	54
50%	97	95	96

Source: *Social Trends* (HMSO 1986)

Britain no longer exhibits the sharp inequalities of wealth and poverty that were to be found in the nineteenth century, and which are to be found today in many western countries. Industrial expansion, and the development of the welfare state have combined to raise general living standards and eradicate the worst poverty. Despite the economic problems of the 1970s and 1980s Britain has become more prosperous and more equitable. An analysis of social and economic trends shows that (after allowing for inflation) real income per-head was 16% higher in 1984 than in 1974. Inequalities in the distribution of wealth have been reduced. Table VII shows that the share of national wealth owned by the richest 1% of the population has declined from about a third in the early 1970s to a fifth today, while the share of the richest 5% of the population has declined from over half to two-fifths. It remains the case, however, that the richest half of the population accounts for over nine-tenths of the wealth, and that this proportion has hardly changed since 1971. What is more, the general rise in prosperity in Britain has not matched that in most other western industrialised countries, and the considerable increase in unemployment in the last ten years has added to the economic inequalities.[1]

In social terms many of the harsh consequences of the industrial revolution are still apparent in the slums of the

[1]See also J. Urry and J. Wakeford, *Power in Britain*, London 1973, pp. 13–65; A. B. Atkinson and A. J. Harrison, *Distribution of Personal Wealth in Britain*, London 1978.

major British cities. These factors are essential limitations on any broad view of Britain as a generally prosperous and egalitarian community. While economically the various sections of the community may be coming closer together, this is not necessarily the case in social terms. With regard to occupations and wealth the main consideration in determining social class is not so much the amount of wealth, but rather how the wealth was acquired, just as with education it is the type of school and University that is significant as well as the level of attainment.

Deference and Consensus

Writing in 1867, Walter Bagehot presented a picture of British society as one that was essentially deferential in its attitudes towards the Monarchy, the Peerage, and the trappings of society. Indeed he argued that the secret of the Constitution was that real power lay with the 'efficient' parts of the Constitution, chiefly the Prime Minister and his Cabinet colleagues, while the Monarchy and the other 'dignified' elements of the Constitution served to mesmerise the mass of the population into a respect for the system as a whole. Thus he claimed that:

> In fact, the mass of the English people yield a deference rather to something else than to their rulers. They defer to what we may call the theatrical show of society . . .[1]

The 'theatrical show of society' survives, in that class-consciousness, a preoccupation with past historical greatness, and the retention of once powerful but now largely symbolic political and social institutions remain as features of Britain today. They help to preserve the impression of the British as a deferential people, satisfied with their institutions and content to be led by a small and self-perpetuating elite.[2] This tradi-

[1] Walter Bagehot, *The English Constitution*, Fontana Library edition, London 1963, p. 248. See also D. Kavanagh, 'The Deferential English: a Comparative Critique', *G and O* 1971, pp. 333–60.

[2] See, for example, W. L. Guttsman, *The English Ruling Class*, London 1969; P. Stanworth and A. Giddens, *Elites and Power in British Society*, London 1974; R. W. Johnson, 'The British Political Elite', *EJS* 1973, pp. 68–77.

tional interpretation, however, has to be qualified today in various ways. In the first place, although traditionally prestigious institutions such as the Monarchy, the House of Lords, the public schools and the ancient Universities survive, and although there still exists a social elite drawn from the remnants of the aristocracy, the military and the senior professions, the social and political status of these institutions and groups is considerably less than in the past. Again, deference to the Conservative Party, as the bastion of the social elite, is less evident than in the past. Although the Conservative Party has won half of the elections in the post-war period, and has regularly been able to attract the support of a third or more of working-class voters, its electoral success has been based as much on secular as on deferential considerations. The change from Old Etonian leaders (such as Macmillan and Douglas-Home) to leaders who are the products of grammar schools (such as Heath and Mrs Thatcher) has certainly not been accompanied by the collapse of the working-class Conservative vote.

Further, the more general deference that, traditionally, the British have shown to the Government of the day has been less evident in recent years. Indeed, a feature of British politics in the 1970s and 1980s has been the willingness of certain groups (most spectacularly, some trade unions and local authorities) to refuse to cooperate in the implementation of policies approved by Parliament. The respect for (and self-satisfaction with) the Constitution and the processes of government that was apparent well into the post-war period has been less evident in recent years. It is still true to say that while there are vocal revolutionary and republican minorities, the vast majority of people still accept the major features of the Constitution such as the Monarchy, the legal system and the Parliamentary-Cabinet system. Nevertheless, governmental explanations have been sought for the economic and political difficulties that Britain has encountered in recent years. In the process, the civil service, the machinery of Cabinet government, Parliament, the party system, the structure of local government and the Constitutional relationship between the component nations of the United Kingdom have all been subjected to scrutiny (sometimes by Royal Commissions) and to considerable criticism. Deference towards, and self-satisfaction with, the political system has been replaced by considerable scepticism about its efficacy.

Britain is also a less consensual society than in the past. For much of the post-war period, as well as wide acceptance of the bases of the Constitution, there was broad agreement about major socio-economic issues, such as the scope of the welfare state, the nature of the mixed economy and the interventionist role of the government in economic affairs.[1] The notion of a broad political consensus among the electorate, and between the parties, seemed to be particularly valid in the 1950s and 1960s. After the ideological debates that took place during the 1945–51 period of Labour rule, over the issues of public ownership, the welfare state and the growth of state authority, the long period of Conservative rule between 1951 and 1964, and then the 1964–70 period of Labour Government, produced merely conflict over details. The acceptance by the Conservatives after 1951 of the bulk of the Labour Government's legislation, the eclipse of extreme left-wing elements from positions of authority within the Labour Party, the growth of material prosperity and of consequent feelings of security and well-being within the community, and the very length of the Conservative period of office with its emphasis on stability, moderation, and preserving the *status quo*, all combined to produce political conflict over details rather than over basic political, economic, or social principles. Thus the phrase 'Butskellism' was coined in the 1950s to describe the essentially moderate policies common to the Conservative Government, in which R. A. Butler was prominent, and the Labour Opposition, led by Hugh Gaitskell. Writing originally in 1955, one authority on the British parties was able to argue forcibly that because of agreement on fundamental issues, there was no real difference between the parties, and that

[1] See J. P. Nettl, 'Consensus or Elite Domination: the Case of Business', *PS* 1965, pp. 22–44; W. G. Runciman, 'A Method for Cross-National Comparison of Political Consensus', *BJS* 1962, pp. 151–5. See also G. A. Almond and S. Verba, *The Civic Culture*, Princeton 1963; B. Jessop, *Traditionalism, Conservatism and British Political Culture*, London 1973; C. W. Chamberlain and H. F. Moorhouse, 'Lower Class Attitudes Towards the British Political System', *SR* 1974, pp. 503–26.

'Two great monolithic structures now face each other and conduct furious arguments about the comparatively minor issues that separate them.'[1]

In 1970, however, it seemed that the consensus that had characterised the 1950s and 1960s might be undermined by the election of a Conservative Government committed to a reversal of many of the policy trends of the post-war period.[2] Included in the Heath Government's initial programme were plans for greatly reduced public expenditure, a reduction in the size of the civil service, a reduced role for the state in many aspects of economic and industrial affairs, and the withdrawal of subsidies from many public services. In fact, many of these policies were abandoned, or were greatly modified in their implementation, and for the most part post-war trends were not put into reverse by the Heath Government. Despite the bitter resentment that was aroused within the Labour Movement by the Industrial Relations Bill at the beginning of the Government's period of office, and by confrontation with the miners at the end of it, the Heath Government proved to be much less ideologically extreme than its opponents feared, or many of its supporters hoped. As so often in the past, performance did not match rhetoric.

In 1979 the Conservatives returned to office with a clear commitment to the principles of economic liberalism. Echoing the Conservative pledges of 1951 and 1979 to 'set the people free', the Thatcher Government indicated that it wished to reduce the role of the State and give the citizens more direct control over their own affairs. To these ends the Government set out to halt the rise in public expenditure, reduce direct taxation and cut the size of the civil service. Through a policy of 'privatisation', the Government returned some nationalised industries and public services to private hands. Reacting against the interventionist tendencies of the previous twenty years, it reduced the role of some of the bodies (such as the National Economic Development Council and the National

[1] R. T. McKenzie, *British Political Parties*, London 1955 (first edition), p. 586.

[2] M. Charlot, 'The Ideological Distance Between the Two Major Parties in Britain', *EJPR* 1975, pp. 173–80; R. Behrens, 'Diehards and Ditchers in Contemporary Conservative Politics', *PQ* 1979, pp. 286–95.

Enterprise Board) that had been created in the 1960s and 1970s, to give the Government greater direct influence over the economy. It attempted to curb the powers of the trade unions and involve members more actively in their union's decision-making processes. More generally, the Government sought to foster an 'enterprise mentality', arguing that only through greater emphasis on self-help and entrepreneurship could Britain's economic difficulties be overcome. Both by their rhetoric and in the policies they pursued, the Thatcher Government sought to be ideologically distinctive and to make a sharp break with what they saw as the debilitating post-war consensus over the welfare state, the extent of public ownership and the Government's economic-management role.[1]

Faced with a clearly ideological Conservative Government, the Labour Party in opposition became more distinctive.[2] The left-wing of the party increased its influence at the constituency level and secured the selection of a greater number of left-wing Parliamentary candidates. The Wilson and Callaghan Governments were criticised for compromising on party policies, and it was demanded that a future Labour Government should be more specifically 'Socialist' in its approach. Conference resolutions called upon the next Labour Government to return denationalised concerns to public hands, increase public spending on the social services and withdraw from the European Community. There were calls also for changes in the machinery of government, including the abolition of the House of Lords, imposition of restraints on the power of the Prime Minister and the appointment of party figures to temporary posts in the civil service. The party's own institutions and practices came under closer scrutiny than at any time since 1945. There were demands for greater party democracy through the election of the leader and deputy leader by the party Conference rather than by the PLP; for the

[1] See P. Jackson (ed.), *Implementing Government Policy Initiatives*, London 1985; W. Keegan, *Mrs Thatcher's Economic Experiment*, London 1984; D. Lewis and H. Wallace (eds), *Policies Into Practice*, London 1984; J. Bruce-Gardyne, *Mrs Thatcher's First Administration: The Prophets Confounded*, London 1984.

[2] See S. Haseler, *The Tragedy of Labour*, London 1980; B. Howell, *British Social Democracy*, London 1980; D. Coates and G. Johnston (eds), *Socialist Strategies*, London 1983.

annual election of a future Labour Cabinet by the PLP; for the mandatory submission of Parliamentary candidates for reselection before each general election.[1]

Given the increased ideological commitment of the Labour and Conservative parties in the 1980s, the defence of the centre-ground and of the post-war consensus has fallen particularly to the Liberals and (since its formation in 1981) the Social Democratic Party. The partners of the Alliance have advocated some new developments, such as more decentralisation of power, electoral and other institutional reforms, and greater consumer participation in the management of public services. Their main characteristic, however, has been a commitment to 'moderation' in face of the new 'extremism' of the Conservative Government and Labour Opposition. Thus they have advocated continued membership of the European Community, the rejection of both privatisation and large-scale nationalisation in favour of a genuinely mixed economy, and the restoration of former levels of public expenditure and taxation. This approach has been condemned by their opponents as a search for 'a better yesterday', and in contrast to the Labour and Conservative parties it clearly does represent an attachment to the consensus politics of the 1950s and 1960s.

As is shown in the next chapter, the differences between the parties emerged clearly in the 1983 general election campaign. The electorate is certainly aware of increased differences between the parties. In public opinion surveys in the 1960s and 1970s normally a third to a half of voters claimed that there was 'a great deal of difference' between the parties, but in 1983 the figure rose to 82%. Survey evidence also suggests that the voters see Labour and the Conservatives as being particularly class-orientated. While two-thirds of voters in 1983 said that the Alliance was 'good for all classes', only a third said this about Labour and the Conservatives. It should be noted, however, that despite the sharper party identities in recent years, and the increased public awareness of policy

[1] See D. Kogan and M. Kogan, *The Battle For the Labour Party*, London 1982; A. Mitchell, *Four Years in the Death of the Labour Party*, London 1983; M. Crick, *Militant*, London 1984; B. Hindess, *Parliamentary Democracy and Socialist Politics*, London 1983; P. Whiteley, *The Labour Party in Crisis*, London 1983.

differences, the electorate has become less predictable in its political behaviour. Electoral volatility has increased in the 1970s and 1980s and the proportion of the electorate that 'identified strongly' with a party has declined (from about two-fifths of the electorate in the 1960s to less than a quarter in 1983). It is clearly ironic that a larger proportion of electors maintained a firm partisan allegiance in the 'consensus years' of the 1950s and 1960s than in the 'conflict years' of the 1970s and 1980s when party images have become more distinctive.

part two

Parties, Pressure Groups and the Electorate

2

Case Study of the British Electoral System: The 1983 General Election[1]

ON MAY 9th 1983 it was announced from 10 Downing Street that a general election would be held on Thursday June 9th. The Parliament that had been elected almost exactly four years previously (on May 3rd 1979) was duly dissolved on May 13th 1983, and the new Parliament assembled on June 15th – just five weeks after the initial announcement. For some weeks there had been considerable speculation as to whether the election would be held in June, or would be postponed until October or perhaps into 1984. At a meeting of senior Cabinet Ministers on May 8th the arguments for a June poll prevailed. In announcing the date Mrs Thatcher said that she had opted for June because it was desirable that the uncertainties be ended. She also freely acknowledged that the Government's prospects of being returned to office in a June election were very good. The popularity of the Government (and particularly of Mrs Thatcher) had slumped in the first three years of the Parliament, but had revived with the Falklands war in 1982. The 'Falklands factor' was still evident in the

[1] See D. E. Butler and D. Kavanagh, *The British General Election of 1983*, London 1984; I. McAllister and R. Rose, *The Nationwide Competition for Votes*, London 1984; A. Ranney (ed.), *Britain at the Polls 1983*, London 1985; J. S. Rasmussen, 'How Remarkable Was 1983?', *Parl. Aff.* 1983, pp. 371–88; I. Crewe and M. Harrop, *Political Communications*, London 1986.

Spring of 1983 and, together with the evident disarray of Labour's ranks, gave the Conservatives great expectations of success. Certainly, economic indicators (especially the retail prices index) were relatively favourable; local government elections on May 4th suggested that the Conservatives had a sizeable (though declining) lead over Labour; and the bookmakers were quoting the Conservatives as clear favourites in a Spring election. In the event, the Government was re-elected with the largest overall majority of seats since 1945, and Mrs Thatcher became the first Prime Minister since Lord Salisbury in 1900 to be returned to office with an increased majority at the end of a Parliament that had run most of its course.

The Dissolution

The freedom to choose the date for a general election is one of the principal weapons in a Prime Minister's political armoury.[1] In the United States, Presidential and Congressional elections are held at fixed intervals, which can be altered only by constitutional amendment, while in most foreign systems where the power of dissolution does exist, as in the German Federal Republic and the French Fifth Republic, it is rarely or never used. Britain is one of the few examples of a political system where the possible use of the power of dissolution plays a vital part in the balance of power between Government and Opposition. In 1979 James Callaghan lost the initiative when the Labour Government was defeated in a vote of confidence in the Commons and was obliged to seek a dissolution. In 1983, however, Mrs Thatcher was able to capitalise on the Prime Minister's ability to seek a dissolution at a politically opportune time.

Historically the power to dissolve Parliament was based on the principle that each Parliament was the Monarch's Parliament, and could therefore be dissolved at his discretion. Until the law was altered in 1867, the death of a Monarch was

[1] See B. S. Markesinis, *The Theory and Practice of Dissolution of Parliament*, London 1972.

TABLE VIII

Gallup Poll: 1979–83 Parliament

Response to question: If there were a general election tomorrow, which party would you support? (In percentages, after excluding 'Don't Knows'.)

Date	Con.	Lab.	Alln*	Con. Lead Over Lab.
1979 June	42.0	43.5	12.0	−1.5
Sept.	40.5	45.0	12.0	−4.5
1980 Jan.	36.0	45.0	16.0	−9.0
May	39.0	43.5	15.5	−4.5
Sept.	35.5	45.0	16.5	−9.5
1981 Jan.	33.0	46.5	18.5	−13.5
May	32.0	35.5	29.0	−3.5
Sept.	32.0	36.5	29.0	−4.5
1982 Jan.	27.5	29.5	39.5	−2.0
May	41.5	28.0	29.0	13.5
Sept.	44.0	30.5	23.0	13.5
1983 Jan.	44.0	31.5	22.5	12.5
May	49.0	31.5	17.5	17.5

* Liberal until May 1981.

Source: Gallup Political Index, Social Surveys (Gallup Poll) Ltd.

followed automatically by the dissolution of 'his' Parliament and the election of a new one for the new Monarch. The last occasion when this happened was in 1837, on the death of William IV, but ceremonial lip service is still paid to this principle in that the Monarch, in person or through Royal Commissioners, still opens, prorogues, and dissolves Parliament.

In modern constitutional terms the dissolution principle is based on the responsibility of the Monarch's Ministers to Parliament, but with the rarity of Government defeats on motions of confidence in the Commons today, and with the recognition of the principle that the Monarch must accept the Prime Minister's advice, the power to request a dissolution has become a practical political weapon in the hands of the Prime Minister. In October 1974, for example, Harold Wilson sought a dissolution of Parliament only eight months after the previous election, at a time of relative Government popularity as reflected in the opinion polls. The Government lacked an overall majority in the Commons, but had not been defeated in a vote of confidence. A dissolution was sought merely in order that the Government's Parliamentary position might be improved. Wilson also used this tactic successfully in 1966, as did Salisbury in 1900, MacDonald in 1931 and Eden in 1955. Early dissolutions were apparently considered but rejected by Disraeli in 1878, after the Congress of Berlin, by Baldwin in 1926, after the general strike, and by Chamberlain in 1938, after his return from Munich.[1] In February 1974 Edward Heath sought a dissolution, though the Parliament still had well over a year to run, while his Government was in the midst of an industrial confrontation with the National Union of Mineworkers. On this occasion, however, the tactic failed and the Government was defeated.

The right to advise the Monarch on the dissolution lies with the Prime Minister, but it is not clear precisely how much influence his Cabinet colleagues may have on the matter. Evidence is scanty about dissolutions in the past, but at least the precise timing of the controversial requests for dissolution by Baldwin in 1923[2] and Attlee in 1951,[3] seem to have been personal decisions. Lord Morrison has declared that the presence of members of the Secretariat at Cabinet meetings precludes the discussion of such matters as the political factors involved in a dissolution,[4] but in 1983, and on other occasions, informal discussions presumably took place between the Prime Minister and at least some colleagues.

Theoretically, an election could have been held at any time after May 1979, but practical considerations limit the choice. A number of months, particularly July, August, and Sep-

[1] For details see C. S. Emden, *The People and the Constitution*, London 1962, p. 269.

[2] K. Feiling, *The Life of Neville Chamberlain*, London 1946, p. 108; C. L. Mowat, *Britain Between the Wars*, London 1956, pp. 165–8.

[3] J. P. Mackintosh, *The British Cabinet*, London 1962, p. 387.

[4] Lord Morrison, *Government and Parliament*, London 1964, p. 24.

tember (summer holiday months) are not normally regarded as being suitable for election purposes. The winter months of November to February are also generally regarded as unsuitable for election campaigning, though in fact nine of the twenty-two elections of this century have been held in this winter period. May and October are usually quoted as the best months and there have been seven October and three May elections this century. Even if his Government avoids defeat in the Commons, the Prime Minister's choice is restricted by practical considerations. As a consequence of a June election in 1983, nine Government Bills had to be abandoned, including major Bills to increase police powers and extend the right of council tenants to buy their houses. The Finance Bill had to be passed hurriedly in a shortened form, and to achieve its passage the Government was obliged to accept Opposition amendments to the Bill. In the midst of the campaign Mrs Thatcher had to visit the USA to attend a previously arranged meeting of Western leaders. She also had to take part in a meeting of the European Council of Ministers in Stuttgart just three days before polling day.

A Prime Minister has to avoid making it appear as though he is seeking to make political capital out of constitutional machinery, as 'sharp practice' could be electorally disadvantageous. In the nineteenth century this mattered less, and Sir Robert Peel argued that as an unsuccessful dissolution was harmful to the Crown, a Prime Minister should only seek a dissolution if he could secure a majority for 'the King's Government'.[1] The Opposition parties may be able to denounce the Government for subjecting the electorate to an 'un-necessary' election, and in 1983 Mrs Thatcher was accused of precipitating a 'cut and run' election. In this respect, however, Opposition parties suffer from the necessity of having to appear eager for an election at any time, regardless of how they may secretly feel about the prospects.

With the exception of the 1945 election, all general election voting has been on the same day since 1918, and since 1935 this has been a Thursday. Notice of a dissolution is not legally necessary. Heath gave only one day's notice in February 1974,

[1] Emden, *The People and the Constitution*, p. 205.

Wilson two days in October 1974, and Mrs Thatcher three days in 1983. Callaghan, however, gave ten days' notice in 1979, as did Wilson in 1970 and 1966, Home in 1964 and Macmillan in 1959.

Often a Government's mid-term unpopularity produces a number of dramatic by-election victories for the Opposition parties. In the 1979–83 Parliament the Conservatives lost four of the seven seats they were defending, while Labour held eight of its nine seats and the Alliance gained four seats. The Alliance victories were particularly spectacular and alarmed Conservative strategists in the south of England particularly. In March 1983, however, the Alliance was placed only third in the Darlington by-election and this was regarded by the Government as a favourable omen. In a Parliament in which the Government has a very small majority, by-elections acquire a special significance. The 1974–9 Parliament (when Labour lost seven of the twenty seats it was defending) was the only one this century when the Government lost its overall majority as a result of by-election defeats.

In assessing the value of by-elections as a mid-term mirror of a Government's popularity it should be remembered that different criteria apply at by-elections than at general elections, and the electors can consider different factors when deciding how (or whether) to vote. The protest vote, whether against the Government or against traditional party loyalties, is more likely to manifest itself in by-elections, and the personal qualities of the candidates probably count for more than they do in general elections. Thus at the 1983 general election, the Conservatives re-gained three of the four seats that they had lost in by-elections in the 1979–83 Parliament. Because by-election results can be unpredictable, and as the party that held the seat determines when the writs for a by-election will be issued, there is often a time lag between a seat becoming vacant and the by-election being held. In 1983, there were two seats vacant at the time of the dissolution.[1]

The 1979–83 Parliament lasted for just over four years (see

[1]C. Cook and J. Ramsden (eds), *By-elections in British Politics*, London 1973; M. Rush, 'The Timing of By-elections', *Parl. Aff.* 1973–4, pp. 44–66; M. Steed, 'My Own By-election', *G and O* 1974, pp. 345–58.

Table IX). Since the Parliament Act 1911, Parliaments have had a maximum life of five years from the date of the issuing of the writs to summon the Parliament, but the average length of Parliaments since 1910 is just under four years – even with the

TABLE IX

General Elections 1900–1983

Parliament	Length of Parliament		Election month at the end of the Parliament	Party in power and Prime Minister at the dissolution		
	Years	Months				
1895–1900	5	1	Oct.	Unionist	Salisbury	a)
1900–6	5	1	Jan.	Lib.	Campbell-Bannerman	b)*
1906–10	3	10	Jan.	Lib.	Asquith	a)
1910		9	Dec.	Lib.	Asquith	a)
1910–18	7	10	Dec.	Coalit.	Lloyd George	a)
1919–22	3	9	Nov.	Con.	Bonar Law	a)†
1922–23	1	0	Dec.	Con.	Baldwin	b)‡
1924		9	Oct.	Lab.	MacDonald	b)
1924–9	4	5	May	Con.	Baldwin	b)
1929–31	2	3	Oct.	National	MacDonald	a)
1931–5	4	0	Nov.	National	Baldwin	a)
1935–45	9	7	July	Con.	Churchill	b)
1945–50	4	7	Feb.	Lab.	Attlee	a)
1950–1	1	8	Oct.	Lab.	Attlee	b)
1951–5	3	6	May	Con.	Eden	a)
1955–9	4	3	Oct.	Con.	Macmillan	a)
1959–64	5	0	Oct.	Con.	Home	b)
1964–6	1	5	March	Lab.	Wilson	a)
1966–70	4	2	June	Lab.	Wilson	b)
1970–4	3	7	Feb.	Con.	Heath	b)
1974		7	Oct.	Lab.	Wilson	a)
1974–9	4	7	May	Lab.	Callaghan	b)
1979–83	4	1	June	Con.	Thatcher	a)

a) Indicates that the Government was returned to power at the election.
b) Indicates that the Government was *not* returned to power.

*The Unionists were in power until December 1905 when Balfour resigned. A Liberal Government was formed, Parliament was dissolved at once, and the Liberals won the election.

†In 1922 the Conservative-dominated Coalition broke up. Bonar Law formed a Conservative Government, Parliament was dissolved, and the Conservatives won the election.

‡The Conservatives remained the largest single party in the Commons, but lost their overall majority.

exceptionally long war-time Parliaments of 1910–18 and 1935–45, which were extended beyond the five-year limit by emergency legislation. Five years is a purely arbitrary limit on a Parliament's life. The Chartists sought annual Parliaments, while in the United States members of the House of Representatives serve for two years, the President for four years, and Senators for six years. The French President is elected for seven years, while the French Assembly serves for five years, the German Bundestag for four years and the Australian House of Representatives for three years. In Britain three distinct time limits have applied over the past three centuries. The Triennial Act 1694 placed a three-year limit upon the life of a Parliament, and in 1716 it was extended to seven years by the Septennial Act. The Parliament Act 1911 amended the Septennial Act to make five years the maximum length of a Parliament, and this is the limit that has applied ever since. Parliaments rarely last this full legal limit.

Between 1715 and 1979 there were sixty full Parliaments, but apart from the two exceptionally long wartime Parliaments of this century, the only Parliaments to extend to the full limit were those of 1715–22 and 1959–64. Some Parliaments were dissolved early because the Government could not continue in office, as in 1924 and (some would argue) in 1951.[1] On other occasions, as in October 1974 or 1966, the Government could have continued, but an early election was sought in an effort to improve the Government's position. On yet other occasions, as in January and December 1910, and February 1974, a dissolution was sought in order that the Government could secure an electoral 'mandate' on a specific issue (though the whole feasibility and desirability of the mandate concept is one that is open to question). A Prime Minister will generally try to avoid waiting until the very end of a Parliament, but will seek a dissolution some months before he is forced to do so, partly in order to keep the Opposition guessing as to the date of the dissolution, and also in order to have some time in which to manoeuvre towards the end of the Parliament. In 1964 Sir Alec Douglas-Home pre-

[1] See, however, Mackintosh, *The British Cabinet*, p. 478, and J. D. Hoffman, *The Conservative Party in Opposition, 1945–51*, London 1964, Ch. 7.

sumably delayed the election until the last possible moment only as the lesser of two evils. As was shown in the 1959–64 Parliament, to delay the dissolution for too long inevitably leaves the Government open to accusations of clinging to office.

The Voters

Those eligible for registration as electors in 1983 were British citizens (or Irish citizens resident in Britain) who were aged over 18, provided they were not Peers or Peeresses in their own right, or lunatics, and provided that over the previous five years they had not been convicted of electoral malpractice.[1] For the June 1983 election the total electorate was 42.2 million. This was an increase of over a million compared with 1979, due partly to the increase in the birth rate in the 1960s and partly to a more comprehensive registration of voters in the eighteen to twenty-one age group than had been achieved in the past. October 10th 1982 was the qualifying date for the register on which the election was fought, and the register came into operation on February 15th 1983. The election was thus fought on a relatively new register, though the 'Attainers' (the special category made up of those who attain the age of eighteen between the qualifying date and the following June 15th) were not eligible to vote because the election was held before their qualifying date of October 2nd 1983. The Representation of the People Act 1948 originally demanded a half-yearly renewal of the register, but in 1949 this was dropped as being impractical. An alternative to the present system would be to have a computerised register which could be kept permanently up to date.[2]

Before 1832 only about 5% of the adult population was eligible to vote, but the Reform Acts of 1832, 1867, and 1884 raised the figure to 28% of the adult population, all voters being male. The Representation of the People Act 1918

[1] For the details of electoral law see A. N. Schofield, *Parliamentary Elections*, London 1959. See also M. Rees, 'Defects in the System of Electoral Registration', *PQ* 1970, pp. 220–3.

[2] C. Smith, 'How Complete is the Electoral Register?', *PS* 1981, pp. 275–8.

changed the voting qualification from the payment of local rates to adulthood (deemed as 21), and also enfranchised women over the age of 30, provided they or their husband owned or occupied property valued at least £5 a year. The 1918 Act thereby rewarded the activities of the Suffragettes, and acknowledged the social changes brought about by the 1914–18 war.[1] In 1928 the voting age for women was lowered to 21, equalising the male and female qualifications and raising the number of eligible voters to 96% of the adult population. The 1918 Act allowed the holders of a business premises qualification to vote in their business constituency as well as their residential constituency (provided they were not the same), and the 1928 Act allowed their wives to vote on this basis also. University graduates also had two votes, one in their University seat and one in their residential constituency.[2] The University representation dates back to the Parliament of 1301, and after 1918 there were twelve University representatives in the Commons. There were unsuccessful legislative attempts to abolish plural voting in 1913 and 1931, and even though the 1944 Speaker's Conference on Electoral Reform advocated its retention,[3] the Representation of the People Act 1948 finally abolished the University and business franchise and established the principle of 'one adult one vote'.

In 1983 the qualifying age for the vote was 18. For the 1918 'Khaki' election the voting age was temporarily lowered to 19, and the 1944 Speaker's Conference considered but rejected the idea of the lowering of the age to 18.[4] In 1969, however, the Representation of the People Act introduced the principle of votes at 18. In favour of this it can be argued that young people are today better educated, mature earlier, are wealthier, and pay more in taxes than at any time in the past, and that in a number of legal and social respects adulthood and maturity are taken to date from the eighteenth rather than the twenty-first birthday. Whatever the qualifying age may be, there is an inevitable time-lag between qualifying for the vote

[1] See D. Morgan, *Suffragists and Liberals*, London 1975.

[2] See T. Lloyd Humberstone, *University Representation*, London 1951.

[3] Report of the Speaker's Conference on Electoral Reform, Cmd. 6534 and 6543 (1944).

[4] Cmd. 6534 (1944).

TABLE X

Stages in the Extension of the Franchise, 1832–1969

1832	Change from corporate to individual basis of representation
1867	Working class enfranchisement
1884	Change from a minority to a majority electorate
1918	Universal Manhood Suffrage
1928	Universal Adult Suffrage (qualifying age 21)
1948	End of Plural Voting
1969	Qualifying age lowered to 18

and having a chance to use it in a general election. Someone who just missed the qualifying date for the 1983 general election may be 22 or 23 before the next general election is held. Because of this, any qualifying age in a sense must be arbitrary, and the limit of 18 is perhaps as logical as any other.

The Constituencies

The United Kingdom is divided into 650 single-member constituencies, most with electorates of around 65,000. The drawing of constituency boundaries is a difficult task, and is more difficult with single-member than with multi-member constituencies, as the greater the number of boundaries the greater the chances of discrepancies. The franchise extensions of 1832, 1867, 1884, and 1918 were accompanied or followed by a redistribution of seats, reducing the ratio between the biggest and the smallest seat from 1 : 60 after the 1832 Act, to 1 : 3 in 1918.[1] Boundary revisions were made in 1944, 1948, 1954, 1971 and 1983. Following the recommendations of the Speaker's Conference in 1944,[2] four permanent Boundary Commissions were created, one each for England, Scotland, Wales, and Northern Ireland. The Speaker of the House of Commons is chairman of each Commission, and appeal from the Commissions is to Parliament, even though electoral malpractice is now tried by the Courts rather than by Parlia-

[1] W. J. M. Mackenzie, *Free Elections*, London 1958, p. 108.
[2] Cmd. 6534 (1944).

ment.[1] The task of the Boundary Commissions is not to try to create constituencies of precisely equal size, as this is virtually impossible to achieve. Every year there are inevitable population movements, particularly from the centres of large cities to the suburbs. Thus at the time of the 1983 revision Glasgow Central had an electorate of 19,000 while Buckingham had 110,000. Between the boundary revisions of 1954 and 1971 the electorate of the Billericay constituency grew from 58,000 to 123,000, while Birmingham Ladywood fell from 47,000 to 18,000. Boundary revisions cannot be made too often as this can cause administrative problems, and hinders the development of party organisations in the constituencies. The Redistribution of Seats Act 1944 stipulated that boundary revisions be made every three to seven years (that is, once per Parliament on average), but in 1958 the period was extended to every ten to fifteen years.

During the 1979–83 Parliament the Boundary Commissions produced proposals for new constituency boundaries, increasing the number of seats from 635 to 650. This revision was the most extensive to date, with only sixty-six constituencies remaining unaltered. Even when constituencies are new, however, equal electoral districts are not achieved. In the 1918 redistribution, precise equality in constituency size was aimed at (though unsuccessfully), but in the redistributions since then regional variations have been recognised as inevitable, and indeed desirable. Certainly, the view that MPs represent not only their own constituents but the whole nation, implies that it is not necessary to have strictly equal districts, as each elector is 'virtually' (or 'communally') represented by all MPs. The Redistribution of Seats Act 1944 recommended that all constituencies be within 25% of the average national size, but in 1948 this recommendation was rejected as impractical.

[1] See D. E. Butler, 'The Redistribution of Seats', *Pub. Admin.* 1955, pp. 125–47; J. T. Craig, 'Parliament and the Boundary Commissions', *PL* 1959, pp. 23–45; V. Vale, 'The Computer as Boundary Commissioner', *Parl. Aff.* 1968–9, pp. 240–9; D. H. McKay and S. C. Patterson, 'Population Equality and Distribution of Seats in the British House of Commons', *Comp. Pol.* 1971–2, pp. 59–76; C. A. Hughes, 'Fair and Equal Constituencies', *JCCP* 1978, pp. 256–71; P. J. Taylor, 'A Fresh Look at the Parliamentary Boundary Commissions', *Parl. Aff.* 1974–5, pp. 405–15.

Today, the task of the Boundary Commissions is to prevent the discrepancies in the sizes of the various constituencies from becoming too big, while at the same time considering administrative convenience and respecting the boundaries of local government, geographical, and natural regions. Thus even with new boundaries in 1983 the Isle of Wight constituency had 94,226 electors while the Western Isles had just 22,822. The Labour Party appealed against the 1983 proposals on the grounds that constituency differences remained too high, but their case was rejected. One consequence of Labour's appeal, however, was that the implementation of the new boundaries was delayed until February 1983, and a number of constituency parties had to select candidates quickly when the election date was announced.

The 1954 redistribution increased the number of seats from 625 to 630. In 1971 the figure was increased to 635 and in 1983 to 650. England has 523 seats, Scotland 72, Wales 38 and Northern Ireland 17. On a strict population basis England is under-represented by 18 seats, while Scotland is over-represented by 12 seats, Wales by 5 seats and Northern Ireland by 1 seat. Similarly the boroughs are under-represented as compared with the counties. In Britain the conscious over-representation of some areas is defended as a safeguard for minority interests, be they national or economic, and as a concession to geographical factors of remoteness and population sparsity. Whatever policy is adopted, however, population ratios inevitably fluctuate markedly between one redistribution and another.

The Candidates[1]

The 1983 election was contested by a record number of 2,579 candidates. This was three more than in 1979 and 300 more than in October 1974. In elections between 1918 and 1959, in most constituencies there was a 'straight-fight' between just two candidates: only in 1929 and 1950 were straight-fights in the minority. Since 1959, however, the number of straight-fights has declined, and in October 1974,

[1]For comments on social background of candidates see below, p. 129.

1979 and 1983 there were none at all. In 1983 the average was four candidates per constituency, but in a number there were six or seven candidates and in Finchley (Mrs Thatcher's constituency) there were eleven. Labour, the Conservatives and the Alliance contested all 633 seats in Great Britain. There were 680 'others' (about a hundred less than in 1979), including 72 SNP (contesting all the seats in Scotland), 38 Plaid Cymru (all the seats in Wales), 109 Ecology Party, 53 British National Party, 60 National Front and 35 Communist Party candidates. The Northern Ireland seats were not fought by any of the Great Britain parties.

Between the wars there were normally 30–50 unopposed candidates at each general election.[1] Since 1951, however, there have been no uncontested seats in general elections, despite the fact that at least two-thirds of the seats are regarded as safe for one of the parties. The new constituencies for the 1983 election mean that it is not possible to assess precisely the number of seats that changed hands. In the 1979 election, however, only 74 seats changed hands, and even in the Labour landslide of 1945 only 227 out of 640 seats changed hands.[2] It seems, however, that while contesting all seats, the parties are concentrating their campaigning efforts more and more into the marginal constituencies.

To be eligible to stand at an election it is necessary to be an elector aged over 21, and have the support of ten electors.[3] In 1983, as in every election since 1918, a candidate had to pay a deposit of £150, which was returned if he received an eighth of the total poll. In all, 739 candidates lost their deposits in 1983 (including a record number of 119 Labour candidates), so that the Treasury benefited by £110,850. To take at least some account of inflation, and to deter the more eccentric candidates, the deposit was raised to £500 in 1984. At the same time, the threshold was reduced to 5% of the poll.

There are a number of factors that disqualify from membership of the House of Commons. Those who do not qualify for the franchise are excluded, as are members of the armed

[1]J. F. S. Ross, *Elections and Electors*, London 1955, pp. 218, 236.

[2]For comments see J. Rasmussen, 'The Implications of Safe Seats for British Democracy', *WPQ* 1966, pp. 517–29.

[3]See A. Barker, 'Disqualification from the House – the "Reverse System"', *Parl. Aff.* 1958–9, pp. 69–74.

forces,[1] the clergy, and holders of 'offices of profit under the Crown' (as defined by the House of Commons Disqualification Act 1957). These disqualifications apply to membership of the Commons, but not to candidature, so that anomalous situations can arise. Anthony Wedgwood Benn was held to be no longer eligible for membership of the Commons when he inherited his father's Peerage in 1960, but he was able to contest and win the by-election caused by his own disqualification, only for a second time to be deemed ineligible to sit in the Commons.[2] Again, the Fermanagh and South Tyrone by-election in 1981 was won by Bobby Sands, standing as an 'Anti H-block' candidate. As he was serving a long prison sentence, he was ineligible to serve in the Commons and a further by-election had to be held. Subsequently, the law was changed by the Representation of the People Act, 1981 to exclude from Parliamentary candidature those serving sentences of more than one year.

In order to have any real chance of being elected, however, it is generally necessary to be an official candidate of one of the main parties. In 1983 only 21 out of 680 'others' were elected, and 17 of these were in Northern Ireland where the Great Britain parties did not compete. In Great Britain only two SNP and two Plaid Cymru MPs broke the dominance of the Conservatives, Labour and the Alliance. Thus while most adults who can raise the £500 deposit are eligible to contest a Parliamentary election, there is clearly a vast difference between being a Parliamentary candidate and being an officially adopted Parliamentary candidate of one of the main parties in one of their winnable seats. The proportion of vacancies that occur in winnable seats is quite low, as the vast majority of incumbent MPs (558 in June 1983) normally seek re-election.[3]

[1] For the peculiar position of servicemen as Parliamentary candidates see A. A. Barrett, 'Service Candidates at Parliamentary Elections 1962–3', *Table*, 1963, pp. 39–43; N. Johnson, 'Servicemen and Parliamentary Elections', *Parl. Aff.* 1962–3, pp. 207–12, and 440–4.

[2] For details of the Wedgwood Benn case see C. O'Leary, 'The Wedgwood Benn Case and the Doctrine of Wilful Perversity', *PS* 1965, pp. 65–79; G. Borrie, 'The Wedgwood Benn Case', *PL* 1961, pp. 349–61.

[3] D. E. Butler, 'The Renomination of MPs', *Parl. Aff.* 1978, pp. 210–12; A. D. R. Dickson, 'MPs Readoption Conflicts', *PS* 1975, pp. 62–70; J. Pentney, 'Worms That Turned', *Parl. Aff.* 1977, pp. 363–72.

Nevertheless the selection of party candidates is of great significance.[1] The choice of candidates eventually determines the make-up of the Parliamentary Party, with all the consequences that this has for party policies, choice of leaders, and general party image.

It has been estimated that between 1950 and 1964 there were only eighteen attempts (twelve of them successful) to force Conservative MPs to retire, and only sixteen attempts (again twelve of them being successful) to force Labour MPs to retire.[2] In 1979, however, Labour adopted new procedures which require Labour MPs to submit themselves for re-selection in each Parliament. As a result, 8 Labour MPs (including ex-Cabinet Minister Fred Mulley) were not re-adopted for the 1983 election. In 1983, however, the re-selection process was complicated by the fact that the boundary revisions abolished some constituencies and created others. Thus a further 12 Labour MPs and 8 Conservative MPs failed to find constituencies.[3] Labour's re-selection process, however, does not necessarily involve a primary contest, and since 1983 most Labour MPs have been re-selected without opposition.

The selection of party candidates is very much an internal party affair, with the public normally taking very little interest. All three main parties apply the same principle of the choice being made by the local constituency party, but with the central party machine supervising the process and retaining the ultimate power to intervene.[4] Within the local parties,

[1] For detailed studies see A. Ranney, *Pathways to Parliament*, London 1965, and M. Rush, *The Selection of Parliamentary Candidates*, London 1969. See also A. Ranney, 'Inter-Constituency Movement in British Parliamentary Candidates 1951–9', *APSR* 1964, pp. 36–45; P. W. Buck, 'First-Time Winners in the British House of Commons Since 1915', *APSR* 1964, pp. 622–7; R. Newman and S. Cranshaw, 'Towards a Closed Primary Election in Britain', *PQ* 1973, pp. 447–52; M. Holland, 'The Selection of Parliamentary Candidates', *Parl. Aff.* 1981, pp. 28–46; J. Hills, 'Candidates: The Impact of Gender', *Parl. Aff.* 1981, pp. 221–8; J. S. Rasmussen, 'Women's Role in Contemporary British Politics', *Parl. Aff.* 1983, pp. 300–15.

[2] Ranney, *Pathways to Parliament*, pp. 74 and 182.

[3] See A. Young, *The Re-selection of MPs*, London 1983.

[4] D. J. Wilson, 'Constituency Party Autonomy and Central Government', *PS* 1973, pp. 167–74; M. Parkinson, 'Central–Local Relations in British Parties: a Local View', *PS* 1971, pp. 440–6.

real power in the selection process lies with the small group of local activists who hold office and serve on the constituency management committee, and their role in the selection process is possibly the most significant contribution that they make to the affairs of their party. None of the parties uses a system of primary elections to choose candidates, though in very rare and exceptional circumstances a ballot of the members of the local association has been used to select Conservative candidates.

In the Conservative Party the process of adopting a new candidate begins with the submission of names to the local party association concerned. Any individual party member can propose himself or suggest someone else, though there is an Approved List of candidates drawn up by the National Union's Standing Advisory Committee on Candidates (SACC). Those who seek to be included on the Approved List are vetted at a Parliamentary Selection Board over a number of days. The Vice Chairman of the party has considerable influence on SACC, and he generally suggests names from the list to the local associations in an attempt to secure seats for particular candidates or particular types of candidate. SACC is also responsible (again under the influence of the Vice-Chairman) for the rules and procedures to be followed in the selection process, and for the granting of final approval to the selected candidate.

From the names that are submitted to the local association a short list is drawn up by a sub-committee of the local association's Executive Council. The power of this body is considerable in that the list can be weighted in favour of one candidate. Those on the short list appear before the Executive Council at a selection meeting (attended also by the Central Office Area Agent), and a choice is made after each contender has addressed the meeting. The Executive Council's decision is presented to the full Association for approval, which is nearly always forthcoming, and though Central Office can veto the decision, it almost never does (there being only one instance of a direct veto since 1945).[1] At this stage the candidate is merely 'prospective', however, and in order to

[1] Ranney, *Pathways to Parliament*, p. 43.

avoid incurring official election expenses, he does not become the official candidate until the election date is named.

Thus the choice of candidate is made locally, with Central Office being able to influence the process, but in practice doing so only to a very limited extent. The same general principle applies with the selection of Labour candidates. The Constituency Labour Party cannot begin to look for a candidate until the Labour Party's National Executive Committee consents, though this consent has not been withheld since 1945. The rules governing the selection procedure are laid down in the party's 'model rules', and the NEC has the power to suspend the normal procedure in an emergency. The NEC also lays down certain very general qualifications for candidates, including acceptance of the policy, principles, and constitution of the party. Unlike the Conservative Party, nominations cannot be made by individual party members, but must come from organisations affiliated to the CLP.[1]

A clear distinction emerges between what are referred to as unsponsored candidates, nominated by a ward committee or socialist society, and sponsored candidates nominated by a trade union which agrees to contribute towards the election expenses of the candidate and to make payments to the CLP's funds. In 1933, in an attempt to reduce the practice of the wealthy unions 'buying' the best seats for their members, limits were placed on the contributions that a union could make to the election expenses and funds of a CLP.[2] Today a union can contribute up to 80% of the candidate's election expenses, plus £350 a year to the funds of the CLP in the case of borough constituencies, and £420 in the case of county constituencies. These are maximum sums, however, and generally the contributions fall short of these figures.

Of the Labour MPs elected in 1983, 115 were sponsored by Trade Unions and eight by the Cooperative Party. Normally the bulk of union-sponsored candidates win their seats, with the largest unions generally being most active in getting them elected. In 1983 twenty-five of the thirty candidates sponsored

[1] See J. Bochel and D. Denver, 'Candidate Selection in the Labour Party', *BJPS* 1983, pp. 45–70.

[2] See T. Park (*et al.*), 'Trade Unions and the Labour Party', *PS* 1986, pp. 306–12.

by the TGWU were elected, as were seventeen of the twenty-seven AUEW candidates and all fourteen NUM candidates. Normally, a half to two-thirds of sponsored candidates are workers or trade officials, but about a quarter are graduates and about a tenth attended public schools.[1]

From the various names that are submitted to the CLP, a short list is drawn up by the CLP Executive Committee. As with the Conservative selection process, this is the vital stage when certain candidates (or types of candidate) can be excluded. The short list has to be approved by the NEC, and then by the CLP's General Management Committee. Although there is no clear evidence of the NEC attempting to alter the short list, unofficial pressure may be exerted at an earlier stage, and the GMC sometimes does seek to remove or add names. Those on the short list then appear before a GMC selection meeting, and the candidate is chosen. The choice has to be endorsed by the NEC. Inclusion on the NEC's lists of approved candidates does not guarantee endorsement, nor does exclusion from the lists necessarily prevent endorsement, and since 1945 there have been only a handful of occasions when this has been refused. In 1981 Michael Foot (then party leader) declared that Peter Tatchell would not be endorsed as Labour candidate for Bermondsey because of his views on extra-Parliamentary action, but subsequently the NEC was obliged to accept his candidature in face of the CLP's insistence. In 1983, however, the NEC refused to accept the last-minute replacement of the sitting MP by Ken Livingstone in Brent East.

In the selection of Liberal candidates, the national party machine exercises even less control over the local parties than is the case with the Labour and Conservative Parties. In general, the Liberal Party is so short of candidates that the local activists are given virtually unlimited freedom to choose whoever they wish. There is an officially approved list of candidates drawn up by the party secretary and a sub-committee of the Liberal Party Organisation, but constituencies are by no means limited to this list in their search for a candidate. The national party machine has no power to veto a

[1]See C. Mellors, *The British MP*, London 1978, pp. 101–5.

constituency party's choice, and has no power to prevent a seat being contested. Also, there are no limits placed on the financial contributions that a candidate can make towards the cost of his campaign.

The SDP differs from the older parties in the extent to which it involves party members directly in the selection of candidates. The party has a Candidates Panel of approved names, and an area committee selects a short-list from the Panel. A general meeting of party members in the area approves or amends the short-list and the choice is then made by the party members through a postal ballot.

For the 1983 election the Liberals and the SDP decided not to oppose each other and between them to contest every seat in Great Britain. It was agreed that seats would be divided evenly between the two parties in the country as a whole and in each of fifty or so broad regions of the country.[1] It was agreed also that in the seats allocated to it the party would select its own candidates. The alternative arrangement of both parties being involved in the joint-selection of an Alliance candidate, was rejected (partly because joint selection was feared by some as a step towards the merger of the parties). Given that the Liberals were well-established in large parts of the country, while the SDP was a newcomer, the electoral arrangement worked extremely smoothly. Initially the Liberals wished to contest the bulk of the seats, but eventually accepted the principle of parity. During 1981 and 1982 regional teams of negotiators from each party managed to achieve agreement about which party would contest particular seats. The process was supervised by a national negotiating team, and towards the end of the exercise a team of assessors was established to arbitrate in the particularly difficult cases. The Liberals secured the 'golden fifty' seats in which they had done best in 1979, while the SDP got two-thirds of the hundred next most promising seats. There were some conflicts, as in West Yorkshire where the Liberals were particularly well-entrenched and resented the arrival of the SDP, and in three seats Liberal and SDP candidates opposed each

[1] See J. Curtice and M. Steed, 'Turning Dreams Into Reality', *Parl. Aff.* 1983, pp. 166–82.

other. Major battles, however, were surprisingly few. Subsequently, the party that was not contesting a seat generally accepted the partner's choice of candidate and, with some exceptions, worked for him during the campaign.

In all the parties the central machine tends to play a bigger role in the selection of candidates for by-elections, partly because the candidate counts for more in by-elections, partly because more national interest is centred on individual constituencies in by-elections, and partly because the central machine is able to devote more time to by-election selections. Whether for by-elections or for general elections, however, the very significance of candidate selection would seem to make inevitable some degree of conflict between national and local leaders. In fact, however, such conflict has been slight, and central interference in the selection process has not been great, no doubt largely because of the desire of the national party leaders not to offend the activists who manage the local electoral machinery.

The Campaign

The campaign began quietly, and it was not until May 18th, just three weeks before polling day, that the Conservative manifesto was published. Entitled 'The Challenge of Our Times' it contained specific pledges to extend denationalisation, abolish the metropolitan councils, restrict rate increases and place further curbs on the trade unions. In general, however, it devoted more space to the Government's past performance than to its future plans. Labour's manifesto, entitled 'The New Hope for Britain', was completed quickly at a joint meeting of the Shadow Cabinet and the NEC. In the manifesto, and throughout the campaign, Labour emphasised the issue of unemployment. The manifesto proposed a policy of expansion through public investment, to be funded largely by borrowing, in order to reduce unemployment to less than one million within five years. It pledged also that a Labour Government would withdraw from the European Community, end the sale of council houses and create a new price commission with powers to order price cuts. The Liberals and SDP produced a joint Alliance document entitled 'Working

Together for Britain'.[1] The document was produced by a joint committee of half-a-dozen MPs. Like Labour, the Alliance advocated public works and borrowing as the means of reducing unemployment. To control inflation the Alliance proposed a statutory incomes policy, supported by a tax on employers who paid more than the annual norm. Labour avoided such a specific commitment, and declared that a Labour Government would achieve a partnership with the unions to plan incomes through an annual 'national economic assessment'.[2]

According to opinion polls, the electorate regarded inflation, defence, law and order and unemployment as the main issues, and saw the Conservatives as having the best policies on each of these issues except unemployment. Unusually for a British election, a great deal of attention was focused throughout the campaign on defence policy. The Labour manifesto indicated that the party was committed to a 'non-nuclear defence policy', but there was confusion over whether this meant that a Labour Government would abandon the Polaris fleet unilaterally and unconditionally. Denis Healey's version of the policy appeared to be different from that of Michael Foot and John Silkin, while James Callaghan spoke out against abandoning the Polaris missile. Throughout the campaign the Conservatives were able to make great capital out of Labour's 'unilateralism', and out of the party's evident division on the issue.

The Conservatives managed to avoid such open conflicts. Nevertheless, Francis Pym was rebuked by the Prime Minister for suggesting that a landslide victory might not be entirely desirable because of the stimulus it could give to backbench dissent, while Conservative attacks on Labour's extremism were undermined when a Conservative candidate was shown to have stood previously for the National Front. More than in most elections, each party sought to concentrate attention on the deficiencies of its opponents, rather than on its own

[1] For details of the parties' proposals see A. Beith, *The Case for the Liberal Party and the Alliance*, London 1983; A. Mitchell, *The Labour Case*, London 1983; C. Patten, *The Tory Case*, London 1983.

[2] See D. Kavanagh, 'The Politics of Manifestos', *Parl. Aff.* 1981, pp. 7–27; M. Laver, 'On Party Policy, Polarisation and the Breaking of Moulds', *Parl. Aff.* 1984, pp. 33–9.

positive proposals. In this strategy, the Conservatives were considerably more successful than Labour, presenting Labour's manifesto as being 'confused, unrealistic, costly and extremist'. For its part, Labour claimed that leaks from secret Government documents revealed that the Government expected unemployment to rise to six million, and had plans to transfer large parts of the National Health Service to the private sector. The Alliance condemned the 'old' two-party system and criticised the Labour and Conservative parties for their extremism.

While Mrs Thatcher was much the most prominent figure in the Conservative campaign Labour sought to present an impression of collective leadership, with Denis Healey and Roy Hattersley being prominent as well as Michael Foot. The media, however, focused attention on the leaders: Mrs Thatcher and Michael Foot received almost half of the television coverage of their parties' campaign, while David Steel and Roy Jenkins received almost three-quarters of the Alliance's coverage. Throughout the campaign Michael Foot lagged well behind Mrs Thatcher in opinion poll ratings: one Gallup survey early in the campaign found that just 19% of respondents felt that he was proving to be a good party leader. David Steel was the party leader who recorded the greatest level of public approval in most polls. The Alliance's strategy of fighting the election under dual leadership, however, caused difficulties. Roy Jenkins (as SDP leader) was the Alliance's 'Prime Minister-designate', but in the last ten days of the campaign David Steel (as Liberal leader) was given more prominence when it appeared that he had more popular appeal than Jenkins.

As in all general elections since 1959, the main contact between the parties and the electorate was through TV and the press.[1] The weekly current affairs programmes (princi-

[1] See D. Glencross, 'Television and the General Election of 1983', *Parl. Aff.* 1984, pp. 267–70; B. Gunter (*et al.*), 'Viewers' Experience of Television Coverage of the 1983 General Election', *Parl. Aff.* 1984, pp. 271–82. See also Blumler and McQuail, *Television in Politics*; Trenaman and McQuail, *Television and the Political Image*; Lord Windlesham, 'Television as an Influence on Public Opinion', *PQ* 1964, pp. 475–85; W. Pickles, 'Political Attitudes in the Television Age', *PQ* 1959, pp. 54–66.

pally 'Panorama', 'TV Eye' and 'Weekend World') examined specific issues and individuals in some depth, while the BBC and ITV evening news programmes examined the progress of the campaign day by day. Throughout the campaign the election accounted for about half of television news time. The parties were allocated time at peak viewing hours on the national networks for party political programmes on a formula that allowed the Alliance four minutes for every five minutes given to each of the two main parties. Although TV coverage placed great emphasis on the activities of the party leaders, there was no TV confrontation between the party leaders (Mrs Thatcher declaring that the object of the election was not to elect a President). The various TV arrangements were mirrored for sound broadcasting, but the parties devoted much less effort to radio than to TV campaigning. There were, however, very successful question and answer programmes on radio, in which party leaders were brought into direct telephone contact with electors. Although all the parties to some extent based their campaign issues on the impact that they would have in the press and on TV, there is little clear evidence that either medium dictated the issues that were to be raised during the campaign.[1] Of the national daily and Sunday newspapers only the *Daily Mirror* and *Sunday Mirror* backed Labour. The other fifteen, with varying degrees of enthusiasm, expressed the hope that the Conservatives would win. Even the *Guardian* backed the Conservatives though it qualified this with the hope that the Alliance would achieve a large representation. In all, about three-quarters of the electorate read a newspaper that was pro-Conservative during the campaign (compared with just over half the electorate in 1970).

A number of public opinion polls appeared in the daily and Sunday papers, and these attracted a considerable amount of comment on radio and television as well as in the newspapers

[1] For the political influence of the press see J. B. Cristoph, 'The Press and Politics in Britain and America', *PQ* 1963, pp. 137–50; D. McLachlan, 'The Press and Public Opinion', *BJS* 1955, pp. 159–68; A. H. Birch, P. Campbell and P. G. Lucas, 'The Popular Press in the British General Election of 1955', *PS* 1956, pp. 297–306.

TABLE XI

*Main Opinion Polls Published During the 1983 General Election Campaign: Size of Conservative Lead**

	May 9th–15th	May 16th–22nd	May 23rd–29th	June 30th–5th	June 6th–9th
Gallup	13	15	17½	17	19
NOP	13	18	19	18	18
MORI	15	11	19	13	18½
Harris	21	10	16	19	21
Marplan	12	13	17	17	20
Audience Selection	—	13	13	14	16

* In percentages, after excluding 'don't knows'. When more than one poll was published in the same week, the average figure is quoted.

Source: Adapted from data quoted in *The Times*, 'Guide to the House of Commons', June 1983, p. 281.

themselves.[1] The polls indicated a clear Conservative lead throughout the campaign (see Table XI), although they differed somewhat over the precise extent of the Conservative advantage. In the last week of the campaign they suggested that the Alliance was overhauling Labour in second place, and this caused the Conservatives some concern about their seats in the south of England. The poll published by MORI in the *London Evening Standard* on polling day was extremely close to the actual result. Each party made considerable use of private polls in formulating its campaign strategy.[2]

[1] For the general influence of the opinion polls on the political process see R. Hodder-Williams, *Public Opinion Polls and British Politics*, London 1970; F. J. Teer and J. D. Spence, *Public Opinion Polls*, London 1974. See also M. Abrams, 'Public Opinion Polls and Political Parties', *POQ* 1963, pp. 9–18; M. Abrams, 'Opinion Polls and Party Propaganda', *POQ* 1964, pp. 13–19; R. Rose, 'Political Decision Making and the Polls', *Parl. Aff.* 1962, pp. 188–202; D. E. G. Plowman, 'Public Opinion and the Polls', *BJS* 1962, pp. 331–49; M. Abrams, 'The Opinion Polls and the British General Election of 1970', *POQ* 1970, pp. 317–24; P. Whiteley, 'Electoral Forecasting from Poll Data', *BJPS* 1979, pp. 219–36.

[2] See D. Kavanagh, 'Election Campaigns and Opinion Polls', *Parl. Aff.* 1982, pp. 267–81.

All three major parties held daily press conferences, conducted by one or more of the leading party figures. A major verbal battleground was also provided by evening meetings which were addressed by the party leaders, and which were covered in some detail by TV and radio news. Also, the three party leaders indulged in 'meet the people' tours, paying flying visits to key constituencies, visiting factories and mixing informally with party workers and electors. In general, however, there was less of this form of campaigning than in some previous elections.

The campaign in the constituencies was directed mainly towards familiarising the electors with the party candidate by means of public meetings, posters, election addresses, and door-to-door canvassing, so as to achieve on polling day a maximum turnout of party workers and voters.[1] Local publicity was aided by the increased coverage of local constituencies by regional TV programmes, although despite this, public attention in the campaign remained centred on the national leaders and national issues. As in all British general elections, the campaign in the constituencies was limited by the fact that there is a legal restriction on the amount of money that can be spent by each candidate.[2] The candidate has to nominate an agent (though he can be his own agent), and all expenditure has to be made through him. On the basis of a formula laid down in 1948, and revised periodically, a candidate can spend £2,700, plus 2.3p per elector in a borough constituency and 3.1p per elector in a county constituency. It is generally accepted, however, that in a number of ways these limits can be evaded, and the situation is somewhat anomalous in that

[1] J. C. Brown, 'Local Party Efficiency as a Factor in the Outcome of British Elections', *PS* 1958, pp. 174–8; J. M. Bochel and D. T. Denver, 'Canvassing, Turnout and Party Support', *BJPS* 1971, pp. 257–70; B. Pimlott, 'Local Party Organization, Turnout and Marginality', *BJPS* 1973, pp. 252–5.

[2] See R. Rose, 'Money and the Election Law', *PS* 1961, pp. 1–15; J. F. S. Ross, 'The Incidence of Election Expenses', *PQ* 1952, pp. 175–81; F. C. Newman, 'Money and the Election Law in Britain – Guide for America', *WPQ* 1957, pp. 582–602; R. J. Johnston, 'Campaign Expenditure and the Efficiency of Advertising at the 1974 Election in England', *PS* 1979, pp. 14–19.

there is no limit on the amount of money that can be spent up to nomination day. Also, while expenditure within each constituency is limited, there is no such limit on the amount of money that can be spent by the central party machine on the *national* campaign, as opposed to the individual *constituency* campaigns. Theoretically the purpose of an election is to choose between individual candidates rather than parties (and thus until 1970 party affiliations were not recorded on the ballot papers). A consequence of this myth is that limits on spending apply only to expenditure by each candidate, and not to party spending on a national scale.[1] One estimate is that on their national campaign in 1983 the Conservatives spent about £3.8 million, Labour £1.8 million and the Alliance £1.0 million.

The significance of any election campaign does not lie solely in the immediate results, in that during a campaign the parties are also concerned with long term education of the electorate, with half an eye being kept on the next general election.[2] At the same time, the part played by individual politicians during an election campaign can be important in the post-election balance of power within the parties.

The Results

At the 1983 election the turnout was 73% of a total electorate of some 42 million. This was the second lowest turnout since the war. It compares with 71% in 1970 and 84% in 1950 (the highest percentage turnout since the 1918 franchise extension). The highest percentage turnout in any one constituency in 1983 was 89% in Fermanagh and South Tyrone,

[1] A. P. Hill, 'The Effect of Party Organization: Election Expenses and the 1970 Election', *PS* 1974, pp. 215–17; A. H. Taylor, 'The Effect of Party Organization: Correlation Between Campaign Expenditure and Voting in the 1970 Election', *PS* 1972, pp. 329–31.

[2] See H. Pollins, 'The Significance of the Campaign in British Elections', *PS* 1953, pp. 207–15; A. Mughan, 'Electoral Change in Britain: the Campaign Reassessed', *BJPS* 1978, pp. 245–52; I. McAllister, 'Campaign Activities and Electoral Outcomes in Britain 1979 and 1983', *POQ* 1985, pp. 489–503.

while Renfrew West had 83%. The lowest turnout was 52% in the City of London and Westminster South.[1]

Voting in Britain is not compulsory. In favour of compulsory voting it can be argued that voting is a duty as much as a right; that everyone in a democratic community should take part in choosing a Government; and that abstention condones bad government. On the other hand, compulsory voting is incompatible with the principle of free elections, while from a practical point of view, expense and administrative problems can be involved in imposing punishments and allowing for genuine excuses. Compulsion inevitably allows martyrs to emerge, and as deliberately spoilt papers cannot be penalized, it is perhaps illogical to punish non-attendance. At present, provision is made for postal votes or proxy votes for those who cannot vote in person, and postal votes generally account for 2% or so of the total electorate. It is generally accepted, however, that the vast majority of postal votes are cast for the Conservatives, and in 1983 there were a handful of seats won by Conservatives with majorities of less than 2%.

The votes and seats won by each party in June 1983 are shown in Table XII. Compared with the 1979 election the Conservatives made a net gain of fifty-eight seats and Labour a net loss of fifty-nine. Labour's share of the vote fell by 9.3%, and the Conservatives' by 1.5%, while the Alliance received 11.6% more votes than the Liberals in 1979 and won twelve more seats. The two main parties' share of the vote (70%), was lower than at any election since the 1920s. There was a mean two-party swing of 6% to the Conservatives – the largest swing of any post-war election. The concept of 'swing' however, assumes that two parties dominate the contest, and it becomes almost meaningless in an election in which 30% of the votes went to the Alliance and 'others'.[2]

[1] D. T. Denver and H. T. G. Hands, 'Marginality and Turnout in British General Elections', *BJPS* 1974, pp. 17–35.

[2] For general comments on the swing concept see J. Rasmussen, 'The Disutility of the Swing Concept in British Psephology', *Parl. Aff.* 1964–5, pp. 443–54. See also G. N. Sanderson, 'The "Swing of the Pendulum" in British General Elections', *PS* 1966, pp. 349–60; I. McLean, 'The Problem of Proportionate Swing', *PS* 1973, pp. 57–63; A. G. Hawkes, 'An Approach to the Analysis of Electoral Swing', *JRSS* 1969, pp. 68–79.

TABLE XII

June 1983 General Election Result

	Votes		Seats	
	N	%	N	%
Conservative	13,012,602	42.4	397	61.1
Labour	8,457,124	27.6	209	32.2
Alliance	7,786,587	25.4	23	3.5
SNP	331,975	1.1	2	0.3
Plaid Cymru	125,309	0.4	2	0.3
Others	963,308	3.1	17	2.6

In Scotland and Wales the Nationalists lost ground, with the SNP vote falling by a third and the Plaid Cymru vote by a smaller amount. The combined Nationalist vote was just under half a million, compared with its peak of over a million in October 1974. Support for independent and fringe party candidates declined throughout Great Britain, even allowing for the fact that there were fewer 'other' candidates than in 1979. Three former Labour MPs, standing as independents, each received only about 10% of the poll. In Northern Ireland Sinn Fein increased its support among Catholic voters at the expense of the SDLP.[1]

Labour's defeat was truly comprehensive. The party won a smaller number of seats than in any election since 1935. While it remained the second party in seats it won only 2% more votes than the Alliance. Labour lost over a third of its 1979 votes, received its smallest ever number of votes per-candidate and recorded its largest ever number of lost deposits (119). Labour's share of the two-party vote was just 40%, and this represented the biggest gap between the two main parties since the 1930s. The elections of 1983 and 1945 represent Labour's post-war low and high points (as is shown in Table XIII). In 1945 Labour won almost two-thirds of the seats and achieved a majority of seats in each broad region of Great

[1] See W. Harvey Cox, 'The 1983 General Election in Northern Ireland', *Parl. Aff.* 1984, pp. 40–58.

TABLE XIII

Regional Distribution of Labour Seats 1945 and 1983

	1945	1983
South	56.3	11.2
Midlands	71.7	29.5
North	74.0	55.0
Scotland	52.1	56.9
Wales	71.4	52.6
Northern Ireland	—	—
United Kingdom	61.4	32.2

Britain. In 1983 it won only a third of the seats, and although in Scotland Labour did better than in 1945, in each other region it did appreciably worse than in 1945.

A major feature of the 1983 result, however, was the extent of the regional variations in party support.[1] As is shown in Table XIV, the Conservatives emerged as much the most successful party in England, but trailed behind Labour in Scotland and Wales. Within England the Conservatives were dominant in the south and midlands but not in the north. In all, three-quarters of Conservative MPs in 1983 came from

TABLE XIV

1983 General Election: Distribution of Votes by Region

	Con.	Lab.	All	Nat.	Other	Turn out
England	46.0	26.9	26.4	—	0.7	72.5
Scotland	28.4	35.1	24.5	11.8	0.3	72.7
Wales	31.0	37.5	23.2	7.8	0.4	76.1
N. Ireland	—	—	—	—	100.0	72.8
UK	42.4	27.6	25.4	1.5	3.1	72.7

[1] See R. J. Johnson, *The Geography of English Politics*, London 1985.

TABLE XV

Conservative Share of Seats by Region: 1935 and 1983 General Elections

	1935	1983	
South	81.9	86.1	+ 4.2
Midlands	77.0	70.5	− 6.5
North	62.0	41.2	−20.8
Scotland	60.6	29.2	−31.4
Wales	31.4	36.8	+ 5.4
Great Britain	68.4	62.7	− 5.7

constituencies in the south and midlands of England, and the Government side of the House was more southern-dominated than in any Parliament this century. For the first time in a hundred years there was no Conservative MP elected in Liverpool or Glasgow. In the south of England, outside London, Labour rarely managed to reach even second place. While in the north of England, Wales and Scotland the battle was still largely between Labour and the Conservatives, in the south the Alliance was the Conservatives' main rival.

The extent of the north-south divide, and its impact on the regional structure of the parties in Parliament, is further illustrated by Table XV, which shows the proportion of seats that the Conservatives won in 1983 and 1935 (the last occasion when the Conservatives achieved a truly landslide victory). In both elections the Conservatives won around two-thirds of the seats in Great Britain. In 1935, however, the Conservatives achieved a substantial majority of seats in each region except Wales, whereas in 1983 they won a majority of seats only in the south and midlands. Compared with 1935 the Conservatives in 1983 did rather better in the south of England and Wales, worse in the midlands and very much worse in Scotland and the north of England.

Electoral Reform

Of the many criticisms that are levelled at the electoral system, two in particular may be noted here – that the winning candidate in a constituency might not have an overall majority of votes, and that in the overall result the relationship between each party's votes and seats is not necessarily a proportional one. The 1983 result provided ample support for each of these criticisms. Over half of the seats in 1983 were won on a minority vote: that is, over half the MPs were elected despite the fact that more people voted against them than for them. In some cases the winner received only around a third of the votes. At Renfrew and Inverclyde, for example, the 1983 result was:

McCurley	Con.	13,669	32.7%
Mabon	All.	12,347	29.5%
Doherty	Lab.	12,139	29.0%
Taylor	SNP	3,653	8.7%

At Leeds West the result was:

Meadowcroft	All.	17,908	38.4%
Dean	Lab.	15,860	34.0%
Keeble	Con.	12,515	26.9%
Braithwaite	BNP	334	0.7%

In such cases the question is raised of what would have been the effect if the contest had been limited to the two main contestants. There need not necessarily have been any change in the constituency result: in the example of Leeds West quoted above, most of the Conservative voters, faced with a straight choice between Labour and Alliance candidates, might well have voted for the Alliance and thus have increased the majority. There is no guarantee that this would have happened, however, and certainly at Renfrew West the majority of SNP and Labour voters would probably have preferred the Alliance to the Conservative candidate.

An absolute majority for each winning candidate could be achieved by limiting the contest in each constituency to two candidates, but this is hardly practical. More practically, the electoral system could be changed to introduce a second ballot if no absolute majority is achieved on the first ballot. At American Party Conventions to select Presidential candidates, an unlimited number of ballots are held until one candidate receives an absolute majority, and the leader of the Labour Party is elected by means of a limited number of ballots, one candidate withdrawing after each ballot, until an absolute majority is achieved.

These systems are perhaps unsuitable for a general election, in that they can involve a considerable number of ballots, but much the same effect as the second ballot can be achieved by means of the Alternative Vote, whereby the elector indicates his order of preference for the candidates by placing numbers opposite their names on the ballot papers. If no candidate receives 50% of the votes on the first count, the bottom candidate is eliminated and the votes that were given to him are re-allocated according to the second preferences among the remaining candidates. This process is continued until an absolute majority for one candidate is achieved. This is more practical for a general election than is the second ballot, in that it involves two or more counts, but only one poll (though it does not allow for second thoughts by the electorate after the initial count). A provision for the introduction of the Alternative Vote was included in the Representation of the People Bill 1918, only to be removed during the passage of the Bill through the Lords. It was discussed but rejected by the Speaker's Conference in 1930,[1] but it was nevertheless included in the Government Bill of that year. The House of Lords opposed the Bill, however, and it was lost with the fall of the Labour Government in 1931.

The Alternative Vote could be grafted on to the present system without too much difficulty, and unlike many proposed electoral reforms, the voting and counting processes are easy for the electorate to understand and are easy to operate. In the present party situation the Alternative Vote would probably benefit the Alliance and the minor parties, in that they would have a better chance than at present of attracting the first preference votes of their potential supporters. A first preference vote for a minor party candidate could be accompanied by a second preference choice between the two major parties, so that no votes would be 'wasted' as was often said of Liberal

[1] Report of the Speaker's Conference on Electoral Reform, Cmd. 3636 (1930).

votes in the past. In those constituencies where an absolute majority was not achieved on the first count, and where the Alliance (or SNP or Plaid Cymru candidate in Scotland or Wales) managed to come second to the Labour or Conservative candidate on the first count, the Alliance would normally take all or most of the second preferences of the eliminated Conservative or Labour candidate. Further, the Labour and Conservative Parties would have to court potential Alliance voters for their second preferences, so that the introduction of the Alternative Vote would probably accentuate tendencies towards moderation in the two main parties – for good or ill. Nevertheless, while ensuring that in each constituency the winning candidate received at least 50% of the votes, the introduction of the Alternative Vote would do nothing to solve the problem of the *Government* elected on a minority vote, and indeed it could well add to the problem by increasing the size of the Alliance vote.[1]

* * *

Under the present system the relationship between a party's overall share of votes and seats is, to say the least, uncertain.[2] In February 1974 the Conservatives received more votes than Labour but won fewer seats, while in 1951 the reverse was the case. Even when the party with most votes does also win most seats, its share of seats is invariably much greater than its share of votes. Indeed, as is shown in Table XVI, it is rare for the winner to achieve an overall majority of votes, but it is equally rare for it to fail to achieve an overall majority of seats. The pattern is for the electoral system to convert a simple majority of votes into an overall majority of seats. In no post-war election has a party won an overall majority of votes, but only in February 1974 did the electoral system fail to produce a party with an overall majority of seats. In 1983 the disproportional features of the electoral system were particu-

[1] See P. M. Williams, 'Two Notes on the British Electoral System', *Parl. Aff.* 1966–7, pp. 13–30.

[2] See G. Gudgin and P. J. Taylor, 'The Decompositional and Electoral Bias in a Plurality Election, *BJPS* 1980, pp. 515–20; J. Curtice and M. Steed, 'Electoral Choice and the Production of Government', *BJPS* 1982, pp. 249–98.

TABLE XVI

*General Elections 1900–83: Winning Party's Share of Seats and Votes**

Overall Majority of Seats and Votes	Overall Majority of Seats But Not Votes	No Overall Majority of Seats or Votes
1900 Con. 60.0 (51.1)	1906 Lib. 59.7 (49.0)	1910 (Jan.) Lib. 41.0 (43.2)
1931 Nat.† 90.1 (67.0)	1918 Coalit. 67.6 (47.6)	1910 (Dec.) Lib. 40.6 (43.9)
1935 Con. 70.2 (53.7)	1922 Con. 56.1 (38.2)	1923 Con. 42.0 (38.1)
	1924 Con. 68.1 (48.4)	1929 Lab. 46.8 (37.1)
	1945 Lab. 61.6 (47.8)	1974 (Feb.) Lab. 47.4 (37.8)
	1950 Lab. 50.4 (46.1)	
	1951 Con. 51.4 (48.0)	
	1955 Con. 54.6 (49.7)	
	1959 Con. 57.9 (49.4)	
	1964 Lab. 50.3 (44.1)	
	1966 Lab. 57.6 (47.9)	
	1970 Con. 52.3 (46.4)	
	1974 (Oct.) Lab. 50.2 (39.2)	
	1979 Con. 53.4 (43.9)	
	1983 Con. 61.1 (42.4)	

* Seats in parenthesis.
† 1931 figures are for the National Coalition: the Conservatives alone received 76.9% of the seats and 55.2% of the votes.

larly marked (as was shown in Table XIV): with just 42% of the votes the Conservatives won 61% of the seats. Labour's share of seats was slightly greater than its share of votes, but the Alliance won only 4% of the seats despite receiving a quarter of the votes.

In many ways the most surprising thing about British general election results is that they are not even more disproportional than they are, as the first-past-the-post system is capable of producing massively disproportional outcomes. If each party's national share of the vote was reproduced fairly closely in each constituency, the leading party could win virtually every seat. Such a grossly disproportional outcome is avoided only because Labour and Conservative support is regionally concentrated. Thus even in its worst years (as in 1983) Labour retains a number of urban seats, while when the Conservatives do particularly badly (as in 1945) they still retain their rural seats. It follows that the system is particularly unrewarding for a party that has a moderate amount of support that is distributed evenly throughout the country (as the Alliance proved in 1983). Equally, however, with a somewhat higher level of evenly-distributed support (say 40% in a three-party contest), a party could well emerge with a disproproportionately *large* share of seats.

For many years it has been argued that the electoral system is so patently unfair and erratic that it ought to be replaced by a system that would produce a truer relationship between a party's share of votes and its share of seats.[1] The Electoral Reform Society and many academic commentators have long advocated this, as have the parties that have been consistently disadvantaged by the established system (particularly the Liberals and now the SDP). The system has also been criticised, especially in recent elections, because of the extent to which it exaggerates the regional differences in party support. Labour voters in the south of England were rather more numerous in 1983 than is suggested by the mere handful of southern seats that Labour won. Similarly, in the large cities Conservative support was rather greater than its representa-

[1] See E. Lakeman, *Power to Elect*, London 1982. See also V. Bogdanor, *What Is Proportional Representation?*, London 1984.

tion indicates. As a consequence of this accentuation of regional partisanship, recent British Governments have been regionally unrepresentative to an exaggerated and undesirable degree.

More fundamentally, the established electoral system has been attacked in recent years because of the contribution that it makes to the adversarial pattern of party competition.[1] By invariably giving the winning party an overall majority of seats that it has not earned in votes, the established system has produced single-party majority governments that are secure in their control of the Commons. The respective merits of 'British' single-party majority governments on the one hand, and 'continental' coalition and minority governments on the other, have long been debated, but (as is discussed in Chapter 15) in the 1970s there emerged particular criticism of the discontinuities involved in majority Labour and Conservative governments following each other at regular intervals. There were calls for electoral reform to achieve a closer relationship between votes and seats, precisely in order to reduce the chances of any party winning an overall majority of seats and to increase the prospects of Coalition or minority Governments being formed.

Thus 'proportional representation' is widely advocated as an alternative to the established system. Proportional representation, however, is a concept, or a value, not a method of election. All electoral systems achieve some degree of relationship between the proportion of votes a party receives and the proportion of seats it wins, but some achieve a closer relationship than others. The ultimate, and only precise, means of achieving proportionality is to have only one constituency composed of the whole country, with the parties presenting national lists of candidates and the electors choosing between the lists as in a referendum. Seats are then allocated in proportion to the votes received by each party list. This system produces a truly proportional result, but it eliminates constituencies, makes no allowance for independent candidates and places great power in the hands of the party

[1] See particularly S. E. Finer, *Adversary Politics and Electoral Reform*, London 1975.

managers who determine the composition of the list. The ultimate situation of having one national constituency applies nowhere in the world at present, though the Israeli system comes close to it.

In Britain the systems advocated most often as means of achieving proportional representation are the Single Transferable Vote (STV) and variations of the West German system.[1] With STV the electorate in multi-member constituencies vote in the same way as with the Alternative Vote, listing the individual candidates in order of preference. In the counting of the votes the principle that applies is that the candidate only needs a certain number, or 'quota', of votes to be elected, and any votes that he receives beyond this figure are surplus, and serve only to build up an unnecessary majority. Once the candidate has received the quota necessary to secure his election, the 'surplus' votes are redistributed among the other candidates according to second preferences. As with the party list system, there are several variations based on the procedures used to determine the quota, count the votes, and redistribute surplus votes.

STV is not designed primarily to produce a proportional relationship between each party's national votes and seats, but to achieve in each constituency the representation of a range of opinions. It does tend, however, to produce fairly proportional results as it increases the chances of smaller parties being elected in at least one of the places available in each multi-member constituency. For the most part, the larger the constituencies the greater the minor party representation and the more proportional the overall result is likely to be. STV is used in the Republic of Ireland and its adoption in the United Kingdom was advocated by the Speaker's Conference on Electoral Reform in 1917.[2] Unsuccessful attempts were made to incorporate it in the Representation of the People Bill 1917, but it was used in some of the University seats between

[1] For an analysis of the different systems see Mackenzie, *Free Elections*; Institute of Electoral Research, *Parliaments and Electoral Systems*, London 1962. For a more detailed analysis see E. Lakeman and J. D. Lambert, *Voting in Democracies*, London 1959; J. F. G. Ross, *Elections and Electors*, V. Bogdanor and D. Butler, *Democracy and Elections*, London 1983.

[2] Report of the Speaker's Conference on Electoral Reform, Cmd. 8463 (1917).

1918 and 1948, and in elections to the Northern Ireland Assembly between 1974 and 1982.[1] The Kilbrandon Commission in 1973 advocated it for elections to Scottish and Welsh Assemblies, and currently it is the system favoured by the Alliance.

In West Germany proportional representation is achieved by a unique system in which the elector is required to record two votes. Half the seats in the legislature are filled (as in Britain) by the first-past-the-post system in single-member constituencies, and the other half by a party list contest. Once the result of the 'constituencies contest' is determined, the seats in the 'party list contest' are distributed so that each party's overall representation (that is, its constituency representatives plus its party list representatives) is in proportion to the support it received in the party list contest. Thus single-member constituencies are combined with the proportional representation of the parties (except that representation in the legislature is confined to those parties that achieved a minimum of 5% of the votes).

The Hansard Society has advocated that a variation of the West German system be used in Britain, with 480 seats in the Commons filled by the present method and 160 on a basis of regional party lists. Initially the SDP favoured this 'additional member' system, but abandoned it in face of the Liberals' preference for the Single Transferable Vote.

The case for the adoption of one of these systems (or one of the many variations of them) is not universally accepted. Even among those who support the principle of proportional representation, there are many who have reservations about the electoral methods that are employed to achieve the desired end. Not least of these limitations is the fact that of the several electoral systems, only the National Party List system can guarantee an outcome in which there is a strict relationship between a party's votes and seats.

Further, the established electoral system has many champions.[2] It undoubtedly has the merit of simplicity, whereas the

[1]See M. Laver, 'On introducing STV and Interpreting the Results: the Case of Northern Ireland 1973–5', *Parl. Aff.* 1976, pp. 211–29.

[2]See J. A. Chandler, 'The Plurality Vote: a Reappraisal', *PS* 1982, pp. 87–94.

counting methods (if not the voting methods) of many of the alternatives are difficult to understand. It is perhaps not absolutely necessary for the voter to be able to understand the counting methods that are used, as he is concerned only with the voting process, but in order that justice may be seen to be done there is much to be said for a system that is simple to understand in all its processes. Also, one merit of single-member constituencies, whatever their drawbacks, is that each member represents a specific constituency. Thus there is achieved in the British system a closer contact between an MP and his constituents than can be achieved with the multi-member constituencies that are necessary for party list or STV systems.

More fundamental than these points, however, is the fact that proportional representation is opposed by some because it would be likely to make hung Parliaments, and thus coalition or minority governments, a lasting feature of British politics. A pattern of coalition and minority governments (it is argued) is less desirable than the established pattern of single-party majority governments, which have the security of tenure that goes with an exaggerated majority in the Commons. A government with a clear majority can survive for a full Parliament, it can be held to account at the subsequent election and the voter can have a clear choice between parties. Thus supporters of single-party majority governments condemn proportional representation for the very reasons that critics of the adversarial system support it. The electoral reform debate is not simply about the fairness and practicality of the various electoral systems, but about the type of Government and the style of Parliamentary party politics that is most desirable today. Ultimately, however, the consideration that militates against any change in the electoral system is the fact that it benefits the two leading parties, and the Government party particularly. It is unlikely that a Conservative or Labour Government would alter a system that works to its advantage unless, in a hung parliament, it was obliged to come to terms with the Alliance and offer electoral reform in return for Alliance support on other issues.

3

The Political Parties: I. Organisation

IN BRITAIN the role of the political parties is not recognised by statute, and an official facade is maintained of non-recognition of the parties. Until 1969 the official regulations relating to Parliamentary and local government elections did not refer to the parties, and ballot papers gave a candidate's name, address, and occupation, but not his party affiliation. Each candidate's personal election expenditure is limited by law, but not the expenditure of the parties on national publicity. Entries in Hansard specify an MP's constituency, but not his party. In these and many other respects the existence of the political parties remains officially unacknowledged. Despite official non-recognition, however, the parties are the backbone of the modern political system. The mass parties represent the main link between the people and their political leaders. General elections today are primarily a contest between political parties, and to have any real chance of election a Parliamentary candidate has to have official party support. In Parliament an MP's activities are dominated by the party Whips. A government's position in Parliament is based to a great extent on the party system and the strength of Parliamentary party discipline.[1]

[1] For general works on the British parties see McKenzie, *British Political Parties*; Beer, *Modern British Politics*; A. Beattie (ed.), *English Party Politics* (2 vols), London 1970; R. Rose, *The Problem of Party Government*, London 1975; J. D. Lees and R. Kimber (eds), *Political Parties in Modern Britain*, London 1972; S. E. Finer, *The Changing British Party System 1945–79*, Washington 1980.

Origins of the Party System

The two main stages in the history of the development of the party system into its modern form were first of all the appearance of 'groups' within Parliament in the seventeenth, eighteenth, and early nineteenth centuries, and then the growth of mass party organisations outside Parliament in the late nineteenth and early twentieth centuries.[1] With regard to the first stage of the development, however, the word 'party' has to be used with caution, at least until the end of the eighteenth century, as these early alignments were merely based upon Parliamentary cooperation between groups of like-minded MPs. During the constitutional and religious conflicts of the seventeenth century, there emerged in Parliament two main elements, the Royalist or Court group, and the Parliamentary or Country group. The Court group became known as the Tories (a 'Tory' being an Irish brigand) because of the willingness of the King's supporters to use Irish troops to secure the succession of James II in 1679. Similarly, the Country group became known as the Whigs (the Whiggamores being Scottish Presbyterian rebels), and these names were retained throughout the eighteenth century. Group organisation in Parliament in the eighteenth and early nineteenth centuries consisted of little more than informal meetings, often over dinner, between MPs of these groups. The late eighteenth century, however, saw the emergence of Whips in Parliament to organise MPs for debating and voting purposes, and the bitter controversies over the 1832 Reform Act led to a hardening of 'party' lines in Parliament.

It was during the nineteenth and early twentieth centuries that the names of the modern parties emerged. The Tory Party became generally known as the Conservative Party following Sir Robert Peel's declaration in his election address to the constituents of Tamworth in 1834, that Tory policy was to 'conserve' all that was good in existing institutions.[2] The repeal of the Corn Laws in 1846 split the Conservative Party,

[1] See A. Ball, *British Political Parties*, London 1981; I. Bulmer Thomas, *The Growth of the British Party System*, London 1965 (2 vols); V. Bogdanor, *The People and the Party System*, London 1982.

[2] See Lord Butler (ed.), *The Conservatives*, London 1977.

one group led by Disraeli (the Protectionists) opposing the repeal, and another group in which Gladstone was prominent (the Peelites) supporting Peel's policy of extending free trade. The Peelites gradually merged with the Whigs and Radicals during the 1850s and 1860s to produce a new Liberal Party.[1] In 1886, however, the issue of Irish Home Rule split the Liberals, Joseph Chamberlain leading a group who favoured the maintenance of Irish union with Britain, into a 'Unionist' alliance with the Conservatives. This was eventually acknowledged by the change of the Conservative Party's name in 1912 to the Conservative and Unionist Party.

Finally, in 1900, in an attempt to get working-class representation in Parliament, the Labour Representation Committee was formed by an alliance between the trade unions and various socialist societies, including the Social Democratic Federation and the Fabian Society. In 1906 the name was changed to the Labour Party, and between 1906 and 1922 the Labour Party grew to replace the Liberals as one of the two major parties.[2] Labour's rise was dependent to a considerable degree on the newly realised wealth of the trade unions, particularly after the Trade Union Act 1913 restored to the unions the right (lost to them through the Osborne Judgement of 1910) to use union funds to support a political party. At the same time, the fairly rapid attainment of a high level of electoral support was helped by the upheaval in the normal party alignments that resulted from the conflicts within the Liberal Party during and after the 1914–18 war.

The great extension of the franchise that took place during the nineteenth century was linked directly with the second main stage in the evolution of the party system – the emergence of mass party organisations outside Parliament. This process began with the 1832 Reform Act, although the

[1] See J. Vincent, *The Formation of the Liberal Party 1857–68*, London 1966.

[2] See H. Pelling, *A Short History of the Labour Party*, London 1985; R. Miliband, *Parliamentary Socialism: A Study in the Politics of Labour*, London 1961; M. Cowling, *The Impact of Labour 1920–24*, London 1971; R. McGibbon, *The Evolution of the Labour Party 1910–24*, London 1975; R. Moore, *The Emergence of the Labour Party 1880–1924*, London 1977; K. D. Brown, *The First Labour Party 1906–14*, London 1985; B. Howell, *British Workers and the Independent Labour Party*, London 1983.

Whig Parliamentary Candidates' Society had been formed before 1832 with the function of 'recommending' to the electorate particular candidates who favoured Parliamentary reform. After 1832 the political clubs, particularly the Tory Carlton Club, founded in 1832, and the Whig Reform Club, founded in 1836, became centres of party loyalties and organisations. Various local Registration Societies were formed after 1832 to persuade the new voters to support particular party candidates, while the growth in the use of election manifestos also dates from this period, the pattern being set by Peel's Tamworth Manifesto of 1834.

It was with the bigger franchise extension of 1867, however, that there occurred the main developments in local party organisation outside Parliament, and the *national* organisations of the Liberal and Conservative Parties also date from this period. The Liberal Registration Association was founded in 1861, and in 1877 Joseph Chamberlain created the National Liberal Federation. Largely on Benjamin Disraeli's initiative, the National Conservative Association (as it is known today) was founded in 1867, and the Conservative Central Office in 1870. At the turn of the century the Labour Party organisation was founded, though, in this case, with the organisation outside Parliament preceding the emergence of the party in Parliament. From these beginnings the parties developed their organisations and increased their membership, until today the Conservative Party, with a membership of about 1,500,000, and the Labour Party with some 6,000,000 individual and trade union members, are among the biggest political parties in the world.

Various factors associated with the franchise extensions contributed to the emergence of these extra-Parliamentary organisations. One interpretation is that the concept of 'popular democracy' contained in the franchise extension, demanded that machinery should be created to make MPs accountable to their supporters outside Parliament, and that the modern mass parties emerged because of this. While this may have been one of the factors involved, it is undoubtedly more accurate to say that the party organisations emerged primarily for more practical and less idealistic reasons. With a larger electorate a need arose for machinery to distribute party propaganda, and provide an organisation for fighting elections. In Birmingham there was a particular need for electoral organisations because in 1867 an electoral experiment with the Limited Vote was introduced, the city being given three MPs but each elector having only two votes. Thus the Birmingham Liberal Association was formed in 1867 to organise (with great success as it turned out) the distribution of Liberal votes so as to achieve the election of all three Liberal candidates. The success of the Liberal organisation in Birmingham proved to be an incentive to the creation of similar bodies elsewhere. The introduction of the secret ballot in 1872, and the imposition in the 1880s of limits on spending at elections, meant that electors had to be persuaded rather than bribed to support party candidates, and therefore a need arose for electoral organisations based on large numbers of voluntary workers. Also, the growth of literacy in this period meant that there was an increased demand for literature as a form of party propaganda, with a consequent need for people to distribute it. Thus the party organisations outside Parliament developed primarily for electoral purposes.

The Party System Today

Traditionally Britain has been described as having a two-party system.[1] Certainly, Whigs and Tories competed for office in the eighteenth and early nineteenth centuries, and Liberals and Conservatives in the late nineteenth and early twentieth centuries, while Labour and the Conservatives have monopolised the roles of Government and main Opposition party since the 1920s. Labour and the Conservatives have won at least 93% of the seats in each post-war election, and over 97% in most of them. Currently they account for over 90% of political party members in Britain (if Labour's affiliated membership is included) and they were responsible for over 80% of campaign expenditure in the 1983 election. Each has enjoyed periods of ascendency in the post-war period. The Conservatives won three successive elections in the 1950s,

[1] See F. O'Gorman, *The Emergence of the British Two-Party System*, London 1982.

while Labour won four of the five elections in the 1960s and early 1970s. Taking the post-war period as a whole, however, they have been relatively evenly matched. They have each won six elections since 1945, and in these elections they have accumulated almost identical total shares of votes (Conservative 44.3%, Labour 42.9%) and of seats (Conservative 49.2%, Labour 47.5%). The Conservatives have a lead in post-war years in office, but it is not overwhelming (Conservatives twenty-four years, Labour seventeen years 1945–86). Such factors underlie the interpretation of Britain as being characterised not by multi-party politics, or by the dominance of a single party, but by relatively even two-party competition.

It is clear, however, that the shape of the British party system has changed considerably in the last thirty years.[1] In the 1951 general election 80% of the seats were contested only by Labour and Conservative candidates, and the Liberals, Communists and 'others' made little impact in the relatively few seats that they did contest. Labour and the Conservatives between them won 97% of the votes in 1951, and won 99% of the seats. Thus the electoral system produced an even more predominantly two-party system in Parliament than existed at the constituency level, but even in the constituencies the pattern was overwhelmingly that of two-party competition.[2]

This situation was repeated in the 1955 election, and to a lesser extent in 1959, but in the 1960s and 1970s the two-party pattern was undermined. The Liberals increased their support, and in the elections of February and October 1974 achieved almost a fifth of the vote (compared with just 2.5% in 1951). Their share of seats rose less dramatically, but with the Nationalists they held the balance of power in Parliament for most of the period 1974–9. In Scotland and Wales the Nationalists emerged as a major force. They won dramatic by-elections in Carmarthen in 1966 and Hamilton in 1967, and increased their vote in the general elections of 1970 and 1974. In October 1974 the SNP achieved almost a third of the votes in Scotland, won eleven of the seventy-two seats and

[1] See A. King, 'Whatever is Happening to the British Party System?', *Parl. Aff.* 1982, pp. 241–51; L. D. Epstein, 'What Happened to the British Party Model', *APSR* 1980, pp. 9–22; P. Norton, 'Britain: Still a Two-Party System?', *WEP* 1984 (IV), pp. 27–45.

[2] See, however, G. Thayer, *The British Political Fringe*, London 1965.

came second in another forty-two.[1] The Ulster Unionists ended their fifty-year pact with the Conservatives in 1972 and have since sat in Parliament as a separate party. They subsequently divided into Official Unionists, Democratic Unionists and a number of other factions, so that recent elections in Northern Ireland have been less predictable than at any time since the 1920s. On the fringes, the National Front,[2] the Ecology Party[3] and a number of left-wing groups appeared in the 1970s and 1980s, although their electoral support was minimal.

Most dramatically of all, the SDP emerged in the 1980s as a new party.[4] In January 1981 four former Labour Ministers (Roy Jenkins, David Owen, Shirley Williams and William Rodgers) issued the 'Limehouse Declaration' in which they criticised recent developments in the Labour Party and announced the formation of the Council for Social Democracy. They were particularly critical of Labour's decision to change the method of selecting the party Leader, and of Conference resolutions supporting unilateral disarmament and withdrawal from the European Community. The original 'gang of four' was joined by thirty or so other Labour MPs and Peers, and by other groups that had emerged on the right of the party. In March 1981 the Social Democratic Party was formally launched and a national and local party organisation was established. Later in 1981 the SDP and the Liberals made an agreement to work together as an Alliance, although a merger of the two parties was rejected.[5]

As is shown in Table XVII, the nature of electoral compe-

[1] See J. Brand (*et al.*), 'The Birth and Death of a Three-Party System', *BJPS* 1983, pp. 463–88; R. Levy, 'The Search for a Rational Strategy', *PS* 1986, pp. 236–48; J. M. Lutz, 'The Spread of Plaid Cymru', *WPQ* 1981, pp. 310–30.

[2] See N. Fielding, *The National Front*, London 1981; S. Taylor, *The National Front in English Politics*, London 1982; C. T. Husbands, 'When the Bubble Burst', *BJPS* 1984, pp. 249–60.

[3] W. Rudig and P. D. Lowe, 'The Withered Greening of British Politics', *PS* 1986, pp. 262–84.

[4] See N. Tracey, *The Origins of the Social Democratic Party*, London 1983; H. Stephenson, *Claret and Chips: the Rise of the SDP*, London 1982; I. Bradley, *Breaking the Mould?*, London 1981; C. Seymour-Ure, 'The SDP and the Media', *PQ* 1982, pp. 433–42.

[5] See G. Pridham, 'Not So Much a Programme – More a Way of Life', *Parl. Aff.* 1983, pp. 183–217.

TABLE XVII

Decline of Two-Party Politics 1945–83

	Lab. + Con. Share of Vote (%)	Lab. + Con. Share of Seats (%)	Seats with More than Two Cands	Average Cands Per Seat (N)	Seats Won On Minority Vote
1945	87.6	94.7	66.4	2.6	29.0
1950	89.6	98.1	81.6	3.0	29.9
1951	96.8	98.6	20.2	2.2	6.2
1955	96.1	98.6	22.4	2.2	5.9
1959	93.2	98.9	40.8	2.4	12.7
1964	87.5	98.6	69.2	2.8	36.8
1966	90.0	97.8	62.9	2.7	29.4
1970	89.5	98.1	70.6	2.9	19.7
1974F	75.1	94.2	94.0	3.4	64.3
1974O	75.0	93.9	100.0	3.5	59.8
1979	80.8	95.7	100.0	4.1	32.4
1983	70.0	93.2	100.0	4.0	51.7

Source: F. W. S. Craig, *British Electoral Facts 1885–1979*, London 1979.

tition has changed considerably as a result of these developments. The number of candidates contesting general elections has increased. In the last two elections there has been an average of four candidates per seat, and there have been no 'straight-fights' between just Labour and Conservative candidates. From its 1951 peak, the Labour and Conservative combined share of the vote declined at almost every election, falling to 70% in 1983. The decline in their share of seats has been less dramatic, and has not fallen below 93%. Nevertheless, in 1983 a total of six parties won seats in Great Britain (Labour, Conservative, Liberal, SDP, SNP and Plaid Cymru), and a further five in Northern Ireland (Official Unionist, Democratic Unionist, Ulster Popular Unionist, Sinn Fein and SDLP). These electoral changes have been accompanied by a fall in the number of electors who, in public opinion surveys, claim to identify 'very strongly' with one or other of the two main parties. In 1964 about 40% of the electorate claimed to have a very strong Labour or Conservative identification, but by 1984 it was only about 20%.

It is not clear whether these changes in the party system simply reflect dissatisfaction with particular parties, or whether they represent a more profound discontent with the two-party system as such. Some developments, of course, have been a consequence of particular regional factors. To some extent the rise of the SNP and PC reflected the surge in cultural nationalism in the 1970s. In the case of the SNP this was reinforced by the North Sea oil discoveries, which stimulated confidence in Scotland's economic prospects and encouraged feelings that Scottish economic assets were being exploited by others. The fragmentation of the Ulster Unionists reflected differences of opinion over Northern Ireland's political and Constitutional future.

More generally, some have seen the decline of Labour and Conservative support as being a consequence of Britain's continuing economic difficulties, and the inability of either Labour or Conservative Governments to establish a lasting image of economic competence. The 'extremism' of the two main parties over the last ten years has also been seen by some as alienating traditional Labour and Conservative voters, and stimulating support for the Liberals in the 1970s and the Alliance as a whole in the 1980s. An alternative explanation, however, is that regardless of the perceived limitations of particular parties and governments, there has emerged in recent years a profound dissatisfaction with the adversarial pattern of party competition, and that a structural change is currently underway from the traditional British pattern of two-party adversarial politics to a European pattern of multi-party coalition politics.

Over the longer-term the British pattern has been that of long periods of two-party ascendency, interspersed with shorter periods of three- or four-party competition. In the mid-nineteenth century, divisions in the Tory Party meant that Protectionists, Whigs and Peelites competed for office until the system evolved into one of Liberal–Conservative confrontation. In the late nineteenth century Liberal divisions over home-rule produced a three-way struggle between Liberals, Liberal Unionists and Conservatives, with Irish Nationalists complicating the scene even further. Earlier this century, as Labour emerged and the Liberals declined, Britain was characterised by three-party politics, until a Labour–Conservative duologue was established.

It may be that the two-party pattern will again reassert itself, either through Labour and the Conservatives regaining the ascendency that they enjoyed in the 1950s and 1960s, or through a new two-party alignment emerging from an interlude of multi-party competition. In the past, it has been argued that there is an 'inevitability' about two-party competition in Britain. In the 1950s the two-party confrontation was often seen as an expression of the 'natural' class conflict between the working class and the bourgeoisie, with Labour and Conservatives representing the two sides of this divide. Such a sociological explanation, however, took no account of the fact that there was a two-party confrontation even in the eighteenth and nineteenth centuries before the extension of the franchise to the working class. What is more, even in the 1950s voting patterns were far from being a reflection of a simple class division: in the elections of the 1950s about a fifth of middle class electors voted Labour, while a third of working class electors voted Conservative.

Some institutional features of the British political system have also been seen as encouraging a two-party, rather than multi-party alignment. In a system of responsible government, major issues in Parliament do tend to become questions of supporting or opposing the Government of the day. This is emphasised by the official recognition that is given to Her Majesty's Loyal Opposition, the Leader of the Opposition and the Shadow Cabinet. Even the shape of the House of Commons, with MPs facing each other across the gangway (rather than being seated in a semi-circle as in many continental legislatures), has been seen as encouraging this adversarial two-party orientation. Above all, however, the electoral system has operated to the advantage of the two main parties in the last twenty years. In the 1950s Labour and the Conservatives were dominant in votes as well as in seats. More recently, however, the fall in these two parties' share of the vote has not been reflected to the same extent in a fall in their share of seats. Thus the electoral system has produced a situation in which there is still a predominantly two-party pattern of

Parliamentary politics, but an increasingly multi-party pattern of electoral politics.

Whether the traditional two-party pattern does reassert itself (as it did after interludes of multi-party politics earlier this century and in the nineteenth century) will depend to a great extent on the issue of electoral reform. A change to an electoral system that produced a close relationship between a party's votes and seats would greatly increase the chances of multi-party politics becoming a lasting feature of the British system. Without such a change the institutional pressures will be towards the preponderance of two parties within Parliament.

* * *

The development of mass parties, based on a wide membership and a large organisation outside Parliament, was deplored by some political writers of the time who argued that mass parties would lead inevitably to 'the tyranny of the masses'. Writing in 1902, Ostrogorski[1] argued that MPs were becoming enslaved by the extra-Parliamentary organisations and that there was a consequent loss of wise leadership and Parliamentary sovereignty. Other writers denied this, however, and claimed that the power structure of the mass parties was based on a pyramid, with a wide membership at the base, but with real power remaining with the leaders at the apex. A. L. Lowell in 1908[2] claimed that a facade of popular control hiding real authority in the hands of a few was inevitable in the British parties, and he argued that the basis of the political system would continue to be that of 'government of the people, for the people, by the best of the people'. Robert Michels, writing in 1911,[3] claimed that the 'iron law of oligarchy' meant that despite mass membership power in political parties would continue to be wielded by an oligarchic group of leaders. In the 1950s, R. T. McKenzie claimed that the need

[1] M. I. Ostrogorski, *Democracy and the Organisation of Political Parties*, London 1902 (first English edition).

[2] A. L. Lowell, *The Government of England*, New York 1912.

[3] R. Michels, *Political Parties*, London 1911. See also J. D. May, 'Democracy, Organization, Michels', *APSR* 1965, pp. 417–29.

to work within the established system of Cabinet government had drawn the two parties into a common power structure, and although big differences between the parties may have existed in the past, the two parties were 'overwhelmingly similar' in their internal distribution of power.[1]

Thus the question is raised of whether the development of mass parties has led in fact to the domination of MPs by the extra-Parliamentary organs of the parties, or whether power remains with the Parliamentary leaders through an oligarchical power structure within each party. It can be argued, of course, that the answer to this question is different for each party, and that in Britain the parties have developed entirely different power structures. While the Conservative Party existed before the developments in the party system that came with the growth of the franchise, the Labour Party emerged after the big franchise extensions. It can be argued that these differences in origin have produced fundamentally different organisations, power structures, and attitudes within the two parties. Certainly, the parties' views of themselves often seem to suggest this. The Labour Party claims to be basically democratic in structure and attitude, while the Conservative Party often seems to suggest by word and action that it is desirable to delegate power to an oligarchy – though of course to a trustworthy oligarchy, that is subject ultimately to control by the party as a whole. It is thus necessary to examine the structures of the parties in some detail, to see whether basic differences do exist between them, or whether the seeming differences between the parties are merely a facade hiding a similar power structure.

[1] McKenzie, *British Political Parties* (1955 edition), p. 582. See also R. T. McKenzie, 'Power in British Parties', *BJS* 1955, pp. 123–32; W. J. M. Mackenzie, 'Mr McKenzie on the British Parties', *PS* 1955, pp. 157–9; S. Rose, 'Policy Decision in Opposition', *PS* 1956, pp. 128–38; R. T. McKenzie, 'Policy Decision in Opposition: a Rejoinder', *PS* 1957, pp. 176–82; G. Loewenburg, 'The British Constitution and the Structure of the Labour Party', *APSR* 1958, pp. 771–91; T. W. Casstevens, 'Party Theories and British Parties', *MJPS* 1961, pp. 391–9; P. Seyd, 'Democracy Within the Conservative Party', *G and O* 1975, pp. 219–39; D. Kavanagh, 'Power In British Political Parties', *WEP* 1985 (III), pp. 5–22.

The Parties in Parliament[1]

Conservative Party. The basis of Conservative Party organisation in Parliament is the 1922 Committee.[2] This body originated in a meeting of Conservative MPs at the Carlton Club in October 1922, which led to the fall of the Lloyd George Coalition and the emergence of Bonar Law as Prime Minister. The 1922 Committee is composed today of all Conservative backbenchers, and it excludes all Ministers when the party is in power. Its meetings are much less formal than those of the PLP. Votes are not taken (the views of the meeting being 'interpreted') and it has less formal power than the PLP. Nevertheless, while its ability to influence party policy is perhaps less than that of the PLP, the power of the 1922 Committee to overthrow Conservative leaders has been amply illustrated this century. It is probably true to say, therefore, that the 1922 Committee has considerable power of appointment and dismissal of Conservative leaders, but that it exercises less control over the party leader when he is in power than is the case with the PLP and the Labour Party leader.

There are various subject committees and regional groups of Conservative backbenchers, but again they tend to be less active and less vocal than their Labour counterparts. When the party is in opposition, a Shadow Cabinet (known as the Leader's Committee or the Consultative Committee) is appointed by the party leader, and these frontbench spokesmen act as chairmen of the backbench subject groups.

In direct contrast to the practice within the Labour Party, the Conservative Whip has not been withdrawn from any MP since 1945, though a number have voluntarily surrendered it. The difference between the two parties in this respect may be because the decision to withdraw the Conservative Whip is

[1] P. Norton, 'Party Organisation in the House of Commons', *Parl. Aff.* 1978, pp. 406–23.

[2] See T. F. Lindsay and M. Harrington, *The Conservative Party 1918–1970*, London 1974; R. Blake, *The Conservative Party from Peel to Thatcher*, London 1985; Z. Layton-Henry (ed.), *Conservative Party Politics*, London 1980; P. Norton and A. Aughey, *Conservatives and Conservatism*, London 1981; F. O'Gorman, *British Conservatism*, London 1986.

made by the party leader, rather than by the Parliamentary Party as is the case with the Labour Party. There is, however, less actual difference between the extent of the parties' control over their MPs than is suggested by this formal difference, and Conservative Party discipline is exerted, informally, as much through the local associations as through the 1922 Committee. Conservatives claim, however, that the Whip has not been withdrawn since 1945 because their party has been more united than the Labour Party in this period, and because the Conservative Party does not fear party rebellions in the way that Labour fears another 1931. In general in the Conservative Party, rebellions tend to be by individuals rather than by groups.

Nevertheless, the Suez Group of right-wing Conservative MPs were prominent in 1954 and 1956,[1] the Common Market issue produced pro- and anti-European groups in the party in the 1960s and 1970s, and there have been clear differences between 'wets' and 'dries' in the 1980s. Lord Salisbury in 1957, and Thorneycroft, Powell, and Birch in 1958, resigned from Macmillan's Government over policy disagreements, while in 1963 Powell and Macleod refused to serve under Home. In opposition in 1965 disagreements appeared within the party over the Rhodesian issue, and in 1968 Powell was dropped from the Shadow Cabinet because of his attitude on racial matters. There were no resignations or dismissals from the 1970–74 Heath Government, but a number of Ministers have been dismissed or have resigned from the Thatcher Government because of disagreements over policy. On none of these occasions, however, did a major party split result.

The Conservative Party leader is chosen by the MPs rather than by the party organisation outside Parliament. A ballot is held of all Conservative MPs, and to be elected on the first ballot a candidate has to receive an overall majority of those qualified to vote, and also has to receive 15% more votes than the runner-up. If this is not achieved, a second ballot has to be held a few days later, for which new candidates can be

[1] See L. Epstein, *British Politics in the Suez Crisis*, London 1964; L. Epstein, 'British MPs and Their Local Parties', *APSR* 1960, pp. 374–91.

nominated. To be successful in this ballot a candidate merely has to have an overall majority of votes. If this is still not achieved, a third ballot is held, restricted to the three leading candidates of the second ballot, and with the voters indicating their first and second preferences on the ballot paper. After the votes have been counted, the third candidate is eliminated, and the votes that were given to him are redistributed, according to the second preferences, between the two remaining candidates. The winner is then presented to a party meeting consisting of Conservative MPs, Peers, prospective candidates, and members of the National Executive Committee.

This process, which was adopted in 1965 and revised slightly in 1975, is thus highly elaborate, though the practice has been less complicated than the theory might suggest. In July 1965, in the ballot to find a successor to Sir Alec Douglas-Home, Edward Heath polled 150 votes, Reginald Maudling 133, and Enoch Powell 15. Although Heath did not have the required 15% lead, Maudling and Powell withdrew from the contest, making a second ballot unnecessary. In March 1975 Margaret Thatcher polled 130 votes in the first ballot, to Edward Heath's 119 and Hugh Fraser's 16. Thus she just failed to obtain the 15% lead, but she was successful in the second ballot a week later, polling 146 votes compared with a total of 128 for the other four candidates.

Before this election process was introduced, Conservative leaders were chosen by a method whereby the Whips and leading party figures sought the opinions of MPs and Peers, and of the party outside Parliament. From these soundings the view of the party was ascertained and a leader 'emerged'. In the changes of leadership in 1957 and 1963, however, the practice had been subjected to much criticism, which in 1963 had extended to suggestions that the Monarch was associated with undesirable procedures. Thus in 1965 the party changed its method of selecting a leader.

Although since 1975 a Conservative leader is required to submit himself (or herself) for annual re-election, he is still in many respects in a more powerful position than a Labour leader. A Conservative leader, for example, appoints personally the senior party officials, in particular the Chairman of the Party, the Chief Whip, and the Deputy Whip. When in opposition he is not faced by an elected Shadow Cabinet. While the significance of these formal factors can undoubtedly be exaggerated, it is probably the case that in policy making and general control over the party, a Conservative leader is subject to less control from the party inside Parliament than is a Labour leader. Thus an impression emerges of a Conservative Party power structure where more freedom and authority is delegated to the leader than is the case with the Labour Party, especially when the comparison is of the parties when in opposition.

Nevertheless, it is also true that the Conservative Party does not hesitate to remove its leaders from power when it is felt that they have become a liability to the party. Of the ten leaders since 1902, five were undoubtedly removed from office by pressure from within the party. A. J. Balfour led the party from 1902 to 1911, when he was forced to resign by those members of the party who felt that his opposition to the Liberal Government was not strong enough. Austen Chamberlain, although never officially appointed to the post, was in fact Conservative leader from March 1921 to October 1922, but was forced from power by members of the party who opposed continued Conservative participation in the Lloyd George Coalition. Neville Chamberlain, party leader and Prime Minister from 1937 to 1940, was forced to resign the Premiership in May 1940 as a result of a loss of support within the party, though he did remain as party leader for a short while after this. Sir Alec Douglas-Home led the party from 1963 to 1965, when he resigned as a result of party pressures. Edward Heath succeeded Douglas-Home, but was defeated when he offered himself for re-election ten years later.

The other five Conservative leaders since 1902 all retired through illness or through their own choice. Bonar Law, party leader 1911–21 and again 1922–3, retired through illness on both occasions. Baldwin (1923–37) and Churchill (1940–55) both retired of their own volition, although Baldwin, and Churchill to a lesser extent, were subjected at various times to pressures from within the party. Eden, 1955–7, and Macmillan, 1957–63, both retired through illness, though their position was being questioned, and it may be doubted whether they could have remained in power if illness had not brought their retirement.

Thus while the Conservative Party may be prepared to grant considerable powers of discretion to its leaders, it is clearly not prepared to allow a leader to remain in power if it is felt that he has not made the best use of his wide powers. As long as he is successful (particularly in an electoral sense), a Conservative leader seems to be in a more powerful position within the party than is a Labour leader, but if his leadership does not bring success for the party, a Conservative leader probably has less security of tenure than has a Labour leader. It may be that as the Conservative Party has been mainly in power this century, and the Labour Party mainly in opposition, the strain of holding the post of Prime Minister has contributed towards the turnover of Conservative leaders. It is probably more true to say, however, that the prestige attached to the office of Prime Minister is an asset in the leader's struggle to retain authority within the party, and that Labour leaders have retained their position despite the fact that they have been so long in opposition, not because of it.

Labour Party. The Parliamentary Labour Party (PLP) is composed of all Labour (and Labour and Co-operative) MPs, including Ministers when the party is in power and Shadow Ministers when the party is in opposition.[1] In 1924 an attempt was made to bring the PLP into line with the Conservative 1922 Committee by excluding Ministers or Shadow Ministers, but the attempt was unsuccessful. When in opposition the PLP normally meets once or twice a week, but generally only fortnightly when the party is in office. It has various backbench committees which discuss policy. These committees are vocal and influential when the party is in opposition, but are less so when the party is in power. When the Labour Governments were formed in 1924 and 1929, a Consultative Committee, consisting of twelve backbenchers and three Ministers, was set up to act as a link between the Government and its

[1]See D. Kavanagh (ed.), *The Politics of the Labour Party*, London 1982; C. Cook and I. Taylor (eds), *The Labour Party*, London 1980; B. Jones and M. Keating, *Labour and the British State*, London 1985.

backbenchers. In 1945 and 1964 smaller and less formal bodies were set up, but in 1974 a Liaison Committee made up of six Ministers and eight backbenchers was created. It is the function of this body to keep a Labour Government informed of backbench opinion, and also to explain and rally support for Government actions.

When the party is in opposition, a Parliamentary Committee is elected by the members of the PLP, and this Committee forms the nucleus of the Opposition frontbench spokesmen.[1] The Committee consists of fifteen members elected annually by the PLP, plus the party leader, the chairman of the PLP (an office separated from that of party leader in 1970), the deputy leader, Chief Whip, and three Peers. It is sometimes claimed that the fact that the Committee is elected rather than chosen by the leader, places a limitation on the freedom of a Labour leader when in opposition that does not apply to a Conservative leader. In practice this seems not to be the case, however, as the leader does not necessarily give the chief shadow responsibilities to Parliamentary Committee members, nor, when the party comes to power, does he necessarily have to give Cabinet posts to those who held shadow responsibilities. The election of the Parliamentary Committee does, however, provide an annual measure of the popularity of senior MPs.

There is generally more independence of spirit to be found among the PLP than among Conservative MPs, and consequently the Labour Whips have had to adopt a more stringent attitude towards the maintenance of party discipline.[2] In the 1951–64 period in opposition the party was divided over a number of fundamental issues, with a powerful 'Bevanite' group questioning official party policy, particularly with regard to defence and public ownership.[3] Bevan resigned from

[1] See R. M. Punnett, *Front-Bench Opposition*, London 1973; J. R. Sibley, 'Labour Party Committee Elections and the Labour Leadership 1945–76', *EJPR* 1978, pp. 71–104.

[2] See R. E. Dowse and T. Smith, 'Party Discipline in the House of Commons – A Comment', *Parl. Aff.* 1962–3, pp. 159–64; R. K. Alderman, 'Discipline in the PLP 1945–51', *Parl. Aff.* 1964–5, pp. 293–305.

[3] See R. E. Dowse, 'The PLP in Opposition', *Parl. Aff.* 1959–60, pp. 520–9; L. Epstein, 'New MPs and the Politics of the PLP', *PS* 1962, pp. 121–9.

the Shadow Cabinet in 1954, and was denied the whip in 1955. Labour disunity reached a peak after the 1959 election defeat, when Anthony Greenwood refused to serve in the Shadow Cabinet under Gaitskell, and he and Wilson challenged Gaitskell for the party leadership.

Differences between 'left' and 'right' over defence policy, incomes policy and membership of the European Community were evident in the Labour Governments of 1964–70 and 1974–9, and have been even more apparent in opposition. The 'soft' left, represented by the Tribune Group, and the 'harder' supporters of Militant Tendency, have been critical of successive leaders in the 1970s and 1980s. Within the PLP's Standing Orders the 'conscience clause' allows MPs to abstain from voting on matters of deep personal conviction.[1] Before 1946 this extended only to questions of religion and temperance, but today it is taken as having a broader meaning. The Labour whip is rarely surrendered (although a total of four MPs resigned the whip in the 1974–9 Parliament), but on a number of occasions the whip has been withdrawn from some of the party's militant and vocal left-wing MPs.

The leader and deputy leader of the Labour Party are chosen at the Party Conference by an electoral college in which the trade unions control 40% of the votes, the constituency parties 30% and the PLP 30%.[2] A candidate is required to receive over half the votes in order to be elected. If no candidate achieves this in the first ballot, the bottom candidate is eliminated and a second ballot is held (and the process is repeated until a winner emerges). This method automatically eliminates a possible compromise candidate who comes bottom of the poll, and it could extend to a number of counts if a number of candidates enter the contest. In fact, it has worked fairly expeditiously. The first time the system was used was to elect a new deputy leader in 1981. On the first ballot Denis Healey received 45% of the votes, Tony Benn

[1] See R. K. Alderman, 'The Conscience Clause of the PLP', *Parl. Aff.* 1965–6, pp. 224–32.

[2] H. M. Drucker, 'Leadership Selection in the Labour Party', *Parl. Aff.* 1975–6, pp. 378–95; H. M. Drucker, 'Changes in the Labour Party Leadership', *Parl. Aff.* 1981, pp. 369–91; H. M. Drucker, 'Intra-Party Democracy in Action', *Parl. Aff.* 1984, pp. 283–300.

37% and John Silkin 18%. Silkin was eliminated, and in the second ballot Healey was elected with 50.4% of the votes to Benn's 49.6%. Following Michael Foot's resignation in 1983 Neil Kinnock was elected leader with 71% of the votes in the first ballot in a four-candidate contest, while Roy Hattersley was elected deputy leader (also in a four-candidate contest) with 67% of the votes in the first ballot.

Prior to 1981 the Labour leader and deputy leader were selected by the PLP. The change to the electoral college system came because it was felt that the extra-Parliamentary party should be allowed to participate in the process, and because the PLP was seen to be dominated by the right of the party. The left felt that the change to the electoral college system would enable it to increase its influence. A proposal that the leader should be chosen by a postal ballot of all party members was rejected, reflecting the view that the choice should reside with the party activists rather than with the MPs or the mass membership.

* * *

Once he is elected, a Labour leader is faced with more limitations on his power than is a Conservative leader. A Labour leader is subject to annual re-election, but in practice he is rarely opposed. In 1960 Gaitskell was opposed by Harold Wilson and in 1961 by Anthony Greenwood. Attlee and Wilson, however, served their long terms (and Callaghan and Foot their short terms) without being opposed. Unlike the Conservative practice, a Labour leader does not appoint party officials, the Transport House organisation being under the control of the NEC. A Labour leader attends PLP meetings and in opposition is faced by a Shadow Cabinet that is elected by the PLP. He attends the party's annual conference and is frequently subjected to strong criticism – as were Hugh Gaitskell at the 1960 Conference and Neil Kinnock at the 1985 Conference. In some ways, however, participation in PLP meetings and Conference debates can be to the leader's advantage, in that he has the opportunity to face and overcome his critics. Certainly, the Conservative leader no longer appears at the Conference only on the final day, but since 1965 has followed the Labour practice of daily attendance.

It is often argued that in formulating policy, a Labour leader and his senior colleagues are more restricted by the views of the PLP and the party outside Parliament than is the case with the Conservative Party. Certainly, for most of its history the Labour Party has been in opposition, and has thus been more concerned with theoretical policies than with the harsh realities of office. Further, the egalitarian ideals of the party, the fear of a repetition of MacDonald's 'betrayal' in 1931, and the unwillingness (at least in the past) to regard the party leader as a potential Prime Minister, have led the Labour Party in Parliament and outside to develop a more critical and less deferential attitude towards its leaders than is the case with attitudes within the Conservative Party.

Despite this, however, whether in power or in opposition, Labour leaders have enjoyed a greater security of tenure over the years than have Conservative leaders. The Labour Party had a total of twelve leaders before Neil Kinnock. Between 1906 and 1921 the post of Parliamentary Spokesman (as the leader was then known) was held by five MPs (Keir Hardie, Arthur Henderson, G. N. Barnes, Ramsay MacDonald, and W. Adamson), each holding the office for two to three years, and each retiring of his own choosing. In 1921 J. R. Clynes became the leader, but with the election of a new group of Labour MPs at the 1922 election, Clynes was defeated in the leadership ballot by Ramsay MacDonald. The title of party leader was officially adopted in 1922, when Labour replaced the Liberals as the main opposition party. As Prime Minister in 1924 and again in 1929, MacDonald was as omnipotent as any Conservative Prime Minister between the wars, but the events of 1931 inevitably produced a reaction within the party against strong leadership.

MacDonald was succeeded as leader by Arthur Henderson who retired after his defeat at the 1931 election. He was followed by George Lansbury, who served until he was forced to resign in 1935 in face of bitter criticism of his pacifist principles. Clement Attlee succeeded him, and although in 1935 Attlee was generally regarded as an unlikely choice, he remained leader until 1955. As Prime Minister, Attlee ignored resolutions passed at the 1933 Conference demanding that when forming a Government a Labour Prime Minister should consult with the Parliamentary Committee, and when deciding when to ask for a dissolution of Parliament he should consult with the Cabinet and the PLP.

On Attlee's retirement in 1955, Hugh Gaitskell was elected leader. Gaitskell led the party only in opposition, and after the 1959 general election his leadership was subjected to severe criticism. He survived this criticism, however, and at the time of his death in 1963 he had restored his prestige. It is doubtful whether a Conservative leader could have survived in the way that Gaitskell did after 1959. Harold Wilson succeeded Gaitskell, and despite spells of unpopularity, retained the leadership for thirteen years before retiring, of his own choosing, in 1976. After relatively short spells as leader James Callaghan in 1980 and Michael Foot in 1983 retired voluntarily after leading the party to electoral defeat.

Thus of the twelve Labour leaders before Neil Kinnock, one died in office, eight retired of their own accord, one broke with the party and only J. R. Clynes and George Lansbury were forced to leave office by party pressures (though had James Callaghan and Michael Foot not chosen to retire it is unlikely that they would have remained unchallenged). Clement Attlee was the longest-serving leader of any of the main parties in this century. The conclusion must be, therefore, that however much criticism a Labour leader may receive from the PLP and the party outside Parliament, and however much these bodies may seek to influence policy making, Labour leaders so far have had a much better record of security of tenure than have Conservative leaders. That security of tenure might be even greater in the future, as the cumbersome nature of the electoral college system may well deter challenges to the established leader.

The Parties Outside Parliament

Conservative Party. The main functions of the Conservative and Labour Party organisations outside Parliament are to nominate Parliamentary candidates, act as election-winning machines, provide a source of finance and party workers, contribute to party policy, and produce and distribute party propaganda. In addition, they provide a means of communication between the Parliamentary leaders and the party supporters. For these purposes the Conservative Party organisation outside Parliament is divided into two distinct sections, the amateur organisation of the National Conservative Association, and the professional organisation of the Conservative Central Office. Both bodies, and the party in Parliament, are, however, under the control of the party leader.

The National Conservative Association (formerly known as the National Union of Conservative and Unionist Associations) was formed in 1867. It represents the mass membership of the Conservative Party, and is a federation of the various constituency associations throughout England and Wales. The Scottish Conservative Association[1] is a separate but parallel body. The National Association has a total membership of about 1,500,000, all on an individual basis. The nominal head of the National Association is the President, and he and the Chairman and the other officers are elected by the Central Council, the governing body of the National Union. The Central Council, which meets in London once a year, is composed of MPs, Peers, prospective candidates, representatives from the constituencies, principal officials of the Conservative Central Office, and the members of the Executive Committee of the National Association, making up a total membership of about 3,000. Its annual meeting is in effect a smaller version of the annual Conference at which policy as well as organisational matters are discussed.

The Executive Committee of the National Association is a body of some 150 members, made up of party officials (including the party leader) and representatives from the local areas. It meets every two months, but most of its functions are delegated to its General Purposes Sub-Committee of about 50 members, which meets monthly. The Executive Committee is also served by various advisory committees, including committees for Publicity and Speakers, Young Conservatives, Political Education, and Local Government. In addition to these committees there are others dealing with policy, finance, and Parliamentary candidates, composed primarily of party

[1] See D. W. Urwin, 'Scottish Conservatism: a Party Organisation in Transition', *PS* 1966, pp. 144–62.

officials and MPs. They are largely under the control of the leader, thereby removing from the National Association control over these vital aspects of party management.

The National Association has twelve Provincial Area Councils, which are made up of representatives from the constituencies in the region. At this level the party organisation follows very closely that of the national structure, and each Area Council is served by officials, an Executive Committee, and various advisory committees directly parallel to the officials and committees that serve the Central Council. Within each area the party is organised into various Constituency Associations.[1] Each Association has a Chairman and other officers, an Executive Committee made up of representatives from the ward and local branches of the association, and a Finance and General Purposes Committee for day-to-day matters. The Constituency Associations are served by about 300 full-time agents (compared with Labour's figure of about 50).

In addition to its fund-raising, propagandising, and election-winning functions, the Constituency Association is responsible for the selection of Parliamentary candidates. If a Conservative MP serves the constituency, the Association has to maintain links between the MP and the electorate, organising meetings with constituents, public meetings, and other like activities for the MP. Within each constituency there are numerous ward or district branches, all with their own officers who serve on the constituency Executive Committee. It is on this final 'grass roots' level that the whole of the National Association's pyramid structure is based. The party relies for its finance on individual membership fees, on local and national fund-raising schemes, and also upon contributions received from business organisations or individuals. This last source accounts for the bulk of the party's income, although the proportion coming from the constituencies has risen in the last ten years to about a fifth of the total. The size and particular sources of the contributions can vary considerably

[1] M. G. Clarke, 'National Organisation and the Constituency Association in the Conservative Party', *PS* 1969, pp. 345–7.

from year to year, so to that extent it is not as reliable as Labour's income from the trade unions.[1]

The other main limb of the Conservative Party structure is the Central Office.[2] This is the professional body, as opposed to the amateur National Association. It is the central administrative structure, and supervises the running of the local organisations. Central Office was established in 1870, after the creation of the Liberal Registration Association in 1861, and following the heavy Conservative defeat at the 1868 election. The Chairman of the party is usually a senior Parliamentary figure and often has a seat in the Cabinet. The Chairman and other leading officers of the Central Office, are appointed by the party leader, and are directly under his control. The leader's powers in this direction are the key to his authority in the party, as the balance of power within the Conservative Party structure lies overwhelmingly with Central Office rather than the National Association. Attached to party headquarters are the Conservative Research Department and the Centre For Policy Studies, which produce literature for policy and propaganda purposes.[3] In each of the twelve provincial areas there is a Central Office Area Agent and an Area Office. This area organisation provides the means of Central Office supervision of constituencies within the area, though some degree of Central Office influence is also exerted through the constituency agents.[4]

* * *

The annual Conservative Party Conference has a potential membership of some 5,600, made up of representatives from

[1] See M. Pinto-Duschinsky, *British Political Finance 1830–1980*, New York 1982; M. Pinto-Duschinsky, 'Trends in British Political Funding 1979–83', *Parl. Aff.* 1985, pp. 328–47; V. Bogdanor, 'Reflections on British Political Finance', *Parl. Aff.* 1982, pp. 367–80.

[2] M. Pinto-Duschinsky, 'Central Office and "Power" in the Conservative Party', *PS* 1972, pp. 1–16.

[3] See J. Ramsden, *The Making of Conservative Party Policy*, London 1980.

[4] D. J. Wilson, 'Party Bureaucracy in Britain: Regional and Area Organization', *BJPS* 1972, pp. 273–80; R. Frasure and A. Kornberg, 'Constituency Agents and British Party Politics', *BJPS* 1975, pp. 459–76; Z. Layton-Henry, 'Constituency Autonomy in the Conservative Party', *Parl. Aff.* 1976, pp. 396–403.

the constituencies and from bodies like the Young Conservatives and the Conservative Trade Union Council. In fact, only about half of this number generally attend. Those who do attend are not instructed delegates, but speak and vote as they think fit. While this is claimed to be a practical arrangement, it means that local constituency workers who do not attend the Conference have no say in its deliberations. It is probably true to say that in general the Conference is attended by the most militant members from the constituencies, but nevertheless the Conference is characterised (certainly in comparison with its Labour counterpart) by a readiness to accept the wishes of the leadership. The Conference, which lasts some two to three days, debates a number of issues, chosen by the General Purposes Sub-Committee of the National Association, but only rarely reveals any serious party divisions. At the 1950 Conference the leadership agreed unwillingly to accept the Conference's proposed target of '300,000 houses a year' as an election pledge, and in 1965 the Conference was critical of party policy towards the Rhodesian independence issue and the record of Conservative Governments on 'law and order' has been attacked at a number of Conferences. In the main, however, the Conservative Conference is tradionally a united and deferential gathering, especially in the flush of electoral success. This annual display of party unity has done much, especially with the televising of party conferences, to enhance the image (however accurate an image) of the Conservative Party as a united and responsible body.

Thus a complicated national and local organisation exists within the National Association and Central Office alike. To a large extent this is accompanied by a clear division of power between the central and local bodies, with the local associations being given a considerable degree of autonomy over their own affairs, including the selection of Parliamentary candidates. Nevertheless, despite this division of power, and despite the complicated nature of party organisation, it must be emphasised that control over party affairs, in other than purely local matters, rests firmly with the party leadership. The diversified formal structure of Conservative Party organisation hides an actual power structure which concentrates power in the hands of the leadership, and of the party leader in particular. To a large extent this is achieved through the willingness of the constituency associations to leave policy matters largely in the hands of the leader and the Parliamentary party, and the overall supervision of the party machine primarily in the hands of the leader and Central Office. The main function of the party organisation outside Parliament is thus not to control the party leaders, but to secure their election to Parliamentary power.

Labour Party. In many ways the most significant aspect of the structure of the Labour Party outside Parliament is the role that is played by the trade unions.[1] The Labour Party was formed in 1900 out of an alliance of trade unions and socialist societies, with the unions forming the dominant numerical and financial element. Today, affiliated membership through the unions accounts for over 90% of the total Labour Party membership, and about 75% of the Labour Party's funds are provided by the unions. The trade unions also contribute additional sums to the party's election-fighting fund, and to the finances of constituency parties that adopt trade union sponsored candidates. The Trade Union Act 1984 required unions to ballot their members to determine whether the union should continue to give financial support to the Labour Party, but all the major unions secured majorities in favour of the political fund. The consequent strength of trade union influence is reflected at various levels throughout the structure of the party.

The NEC of the Labour Party, which normally meets monthly, supervises the whole party organisation outside Parliament.[2] The General Secretary, and other senior members of the party bureaucracy, are appointed by, and are answerable to, the NEC, and not to the party leader as is the case with the Conservatives. Since 1900 there have been only

[1] See M. Harrison, *The Trade Unions and the Labour Party since 1945*, London 1960; R. Taylor, 'The Uneasy Alliance – Labour and the Unions', *PQ* 1976, pp. 398–407; M. Shanks, 'Politics and the Trade Unionist', *PQ* 1959, pp. 44–53; B. Simpson, *Labour: the Unions and the Party*, London 1973; A. Taylor, *The Trade Unions and the Labour Party*, London 1986; K. D. Ewing, *Trade Unions, the Labour Party and the Law*, London 1982.

[2] See R. T. McKenzie, 'The Wilson Report and the Future of Labour Party Organization', *PS* 1956, pp. 93–7.

eight party Secretaries, and while the first two (Ramsay MacDonald and Arthur Henderson) were powerful and independent figures within the party, the others (most recently Ron Hayward and Larry Whitty) have been rather more subject to NEC control. Under the Secretary, the Transport House organisation is divided into various departments, including Research, Press and Publicity, and Finance, and these departments are supervised by sub-committees of the NEC. The NEC is composed of twenty-nine members. These are the leader and deputy leader of the party, twelve members elected by the trade union delegates to the annual party Conference, seven elected by the constituency party delegates, one by the Young Socialists, one by Socialist and Co-operative Societies, and five women members and the Treasurer elected by the whole Conference (where the trade union delegates have a majority of votes). The Secretary is also a member of the NEC, but he does not vote. The NEC elects a chairman and vice-chairman from its own number, and generally the longest-serving members are chosen.

Normally, MPs are in a clear majority on the NEC, as usually most of the five women members, most of the seven members elected by the constituency parties, and at least some of the twelve members elected by the trade unions, are MPs. The domination of the composition of the NEC by trade union votes, and the overlap between the NEC and the PLP, are the most important features of the structure of the committee, and provide the key to the distribution of power within the Labour Party. In a notable dispute in 1945 with Harold Laski, then chairman of the NEC, Attlee emphasised the need for the Parliamentary leaders to be free from domination by the NEC or its chairman. This issue comes to the fore regularly, particularly when the party is in opposition. The authority of the Parliamentary leaders on the NEC is strengthened by the provision in the party constitution which makes members of the TUC General Council ineligible for membership of the NEC. In most cases the most prominent union leaders have preferred service on the General Council, leaving the second rank of union officials to serve on the NEC. Also, until the 1960s the Parliamentary leaders were generally able to control the NEC through the support of the most powerful trade unions, which were traditionally loyal to the party leadership. In the last twenty-five years, however, this support has been less automatic, and the party leader has often been faced with an alliance (sometimes in the majority) of left-wing trade unionists and MPs.

* * *

The Labour Party has eleven Regional Councils throughout England, Wales, and Scotland. The Regional Council, which meets annually, is made up of members drawn from the constituencies, trade union organisations, cooperative societies, and socialist societies within the region. These bodies are also represented on a federal basis on the Council's Executive Committee, which meets generally every two months. In each region there is a Regional Organiser, who has the task of supervising the party machine throughout the region. The Regional Organisers are responsible to party head office rather than to the Regional Council, and this follows the pattern that applies within the Conservative Party.

At a local level there is a committee for each ward or district, and these committees join with the unions and other affiliated bodies to create a constituency organisation.[1] The General Management Committee is the controlling body of this organisation. The delegates from the affiliated organisations constitute a numerical majority on the GMC, but most attend its meetings only rarely. The GMC appoints an Executive Committee for day-to-day business, and there are various sub-committees of the Executive Committee for the several aspects of constituency affairs. Only a small number of constituencies have an agent, and at this level Labour organisation is generally smaller, less wealthy, and less effective than Conservative organisation. Although the constituencies are largely free to manage their own internal affairs, they are subject to rather more central control than is the case with the Conservative constituency associations.

The annual Labour Party Conference generally lasts for five

[1]See H. J. Hanham, 'The Local Organization of the British Labour Party', *WPQ* 1956, pp. 376–88; J. Blondel, 'The Conservative Association and the Labour Party in Reading', *PS* 1958, pp. 101–19.

days, the bulk of the time being devoted to debating resolutions proposed by the NEC or the delegates.[1] It has a smaller attendance than the Conservative Conference. Each trade union, affiliated organisation, and constituency association is entitled to send one delegate for every 5,000 of its party members, and these delegates, plus various ex-officio members of the Conference, make up a total potential attendance of about 2,500. In fact, the actual attendance is usually only about 1,100. The unions in particular normally send only about half the numbers they are entitled to, and they are generally outnumbered by the constituency delegates. The constituency delegates are also usually much more vocal than those union delegates who do attend. However, the union delegates have a much greater voting strength than those from the constituencies, as each delegation has a 'block vote' equivalent to the total number of party members that it is representing. As the unions account for the bulk of the membership of the Labour Party, they control the bulk (about five-sixths) of the votes at the Conference.

There is no general rule as to how far Conference delegations receive prior instructions from their unions and associations on how to vote on the various Conference issues, but in most cases the decisions are made by the delegations themselves. A delegation may divide its total number of votes if it so wishes, but it is an accepted convention that the various delegations cast their votes as a block. The four biggest unions account for about half of the total Conference votes, while the TGWU and the AUEW each have more votes than all the constituency delegates put together. The voting power of the big unions is thus vital to the control of Conference decisions.

In the past a picture was often presented of the union delegates representing the right wing of the party, and the constituency delegates the left wing, with the ever-moderate union leaders supporting the party leadership against left-wing extremists. As a generalisation, however, it is probably more true to say that on most Conference issues the opposition to the party leadership comes both from trade unionists and constituency associations alike, with the precise extent of the opposition varying with the issue. Studies of the type of

[1] L. Minkin, *The Labour Party Conference*, London 1980.

Conference resolutions proposed by the various delegations suggest that this is probably a more accurate generalisation than any straight division into trade unions versus constituency associations.[1]

The Conference, as well as being a rally and an annual meeting ground for MPs and party workers, has the twin functions of proposing party policy, and of considering policies that have been drawn up by the PLP and the NEC. The precise interpretation and extent of these powers, however, has frequently caused controversy in the past. The whole question of the extent to which the organisation outside Parliament is able to determine Labour Party policies, is to a considerable degree bound up with the interpretation of the precise nature of the power and authority of the Conference. It has been noted above that the party leader and his senior Parliamentary colleagues are generally in a position to influence the NEC, and that with the support of the majority of the big unions, the leadership is often able to control conference decisions. It is less clear, however, to what extent the NEC, the PLP, and the party leader are limited in their power when the Conference passes policy resolutions of which the leadership does not approve.

On the one hand it has been claimed that the Conference is 'the final authority of the Labour Party . . . [It] lays down the policy of the party, and issues instructions which must be carried out by the Executive, the affiliated organisations, and its representatives in Parliament and on local authorities'.[2] The Labour Party Constitution stipulates that a Conference resolution becomes party policy if it is approved by a two-thirds majority. The Constitution, however, also gives the Parliamentary leaders the power to implement the party's programme 'as far as may be practicable', and in practice the Parliamentary leaders have sought to retain the power to decide policy issues themselves, regardless of Conference

[1] See R. Rose, 'The Policy Ideas of English Party Activists', *APSR* 1962, pp. 360–71; K. Hindell and P. Williams, 'Scarborough and Blackpool: An Analysis of Some Votes at the Labour Party Conferences of 1960 and 1961', *PQ* 1962, pp. 306–20.

[2] C. R. Attlee, *The Labour Party in Perspective: and Twelve Years Later*, London 1949, p. 93.

decisions. As early as 1907, Keir Hardie and Arthur Henderson resisted Conference attempts to 'instruct' Labour MPs to introduce particular legislation, and insisted on the right of MPs to decide legislative priorities. At the 1960 and 1961 Conferences, Hugh Gaitskell defended the right of the Parliamentary leaders to decide policy issues irrespective of Conference decisions,[1] and in 1968 when the Conference opposed (by a majority of five to one) the Government's prices and incomes policy, Harold Wilson declared that he would note the decision but could not accept it as an instruction. In 1975, at the special Conference called to debate the party's attitude towards the EEC referendum, the Government's recommended policy was clearly defeated, but this did not result in any change in Government policy. Recent Conference resolutions on defence policy have been ignored, or 'interpreted loosely', by the Parliamentary leadership.

As well as the arguments that Conference resolutions are frequently vague and often contradictory, and that for practical reasons the Parliamentary leaders should be the ones to decide precisely what legislation a Labour Government should seek to introduce, the doctrine of Parliamentary Sovereignty makes it unconstitutional for the Conference to attempt to dictate to the PLP. Thus MPs claim that they should be free from outside party pressures in the same way that Burke's interpretation of the MP's role demands that he be free from constituency pressures. It is probably true to say that the Conference was intended to play a much more important part in party affairs than it does at present, and it is probably also true that to outside observers and Conference delegates alike, it seems to have more power and influence than it actually does have. When a Labour Government has been in power the Conference has possibly been even more submissive to the wishes of the Prime Minister than has the Conservative Conference to Conservative Prime Ministers. It is when the Labour Party has suffered a major setback, as at the 1918, 1931, 1959, 1979 and 1983 elections, that there have occurred open disputes between the Conference and the party

[1] S. Haseler, *The Gaitskellites: Revisionism in the British Labour Party 1951–64*, London 1969.

leadership, and it is at times such as this that the Conference emerges as a limiting force on the authority of the leader and the Parliamentary party. Certainly, the Conference retains ultimate control of the party organisation and procedures. Thus the 1979 Conference introduced the requirement that MPs submit themselves for re-selection in each Parliament, and the 1981 special Conference devised the electoral college method of selecting the party leader – both changes being contrary to the wishes of the majority of MPs. In this respect the power of the Conference represents a difference between the power structures of the Labour and Conservative Parties.

Liberal Party.[1] The leader of the Liberal Party is chosen, not by the MPs, but by an electoral college composed of representatives of the Labour constituency associations. This procedure was used for the first time in 1976, when David Steel was elected. The number of Liberal MPs has been so small in recent years that Liberal organisation in Parliament can be very informal, but Liberal MPs and Peers are allocated to 'shadow cabinet' responsibilities by the leader. The power of the leader is considerable both inside and outside Parliament. In 1981 the Liberal Assembly opposed the introduction of Cruise missiles into Britain, but David Steel declared that he would not include this as party policy in the election manifesto. In 1983 the Assembly upheld the leader's right to determine party policy in this way.

The Liberal Party Organisation outside Parliament is headed by a President and officers elected by the annual Assembly. The Assembly is attended by MPs, Peers, party officials, and representatives from the constituencies, making a total of about 800. This body elects representatives to the Liberal Council of some 150 members, which meets quarterly and which decides policy issues when the Assembly is not in session. The Council delegates authority to an Executive Committee which meets monthly, and this body in turn elects an Organising Committee which controls party headquarters and is responsible for day-to-day matters. In addition, there is

[1]See V. Bogdanor, *Liberal Party Politics*, London 1983; C. Cook, *A Short History of the Liberal Party 1900–1984*, London 1984; J. Rasmussen, *The Liberal Party*, London 1965; R. Douglas, *The History of the Liberal Party 1895–1970*, London 1971.

a Liberal Party Committee, composed of the fifty or so senior figures and officers of the Liberal Party in and out of Parliament. This Committee is responsible for the overall supervision of Liberal Party affairs, but its existence does not remove autonomy from the Parliamentary Party.

At a local level the constituency associations are organised in much the same way as the Conservative and Labour Parties, with an Executive Committee controlling affairs. The local party has, if anything, more independence from central control than is the case in the Conservative Party. At a regional level there are Area Federations, and party headquarters appoint organisers in the Areas, and agents in some of the constituencies.

Social Democratic Party. Unlike the Labour Party, but like the Liberal and Conservative Parties in the nineteenth century, the SDP emerged as a Parliamentary party and then subsequently developed an extra-Parliamentary organisation. The party leaders sought to devise a structure that emphasised the role of the MPs and party members rather than the party activists. Thus the Parliamentary leaders have a guaranteed place in the management and policy-making machinery of the party, while the members are directly involved in the process of selecting the leader of the party. The leader is chosen through a postal ballot of party members, with the leadership candidates being nominated by the MPs from among their own number. In the first leadership contest in 1982 Roy Jenkins received 56% of the votes to David Owen's 44%. When Jenkins retired from the leadership after the 1983 election, David Owen was elected unopposed.

The party also has a President (again elected by a postal ballot of party members) who heads the organisation outside Parliament. The party's management body is the National Committee, drawn almost equally from MPs and Peers on the one hand, and party activists and members on the other. The policy-making body is the Council for Social Democracy, which meets three or four times a year. It has some 400 members drawn principally from the local parties. Much of its detailed work is delegated to a policy sub-committee on which the MPs have a dominant influence. There is also a Consultative Assembly, though its functions are very limited. At the local level emphasis is placed on 'areas' rather than on individual constituencies, with each area consisting of groups of up to seven constituencies. Area parties combine to form Regional Committees for policy purposes, and they feed proposals to the Council for Social Democracy.

In the 1983 election the SDP cooperated closely and successfully with the Liberals. The partners agreed on a single Alliance manifesto, divided the seats between them with only a limited number of conflicts and agreed that Roy Jenkins be the Alliance's 'Prime Minister-designate'. A post-election survey felt that the Liberals had 'good or excellent' relations with the SDP (compared with just 42% that felt this before the election). The relative success of this cooperation was seen as a prelude to the merging of the two parties. Those Liberals and Social Democrats who favoured this argued that only through unification could the full potential of the 'third force' be realised, and that there was sufficient agreement about ends and means to justify a merger. They maintained that a single party would be more credible as an alternative Government, that continuing debate about the Alliance's future was damaging and that as long as they remained as separate units disagreements over policy, strategy or the allocation of seats would become institutionalised and thereby magnified.

It is the case that the two parties do complement each other in some respects. In the 1983 election the Liberals provided some 60% of the Alliance's workforce while the SDP provided two-thirds of the finance. Some SDP leaders have extensive Ministerial experience while the Liberals have been active in local and community politics. There remains, however, considerable resistance to a merger of the Liberals and the SDP. In each party there is a body of opinion that unification would involve, in effect, absorption by the partner. While the two parties have much in common, disagreements remain. They agree about the desirability of electoral reform, devolution and the maintenance of a wholehearted commitment to the European Community, but there are other areas of policy (notably defence) where they disagree.[1] The two parties have very

[1] See J. M. Bochel and D. T. Denver, 'The SDP and the Left–Right Dimension', *BJPS* 1984, pp. 386–92.

different structures. The SDP was formed 'from the top down' and is a more centralised party than the Liberals. While the Liberals' organisation is based on the constituencies, the SDP is organised on an area basis. These factors have delayed a merger and may prevent it.

These uncertainties about the future of the Alliance reflect broader questions about the future of the whole party system. There is clearly a variety of ways in which the party system might develop in the next few years, but four particular possibilities may be noted here. First, the Alliance, as a single entity or as two separate parties, may come to form part of a multi-party system (maybe also with revived nationalist parties in Scotland and Wales). Such a pattern could be underpinned by a reformed electoral system that gave each party Parliamentary representation in proportion to its electoral support. With such a development a succession of minority or coalition governments would be likely to emerge. Second, it may be that the Liberals and SDP will merge and come to replace one or other of the two main parties, leaving Labour or the Conservatives as a declining rump on the fringe of a new two-party system. Third, support for the Alliance might well fade, and the Conservatives and a revived Labour Party might re-establish the ascendency they enjoyed earlier in the post-war period with each experiencing periods in office as a single-party majority government. Fourth, it may be that the pattern that emerged in the 1983 election will persist for some years, with a dominant Conservative Party (at least in terms of Parliamentary seats) facing a highly divided Opposition. With such a pattern it would be possible for the Conservatives to maintain an unbroken spell in office well into the 1990s on the basis of no more than two-fifths of the vote. Not for many years has the future of the party system been so uncertain, with not just the prospects for individual parties but the very shape of the party system, and the type of government it produces, being in doubt.

4

The Political Parties: II. Social Structure

For the vast majority of people in Britain political participation extends only to voting in Parliamentary elections. Some do not participate even to this extent, in that about a quarter abstain in any particular general election and some of these are consistent abstainers. In local government elections, generally half to two-thirds of electors abstain. Of those who do vote regularly, only a relatively small proportion are members of political parties. Currently, about 1.5 million are members of the Conservative Party, some 6.25 million are individual or affiliated members of the Labour Party, about 250,000 are members of the Alliance parties, and perhaps another 50,000 are members of the several minor parties. Thus in all, roughly a fifth of electors are party members. Membership of a party, however, need not entail political activity, while among members who are 'active', participation may extend to a leadership role at a constituency, area or national level, or may merely involve attendance at party meetings. One estimate is that less than 4% of electors are party activists in any real sense, and only about half of these take any regular part in party affairs. A small proportion of party activists seek (and an even smaller proportion achieve) elected office in national or local government. There are 650 MPs, about 26,000 councillors in the main local government units and a further 75,000 parish and community councillors. These national and local representatives constitute some 0.2% of the electorate, although if the many non-partisan local councils are excluded the number of party representatives falls to less than 0.1% of the electorate. Given these several forms and degrees of political participation, an examination of the social structure of the parties has to range from the voters, to party members, activists and local leaders, and to the parties' candidates, MPs and Parliamentary leaders.

The Electors[1]

A person's voting decision is a product partly of sociological considerations (particularly the social class, sex and age group to which he belongs) and partly of consumer-choice considerations (such as the attractiveness of the parties' policies and general image). The relative importance of these factors is a matter of much debate among students of voting behaviour.[2] It has been argued by some that in Britain in recent years sociological divisions have become less significant as determinants of voting behaviour, and that voters have become much more rational in their approach, basing their voting decision increasingly on their assessment of the parties' programmes. Whatever the nature and extent of such a change over the longer term, it remains the case that voting behaviour in Britain is determined by a combination of sociological and consumer-choice considerations. As one recent study of voting behaviour has expressed it: 'It is the interaction between the social and the political that determines how people vote'.[3]

[1] For studies of electoral behaviour see D. E. Butler and D. Stokes, *Political Change in Britain*, London 1974; A. Heath (*et al.*), *How Britain Votes*, London 1985; W. L. Miller, *Electoral Dynamics In Britain Since 1918*, London 1977; B. Sarlvik and I. Crewe, *Decade of Dealignment*, London 1983; K. Wald, *Crosses on the Ballot*, New York 1983.

[2] See H. Himmelweit (*et al.*), *How Voters Decide*, London 1981; M. Franklin, *The Decline of Class Voting in Britain*, London 1985; R. Rose and I. McAllister, *Voters Begin to Choose*, London 1986; I. Crewe (ed.), *Electoral Change in Western Democracies*, London 1985; M. N. Franklin and E. C. Page, 'A Critique of the Consumption Cleavage Approach in British Voting Studies', *PS* 1984, pp. 521–36; P. Whiteley, 'Predicting the Labour Vote in 1983', *PS* 1986, pp. 82–98.

[3] Heath (*et al.*), *How Britain Votes*, p. 10. See also A. Heath (*et al.*), 'Understanding Electoral Change in Britain', *Parl. Aff.* 1986, pp. 150–64.

The personal qualities of a candidate would not seem to be major factors in determining voting behaviour. In by-elections, when a Government is not being elected, the qualities of the candidates can be important, and in the 1983 general election the Conservatives won a number of seats with above-average swings (including Basildon, Barrow, Amber Valley and Nottingham North), while Labour held Birmingham Perry Barr with a swing against the general Conservative tide. It is not clear, however, whether such results are produced by the appeal of particular candidates or by other local circumstances, and on the whole it is probably true that the personal appeal of a candidate is worth less than a thousand votes in most constituencies.[1] The personal appeal of the party leader would seem to be of greater significance for a party's electoral success, however. This is perhaps epitomised in the personal appeal of Harold Macmillan in 1959, Harold Wilson in 1966 and Mrs Thatcher in 1983. One survey in 1983 indicated that while 90% of voters regarded Mrs Thatcher as an effective Prime Minister, only 29% felt that this would be the case with Michael Foot. In 1979 on the other hand Mrs Thatcher's appeal was less positive, and it almost certainly was the case that Labour lost in 1979 (and the Conservatives in 1945) despite having more personally-popular leaders than the Opposition.

Linked with this factor is the impression that the electorate has of the general competence of the Government and Opposition leaders as a whole. Specific policy issues, however, are probably not of major significance in determining electoral support, whether the issues be long-established aspects of party policy, or merely transitory issues that emerge during an election campaign.[2] It is unlikely that a voter will agree with every aspect of the policy of the party he supports, and surveys have revealed that a voter may support a party while disagreeing with some fundamental aspect of its policy. In 1983 only

[1] See I. Robinson, 'The Candidate's Share of the Vote', *PS* 1971, pp. 447–54.

[2] J. E. Alt (*et al.*), 'Partisanship and Policy Choice', *BJPS* 1976, pp. 273–90. D. T. Studlar, 'Policy Voting in Britain', *APSR* 1978, pp. 46–64; W. L. Miller, 'The Connection Between SNP Voting and the Demand for Scottish Self-Government', *EJPR* 1977, pp. 83–102.

about half of Conservative voters felt that their party had the best policy for dealing with unemployment (which was one of the main issues in the campaign). Often a voter will change his own view to conform with party policy, rather than change his party allegiance.

Of much greater significance in Britain is the question of party 'image'.[1] The general impression that an elector has of a party is based on the party's attitudes to an accumulation of issues. It may be felt for example that the Labour Party is 'soft' and the Conservative Party is 'tough' on law and order or defence policy, or that the Labour Party is 'for the working man', while the Conservatives are 'for big business'. Nevertheless, no matter how vague or general the elector's impression of a party may be, this image is readily accepted today as being of much greater significance in determining electoral loyalties than any identification of the parties with individual policy issues.

The forces that mould an elector's attitude to a party, and which cause him to prefer the image of one party to that of another, arise from various social, economic, demographic, regional, and religious considerations. In Britain the chief long-term determinants of voting behaviour would seem to be family and social factors, and it is generally accepted that the most significant division in electoral loyalties is that the well-to-do members of the community predominantly vote Conservative, while those of a lower social status and a lower income group tend to vote Labour.[2] Findings in recent elections suggest that the Conservatives have the support of the vast majority of middle- and lower middle-class voters (who make up about a third of the electorate), while Labour has more support than the Conservatives among the skilled and unskilled working class (who make up about two-thirds of the electorate).

[1] P. Crane, 'What's in a Party Image?', *PQ* 1959, pp. 230–43; M. P. Wattenberg, 'Party Identification and Party Images', *CP* 1982–3, pp. 23–40.

[2] See D. Robertson, *Class and the British Electorate*, London 1984; M. Abrams, Social Class and British Politics', *POQ* 1961, pp. 342–51; M. Abrams, 'Social Trends and Electoral Behaviour', *BJS* 1962, pp. 228–42; J. W. Books and J. B. Reynolds, 'A Note on Class Voting in Great Britain and the United States', *CPS* 1975–6, pp. 360–76.

TABLE XVIII

*Voting Intention, 1983 General Election: by Social Class**

	All	Middle Class ABC 1	Skilled Workers C 2	Semi- and Unskilled DE
% of all voters	100	40	31	29
Con.	44	55	40	33
Lab.	28	16	32	41
Alln.	26	28	26	24
Others	2	1	2	2

* Social class groupings used by Registrar General in Census returns.

Source: Butler and Kavanagh, *The British General Election of 1983*, p. 296.

Using general elections as case studies of voting behaviour can be dangerous, in that voting intentions fluctuate to some extent from one general election to another. At the same time, comparisons between one general election and another are complicated by the changes that inevitably occur over the years in the social structure of the community. Nevertheless, Table XVIII suggests that in 1983 the broad pattern of voting was that the Conservatives did best among socio-economic groups A, B and C1, and worst among groups D and E, with the Labour pattern being the precise reverse of this. Alliance support was drawn fairly evenly from all social groups. Longer-term comparisons suggest that these broad patterns of support have been fairly constant over the last thirty years, although the extent of the parties' support in a particular group has varied from election to election. Specifically, in 1983 as compared with 1964 Labour support was lower, and Alliance support was greater, across all the social groups.

Although Table XVIII suggests that electoral divisions along class lines are quite distinct, it is also the case that a minority (about 20%) of the middle class normally vote Labour, while a more substantial minority of the working class normally vote Conservative. In 1983 the middle-class Labour vote was smaller, and the working-class Conservative vote was larger, than in elections of the 1960s and 1970s, while the Alliance thrived as an 'all-class' force. These exceptions to rigid class voting alignments prevent a strictly Marxist interpretation of British electoral behaviour. Some opponents of the nineteenth-century franchise extensions argued that as the working class made up the vast majority of the population, any party that had complete, or almost complete, working-class electoral support could expect to be permanently in power. In fact, however, the retention of a large proportion of working-class support by the Conservative Party (supplemented in 1983 by appreciable working-class support for the Alliance) has prevented any such development in modern Britain.

The existence of a substantial working-class Conservative and Alliance vote enables these parties to claim that they are more truly representative (at least at an electoral level) of the different social groups within the community than is the Labour Party. While the middle-class Labour vote accounts for only a small proportion (about 15%) of the total Labour vote, the working-class Conservative and Alliance vote accounts for about 50% of their total vote. Thus the vital factor in electoral behaviour in Britain is the extent to which electoral support for the parties does *not* follow rigid class lines.

Various considerations can be advanced to explain these deviations from a strict class-party voting alignment in Britain.[1] The Conservative working-class vote is to some extent a product of feelings of deference among some members of the working class towards the Conservative Party. British society is notoriously more class-conscious in its social and political attitudes than are most comparable nations,[2] and clearly the Conservative Party has benefited from the view held by some

[1] See, for example, J. Bonham, *The Middle Class Vote*, London 1954; Rose, *Studies in British Politics*, Ch. 1; H. J. Eysenck, *The Psychology of Politics*, London 1954.

[2] See Alford, *Party and Society*, Ch. 6; E. A. Nordlinger, *The Working Class Tories*, London 1967; R. T. McKenzie and A. Silver, *Angels in Marble*, London 1968; F. Parkin, 'Working-Class Conservatives', *BJS* 1967, pp. 278–90; S. Taylor, 'Parkin's Theory of Working-Class Conservatism', *SR* 1978, pp. 827–42.

working-class voters that the party's public school–Oxbridge–big business image gives it a monopoly of talent and of political expertise. At the same time, many Conservative policy attitudes are more attractive to members of the working class than are Labour attitudes. On subjects like legal reform and crime generally, the 'firm' line that the Conservative Party tends to adopt can have much more appeal for working-class voters than Labour's 'mild' or 'intellectual' approach. Further, the voting habits of many older working-class voters were formed in the years before the Labour Party emerged as a party of government. In the 1950s the identification of Conservative Governments with the growth of material prosperity provided an additional basis for working-class Conservative support, as did the Conservative record on taxation, prices and incomes (though not employment) in 1983.[1]

Self-assigned social position can be very different from actual social position, and many actual members of the working class regard themselves as belonging to the middle class, and adopt middle-class attitudes (including political attitudes) as a consequence.[2] Also, the borderlines between social classes are inevitably blurred, and those situated on the social or economic borderline between the working class and the middle class often tend to adopt middle-class attitudes (such as voting Conservative) in an attempt to identify themselves with that class rather than with the working class. In this sense, voting Conservative can be seen as a means of gaining social prestige.

Pressures provided by family background, neighbourhood, and place of employment are also significant in this context. Working-class Conservative parents inevitably seek to per-

[1] J. Hudson, 'The Relationship Between Government Popularity and Approval for the Government's Record in the UK', *BJPS* 1985, pp. 165–86; G. Husbands, 'Government Popularity and the Unemployment Issue 1966–83', *Soc.* 1985, pp. 1–18.

[2] J. H. Goldthorpe, 'The Affluent Worker and the Thesis of Embourgeoisement', *Soc.* 1967, pp. 11–32; W. G. Runciman, '"Embourgeoisement", Self-Rated Class and Party Preference', *SR* 1964, pp. 137–54; I. Crewe, 'The Politics of "Affluent" and "Traditional" Workers in Britain', *BJPS* 1973, pp. 29–52.

suade their children to vote Conservative. Surveys have suggested that a member of the working class who lives in a predominantly middle-class area is less likely to vote Labour than a worker who lives in a working-class area. In 1983 almost two-thirds of working-class council house tenants voted Labour compared with only about a third of working-class home owners. Similarly factory-workers have been found to be more likely to vote Labour than workers who do not work in close proximity to large numbers of other workers. Traditionally, workers who belong to a trade union have been much more likely to vote Labour than those who do not, although in 1983 Labour received the votes of only about two-fifths of trade unionists while the Conservatives received almost a third.

Demographic factors in voting behaviour can cut across class alignments, and thus help to explain the source of the working-class Conservative vote. As is shown in more detail below,[1] women are more inclined to vote Conservative than are men, while middle-aged and older electors are more likely to vote Conservative than are the younger voters – and this applies to the working class as well as to voters in general. Again, Anglicans (including working-class Anglicans) have been found to be more likely than Nonconformists to vote Conservative, while electors (and thus workers) in the midlands and south of England, have been found to be more likely to vote Conservative than workers in Wales, Scotland, or northern England. In Northern Ireland, religious divisions override class divisions.

Thus various factors can be advanced to explain the Conservative Party's working-class support, and many of these factors can also be used in reverse to explain the middle-class Labour vote.[2] A member of the middle class whose parents were working class, or who lives in a predominantly working-class area, is more likely to vote Labour than someone with a completely middle-class background. Some members of the middle class, like school teachers or welfare officers, who are

[1] p. 118.

[2] See C. S. Rallings, 'Two Types of Middle-Class Labour Voter?', *BJPS* 1975, pp. 107–12; C. Chamberlain, 'The Growth of Support for the Labour Party in Britain', *BJS* 1973, pp. 474–89.

employed in working-class surroundings and are thus subject daily to working-class influences, are more likely to vote Labour than are members of the middle class who come in contact with no such influence. At the same time, many of the policy attitudes of the Labour Party that antagonise some sections of the working class, prove to be more acceptable to liberal-minded members of the middle class. Also, as is discussed below,[1] although the Labour Party derives its electoral support primarily from the working class, the middle class is in a majority within the Labour Party at a Parliamentary and Ministerial level, where most policies are formulated.

Long-term changes in class voting patterns are difficult to detect. In the early-1960s some electoral studies suggested that with the increase in working-class affluence under Conservative Governments, Labour's electoral support had declined and would continue to do so. In the late-1960s, on the other hand, it was claimed that Labour's greater strength among young voters would give it an increasing electoral advantage over the years. More recent electoral studies have pointed to a general decline in class voting, with a growing number of electors moving away from their 'natural' class party. In the elections of 1945 and 1966 something like two-thirds of manual workers voted Labour and two-thirds of non-manual workers voted Conservative. In 1983, however, less than half of the electorate voted for 'their' class party: only 42% of manual workers voted Labour and 55% of non-manual workers voted Conservative. It is also the case that the social structure of the country has changed considerably in the last twenty years. The proportion of blue-collar workers has declined from about half of the electorate in the mid-1960s to about a third today, while the proportion of people who own their own homes has risen from under half twenty years ago to almost two-thirds today. Thus Labour's 'natural' working-class base has shrunk appreciably.[2]

* * *

[1] p. 138.

[2] See I. Crewe (*et al.*), 'Partisan Dealignment in Britain 1964–74', *BJPS* 1977, pp. 129–90; M. N. Franklin and A. Mughan, 'The Decline of Class Voting in Britain', *APSR* 1978, pp. 523–34; B. E. Cain, 'Dynamic and Static

Traditionally men have been more inclined to vote Labour than have women, and in the elections of the 1950s and 1960s (and in 1974) a majority of men voted Labour while a majority of women voted Conservative. In 1970, 1979 and 1983 the Conservatives were preferred by men and women alike, although the Conservative lead over Labour was somewhat greater among women, and more women voted for the Alliance than voted Labour.[1] It may be that women are more attracted than men towards the Conservative Party for social reasons, or are more conservative by nature than are men. Again, women are not subject to the same extent as men to the pressures of factory working conditions and trade union membership, which are major factors determining Labour's electoral support. Also, women tend to live longer than men, and the older age groups tend to be relatively more conservative than the younger age groups. Surveys suggest that in 1979 and 1983 the Conservatives, with a woman as leader, had an even greater than usual appeal for women voters.

With regard to the relationship between age and voting, Table XIX shows that in 1983 the Conservatives led in each age group but did slightly better among those aged over 35 than among the youngest voters. Labour and the Alliance shared second place in each age group beyond 25, but in the 18 to 24 group Labour did rather better than the Alliance. These differences across age groups were less marked than in past elections. In the 1960s and early 1970s Labour generally had appreciably more support than the Conservatives among the younger voters, while the Conservatives' advantage among the older voters was more pronounced than in 1983. It

[1] See P. Norris, 'The Gender Gap in Britain and America', *Parl. Aff.* 1985, pp. 192–201.

Components of Political Support in Britain', *AJPS* 1978, pp. 849–66; W. L. Miller, 'Social Class and Party Choice in England', *BJPS* 1978, pp. 257–84; P. R. Abramson, 'Generational Change and Continuity in British Partisan Choice', *BJPS* 1976, pp. 364–8; H. D. Clarke and M. C. Stewart, 'Dealignment of Degree', *J of P* 1984, pp. 689–718; M. N. Franklin, 'How the Decline of Class Voting Opened the Way to Radical Change in British Politics', *BJPS* 1984, pp. 483–508; R. Pinkney, 'Dealignment, Realignment or Just Alignment?', *Parl. Aff.* 1986, pp. 47–62.

TABLE XIX

Voting Intention, 1983 General Election: by Sex and Age Group

	All	Men	Women	18–24	25–34	35–54	55+
% of all voters	100	48	52	13	20	32	34
Con.	44	42	46	42	40	44	47
Lab.	28	30	26	33	29	27	27
Alln.	26	25	27	23	29	27	24
Others	2	2	2	2	2	2	2

Source: Butler and Kavanagh, *The British General Election of 1983*, p. 296.

was widely assumed in the 1960s that voting habits acquired early in life were retained for a lifetime, and that the Conservatives' strength among older voters was attributable to influences to which this age group had been subjected in the period of Conservative ascendency and Liberal and Labour failure before 1939. It was also predicted that 'time was on Labour's side' in that younger voters would retain their Labour allegiance as they grew older.[1] The electoral volatility of the 1970s, however, clearly undermined notions of long-term partisan allegiance, and the 1983 voting figures offer no long-term comfort to Labour.

While religion is not a major political issue in Great Britain as a whole, in certain areas religion is a big factor (and in some cases is the biggest factor) in determining voting behaviour.[2] In Wales, the strength of religious nonconformity accounts to some extent for Labour and Liberal success there, with the Labour Party to some extent inheriting the Liberals' nineteenth-century nonconformist traditions. In Ulster particularly, but also in cities like Glasgow and Liverpool, where

[1]See E. T. Zureik, 'Party Images and Partisanship Among Young Englishmen', *BJS* 1974, pp. 179–200; R. E. Dowse and J. A. Hughes, 'Girls, Boys and Politics', *BJS* 1971, pp. 53–67; J. G. Francis and G. Peele, 'Reflections on Generational Analysis', *PS* 1978, pp. 363–74.

[2]See W. L. Miller and G. Raab, 'The Religious Alignment at English Elections Between 1918 and 1970', *PS* 1977, pp. 227–51; W. L. Miller, 'The Religious Alignment in England', *Parl. Aff.* 1974, pp. 258–68.

large sections of the population are of Irish–Catholic descent, religious factors cut across class factors in determining party alignments. Surveys in Glasgow, for example, found that Catholics of all social classes vote predominantly Labour, while working-class Protestants tended to vote Conservative in much greater proportions than in the United Kingdom as a whole.[1] In the rest of Britain, and especially in the south of England, religion is of less electoral significance. Nevertheless, to some extent the relationship between religion and voting reflects the traditional picture of the Conservative Party as the party of the Established Church, and the Labour Party as the party of Nonconformity and of those of no religion.

There are distinct variations in party strength from one part of the country to another.[2] Labour invariably wins a much bigger proportion of votes and seats in Scotland and Wales than in England, and a bigger proportion in the north of England than in the south. In the 1970s regional differences became more pronounced. The 1970 and 1974 elections were characterised by the success of the Nationalists in Scotland and Wales, the advance of the Liberals in some regions of England, and the particularly localised nature of the parties and issues in Northern Ireland. In 1979 the Nationalist and Liberal vote declined, but the swing from Labour to the Conservatives varied dramatically from region to region, with the general trend being for the Conservative performance to improve considerably from north to south.

In 1983 regional variations in party support were even greater than in the 1970s. The Conservatives received over half the votes in the south and midlands of England, but only about 40% in the north of England, a third in Wales and under a quarter in Scotland. The Labour vote showed the reverse north to south pattern. To some extent such regional variations reflect differences in the social structures of the regions, with Scotland and Wales having a larger proportion of working-class electors than the south of England. The

[1] I. Budge and D. W. Urwin, *Scottish Political Behaviour*, London 1966.

[2] See W. L. Miller, *The End of British Politics*, London 1981; R. Waller, *The Atlas of British Politics*, London 1985; D. Balsam (*et al.*), 'The Red and the Green: Patterns of Partisan Choice in Wales', *BJPS* 1983, pp. 299–326.

regional variations in the Labour and Conservative vote in 1983, however, were very much greater than can be accounted for by regional variations in the distribution of social groups. Thus the Conservatives in 1983 received 40% of working-class votes in the south of England, but under a quarter in the north: Labour received only a third of working-class votes in the south but 60% in the north. It can be seen in Table XX how much weaker was Labour's working class support in each region in 1983 compared with 1964, and how much greater was the difference between Labour's performance in its best and worst regions in 1983 compared with 1964.

Just as the Alliance's 1983 vote was drawn almost equally from each sex, age group and social group, so the regional variations in its support were slight. The Alliance did rather better in the south of England than in the other parts of the country, but the over-riding characteristic was the evenness of the spread. The highly disproportional relationship between the Alliance's votes and seats was a direct consequence of this regionally-even distribution of its support. Its 25% of the poll was not sufficiently concentrated to enable it to capture any more than 4% of the seats. It should be noted, however, that the established electoral system can also greatly over-represent a party that is characterised by the even distribution of its support – provided that the level of its support is sufficiently high. In a future three-party contest, with (say) 40% of the vote distributed evenly throughout the regions, the Alliance could well win the vast majority of seats under the

TABLE XX

Size of Working Class Labour Vote by Region: 1964 and 1983 General Elections

	South	Midlands	North	Scotland
1964	62	70	72	83
1983	34	39	60	64
Change	−28	−31	−12	−19

Source: Based on figures quoted in Heath (*et al.*), *How Britain Votes*, p. 86.

established electoral system, and thus be as grossly over-represented as it was under-represented in 1983.

Floating Voters and Non-Voters

General elections can be won and lost by the transfer of allegiance of a comparatively limited number of 'floating' voters.[1] The size of the floating vote is much bigger than is suggested by the parties' overall share of the vote, as some electors change their voting habits against the general tide, and thus reduce the size of the overall swing. In the 1960s, during a period of comparatively stable party loyalties, it was authoritatively argued that as many as a quarter of the electorate change their allegiance from one general election to another.[2] In the 1970s and in 1983 the number of floating voters increased, as considerable inroads were made into traditional Labour and Conservative support by the Liberals (and then the Alliance), the Nationalists and others. In 1983 Labour managed to retain only about two-thirds of its 1979 voters, while the Conservatives and the Alliance retained about three-quarters of their 1979 support. Even so, of the Alliance voters in 1983 only about two-fifths had voted Liberal in 1979: about a quarter had voted Labour, a fifth had voted Conservative, and another fifth had voted for other parties or had not voted at all.

In addition to the people who do change their party allegiance from one general election to another, there are many others who may well change their loyalties at a by-election or a local government election, and who may tell public opinion pollsters that they intend to change their loyalties at a general election, but who return to their original voting habits when polling day arrives. Death and other factors produce a change in the electoral register of about

[1] See R. S. Milne and H. C. Mackenzie, 'The Floating Vote', *PS* 1955, pp. 65–8; W. H. Morris Jones, 'In Defence of Apathy: Some Doubts on the Duty to Vote', *PS* 1954, pp. 25–37; R. J. Benewick (*et al.*), 'The Floating Voter and the Liberal View of Representation', *PS* 1969, pp. 177–95; D. Denver and G. Hands, 'Marginality and Turnout in General Elections in the 1970s', *BJPS* 1985, pp. 381–7.

[2] See Blondel, *Voters, Parties and Leaders*, p. 71.

one-sixth every ten years, so that the personnel of the Conservative vote in 1983 was substantially different from the personnel of the 1970 Conservative vote. Thus behind the stability and consistency of British voting behaviour, it is necessary to recognise the existence of the floating voters, the 'almost floaters', and the presence of new voters on the electoral register each year.

Non-voters are often closely linked with the floating voters. In the 1983 election over a quarter of the electorate did not vote, and at general elections since 1945 the proportion of non-voters has ranged from 16% to 28%. Some abstentions can be accounted for by the limitations of the electoral register, which is inevitably out of date as soon as it is compiled, and by the new voters who are included on the register but who cannot vote if the election is held before October 2nd. These administrative factors can account for some 5% to 10% of the non-voters. Others can perhaps be accounted for by minor party supporters who prefer to abstain rather than vote for another party's candidate in constituencies which their party does not contest.

Some uncommitted electors abstain merely because they cannot decide whom to support. Others abstain because they are politically disillusioned, either permanently, like those who reject the whole political system, or temporarily, like some Conservatives in 1974 and some Labour supporters in 1983, who felt that on that particular occasion their party did not deserve their vote. Other abstentions can be accounted for by people who cannot be bothered to vote, perhaps because of bad weather on polling day, or are prevented from voting by ill health or other accidental factors (although postal and proxy voting reduces the effect of this). Undoubtedly some people abstain because they feel that their vote is not needed as the election result is certain, either nationally or in their constituency. In more recent elections the forecasts of the opinion polls have probably added to this, especially in elections like 1983 when a clear Conservative victory seemed likely during the campaign. Again, in 1970 the Conservatives probably benefited from an assumption among some Labour supporters that their party could win without their support. A low turnout in safe constituencies can be partly a result of less activity on the part of party election machines in getting supporters to the poll. Finally, it may be noted that surveys have revealed that in general, abstentions are more numerous among women than among men, more numerous among the youngest age groups than among the middle-aged, more numerous among non-churchgoers than among churchgoers, more numerous among the working class than the middle class, and more numerous among Labour supporters than among Conservatives.

Party Members and Activists[1]

Much less information is available about party members and activists than about voters. In addition, such studies as have been made of the backgrounds and opinions of members and activists, have revealed that considerable variations exist in party composition from one area to another. A Conservative constituency party in a northern industrial town, for example, can be very different in social composition and attitudes from a Conservative constituency party in northern Scotland or in Sussex. From the limited amount of information that is available, it is thus difficult to make assumptions that could apply to the whole country, although some general conclusions can be drawn.

Although the Labour and Conservative parties are among the biggest mass parties in the western world, the proportion of active party members is small, and it has been claimed that the proportion of active party members today is no greater than it was before 1867.[2] Both parties have a large number of passive members. This is especially true of the Labour Party, with its big but largely inactive affiliated trade union membership. Indeed, of the 6 million trade unionists affiliated to the Labour Party, less than two-thirds even voted Labour in 1983. Among the 250,000 individual Labour Party members the *proportion* of active members is higher than among the

[1] See D. R. Berry, *The Sociology of Grass Roots Politics*, London 1970; I. Budge (*et al.*), *Political Stratification and Democracy*, London 1972.

[2] Rose, *Politics in England*, p. 93. See also C. Martin and D. Martin, 'The Decline of Labour Party Membership', *PQ* 1977, pp. 459–71.

1,500,000 Conservative Party members, although the Conservatives still remain with the larger absolute number of activists.[1]

The distinction between the individual constituency party membership of the Labour Party and the affiliated trade union membership, manifests itself in a great number of ways within the party. The trade union membership is large but mainly passive, the individual membership is small but more active. Although trade unionists can 'contract out' of any affiliation with the Labour Party, many who have no real Labour Party sympathies do not bother to contract out, so that among the affiliated members there are many who are apathetic, and some who are hostile. The trade union membership is predominantly working class, while the individual membership contains a proportion of the middle class. To a large extent the trade union membership provides the party finances, while the individual membership provides the intellectual leadership. The individual members are often thought of as being more ideological in their political attitudes than the trade union members. Thus the original fusion of the unions and the socialist societies to form the Labour Party in 1900 is still reflected today in the composition of local Labour Parties.

It is sometimes assumed that the political attitudes of party members, and of party activists in particular, will tend to be more extreme than the attitudes of the mass of the party voters who are not sufficiently interested to join a party. Studies of the political attitudes of party members, however, tend not to confirm this view. In Glossop, Derbyshire, it was found that Labour members tended to be slightly more 'left wing' than Labour voters, in that the party membership contained a higher proportion of supporters of CND and public ownership than was found among Labour voters, but extreme views were not dominant.[2] Among Conservative members there was no evidence that they were markedly more 'right wing' than Conservative voters. In Newcastle-under-Lyme a survey

[1] See P. Whiteley, 'Who Are the Labour Activists?', *PQ* 1981, pp. 160–70.

[2] A. H. Birch, *Small Town Politics*, London 1959, p. 82. See also S. Welch and D. T. Studlar, 'The Policy Options of British Political Activists', *PS* 1983, pp. 604–19.

found that the Conservative members tended to be basically 'moderate' in their attitudes, with Labour Party members being only slightly less so, despite being served by a left-wing Labour MP.[1] Studies of the type of resolution proposed by constituency party leaders at party conferences (which can perhaps be taken as indicative of the attitudes of party activists), also indicate that the constituency party leaders are not as extreme in their political attitudes as is often thought.[2]

Studies of the social structure of party membership have revealed that with the Labour Party the members tend to be drawn from the various social classes in much the same proportion as are Labour voters, with the working class being predominant and with the middle class being represented only by a minority. In Glossop, for example, it was found that industrial workers made up 77% of Labour voters and 76% of Labour Party members, while business proprietors and professional or managerial workers accounted for 5% of Labour voters and 7% of Labour Party members. Similarly, in Newcastle-under-Lyme, it was found that 77% of Labour Party members were manual workers, 13% were clerical workers, and only 10% were business proprietors or professional or managerial workers.

With the Conservative Party, on the other hand, businessmen, professional men and managers tend to make up a much bigger proportion of party members than of Conservative voters. In Glossop they accounted for only a quarter of Conservative voters, but almost half of Conservative Party members. White collar workers and industrial workers, on the other hand, made up almost three-quarters of Conservative voters in Glossop, but they were only half of Conservative members. Thus these surveys suggest that the electoral support that the Conservative Party has among the working class does not extend to the same extent to membership of the

[1] F. Bealey, J. Blondel, and W. P. McCann, *Constituency Politics*, London 1965, p. 274.

[2] R. Rose, 'The Policy Ideas of English Party Activists', *ASPR* 1962, pp. 360–71; K. Hindell and P. Williams, 'Scarborough and Blackpool: Analysis of some Votes at the Labour Party Conferences of 1960 and 1961', *PQ* 1962, pp. 306–20; S. Welch and D. T. Studlar, 'The Policy Options of British Political Activists', *PS* 1983, pp. 604–19.

party, and at a membership level the Conservative Party is not as representative of the various social groups of the community as it is at an electoral level.

Many of the other differences of background that have been noted between Labour and Conservative voters are mirrored among party members. Just as Labour's voting strength is greater among men than among women, so it was found at Newcastle-under-Lyme that men made up 54% of Labour Party members, compared with 45% of Conservative members. In both parties, however, the party members tend to be drawn mainly from the older age group, and despite the extent of Labour's support among young voters, all the surveys suggest that the Labour Party does not have any markedly greater number of young members than does the Conservative Party. In some ways this perhaps reflects Labour's longstanding failure to develop a youth movement as successful as the Young Conservatives.[1]

Among the active Conservative Party officers, the middle class tends to be even more strongly represented than among the mass of Conservative members. In Glossop, the proportion of businessmen, professional men and managers was found to be over three-quarters of Conservative activists, compared with half party members and a quarter of Conservative voters. Again, in Greenwich the middle class accounted for three-quarters of Conservative party members but 90% of party officers. In these constituencies, then, working-class deference towards the Conservative Party extended to the abdication of almost all control over the party's local affairs to the middle class. It was also found in Greenwich that although 57% of Conservative Party members were women, only 25% of the party officers were women.

The similarity between the social composition of Labour voters and Labour Party members is not repeated in the case of Labour Party activists, and the middle class tends to be better represented among Labour leaders than among the rank and file of Labour Party members. Although industrial

[1] P. Abrams and A. Little, 'The Young Activist in British Politics', *BJS* 1965, pp. 315–32; Z. Layton-Henry, 'Labour's Militant Youth', *PQ* 1974, pp. 418–25.

workers accounted for three-quarters of Labour voters and party members in Glossop, they accounted for only one-third of the party leaders. White collar workers in Glossop were only one-sixth of Labour voters and members, but they accounted for a third of the activists. Professional and managerial workers made up another third of the activists, although they were less than one-tenth of Labour voters and members. Similar trends were found at Greenwich, although the workers made up a bigger proportion (almost half) of the activists.

Thus the social composition of both parties changes considerably from the electoral level to the local leadership level. In both parties the middle class forms a much bigger proportion of the local leaders than of the electors, and this tendency for the middle class to increase towards the top of the leadership hierarchy is continued among area and regional leaders. Having acknowledged this, however, the difference between the social composition of the two parties remains pronounced at the local leadership level. The vast majority of the Conservative middle-class activists are businessmen, while the Labour middle-class element consists primarily of professional men and managers. In particular, teachers and journalists tend to form a large proportion of Labour's local leaders, as they do of Labour MPs, and the Labour Party's intelligentsia is thus very different in composition from the middle-class leadership of the Conservative Party.

The extent of middle-class representation among the Labour Party's local leadership perhaps gives an overall impression of the mass membership of the Labour Party being led by the party's intellectuals. It must be emphasised, however, that in examining the social structure of the CLPs, only one part of the Labour Party structure is being dealt with. Although the trade unions play an important part in constituency party activities, they also remain as a separate part of the Labour Party structure at all levels of the party organisation. The unions, which are overwhelmingly working class at a leadership level as well as a membership level, remain as a counterbalance to the middle-class members and activists in the constituency parties.

It might perhaps be expected that in socio-economic respects the background of Liberal Party and SDP members would be closer to that of Conservative Party members than of Labour Party members. Certainly in Glossop it was found that the occupational background of Liberal Party members was predominantly middle class, and the proportion of industrial workers fell from two-thirds of Liberal voters, to a third of party members and just 6% of party leaders. Compared with Conservative activists, however, there was among Liberal activists a bigger proportion of professional, managerial, and white collar workers (61% to 30%), and a smaller proportion of businessmen (33% to 62%). At the same time, in Newcastle-under-Lyme men formed an even bigger proportion of Liberal members than of Labour members, and the Liberal Party had an even bigger proportion of Nonconformist members than did the Labour Party. Also, in Newcastle-under-Lyme the Liberals were the 'youngest' party, having a smaller proportion of members aged over 60 and a larger proportion aged under 30, than either of the other parties.

The SDP membership is predominantly male, middle class and suburban. A survey of members soon after the party's formation showed that some two-thirds were men, over four-fifths were in middle-class occupations (mainly in the public sector), and over half lived in residential suburbs rather than the inner cities or rural areas.[1] Over half were aged between 25 and 45, and only a third had previously belonged to another political party.

Parliamentary Candidates and MPs

Considerably more information is available regarding the relatively small number of party members who become Parliamentary candidates, than about the party membership as a whole. Table XXI shows that in June 1983, as in most recent general elections, almost two-thirds of Conservative candidates had attended public schools. About the same proportion had attended University, most of them Oxford or Cambridge. It is the predominance of public school and Oxbridge pro-

[1] See *The Times*, September 8th 1983. See also T. Barton and H. Daring, 'The Social and Attitudinal Profile of Social Democratic Party Activists', *PS* 1986, pp. 296–305.

TABLE XXI

Educational and Occupational Profile of Parliamentary Candidates, 1983 Election

	Con. (%)	Lab. (%)	Alln. (%)
Public School	59	12	29
University	66	57	72
Professions	44	49	56
Business	36	9	21
Misc. white collar	18	21	21
Workers	2	21	2
N	633	633	633

Source: Butler and Kavanagh, 1983, pp. 235–7.

ducts that is the most characteristic social feature of Conservative candidates (and Conservative MPs and Ministers). In contrast, in 1983, as in most recent elections, only about an eighth of Labour candidates were from public schools. Also, although well over half of Labour candidates were graduates, the vast majority of these were from Universities other than Oxford or Cambridge. This is clearly very different from the predominantly public school and Oxbridge pattern of Conservative candidates. At the same time it is also very different from the educational pattern of the mass of the population, of whom only about 5% attend public schools, and under 10% attend University.

Similar differences between the parties emerge with regard to the occupational background of the candidates. In making comparisons between occupational backgrounds, however, some allowance has to be made for the fact that the divisions into occupational groups must be somewhat arbitrary. A candidate may have had more than one occupation, and there is, for example, frequently a big overlap between business and the professions, and in particular between big business and the legal profession. In this context, however, it is only the first occupation that is referred to. On this basis, four-fifths of Conservative candidates in 1983 were drawn from business or the professions, while only about 2% were workers. Of Labour candidates on the other hand, about a fifth were workers, and almost two-thirds were from the professions or business. In so far as information is available regarding the religious convictions of the candidates, about a quarter of Labour candidates belong to 'Nonconformist' religious groups (in the broadest sense[1]), as compared with only an eighth of Conservative candidates. This mirrors the general impression gained at an electoral and party membership level of the links between religion and voting patterns, and between religion and party membership.

In educational and occupational terms, Alliance candidates in 1983 tended to fall between the extremes of the two main parties. The Alliance had more public school products than Labour, and more graduates than either party. As with the Conservatives, the Alliance candidates had almost exclusively middle-class occupations, though rather more were from the professions, and fewer were from the business world, than was the case with the Conservatives.

As might be expected, many of the patterns that apply to the social backgrounds of the candidates of the respective parties are repeated in the case of the MPs. Thus the majority of the 397 Conservative MPs elected in 1983 had a public school and University education. About an eighth attended Eton and another half attended other public schools. Just under half of Conservative MPs had been to Oxford or Cambridge Universities, and a further quarter had attended other Universities. Of Labour MPs, on the other hand, 6% had only an elementary school education, half attended grammar or secondary schools, and less than an eighth attended public schools. Under a fifth of Labour MPs had been to Oxford or Cambridge Universities, and a third to other Universities.

Similarly, as is shown in Table XXII, the vast majority of Conservative MPs elected in 1983 had middle-class or upper-class occupational backgrounds. A third were in business before entering Parliament, and over a fifth were barristers or

[1] That is, Jews, Roman Catholics, and Quakers as well as Methodists and other Protestant Nonconformist groups.

TABLE XXII

The House of Commons, 1983 Parliament

	Labour	Conservative	Alliance
Professions			
Barrister/Solicitor	17	82	5
Doctor/Dentist	2	2	1
Architect/Surveyor/Engineer	1	13	2
Chartered secretary/Accountant	3	19	1
Civil servant/Local government	10	16	1
Armed services	—	18	1
University and adult educ. teachers	25	6	1
School teachers	27	14	2
Other consultants/Research	2	7	—
Total	87	177	14
Percentage	42	45	61
Business			
Company director/executive	5	100	—
Commerce/Insurance	4	31	—
Management/Clerical	8	4	1
Small business	2	7	—
Total	19	142	1
Percentage	9	36	4
Miscellaneous			
Miscellaneous white collar	14	6	1
Politicians/Political organisers	7	12	1
Publisher/Journalist	9	31	5
Farmer	1	19	1
Housewife/Private means	2	6	—
Total	33	74	8
Percentage	16	19	35
Workers			
Miner	20	—	—
Skilled worker	35	4	—
Semi/Unskilled worker	15	—	—
Total	70	4	—
Percentage	33	1	—
Grand Total	209	397	23

Source: Based on a table in Butler and Kavanagh, 1983, pp. 235–7.

solicitors. There were also a large number of farmers, publishers and journalists, while chartered secretaries, accountants, other professional consultants and members of the armed forces accounted for about 15% of the total. Only four of the 397 had manual occupations. In marked contrast, a third of Labour MPs elected in 1983 were manual workers, and about a quarter were teachers or lecturers. At the same time, a large number of barristers, solicitors, professional consultants, journalists and publishers are to be found among Labour MPs, although not quite in the same proportion as among the Conservatives.

Two more general contrasts between the two parties' social structures may be noted. First, greater differences are to be found between the educational and occupational background of Labour and Conservative MPs than of their candidates. Secondly, there are many more differences between the various elements that make up the PLP, than between the members of the Conservative Parliamentary Party, who constitute a much more homogeneous social unit. With the Conservative Party the proportion of those with an 'exclusive' background (public school, Oxbridge, and the professions or business) was greater among the MPs than among the mass of the candidates. With the Labour Party, on the other hand, the proportion of those with a University education and a middle-class occupation was not quite as high among MPs as it was among the candidates. This is largely because trade union sponsorship of candidates means that a large proportion of working-class candidates with trade union connections acquire safe Labour seats, while a correspondingly large proportion of middle-class Labour candidates are left to contest the hopeless seats. The 'failure rate' among Labour's working-class candidates is thus much lower than among the party's middle-class candidates. This factor has been reduced somewhat, in that in the last ten years the unions have shown more willingness to sponsor candidates who have no actual union connections, although workers continue to account for the vast proportion of union sponsorships.

Despite its several diverse social elements, however, the PLP is still very far from being a mirror of society. The middle class is represented in much bigger proportions among

Labour MPs than among Labour Party members or voters, or in society as a whole. It may also be noted that the middle-class membership of the PLP is increasing, and that the educational and occupational background of the two parties' MPs are coming a little closer together. It can be seen from Table XXIII that in the post-war period there has been a marked increase in the proportion of graduates and of teachers and lecturers among Labour MPs. The proportion of Labour MPs with only an elementary or secondary education has declined, as has the proportion of former manual workers (though with a slight reversal of the trend in 1979 and 1983). Among Conservative MPs the proportion from public schools has declined, with the proportion of Old Etonians falling from a quarter in 1945 to an eighth in 1983. The proportion of Conservative graduates has increased slightly, with Universities other than Oxbridge now accounting for a third of them. Indeed, of the Conservative MPs elected for the first time in 1983, less than half had attended public schools, only a third had attended Oxbridge and a larger number had attended 'other' Universities. While the precise balance between the business world and the professions has varied, there has been no increase at all in the minute proportion of Conservative MPs with working-class occupations. There has been no increase in the small number of women MPs in either party.

Variations occur from one election to another partly because a large proportion of the 'old guard' of both parties (Labour's trade unionists and the Conservatives' public school elite) represent safe seats, and thus tend to be re-elected no matter how the party's fortunes may fluctuate from election to election. On the other hand, a big proportion of the 'new wave' of MPs of both parties are often in marginal seats, and thus lose their seats if the party suffers a heavy defeat – as did Labour in 1983 and the Conservatives in 1966. Despite this, however, an overall picture can still be obtained, and the trends that have been noted as emerging in the post-war period are even more pronounced if comparisons are made with pre-war MPs.[1]

[1] J. F. S. Ross, *Parliamentary Representation*, London 1948, and *Elections and Electors*, London 1955, for a detailed examination of the backgrounds of pre-war MPs.

TABLE XXIII

Changing Social Structure of the Parties in Parliament 1945–83

	1945	1950	1951	1955	1959	1964	1966	1970	Feb. 1974	Oct. 1974	1979	1983
	(in percentages)											
Conservatives												
Eton	27	27	24	23	19	22	22	19	18	17	15	12
All Public Schools	83	83	70	80	76	78	79	74	75	75	73	64
Oxbridge	53	54	54	54	51	54	57	51	56	55	49	46
All Universities	65	65	65	65	61	64	67	64	67	67	68	72
Women MPs (N)	1	6	6	10	12	11	7	15	9	7	8	13
Labour												
Public Schools	19	22	23	24	25	24	23	19	16	16	17	13
All Universities	34	38	39	38	40	44	49	51	53	56	57	54
Manual Workers	28	28	26	25	21	18	17	13	12	12	20	15
Teachers and Lecturers	12	14	15	14	15	17	20	21	26	28	24	26
Women MPs (N)	21	14	11	14	13	18	19	10	13	18	11	10

Source: Based on data in C. Mellors, *The British MP*, London 1978; M. Burch and M. Moran, 'The Changing British Political Elite 1945–1983', *Parl. Aff.* 1985, pp. 1–15.

It is easy to exaggerate the extent to which the social composition of the two main parties in Parliament is changing. There has been some convergence, but there remain major contrasts. Conservative MPs are now less predominantly public school and Oxbridge products than in the 1950s, but they remain essentially middle class in their occupational characteristics. The PLP in the 1980s is much more of a 'white collar' body than thirty years ago, but there is still a significant proportion of former manual workers in the ranks of Labour MPs. What is more, many of the Labour MPs with a University education and middle-class occupations came originally from working class homes.

Other differences in the backgrounds of the MPs of the two parties may also be noted. The median age for Labour MPs elected in 1983 was 51 compared with 47 for the Conservatives: almost a fifth of Labour MPs were aged over 60 compared with a tenth of Conservative MPs. The Conservative Parliamentary Party thus tends to be 'younger' than the PLP, and this coincides with a general tendency for middle-class parties to be younger in composition than are working-class parties. In Britain this may be attributable in part to the fact that many Labour MPs, particularly the trade unionists, often had to serve a long apprenticeship in the Labour Movement before having their services rewarded with a seat in Parliament. In the Conservative Party, on the other hand, youth has been less of a barrier to a Parliamentary candidature than have social and educational factors. It may be noted that between 1951 and 1964 there was no marked change in the median age of the MPs of the two parties, but in 1966 there was a big influx of Labour MPs aged under 40, and this brought the median age for Labour MPs a little closer to that of the Conservatives. Almost two-thirds of MPs elected in 1983, however, were aged between 40 and 60, thus emphasising that service in Parliament is very much a middle-aged occupation. It is thus misleading to think of Parliamentary service as a permanent career. While some MPs, particularly Labour MPs, may devote themselves almost completely to Parliamentary service over a period of many years, many others, and Conservative MPs in particular, tend to retain their professional or business contacts, and return to their former careers (or start a new career) after some years in Parliament.

In 1983, for only the second time since 1945, there were more women among Conservative MPs (thirteen) than among Labour MPs (ten). All the Alliance, SNP, Plaid Cymru and Irish MPs were men. There has been a big increase in the number of women contesting elections. In the elections of 1964–74 about 5% of the candidates were women, but the proportion was 9% in 1979 and 11% in 1983. Women have been no more successful in getting elected, however, and the total of twenty-three in 1983 is no better than average for the post-war period.[1]

The number of Alliance and Nationalist MPs in 1983 was too small to justify any detailed comparisons with the two main parties in terms of social background. Nevertheless it may be noted that of the twenty-three Alliance MPs, fifteen were graduates (seven of them from Oxbridge), all had middle-class occupational backgrounds, and sixteen were aged under 50. The Nationalist MPs were similarly middle-aged and middle class in occupational background. The Alliance and Nationalists tended, therefore, to come closer to the pattern of Conservative MPs than of Labour MPs, and in this they followed much the same pattern as Liberal MPs elected for each Parliament since 1951.

It can be seen that the Conservative Party in Parliament is a remarkably homogeneous body, while Labour MPs are drawn from a variety of social backgrounds. It is possible to discern three broad groups within the PLP. One group is made up of those MPs who had only an elementary or secondary school education, and who were manual workers before entering Parliament. A second group consists of the journalists, teachers, and various other white collar workers, most of whom were educated at grammar schools and provincial universities. In the main, they are sponsored by the constituency parties or the Cooperative Party, rather than the unions, and they tend to be the youngest and shortest serving

[1] See J. Rasmussen, 'Female Political Career Patterns and Leadership Disabilities in Britain', *Polity* 1980–1, pp. 600–20; J. Rasmussen, 'The Electoral Costs of Being a Woman in the 1979 British General Election', *CP* 1982–3, pp. 461–75.

of Labour MPs. A third group is made up of those Labour MPs who are drawn from the older professions like the law and medicine, who often had a public school and Oxbridge education, and who also tend to be sponsored by the constituency parties. These groupings are clearly not watertight compartments, and some Labour MPs do not fit precisely into any one group, but in general terms they do give a broad picture of the social structure of the PLP.

Ministers

Some indication of the social background of Labour and Conservative Ministers can be obtained by comparing the composition of the last Labour Cabinet at the time of the May 1979 election, with the latest Conservative Cabinet.[1] This is done in Table XXIV, and it can be seen that the proportion of public school and Oxbridge products tends to be even greater among Conservative Cabinet Ministers than among the mass of Conservative MPs. Even though the Prime Minister herself (like her predecessor as Conservative party leader) was a grammar school product, fifteen of the twenty-two members of her Cabinet in October 1986 were from public schools. Four had attended Eton – a much smaller proportion than in Douglas-Home's Cabinet twenty years earlier, when almost half were Old Etonians. Eight were Cambridge graduates, and another seven were from Oxford.

Thus the proportion of Oxbridge products increases towards the top of the Conservative Party hierarchy, rising from just over a third of Conservative candidates, to around half of Conservative MPs, and three-quarters of Cabinet Ministers. Similarly, the top professional and business elements predominate among Conservative Ministers to an even greater extent than among Conservative MPs. Over a third of the Thatcher Cabinet in 1986 had backgrounds in business, another quarter were lawyers and the rest had farming,

[1]For earlier Labour Governments see J. Bonnor, 'The Four Labour Cabinets', *SR* 1958, pp. 37–47. See also W. W. Lammers and J. L. Nyomarkay, 'Socialist Elites and Technological Societies', *Polity* 1984–5, pp. 40–65.

TABLE XXIV

Social Structure of the Callaghan (May 1979) and Thatcher (Oct. 1986) Cabinets

	Age (Years and months)	School	University	Occupation
Callaghan Cabinet				
Callaghan	67.2	Secondary	None	Civil Servant
Foot	65.10	Grammar	Oxford	Journalist
Lord Elwyn-Jones	69.6	Grammar	Wales & Cambridge	Barrister
Healey	61.8	Grammar	Oxford	Party Officer
Rees	58.5	Grammar	London	Lecturer
Owen	40.10	Bradfield	Cambridge	Doctor
Mrs Williams	48.9	St Paul's	Oxford	Economist
Benn	54.2	Westminster	Oxford	Journalist
Varley	46.8	Secondary	None	Miner
Shore	55.0	Grammar	Cambridge	Economist
Mason	55.0	Elementary	None	Miner
Millan	51.7	Grammar	None	Accountant
Morris	48.6	Grammar	Wales & Cambridge	Barrister
Mulley	60.10	Grammar	Oxford	Barrister
Booth	51.0	Secondary	None	Engineer
Ennals	56.9	Grammar	None	UN officer
Lord Peart	65.0	Grammar	Durham	Teacher
Barnett	55.10	Grammar	None	Accountant
Silkin	56.2	Dulwich	Wales & Cambridge	Solicitor
Hattersley	46.5	Grammar	Hull	Civil Servant
Rodgers	50.8	Grammar	Oxford	Economist
Orme	66.0	Elementary	None	Engineer
Smith	40.8	Grammar	Glasgow	Advocate
Lever	65.4	Grammar	Manchester	Barrister
Thatcher Cabinet				
Thatcher	61.0	Grammar	Oxford	Barrister
Lord Hailsham	79.0	Eton	Oxford	Barrister
Howe	59.9	Winchester	Cambridge	Barrister
Lord Whitelaw	68.4	Winchester	Cambridge	Army
Moore	48.11	Grammar	LSE	Business
Younger	55.1	Winchester	Oxford	Business
Edwards	52.8	Westminster	Cambridge	Business
Biffen	55.11	Grammar	Cambridge	Economist
Walker	54.7	Latymer Upper	None	Business
Rifkind	40.4	George Watson's	Edinburgh	Advocate
Lawson	54.7	Westminster	Oxford	Journalist
Hurd	56.7	Eton	Cambridge	Civil Servant

TABLE XXIV (*continued*)

	Age (Years and months)	School	University	Occupation
Fowler	48.8	Grammar	Cambridge	Journalist
Tebbit	55.7	Grammar	None	Airline pilot
King	53.4	Rugby	Cambridge	Business
Jopling	55.9	Cheltenham	Durham	Farmer
Ridley	57.8	Eton	Oxford	Business
Lord Young	54.8	Grammar	London	Business
Baker	52.0	St. Pauls	Oxford	Business
Clarke	46.4	Grammar	Cambridge	Barrister
McGregor	49.8	Merchiston	St. Andrews & London	Journalist
Channon	51.0	Eton	Oxford	Business

Source: Biographies of MPs in *Dod's Parliamentary Companion*, 1986.

military or professional backgrounds. It must be emphasised, however, that the distinction between the professions and business can be misleading, as many professional men also have close and active connections with the business world.

Of the Callaghan Cabinet in May 1979, three-quarters had attended grammar schools, and only four had attended public schools. Three-quarters were graduates, compared with just over half of the PLP and just under half of Labour candidates. Again, most of the Cabinet's graduates were from Oxbridge, whereas among Labour candidates and MPs as a whole, a big majority were from Universities other than Oxbridge. Nevertheless, the Callaghan Cabinet did contain a larger number of graduates from Universities other than Oxbridge than did the Thatcher Cabinet.

These educational patterns are reflected in the fact that the proportion of manual workers tends to be smaller among Labour Ministers than among the PLP as a whole, while the proportion of middle-class professional and white collar workers tends to be greater. Half of the Labour Cabinet Ministers in 1979 had been journalists, teachers or lawyers before entering Parliament, and most of the others had held professional posts. Only Roy Mason, Albert Booth, Stanley Orme and Eric Varley had been 'workers'.

The age differences that were noted as existing between Labour and Conservative MPs are not mirrored in the age differences between the Ministers of the two parties. The median age for Labour Cabinet Ministers in May 1979 was fifty-five and a half while the Conservative figure in October 1986 was fifty-six. Thus, as might be expected, in both parties the younger MPs tend to be under-represented among the Ministers. Finally, it may be noted that each Cabinet contained only one woman, although in the Conservative case she held the all-important post.

Thus the diverse social structure of the PLP, and the relatively homogeneous social structure of the Conservative Parliamentary Party are reflected at Ministerial level. Even though the differences may not be as marked among Ministers as among MPs, and even though in some respects the social structures of the parties seem to be coming rather closer together, clear differences still remain.

Studies of the social composition of the Cabinet over the longer term show that while recent Conservative Cabinets are less aristocratic, and more middle class, than before 1955, they are no more proletarian than they have ever been.[1] Indeed, Conservative Cabinets in the 1955–84 period had a larger proportion of public school and Oxbridge products than did Conservative Cabinets of 1916–55. It remains to be seen whether those members of the 1983 intake of Conservative MPs who do not have a public school and Oxbridge background will work their way into the party hierarchy in the 1990s, or whether they will find themelves excluded in favour of colleagues with more traditional backgrounds. Certainly, among Mrs Thatcher's junior Ministers in 1986 about a quarter were Old Etonians, and no doubt a good proportion of these will find their way into Conservative Cabinets of the future.

Party and Society

On the basis of this survey of the composition of the parties inside and outside Parliament, their social structure can be

[1]See M. Burch and M. Moran, 'The Changing British Political Elite 1945–1983', *Parl. Aff.* 1985, pp. 1–15.

likened to a pyramid built in six steps, with the voters, party members, party activists, Parliamentary candidates, MPs, and Ministers representing the six steps. In both parties the middle class is much more in evidence at the top of the pyramid than at the bottom, and it constitutes a clear majority in the top levels of both parties. Apart from this general similarity, however, the social pyramids of the two parties are very different. The Conservative structure has a broad social base, in that in addition to the large middle-class Conservative vote the Conservative Party has a sizeable electoral following among the working class. The working class is much less in evidence among Conservative Party members, however, and is even less in evidence among the local activists. The upper- and upper-middle-class element within the Conservative Party becomes increasingly preponderant at the Parliamentary and Ministerial level, until at the top of the structure Conservative Cabinet Ministers tend to be drawn predominantly from the most exclusive sections of society.

The Labour structure is considerably more complicated. It has a narrower social base than the Conservative Party, in that the Labour Party's electoral support is predominantly working class, with the middle class forming only a small part of the Labour vote. The same thing applies to party membership, but among Labour's local activists the middle-class element is much more in evidence, and constitutes a big majority among Labour's Parliamentary candidates. At a Parliamentary level, however, the trend in favour of the middle class is reversed, and the middle class forms a smaller proportion of Labour MPs than of Labour candidates. The pattern is further complicated at a Ministerial level, in that the middle-class element again increases towards the top of the Ministerial hierarchy. At the same time, the PLP has included over the years a growing element drawn neither from the upper middle class, nor from the trade unions, while the Conservative Party has also included a small proportion of MPs whose backgrounds were not exclusively upper middle class.

No matter how different the social structures of the parties may be, in combination they are still very far from being an educational, occupational or social reflection of the country as a whole. MPs are preponderantly male, middle-aged and middle class, and are better educated than the population as a whole (at least as measured by the number of years of formal education). Despite the changes that have taken place in the ethnic composition of the United Kingdom, the House of Commons (though not the House of Lords) remains exclusively 'white'. Party members and activists are rather more socially representative of the community than are the Parliamentary leaders, but even here the middle class, the middle-aged, the better-educated and males are over-represented. At the electoral level, of course, the parties in combination reflect broadly the electorate as a whole. Even here, however, the non-voters tend to come disproportionately from the youngest, oldest and most disadvantaged sections of society; the electoral system distorts the Parliamentary representation of the parties; and the fact that each party draws its support disproportionately from different sections of society means that at any one time particular groups and regions will be under-represented on the Government side of the House.

It is easier to describe this situation than to assess its consequences. While it is a basic principle of social psychology that social origins affect attitudes and behaviour, the precise effect is not predictable in individual cases. There is certainly no guarantee that a particular educational and occupational background will produce standard political attitudes. In the 1930s the public schools and Oxbridge produced Soviet spies as well as Conservative, Labour and Liberal party leaders. Today, some of Labour's most militant members are products of the more exclusive public schools, while many of the Conservative Party's staunchest supporters are found among the working class. Nevertheless, despite the difficulty of making firm predictions about political behaviour on the basis of social backgrounds, it can at least be questioned whether the social homogeneity of the Conservative Party in Parliament helps to foster ideological cohesiveness, while the more heterogeneous social structure of the PLP exacerbates Labour's ideological conflicts. Some studies have established correlations between the social groups of the PLP and attitudes to party policy.[1] More broadly, it can be questioned whether the middle-class dominance in both parties in Parliament is prejudicial to the interests of the working class; or whether the interests of women are neglected as a result of the predominance of men; or whether the interests of the young and the old suffer through the over-representation of the middle-aged in Parliament; or whether particular regions suffer from their under-representation on the Government side of the House. The consideration of these broad issues, however, is beyond the scope of this chapter.

[1] S. E. Finer, H. B. Berrington, and D. J. Bartholomew, *Backbench Opinion in the House of Commons, 1955–9*, London 1961. See also H. Berrington, *Backbench Opinion in the House of Commons*, London 1973; R. C. Frasure, 'Backbench Opinion Revisited: the Case of the Conservatives', *PS* 1972, pp. 325–8; A. Kornberg and R. C. Frasure, 'Policy Differences in British Parliamentary Parties', *APSR* 1971, pp. 694–703; P. Seyd, 'Factionalism Within the Conservative Party: the Monday Club', *G and O* 1972, pp. 464–87.

5

Pressure Groups

THE BASIS of the electoral system in Britain is territorial representation, whereby an MP serves a geographical constituency, rather than functional representation, whereby members of the legislature are elected directly by sectional interests based on social, economic, ethnic, or other groupings within society. Nevertheless, sections of the community are directly represented within the British political system by the activities of pressure groups. Through the trade unions, employers' associations, religious and educational bodies, recreational and welfare societies, and innumerable organisations capable of exerting political pressure, the opinions and interests of sections of the community are brought to bear on the political process. At the same time, the political parties indirectly represent social and economic interests within the state. MPs are drawn from various sections of the community, and while representing a geographical constituency, an MP may also be a member (and thus potentially a representative) of a trade union, while another may be associated with an industrial or commercial interest. In practice, therefore, functional representation exists side by side with territorial representation.

Pressure Group Politics

Pressure group politics has been defined as 'the field of organised groups possessing both formal structure and real common interests, in so far as they influence the decisions of public bodies',[1] or alternatively, '. . . in so far as they seek to

[1] W. J. M. Mackenzie, 'Pressure Groups in British Government', *BJS* 1955, p. 137.

influence the process of government'.[1] In detail this means influencing the formation, passage through Parliament, and administration of policy by means of contact with Ministers and civil servants, the political parties, individual MPs, and the public. In Britain today there are literally thousands of organised groups of varying size, structure, functions, and influence, from the powerful Confederation of British Industry and the TUC on the one hand, to relatively insignificant social and cultural groups on the other. As a political study, however, interest lies primarily with those bodies that seek to affect public policy, for as long as they do so. Pressure groups are not themselves political parties, as they do not seek office, or control over the whole process of government. They are concerned with only a limited aspect of the field of public policy, and their efforts are more concentrated, and perhaps more effective, as a result. The term 'pressure group' is sometimes objected to because it implies coercion, and because many groups have functions other than the influencing of public policy. Thus the term 'lobby' can be an alternative.[2]

Pressure groups are certainly not a new political phenomenon in Britain.[3] The issues with which groups are concerned, and many of the tactics that they use in pursuit of their aims, have changed over the years, but the broad principles of pressure group politics are unchanging. In the eighteenth century there emerged a number of political associations that agitated for the reform of Parliament.[4] These associations were largely unsuccessful, but the Committee for the Abolition of the Slave Trade, formed in 1807, was a much more successful body. In the middle of the nineteenth century the lack of party cohesion allowed scope for activity by pressure groups in Parliament, and the Anti-Corn Law League was an outstandingly successful pressure group in this period. Later in the nineteenth century there emerged a close identification between the Liberal Party and the temperance movement, while the Conservative Party formed (and retains) close ties with

[1] J. D. Stewart, *British Pressure Groups*, London 1958, p. 1.

[2] S. E. Finer, *Anonymous Empire*, London 1965, for the use of this term.

[3] See W. J. M. Mackenzie, 'Pressure Groups: the Conceptual Framework', *PS* 1955, pp. 247–55, for an early analysis.

[4] E. C. Black, *The Association*, Harvard 1963, for details of these bodies.

brewing interests.[1] At the turn of the century the Labour Party emerged as a combination of various pressure groups from the trade union and socialist movements.

Though pressure groups are not a new phenomenon, they are a growing force in Britsh politics. In the post-war period when government activity has spread into the spheres of social welfare, industry, and economic planning, the state has been inevitably drawn into closer direct contact with more people, and more groups of people, thus giving a greater impetus to the activities of organised groups. Similarly, as the work of government extends into technical fields, the administrators have to turn for expert advice to bodies outside the Civil Service, again creating opportunities for pressure group influence. Each pressure group that emerges tends to produce a counter pressure group, thereby causing a snowball effect. The ease of communication within society today, with more and more advertising through the mass media, and the growth in the efficiency and respectability of 'public relations', means that pressure groups have greater facilities for influencing public opinion. In this respect it is often claimed that in many ways Britain is the most 'organised' country in the world, with much more scope for activity by pressure groups than in the USA.[2]

Certain features of the British political system contribute to this. The unitary nature of the British system, with the concentration of constitutional authority in the hands of the central government, means that pressure groups can direct their activities towards the machinery of a single central government.[3] At the same time, there is in Britain a historical tradition of contact between MPs and outside bodies, which helps to legitimise the close contact that exists in Britain today between the parties and some pressure groups. After the ideological disputes of the 1945–50 Parliament, the emphasis

[1] J. M. Lee, 'The Political Significance of Licensing Legislation', *Parl. Aff.* 1960–1, pp. 211–28.

[2] S. H. Beer, 'Pressure Groups and Parties in Britain', *APSR* 1956, pp. 1–23, for comments on this. See also S. H. Beer, 'Representation of Interests in British Government', *APSR* 1957, pp. 613–51.

[3] See R. T. McKenzie, 'Parties, Pressure Groups, and the British Political Process', *PQ* 1958, pp. 5–16.

on details rather than ideological principles in British politics in the 1950s, 1960s and 1970s provided pressure groups with a fruitful field in which to work. By the very nature of their function pressure groups can be much more effectively concerned with the details of policy than with general principles, and thus the 'politics of details' enables the influence of pressure groups to increase. To a certain extent, however, the politics of details is the result as well as the cause of increased pressure group activity, in that the awareness of Conservative Governments of the need to come to terms with the unions, and the parallel awareness of Labour Governments of the importance of big business, means that all Governments are constrained to some extent by these powerful industrial interests.

Classification of Pressure Groups[1]

In the classification of pressure groups an initial distinction can be made between sectional interest groups (like the Automobile Association or the Police Federation), which exist for other purposes as well as lobbying, and cause groups (like the Abortion Law Reform Association[2] or the National Viewers and Listeners Association), which are bodies created specifically to lobby on behalf of some cause, and have no function other than this. Cause groups are the oldest type of pressure group, and the political activities of sectional interests are a much more recent phenomenon. Sectional interest groups are generally formed initially for some purpose other than lobbying, and their role as a political pressure group

[1] For a detailed examination and classification see A. M. Potter, *Organized Groups in British National Politics*, London 1961. See also R. Kimber and J. J. Richardson, *Pressure Group Politics in Britain: a Reader*, London 1973; P. S. Shipley (ed.), *The Guardian Directory of Pressure Groups and Representative Associations*, London 1976; A. R. Ball, *Pressure and Politics in Industrial Societies*, London 1986; D. Marsh (ed.), *Pressure Politics: Interest Groups in Britain*, London 1983; G. Alderman, *Pressure Groups and Government in Great Britain*, London 1984.

[2] J. Chapman, 'The Political Implications of Attitudes to Abortion in Britain', *WEP* 1986 (I), pp. 7–31; D. Marsh and J. Chambers, *Abortion Politics*, London 1981.

often remains a relatively minor aspect of their activities. Because they are something more than pressure groups, and because they are often able to provide the Government with expert advice, sectional interest groups are quite likely to be consulted by the Government in matters affecting their members, provided that they are authoritative and representative of their interests. They have a potential membership limited to the sectional interest they represent, and their percentage membership is an important factor in determining their strength and authority. For example, some 90% of farmers are members of the National Farmers Union, so that this body can claim to be highly representative and authoritative when speaking on behalf of the interests of farmers.[1] In contrast, only about 10% of the war wounded are members of the British Legion, so that this body cannot claim to be highly representative of wounded veterans. Unity of purpose is also an important factor. The TGWU has the largest membership of any trade union in Britain, with almost two million members. Because 'General Workers' covers so many categories of employment, however, and the TGWU contains so many diverse elements, a unified purpose is often lacking. Thus the NUM, though smaller in membership (250,000 members), has in the past been capable of much more concerted action because it is concerned only with one class of workman and one employer.

Any sub-division of sectional interests into categories according to the interests they represent, must to a very large extent be arbitrary, but a basic four-fold classification can be made into business groups, labour groups, professional groups, and miscellaneous groups. The business groups include the vast number of industrial, commercial, and managerial bodies such as, for example, the Institute of Directors, the Retail Consortium, the Confederation of British Industry, the British Bankers' Association, the Association of British Chambers of Commerce, the National Federation of Building

[1] See P. Self and H. Storing, *The State and the Farmer*, London 1962; J. R. Pennock, 'Agricultural Subsidies in England and America', *APSR* 1962, pp. 621–33; R. W. Howarth, 'The Political Strength of British Agriculture', *PS* 1969, pp. 458–69.

Trade Employers.[1] The labour groups are primarily the TUC and the individual Unions. Although there are about a hundred unions affiliated to the TUC, the six largest account for almost half of the twelve million trade unionists.[2] The Cooperative Movement, under the leadership of the Cooperative Union, can also be included among the labour groups, although there is not the same concentration of influence in the Cooperative Movement as in the TUC. While many business groups tend to be associated with the Conservative Party, and most labour groups are formally affiliated to the Labour Party, the professional groups are largely free from direct ties with any one particular party. Bodies like the British Medical Association, the Society of Civil Servants, and the Association of University Teachers are not affiliated to a political party, and remain aloof from close and formal party ties.[3] There are also a multiplicity of miscellaneous groups which may be further subdivided under various other headings. There are welfare groups (the Royal Air Force Association), ethnic groups (the New Zealand Society), church groups (the Free Church Federal Council), property groups (the National Federation of Property Owners), and any number of other groupings.

Cause groups are formed for no other purpose than to promote some particular objective, such as the abolition of capital punishment, the preservation of rural England, the reform of the electoral system, or the introduction of a simplified alphabet, and such groups disband or change their nature if their objective is achieved. Thus the National Union of Societies for Equal Citizenship changed into the National Union of Townswomen's Guilds once the Suffragette cause

[1] See S. E. Finer, *Private Industry and Political Power*, London 1958; S. E. Finer, 'The Political Power of Private Capital', *SR* 1955, pp. 279–84, *and* 1956, pp. 5–30; S. E. Finer, 'The Federation of British Industries', *PS* 1956, pp. 61–85; F. G. Castles, 'Business and Government: A Typology of Pressure Group Activity', *PS* 1969, pp. 160–76; S. Blank, *Government and Industry in Britain: the FBI in Politics 1945–65*, London 1973; W. Grant and D. Marsh, *The CBI*, London 1977; M. Moran, 'Finance Capital and Pressure Group Politics in Britain', *BJPS* 1981, pp. 381–404.

[2] K. Middlemas, *Industry, Unions and Government*, London 1983; R. M. Martin, *TUC*, London 1980.

[3] P. R. Jones, *Doctors and the BMA*, London 1981.

was won by 1928. Such bodies are less likely than sectional interest groups to be consulted by the Government, unless, like the Howard League for Penal Reform, they are able to offer specialised advice on technical matters. Cause groups tend to be organised as a committee, often with a large but passive membership, or with supporters rather than members.

A certain distinction may be noted among cause groups between what may be termed 'interested parties' and 'promoters of good causes'. Aims of Industry and the Economic League are bodies which seek to promote the interests of private enterprise, and they are composed primarily of individuals who have a direct financial interest in the prosperity of private enterprise. On the other hand, bodies like the Royal Society for the Prevention of Cruelty to Animals, or the National Society for the Prevention of Cruelty to Children, seek to promote 'good causes'. The dividing line between interested parties and the promoters of good causes is an arbitrary one, however, and to some extent both elements are to be found in most groups, though in differing degrees. Cause groups can be listed under numerous different categories, and there are, for instance, animal welfare groups (the League against Cruel Sports), religious and moral groups (the Lord's Day Observance Society[1]), social health groups (the National Society for Clean Air[2]), internationalist groups (the English Speaking Union), and feminist groups (the Fawcett Society). As with the classification of sectional interests, however, this is an arbitrary and incomplete categorisation, and is intended only to illustrate the wide variety of bodies that exist.[3]

Pressure Group Acitivity

The methods by which pressure groups seek to influence the process of government vary from country to country according

[1] B. A. Pym, 'Pressure Groups on Moral Issues', *PQ* 1972, pp. 317–27.

[2] E. Ashby and M. Anderson, *The Politics of Clean Air*, London 1982; J. B. Sanderson, 'The National Smoke Abatement Society and the Clean Air Act', *PS* 1961, pp. 236–53.

[3] See also R. Wraith, *The Consumer Cause*, London 1976; S. K. Brookes and J. J. Richardson, 'The Environmental Lobby in Britain', *Parl. Aff.* 1974–5, pp. 312–28; P. Lowe and J. Goyder, *Environmental Groups in Politics*, London 1983.

to the nature of the political system, but in Britain it is possible to distinguish between pressure group activity directed towards the executive, towards Parliament, and towards the public.[1] Of these three levels of activity, pressure on the Government and the Civil Service is the most direct and most important sphere of influence, as the concentration of constitutional authority in the hands of the central government means that pressure on Parliament and the public is used only as a means of indirectly influencing the Government. Also, the most likely success for most pressure groups is in the field of administrative and legislative detail, and here it is influence with the executive that is most valuable.

Some groups are 'insiders' in the sense that they are consulted regularly by the Government on aspects of policy. The BMA, NFU and CBI fall into this category. Other groups are 'outsiders' with no established contacts with Ministers and civil servants.[2] Some groups will be outsiders because they have not yet been accepted by the Government, or because they have not yet developed the skills required to establish contacts with the Government. Others, however, will be outsiders because they are ideologically at odds with the Government. While it will normally be a great advantage for a pressure group to have formal contacts with the Government, it has been pointed out[3] that some insider groups become 'prisoners' of the Government in the sense that they become so closely involved with the departments that their ability to resist Government policies is limited. Contacts between the Government and some insider groups are institutionalised through bodies such as the Advisory, Conciliation and Arbitration Service (which seeks to help to resolve industrial disputes) and the Manpower Services Commission (which promotes job creation and training schemes).

In Britain there is a direct overlap between pressure group politics and party politics, in that there is a close link between

[1] See D. Wilson, *Pressure: the A to Z of Campaigning in Britain*, London 1984; S. Ward, *Organising Things*, London 1984.

[2] For the distinction between 'insider' and 'outsider' groups see W. Grant, 'The Role and Power of Pressure Groups', in R. L. Borthwick and J. E. Spence (eds), *British Politics in Perspective*, London 1984.

[3] Ibid.

some pressure groups and the two main political parties.[1] The general influence of the trade unions over the Labour Party is clear.[2] The Labour Party is a product of the trade union movement, and today twelve of the twenty-nine seats on the party's NEC are filled directly by the unions. About half of the Labour MPs elected in 1983 were directly sponsored by the unions, and many others had trade union links. Direct sponsorship means that 80% of the election expenses of the candidate are paid by the union, and contributions are also made to the constituency party's funds. In this and other ways the trade unions provide the Labour Party with most of its finance, while the votes of the trade union delegates are a vital factor in disputes at the Labour Party Conference. Similarly, the Cooperative Movement is linked directly with the Labour Party through the Labour and Cooperative Party. The links between the Conservative Party and the business community are also strong, though less formal than the Labour Party's ties with the unions. A vast number of Conservative Members of Parliament have industrial, commercial or farming links, and there is considerable interchange of personnel between the business world and the Conservative Party in Parliament. Even though candidates may not be sponsored or officially supported, business and commercial pressure groups have a stake within the Conservative Party merely because they have members or former members among the ranks of Conservative MPs, and the Conservative Party receives considerable financial contributions from big business.

Thus there is an important relationship between the main parties and powerful sectional interests within the community. When their party forms the Government, particular advantages can accrue to these interests, just as can disadvantages when their party is in opposition. However, the dependence of both parties when in power today upon cooperation with trade union and business interests alike, perhaps tends to nullify this factor to a large and growing extent. A Labour Government,

[1] For an appraisal of this see Beer, *Modern British Politics*.

[2] I. Richter, *Political Purpose in Trade Unions*, London 1973; S. E. Finer, 'The Political Power of Organized Labour', *G and O* 1973, pp. 391–406; D. Farnham, 'The Labour Alliance', *Parl. Aff.* 1976, pp. 37–46; L. Minkin, 'The Party Connection', *G and O* 1978, pp. 458–84.

for example, needs the cooperation of both employers and employees in any 'social contract' type of policy, so that the party's special relationship with the unions has to be tempered by close cooperation with business interests. Similarly, the trade unions' ties with the Labour Party do not prevent the unions from being able to influence Conservative Governments when they are in office,[1] nor do they guarantee favourable treatment for the unions from a Labour Government.

What has been referred to as 'quasi-corporatism',[2] the inter-dependence between the Government and many outside bodies, means that many interests have regular and direct dealings with the executive machine. In that respect, contact with the executive may be all that is needed to secure a pressure group's ends, but even when wider activity is thought to be necessary, a pressure group will often approach the executive as a first step before seeking to influence Parliament or public opinion. Pressure at Government level can be discreet and hidden, and with pressure group politics a valid general principle is that most noise equals least success.

In the 1960s and 1970s the CBI and TUC were drawn directly into the policy-making process as Labour and Conservative Governments alike sought to achieve a consensus on social and economic policy. The National Economic Development Council was formed in 1961 to bring the Government, trade unions and employers into formal and regular consultations about industrial policy. In the 1970s the creation of bodies such as the Health and Safety Commission, the Manpower Services Commission and the Advisory, Conciliation and Arbitration Service brought the two sides of industry into direct contact with departments of state and involved them in the decision-making process. The 1974–9 Labour Government, as part of its battle against inflation, attempted to maintain an agreement with the unions on incomes in return for Government commitments on taxation and expenditure on social services.

In the 1980s there has been a reaction against such direct

[1] M. Moran, 'The Conservative Party and the Trade Unions Since 1974', *PS* 1979, pp. 38–53; R. Behrens, 'The Conservative Party and the Trade Unions', *PQ* 1978, pp. 457–66.

[2] Beer, *APSR* 1956, p. 7.

involvement of interest groups in the policy-making process. Nevertheless, all Governments rely to some extent on outside bodies for technical advice and information, for cooperation in the framing of legislation, and for help in the administration of policy. There exist numerous permanent advisory committees to provide the Civil Service with expert information, and pressure groups provide members for these committees. The Ministry of Agriculture, for example, relies heavily upon the NFU for membership of some fifty agricultural advisory committees, from the Bees' Diseases Advisory Committee to the National Food Survey Committee. Expert advice is given in return for the recognition of interests. The Government consults with interested parties before legislation is produced, and the information provided by these interests is often essential in the preparation of a Bill. Pressure groups cannot be made aware of the precise text of a Bill before it is revealed to Parliament, as this would be a breach of Parliamentary privilege, but the general proposals have often to be revealed in order to secure cooperation from interested parties. The Government cannot ignore bodies that execute legislation, as with local government organisations such as the County Councils Association and the Association of Metropolitan Authorities over the reform of local government. This factor is especially important with the growth of delegated legislation. Some bodies actually administer legislation on behalf of the Government; for example, the Law Society administering Legal Aid, and the Royal Society for the Prevention of Accidents acting as a Government agent.

This type of direct involvement in the process of legislation or administration is open only to bodies that are able to speak authoritatively on behalf of some association, trade, profession, or interest in the community. This is an incentive to amalgamation between groups of like nature, and to the concentration of authority within an organisation. In this respect the doctors, through the BMA, are more cohesive and better organised, and are thus more likely to be consulted by the Government, than are the teachers with their numerous factious organisations. In this context a pressure group has to be responsible if it is to retain its influence within the executive machine, and this can place limitations upon its ability to conduct campaigns to influence Parliament or the public, if this becomes necessary.

In addition to the formal machinery for contact between the Government and outside bodies, pressure groups are able to exert influence upon individual Ministers and civil servants in less formal ways. Many Ministers are themselves members or former members of pressure groups, and these groups are thereby able to exert influence upon Ministers in much the same way as they can upon individual MPs with whom they have connections. Here a Minister may be divided between loyalty to the Government and loyalty to the interest group. There is often informal contact between Ministers, top civil servants, and the leaders of many pressure groups, so that 'the personal touch' is of great significance in this context. As with direct participation in the process of government, this form of influence is open to only a limited number of interests, and this perhaps represents the most criticised aspect of pressure group activity in Britain. It cannot be known, for instance, how many Ministers or civil servants are influenced in their contact with powerful business pressure groups by the possibility of acquiring top posts in industry or commerce at some later date.[1] Certainly in 1984 the House of Commons Select Committee on the Treasury and Civil Service expressed concern at the number of Permanent Secretaries who were leaving the civil service to take up posts with banks, insurance companies and other private firms.

* * *

The second level of pressure group activity is through Parliament. Bodies that do not have the direct links with the departments of state that are enjoyed by some pressure groups, have to seek other means of establishing contact with the parties or with individual MPs.[2] In the main they seek to infiltrate the established parties rather than promote independent candidates dedicated solely to the interests of one pressure group, as today independent candidates stand little or no chance of election, and even if elected would be swamped by

[1]See D. C. M. Platt, 'The Commercial and Industrial Interests of Ministers of the Crown', *PS* 1961, pp. 267–90.

[2]G. Jordan, 'Parliament Under Pressure', *PQ* 1985, pp. 174–82.

the party machines in Parliament. Candidates supporting individual interests sometimes do seek election, particularly in by-elections, but their object as a rule is merely to secure publicity for their cause, and they generally receive only a small number of votes. In the 1983 general election the Ecology Party (dedicated to a variety of environmental causes) put up over a hundred candidates, but they averaged only about 1% of the vote in the seats they contested.

Pressure groups without direct party ties may still attempt to influence one party in particular, or they may attempt to infiltrate both main parties equally. The National Union of Teachers, for example, is allowed by its Constitution to offer official support at a general election to candidates from each of the main parties, although in practice far more Labour MPs than Conservative MPs are ex-teachers. Other groups ignore the party organisations as such, and seek to influence individual MPs regardless of their party affiliations, often recruiting existing MPs into their ranks, perhaps as honorary office holders.

Even where this degree of contact does not exist between a pressure group and MPs, the pressure group can still exert influence by offering 'votes for causes' at elections. Some constituencies are dominated by a particular interest, such as the car workers' vote in Coventry, or the farmers' vote in many rural constituencies. Interest groups may send questionnaires to the candidates in an election to ascertain their views on particular issues, or they may organise special meetings of their members, at which the candidates are given an opportunity to present their case and respond to questions. To some extent the degree of pressure to which an MP is subject in this way depends on the size of his majority, MPs in marginal seats being more susceptible to such pressures. Between elections, however, pressure groups are still free to 'lobby' backbench MPs and Ministers alike, and even if a candidate does not have a direct affiliation with the interest that dominates his constituency, he has to take some heed of this interest between elections.

Pressure groups often use gimmicks to draw attention to their cause. They may organise a mass lobbying of an MP by his constituents, or a mass demonstration at Westminster.

Contact can be made by letter and telegram. On December 17th 1946, MPs received 2,500 telegrams in opposition to the nationalisation of road haulage (although to no avail), while on one occasion a vast number of valentine cards were sent to MPs in the cause of equal pay for women.[1] Dinners, gifts, expense-free tours in Britain and abroad, and other perhaps rather dubious forms of contact through the 'personal touch' can also be employed. Ultimately pressure groups and individuals with grievances can withdraw electoral support from an MP, but it is very easy to exaggerate the influence that pressure groups have in individual constituencies. Also, to threaten to withdraw electoral support from an MP as a means of persuasion is a breach of Parliamentary privilege. In 1947 the Civil Service Clerical Association was censured by the House of Commons' Committee of Privileges for threatening to withdraw official support from W. J. Brown, Independent MP for Rugby, who was sponsored by the Association. It was deemed that pressure of this kind on an MP was undesirable and unconstitutional.

Within Parliament, groups such as the Parliamentary Panel of the Institute of Directors exist as a focus for pressure group interests. Some pressure groups hire the services of professional lobbyists, called Parliamentary Agents.[2] Other bodies, like the NFU, have local Parliamentary correspondents to maintain contact with their local MPs. By these various methods pressure groups can prevail upon MPs to use the Parliamentary timetable to call attention to their interests.[3] Question Time, the daily Adjournment Debate, Private Members' time, and other parts of the Parliamentary timetable can be used for this purpose. Amendments to Government Bills can be made at the instigation of pressure groups, with the Confederation of British Industry and other business groups being particularly active with regard to the passage of the Finance Bill through the Commons each year. The Com-

[1] See A. M. Potter, 'The Equal Pay Campaign Committee', *PS* 1957, pp. 49–64.

[2] D. C. M. Yardley, 'The Work and Status of the Parliamentary Agent', *Parl. Aff.* 1964–5, pp. 162–6.

[3] J. H. Millett, 'The Role of an Interest Group Leader in the House of Commons', *WPQ* 1956, pp. 915–26.

mittee stage of this and other Bills, when the details of the legislation are under consideration, provides scope for the furtherance of a pressure group's cause, and this form of pressure group activity is perhaps second in importance only to direct contact with the executive.

Pressure groups have the greatest chance of influencing legislation in Parliament when the normal party alignment is broken. If there is dissension among Government backbenchers with regard to a particular aspect of Government policy, this can be exploited by the opponents of the policy. Thus in the 1964–6 Parliament the interests opposed to steel nationalisation benefited from the dissent among Labour backbenchers over the Government's proposals. During the 1974–9 Parliament the anti-devolutionists succeeded in destroying the Scotland and Wales Bill in 1976, and secured major amendments to the Scotland Bill and the Wales Bill in the following session. In 1986 trade unions and Church organisations that were opposed to the Government's proposals for Sunday trading, contained in the Shops Bill, were able to capitalise on divisions among Conservative backbenchers to secure the defeat of the Bill in the Commons. In the passage of legislation through Parliament the Government may make concessions to the views of interested parties in order to placate the interest groups, or through fear of losing electoral or financial support. On the other hand, it may be that during the passage of a Bill the Government may become convinced that the pressure group's case is a valid one.

* * *

The final level of pressure group activity is through public opinion, in the hope that this will lead ultimately to influence on Parliament, or directly on the Government. This is the most conspicuous, but at the same time the least rewarding, activity. In the main it is undertaken as a last resort, as pressure directly on the executive (or if this is not possible, pressure directly on Parliament) can bring results much more quickly and much more cheaply. Also, interest groups that have established contacts with the executive have to present an image of responsibility if these contacts are to be maintained, and this can inhibit contact with the public through publicity campaigns. Some bodies, however, particularly cause groups, have to resort to pressure on public opinion because they have only limited means of lobbying at Government or Parliamentary level.

With publicity campaigns that seek to influence public opinion, it is necessary to distinguish between the long-term educational campaign and the short-term propaganda campaign. Bodies such as Aims of Industry and the Economic League have conducted campaigns over a long period designed to educate public opinion in favour of free enterprise, and similar work in defence of Socialism has been attempted by the Fabian Society.[1] The National Union of Teachers has attempted over a long period to present a favourable picture of the teaching profession,[2] while the Hunt Saboteurs' Association has used direct action to draw public attention to the activities of the fox-hunters. The object of such long-term campaigns is gradually to cultivate in the minds of the public an image, favourable or unfavourable, of private enterprise, economic planning, nationalisation, trade unions, a particular profession, or whatever the cause may be. The short-term propaganda, or 'fire-brigade' type of campaign, seeks to achieve particular *ad hoc* goals in a shorter space of time, and by means of much more concentrated activity. Thus in the late 1940s and before the 1959 and 1964 general elections, campaigns against the nationalisation of the iron and steel industry were mounted by the steel firms, while before the 1979 election the Police Federation mounted a campaign for greater public expenditure on the police force, in the interests of law and order. The effectiveness of such electoral campaigns, however, depends largely on current public sensitivity about the issue.

The methods that are used in long- and short-term campaigns are similar, though the fire-brigade type of campaign generally uses more gimmicks. Press advertisements offer a wide scope for such campaigns, and the press is all the more important because TV and radio cannot be used for these

[1] J. F. Milburn, 'The Fabian Society and the British Labour Party', *WPQ* 1958, pp. 319–39.

[2] R. D. Coates, *Teachers' Unions and Interest Group Politics*, London 1973; R. A. Manzer, *Teachers and Politics in England and Wales*, London 1970.

purposes in Britain. The Institute of Public Relations, formed in 1948, has widened the scope of advertising, with prestige advertising being more widely undertaken. Some industrial and business concerns issue publications which present an image of an advanced and progressive enterprise. Direct contact with the public can be achieved through meetings, demonstrations, petitions, and opinion surveys. In 1946 dentists were urged to present to their patients the case against state medicine – the dentist's chair being seen as a highly effective place for influencing opinion. Much propaganda on behalf of the Campaign for Nuclear Disarmament has been achieved through novels, films, and plays.[1]

These different forms and different levels of pressure group activity are not necessarily mutually exclusive. An interest group may be engaged in negotiations with a Government department about the details of legislation, and at the same time be attempting to influence MPs and public opinion against that piece of legislation. There can be conflict within a pressure group, the rank and file calling for a public campaign while the leaders seek to pursue only the more discreet methods.

Pressure Groups in Action

In 1972 the National Association of Bookmakers achieved considerable success in defence of their members' interests when they mounted a successful Parliamentary lobby against a Government Bill.[2] The Totalisator Board, which runs 'the Tote' on behalf of the State, was in financial difficulties in the early 1970s and the Conservative Government had been persuaded to come to its assistance. The Home Secretary, Reginald Maudling, introduced the Horserace Totalisator and Betting Levies Boards Bill, which sought to provide the Tote with financial assistance and enable it to expand its activities. The most controversial proposal, contained in Clause Three of the Bill, was that the Tote should be allowed

[1] R. Taylor and C. Pritchard, *The Protest Makers*, London 1982; T. Chafer, 'Politics and the Perception of Risk', *WEP* 1985 (I), pp. 5–28.

[2] See *The Guardian*, May 11th 1974.

to open betting shops, in competition with the bookmakers, under very favourable conditions. Whereas bookmakers were required to prove that there was a demand before they could open a shop in a particular area, the Tote was to be free from this restriction.

In opposition to the Bill as a whole, and Clause Three in particular, the National Association of Bookmakers organised a Parliamentary Action Committee and presented their case to backbench MPs vigorously and flamboyantly. A series of lunches in the better hotels, and receptions in the House of Commons, were organised, and bookmakers were organised to lobby their constituency MPs. Given the ideological climate of the early 1970s, Conservative MPs were encouraged to regard the Tote as a 'lame duck' unworthy of public assistance. Among Labour backbenchers Brian Walden was prominent in opposition to the Bill. At the time he had no formal connections with the National Association of Bookmakers, but he subsequently accepted a lucrative contract as their Parliamentary consultant. Lord Wigg, the Chairman of the Horserace Betting Levy Board, originally supported the Bill, but became an influential critic when he was persuaded by the campaign that the financial position of the Tote was less precarious than the Government had indicated. The opponents of the Bill concentrated their attack at the committee stage in the Commons. After an unusually large number of sittings the Government agreed to a 'compromise' which in effect emasculated the Bill. The Government agreed not to implement the key Clause Three, in return for an undertaking by the bookmakers to give facilities to the Tote in existing betting shops. Thus very much 'against the odds', the bookmakers' lobbying had produced a major concession from the Government.

* * *

The Independent Television Authority Act 1954 was essentially a triumph for pressure group activity by the radio and TV industry, advertising interests, and finance houses.[1] After 1945 the BBC was criticised in some quarters on account of its monopolistic and non-commercial basis. There were demands

[1] See H. H. Wilson, *Pressure Group*, London 1961.

for a commercial radio and TV concern to compete with the BBC. The 1945 Labour Government favoured the existing system, and the Beveridge Committee on Broadcasting set up in 1949 was opposed to the idea of a commercial rival for the BBC. Even when the Conservative Government was formed in 1951 there was at first no obvious alignment between the Government and commercial radio and TV interests, and the Conservative leadership seemed either to favour the existing system or to be non-committal. There was soon a rapid change. A Conservative backbench group was formed, led by John Profumo and Ian Orr-Ewing, to agitate for commercial broadcasting. At the same time, Lord Woolton was put in charge of Government broadcasting policy, and as he was one of the few members of the Government who actively favoured commercial TV, the door was open for influence by 'the group'. Churchill was concerned primarily with foreign affairs, and was content to leave domestic matters to other members of the Government, while the narrow Parliamentary majority on which the Government was based perhaps made Ministers more open to outside pressure.

Two main pressure groups emerged, the National TV Council, led by Christopher Mayhew (a Labour MP and at that time a BBC personality), to oppose commercial TV, and the Popular TV Association, in which Lord Derby was prominent, to agitate for commercialism. There followed a campaign to convert the Conservative Government to commercialism, and at the same time a 'grassroots' campaign was aimed at public opinion. The Government and most Conservative backbenchers were persuaded to accept commercial TV during 1953, and a White Paper was introduced in November 1953, and then a Bill in January 1954. The Bill passed the Commons despite vigorous Labour opposition, but was only passed through the Lords with the assistance of Conservative 'backwoodsmen' after Lord Hailsham had led strong opposition to the measure.

Thus in this particular instance pressure group activity was directed towards public opinion on the one hand, and the top levels of the Conservative Government on the other. As the issue involved was one of principle rather than details, contact with the Civil Service was not necessary. The episode shows how quickly a pressure group can achieve its ends if it can convert to its cause influential elements in the Government of the day. Once the Conservative Government was committed to the cause of commercial TV, Parliament and the legislative process proved to be no barrier, and the delaying power of the Lords was not applied in this instance.

* * *

The Murder (Abolition of the Death Penalty) Act 1965, which suspended the operation of the death penalty for an experimental period of five years, came after many years of activity by abolitionist cause groups, and represents a triumph for pressure group politics.[1] As early as 1810 the Society for the Diffusion of Knowledge upon the Punishment of Death was formed as a reaction against the big increase in the use of the death penalty. This society was followed by many others in the nineteenth century which sought, with some success, to reduce the number of capital crimes. In the revival of reformist interest in capital punishment after 1918, the Howard League for Penal Reform was formed in 1921.[2] The Howard League's concern was with all forms of legal reform, and it has formed over the years a close relationship with the Home Office. Thus, like the BMA, it must maintain a responsible attitude, and this inhibited its activities in public campaigns against the death penalty. On the other hand, the National Council for the Abolition of Capital Punishment, formed in 1925, and its successor, the National Campaign, formed in 1955, though less wealthy and less well established than the Howard League, were concerned only with capital punishment and were able to mount campaigns without worrying about Home Office attitudes. The counter-lobby was badly organised in the main, but as it was made up primarily of the Home Office, prison officers, and sections of the Conservative Party, its powerful position made up for this.

[1] See James B. Cristoph, *Capital Punishment and British Politics*, London 1962; James B. Cristoph, 'Capital Punishment and British Party Responsibility', *PSQ* 1962, pp. 19–35; E. O. Tuttle, *The Crusade Against Capital Punishment*, London 1962.

[2] See G. Rose, *The Struggle for Penal Reform*, London 1962; G. Rose, 'Some Influences on English Penal Reform 1895–1921', *SR* 1955, pp. 25–43.

As this was an emotional not a technical issue, largely beyond party politics, pressure group activity was directed towards individual MPs and public opinion (which for most of the period after 1945 opposed abolition). Neither Labour nor Conservative Governments were prepared to take abolition upon themselves, but on occasions they did allow time and free votes in the Commons for the consideration of Private Members' proposals for abolition. Thus ultimately the success of the abolitionist cause depended at least on the neutrality of the Government of the day. In 1948 a free vote was allowed in the Commons on an abolitionist amendment to the Criminal Justice Bill, although the Home Secretary, Chuter Ede, was opposed to abolition. The amendment was carried, but was rejected by the Lords, and the Government was not prepared to oppose the Lords' action. In 1956 a Private Member's Bill, introduced by Sidney Silverman, passed the Commons, but again the Lords opposed abolition. On this occasion the Conservative Government introduced its own compromise Bill, retaining capital punishment for some crimes. Finally, in 1965 a Private Member's Bill, again introduced by Sidney Silverman, was accepted by the Commons and the Lords with the tacit approval of the Labour Government, and in 1970, after an experimental period of five years, the provisions of the Act were put onto a permanent basis.

* * *

As a result of pressure group activities, the form of the Race Relations Bill, introduced by the Labour Government in 1965, was altered quite considerably during its passage through Parliament.[1] In 1964, when still in opposition, Harold Wilson called upon the Society of Labour Lawyers to prepare a Race Relations Bill to make illegal racial discrimination and incitement to racial hatred in public places. The Labour lawyers advocated the application of criminal law sanctions to those guilty of racial incitement, and this was approved by the Labour Party's NEC and was incorporated in the Bill when it was presented initially to Parliament. Among some Labour

[1] See K. Hindell, 'The Genesis of the Race Relations Bill', *PQ* 1965, pp. 390–405.

lawyers and some backbench Labour MPs the view emerged that criminal law sanctions were too rigid and therefore too limited in application, and moves were made to replace criminal law sanctions by conciliation machinery, supported by legal sanctions when necessary. Such machinery could be applied to a much wider field of racial problems. The Campaign against Racial Discrimination (CARD) sought to persuade backbenchers of both parties, the Society of Labour Lawyers, and the Cabinet sub-committee in charge of the Bill, that conciliation machinery was practical and was preferable to criminal law sanctions.[1] The views of CARD were widely publicised in the press, and many Labour MPs expressed dissatisfaction with the Government's restrictive attitude towards the immigration question.

At first the Minister coordinating Government policy on immigration, Maurice Foley, and the Home Secretary, Sir Frank Soskice, supported the attitude of the Home Office advisory committee, which was that changes in the Bill were not practical. However, the activities of CARD in Parliament and in the press produced a change in attitude in the Cabinet sub-committee, and at the Committee stage in the Commons conciliation machinery was substituted for criminal law sanctions as the means of dealing with racial incitement.

* * *

The impact that pressure groups can have on administrative procedures is illustrated by difficulties encountered by the Efficiency Unit that was established in 1979 to achieve economies in the administration of the departments of state. As one of its first enquiries the Unit examined the methods used to distribute pensions, child benefit and other social security payments.[2] The established system was, for the most part, that of weekly cash payments at post offices. After examining the procedures, and taking stock of civil service and some consumer opinion, the Efficiency Unit concluded that

[1] B. W. Heineman, *The Politics of the Powerless: a Study of the Campaign Against Racial Discrimination*, London 1972.

[2] See N. Warner, 'Raynerism in Practice: Anatomy of a Rayner Scrutiny', *Pub. Admin.* 1984, pp. 6–22.

the system was inefficient and extremely costly, and that considerable economies could be achieved if a system was adopted of monthly payments directly into bank accounts. The enquiry also revealed ways in which economies could be made in the production and distribution of order books. Were these changes to be introduced, it was estimated that administrative costs could be reduced by about £50 million per year. What appeared to be an administratively and financially sound recommendation was welcomed by the Department of Health and Social Security, and initially the Cabinet favoured implementation. The attitude of Ministers changed, however, in face of a campaign mounted by a variety of interests. Pensioners' associations resisted the change, arguing that many pensioners did not have bank accounts and that weekly payments were especially desirable for the poorer recipients. The National Federation of Sub-Postmasters expressed concern about the effect that the new payment procedure would have on post offices. They pointed out that about a third of the time of post office counter staff was devoted to the payment of social security benefits and that the loss of this function would threaten the livelihood of many of their members.

A lobby of Parliament by post office staff was organised. Several hundred letters and a number of petitions opposing the proposals were sent to the Minister. The National Council for Voluntary Organisations was drawn into the campaign in defence of rural post offices. Rural MPs were alerted and a number of Early Day Motions were put down. A Parliamentary debate on the proposals was granted and the new House of Commons Select Committee on Social Services took up the issue. As well as this Parliamentary activity the media took an interest in the Efficiency Unit in general, and in this enquiry in particular.

In face of this Parliamentary and public campaign the Government decided to implement the Efficiency Unit's recommendations only in part. A system of monthly payments into bank accounts was made available to those who wished it, but the new system was not made obligatory. Financial compensation was made available to the rural post offices for loss of business that might result from the new arrangements. Thus a modest reform that was widely regarded as sensible and cost-effective, which was approved by civil servants, Ministers and the prestigious Efficiency Unit, and which had been preceded by surveys of consumer opinion, was undermined by resistance from pressure groups that are not normally regarded as especially politically powerful.

Pressure Group Politics: an Assessment

Pressure groups can be seen as performing a valuable function within the political system in a number of ways. Pressure group activity provides participation in the decision-making process between elections, and this is perhaps particularly important in a situation (as in Britain) of Government domination of Parliament. A bigger proportion of the population is active in pressure groups than in the political parties, and this has led Professor S. E. Finer to make the claim that 'For better or for worse such self-government as we now enjoy today is one that operates by and through the Lobby.'[1] In return for the acknowledgement of their interests, and for the influence and status that comes through involvement in the process of Government, pressure groups provide information, administrative cooperation, and public and political support. It can be argued that those who are most closely affected by Government activity should be most closely consulted, and should be able to influence policy. Indeed pressure groups are indispensable to the executive for the part they play in policy making and in administration. Thus pressure groups draw people into the process of government and at the same time break down party domination of the political process, bringing to the fore issues, like capital punishment and moral questions, which might otherwise lie outside the sphere of party politics.

The basic objection, however, to the influence of pressure groups is that not all sections of the community are equally capable of exerting influence. Though virtually everyone is able to join an organisation that can influence the process of government to some degree, some organisations are clearly more powerful than others. Consumers, for example, lack the

[1] Finer, *Anonymous Empire*, p. 120.

formal contact with the centres of political power that is enjoyed by business and commercial interests. The rich, the powerful and the well organised can acquire an excessive degree of influence, and sectional interests can thereby override national interests. The 'concurrent majority' as represented by the powerful pressure groups, is seen as having too much power as compared with the 'numerical majority' as represented in Parliament.[1] Thus the rise in the importance of pressure group politics has led to the emergence of a new hierarchy of political influence, based on the organisation of group interests, producing what has been described as a 'new Medievalism',[2] whereby a person is politically important only in so far as he belongs to a group. The leadership of pressure groups is often unrepresentative and authoritarian, as it has to be powerful if it is to be in a position to negotiate. Thus secrecy in decision making is to a large extent inevitable. In these various respects, therefore, pressure group politics, as opposed to party politics, are perhaps to be deplored.

Various factors within the political system, however, can limit the power of pressure groups. Within the central government the independence and political neutrality of the Civil Service acts as something of a counterbalance to political pressure of all kinds, including the activities of interest groups. The collective view of the Cabinet can counter influence on individual Ministers, while the pressure that may be exerted on individual MPs is countered by the forces for party unity. Parliamentary debates can be used to give publicity to seemingly dubious relationships between interest groups and an MP or Minister, a party or a Government. In this respect the Parliamentary privilege of free speech is important. Despite the close and direct ties that exist between some interest groups and the political parties, party politics can at times be seen to be in direct conflict with pressure group influence. If a pressure group seeks to influence one party particularly, as do the trade unions and big business, it encounters concerted opposition from the other main party. If, on the other hand, it seeks to infiltrate both main parties, as do bodies like the

[1] Ibid., p. 108.
[2] Mackenzie, *BJS* 1955, p. 146.

RSPCA and other 'non-political' organisations, the pressure group can expect to be only one of the lesser forces and influences within the parties. In Britain no pressure group is capable of dominating both main parties, although many powerful groups do have considerable influence on Governments of all political complexions.

Each lobby tends to be faced by a counter-lobby, the emergence of a new pressure group tending to produce a rival group (although not necessarily of equal strength). The brewers are matched with temperance interests, the League against Cruel Sports with the British Field Sports Society,[1] the Lord's Day Observance Society with advocates of a continental Sunday. Sometimes there is hostility and conflict between groups pursuing similar ends (as with the AA and RAC) while divisions will often exist within a particular body (as between big business and small business interests within the CBI). Often two conflicting forces emerge within one political party, as with the emergence of pro- and anti-European groups in both main parties in the 1960s and 1970s, and of pro- and anti-devolution groups in the parties in Scotland and Wales in the 1974–9 Parliament. It does not necessarily follow that rival interests are equally matched, but a certain natural balance of forces often does emerge, as between the trade unions and big business.

Pressure groups that have contacts with the executive have to be responsible and co-operative if they are to remain influential, and this applies to the most powerful interests. Wholly exceptional in this respect were the direct clash between the TUC and the Government in the General Strike of 1926, and the conflict between the National Farmers' Union and the Government over agricultural policy in 1943–4. The general concept of 'the public interest' or 'the general good of the nation' acts as a counter to pressure group influence, a pressure group's case being considerably weakened if it can be shown by the Government or by its opponents to be a threat to national interests. Thus in recent years the trade unions have

[1] R. H. Thomas, 'Hunting as a Political Issue', *Parl. Aff.* 1986, pp. 19–30; R. H. Thomas, *The Politics of Hunting*, London 1983.

suffered through the publicity given to industrial strikes. Much pressure group advertising is designed, like the steel industry's campaign in 1959 and 1964, to convey the impression that the interests of one section of the community coincide with the interests of the nation as a whole.

Despite these limitations, critics of the existing degree of power enjoyed by pressure groups argue that changes should be made within the political system to reduce the scope for pressure group influence. It is argued that the structure of the Civil Service should be reformed to bring into the service more specialists and technical experts, and thereby reduce the need for advisory committees through which pressure groups have so much influence. Opponents of the power that the trade unions have in the Labour Party have argued for a reduction in the union numbers on the party's NEC, and for a weakening of union voting power at party Conferences. It has been suggested also that primary elections should be introduced as the means of choosing party candidates so as to weaken trade union influence at this level. Similarly, the opponents of big business have claimed that there should be more publicity given to the connections between the Conservative Party and the business world. In 1975 a House of Commons register of the outside interests of MPs was established, following the recommendation of a Select Committee. MPs are requested to record in the register the source (though not the amount) of income they receive from directorships, consultancies and other outside sources. However, just as important as present and past connections, are the positions that MPs and Ministers may hope to take up on leaving Parliament. This type of potential influence can only be restricted by increasing the existing limitations on former Ministers taking up appointments with commercial concerns with which they had dealings as Ministers.

These and many other proposals for reducing or publicising pressure group influence have been made from time to time. It has been argued (and not only by MPs) that higher salaries would make MPs less dependent upon outside interests, but it is difficult to judge whether salary increases have such an effect. Similarly it is difficult to ascertain whether the revelation of contributions by firms to political party funds has in any way reduced the influence of big business upon the Conservative Party. These and any other similar changes, foreseeable in the near future, can have only a minor effect on the vast power and influence of pressure groups in the political system.

part three

Government and Parliament

6

The Constitution

THE ESSENTIAL feature of the Constitutional machinery of British government is the formal concentration of authority, rather than any separation or diffusion of powers. The various legal features of the Constitution, combined with the practical features of the party and Parliamentary systems, give to the Government of the day, and particularly to the Prime Minister, a power and control over the Constitutional machinery that is not to be found in systems where Constitutional checks and balances are designed to prevent any one element in the government process from exercising too much power. The features of the Constitution that help to create this concentration of authority are its antiquity and its unwritten, flexible, and unitary nature. In each of these respects the British Constitution is in marked contrast to that of the USA.

The Unwritten Constitition[1]

The British Constitution is old by any standards, in that the origins of the present system can be traced back at least to the

[1] For works on the Constitution see A. V. Dicey, *Introduction to the Study of the Law of the Constitution*, London 1964; Sir Ivor Jennings, *The Law and the Constitution*, London 1959; E. C. S. Wade and G. G. Phillips, *Constitutional Law*, London 1977; O. Hood Phillips, *Constitutional and Administrative Law*, London 1962; H. W. R. Wade, *Constitutional Fundamentals*, London 1980. See also O. Hood Phillips, *Reform of the Constitution*, London 1970; P. Bromhead, *Britain's Developing Constitution*, London 1974; N. Johnson, *In Search of the Constitution*, London 1977; P. Norton, *The Constitution in Flux*, London 1982; J. Jowell and D. Oliver, *The Changing Constitution*, London 1985.

period after the Norman Conquest.[1] The political system has evolved slowly, and Constitutional developments have tended to come only gradually. It is necessary to emphasise, however, that though many of the institutions of the present system of government in Britain have medieval origins, the role that these institutions play is constantly changing as the substance of the Constitution evolves. The danger of stressing and perhaps glorifying the ancient origins of some Constitutional features is that the role that these features play in the modern Constitution is often misunderstood.

Partly because of its ancient origins, the British Constitution is largely unwritten and unsystematic, in the sense that there is no Fundamental Law of the Constitution and there has been no attempt to codify the various rules and conventions that make up the Constitution. The sources of modern Constitutional practice are thus numerous and varied. The Constitution has some written aspects, just as the written Constitution of the United States has been modified by some unwritten conventions. The parts of the British Constitution that are written, however, such as Acts of Parliament relating to Constitutional machinery, do not require any special legislative process for enactment. The Act of Settlement 1701, the Parliament Acts 1911 and 1949, the Representation of the People Act 1949, the European Communities Act 1972, and the Peerage Act 1963, are all examples of legislation that creates or modifies some aspect of the Constitution. Also in this category can be included Constitutional documents such as Magna Carta 1215, and the Petition of Rights 1628. Some classic writings on the Constitution have acquired the status of Constitutional documents themselves. Probably the most authoritative of such works is Erskine May's *Treatise on the Law, Privileges, Proceedings, and Usage of Parliament*.[2] This is the classic guide to the procedure and privileges of Parliament, and is constantly referred to by Speakers of the House of Commons in the formulation of their rulings on questions of

[1] For the history of Constitutional development see J. E. A. Jolliffe, *The Constitutional History of Medieval England*, London 1961; D. L. Keir, *The Constitutional History of Modern Britain*, London 1964.

[2] Sir T. Erskine May, *Treatise on the Laws, Privileges, Proceedings, and Usages of Parliament*, London 1983 (20th edition).

privilege and procedure. Also (although to a much lesser extent) A. V. Dicey's *Law of the Constitution* has acquired over the years an authority that makes it more than merely a commentary on constitutional practice.[1]

The exercise of the Royal Prerogative forms another aspect of Constitutional practice. The power to declare war, make treaties, pardon criminals, and dissolve Parliament are vital functions performed by Royal Prerogative, and are executed through Orders in Council or through proclamations and writs under the Great Seal. Today, these functions are performed by Ministers acting on behalf of the Monarch, so that this gives to Ministers a sphere of activity in which the authority for the decision comes from the Crown rather than from Parliament. Decisions made by the Courts form a further source of Constitutional authority, many of the privileges of Parliament being based on nineteenth-century judicial decisions. Thus the decision in the case of the Sheriff of Middlesex in 1840 established the principle that Parliament had the right to punish its own members for a breach of privilege, no other legal authority being necessary,[2] while the judgement of Mr Justice Stephen in *Bradlaugh* v. *Gossett* in 1884 established the supremacy of Parliament over the Courts in all matters concerning the internal affairs of Parliament.[3]

The bulk of Constitutional practice, however, is based on conventions that have emerged and evolved through time.[4] Doctrines such as the impartiality of the Speaker of the House of Commons, the collective responsibility of the Cabinet, and the individual responsibility of Ministers, are not based on statutes, documents, or judicial decisions, but on the acceptance of a general practice over the years. Conventions are continually evolving, and there is no guide as to what forms a Constitutional convention other than what is generally regarded as normal practice at any given time. Lord Salisbury,

[1] V. Bogdanor, 'Dicey and the Reform of the Constitution', *PL* 1985, pp. 652–78.

[2] Court of Queen's Bench 27.1.1840.

[3] Queen's Bench Division 9.2.1884.

[4] G. Marshall, *Constitutional Conventions*, London 1984; C. Munro, 'Dicey on Constitutional Conventions', *PL* 1985, pp. 637–51; G. Marshall, 'What are Constitutional Conventions', *Parl. Aff.* 1985, pp. 33–9.

for example, was Prime Minister from 1895 to 1902, but today it is generally accepted that the Prime Minister must serve in the House of Commons, and thus in 1963 Lord Home had to disclaim his Peerage on becoming Prime Minister. In Britain, proper Constitutional conduct merely involves the interpretation of such written documents as there are, and the acceptance of the current conventions. The Constitution is flexible, in that there is no special machinery, or special procedures, for the passage of Constitutional legislation. A Bill to abolish the House of Lords, increase the franchise or alter the number of MPs passes through the same legislative stages as any other Bill. This, and the absence of Constitutional Courts to adjudicate on Constitutional conflicts, gives the British Constitution great legal flexibility. The Constitution can be adapted to new developments unhampered by legal formalities. Thus the old, unwritten, and flexible characteristics are interrelated.

As a safeguard against the considerable powers that such a flexible Constitution confers upon the Government of the day, it has been argued that the principal freedoms that citizens enjoy should be codified in a Declaration of Rights or Bill of Rights.[1] The formal codification of individual freedoms, it is argued, would provide a yardstick against which the activities of central and local government could be assessed. It would focus public attention on the importance of civil liberties, and could inhibit a government that sought to extend the power of the state at the expense of the individual.

There are, however, a number of practical difficulties associated with a Bill of Rights that have prevented its adoption. In the first place, the question of precisely what should be included in a list of 'inalienable rights' raises ideological issues that might not be readily resolved. While there could be little argument that 'freedom of speech' should be included in any list of basic rights, there might be more controversy about 'the right to strike'. One possibility would be to adopt the European Convention on Human Rights as a ready-made Bill

[1]See M. Zander, *A Bill of Rights?*, London 1985; J. A. G. Griffith, *The Politics of the Judiciary*, London 1978; C. Campbell (ed.), *Do We Need a Bill of Rights?*, London 1980; J. Jacanelli, *Enacting a Bill of Rights*, London, 1980.

of Rights for Britain. At present the Human Rights Commission in Strasbourg hears complaints about alleged breaches of the European Convention and British citizens are able to take their grievances to the Commission. If the European Convention was adopted in Britain, British citizens would be able to take their complaints to the British courts.

A major problem with any Bill of Rights, however, is that judges are inevitably drawn into politically controversial disputes over civil liberties, with their interpretations perhaps clashing with those of the electorate's political representatives in Parliament. What is more, a Bill of Rights could provide safeguards against arbitrary rule only if it was entrenched, in the sense that it could not be repealed or suspended by the Government. The concept of an entrenched Bill of Rights, however, conflicts with the basic Constitutional principle that each new Parliament is free to adopt any measures it inherits from preceding Parliaments. For these reasons the adoption of the European Convention on Human Rights, or the creation of a home-grown Bill of Rights, have been resisted.

Unitary Government

The second main legal feature of the Constitution is that it is unitary, there being only one sovereign body in the state.[1] The central government, taking its authority from Parliament, is constitutionally supreme, and the local government machine is merely an agent for the central government. Within the unitary structure of the Constitution, some areas do enjoy a degree of regional independence. In no case, however, does this extend to the creation of a federal relationship.[2] The Channel Islands and the Isle of Man have their own Parliaments, and they are largely self-governing in internal affairs.[3] Nevertheless, they are ultimately subject to the legislative

[1] D. E. Ashford, 'Are Britain and France Unitary?', *CP* 1977, pp. 483–99.

[2] W. D. Birrell, 'The Stormont–Westminster Relationship', *Parl. Aff.* 1972–3, pp. 471–91; W. D. Birrell, 'The Mechanics of Devolution', *PQ* 1978, pp. 304–21; P. Arthur, 'Devolution as Administrative Convenience: a Case-Study of Northern Ireland', *Parl. Aff.* 1977, pp. 97–106.

[3] D. G. Kermode, 'Regional Self-Government: a Case-Study of the Isle of Man', *Pub. Admin.* 1974, pp. 161–78.

TABLE XXV

Legislative, Executive and Administrative Devolution Within the United Kingdom

	MPs at Westminster	Own Legislature	Own Cabinet	Own Department of State
England	*			*†
Scotland	*			*
Wales	*			*
Northern Ireland	*	*	*	*
Isle of Man		*	*	
Channel Islands		*	*	

† That is, the Home Office.

supremacy of the United Kingdom Parliament, even though they are not represented at Westminster.

Scotland enjoys a considerable degree of administrative devolution in that the Scottish Education, Agriculture and Fisheries, Industry and Home and Health Departments, under the direction of the Secretary of State for Scotland, are situated in St Andrew's House, Edinburgh.[1] The 1603 union of the crowns of England and Scotland left separate Parliaments for the two countries, but the 1707 Act of Union dissolved the Scottish Parliament, and Scotland has since sent representatives to Westminster. In the House of Commons, however, the Scottish Grand Committee debates the Scottish Estimates, Scottish affairs in general, and the Second Reading of Bills relating exclusively to Scotland. The Committee Stage of Scottish legislation is taken in a special Standing Committee on which there is a majority of MPs from Scottish seats, and there is a Select Committee on Scottish Affairs that examines the activities of the Scottish Office.

The administration of Welsh affairs is centred on the Welsh Office in Cardiff.[2] In 1957 the post of Minister of State for

[1] See J. G. Kellas, *The Scottish Political System*, London 1984; M. J. Keating and A. Midwinter, *The Government of Scotland*, London 1983.

[2] P. J. Randall, 'Wales in the Structure of Central Government', *Pub. Admin.* 1972, pp. 353–72; E. Rowlands, 'The Politics of Regional Administration: the Establishment of the Welsh Office', *Pub. Admin.* 1972, pp. 333–52.

Wales was created, and in 1964 there was appointed a Secretary of State for Wales with a seat in the Cabinet. There is also a Welsh Grand Committee, and Welsh Standing and Select Committees on similar lines to the Scottish Committee. In the 1974–9 Parliament proposals were made for the creation of Scottish and Welsh Assemblies, but they were within the context of the supremacy of the Westminster Parliament.

From 1922 to 1972 Northern Ireland had its own Parliament and Cabinet. In 1920 this was envisaged as applying to the whole of Ireland, but it was rejected by the south in favour of full independence. While in internal matters Northern Ireland was virtually self-governing, the relationship between Northern Ireland and Westminster was not a federal one in that Northern Ireland was ultimately subject to the legislative supremacy of Westminster, and the authority enjoyed by the Northern Ireland Parliament and executive could be (and eventually was) withdrawn by the United Kingdom Parliament. In 1972, in face of the civil unrest in Northern Ireland and the refusal of the Protestant majority to accept reforms proposed by the Heath Government, the Northern Ireland Parliament and executive were suspended and direct control of Northern Ireland's affairs from London was established. A Secretary of State for Northern Ireland was appointed and a Northern Ireland Office created with departments for Agriculture, Commerce, Education, Environment, Manpower and Health and Social Services.

Direct rule was intended to be a temporary arrangement, but subsequent attempts to re-establish a degree of self-government in Northern Ireland have failed in face of the difficulty of producing a formula acceptable to majority and minority groups. In 1974 an Assembly elected by the Single Transferable Vote, and an executive drawn from all the main parties, were set up, but had to be abandoned in face of Protestant resistance. In 1975 a constitutional convention was elected, but the Government was not prepared to accept its recommendation that an executive be drawn from the majority party. In 1982 an Assembly was restored, and proposals made for the gradual re-introduction of devolved powers, but the Assembly was boycotted by the Catholic parties. Had any one of these initiatives succeeded it would have constituted only a degree of devolved power within the United Kingdom.

Despite the several forms of devolution for Scotland, Wales and Northern Ireland the Constitution remains unitary, and the United Kingdom Parliament retains ultimate sovereignty over the whole of Great Britain and Northern Ireland.

The Evolution of Parliament and the Cabinet

The evolutionary nature of the British Constitution is well illustrated by the history of Parliament and the Cabinet.[1] Parliament emerged after 1066 from the Magnum Concilium, or Great Council, of the Norman Kings of England, although even before this, the Saxon Kings had been advised by an assembly of wise men (the Witangemot). The Norman Great Council was made up of the barons who, under the feudal system, held land directly from the King. It met three or four times a year when summoned by the King, and its task was to give advice and support to the King and to provide money when he was unable to live from his own finances. During the thirteenth century the King found it increasingly difficult to live off his own money, or the money provided by the barons, and in years when the King was particularly short of finance members of the new rich trading classes were added to the baronial members of the Great Council. In 1213 King John summoned four knights from each county, selected by the Sheriff, and in 1254 Henry II summoned from each county two knights who were chosen by their colleagues. In 1265 Simon de Montfort summoned as well as the knights from the counties two burgesses from the independent towns with Royal charters, and in the 1295 'Model Parliament' of Edward I, barons, knights, burgesses, senior clergy, and lower clergy were all summoned on the principle that 'what touches all should be approved by all'.

The influence of Parliament, and particularly of the Commons, grew during the fourteenth century with the growing reliance of the Monarch on the taxes paid by the trading classes. The principle was established that taxation would

[1] For the history of Parliament see A. F. Pollard, *The Evolution of Parliament*, London 1964; K. R. Mackenzie, *The English Parliament*, London 1959. See also Sir R. S. Rait, *The Parliaments of Scotland*, Glasgow, 1924.

only be granted after grievances had been redressed, and this principle remained the basis of Parliamentary development during the fifteenth and sixteenth centuries. The growth in Parliament's influence led inevitably to conflict between the Monarch and Parliament over the extent of Parliament's powers, and this culminated in the constitutional conflicts of the seventeenth century. After Royal attempts to rule without Parliament, the 1688–9 settlement established a 'separation of powers' between the executive authority of the Monarch and the legislative power of Parliament. Constitutional developments in the eighteenth and nineteenth centuries, however, led to a complication of this situation, with Ministers drawn from Parliament exercising more and more executive authority on behalf of the Monarch. Thus the earlier Constitutional conflicts between the King and Parliament were followed in the modern period by conflicts between Parliament and Governments drawn from Parliament.

As with Parliament, the origins of the Cabinet can be traced back to the period following the Norman Conquest.[1] All Monarchs, even in medieval times, tended to surround themselves with close advisers, and very often with one adviser in particular. The Norman Kings looked for advice to the Curia Regis, a gathering of leading figures within the Magnum Concilium. During the thirteenth century the Curia Regis developed into the Privy Council composed of Royal officials like the Justiciar, the Chancellor, the Treasurer, and the Secretary (later to be known as the Secretary of State), and the medieval Monarchs relied on the Privy Council for advice on administration and the implementation of policies. By the middle of the seventeenth century the Privy Council had grown into a body of thirty or forty members, and an inner committee of advisers emerged, known variously as the Junto, Cabal, or Cabinet Council. Under William and Mary, and then Queen Anne, the Privy Council remained nominally as the body of King's advisers, but more and more influence passed to the Cabinet Council of about ten advisers.

In its turn, this body grew in numbers, and during the course of the eighteenth century there emerged a smaller

[1] For a history of the Cabinet see Mackintosh, *The British Cabinet*.

group within the Cabinet Council known at different times as the Lords of the Committee, the Select Lords, or the Inner Cabinet of senior advisers. By the middle of the eighteenth century the full Cabinet Council had ten to thirteen members, while the Inner Cabinet had from five to eight members. The King tended to refer primarily to the Inner Cabinet, and it thus grew in status. It superseded the larger body, and in its turn became known as the full Cabinet. By 1832 this Cabinet had grown to about a dozen members, and to about fifteen by the middle of the century. This was a result partly of the growth in the number of administrative departments, and partly a result of Parliamentary demands for all government agencies to have heads in Parliament so that they could be held responsible to Parliament.

Among the King's advisers there often tended to be a predominant figure, and in medieval times this was often the Chancellor. Even after 1660 Clarendon under Charles II, and Harvey and Godolphin under Queen Anne, were powerful figures. It is only with Sir Robert Walpole, however, towards the middle of the eighteenth century, that the title of Prime Minister is used to describe the King's chief Minister. Walpole, appointed First Lord of the Treasury in 1721, at first shared power with Townshend, but with Townshend's retirement in 1729 Walpole became supreme, and remained so until his resignation in 1742.

The power that Walpole possessed between 1729 and 1742 stemmed largely from his personal influence with the Monarch, but also from the fact that as First Lord of the Treasury he had the national finances at his disposal for patronage purposes, and in the eighteenth century this became essential for the management of Parliamentary elections on the King's behalf. The ability to secure through bribery the return of the King's candidates at elections gave Walpole power and influence in the Court. Similarly, he was able to command support in Parliament, and it is the fact that he was the direct link between the Monarch and Parliament that distinguishes Walpole from previous Royal advisers, and justifies his description as the first Prime Minister. After 1717 the Hanoverian Monarchs tended less and less to attend Cabinet meetings, largely because they preferred to consult their Ministers informally. This added to the influence that Walpole and his successors were able to exert as the link between King, Cabinet, and Parliament, while later in the century the Cabinet strengthened its authority in face of the Monarch and Parliament by presenting Cabinet decisions as a common view through the doctrine of collective responsibility.

* * *

The acceptance of the responsibility of Ministers to Parliament as well as to the King, forms the other main aspect of Cabinet development in Britain. Today Ministers individually, and the Government collectively, must have the support of the majority of the members of the House of Commons, with the resignation of the Government or the dissolution of Parliament being required if this support is lost. Support for the Government in the House of Commons has been achieved by different factors at different times. In an attempt to maintain harmony with Parliament, the Monarchs after 1688 tended to choose as Ministers some figures who were influential in the Commons. In 1694 and 1708 the Cabinet was composed entirely of Whig Ministers, and in this can perhaps be seen the beginning of party ties as the basis of Government strength in the Commons. In the eighteenth century, however, support for the Cabinet in the Commons was assured largely because the Monarch and his Prime Minister could use patronage and financial bribery to manipulate elections so as to produce a House of Commons favourable to the Cabinet.

The Reform Act 1832, by extending the franchise and destroying the rotten boroughs, destroyed this Royal control over elections. In the modern period, largely since the growth of mass parties after the 1867 franchise extension, the support of the House of Commons for the Government has been achieved primarily by the strength of party discipline within the modern party system. In the middle of the nineteenth century, however, with the elimination in 1832 of Royal manipulation of elections, but before the emergence of the modern party system, support for the Government in Parliament was based on a number of factors, including personalities, some degree of party loyalty, and the fear of MPs that unless an alternative Government was available, defeat for the Government would lead to dissolution. It is only this comparatively short period of some forty years following the first Reform Act that represents Parliament's 'Golden Age', when Governments were made and unmade largely at the will of individual MPs.

The British Parliamentary system requires, however, that as well as being responsible *to* Parliament, Ministers must be drawn *from* Parliament. This requirement is not found in all Parliamentary systems. A Parliamentary system, as opposed to a Presidential system, is one in which the executive is responsible to the legislature, in the sense that the executive must have the support (or the 'confidence') of a majority of the members of the legislature. Within this broad principle, however, there are variations in the physical relationship between the executive and the legislature. In some Parliamentary systems, such as West Germany and Italy, Ministers may, but are not obliged to, serve in Parliament. In others, such as Norway and Luxembourg, Ministers are specifically excluded from serving in Parliament, though they may attend its deliberations. In the Netherlands, Ministers may not even attend Parliament.

In Britain, the principle emerged in the eighteenth century that the King's Ministers *could* be drawn from Parliament, and then later that they *must* be drawn from Parliament (or must become members of one of the Houses). At first, limitations were placed on the right of members of the House of Commons to hold Ministerial office for fear that the Monarch might exercise too much influence over the Commons through the power of patronage. Thus the Act of Settlement 1701 contained a clause that excluded entirely from the Commons anyone who held an office of profit under the Crown. Had this rigid separation of the executive from the legislature been implemented to the full, the whole nature of British Constitutional development would have been fundamentally altered. The exclusion of Ministers from Parliament might limit executive control over the legislature, but by the same token it would limit the capacity of the legislature to influence the executive. Before the 1701 Act could be brought into operation, however, the attitude of the Commons softened, and the Succession to the Crown Act 1705 (re-enacted after the union with Scotland as the Regency Act 1707) drew a distinction between some posts which members of the Commons could not hold, and others to which members of the Commons could be appointed, subject to the provision that any such Ministers resign their House of Commons seats and seek re-election in by-elections.

This system operated throughout the eighteenth and nineteenth centuries, though some junior posts were excluded from the re-election requirements, and the list of posts that members of the Commons could not hold was gradually whittled away. The Reform Act 1867 also modified things slightly by allowing Ministers to change from one post to another without involving re-election. In the main, however, the appointment of an MP to a Ministerial post was automatically followed by a by-election to re-establish his place in the House. Legislation in 1919 and 1926 finally got rid of the re-election requirement. At times someone from outside Parliament is appointed to Ministerial office and is then found a seat in the Commons through a by-election (as with Frank Cousins in 1965), or is given a Peerage (as with Lord Bellwin in 1979, and Lord Young in 1984). In such cases, however, membership of one of the Houses must be attained, and in 1965 Patrick Gordon Walker had to resign his post as Foreign Secretary after failing to be elected to the Commons in a by-election.

Government and Parliament Today

The doctrine of the Sovereignty or Supremacy of Parliament means the absolute legal power of Parliament to make or unmake any law whatsoever, Parliament being 'the Crown, Lords and Commons in Parliament assembled'.[1] The four essential features of the doctrine are that there is no higher legislative authority; no court can declare Acts of Parliament to be invalid; there is no limit to Parliament's sphere of legislation; and no Parliament can legally bind its successor, or be bound by its predecessor. A feature of membership of the

[1] See R. S. Allan, 'The Limits of Parliamentary Sovereignty', *PL* 1985, pp. 614–36.

EEC is that Community laws apply to all member countries and take precedence over domestic laws. This is acknowledged in the European Communities Act 1972.[1] This factor aside, there are no limits to Parliament's sphere of legislative authority, other than those of physical possibility and practical politics. Thus whoever controls Parliament has supreme legislative authority. Though in strict terms Parliament means Crown, Lords and Commons, in practical terms Parliament means the House of Commons. The power of the Crown is limited by convention, and the power of the House of Lords by statute and convention. Thus it may be said more truly that whoever controls *the Commons* has supreme legislative authority, other than in those rare cases when the power of the Crown or the Lords is invoked to oppose the Commons.

The practical working of the Cabinet system and the two-party system in Britain means that this control over the House of Commons is exercised by the Government of the day. The Government is drawn from the Commons and the Lords, and is maintained in power by the support of the majority of the members of the Commons. The two-party system, in the context of the existing electoral system, means that generally one party has an overall majority in the Commons, while the nature of intra-party relationships means that usually the Government can secure the support of its own MPs. The Government is thus in a dominant position of control over the House of Commons, and thus (in most circumstances) over the whole of Parliament. In this situation, the Government is constitutionally omnipotent.

The unwritten, flexible, and unitary nature of the Constitution, and the doctrine of Parliamentary Sovereignty, mean that the Constitution can be readily amended, and any legislative change is legally possible. Thus the Government in 1914 assumed almost dictatorial powers through the Defence of the Realm Act, and in 1939 through the Emergency Powers Act.

[1] See J. Taylor, 'British Membership of the European Communities: the Question of Parliamentary Sovereignty', *G and O* 1975, pp. 278–93; J. D. B. Mitchell (*et al.*), 'Constitutional Aspects of the Treaty and Legislation Relating to British Membership', *CMLR* 1972, pp. 134–66; H. W. R. Wade, 'Sovereignty and the European Communities', *LQR* 1972, pp. 1–5; J. Forman, 'The European Communities Act', *CMLR* 1973, pp. 39–55.

In 1972 a Bill giving the Government wide powers to deal with a crisis in Northern Ireland was passed through all of its stages in just four hours. The Government controls and dominates the Parliamentary timetable, and the rules of the House of Commons (the Standing Orders) can be altered by the House itself. By Act of Parliament the Government can perpetuate the life of the Parliament (and thus its own life), as happened during the two world wars. Thus with a secure majority in the Commons, a Government, in legal and Parliamentary terms, can achieve anything.

The traditional explanation of the strength of the Government's position in the House of Commons is the very fact that the Government requires the support of the Commons in order to remain in office.[1] This seeming weakness of the Government's position is seen as its real strength, in that rebellion against the Government is deterred by the fact that it could precipitate the resignation of the Government or a dissolution of Parliament.[2] In the subsequent election the rebellious MPs might lose their seats and the party might lose office. It is true that most MPs are in safe seats and incur little personal expense in an election campaign. Nevertheless, the number of truly safe seats has declined in recent years, the discomforts of a campaign can be considerable and the possibility of the party's electoral defeat remains as the ultimate spur to party loyalty.

As well as this basic constitutional factor, however, other considerations help to preserve the Government's position in Parliament. Backbenchers will normally support their Government, in debates and votes, because of their general loyalty to the party. Even if an MP dislikes a particular item of policy he may still be inclined to support it because he feels that, on

[1] P. Norton, *Dissension in the House of Commons 1945–74*, London 1975; P. Norton, *Conservative Dissidents*, London 1978; P. Norton, *Dissension in the House of Commons 1974–79*, London 1980; P. Norton, 'Intra-Party Dissent in the House of Commons', *Parl. Aff.* 1976, pp. 404–20; E. W. Crowe, 'Cross-Voting in the British House of Commons', *J of P* 1980, pp. 487–510.

[2] See W. G. Andrews, 'Some Thoughts on the Power of Dissolution', *Parl. Aff.* 1959–60, pp. 286–96; W. G. Andrews, 'Three Electoral Colleges', *Parl. Aff.* 1960–1, pp. 178–88; G. Marshall and G. C. Moodie, *Some Problems of the Constitution*, London 1961, Ch. 3.

the whole, the party is well-led and is pursuing acceptable policies. In this respect an important consideration will be the desirability of the party presenting an image of unity in order to maintain its electoral prospects. An MP will also be aware that persistent dissent, or failure to support the Government in an especially important vote, could lead to his expulsion from the party, or at least to a setback in his political career. The Prime Minister's power of patronage is particularly important in this context.

Although the Government can rely to some extent on MPs' loyalty to their party and their fears of the consequences of dissent, it also secures the support of backbenchers by accommodating their views as it formulates its policies. In this the role of the party Whips is crucial. As well as serving as the means through which party discipline is enforced, the Whips act as channels of communication, reporting backbench views to Ministers and indicating the strength of backbench feelings. Thus Government defeats in Parliament are relatively rare partly because the Government knows what its backbenchers will accept, and tends only to introduce measures that it knows to be acceptable to them. Party unity and docility in public is often the product of discord and dissent in caucus meetings.

In the last fifteen years backbenchers have been more willing than previously to take their dissent beyond the caucus meeting and to abstain or vote against the Government in divisions. On a number of occasions backbench defections have led to the defeat of the Government. In 1972 the Heath Conservative Government was defeated on its immigration policy as a result of a combination of abstentions and cross-voting by Conservative backbenchers. Other defeats followed, and in all the Heath Government was defeated on six occasions in the 1970–4 Parliament. The 1974–9 minority Labour Government suffered a number of defeats when the opposition parties combined against it, but it was also defeated on more than twenty occasions specifically because Labour MPs declined to support it in divisions. Some of these defeats were on major items of policy. The Scotland and Wales Bill was effectively destroyed in 1977 when Labour MPs combined with the opposition parties to reject the Government's Parliamentary timetable for the Bill. The Scotland Bill and the Wales Bill (that the Government then introduced to replace the original measure) were amended in major ways, against the wishes of the Government, as a result of Labour MPs combining with the opposition parties. Other measures on which the Labour Government was obliged to accept changes, against its will, included the Social Security Benefits Bill 1975, the Dock Work Regulation Bill 1976 and the Criminal Law Bill 1977. As well as defeats on the floor of the House the Labour Government was defeated on a number of occasions in Standing Committees as a result of Labour defections.

Since 1979 the size of the Government's majority has generally been large enough to absorb cross-voting by Conservative backbenchers, but in 1986 the Shops Bill was defeated at second reading when sixty-eight Conservative MPs voted against the Government. On a number of other occasions the Thatcher Government has been severely embarrassed by the number of Conservative MPs who have refused to support it in divisions. In 1984 the Civil Aviation Bill was withdrawn in face of opposition from Conservative MPs at the committee stage, and (also in 1984) the Government's plans to increase parental contributions towards their children's higher education costs were amended after resistance by Conservative MPs.

There are a variety of factors that help to explain the more aggressive behaviour by backbench MPs in the last fifteen years or so. Those entering the House since the 1960s have been somewhat more ambitious and assertive than their predecessors, and have been more anxious to have a direct influence upon policy. The failure of successive governments to solve major social and economic problems may have helped to undermine their authority with their own supporters. Certainly, the Heath, Wilson and Callaghan Governments were ideologically disappointing to many of their supporters inside and outside Parliament. The 1974–9 Labour Government had particular difficulties because it lacked an overall majority for most of the time and thus was subject to minor party pressures as well as backbench pressures. In the past, party leaders were able to use an MP's constituency party as a means of influencing his behaviour, but the increasing influence of extremist groups in some constituencies has meant that (especially in the Labour Party) constituency pressures have encouraged rebellion rather than conformity. In this respect, then, the greater tendency for backbenchers to vote against their Government is part of the general decline of the disciplined two-party system.

A major consequence of the increased number of Government defeats on the floor of the House of Commons has been the clarification of the question of just when the Government is obliged to resign or seek a dissolution. In the past the convention was that a Government would resign or seek a dissolution only if defeated 'on a major issue', but the question of what constituted a major issue was unclear. In the 1970s, however, it became established that only a defeat in a vote on a specific motion of confidence would be recognised as necessitating a resignation or dissolution. Thus the Conservative and Labour Governments 'accepted' the several defeats they suffered on their legislation, and the Callaghan Government eventually sought a dissolution in March 1979 only after being defeated on a motion of confidence.

As a result of this clarification of the circumstances under which a Government will fall, the position of backbench MPs has been strengthened. A Government's legislative proposals can be rejected without the Government itself being brought down. If the normal processes of intra-party discussion fail to produce a formula that Ministers and backbenchers can accept, the backbenchers can press their case to the extent of defeating the Government without precipitating its fall. The recognition of this new flexibility in the Government's Constitutional position, of course, is itself an encouragement to rebellion, and helps to explain the greater willingness of backbenchers to defy the Whips.

* * *

The 'normal' situation of a Government based on a clear party majority does not emerge in every instance.[1] A majority for a Government can be achieved in a number of different ways. A Government may be a Coalition with the support of

[1] See above, pp. 66–7.

all the parties in the Commons (as with the two wartime Coalitions), or of just some party elements (as with the National Government formed in 1931). A Government can be drawn from one party but with the support necessary for a majority in the Commons coming from more than one party, as was the case with the Liberal Government of 1910–15 and the Labour Governments of 1924, 1929–31, and (for a good part of its life) 1974–79. Either a coalition or a minority government is inevitable if an election does not produce an overall majority for one party. Of the twenty-three elections this century, eighteen did produce an overall majority in the Commons for one party (though Labour's majorities in 1950, 1964 and October 1974 were small), while in the elections of 1910 (January and December), 1923, 1929 and February 1974 no party won an overall majority.

Just as a Government that lacks an overall majority in Parliament still has a number of weapons at its disposal, so a Government that does have a clear overall majority is not entirely free from Parliamentary constraints. The 'rules of the game' and the 'customs of the House' demand that the Opposition cannot be ignored or steam-rollered, and this is not merely to avoid bad public reactions. To a large extent the effective working of the Parliamentary machine is dependent upon the cooperation and mutual accommodation of the Government and Opposition Whips. A Government with a very small majority in the Commons can have this destroyed in by-elections, as happened to the Labour Government during the 1974–9 Parliament. Also, Governments secure in the Commons can be destroyed by an internal Cabinet split, as happened with the Unionist Government in 1905, the Coalition Governments in 1916 and 1922, and the Labour Government in 1931.

Ultimately a Government could conceivably be overthrown by a defeat in the House of Commons on a vote of confidence caused by a breakdown in party loyalty on the backbenches. In practical terms, however, no Government with a clear party majority in the Commons has been destroyed by a defeat in a division in the House since Gladstone resigned after a defeat on the Finance Bill in 1885. This forms the basis of the claim that today Governments are not created and destroyed by the House of Commons, as they were in the nineteenth century, but by the electorate at general elections, and by the leaders of the party that is in power between elections.

As can be seen from Table XXVI, there have been twenty-five changes of Government this century and on most occasions the change came as a result of factors unconnected with defeat in the House. On five occasions the Government was defeated in a general election towards the end of a full Parliament, and on four occasions the Government fell because of Cabinet discord. In 1915 the Liberal Government gave way to a wartime coalition, and in 1945 the coalition was replaced by a 'caretaker' Conservative Government. On nine occasions the Prime Minister was replaced by another member of the Government. There were five other occasions this century, however, (in January 1924, October 1924, 1940, 1951 and 1979) when the House of Commons was involved to some extent in the fall of the Government, though there were complicating factors on each occasion.

In the 1923 general election the Conservatives lost their overall majority, but remained the largest single party. Baldwin did not resign at once, but met Parliament in January 1924, only to be beaten by the combined Liberal and Labour votes in the Commons. Thus, technically, the Government was overthrown by the House of Commons, but in fact the Government's fate had been sealed at the general election.

MacDonald in October 1924 and Callaghan in 1979 asked for dissolutions (and lost the consequent elections) when their Labour Governments were beaten in divisions in the Commons. The MacDonald and Callaghan Governments, however, were both minority Governments. They were dependent on the support of the minor parties, which was not forthcoming on the occasions of their defeats. In 1979 the Welsh Nationalists voted with the Government in the vote of confidence, but the Scottish Nationalists, Ulster Unionists, Liberals and Conservatives combined to defeat the Government by one vote.

In 1940 the Chamberlain Government fell after a censure debate in the Commons on the Government's handling of the war. The Government was not defeated in the division, but its

TABLE XXVI

Governments and Prime Ministers this Century

Prime Minister			Reason for the change of Government A. Voluntary retirement of the Prime Minister (that is, for health or similar reasons) B. Electoral defeat C. Resignation of the Prime Minister or the whole Government for reasons other than electoral defeat D. Wartime emergency
Salisbury	Con.	1895–1902	A
Balfour	Con.	1902–5	C
Campbell-Bannerman	Lib.	1905–8	A
Asquith	Lib.	1908–15	D
Asquith	Coalition	1915–16	C
Lloyd George	Coalition	1916–22	C
Bonar Law	Con.	1922–3	A
Baldwin	Con.	1923–4	B
MacDonald	Lab.	1924	B
Baldwin	Con.	1924–9	B
MacDonald	Lab.	1929–31	C
MacDonald	National	1931–5	A
Baldwin	National	1935–7	A
Chamberlain	National	1937–40	D
Churchill	Coalition	1940–5	C
Churchill	Con.	1945	B
Attlee	Lab.	1945–51	B
Churchill	Con.	1951–5	A
Eden	Con.	1955–7	A
Macmillan	Con.	1957–63	A
Home	Con.	1963–4	B
Wilson	Lab.	1964–70	B
Heath	Con.	1970–4	B
Wilson	Lab.	1974–6	A
Callaghan	Lab.	1976–9	B
Thatcher	Con.	1979–	—

majority was so much smaller than its normal majority, and criticism of Chamberlain was so severe in the debate, that the Prime Minister felt obliged to resign. This, however, was a peculiar wartime situation, and a Conservative Prime Minister and Government was merely replaced by another Conservative Prime Minister and a Conservative dominated coalition. It has also been argued that Chamberlain's resignation came as a result of the pressure of public opinion rather than the House of Commons division.[1]

In 1951 Attlee asked for a dissolution after his Government (left with an overall majority of only six at the 1950 election) had been subjected to eighteen months of vigorous Opposition pressure. The Government lost the consequent election, and there has been much argument as to whether Attlee need have sought a dissolution when he did.[2] Attlee was not forced to seek a dissolution as a result of any specific Government defeat, and in the final analysis the Government could have carried on. Indeed, it can be argued that the 1950–1 Parliament, and more particularly that of 1964–6, illustrate how a Government can survive in the Commons with a very small majority, provided that it avoids as far as possible issues that are likely to cause dissent among its own backbenchers. This suggests that a Government with a very small majority is in some ways more secure than a Government with a large majority, potential rebels being less likely to show dissension if the Government appears to be in a precarious position.

Despite these five instances, it remains true that on no occasion this century has a Government based on a workable party majority been overthrown by the House of Commons. The January 1924 incident merely involved a technicality, in that Baldwin's defeat in the Commons was inevitable after his overall majority had been destroyed at the election; in October 1924 and 1979 the Government party was in a minority in the House; in 1940 and 1951 the Government's fall did not come as a result of any specific defeat in a division in the Commons. While these episodes illustrate how the House

[1] See Jennings, *Cabinet Government*, p. 478. See also J. S. Rasmussen, 'Party Discipline in War-Time: the Downfall of the Chamberlain Government', *J of P* 1970, pp. 379–406.

[2] See Hoffman, *The Conservative Party in Opposition, 1945–51*, Ch. 7.

of Commons can be involved in the circumstances surrounding the fall of a Government, the general principle remains that today Governments are made and unmade by the electorate and the party leaders rather than by the House of Commons. The point is reinforced by the defeats that Labour and Conservative Governments in the 1970s and 1980s have suffered in the Commons on (often significant) items of policy. The Governments have chosen not to resign or seek a dissolution of Parliament, but to live with these setbacks and leave the electorate to decide their fate in due course.

Ministerial Responsibility

The term 'responsible government' can be applied to the British system in three main respects.[1] First of all, it may be regarded as a characteristic feature of the British system that Governments act in a responsible manner, in the sense that they do not abuse the wide legal powers that they possess as a result of the various features of the Constitution which concentrate considerable power in the hands of the Government of the day. In this sense, responsible government means 'trustworthy' government, and is a general feature of the British political culture. Secondly, responsible government can be taken to mean that the Government is responsive to public opinion, and acts in accordance with what it judges to be the wishes of the majority of the people. There is a certain overlap between this meaning and the first meaning, in that today we assume that in order to be regarded as trustworthy, a Government has to be responsive to public opinion. Clearly, however, there can be conflict between these meanings, in that at times a Government may have to ignore current public opinion if it is to act in what it regards as the long-term interests of the country.

The third and most specific meaning of responsible government is that the Government is accountable to Parliament. This meaning is based on the principle that the Government has to have the support of the majority of the members of the House of Commons. The modern application of this third

[1] See Birch, *Representative and Responsible Government*.

meaning of responsible government has been considered above, but it is necessary here to consider two doctrines that stem from it – the principles of collective Government responsibility and individual Ministerial responsibility to Parliament.[1]

The doctrine of collective responsibility means that all members of the Government, and not just the departmental Ministers most directly involved, are collectively responsible for the successes or failures of the Government's policies. Implicit in the doctrine is the notion that all Ministers are bound to support Government decisions before the public, Parliament, and the party, and at the very least must refrain from openly criticising Government policy. This doctrine also implies that a Minister who dislikes a particular Government policy must reconcile his differences or resign from the Government. The principle is perhaps aptly summed up by Lord Melbourne's comment to his Cabinet colleagues that 'it doesn't matter a damn which line we take but we had better all be in one story'.[2]

Collective responsibility had its origin in the need for Ministers in the eighteenth century to present a united front to the Monarch on the one hand, and to Parliament on the other.[3] Today, collective responsibility enables the Government to present a common face to its party inside and outside Parliament, and to the electorate generally – the maintenance of a united front being an essential prerequisite of the preservation of party discipline in the House, and to the answering of Opposition and public criticism of Government policy. In this respect it also serves as a means of suppressing differences of opinion within the Government itself.

The doctrine applies to all Ministers, from senior Cabinet Ministers to junior Ministers. It would also seem to apply to the unpaid Parliamentary Private Secretaries, in that in 1967 the Prime Minister forced a group of Parliamentary Private

[1] See G. Marshall, 'Ministerial Responsibility', *PQ* 1963, pp. 256–68; Marshall and Moodie, Ch. 4.

[2] Quoted in Lord Fitzmaurice, *Life of Lord Granville*, London 1906 (2 vols), II, p. 469.

[3] See D. L. Ellis, 'Collective Ministerial Responsibility and Collective Solidarity', *PL* 1980, pp. 367–96.

Secretaries to resign when they declined to support specific aspects of Government economic policy. On some issues where there is no clear party line, the members of the Government are sometimes allowed to join in the 'luxury' of a free vote in Parliament, uninhibited by the party Whips or by the doctrine of collective responsibility. Even on some occasions when backbenchers are allowed a free vote, however, the Government's collective view is often made clear. The Government is expected to give a lead on practically all issues, and for the Government not to do so can be seen as an abdication of its duty.

In the National Government formed in 1931 there was an open 'agreement to differ' among Ministers in their attitude towards tariff policy.[1] The Government contained Conservative, Liberal, and Labour members, who had fundamentally opposed attitudes towards the question of protective tariffs, and this was felt to be justified in order that the Government might maintain its broad all-party nature. The agreement only operated from January to September 1932, when the free-traders primarily concerned (Snowden, Samuel, and Sinclair) resigned from the Government.

In 1975 the 'agreement to differ' principle was revived, in the context of the national referendum on the question of Britain's continued membership of the European Community. Anti-marketeers among Labour Ministers were allowed to express their views in public during the referendum campaign, even though the 'official' Government policy was that Britain should remain within the Community. The Prime Minister insisted, however, that the freedom of dissent did not extend to debates within Parliament, and in April 1975 Eric Heffer was asked to resign his post as Minister of State for Industry after speaking in the Commons against the policy of remaining within the Community. Labour Ministers were again given the freedom to differ in 1977 in face of their disagreements over the choice of the electoral system for direct elections to the European Parliament.

Although in strict theory today the doctrine of collective responsibility demands support from all Ministers for Gov-

[1] For comments see Jennings, *Cabinet Government*, p. 278.

ernment policies, there are obvious practical difficulties in applying such a principle in modern Governments which contain about one hundred members. The British parties, and thus British Governments, are made up of many diverse elements. Within any Government there will be a number of important policy disagreements which are not publicly revealed, and it is necessary to discount the notion that collective responsibility involves genuine agreement by all Ministers on all aspects of Government policies. Certainly, in the eyes of the public some Ministers are held to be 'more responsible than others', and thus open to more blame (or in some cases, more praise) than their colleagues. The 'Guilty Men of Munich' in 1938, and the 'Suez Ministers' in 1956, were small groups of Ministers who received particular blame for the Government's policies. Similarly, individual Ministers often attract criticism rather than the whole Government. Sir Keith Joseph, as Secretary of State for Education in the Thatcher Government, received particular criticism from teachers and students, while the Chancellor of the Exchequer is always singled out for particular criticism in times of wage restraint. The Government can often use individual Ministerial unpopularity as a means of escaping from collective responsibility. Thus in 1962 Selwyn Lloyd was asked to resign after his incomes policy, which had previously been endorsed by the whole Government, proved to be unpopular and ineffective.

The degrees of responsibility that exist within the Government are thus often known to the public, and are sometimes used as a means of sacrificing one Minister in order to relieve the whole Government of responsibility. A general basis of unity has to be maintained, however, in that if disagreements become too acute, and become too well known, the Government's Parliamentary and electoral security is threatened. To this end, collective responsibility, despite its practical limitations, remains as a device that is used to curb excessive disagreements among Ministers, and to hide such disagreements as do exist.

* * *

The doctrine of individual responsibility has a number of meanings. In the legal sense it means that the Minister, not the Monarch, is responsible for a particular aspect of governmental activity, and in this sense it is the logical expression of the principle that the Monarch exercises his powers only on the advice of Ministers. In relation to Parliament, Ministerial responsibility means that the Minister has to answer, in the informative sense, for the activities of the department of which he is in charge. He has to answer questions and contribute to debates in Parliament, providing information about the matters of activity for which he is responsible. Further, as indicated above, individual Ministerial responsibility can mean that within the doctrine of collective Government responsibility an individual Minister is particularly responsible for his own department or his own sphere of activity. Theoretically this can be taken to mean that the Minister, and not his departmental officials, is responsible for the mistakes made by the department, with the Minister's resignation being necessary in the event of a serious error by the Minister's department.

The precise extent of a Minister's responsibilities in this direction is not clear, nor are the consequences of the acknowledgement by Ministers of responsibility for departmental errors. It has been argued that the Minister is held to be responsible and accountable for all mistakes by his subordinates, even though the Minister may not have known about them, and could not have prevented them. Thus Sir Ivor Jennings talks of 'the responsibility of the Minister for every act done in his department',[1] while Lord Morrison has said that the Minister 'must accept responsibility as if the act were his own'.[2]

The practical limitations of this interpretation, however, were illustrated by the 'V and G affair' in 1971.[3] The Department of Trade and Industry (and its predecessor the Board of Trade) had a general responsibility for supervising the affairs of insurance companies, in the public interest, but failed to anticipate the collapse of the Vehicle and General Insurance Company in March 1971. A Tribunal that examined the affair censured the department. Particular civil servants were

[1] *Cabinet Government*, p. 499.

[2] *Government and Parliament*, p. 329.

[3] R. A. Chapman, 'The Vehicle and General Affair', *Pub. Admin.* 1973, pp. 273–90.

accused of incompetence and negligence, and subsequently were removed from their posts. The Secretary of State for Trade and Industry, however, did not accept responsibility. There was no question of a Ministerial resignation, and the Minister even argued that the civil servants involved should defend themselves in public. In support of the Minister's attitude it was pointed out that the department's involvement with the insurance company extended over a number of years, that in this time six different departmental Ministers had held office, and that the matter had been handled quite far down the departmental hierarchy.

Ministers resign from the Government for a variety of reasons. Some resign because they cannot accept collective responsibility for an aspect of government policy, or because they are generally at odds with their colleagues. Thus in 1985 Ian Gow resigned as Minister of State at the Treasury because he disagreed with changes in Government policy towards Northern Ireland, while in 1986 Michael Heseltine resigned as Secretary of State for Defence over the manner in which Cabinet business was conducted. Some Ministers give up their posts for reasons of age, health or other personal considerations, and others are asked to resign because the Prime Minister feels that they are no longer suitable. After the 1983 election Francis Pym and David Howell were asked to 'return to the backbenches', and in all about a dozen Ministers (and a greater number of junior Ministers) were removed from office in this way between 1979 and 1986.

Few Ministers, however, resign or are asked to resign because of specific errors by them or their departments. Indeed, between 1855 and 1955 there were only twenty such resignations, and there have been few in the last thirty years. Following the invasion of the Falkland Islands in 1982 Lord Carrington resigned as Foreign Secretary (together with two junior Ministers, Humphrey Atkins and Richard Luce), while in 1986 Leon Brittan resigned as Secretary of State for Trade and Industry after he was criticised for authorising the disclosure of confidential matters to the press. These, however, are rare examples: resignation in acknowledgement of specific Ministerial errors is unusual.

A number of factors are responsible for the comparative rarity of such Ministerial resignations.[1] The Minister may be shielded by the collective responsibility of the whole Government, or a small group of Ministers can assume a collective responsibility, making it difficult to apportion specific blame. Even when criticism is clearly levelled at one Minister, as with the Minister of Food, John Strachey, over the failure of the groundnut scheme in 1947, the Prime Minister may support the Minister and help him to weather the storm. A Minister who offers to resign may be persuaded to remain in post, as when the Prime Minister refused to accept John Nott's resignation as Secretary of State for Defence following the invasion of the Falklands in 1982. Alternatively, the Minister may be moved to another department in a Ministerial reshuffle, as were Shinwell after the fuel crisis of 1947, and Callaghan after the 1967 devaluation. A Minister who does resign may, of course, return to the Government in another post at a later date (as did Richard Luce in 1984).

Thus there is a clear overlap between individual Ministerial responsibility and collective Government responsibility, in that at times a Minister's individual responsibility is used as a means of avoiding the Government's collective responsibility for an error, while on other occasions an individual Minister can be shielded behind the collective responsibility of the whole Government. As the scope of government activity has grown over the last fifty years, Ministers must inevitably find it difficult to keep in touch with the technical details of their departments' work. It has also become harder to keep the Government as a collective body responsible for the whole range and depth of executive actions. Thus both doctrines have become more and more difficult to apply in their strict meaning, and there must inevitably be a large and growing difference between their theory and practice.

[1] S. E. Finer, 'The Individual Responsibility of Ministers', *Pub. Admin.* 1956, pp. 377–96. See also G. K. Fry, 'Thoughts on the Present State of the Convention of Ministerial Responsibility', *Parl. Aff.* 1969–70, pp. 10–20; L. A. Gunn, 'Politicians and Officials: Who is Answerable?', *PQ* 1972, pp. 253–60; G. K. Fry, 'The Sachsenhausen Concentration Camp Case and the Convention of Ministerial Responsibility', *PL* 1970, pp. 336–57.

Constitutional Authority and Political Power

In this chapter, emphasis has been placed on the almost unlimited Constitutional authority of Governments in Britain. It has been pointed out that the Constitution is largely unwritten and essentially flexible; that its unitary nature means that the Government is not faced by sovereign States; that Parliamentary supremacy, and the dominance of the Commons within Parliament, gives vast legislative scope to a Government that has a majority in the Commons; that in addition Ministers enjoy considerable prerogative powers that they exercise in the name of the Crown. In previous chapters it was noted that in the past the party system and the electoral system have generally combined to produce a Government with a clear working majority in the Commons, and that Parliamentary party discipline has normally allowed a Government to preserve its majority from one election to the next. Thus there is considerable justification for Bernard Crick's observation that 'Of all governments of countries with free political institutions, British government exhibits the greatest concentration of power and authority'.[1]

There is a fundamental distinction, however, between what is Constitutionally legitimate and what is politically feasible: although there may be few Constitutional constraints on British Governments' authority, there are innumerable practical constraints.[2] Four main types may be noted. Firstly, there are constraints within the machinery of central government itself. The efficiency of any Government is affected by structural factors such as its size, the effectiveness of its decision-making machinery, the channels for the coordination of this machinery, and the efficiency of the bureaucracy that surrounds it. The nineteenth-century Cabinet, for example, had little or no machinery for preparing Cabinet papers, recording decisions and ensuring that they were executed. In this

[1] B. Crick, *The Reform of Parliament*, London 1964, p. 16.

[2] See W. A. Robson, 'The Constraints on British Government', *PQ* 1973, pp. 117–26; N. H. Keehn, 'Great Britain: the Illusion of Governmental Authority', *WP* 1977–8, pp. 538–62; J. Douglas, 'The Overloaded Crown', *BJPS* 1976, pp. 483–506; A. S. Klieman, 'Emergency Powers and Liberal Democracy in Britain', *JCCP* 1978, pp. 190–211.

century the Cabinet Office has developed in size and scope, but the coordination of the machinery of government has been made difficult by the big increase in the number of Ministerial posts. The efficiency of the Government is affected even more fundamentally by personnel factors such as the availability of talented people to fill Ministerial posts, the turnover rate among Ministers, or the degree of ideological and personal animosity within the Government. As is discussed in the next chapter, Ministers are drawn from a fairly limited pool. There is a wide variety of considerations other than 'ability' that affect the Prime Minister's choice, and the impact that Ministers are able to have on their departments is limited by a range of factors. Though ideological differences among Ministers may be hidden beneath a blanket of collective responsibility, they can nevertheless paralyse a Government and restrict the emergence of agreed policies.

Secondly, there are constraints that are imposed by other institutions of government with which Ministers have to deal, such as the Civil Service, Parliament, local authorities and nationalised industries. The relationship between Ministers and civil servants is complex, and is considered in detail later. In this context, however, it is necessary to emphasise the fallaciousness of the view that the civil servants' role is merely to administer policies that are devised exclusively by Ministers. The 'departmental point of view' on a particular issue is normally very clearly defined. Equally, a much broader 'Civil Service point of view' invariably emerges towards the overall policy and strategy of the Government. Individual Ministers, and the Cabinet collectively, have to recognise and accommodate these influential views if they are to avoid a succession of confrontations with the Civil Service. In Parliament the Government has to contend with opposition from the main Opposition party, the minor parties, and from its own backbenchers. Government control of the Parliamentary timetable, and party discipline enforced through the Whips, mean that ultimately the Government has the means to overcome resistance to its legislation in the Commons. The Government also has the Constitutional means, through the Parliament Acts 1911 and 1949, to overcome the rejection of legislation by the House of Lords. It is often more politically sensible, however, for the

Government to seek to compromise with its opponents in the Commons and the Lords than to make continual use of its ultimate powers. Similarly, in their dealings with local authorities and nationalised industries, Ministers possess ultimate powers of coercion which, nevertheless, they will use with caution, not least because of the considerable political benefits to be gained from the preservation of harmonious relations with the bodies concerned.

Thirdly, there are numerous constraints imposed by the need for the Government to come to terms with powerful interests within the State. The strength of business interests on the one hand, and trade unions on the other, is universally recognised, and a Government ignores these bodies at its peril. There are, however, many other less conspicuous organisations and interests that are capable of bringing considerable pressure to bear on Ministers, and of obliging them to take note of their particular interests in the formulation of public policy. Ultimately, of course, a Government is limited in what it can achieve by the threat of civil strife, but long before that stage is reached the pressure of public opinion limits considerably what a Government can achieve. Precisely what constitutes 'public opinion', and how it makes itself felt, is difficult to define, but several forces including the press, radio and television, the local organs of the political parties, and pressure groups all help in the formulation of public attitudes, and at the same time provide channels for the expression of these attitudes. Given that a Government wishes to win the next election (it being assumed that Governments do strive to retain office), it cannot afford to ignore entirely, in the years before the election, the opinions that are expressed by pressure groups, the press, and all the other outlets for public attitudes. More than this electoral consideration, however, Governments prefer, in general, to achieve their ends through persuasion rather than coercion. While it may possess the ultimate Constitutional authority to pursue a particular policy, a Government may be deterred from exercising its ultimate power of enforcement by the political and social costs of such a step. Indeed, some policies will succeed only if they are launched against a background of favourable public opinion.

Finally, there are a vast number of constraints that are

imposed by economic, administrative, diplomatic and other practical facts of political life. A Government's legislative ambitions are conditioned by what the Parliamentary timetable can accommodate, and by what is administratively possible. While a determined Minister may be able to galvanise his civil servants to achieve administrative miracles, there are limits to the ability of even the most dynamic and persuasive Ministers. Foreign crises, economic difficulties or industrial unrest can undermine a Government's plans and limit its ability to fulfil its intentions. Economic conditions affect the performance of Governments in all countries, and this has been especially the case in post-war Britain. With an economy that depends particularly heavily on the import of raw materials and the export of manufactured goods, Britain is especially vulnerable to international conditions. Increases in the price of basic commodities, international trade recessions, and inflation stimulated by world-wide economic conditions are all factors that British Governments are able to influence only marginally, but which can affect a Government's economic strategy in fundamental ways. Britain's involvement with, and dependence upon, foreign governments and international organisations, is considerable. The attitudes of the International Monetary Fund and overseas investors have to be considered in the formulation of economic policy, especially (but not only) during sterling and balance of payments crises. Trade policy is affected by the many international agreements that are a consequence of membership of the European Community. Defence policy involves membership of NATO and various other mutual-aid agreements. Foreign policy is conditioned by the attitudes of Britain's allies, particularly the USA (with the 1956 Suez crisis providing the most dramatic post-war example of Britain's dependence on American attitudes).

Politics is essentially the art of the possible, and numerous practical difficulties can limit the ability of a Government to implement its intentions. To quote examples of widely unpopular actions that Governments could take, or have taken in the past, detracts from the essential fact that, in the main, and for a variety of reasons, Governments do not abuse the wide Constitutional powers that they possess. Indeed, in the 1970s British Governments were characterised more by their failure to act decisively in the face of a variety of economic, social and Constitutional problems, than by any excessive use of executive authority. Thus a picture emerges of British Governments having almost unlimited legal power, but exercising this power in a spirit of restraint. They are not limited in the scope of their authority by written Constitutional checks and balances, but rather by various practical considerations, by the nature of British society, and by an unwritten code of behaviour. It has been said of the British Constitution that it is 'no more than the current notion of politicians about proper conduct'.[1] This essentially vague and nebulous feature of the British political system, with the consequent differences between what the Constitution theoretically allows and what is actually practised, means that the British system can easily be misinterpreted. It is thus necessary to emphasise the very real checks that are imposed on the activities of Government by practical politics and by the traditional acceptance of the need for moderate and reasonable government.

[1] D. E. Butler, *The Study of Political Behaviour*, London 1959, p. 17. See also D. B. Searing, 'Rules of the Game in Britain', *APSR* 1982, pp. 239–58.

7

The Structure of Government

WRITING IN 1867, Walter Bagehot, in *The English Constitution*,[1] declared that the two characteristic features of Cabinet Government in Britain were, firstly, that the Cabinet was a collective executive body, and secondly, that it was answerable to Parliament (rather than directly to the electorate) for its authority and very existence. This, observed Bagehot, was in direct contrast with the features of Presidential Government in the United States where the executive was the single figure of the President, who was directly elected and was thus not responsible to the legislature. It is often argued today, however, that Constitutional developments in Britain in the last one hundred years have largely removed from our system the classic features attributed to it by Bagehot: that a Government's position in Parliament is now normally so secure between general elections that, in effect, it is answerable directly to the electorate rather than to Parliament, and that the personal power of the Prime Minister within the Government has increased to such an extent that the system has acquired Presidential characteristics. The modern relationship between the Government and Parliament was discussed in the previous chapter. Relationships within the Government, and particularly that between the Prime Minister and his Ministers, will be considered in this chapter.

[1] Fontana Library edition 1963, London, pp. 59–81.

Government Structure

The general term 'Minister' covers a number of categories.[1] Each department of state is presided over by a Minister or Secretary of State, the distinction between the two titles being largely historical. They have the same salary (£42,980), though Secretaries of State do tend to be in charge of the most important departments. The law officers are the Attorney-General, Solicitor-General, Lord Advocate, Solicitor-General for Scotland, and Lord Chancellor. As the chief law officer the Lord Chancellor has an even higher salary (£65,900) than the Prime Minister (£53,600). There are a number of posts that have historical significance and at one time carried important responsibilities, but which today are largely free from specific duties. In this category are the posts of Lord President of the Council, Lord Privy Seal, Paymaster-General and Chancellor of the Duchy of Lancaster. Today these offices are either held in conjunction with some other Ministerial office, or are included in the Government in order that the holder may perform some general function. Thus in the Conservative Cabinet in 1986, Lord Whitelaw as Lord President of the Council was Government Leader in the House of Lords and Norman Tebbit as Chancellor of the Duchy of Lancaster was Chairman of the Conservative Party. A Minister Without Portfolio is also sometimes appointed to perform some general role.

Each departmental Minister is normally assisted by one or more junior Ministers who may have the title of Parliamentary Secretaries, Under Secretaries or Ministers of State.[2] The distinction between Parliamentary and Under Secretaries is again largely that of title, and they receive the same salary

[1] For a detailed analysis of government structure see F. M. G. Willson and D. N. Chester, *The Organization of British Central Government*, London 1957. See also D. C. Pitt and B. C. Smith, *Government Departments*, London 1981; C. Pollitt, *Manipulating the Machine*, London 1984; C. Hood (*et al.*), 'Scale Economies and Iron Laws', *Pub. Admin.* 1985, pp. 61–78; F. M. G. Wilson, 'The Organization of British Central Government 1955–61 and 1962–4', *Pub. Admin.* 1962, pp. 159–206, *and* 1966, pp. 73–101; W. A. Robson, 'The Reform of Government', *PQ* 1964, pp. 193–211.

[2] See K. Theakston, 'The Use and Abuse of Junior Ministers', *PQ* 1986, pp. 18–35.

(£28,120). Ministers of State are subordinate to Ministers and Secretaries of State, but have more status and salary (£33,590) than the other junior Ministers. The post of Minister of State was introduced in its modern form in 1955, and was at first confined to departments with wide geographical commitments that involved a Minister being away from London for long periods. For this reason Ministers of State tended to be Peers. More recently the post of Minister of State has been extended to almost all departments.

The Treasury in 1986 had a total of twelve Ministers, including the Prime Minister whose formal title is First Lord of the Treasury. Other Treasury Ministers have the distinctive titles of Chancellor of the Exchequer, Chief Secretary (both included in the Cabinet in 1986), Parliamentary Secretary (the formal title of the Chief Whip), Economic Secretary, Financial Secretary and Lord Commissioners (the assistant whips). Other assistant whips have formal titles as members of Her Majesty's Household.

The ratio of full Ministers to junior Ministers has changed in the last twenty-five years with the merger of some departments of state to create fewer but larger 'super departments'. The number of full Ministers was thereby reduced, but the number of Ministers of State and Parliamentary Secretaries and Under Secretaries attached to the enlarged departments was increased. Thus in January 1960 Harold Macmillan's Government contained thirty-five Ministers or Secretaries of State, seven Ministers of State, and thirty-seven Parliamentary Secretaries or Under Secretaries. Margaret Thatcher's Government in 1986, however, consisted of just thirty Ministers or Secretaries of State, but twenty-four Ministers of State and forty-five Parliamentary Secretaries or Under Secretaries (as shown in Table XXVII).

In its broadest sense the Government also includes the Parliamentary Private Secretaries who act as unpaid assistants to Ministers, fulfilling the role of general assistants in Parliamentary matters.[1] A classic line of promotion would be through the various levels of Parliamentary Private Secretary,

[1]See R. K. Alderman and J. A. Cross, 'The Parliamentary Private Secretary', *PS* 1966, pp. 199–207.

TABLE XXVII

Structure of the Thatcher Government, Oct. 1986

Department	Secretary of State or Minister	Minister of State	Under Secretary	Total
Agriculture, Fisheries and Food	1	2	1	4
Arts	1	–	–	1
Defence	1	2	2	5
Duchy of Lancaster	1	–	–	1
Education and Science	1	1	2	4
Employment	2†	–	2	4†
Energy	1	1	2	4
Environment	1	3	3	7
Foreign and Commonwealth	2	3	1	6
Health and Social Security	1	2	3	6
Home Office	1	3	1	5
Law Officers' Department	2	–	–	2
Lord Advocate's Department	2	–	–	2
Lord Chancellor	1	–	–	1
Lord President	1	–	–	1
Lord Privy Seal	1	–	–	1
Northern Ireland	1	1	4	6
Paymaster-General	1†	–	–	1†
Scottish Office	1	1	3	5
Trade and Industry	1	3	3	7
Transport	1	1	3	5
Treasury	5*	1	6	12*
Wales	1	–	2	3
Her Majesty's Household	–	–	7	7
Total number of posts	31	23	45	100
Total number of Ministers	30†	23	45	99†

* Includes the Prime Minister.

† Paymaster-General was also Minister for Employment.

Parliamentary Under Secretary, Minister of State, non-Cabinet Minister, Cabinet Minister, senior Cabinet Minister – and perhaps ultimately Prime Minister. It is unlikely, however, that promotion would be as laborious or as precise as this. Sometimes appointments are made to full Ministerial office, and perhaps even Cabinet office, without any previous junior Ministerial experience, especially if a party comes to power after a long period in opposition. Alternatively, some members of the Government may never rise above the rank of junior Minister.[1]

The overall size of the Government (excluding Parliamentary Private Secretaries) has more than doubled this century, rising from about forty-five in the Governments of Balfour, Campbell-Bannerman and Asquith before 1914, to more than one hundred in the Wilson Government formed in 1964. In 1970, Heath formed a Government of less than eighty members, but it grew to over ninety by 1974. The Thatcher Government in May 1979 had just under a hundred members, and has remained broadly the same size since then. The danger of excessive domination of the legislature through the 'payroll vote' (that is, members of the Government voting for their own policies in the House) is one of the problems involved in a large executive machine. In the House of Commons elected in February 1974, for example, about half of the Labour MPs held posts either as Ministers, Whips or Parliamentary Private Secretaries.

The eighteenth-century Parliamentary fear that the Monarch would dominate Parliament if the King's Ministers were drawn from Parliament, is thus echoed today in the fear of Government domination of Parliament. This led to criticism of the trend in the post-1945 period that produced a marked increase in Ministerial numbers in the Commons. Although members of the Commons appointed to Ministerial office no longer have to secure re-election to the Commons, there do exist statutory limits on the number of Ministers allowed to serve in the Commons at any one time. One of the

[1]See P. W. Buck, 'The Early Start Towards Cabinet Office 1918–55', *WPQ* 1963, pp. 624–32; P. W. Buck, 'MPs in Ministerial Office 1918–55 and 1955–9', *PS* 1961, pp. 300–6; D. J. Heasman, 'Parliamentary Paths to High Office', *Parl. Aff.* 1962–3, pp. 315–39; F. M. G. Willson, 'Routes of Entry of New Members of the British Cabinet 1868–1958', *PS* 1959, pp. 222–32; F. M. G. Willson, 'Entry to the Cabinet 1959–68', *PS* 1970, pp. 236–8; E. G. Frankland, 'Parliamentary Career Achievement in Britain and West Germany', *LSQ* 1977, pp. 137–54; R. K. Alderman and J. A. Cross, 'Patterns of Ministerial Turnover in Two Labour Cabinets', *PS* 1981, pp. 425–30.

first pieces of legislation introduced by the new Labour Governments in 1964 and 1974 was a Ministers of the Crown Bill, to increase the number of Ministers allowed to sit and vote in the House of Commons. Legislation was necessary because the new Ministries and posts created in the two Wilson Governments increased the number of Ministers serving in the Commons beyond that allowed by existing legislation.

Ministerial Recruitment

The basic Constitutional principle governing the selection of Ministers is that the choice is made by the Prime Minister from among the ranks of MPs and Peers.[1] Normally the choice is confined to one party, though it is wider when, as in 1915, 1931 and 1940, a Coalition Government is formed. From time to time (and especially after major electoral setbacks as in 1931 and 1979) sections of the Labour Party demand that Labour Cabinets should be *elected* by caucus rather than *selected* by the Prime Minister. The Australian and New Zealand Labour Parties pioneered the election of Ministers by caucus, and when in opposition the British Labour Party elects its Shadow Cabinet, but so far all Labour Prime Ministers, like their Conservative counterparts, have exercised a personal choice. Normally, however, a Prime Minister will consult the Chief Whip and may seek the advice of his senior colleagues or his personal advisers.

There are a number of restrictions on the Prime Minister's choice of Ministers. The most fundamental restriction is the Constitutional requirement that Ministers must be members of the Commons or the Lords, or must become members soon after appointment (though a convention has now emerged that the Scottish Law Officers may be excluded from this requirement). As single-party governments, rather than Coalitions, are the norm in Britain, the Prime Minister's field of

[1]See R. Rose, 'The Making of Cabinet Ministers', *BJPS* 1971, pp. 393–414; R. K. Alderman, 'The Prime Minister and the Appointment of Ministers', *Parl. Aff.* 1976–7, pp. 101–34; M. Dogan (*et al.*), 'The Selection of Cabinet Ministers in Contrasting Political Systems', *IPSR* 1981, pp. 125–234; M. Steed, 'The Formation of Governments in the United Kingdom', *PQ* 1983, pp. 54–65.

choice is thus confined to those members of his party (normally 300 to 400) who have seats in the Commons, plus such Peers as he may wish to appoint. With about a hundred posts to fill, the Prime Minister thus has a theoretical average of three or four candidates for each post. In reality, however, this theoretical average is reduced by a variety of practical considerations.

In the first place, the pool of potential Ministers is reduced by the fact that not all MPs will be sufficiently able, or sufficiently experienced, to hold even a junior Ministerial post. Ministers are rarely appointed without some prior Parliamentary experience (though the appointment of Frank Cousins in 1964 and John Davies in 1970 are exceptions to this general principle). A minimal requirement for all Ministers is the ability to perform competently on the floor of the House, in debates and at Question Time, and a Prime Minister generally requires some evidence that a potential Minister possesses basic Parliamentary skills. Thus junior Ministers usually will have served a few years on the backbenches before being appointed, while over the last hundred years Ministers have had, on average, about fifteen years of Parliamentary experience before reaching Cabinet rank. For senior posts some previous Ministerial experience is normally seen as desirable, but when a party has been out of office for some time the Prime Minister may have few ex-Ministers available.

Some MPs will be disqualified because they are now too old, or as yet too young, to hold Ministerial office. Others will be excluded because they have been guilty of indiscretions – political or personal. Again, some MPs who may otherwise be acceptable for a Ministerial appointment may not wish to hold office. Some may be deterred by financial considerations, preferring to maintain lucrative careers outside Parliament. Others may be deterred by the disciplines of office, preferring the relative ideological freedom of the backbenches to the restrictions of collective responsibility. Yet others may be unwilling to settle for the particular post that the Prime Minister is prepared to offer. Factors such as these will reduce quite considerably the list of 'available' MPs.

From the list of available MPs the Prime Minister has to select a team that, to some degree, is representative of the various elements that make up the Parliamentary party. Regional, religious and social considerations are important to some degree (and the Labour Cabinets in the 1960s and 1970s were criticised for becoming 'too middle class'), but ideological considerations are more important. Labour Cabinets normally will contain at least one prominent Trade Union figure, a Cooperative MP, and spokesmen of 'left', 'right' and 'centre' factions of the party. Conservative Cabinets may be less obviously coalitions of factions, but a Conservative Prime Minister does have to come to terms with the ideological groupings of the party. Thus in 1979 Mrs Thatcher included in her Cabinet members of the 'left' and 'centre' of the Conservative Party, such as Peter Walker and James Prior, as well as 'right-wingers' such as Sir Keith Joseph (though subsequently the right-wing became predominant).

Faced with a prominent but potentially rebellious faction leader, the Prime Minister has to choose between including him in the Cabinet, and thereby straining the Cabinet's unity, or excluding him, and thereby creating a possible centre of backbench discontent. Thus Attlee in 1945 included Aneurin Bevan, and in 1974 Wilson included Tony Benn, but Heath in 1970 excluded Enoch Powell, and was himself excluded by Margaret Thatcher in 1979. A recently appointed party leader may feel obliged, in the interests of party unity, to give prominent posts to those who opposed him in the leadership contest. Thus in 1964 Wilson gave key posts to James Callaghan, George Brown and Patrick Gordon Walker. A Prime Minister also has to reward friends, and may well have various debts that can best be settled through the distribution of Ministerial rewards. Precisely because it may be necessary to appoint some political enemies and ideological mavericks, the Prime Minister also has to ensure that the Cabinet contains a proportion of figures whose loyalty is assured.

On the principle of 'horses for courses', Cabinet formation involves not simply the selection of individuals, but the equally delicate allocation of individuals to specific departmental slots. An MP's particular skills and interests may qualify him for one department but not for another. Key figures may seek particular posts as a condition of joining the team, and former Ministers will have particular claims to their old posts, or to more senior posts. Some MPs may have become associated with certain policy areas, or laid claim to particular posts, through work in opposition. Thus Iain Macleod in 1970 and Sir Geoffrey Howe in 1979 were virtually assured of the post of Chancellor of the Exchequer because of their work in opposition on Conservative taxation policy.

* * *

Ultimately the Prime Minister's choice of Ministers is conditioned by the nature of the tasks that they will be required to carry out. Ministers perform a considerable range of functions within the machinery of government.[1] A departmental Minister is head of a large administrative organisation, and as such he is required to perform the managerial functions of organising, motivating and controlling the large number of civil servants who staff his department.[2] The Department of the Environment has some 6,000 civil servants in Whitehall, and a staff of several thousand throughout the country. The Permanent Secretary is the senior civil servant in a department, and he performs the tasks of day-to-day management, but the Minister retains ultimate responsibility for the conduct of affairs in his department. The Minister is also responsible for coordinating the activities of the department's junior Ministers, and in the large departments a number of Ministers will be involved. The Departments of the Environment and Trade and Industry in 1986 each had a team of seven Ministers or junior Ministers, while the Treasury had eleven (excluding the Prime Minister and five Assistant Whips). Thus the Prime Minister normally will try to ensure that whoever is put in charge of a large department of state has a certain amount of managerial competence. Peter Walker's experience in big business perhaps helped to persuade Edward Heath to make him, in 1970, the first Secretary of State for the Environment.

[1] G. Kaufman, *How To Be a Minister*, London 1980. See B. W. Headey, *British Cabinet Ministers*, London 1974; B. W. Headey, 'The Role Skills of Cabinet Ministers: A Cross-National Review', *PS* 1974, pp. 68–87; J. Blondel, *Government Ministers in the Contemporary World*, London 1985.

[2] See Sir P. Nairne, 'Managing the Elephant', *PQ* 1983, pp. 243–56; J. Radcliffe, 'The Role of Politicians and Administrators in Departmental Reorganisation', *Pub. Admin.* 1985, pp. 201–18.

The Minister is ultimately responsible for the policy that emerges (or fails to emerge) from his department. His involvement in departmental policy, however, can take various forms. The Minister may initiate policies, introducing new ideas and persuading the civil servants to accept and implement them. Such initiatives will be particularly evident when a Government has newly come to office, and is anxious to implement policies conceived in opposition and submitted to the electorate in the manifesto. Such Ministerial policy initiatives may involve the coercion of an unwilling department, and one of the recurring conflicts within the machinery of government is between an innovative Minister and reluctant departmental officials. In such conflicts, however, it can be arguable whether the civil servants' resistance is based on natural conservatism, on ideological opposition, or on the appreciation of factors that have escaped an enthusiastic but inexperienced Minister.[1]

Alternatively, rather than initiating policy the Minister may be called upon to select policies from a range of possibilities submitted by his civil servants. In this case the civil servants' role is to gather information on the possible consequences of different courses of action, and present the information for the Minister to assess. The Minister's choice of policy may be governed by his interpretation of the Government's strategy and priorities, by his own ideological inclinations, by guidelines laid down by the Cabinet or its committees, or by some combination of such considerations. Whatever the determining factors may be, the Minister is required to possess a degree of political judgement, and to contribute this to the policy-making exercise within his department. This contribution is not necessarily a positive one, however, and the Minister's political judgement may require the rejection of all the options that the civil servants present, either in face of

[1]See D. Wass, *Government and the Governed*, London 1984; D. Allen, 'Ministers and their Mandarins', *G and O* 1977, pp. 135–49; M. Wright, 'Ministers and Civil Servants: Relations and Responsibilities', *Parl. Aff.* 1977, pp. 293–313; M. R. Gordon, 'Civil Servants, Politicians and Parties', *Comp. Pol.* 1971–2, pp. 29–58; Sir E. Boyle (*et al.*), 'Who Are the Policy Makers?', *Pub. Admin.* 1965, pp. 251–88; R. K. Alderman and J. A. Cross, 'Ministerial Reshuffles and the Civil Service', *BJPS* 1979, pp. 41–65.

ideological opposition from his Ministerial colleagues, or because of shortage of legislative time, or for financial considerations.

Again, the Minister's policy role may merely be as an exponent of departmental proposals. Civil servants are required to be anonymous, and the Minister is the public spokesman for his department. Whatever the source of a particular policy, and whether or not he has been closely involved in its initiation or selection, the Minister has to explain and justify the policy in Cabinet, in Parliament and in public. At the public level he will appear on television and radio, hold press conferences, address public and party gatherings, and receive pressure group deputations. In Parliament he will defend his department at Question Time, before Select Committees, and in general debates, and will steer the department's Bills through the various stages of the legislative process. On occasions he will be called upon to secure the acceptance of an unpopular policy by the Cabinet, his party or the public in general. On other occasions he will have to publicise an important but little-known departmental initiative. For these several public relations activities he has to be skilled in the public presentation of a case before a wide variety of audiences. It is for this highly visible aspect of the Minister's job that his experience as an MP and party politician will be particularly valuable.

In addition to specific responsibility for their departments, the twenty or so Ministers who are members of the Cabinet also have a general responsibility for the Government's performance as a whole. They will attend meetings of the full Cabinet (normally on Thursdays from 11.00 a.m. until 1.30 p.m. at 10 Downing Street) and of Cabinet committees of which they are members.[1] Meetings of the Cabinet and its committees are the principal occasions when conflicting departmental interests are reconciled. The Minister is required to fight to obtain financial resources and legislative time for his department, and to present his department's view on any general item of policy. He is also required to contribute

[1]For accounts of the Cabinet at work see P. Gordon Walker, *The Cabinet*, London 1970; V. Herman and J. Alt (eds), *Cabinet Studies*, London 1975; P. Hennessy, *Cabinet*, London 1986.

his own personal views on Government policy as a whole, and on the Government's overall strategy and performance. A major contrast between the modern Cabinet and the nineteenth-century Cabinet, however, is that Ministers today are so bound up in their roles as departmental Ministers that they have little time to devote to the consideration of the Government's performance in general. The Prime Minister or such non-departmental Ministers as are included in the Cabinet, may be able to concern themselves with the Government's overall performance and long-term strategy, but for departmental Ministers the smaller-scale interests of their own departments are likely to be paramount. The amount of influence that a Minister is able to exert in Cabinet will depend partly on the size and weight of the department he represents (with the Treasury and the Foreign Office being the most weighty of all) and partly on his own personal authority. This in its turn will be determined by his Ministerial experience, his past record in giving advice, his persuasiveness and skill in committee, and his general status in the party and in Parliament. From the civil servant's point of view it is highly desirable that their Minister be sufficiently authoritative and skilful in Cabinet to be able to defend the department's interests, especially when financial economies are being sought.

Thus the Minister performs a number of roles and makes a variety of contributions to the machinery of government. He contributes the skill of public persuasion. He personalises the process of government, symbolising and personifying the particular department to which he is attached. He thereby legitimises the activities of the anonymous civil servants for whom he is Constitutionally responsible. He contributes political sensitivity to the department. While civil servants are not political innocents, the Minister's experience as a party politician makes him particularly well qualified to assess political possibilities and impossibilities in a given situation. In policy terms the Minister may initiate policies himself, he may select them from options presented by his officials, he may secure political acceptance for them, or he may advertise and explain them. While a Minister may be able to make a contribution in all of these ways, it is likely that he will be more competent in some roles than in others. The Ministerial team of a large department, and the Government as a whole, has to be constructed in such a way that Ministers with different specialised skills complement each other and a balanced team is produced.

The Cabinet's Role and Structure

The Government and the Cabinet are not synonymous terms.[1] The Government is all-embracing, covering the various grades of Ministers and junior Ministers described earlier. The Cabinet is a committee of the Government, consisting of the twenty or so senior members of the Government who meet together to supervise and coordinate the work of the whole governmental machine. In 1918 the committee that had been established to review the machinery of government in Britain (the Haldane Committee) defined the functions of the Cabinet as being:

1. The final determination of the policy to be submitted to Parliament;
2. The supreme control of the national executive in accordance with the policy prescribed by Parliament;
3. The continuous coordination and delimitation of the activities of the several Departments of State.

Today the Cabinet remains at the centre of the machinery of British government, acting as a final court of appeal in disputes between departments and between individual Ministers, overseeing and coordinating government policy and political strategy, and taking final decisions on the most important matters of policy and on politically controversial issues. Many of these tasks, however, are performed not by the Cabinet as a whole, but by sub-divisions of it – by formal committees of the Cabinet, by informal groups of senior Ministers and by the Prime Minister.

[1]See H. Daalder, *Cabinet Reform in Britain 1914–63*, London 1964; W. Thornhill (ed.), *The Modernization of British Government*, London 1975, Chs 3 and 4.

TABLE XXVIII
Cabinet Appointments Made by New Prime Ministers, January 1957–May 1979

	Jan. 1957	Oct. 1963	Oct. 1964	June 1970	March 1974	April 1976	May 1979
Prime Minister	✓	✓	✓	*1	*1	*1	*1
Lord Chancellor	✓	✓	✓	✓	✓	✓	✓
Lord President of the Council	✓	*1	✓	✓	✓	✓	✓
Lord Privy Seal	*1	✓	✓	✓	✓	✓	✓
Chancellor Duchy of Lancaster	✓	✓		✓	✓	✓	✓
Paymaster-General		*2				*2	✓
Chancellor of the Exchequer	✓	✓	✓	✓	✓	✓	✓
Chief Secretary to Treasury		*2					✓
First Secretary of State			*1				
Minister Without Portfolio		✓†	✓				
Secretary of State (or Minister) for:							
Foreign Affairs	✓	✓	✓	✓	✓	✓	✓
Home Affairs	*1	✓	✓	✓	✓	✓	✓
Colonies	✓	*3	✓				
Commonwealth	✓	*3	✓				
Scotland	✓	✓	✓	✓	✓	✓	✓
Education	✓	✓	✓	✓	✓	✓	✓
Defence	✓	✓	✓	✓	✓	✓	✓
Agriculture	✓	✓	✓	✓	✓	✓	✓
Labour (Employment)	✓	✓	✓	✓	✓	✓	✓
Housing	*2	*4	✓	✓			
Wales	*2	*4	✓	✓	✓	✓	✓
Trade	✓	*5	✓	✓	✓	✓	✓
Transport	✓	✓	✓				
Power (Energy)	✓	✓	✓		✓	✓	✓
Northern Ireland					✓	✓	✓
Science		*1					
Industry		*5			*2	✓	✓
Health		✓					
Public Building and Works		✓					
Technology			✓	✓			
Overseas Development			✓			✓	
Environment					✓	✓	✓
Civil Service				*1	*1	*1	*1
Economic Affairs			*1				
Prices					✓	*2	
Social Services				✓	✓	✓	✓
Posts and Telecommunications					*2		
Planning						✓	
Number of posts	20	28	24	19	23	25	23
Number of Ministers	18	23	23	18	21	23	22

*Where a Minister held more than one post, the posts are marked by an asterisk and a number, e.g. in January 1957 the Home Secretary was also Lord Privy Seal.

† In October 1963, Home appointed two Ministers Without Portfolio.

The precise size and composition of the Cabinet is determined by the Prime Minister within certain general principles. Some departmental posts such as Foreign Secretary, Chancellor of the Exchequer and Home Secretary, would be included in any conventional Cabinet. Added to these are the most important posts of the day, and also some posts, such as perhaps the Secretaries of State for Scotland and Wales, which are included largely for reasons of regional representation. Balanced with these departmental posts will normally be some Ministers free from departmental ties who can undertake the tasks of policy coordination, long-term planning, and general administrative functions not attached to specific departments. Posts like Lord Privy Seal, Lord President of the Council, Chancellor of the Duchy of Lancaster can be included in the Cabinet in order that their holders may perform these non-departmental functions.

The Prime Minister also has to take into account certain structural considerations. If too many Ministers are included in the Cabinet it will be an unwieldy body and will breach the general principle that the task of decision-making is most effectively performed by a small group. If too few Ministers are included it will be difficult for the Cabinet to keep in touch with the other members of the Government and with the departments of state, backbench MPs and the party outside Parliament. In practical terms the problem is whether the Cabinet should contain all full Ministers, most Ministers, or merely a few very senior Ministers. In the nineteenth century this question largely resolved itself, in that it was possible to include all full Ministers and still keep the Cabinet a reasonably small and workable unit. Before 1867 Cabinets generally contained thirteen to sixteen members, and in 1914 it was still possible, with a cabinet of twenty, to include virtually all full Ministers. Even in 1939, Chamberlain's Cabinet of twenty-three excluded only a few relatively minor posts.

Since 1945, however, the vast increase in the range of Government activities, and the consequent growth in the number of departments and Ministers, has meant that a Cabinet composed of all Ministers would be impractical.[1] By

[1] See, however, R. V. Clements, 'The Cabinet', *PS* 1965, pp. 231–4.

1960 a Cabinet that included all full Ministers would have had thirty-five members. The merger of some departments in the 1960s and 1970s to create 'super departments' eased the problem of Cabinet size to some extent. One Secretary of State for Foreign and Commonwealth Affairs could be included in the Cabinet rather than (as in the 1950s) separate Ministers for Foreign affairs, Commonwealth affairs and Colonial affairs. Despite the merging of departments, however, there were still more full Ministers than was desirable for a working committee and the practice continued of excluding some full Ministers from the Cabinet. In 1986 there were thirty full Ministers, with twenty-two of them having seats in the Cabinet.

Within the concept of the Cabinet composed of not all Ministers but of most of them, opinions vary as to what is the ideal number to include. Lord Morrison has advocated a Cabinet of sixteen to eighteen members;[1] D. N. Chester, eighteen to twenty;[2] Harold Laski, little more than fifteen members;[3] Harold Wilson, fifteen to twenty members[4] – though Wilson's actual Cabinets had more than twenty members. Cabinets since 1945 have in fact ranged from sixteen to twenty-four members, with a general tendency over the years for them to increase in size. In 1970, Heath temporarily reversed this trend with a Cabinet of only eighteen members, and of only seventeen after the Ministerial re-shuffle in October 1970. By 1974, however, it had increased to twenty-one. The Wilson and Callaghan Cabinets of 1974–9, and the Thatcher Cabinet since 1979, have contained over twenty members.

An alternative to the normal Cabinet of twenty or so Ministers would be a Cabinet composed of only a handful of very senior Ministers. Such a Super Cabinet has been formed in periods of crisis in the past, but has been advocated as a permanent alternative to the conventional system.[5] A Cabinet of perhaps half a dozen members could be made up entirely of

[1] *Government and Parliament*, p. 44.
[2] Sir John Anderson, *British Government Since 1918*, London 1950, p. 36.
[3] H. J. Laski, *Reflections on the Constitution*, London 1963, p. 178.
[4] BBC Publications, *Whitehall and Beyond*, London 1964, p. 26.
[5] See Daalder, *Cabinet Reform in Britain 1914–63*.

non-departmental Ministers who could act solely as coordinators and planners, or it could be composed of the six or so senior departmental Ministers, or it could be made up of a mixture of the two types of Minister. The Cabinet formed by Lloyd George when he became Prime Minister in 1916 was composed of only five Ministers, four of them without specific departmental duties, and in 1918 a fifth non-departmental member was added. Departmental Ministers and service chiefs were often called upon to attend War Cabinet meetings, however, and it has been calculated that in the final year of the Cabinet's life a total of 248 non-Cabinet personnel attended its meetings.[1]

With the outbreak of war in 1939, Neville Chamberlain formed a Cabinet of nine members, including four non-departmental Ministers. When Churchill succeeded him in 1940 he formed a Cabinet composed of himself, the Foreign Secretary, and three Ministers without departmental duties. In August 1942 Churchill increased the Cabinet size to eight by adding three more departmental Ministers. The conflict that arose within the Cabinet between Ernest Bevin as Minister of Labour, and Lord Beaverbrook as Minister of Production, illustrates the problems that can arise in a small Cabinet made up of senior departmental Ministers, and a change to an entirely non-departmental Cabinet was urged on Churchill, but to no avail. It is probably true to say, however, that Churchill's Cabinet was based more on personalities than on theories of departmental or non-departmental Cabinets.

As well as these actual examples of small Cabinets, theoretical support for the idea of Super Ministers came from the Machinery of Government Committee in 1918.[2] The Committee reported on the theoretical principles of Cabinet Government and their practical application, and it advocated a Cabinet of ten to twelve Super Ministers, though it avoided the question of whether or not they should be departmental Ministers. Super Cabinets have been advocated in other academic studies, and L. S. Amery proposed a small Cabinet

[1] Ibid., p. 54.

[2] Cmd. 9230 (1918). See also H. Daalder, 'The Haldane Committee and the Cabinet', *Pub. Admin.* 1963, pp. 117–36; Lord Bridges, 'Haldane and the Machinery of Government', *Pub. Admin.* 1957, pp. 254–66.

of six non-departmental Ministers to decide broad policy, with departmental committees for administrative supervision under the chairmanship of Cabinet Ministers.[1]

Thus the concept of a Super Cabinet involves, firstly, the question of whether a small Cabinet of six or so members is to be preferred to the conventional larger Cabinets, and secondly, if a small Cabinet is preferred, whether or not it should be composed of Ministers free from departmental duties. Theoretical proposals and the wartime precedents offer different examples of attempts to resolve these questions. The basic argument used by those who favour the concept of a Super Cabinet, is that with the gradual increase in the number of Ministers both inside and outside the Cabinet, the present system has got out of hand. It is often argued, for example, that under the present system the long-term policy-making function of the Cabinet is neglected because of the pressure of departmental business on Ministers. As Ministers are increasingly bound up with the details of their own departments, they have less and less time to devote to the general supervision of the whole field of government. Thus it is maintained that it is necessary to distinguish more clearly between policy-making and administration, and to create a new category of Super Ministers who would, with the Prime Minister, devote their attention primarily to broad policy, leaving the details of administration largely to Ministers outside the Super Cabinet.

A small Cabinet could meet more often and deal with business much more expeditiously than the existing Cabinets of twenty or more members. With a small Cabinet linked with the rest of the Government through a system of committees, the number of departmental and junior Ministers could increase without affecting Cabinet size. As with the wartime Cabinets, and as indeed with the present system, non-Cabinet Ministers could be called to attend Cabinet meetings when their presence was required, so that the small Cabinets need not become too remote from the rest of the Government. A Cabinet made up of six senior Ministers would be a much more effective check on the personal authority of the Prime Minister than is the present system. The idea of a Super

[1] L. S. Amery, *Thoughts on the Constitution*, London 1964.

Cabinet is thus favoured by those who argue that the Prime Minister's authority within the present system is excessive and ought to be curbed.

The idea of a Super Cabinet, however, can be objected to on a number of grounds.[1] It is not always practical to separate the functions of policy-making and administration in the way envisaged with a Super Cabinet, and such a body could become too far removed from the administrative facts of life, and too theoretical in its thinking. Similarly, a Cabinet of only a few senior Ministers could become too remote from the party, from the rest of the Government, and from Parliament. The present difficulties experienced by the Cabinet in keeping in touch with the party, and with junior and non-Cabinet Ministers, would be magnified, and the authority of Ministers who were not included in the Cabinet would be reduced. The wartime Cabinets which are quoted as examples of small Cabinets working effectively, are not necessarily good precedents, in that in wartime, Ministers, Parliament, and the political parties are prepared to delegate power to a few powerful figures. What is more, as the wartime Governments were Coalitions, they were not precedents for *party* government through a small Cabinet. While the wartime Cabinets were theoretically small, in Lloyd George's Cabinet meetings additional Ministers and service chiefs were normally present, and in Churchill's Government the Lord President's Committee acted almost as a second Cabinet responsible for home affairs.

* * *

Thus the existing system, with all its limitations, is perhaps a more practical system than that of a Super Cabinet. In practice it may be that the two systems are not so very different. Even with a Super Cabinet other Ministers would at times attend Cabinet meetings, and within the existing system most Governments tend to contain a group of senior Ministers who have more authority than their colleagues, and upon whom the Prime Minister particularly relies – although whether the Prime Minister's closest colleagues can be said to

[1] See, for example, Laski, *Reflections on the Constitution*, Chs 8, 9 and 10.

make up a formal 'Inner Cabinet' is a matter of debate.[1] Certainly, the work of any Government falls into the four general categories of external affairs, defence, home affairs, and financial and economic affairs, and the Ministers in charge of these fields must inevitably form an inner group of particularly influential Ministers.

Most Governments over the past fifty years seem to have contained their inner circles. In MacDonald's two Labour Governments, for example, Clynes, Henderson, Snowden and J. H. Thomas were particularly influential, and in the 1931 crisis, MacDonald, Snowden and Thomas worked particularly closely together – to the detriment of the collective responsibility of the Cabinet. The 'Guilty Men' of Chamberlain's Government in the prelude to the second world war were Lord Halifax, Hoare, Simon and Chamberlain himself, and as with MacDonald in 1931, the advent of a crisis seemed to produce more frequent consultations between senior Ministers. Attlee relied particularly on Bevin, Cripps and Morrison, and later on Ede, Griffiths and Morrison. Churchill, despite the impression of personal rule, had his circle of particular friends during the war, and in his 1951 Government he often met for informal 'conversations' with his chief Ministers and friends. In the Eden Government the men particularly responsible for the Suez policy were Eden, Macmillan, Anthony Head, Lord Hailsham and Selwyn Lloyd, with Butler being close to the Prime Minister at other times. Macmillan seems to have relied on Lord Home, Butler, Macleod and Selwyn Lloyd for much of the time. Bonar Law and Baldwin, however, are thought to have had no Inner Cabinet. In 1964, when still in opposition, Harold Wilson declared that he was opposed to the idea of chief advisers meeting as an Inner Cabinet.[2] In 1969, however, he formed a 'Management Committee' of six senior Cabinet Ministers, plus himself as chairman, which met weekly, and this was widely interpreted as representing the formal creation of an Inner Cabinet.

Even if a formal Inner Cabinet is not appointed, informal

[1] See G. Jordan, 'Central Coordination, Crossman and the Inner Cabinet', *PQ* 1978, pp. 171–80.

[2] *Whitehall and Beyond*, p. 27.

groups of senior Ministers will take many of the key decisions. Patrick Gordon Walker has drawn a distinction between an 'Inner Cabinet', with a fixed membership, and a 'Partial Cabinet', the composition of which will vary from issue to issue. Partial Cabinets, he claims, are an 'accepted and established part of the Cabinet system'. Under Mrs Thatcher the Government's Parliamentary strategy is determined at weekly meetings of the Prime Minister, the Leader of the Commons, the Chief Whip, the Leader of the Lords and the chairman of the Conservative Party. In 1981 the final decision to purchase the Trident missile was taken not by the Cabinet as a whole, but by a small group of Ministers, as was the 1984 decision to ban trade unions membership among civil servants at the Government's communications headquarters at Cheltenham. During the Falklands war in 1982 military and diplomatic strategy was determined largely by the Defence Committee of the Cabinet. It met on an almost daily basis, only rarely referred issues to the full Cabinet and was known popularly (though not officially) as the 'War Cabinet'. Its political significance was emphasised when the chairman of the Conservative Party (Cecil Parkinson) became a member for the duration of the crisis.[1] The extent to which a Prime Minister does rely on such machinery to bring senior colleagues into an inner group bridges the gap between the structure of the existing Cabinet system and the idea of a small Super Cabinet.

Government Coordination

In post-war Governments the problem of keeping the Cabinet in touch with other Ministers and junior Ministers has been tackled in various ways.[2] A degree of coordination

[1] C. Seymour-Ure, 'British "War Cabinets" in Limited Wars', *Pub. Admin.* 1984, pp. 181–200.

[2] For studies of British governments 'at work' see J. M. Lee, *The Churchill Coalition*, London 1980; K. O. Morgan, *Labour in Power 1945–51*, London 1984; H. Pelling, *The Labour Governments 1945–51*, London 1984; A. Seldon, *Churchill's Indian Summer*, London 1981; M. Holmes, *Political Pressure and Economic Policy – British Government 1970–74*, London 1982; M. Holmes, *The Labour Government 1974–79*, London 1985; D. Coates, *Labour in Power?*, London 1980; P. Riddell, *The Thatcher Government*, London 1985; D. S. Bell (ed.), *The First Thatcher Government 1979–84*, London 1985.

can be achieved by making one Minister responsible for two departments, as with the appointment of one Secretary of State for Colonial and Commonwealth Affairs from 1962 to 1964.[1] There are clearly limits to this type of Ministerial reorganisation, however, and as it involves an increased burden on the Minister it could make him less effective. Again, it is possible to create the formal post of coordinator, without a department of his own, to supervise and coordinate the work of a number of other Ministers. Thus in 1936 a Minister for the Coordination of Defence was appointed, and in his 1951–5 Government Churchill experimented with a number of Overlords to supervise various departmental Ministers. By these means it is possible to leave out some Ministers from the Cabinet by including only the coordinating Minister, although the creation of a new Ministerial post adds to the original problem of an ever-increasing Government machine.

Alternatively, an entirely new large department can be formed through the amalgamation of two or more small departments. In 1955 the Ministry of Agriculture and Fisheries was merged with the Ministry of Food, and in the 1960s and early-1970s new 'super departments' were formed through departmental mergers.[2] In 1964 the departments of War, Air, Admiralty and Defence were merged into a new large Defence Department. In 1968, under Harold Wilson, the Foreign and Commonwealth Office replaced the previously separate departments for Foreign, Commonwealth and Colonial affairs, while the Department of Health and Social Security was formed through the merger of the departments of Health and of Pensions and National Insurance. In 1970, under Edward Heath, the departments of Trade, Power and Aviation were merged into a new Department of Trade and Industry, and the departments of Transport, Works and Housing and Local Government merged into a new Department of the Environment. Subsequently, Transport was

[1] See M. Beloff, 'The Foreign and Commonwealth Services', *Pub. Admin.* 1964, pp. 415–22; B. Miller, 'The Colonial Office and the Estimates Committee', *Pub. Admin.* 1961, pp. 173–80.

[2] Sir R. Clarke, 'The Number and Size of Government Departments', *PQ* 1972, pp. 169–86; A. Clark, 'Ministerial Supervision and the Size of the Department of the Environment', *Pub. Admin.* 1977, pp. 197–204.

detached from the Department of the Environment, and Energy from the Department of Trade and Industry, but the other giant creations survived. The creation of super departments was stimulated partly by the many mergers that were taking place in private industry in that period, and by the attractions of the economies of scale and other assumed advantages of large organisations. It was also, however, an attempt to deal with the problem of coordinating a large Ministerial team, a problem that had increased considerably in the 1950s and 1960s with the emergence of new departments, and thus new Ministers.

In the main, however, the coordination of the Government departments in Britain in the post-war period has been achieved through a system of Cabinet committees.[1] The origins of the system of Cabinet standing committees can be traced back to the Committee of Imperial Defence, which was formed in 1902 as a permanent committee to supplement the Cabinet's general responsibility for defence.[2] Ad hoc Cabinet committees had been formed before this to deal with particular questions, but this was the first standing committee of the Cabinet. The Defence Committee was retained during and after the first world war, though with a frequently changed name and status, and in 1919 there was also created a Home Affairs Committee. More standing committees emerged in the inter-war period, and with the second world war an extensive committee system was adopted. This was retained by Attlee in 1945, and he had some fifteen committees composed of Cabinet and non-Cabinet Ministers and presided over by senior members of the Cabinet.[3]

Considerable secrecy surrounds the composition and functions (and even the existence) of the committees. Standing committees deal with particular areas of government business,

[1] T. T. Mackie and B. W. Hogwood, 'Decision Arenas in Executive Decision Making', *BJPS* 1984, pp. 285–312.

[2] See F. A. Johnson, *Defence by Committee*, London 1960; F. A. Johnson, 'The British Committee of Imperial Defence', *J of P* 1961, pp. 231–61.

[3] For a list see Walker, *The Cabinet*, Appendix I. See also M. Cockerell (*et al.*), *Sources Close to the Prime Minister*, London 1984; T. T. Mackie and B. W. Hogwood, *Unlocking the Cabinet*, London 1985; B. Page, 'The Secret Constitution', *New Statesman*, 21st July 1978, p. 72.

such as economic strategy, future legislation, home affairs or foreign and defence policy. In addition, ad hoc or miscellaneous committees ('MISCs') are set up to deal with specific issues and problems. Thus under Mrs Thatcher a MISC has been formed each autumn to determine the level of the rate support grant to be paid to local authorities, and another (referred to as the Star Chamber) has settled disputes between the Treasury and the departments over levels of expenditure. As well as committees composed entirely of Ministers, there are committees composed of senior civil servants, and others with a mix of Ministers and civil servants. In the Callaghan Government there were some twenty-five standing committees and well over a hundred MISCs. Mrs Thatcher is thought to have operated a similar structure, though with fewer standing committees and more MISCs than her immediate predecessors. A major consequence of the development of the committee system in the post-war period is that business that at one time would have been dealt with in full Cabinet is now handled in committee. Even the Cabinet's role as a final court of appeal has been reduced, in that since the 1960s the usual practice has been that decisions taken in committee cannot be re-opened in Cabinet unless the committee chairman agrees.

* * *

Apart from the Cabinet committees and the creation of super departments, the most ambitious post-1945 experiment in the coordination of Government departments was the system of 'Overlords' introduced by Churchill in his 1951–5 Government.[1] In October 1951 Churchill formed a Cabinet of sixteen Ministers, including six peers, three of whom were Overlords with the task of coordinating various departments. Lord Leathers was Minister for the Coordination of Transport, Fuel and Power; Lord Cherwell, as Paymaster-General, was to coordinate scientific research and development; Lord Woolton, as Lord President of the Council, was to coordinate the work of the Ministry of Agriculture and Fisheries and the

[1] See R. S. Milne, 'The Experiment With "Coordinating Ministers" in the British Cabinet 1951–3', *CJEPS* 1955, pp. 365–9; Morrison, *Government and Parliament*, Ch. 3.

Ministry of Food. Churchill, as Minister of Defence as well as Prime Minister, was at first responsible for the coordination of the service departments, but in January 1952 Lord Alexander was made Minister of Defence, increasing the number of Overlords to four. Sir John Anderson was to have been given a Peerage and the post of Chancellor of the Duchy of Lancaster to coordinate Treasury, Board of Trade, and Ministry of Supply policy, but he declined.

The object of the scheme was to group and coordinate the departments by some means other than the Cabinet committee system, and to reorganise the nature and structure of Cabinet composition. A number of weaknesses of the scheme soon emerged, however. In the first place, the size of the Cabinet was not really reduced. Although the presence of the coordinating Ministers meant that five Ministers (Agriculture and Fisheries, Food, Transport, Civil Aviation, and Fuel and Power) did not need to be in the Cabinet, four of them had not been in the Attlee Cabinet in 1951 either, and in fact the Lord Leathers appointment made up for this saving of one departmental Minister. Churchill did reduce his Cabinet size by holding the post of Minister of Defence himself, but this only meant a Cabinet of sixteen members as compared with Attlee's Cabinet of seventeen in 1951, and by December 1952 Churchill had increased his Cabinet numbers to nineteen.

A second fundamental criticism of the experiment was that whereas the chairmen of the Cabinet committees had been unannounced, the Overlords held formal posts, and this led to confusion as to who was the responsible Minister, the Overlord or the departmental Minister. The situation was further complicated by the fact that the Overlords were indeed Lords, and were thus not answerable to the House of Commons. The Opposition attacked this as a threat to the authority of the House of Commons, and argued that it added to the general confusion over the respective responsibilities of the Ministers.

Early in 1952 there was Ministerial confusion over a decision not to extend to the rest of the country increases in rail fares that had been made in the London area. There was some doubt as to who was responsible for Government policy in this matter, Lord Leathers as Overlord, or the Minister of Transport. After this, the experiment was gradually abandoned and

Churchill returned to the system of Cabinet committees for the coordination of policy. Had the coordinators been drawn from the Commons, their authority might have been greater, and the pattern of responsibility rather more clear. As well as this, however, there remained a fundamental difference between informal coordination within the Government through unnamed Ministers, and the formal coordination that Churchill attempted through his openly announced coordinating Ministers.

Cabinet Supports and Services

Before 1914 no minutes of Cabinet meetings or records of Cabinet decisions were kept, though occasionally written memoranda were made, as with the request to the Queen in 1870 to abolish the purchase of Commissions, and the requests made to Edward VII and George V during the Constitutional crisis in 1910, for the creation of Liberal Peers. In 1916, under the pressure of wartime conditions, the Secretariat that under Sir Maurice Hankey had served the Committee of Imperial Defence, was transferred by Lloyd George to the wartime Cabinet, and was retained throughout the war.[1] In 1918 the Haldane Committee recommended that it be retained in peacetime, and despite the claim that it was a threat to the principle of Cabinet secrecy, the Secretariat was retained after the break-up of the Coalition Government in 1922 (though with a cut in staff from 144 to 38).[2]

Today the Secretariat, or Cabinet Office, is an essential part of the Cabinet system, and is even more necessary as a result of the development of the system of Cabinet committees.[3] It is headed by the Secretary of the Cabinet who attends Cabinet meetings and records its deliberations. The Cabinet Secretary and his staff prepare the agenda for meetings of the Cabinet and its committees, and follow-up the decisions of the meetings by informing the relevant departments of state and ensuring that appropriate action is taken.

[1] J. Turner, *Lloyd George's Secretariat*, London 1980; J. F. Naylor, *A Man and an Institution*, London 1984.

[2] Daalder, *Cabinet Reform in Britain 1914–63*, p. 60.

[3] See R. K. Mosley, *The Story of the Cabinet Office*, London 1969.

Since 1916 the post of Secretary to the Cabinet has been filled only by Lords Hankey, Bridges, Normanbrook, Trend and Hunt, and the present Secretary, Sir Robert Armstrong. Until 1962 the Cabinet Secretary was also one of the two joint Permanent Secretaries to the Treasury, but in the reorganisation of the Treasury in 1962 the Secretary of the Cabinet was relieved of his other Treasury duties.[1] The 'number 10 network' of secretarial organisation and communication is widely recognised as being ultra-efficient. The Secretariat also helps in the coordination of Government business in that it keeps non-Cabinet Ministers informed of Cabinet decisions, prepares the ground for Cabinet meetings by circulating memoranda beforehand, and performs this function also for the committees of the Cabinet.

When the Heath Government was formed in 1970, a Central Policy Review Staff (or 'Think Tank') was set up as part of the Cabinet Office.[2] It survived the changes of Government in 1974 and 1979, but was abolished in 1983. Consisting of a staff of about a dozen administrators, economists, statisticians and sociologists, its general image was of a youthful intellectual hothouse. Its function was to undertake in-depth studies of particular aspects of policy, free from any specifically departmental point of view, and it made extensive use of consultants from outside the civil service. It was probably most effective when dealing with topics that cut across various departmental responsibilities, and least effective when confronting one particular department.

The Cabinet Office is not a Prime Ministerial agency but serves the Cabinet as a whole. The Prime Minister, however, requires specifically personal assistance, both of a secretarial nature, to make the daily routine run more smoothly, and of a policy nature, to provide information and advice on current issues.[3] The secretarial assistance is provided by the Prime Minister's Private Office. Recently this has had a staff of about fifty, mainly in clerical posts but also including particu-

[1] See below, p. 322.

[2] See C. Pollitt, 'The Central Policy Review Staff 1970–4', *Pub. Admin.* 1974, pp. 375–94; M. Beloff, 'The Think Tank and Foreign Affairs', *Pub. Admin.* 1977, pp. 435–46.

[3] See G. W. Jones, 'The Prime Minister's Advisers', *PS* 1973, pp. 363–75.

larly close senior advisers such as the Personal Political Secretary and the Press Officer. In the 1974–9 period of Labour Government personal advice on domestic policy was provided for the Prime Minister by the Policy Unit. This consisted of a handful of Labour Party researchers located in 10 Downing Street. While they were civil servants paid out of public funds, they were temporary and essentially partisan. Their allegiance was specifically to the Prime Minister, and their function was to free him from dependence on civil service sources of advice and information. Mrs Thatcher has also had a team of personal advisers, drawn from various sources including the civil service, the diplomatic service and the business world. In effect, the Policy Unit and the Private Office are the successors to Churchill's wartime personal advisers, and Lloyd George's 'Garden Suburb', which was a body of advisers housed in the garden of 10 Downing Street, serving as a personal office for the Prime Minister.

Thus the Cabinet Office provides a high-powered Secretariat for the Cabinet, the Prime Minister receives a personal administrative service from his Private Office, while the Policy Unit gives the Prime Minister information and advice on current issues. These bodies are all of relatively recent origin, the oldest (the Cabinet Secretariat) dating only from the first world war. The modern Cabinet, with its elaborate support system, thus provides a stark contrast with the informality of the pre-1914 Cabinet. Nevertheless, while the Private Office and the Policy Unit can provide the Prime Minister with information and advice on a range of matters, the Prime Minister does not enjoy the extent of support that each Minister receives from his department of state. It has been argued, therefore, that the Private Office and Policy Unit should be expanded into a Prime Minister's Department, with a large staff of civil servants covering the full range of policy areas, to provide a more effective counter-balance to the weight of the Treasury, the Foreign Office and other departments of State. The case for such a department has been strengthened in recent years by the increased need for the Prime Minister to maintain control over the Government's broad strategy, and by the Prime Minister's greater involvement with European and other heads of government on issues that cut-across the responsibilities of a number of departments.[1] The advice that the Prime Minister receives from close personal advisers in the Private Office and the Policy Unit may well conflict with the views expressed by the civil servants of the Cabinet Office, while each of these bodies may come into conflict with the departments of state and individual Ministers. The Secretary to the Cabinet, as the principal civil servant, may see his position threatened by the partisan political figures who are close to the Prime Minister, while they in turn may feel that the Prime Minister relies too heavily on the Whitehall machine to the detriment of friends and party colleagues.[2] Much of the Prime Ministerial art lies in the ability to balance these several conflicting interests.

* * *

Despite the work of the Cabinet Office in preparing an agenda and drawing up minutes or 'conclusions' of Cabinet meetings, Cabinet proceedings remain essentially secret.[3] The conclusions of Cabinet meetings are bare and factual, and in a sense are a distortion of the truth, in that all discussion is summarised and clarified. The agenda and conclusions are circulated to all Cabinet Ministers, but remain top secret. This Cabinet secrecy is based formally on the Privy Councillor's Oath, the Official Secrets Act, and the Constitutional principle that Cabinet decisions are advice to the Monarch, so that Royal permission is required for their disclosure. In practical terms, however, the essence of Cabinet secrecy is that free discussion is possible only in secret, and only through the secrecy of Cabinet discussion can any semblance of collective responsibility be maintained. Complete secrecy is limited by the guidance that is sometimes given to the press, and by the revelations that occasionally appear in the writings of

[1] P. Weller, 'Do Prime Ministers' Departments Really Create Problems?', *Pub. Admin.* 1983, pp. 59–78.

[2] See, for example, the views expressed in Marcia Williams, *Inside No. 10*, London 1973; J. Haines, *The Politics of Power*, London 1975.

[3] See J. Jacob, 'Some Reflections on Governmental Secrecy', *PL* 1974, pp. 25–49; K. E. Middlemas, 'Cabinet Secrecy and the Crossman Diaries', *PQ* 1976, pp. 39–51.

former Cabinet Ministers. Also, 'unattributable leaks' occur. For example, the press and public became aware of clear divisions in the Labour Cabinet in 1969 over Government policy towards the trade unions, and of differences of opinion in the Conservative Cabinet in 1985 over the future of the Westland Company. In 1975 the division in the Labour Cabinet over the Common Market issue was publicly revealed by the Prime Minister himself. From these sources it is possible to gain some idea of the nature of the internal workings of the Cabinet.

The agenda for Cabinet meetings, and any papers that are to be dealt with, are circulated beforehand so that prior consideration can be given to the issues. In this way Cabinet approval is no doubt often a formality, while Cabinet meetings are very often merely a report on progress and a forum for interdepartmental disputes. The Chancellor of the Exchequer and the Law Officers see the Cabinet papers before other Ministers in order to look for legal and financial snags. Formal votes are rarely taken in Cabinet meetings, partly because the Ministerial hierarchy means that opinions have to be weighed as well as counted. The meeting comes to decisions under the guidance of the Prime Minister's chairmanship, but the nature of Cabinet meetings, and the method of reaching decisions, must depend upon the Prime Minister and his handling of his colleagues – a factor that must inevitably vary according to the personalities involved. Cabinet Ministers have attested to the grandeur of the Cabinet room and to the importance of the Prime Minister's role, while non-Cabinet Ministers have revealed that it can be an awesome experience to be 'summoned' to Cabinet meetings. Senior civil servants are occasionally called upon to attend, especially Foreign Office and Treasury officials, and service chiefs. Their presence, and the permanent presence of the Cabinet Secretary and his assistant, must inevitably reduce the specifically partisan content of Cabinet discussions.

Despite the vast increase in the scope of Government activity in this century, the volume of work undertaken by the Cabinet has not markedly increased. The Cabinet meets normally only once each week, for some two hours at a time, though in times of crisis there may be longer and more frequent meetings. The nature of the work undertaken by the Cabinet, however, has changed considerably, with the full Cabinet inevitably being much less concerned with details and much more concerned with making and approving top-level decisions. Under recent Prime Ministers, Cabinet meetings have been concerned primarily with the forthcoming Parliamentary business, foreign affairs, any major issue of the day and such matters as have been referred to full Cabinet from its committees. This change in the nature of Cabinet proceedings has been made possible only through the work of the Secretariat in preparing and circulating material for Cabinet meetings, through the delegation of much work to Cabinet committees and individual Ministers, and through informal contact between the Prime Minister and other Ministers outside full Cabinet meetings.

The Prime Minister and the Cabinet

The traditional description of the Prime Minister's role in the Cabinet is that of *primus inter pares*, but it is widely claimed that the power of a modern Prime Minister within the Cabinet is such that he is much more than 'first among equals'.[1] The general basis of the Prime Minister's authority is wide. As the Monarch's principal adviser, he is the chief inheritor of the Monarch's powers and prerogatives. The Prime Minister, for example, personally advises the Monarch on the date of the dissolution of Parliament:[2] it is not a matter for Cabinet decision, though it is not clear to what extent the Prime Minister would consult his colleagues informally. The Prime Minister has wide powers of patronage, including the

[1] See Mackintosh, *The British Cabinet*; A. H. Brown, 'Prime Ministerial Power', *PL* 1968, pp. 28–51, *and* 96–118; G. W. Jones, 'The Prime Minister's Power', *Parl. Aff.* 1964–5, pp. 167–85. See also A. King (ed.), *The British Prime Minister*, London 1985; R. H. S. Crossman, *Inside View*, London 1972; P. Weller, *First Among Equals*, London 1985; P. Weller, 'The Vulnerability of Prime Ministers', *Parl. Aff.* 1983, pp. 96–117; Tony Benn, 'The Case for a Constitutional Premiership', *Parl. Aff.* 1980, pp. 7–22.

[2] See R. K. Alderman and J. A. Cross, 'The Prime Ministers and the Decision to Dissolve', *Parl. Aff.* 1974–5, pp. 386–404; D. J. Heasman, 'The Monarch, the Prime Minister and the Dissolution of Parliament', *Parl. Aff.* 1960–1, pp. 94–107.

appointment and dismissal of Ministers. In 1962 Macmillan dismissed a third of his Cabinet, and in an age when professional politicians predominate, the Prime Minister's ability to affect directly the careers of ambitious MPs inevitably gives him considerable influence over his colleagues. The distribution of general patronage through the Honours List also gives the Prime Minister an influence in many sectors of national life. To a certain extent Lloyd George's abuse of patronage discredited the whole system, and now all proposed awards are vetted by the Political Honours Scrutiny Committee, composed of respected public figures. Nevertheless, the Prime Minister can insist on certain awards (as did Harold Wilson with his controversial resignation honours list in 1976), and patronage remains a valuable political weapon in the Prime Minister's hands.[1]

Within the structure of the Government the Prime Minister has a special place, in that he has no department of his own and he acts as coordinator-in-chief. In the past, departmental responsibilities were sometimes combined with the Premiership. Lord Salisbury was Foreign Secretary 1895–1900 as well as being Prime Minister. Asquith, when Prime Minister in 1914, also temporarily assumed the post of Minister of War. Baldwin was Chancellor of the Exchequer as well as Prime Minister as a temporary expedient in 1923, and MacDonald in 1924 assumed the office of Foreign Secretary. Attlee, 1945–6, and Churchill, 1940–5 and 1951–2, combined the Premiership with the post of Minister of Defence. Between 1968 and 1981 successive Prime Ministers headed the Civil Service Department, and with its abolition in 1981 Mrs Thatcher assumed responsibility for the Management and Personnel Office that took over some of its functions.

These, however, may all be regarded as exceptions to the general rule that the Prime Minister is free from departmental responsibilities and is thus able to choose the areas of policy with which he will become involved at any particular time. The Prime Minister has the special authority that goes with

[1]See P. G. Richards, *Patronage in British Government*, London 1963; K. Sainsbury, 'Patronage, Honours and Parliament', *Parl. Aff.* 1965–6, pp. 346–50; R. S. Goldston, 'Patronage in British Government', *Parl. Aff.* 1977, pp. 80–96.

being Chairman of the Cabinet and of its most important committees. As votes are rarely taken at Cabinet meetings, the Prime Minister's power to sum up in Cabinet discussions is very important, though the ability to handle Cabinet meetings must, like any chairmanship, vary from one Prime Minister to another. The Prime Minister also enjoys the natural authority that goes with being party leader (although MacDonald's position in the National Government in 1931, and for a while Churchill's position in the wartime Coalition, were exceptions to this).

These several aspects of the Prime Minister's position within the political system are all of quite long standing, most of them emerging during the constitutional developments of the nineteenth century. A number of more recent developments, however, have added to the Prime Minister's historically based power. In many ways the structure of the expanded Government machine of recent years can be likened to a pyramid with the Prime Minister at the apex, performing the vital role of principal coordinator of the whole machine. Similarly, the Prime Minister can be seen as the head of a Civil Service elite of Permanent Secretaries who, since 1920, have moved from department to department, answerable not so much to individual departments as to the Cabinet Office, the Treasury and the Prime Minister. The Prime Minister vets all appointments to top Civil Service posts and thus can influence the complexion of the Higher Civil Service. Even by 1983 most of the Permanent Secretaries then in post had been appointed by Mrs Thatcher. Thus, as with the Ministerial hierarchy, the Prime Minister can be seen as the head of the permanent administrative structure.

Ministers are today more bound up with departmental duties than at any time in the past, so that the planning and coordinating function of government is left increasingly in the hands of the few non-departmental Ministers of the Cabinet, and the Prime Minister in particular. In this sense the role that the Cabinet played in the nineteenth century, of discussing and deciding on general policies, has to a large extent given way to the more automatic function of approving policies that are largely decided elsewhere. The inability of departmental Ministers to probe into the details of their colleagues' work, suggests that policies frequently receive Cabinet approval on the strength of an alliance between the departmental Ministers most directly concerned and the Prime Minister.

The Prime Minister is no longer tied to the Commons as Leader of the House. Asquith separated the offices of Prime Minister and Leader of the Commons in 1915 when he appointed Lloyd George to this office. This precedent was followed with Bonar Law and Austen Chamberlain as Leader of the Commons under Lloyd George's Premiership, and with Clynes and then Baldwin under MacDonald. Since 1945 no Prime Minister has attempted to combine the two roles, so that the Prime Minister is left with more time to devote to his task of coordinating the Government machine.

Since 1945 the Cabinet Office has developed as a body of officials largely under the Prime Minister's control. When a Prime Minister wishes to take particular note of a department or a Minister, he can create a special Cabinet Committee to perform the task of supervision. Normally the Prime Minister will take a special interest in the Treasury, and often Budget policy will be decided by the Prime Minister and the Chancellor of the Exchequer, rather than by the whole Cabinet. The Prime Minister also normally involves himself with foreign affairs, sometimes to the exclusion of the Foreign Secretary's own authority. Mrs Thatcher was critical of the Foreign Office and took a close interest in foreign affairs, especially during and after the Falklands war. Lord Salisbury, 1895–1900, and MacDonald in 1924 were literally their own Foreign Secretaries. In the main, the nature of international relations today, with 'summit meetings' of heads of state and the need for speedy military decisions in a nuclear age, means that the Prime Minister's involvement in foreign affairs, and particularly European affairs, is personal and direct.

In general elections today great emphasis is placed on the 'image' of the Prime Minister and the other party leaders. In particular, the effect of the mass media on elections has been to concentrate the electorate's attention on personalities, and the personalities of the party leaders in particular. This process, perhaps beginning with Gladstone's Midlothian Campaign in 1880, and culminating with the impact of television on general elections since 1959, has had the effect of increasing the influence that a successful leader can exert over his own party, in that the leader has become the hub of the party's electoral appeal and the centre of party loyalty. This must inevitably help an electorally successful Prime Minister to command the support of his party's MPs in Parliament.

* * *

These several developments in the political process can all be advanced as factors that have increased the individual authority of the Prime Minister in this century. They underlie the claims made by Richard Crossman[1] that '. . . The post-war epoch has seen the final transformation of Cabinet Government into Prime Ministerial Government . . .', and by J. P. Mackintosh[2] that '. . . Now the country is governed by a Prime Minister, his colleagues, junior ministers and civil servants, with the Cabinet acting as a clearing house and court of appeal.' Nevertheless, there are various other considerations which still limit the power of the Prime Minister. The Prime Minister's authority has no legal basis, in that it is not based on statute, and his Constitutional role is purely that of principal adviser to the Monarch. Whatever may be the power of Prime Ministers when in office, their security of tenure does not seem to be particularly strong. Asquith, Churchill and Wilson each served for a total of nearly nine years as Prime Minister, but most tenures of office have been much shorter than this: the average this century is under five years. Between elections the Prime Minister is dependent upon the support of his Ministers and his party to an extent that a popularly elected leader is not. This support can be withdrawn and very often is. The Prime Minister can survive the resignation of a leading Minister, but a Prime Minister can be forced from office when faced with a substantial body of discontent in his Cabinet or his party. The resignations of Asquith in 1916, Lloyd George in 1922, MacDonald in 1935, and Chamberlain in 1940 came primarily as a result of discontent within the Government, while Eden in 1957 and Macmillan in 1963 were

[1] Introduction to *The English Constitution*, p. 51.
[2] *The British Cabinet*, p. 524.

widely criticised within the party before illness brought their resignations. Unpressured retirements, like that of Wilson in 1976, are rare.

The wide powers of appointment and dismissal that the Prime Minister enjoys inevitably are limited by personal and practical factors. As noted earlier in the chapter, Cabinet and Government formation is complicated by factors of maximum and minimum numbers, the temperament and party standing of potential Ministers, the availability of talent, and even geographical considerations. Equally, it is debatable to what extent the Prime Minister's power to dismiss Ministers extends to his closest colleagues. Certainly, between 1979 and 1986 Mrs Thatcher dismissed a number of Cabinet Ministers or senior non-Cabinet figures. In general, however, there is an inner circle of senior Ministers with a security of tenure that normally a Prime Minister would find very difficult to shake. This, and the several other factors already noted, are restrictions upon the Prime Minister's absolute powers of appointment and dismissal.

With regard to the personality cult in modern elections, 1945 is often quoted as an example of an election when the undoubted prestige and personality of Winston Churchill did not bring electoral advantage for his party. Again, the Conservatives won the 1979 election despite the fact that (according to opinion polls) Margaret Thatcher had much less electoral appeal than James Callaghan. The importance of image can rebound on a party leader, in that just as a good image may be an electoral advantage, so a bad image can be fatal to a leader's standing within his party. Before their replacement as leaders of the Conservative Party, the prestige of Eden, Macmillan, Home and Heath had probably suffered because it was thought that they were an electoral disadvantage to the party.

The power exercised by Lloyd George and Churchill during the two wars was in some ways exceptional, and it is easy to exaggerate the extent to which this wartime authority was carried over into peacetime. It is possible to find in the nineteenth century evidence of Prime Ministers who dominated their parties and their Governments. Disraeli's purchase of the Suez Canal shares for Britain in 1878, without prior Cabinet approval, was a major example of the exercise of individual authority, while Disraeli and Gladstone together dominated their parties, and the whole of the political arena, for almost twenty years. It is doubtful if any modern Prime Minister has had the authority and control over the entire government process that was enjoyed by Sir Robert Peel in the 1840s.

Indeed, the extent of modern government is such that no Prime Minister can be expected to grasp all the intricacies of his Ministers' work. Despite the development of the Cabinet Secretariat no modern Premier can hope to be in touch with all aspects of policy and administration in the Peelite tradition. Today a Prime Minister's activities are bound to be limited and specialised to a certain extent, and some Foreign Secretaries like Ernest Bevin, or some Chancellors of the Exchequer under non-economist Prime Ministers like Douglas-Home, can be largely free to pursue their own activities without direct interference from the Premier. Also, as has been noted above, the presence within every Cabinet of a group of senior Ministers (whether or not they form an 'Inner Cabinet') who are of particular authority in the Government and the party, means that there is formed a counter-balance to the individual power of the Prime Minister.

* * *

The picture that emerges from this consideration of Prime Ministerial powers and constraints is that of the Prime Minister as a powerful but not overwhelmingly supreme figure. While normally there will be no other single figure who is more powerful than the Prime Minister, and while to a great (and probably growing) extent the Prime Minister symbolises the Government of the day, the Prime Minister is less dominant within the British system of government than is suggested by the amount of attention that is focused on the office and its incumbent. Lord Morrison[1] has written that the Prime Minister '. . . ought not to, and usually does not, presume to give directions or decisions which are proper to the Cabinet or one

[1] *Government and Parliament*, p. 52.

of its Committees.' Similarly Patrick Gordon Walker[1] has argued that '. . . Despite the rise of the Prime Minister there are restraints on him that make Prime Ministerial government impossible.'

Of the several interpretations of the decision-making process that have been advanced by former Ministers and political commentators, the most convincing is perhaps Gordon Walker's view that key decisions are made, not by the Prime Minister alone, but by groups of Ministers (or 'Partial Cabinets'), with the composition of the group varying from issue to issue. The Prime Minister will usually be at the centre of such a group of Ministers, but will be obliged to come to terms with the Ministers (and the civil servants, service chiefs and other specialist advisers) most directly concerned with the issue in question. Thus, says Gordon Walker,[2] 'Partial Cabinets, but not Prime Ministerial government, have become an accepted and established part of the Cabinet system. . . . a partial Cabinet is the very opposite of Prime Ministerial government: it presupposes that the Prime Minister carries influential Cabinet colleagues with him, and that these will, with the Prime Minister, convince the Cabinet if policy is questioned when the Cabinet is informed.'

Certainly, descriptions of the Prime Minister's authority as being 'Presidential' in scope are essentially misleading. The most relevant examples of Presidential systems are those of the United States and France, and there are at least three fundamental respects in which the British Prime Minister is at a disadvantage when compared with an American or French President. In the first place, unlike a British Prime Minister the President of the United States or France is head of state as well as head of the government, and is able to capitalise on all the prestige that goes with that fact. Second, the British Prime Minister retains office only so long as he preserves the support of his party colleagues, whereas the American or French President is directly elected for a fixed term and can be removed from office only in the most exceptional constitutional circumstances. Third, while the British Prime Minister

[1] *The Cabinet*, p. 91.
[2] Ibid.

has to appear before the House of Commons on a regular basis, and is subject to rigorous scrutiny, the separation of powers in the United States and France means that the President is spared that requirement. It is the case, of course, that an American or French President may be obliged to live with a legislature that is controlled by an opposing party, while the federal nature of the American Constitution limits the President's sphere of authority. That said, the Monarchical and Parliamentary features of the British system impose major limitations on a Prime Minister's authority that do not apply in the case of an American or French President.

8

Parliament: I. The House of Commons

THE TERM 'Parliament' is used in Britain in at least four distinct senses. First, Parliament is a legal term. The concept of the Queen in Parliament embraces the three estates of Monarch, Lords and Commons which, when acting together, constitute the supreme legal authority in the United Kingdom. Second, Parliament is a structural term that describes the Palace of Westminster in which the House of Commons and House of Lords are located. Third, a Parliament is a period of time between general elections, with a general election bringing a new Parliament into existence and a dissolution ending its life. Fourth, Parliament is often used synonymously with the House of Commons. While it is incorrect to equate the Commons with Parliament in either the legal or structural senses, in practical terms the role of the Monarch in Parliament is largely formal, and the legal power and political authority of the House of Lords is subservient to that of the Commons. Today, the House of Commons, composed of the 650 elected representatives of the people, is the dominant element in Parliament.

Functions and Timetable of the Commons[1]

The main role of the House of Commons is as a publicist and critic of Government activities, though within this overall

[1] For general works on the House of Commons and Parliament see P. Norton, *The Commons In Perspective*, London 1981; P. Norton (ed.), *Parliament*

role it is possible to distinguish between three main forms of Parliamentary activity. In classical Constitutional terms the functions of the Commons are to legislate, to approve the granting of finance to the Government, and to examine and criticise the activities of the Government. The legislative function of the House of Commons (as of the House of Lords) extends to the introduction of legislation, and the approval of all legislation before it becomes law. Generally, however, Government control of the Commons' timetable, and the assured Government majority in the House, means that the legislative function of the Commons is limited mainly to the discussion, perhaps the amendment, and then the final approval of Bills that are introduced by the Government (although Private Bills and Private Members' Bills remain as exceptions to this). The details of the financial powers of the House of Commons are examined elsewhere,[1] but it may be noted here that as with other Government legislation, the granting of supply and the approval of the Government's financial proposals are largely automatic today, with financial debates being used primarily as a further opportunity to comment in general upon Government activities. Thus the deliberative function of the Commons, the probing and criticism of the Government actions, is today not limited merely to questions and general debate, but is exercised also through the examination of Government legislation and financial proposals.

A Parliament, in the sense of a Parliamentary period, lasts for a maximum of five years before it is dissolved and a general election held (unless, as during the two world wars, the life of

[1] See below, Ch. 10.

---

in the 1980s, London 1985; R. Needham, *Honourable Member*, London 1983; P. G. Richards, *The Backbenchers*, London 1972; Sir Ivor Jennings, *Parliament*, London 1957; A. H. Hanson and H. V. Wiseman, *Parliament at Work*, London 1962; Eric Taylor, *The House of Commons at Work*, London 1981; S. A. Walkland and M. Ryle (eds), *The Commons Today*, London 1981; J. P. Mackintosh (ed.), *People and Parliament*, London 1977. See also G. Marshall, 'Parliament and the Constitution', *PQ* 1965, pp. 266–76; A. H. Hanson, 'The Purpose of Parliament', *Parl. Aff.* 1963–4, pp. 279–95; P. Norton, 'The Changing Face of the British House of Commons in the 1970s', *LSQ* 1980, pp. 333–58.

the Parliament is extended by special legislation). Each Parliament is divided into sessions, which are terminated by prorogation.

Each session is self-contained, in that uncompleted business cannot be carried over from one session to another.[1] Until 1920, sessions generally began in February, but today sessions normally run from October to October. In election years when (as on five of the last six occasions) the election is not held in October, this pattern is upset, and an especially long or short session is necessary in order to return to the October prorogation. The legislative business of a normal session is usually completed by the end of July, before the long summer recess begins. In order, however, that Parliament may be recalled if necessary during the summer, with the minimum of procedural fuss, Parliament is not prorogued until the end of the summer recess in October or November, and the new session then begins almost at once.

The House of Commons generally sits for about 170 days in each session, and there has been no marked increase in this number as compared with the inter-war years. The average length of each day's sitting, however, has increased compared with pre-1945 sessions, so that today the Commons does spend rather more hours in session than it did in the past. The House normally sits from 2.30 p.m. to 10.30 p.m. from Monday to Thursday, and from 11.0 a.m. to 4.30 p.m. on Fridays, although in recent years a third or more sittings have extended beyond midnight. In 1967 morning sessions were introduced on Monday and Wednesday mornings as an experiment, but now the House sits in the mornings only very rarely, to deal with unfinished business from the previous evening. Normal hours can be exceeded on days when certain types of business are being discussed, and on any day if the House agrees to suspend Standing Orders. The last Saturday sitting was on April 3rd 1982, at the beginning of the Falklands crisis, and the last Sunday sitting was on September 3rd 1939.

This distribution of time is often seen as inadequate. It is

[1]For Parliamentary procedure see Lord Campion, *Introduction to the Procedure of the House of Commons*, London 1958; J. Redlich, *The Procedure of the House of Commons*, London 1908; R. A. Chapman, 'The Significance of Parliamentary Procedure', *Parl. Aff.* 1962–3, pp. 179–87.

suggested, for example, that the House should sit for at least another fifty days in each session; that there should be more frequent and longer morning sittings; and that the sittings should be spread more evenly over the year, with perhaps a mid-week recess rather than the long holiday recesses.[1] Such proposals are resisted, however, on the grounds that they would impose too great a burden on members of the Government. This is a major problem in a system of government where Ministers are members of the legislature. Morning sittings for each day of the week are opposed because they might interfere with the work of the Standing Committees, which at present meet in the mornings. Longer hours are also objected to by those who argue that MPs should retain interests, and even employment, outside the House. Thus, here, as in so many aspects of the activities of the Commons, the question is raised of whether the role of an MP should or should not be a full-time one.

Each day's sitting in the Commons begins, appropriately enough, with prayers. This is followed (except on Fridays) by Question Time, which lasts an hour. After Question Time a number of matters may be dealt with, including Ministerial statements, Urgency Motions, and the formal First Reading of Bills. Then follows the main business of the day (the Orders of the Day), be it legislation, finance, or the consideration of some motion. The final half-hour of the sitting is devoted to the Adjournment Debate, when backbenchers can raise constituency or personal grievances. In the main, Fridays are devoted to Private Members' Bills and Private Members' Motions, though this can vary from session to session. On other days the business to be considered is determined by the

[1]For general works on Parliamentary reform see D. Judge (ed.), *The Politics of Parliamentary Reform*, London 1983; B. Crick, *The Reform of Parliament*, London 1964; Hansard Society, *Parliamentary Reform 1933–60*, London 1961; M. Foot, *Parliament in Danger!*, London 1959; A. Hill and A. Whichelow, *What's Wrong With Parliament?*, London 1964; P. Bromhead, 'How Should Parliament Be Reformed?', *PQ* 1959, pp. 272–82; S. A. Walkland, 'A Liberal Comment on Recent Proposals for Parliamentary Reform', *Parl. Aff.* 1962–3, pp. 338–42; B. Crick, 'The Prospects for Parliamentary Reform', *PQ* 1965, pp. 333–46; H. V. Wiseman, 'Parliamentary Reform', *Parl. Aff.* 1958–9, pp. 240–54; S. A. Walkland, 'The Politics of Parliamentary Reform', *Parl. Aff.* 1975–6, pp. 190–200.

two frontbenches. The Leader of the House of Commons and the Government Whips consult with the Opposition Whips about the timetable and try to meet Opposition wishes, but the final control of the timetable lies with the Government.

In 1800 Government time involved only one day per week, but this was increased to two days in 1837, three days in 1892, and four days in 1902, while Governments with a particularly heavy programme have in some sessions suspended private members' business altogether. Excluding the daily Question Time and Adjournment Debate, roughly 35% of the time of the House is normally devoted to the consideration of motions, roughly 45% to the consideration of Government legislation, and roughly 5% is taken up in incidental business. Thus about 85% of the House's time is devoted to matters determined by the Government and Opposition frontbenches. The 15% that remains for backbenchers' topics is made up of ten or so days for Bills and ten or so days for motions, with some of the time that is devoted to the consideration of the annual Estimates, and part of the first day's debate on the Speech from the Throne, also being devoted to private members' topics.

Backbenchers criticise this distribution of time as devoting too much attention to matters raised by the two frontbenches, at the expense of constituency matters. From another standpoint, the timetable can be criticised for devoting too much time to the consideration of Government *legislation*, and the Finance Bill in particular, as these debates often involve long hours spent on points of detail which are incomprehensible to most MPs and outside observers. The details of legislation and of finance are probably better considered in committee away from the floor of the House. Certainly, the main function of the House, of drawing the attention of the public to Government activities, can be much better achieved by debating issues and principles, rather than by examining financial and legislative details.

Given that Parliament's central function is to publicise the activities of the Government, it is surprising that its proceedings are not televised. The State Opening of Parliament has been televised, the proceedings of the House of Lords have been televised since 1985 and excerpts from House of Commons business have been broadcast on radio since 1978, but there has been no live televising of the Commons. The continuous televising of the Commons on a special channel, or a programme of selected parts of the day's business, might make the public more aware of Parliamentary activities. It might also produce better attendance in the House, and better speeches, though opponents argue that it might lead to greater exhibitionism and a tendency to play to the cameras. It could also remove some of Parliament's mystique (for good or ill), and this is perhaps a major reason why the Commons, in free votes in 1966, 1975 and 1985, rejected proposals for the televising of proceedings for experimental periods, even though Select Committees have reported in favour of such an experiment.[1]

Parliamentary Procedure

The principles governing the conduct of business in the House are based partly on the 'practice of the House' (which consists of conventions and traditions of behaviour which have developed over the years), and partly on Standing Orders, which are the written rules that have been formulated in the modern period, particularly over the past century. The interpretation and application of the various conventions and Standing Orders is the responsibility of the Speaker or his deputy. In this task he is aided by 'the Bible' of Parliamentary practice, Erskine May's *Law, Privileges, Proceedings and Usage of Parliament*, which is regularly brought up to date by succeeding Clerks of the House.[2]

The office of Speaker originated when the Commons elected one of its own number to report proceedings to the Monarch.[3] Sir Peter de la Mare in the 1376 Parliament is usually

[1] See B. Franklin, 'A Leap in the Dark', *Parl. Aff.* 1986, pp. 284–96; J. G. Blumler, 'The Sound of Parliament', *Parl. Aff.* 1984, pp. 250–66; B. Gould, 'Televise Parliament to Revive the Chamber', *Parl. Aff.* 1984, pp. 243–9.

[2] 20th edition, 1983.

[3] See P. Laundy, *The Office of Speaker in the Parliaments of the Commonwealth*, London 1984; P. Laundy, 'The Speaker of the House of Commons', *Parl. Aff.* 1960–1, pp. 72–9; J. E. Powell, 'A Speaker Before "The First"', *Parl. Aff.* 1964–5, pp. 20–2; J. A. Cross, 'Deputy Speakers and Party Politics', *Parl. Aff.* 1964–5, pp. 361–7; W. S. Livingston, 'The Security of Tenure of the Speaker of the House of Commons', *Parl. Aff.* 1957–8, pp. 484–504.

TABLE XXIX

Sessional Timetable 1984–5

	Number of Sittings	
	House of Commons	House of Lords
Legislation	*71½ (41.6%)*	*93 (61.6%)*
Government Bills introduced in Commons	52½	60
,, ,, ,, ,, Lords	5	21
Private Members' Bills ,, ,, Commons	11	2
,, ,, ,, ,, ,, Lords	1	10
Opposed Private Bills	2	
General Debates (initiated by)	*87½ (50.9%)*	*57 (37.7%)*
Speech From the Throne	6	4
Government or Opposition Motions	44½	22½
Opposition Days	18½	
Adjournment Motion for Recess	4	
Private Members Motions	14½	
Motion for Papers*		24
Questions		6½
Finance	*12 (7.0%)*	*1 (0.7%)*
Budget Statement	4	
Finance Bill	5	1
Estimates	3	
Incidental Business	*1 (0.5%)*	
Prorogation	1	
Total sittings	172	151
Total hours	1,593	1,023
Average length of sittings	9¼ hrs	6¾ hrs
Longest sitting	30¼ hrs	11½ hrs

*A procedure, peculiar to the Lords, that reserves for the proposer the right to make the final contribution in the debate.

regarded as the first Speaker, but it was not until the Constitutional struggles of the seventeenth century that the Speaker emerged as the champion of Parliamentary rights against Royal authority. The independence of the Speaker was established in the eighteenth and nineteenth centuries, when he was given a salary (now £44,560) and a pension, and was required to sever his party connections on taking office. The convention also emerged in the nineteenth century that the Speaker was not opposed at a general election, but this has not always been observed this century. A special Speaker's constituency of St Stephen's, made up only of MPs, has been advocated at various times, but it has been resisted partly on the grounds that if the Speaker was not re-elected to office he would be without a seat in the House. The Speaker serves for a full Parliament, and since 1935 all Speakers have been re-appointed if they so desired. The choice of Speaker is not normally contested, as this would be seen as weakening his impartiality, and any disagreements over the choice of Speaker are generally settled by the Whips behind the scenes. In 1951, however, there was a division on the choice of Speaker for the first time since 1895, and the 1951 situation was further unusual in that the choice of a new Speaker had to be made immediately after a general election rather than in the middle of a Parliament.

As well as being responsible for the maintenance of order and the general conduct of debates, the Speaker has control over such matters as the acceptance or rejection of Urgency Motions, motions for the Closure, the selection of amendments for debate, and the limitation of supplementary questions at Question Time. The Speaker is also the initial judge of whether there has been a breach of House of Commons privilege, though in matters of privilege the ultimate judges are the House itself and the Committee of Privileges.[1] Most of the 'ancient and undoubted rights and privileges' of the House are now largely of historical significance, having arisen from a desire in the past to protect MPs from outside interference (primarily Royal interference), and from a desire to allow freedom of speech and activity in the House. Thus Parliamentary privilege includes freedom of speech, so that MPs cannot be prosecuted for sedition or sued for libel or slander for anything said in the House or reported in Parliamentary publications.[2] The House is also protected from criticism that

[1] G. Marshall, 'Privilege and "Proceedings in Parliament"', *Parl. Aff.* 1957–8, pp. 396–404.

[2] P. M. Leonard, 'Freedom of Speech in Parliament – its Misuse and Proposals for Reform', *PL* 1981, pp. 30–51.

affronts 'the dignity of the House', and can deal internally with matters affecting its own privileges and conduct. In 1947 Garry Allighan was expelled from the House on account of critical articles he had written about Parliament, and at times, outside offenders against privilege are summoned to the House and reprimanded.

Privileges of the House also include the right of access to the Crown through the Speaker; the general right to have its activities favourably construed by the Monarch; the right to judge cases of electoral malpractice (though today this is handled by High Court Judges); the right to fill casual vacancies (which gives the Whips of the party that holds the seat the right to determine by-election dates); and the right of freedom from civil arrest, which in its practical application today means freedom from jury service and subpoena.

While these privileges were perhaps desirable in the constitutional conflicts of the past, it may be questioned whether these are necessary today.[1] The ancient Parliamentary privileges are also often linked in criticism and ridicule with the time-honoured ceremonial of Parliament, such as the Speaker's traditional reluctance to take office; the ceremonial attached to the opening of a new Parliament; Black Rod's summoning of the Commons to the Lords to hear the Royal Assent to legislation; the Royal Assent being given in Norman French; the reference to Honourable, Right Honourable, Honourable and Gallant, and Honourable and Learned Members. These aspects of traditional Parliamentary practice are frequently attacked as archaic mumbo-jumbo.

The defenders of 'the glory of Parliament', however, reject these criticisms and claim that Parliament's traditional practices are a colourful part of a Parliamentary and national heritage of several hundreds of years, which (they claim) produces respect for Parliament and the dignity of its proceedings.[2] They argue that the ancient practices of Parliament

[1] Lord Kilmuir, *The Law of Parliamentary Privilege*, London 1959; D. C. M. Yardley, 'The House of Commons and its Privileges since the Strauss Affair', *Parl. Aff.* 1961–2, pp. 500–10; C. Seymour Ure, 'Proposed Reforms of Parliamentary Privilege', *Parl. Aff.* 1969–70, pp. 221–31.

[2] See, for example, H. Boardman, *The Glory of Parliament*, London 1960; S. Gordon, *Our Parliament*, London 1964; Sir H. Dunnico, *The Mother of Parliaments*, London 1951; H. King, *Parliament and Freedom*, London 1962.

serve in general to emphasise the stability and continuity of the political system, and that in countries where such traditions do not exist, they are often invented. The debate is an old and frequently repeated one, and is linked very closely with the debate over the ceremonial value of the Monarchy. To some extent the debate cuts across party lines, though in general Conservative MPs tend to be more 'traditionalist' in outlook, while Labour and Liberal MPs tend to be less so.

The Legislative Process

The legislative function of Parliament embraces various types of Bill. There is an initial distinction between Public Bills, which concern the whole community, Private Bills, which affect only a section of the community (be it a local authority, a business company, or an individual), and Hybrid Bills, which are Public Bills that are classified by the Speaker as having a particular effect on one section of the community. Most Public Bills are Government Bills, introduced by a Minister as official Government policy, but Public Bills may also be introduced by backbench MPs as Private Members' Bills.[1]

These formal classes of legislation can be further subdivided according to their precise source. Government Bills may stem from the party electoral programme, particularly after a general election, and especially if a party has been out of office for some time and comes to power with a big legislative programme. Such legislation tends to attract attention because it is often contentious, but in the main this type of legislation forms only a small part of a Government's legislative programme for a session. Some Government Bills, like the Finance Bill and the Consolidated Fund Bills, have to be introduced every session. A Government may also be called upon to introduce emergency legislation to meet an immediate crisis at home or abroad, while the findings of Select Committees, Royal Commissions, or other committees of enquiry may

[1] See I. Burton and G. Drewry, *Legislation and Public Policy*, London 1981; I. Burton and G. Drewry, 'Public Legislation: A Survey of the Sessions 1981–2 and 1982–3', *Parl. Aff.* 1985, pp. 219–52 (and for earlier sessions in each annual volume of *Parl. Aff.*); D. A. Miers and D. C. Page, *Legislation*, London 1982.

produce a need for legislation. Pressure groups may be able to influence a Government to introduce a particular piece of legislation, while 'departmental Bills' can stem from the administrative needs of the departments of State. Legislation that applies to England and Wales has sometimes to be introduced separately for Scotland, and some Bills arise from the need to supplement the work of previous legislation. Similarly, Consolidation Bills are frequently introduced to gather existing legislation into one general statute. These various factors inevitably reduce the party political content of a Government's legislative programme. One estimate is that in the 1970s over three-quarters of all Government Bills were 'Whitehall Bills' (in the sense that they emerged from the demands of the departments of state), another tenth emerged from the Government's reaction to unexpected events, and only about an eighth arose from party manifesto commitments.[1]

Private Members' Bills also may have various sources. A Bill may be the result of the initiative of the MP concerned, or one backbencher may persuade another to introduce a measure on his behalf. A pressure group may persuade a backbencher to introduce a Private Member's Bill, while the Government or Opposition Whips may prevail upon a backbencher to adopt a Bill that they wish to see introduced but cannot accommodate in Government time.

Whatever its source, however, to become law a Bill has to be approved by both Houses of Parliament (other than under the terms of the Parliament Acts 1911 and 1949), and must receive the Royal Assent. Bills may be introduced into either House, though politically controversial legislation, financial legislation (particularly the annual Finance Bill and Appropriations Bill), and electoral legislation normally begins in the House of Commons. The procedure for Public Bills is basically the same in both Houses. The Bill is drafted by Parliamentary Counsel. If it is a Government Bill, before it is presented to Parliament its proposals will be examined by the Cabinet, a Cabinet committee, the department of state concerned, and any sectional interests who may be affected. These discussions behind the scenes may be continued during

[1] R. Rose, *Do Parties Make a Difference*, p. 70.

much of the Bill's passage through Parliament, and in many cases they are of more practical significance than is the Parliamentary process.

The Bill is introduced into one of the Houses and is given a formal First Reading. It is then printed, and normally after two or three weeks the Second Reading debate takes place, when the general principles and merits of the Bill are considered. The Second Reading can be taken on the floor of the House or in a Standing Committee. The opponents of the Bill may choose not to vote against it at this stage (especially in the Lords), but may seek to make amendments at the committee stage. If the Bill involves the spending of public money, it is accompanied by a financial resolution which is considered after the Second Reading. The Bill goes to a Standing Committee for detailed consideration, clause by clause, though for some Bills this stage is taken in a Committee of the Whole House. The Report stage then follows, when the amendments made in committee are considered and perhaps altered, but if further detailed amendments are sought, the Bill has to be returned to the Committee. With non-controversial Bills the debate at the Report stage can be dispensed with. Finally, the Bill is debated once more in general terms, with only verbal amendments allowed, and is given a Third Reading. The Bill then passes to the other House, where the process is repeated. Any amendments made in the second House have to be considered by the original House, and deadlock may result. Generally, however, agreement is reached, and the Bill goes for Royal Assent. This is given by Lord Commissioners, as not since 1854 has the Royal Assent been given by the Monarch in person.

The vast majority of changes that are made to Government Bills during their passage through the Commons are a result of amendments proposed by Ministers themselves. In the 1970–71 session, for example, all 974 amendments proposed by Ministers at the Committee and Report Stages of Government Bills were accepted, compared with just 74 of the 1,008 amendments moved by Opposition MPs and Government backbenchers.[1] What is more, of the Opposition or Govern-

[1] J. A. G. Griffith, *Parliamentary Scrutiny of Government Bills*, London 1974, Ch. 6.

ment backbench amendments that were successful, the vast majority were changes that Ministers were quite happy to accept.

All Bills are sessional, in that if they are not passed in one session they cannot be taken up in the next session from where they left off. Thus in the 1973–4 session a number of Government Bills were lost as a result of the 'early' dissolution of February 1974, while even in 1983 nine Bills (including the Data Protection Bill and the Police and Criminal Evidence Bill) were lost through the May dissolution. The timetabling of legislation is arranged by the Leader of the House in consultation with the Government and Opposition Whips. Some Bills pass through all their stages in only a few hours while others are considered at great length. The 1974 Finance Bill was examined for 150 hours in Standing Committee alone, while in 1971 the Report Stage of the Industrial Relations Bill extended to five days. In the Commons, all the stages of a Bill can be taken on one day, as was illustrated with the Rhodesia Bill in 1965, and though the Lords' Standing Order No. 41 prevents two stages being taken on one day, in practice this Standing Order is frequently suspended. Thus in December 1972 the Pensions Bill passed all its stages in the Lords in just four minutes.

In the Commons, three particular procedures can be used to overcome attempts to disrupt the timetable. The Closure (first applied voluntarily by Speaker Brand to end a 41½-hour sitting, January 31st to February 2nd 1881) can end a debate at any stage if the Speaker accepts a Motion of Closure supported by a hundred members. Secondly, 'the Guillotine', or closure by compartments, also introduced in 1881, enables the Government to allocate a specific timetable for the consideration of each section of a Bill. A logical extension of this would perhaps be a Rules Committee to timetable the committee stage, or perhaps all stages of all Bills.[1] Thirdly, 'the Kangaroo', introduced in 1909, gives the Speaker the power to select for consideration a few representative amendments from a long list, in order to prevent repetitive debating. These three

[1]J. Palmer, 'Allocation of Time: the Guillotine and Voluntary Timetabling', *Parl. Aff.* 1969–70, pp. 232–47.

devices apply to the committee stage as well as to debates on the floor of the House.

* * *

In most sessions the number of Private Members' Bills that is introduced equals or exceeds the number of Government Bills, but whereas Government Bills are almost certain to be passed, the majority of Private Members' Bills are lost.[1] Thus of the 117 Private Members' Bills that were introduced during the 1981–2 session, only 10 received the Royal Assent, compared with 45 of the 46 Government Bills that were introduced (see Table XXX). An MP who wishes to introduce a Bill is faced with a number of problems. In the first place, little time is available. In recent sessions twelve or sixteen Fridays (when sittings only last five hours) have been allocated to Private Members' Bills. The Government may allocate additional time, but this depends on the Government's goodwill. One

TABLE XXX

Legislation 1981–2 and 1982–3

	Total Introduced		Enacted	
	1981–2	1982–3	1981–2	1982–3
Government Bills	46	50	45	42
Non-Government Bills	117	101	10	11
Private Members' Ballot	20	20	7	6
Ten Minute Rule	58	36	0	2
S.O. No. 37	14	24	1	1
Private Peers	25	21	2	2

Source: Based on a table contained in I. F. Burton and G. Drewry, 'Public Legislation: A Survey of the Sessions 1981–2 and 1982–3', *Parl. Aff.* 1985, pp. 219–52.

[1]See P. Bromhead, *Private Members' Bills*, London 1956; E. Davies, 'The Role of Private Members' Bills', *PQ* 1957, pp. 32–9; J. Gray, 'The Unsolicited Goods and Services Acts 1971 and 1975', *PL* 1978, pp. 242–63; A. Mitchell, 'A House Buyers Bill: How Not to Pass a Private Member's Bill', *Parl. Aff.* 1986, pp. 1–18; D. Marsh, 'Private Members' Bills and Moral Panic', *Parl. Aff.* 1986, pp. 179–86.

Standing Committee, however, gives precedence to Private Members' Bills. A ballot at the beginning of the session determines which MPs will be given time. Many enter the ballot without having a Bill to promote, and then adopt some measure (perhaps on the advice of the Whips) if they are successful in the ballot. It has been suggested that MPs should have a Bill before being allowed to enter the ballot, or that the ballot should be abolished and precedence given to Bills that received most support among MPs, perhaps in the form of MPs' signatures appended to the Bills.

If an MP is successful in the ballot, and if he overcomes the problems of drafting the Bill, he may have difficulty in maintaining a quorum of forty members for a non-controversial measure. Alternatively, if his Bill is controversial he may find that it is obstructed. The usual means of killing a Bill is to 'talk it out' by using up the time allotted to it, perhaps because it is controversial itself, or perhaps because it is due to be followed by a controversial measure on which some MPs wish to avoid a debate. In 1985 the Unborn Children (Protection) Bill, introduced by Enoch Powell, was 'talked out' at the report stage, while in order to delay the Water (Fluoridation) Bill Ivan Lawrence spoke for a twentieth-century record of four hours and twenty-three minutes on March 6th 1985. A further complication for a backbencher is that he cannot initiate a Bill, the main purpose of which is financial, and any Bill that involves the spending of public money has to be accompanied by a financial resolution introduced by a Minister. Any Bill that passes all its stages in the Commons has a very good chance of being given time in the Lords, but Bills that have passed first through the Lords cannot always be accommodated in the more crowded Commons' timetable.

In addition to Private Members' Fridays, other means of introducing a Bill are open to MPs. Under Standing Order No. 37, a member at any time may ask the House for leave to introduce a Bill for an unopposed Second Reading, but this is killed at once if there is any objection. Further, under the 'Ten-Minute Rule', at certain limited times in the week's timetable, a backbencher may make a ten-minute speech in defence of a Bill he wishes to introduce. This is followed by a ten-minute speech in opposition, and then a vote on whether the Bill may be introduced. Few Bills do materialise from this procedure, however, and it is used mainly to draw attention to an issue, though without much real hope of legislative success.

Thus there are great difficulties facing backbenchers who seek to introduce legislation, and there is some doubt as to the overall value of Private Members' time. Most Bills deal only with relatively minor matters, and generally debates are poorly attended. With an overcrowded timetable the time that is devoted to Private Members' Bills could perhaps be better used in considering Government policies, and during the wars, and from 1945 to 1948, Private Members' time was suspended. Backbenchers are able to propose amendments to Government Bills, and many amendments can have the force of separate legislation. Further, for some MPs the prime value of Private Members' time is that it occupies Fridays, and thus enables them to go home for a long weekend beginning on Thursday night.

In Defence of Private Members' Bills, however, it is undoubtedly the case that there are some sensitive issues such as animal welfare, some legal matters, and moral questions, about which Governments will not legislate for fear of offending some sections of the community. Thus important Private Members' Bills have been the Matrimonial Causes Act 1937,[1] the Obscene Publications Act 1959, the Murder (Abolition of the Death Penalty) Act 1965, the Termination of Pregnancy Act 1967, and the Divorce Reform Act 1969. Similarly, Private Members' Bills may reveal otherwise unpublicised issues and thereby stimulate the Government into action, as with the 'clean air' campaign. In this sense Private Members' legislation is another means of publicising Government activity or inactivity. Private Members' time can also be defended as being one of the rare occasions when Parliament is acting largely free from the control of the Government and the Whips, though at times the Government Whips persuade backbenchers to introduce measures that cannot be accommodated in the official Government legislative programme. Ultimately, however, the question is whether it is worth while spending time debating legislative proposals that in the main

[1] See A. P. Herbert, *The Ayes Have It*, London 1937.

are comparatively insignificant, or whether it would be better to devote the time to a fuller discussion of Government policies.

* * *

Private Bills are promoted in the main by local authorities which seek to acquire powers additional to those granted by general legislation, or by private firms and interests that wish to acquire land or property.[1] Many matters which in other countries might be settled by the Law Courts, are in Britain settled by an approach to Parliament. Only rarely do Private Bills arouse general interest, although some prove to be controversial, as with the Calderdale Water Bill in 1970 and the Burmah Refineries Trust Bill 1974 (which were both rejected against the advice of the Government). As with Public Bills, Private Bills must pass both Houses and receive the Royal Assent to become law, and the procedure involves three Readings, a committee stage, and a Report stage. In practice, however, the procedures for Public and Private Bills are very different, and almost all of the work on Private Bills is done in committee, or before the Bill ever reaches Parliament. Private Bill proposals have to be advertised widely in the press, and are presented to Parliament as a petition. The Bill is examined by the Examiners of Petitions for Private Bills to see that Standing Orders are complied with, and it is allocated to the Commons or Lords for introduction. Greater use is made of the Lords today than in the past, and about half of the Bills begin in the Lords. Any petitions opposing the Bill must be presented by the end of January, and after this the Bill is given a formal First Reading, and a Second Reading when its principles are debated. It then goes to the Private Bill Committee, composed of only four MPs, where, as in legal procedure, witnesses are called, evidence is examined, and legal counsel make pleas for and against the Bill. This process may last four or five days. Bills that are unopposed go to the Unopposed Private Bill Committee, made up of five MPs.

[1] See H. V. Wiseman, 'The Leeds Private Bill 1956', *Pub. Admin.* 1957, pp. 25–44; 'Promotion of Private Bills by Local Authorities', *Pub. Admin.* 1960, pp. 72–3; P. G. Richards (*et al.*), 'Private Bill Procedure: A Case for Reform', *PL* 1981, pp. 206–27.

Then follows a Report to the House, Third Reading, and transfer to the other House where the procedure is repeated.

A joint committee of both Houses has been suggested for Private Bills, as has a committee to take the Second Reading. A more radical reform that would make much private legislation unnecessary, would be to set up a committee with the authority, when petitioned, to grant to local authorities powers that had already been granted to other local authorities. As it is, however, less use is made of Private Bills than in the past. In the eighteenth and nineteenth centuries the enclosure movement and the purchase of land by the railway companies were largely achieved through Private Bills. Today, however, Government legislation has wider scope than in the past, while the cost of private legislation is often prohibitive, sometimes involving several thousands of pounds.

Finally in this context may be noted the procedure for Hybrid Bills.[1] They follow the same course as Public Bills, except that they are presented to the Examiners of Petitions for Private Bills who decide whether Private Bill Standing Orders are applicable, and have been complied with. Also, after Second Reading, the Bill goes to a small Select Committee where a procedure is followed that is similar to that of the Private Bill Committee. The Bill then reverts to the normal Public Bill procedure. The opportunities for delay and opposition are greater with Hybrid Bills than with Public Bills. In 1976 a major Parliamentary controversy developed when the Speaker ruled the Government's Aircraft and Shipbuilding Bill to be a Hybrid Bill, thereby complicating its passage through Parliament.

Questions and Debates

The Commons' function of scrutinising and publicising the executive is achieved through the questioning of Ministers in the House, through the consideration of Government policy in general debates, and through the work of the committees of the House. There are a number of different ways in which

[1] See G. W. Jones, 'A Forgotten Right Discovered', *Parl. Aff.* 1965–6, pp. 363–72.

MPs can ask questions of members of the Government.[1] Ministers can be questioned orally in Question Time in the Commons on Mondays to Thursdays from 2.30 p.m. to 3.30 p.m. Alternatively, questions may be submitted for a written answer in Hansard, and in addition, any oral questions that are not dealt with in Question Time are given a written answer. In the region of 3,000 oral answers to questions, and something like 40,000 written answers, will be given in an average year. Private Notice Questions on urgent matters may be submitted for oral answer on the same day, but the Speaker determines whether the matter is urgent enough to merit this, and less than fifty a year are granted. In addition to these public questions, MPs can write directly to Ministers for information.[2]

The daily question hour is a product of the specifically British Parliamentary system, with Ministers drawn from and answerable to Parliament. The practice emerged in the eighteenth century and developed in the nineteenth century, partly as a result of the activities of the Irish MPs in the 1880s, who were determined to draw attention to the Irish problem, but also as a result of the increased awareness of MPs of their responsibilities to their constituents, and of the growth in the extent of state activity. As well as increasing the number of questions asked in the House, however, the growth in the scope of governmental activity increased other pressures on Parliamentary time, and legislation, general debates, and questions competed for priority. In 1901 Government business was delayed by the number of questions asked in the Commons, and thus in 1902 Balfour introduced a procedure for questions, which, as modified in 1906 and on occasions since then, has survived as the basis of the existing procedure.

Today, Question Time is limited to one hour (there being

[1] D. N. Chester and N. Bowring, *Questions in Parliament*, London 1962; P. Howarth, *Questions in the House*, London 1956; D. Judge, 'Backbench Specialisation – a Study of Parliamentary Questions', *Parl. Aff.* 1973–4, pp. 171–86.

[2] K. E. Couzens, 'A Minister's Correspondence', *Pub. Admin.* 1956, pp. 237–44; D. Thompson, 'Letters to Ministers and Parliamentary Privilege', *PL* 1959, pp. 10–22; P. Norton, '"Dear Minister" – The Importance of MP-to-Minister Correspondence', *Parl. Aff.* 1982, pp. 59–72.

no increase or reduction in this time since 1906), and at least two days' notice of a question must be given. Generally about sixty to one hundred questions are submitted for oral answer each day, and about fifty of them are answered in the hour, though this can vary according to the time allowed by the Speaker for each answer. There is a limit on the number of questions that each MP can ask. Since 1960 this limit has been two questions per day and eight in any ten days. In fact, however, Question Time tends to be dominated by a few MPs, with Labour members generally asking more questions than Conservative members, whether a Labour Government is in office or not. There is no limit (other than the Speaker's discretion) on the number of supplementary questions that may be asked, and supplementaries are not limited to the original questioner. In 1908 some 42% of the questions were followed by supplementaries, while more recently the proportion has been over 90%. It is, of course, debatable whether it is better to have a few questions answered in detail, with perhaps even a short debate on five or six questions each day, or whether it is better to have a lot of questions answered briefly with distinct limits on supplementaries.

On Tuesdays and Thursdays, fifteen minutes of the hour are devoted to questions to the Prime Minister.[1] Other Ministers answer questions in turn on a complicated rota system, that attempts to ensure that each Minister will appear fairly regularly. Specific times on the rota are allocated to questions about the European Community and to questions addressed to the smaller departments. A particular Minister can be 'sheltered', however, by his supporters putting down a large number of questions for the Minister who precedes him on the rota. MPs also often hand in a question well in advance to try to ensure that it will be high on the list, or perhaps in order to exclude other questions, although questions may not now be submitted more than three weeks in advance. The Speaker determines whether a question is 'out of order'. As general guides, a question must be concerned with fact and not merely opinion, it must be an enquiry and not a statement, and it

[1] G. W. Jones, 'The Prime Minister and Parliamentary Questions', *Parl. Aff.* 1972–3, pp. 260–73.

must be couched in 'proper' language. A question must be within a Minister's sphere of responsibility, and there can be disagreement over the precise extent of a Minister's responsibility, as with disputes over Ministers' responsibilities with regard to the public corporations.

Questions may be motivated by a number of different considerations. An MP may seek information that he cannot otherwise obtain for himself. In such a case a question for a written answer or a letter to a Minister is often best, as this allows for a more detailed answer. MPs argue, however, that this type of enquiry would be less necessary if the House had better research facilities. An oral answer is most likely to be sought not so much for information, but in order to voice a grievance or embarrass the Minister. Similarly, an oral question, or the threat of an oral question, can be used to stimulate action by a Minister. Not all questions are hostile, however. A question may be asked by Government backbenchers in order to reveal Government achievements, while some questions are asked merely in order to gain publicity for the questioner.

Question Time generally receives good coverage in press reports of Parliament as it tends to be livelier and more topical than other Parliamentary proceedings,[1] and also because it comes early in the day and thus can be reported in the evening and morning newspapers. Radio coverage of Parliament originally concentrated on Question Time as one of the livelier Parliamentary occasions. A supplementary question can turn a seemingly innocent enquiry into a much more meaningful issue, and Question Time is very much a battle of wits between Ministers and questioners, with some Ministers clearly being much more adept than others at dealing with questions. A Minister can develop evasive techniques. Ultimately, of course, he can decline to answer 'in the public interest', or because the information would be too costly to obtain, but excessive reliance on this would eventually discredit the Minister. An MP who is not satisfied with an

[1]For relations between Parliament and the press in general see A. Butler, 'The History and Practice of Lobby Journalism', *Parl. Aff.* 1959–60, pp. 54–60; P. Bromhead, 'Parliament and the Press', *Parl. Aff.* 1962–3, pp. 279–92; A. E. Musson, 'Parliament and the Press', *Parl. Aff.* 1955–6, pp. 277–88.

answer can seek to develop the issue through an Adjournment Debate, an Urgency Motion, or by further questions. It has been suggested that, given the limitations of Question Time, a Prime Ministerial or Ministerial Press Conference should be introduced to supplement Parliamentary questioning. Despite its limitations, however, Question Time remains an important weapon that MPs have for probing the activities of the executive.

* * *

Government policy and actions can be the subject of general debates on various different occasions during the Parliamentary session. At the beginning of each session the Queen's Speech, containing the Government's legislative proposals, is followed by five or six days of debate. The first of these days is devoted primarily to speeches by backbenchers on constituency issues, but the other days are spent in debating more specific aspects of Government policy as agreed by the Whips. In addition, a further fifteen or so days in a normal session are devoted to general debates on topics chosen by the Government, after consultation with the Opposition. The Government sometimes uses these debates to test the attitude of the House and the public on some aspect of policy, perhaps as contained in a Government White Paper, and this may be used as a preliminary to future legislation.[1] Motions of censure also come into this category, and the Government will always find time for such a motion. On nineteen days the topics for debate are chosen by the Opposition.

Ministerial statements after Question Time cannot develop into full-scale debates, but very often lengthy statements and counter-statements continue for half an hour or so after Question Time. Under Standing Order No. 10, the House may adjourn in order to debate 'a specific and important matter that should have urgent consideration'.[2] This motion is proposed after Question Time, and needs the support of forty

[1] A. Silkin, 'Green Papers and Changing Methods of Consultation in British Government', *Pub. Admin.* 1973, pp. 427–48.

[2] See H. V. Wiseman, 'Private Members' Opportunities and Standing Order No. 9', *Parl. Aff.* 1958–9, pp. 377–91; W. H. Greenleaf, 'Urgency Motions in the Commons', *PL* 1960, pp. 270–84.

members and the agreement of the Speaker. Only two or three of the several requests for emergency debates each year are approved. Such debates last for three hours, and then the business of the day resumes from where it was interrupted. The Government may propose the adjournment of the House at the beginning of the day's business in order to debate a particularly urgent matter. The historic debate in 1940 that led to Chamberlain's resignation was of this type, but such debates are extremely rare.

These are all occasions when MPs have an opportunity to debate Government policy, but the topics are controlled by the two frontbenches. In these debates backbenchers are at a disadvantage when wishing to speak, in that Privy Councillors are given precedence over other MPs. Also, the Whips may discourage backbenchers from speaking in order that the frontbenchers may present the party case, and Government backbenchers are probably in the worst position of all in this respect. The Speaker usually allows minority opinions to be heard, however, so that minor party MPs have an advantage here. There are other occasions when backbenchers are given the chance to raise their own topics. Some Fridays are allocated to Private Members' Motions, MPs being selected by ballot. A number of motions are allocated to each day, though in practice only one is generally dealt with. Very often, Government policies rather than constituency topics are raised, and many MPs enter the ballot merely to prevent it being dominated by their opponents.

The final half-hour of each day's sitting is devoted to an Adjournment Debate on a topic initiated by a backbencher, on the historically based principle that the House should not rise without debating outstanding grievances.[1] The MPs to raise topics in an Adjournment Debate are chosen partly by ballot and partly by the Speaker. The matters raised are primarily constituency issues, and often arise from unsatisfactory answers at Question Time. The Adjournment Debate is a useful means of probing executive action, in that the enquiries can be more detailed than at Question Time. The Minister

[1] V. Herman, 'Adjournment Debates in the House of Commons', *Parl. Aff.* 1972–3, pp. 92–104.

has to state his case more fully, and it is harder to evade the issue than it is in Question Time. The debate often fails to attract attention, however, because the House tends to be empty by the end of the day, and except on Fridays the debate comes too late to receive good press and news coverage.

In addition to the daily Adjournment Debate, the final day before the House adjourns for the recess at Christmas, Easter, Whitsun, and summer, is devoted to general debates on topics decided by the Speaker in consultation with the Whips. It may also be noted in this context that an MP can draw attention to an issue by tabling a motion for debate 'on an early day'. Such Early Day Motions are very unlikely to be debated, but they are a means of publicising an issue and indicating the strength of Parliamentary feeling about it (as measured by the number of MPs who add their names to the motion).

The Committee System

Much of the work of the House, both legislative and deliberative, is done through committees.[1] The committee system has been reformed regularly over the last twenty years, but it is still widely criticised. There is a basic distinction between the committees that exist to consider legislation, and those that exist for purposes of general enquiry. The committee stage of all legislation is taken either in a Standing Committee or a Committee of the Whole House. A Committee of the Whole is made up of the House minus only the Speaker and the mace – the symbol of Royal authority. Originally the House met as a committee in this way in order to exclude the influence of the King through the Speaker. In the eighteenth century the practice also developed of allowing all who wished to do so to attend Select Committee meetings, so that on occasions these committees were made up of virtually the full House. Today the significance of a Committee of the Whole is not merely historical, in that the rules of debate and the

[1]See K. C. Wheare, *Government by Committee*, London 1955; M. Ryle, 'Committees in the House of Commons', *PQ* 1965, pp. 295–308; D. Pring, 'Standing Committees in the House of Commons', *Parl. Aff.* 1957–8, pp. 303–17; A. H. Hanson and H. V. Wiseman, 'The Use of Committees by the House of Commons', *PL* 1959, pp. 277–92.

general atmosphere in a Committee of the Whole are less formal than in the House with the Speaker. The Bills that are taken in a Committee of the Whole are either 'one-clause Bills' which can be passed very quickly, or Bills of first-class constitutional or political importance. In addition, the money resolution that accompanies any Bill that proposes an increase in public spending, is considered between the Second Reading and the committee stage by the House sitting as a Committee of the Whole. As well as this legislative function, some aspects of financial procedure are also considered by the whole House.

The Committee stage of most Bills, however, is taken in one of the Standing Committees. These Committees also take the Second Reading of some Bills. The first Standing Committee emerged at the end of the last century, and in most sessions before 1945 three to five Standing Committees were normally appointed. Today there are ten in most sessions, including two for Scottish Bills and one where precedence is given to Private Members' Bills. Each committee is normally made up of sixteen to fifty members, chosen roughly in proportion to party strength in the House, and according to their particular knowledge of the piece of legislation to be considered. A committee may deal with a number of Bills in a session, and until 1960 each committee had a nucleus of twenty members with an additional thirty or so who were chosen according to the Bill to be considered. Since 1960, however, committee members have been chosen because of their knowledge of the particular Bill to be dealt with. The relevant Minister, or his deputy, and a Government whip will invariably be members.

The Standing Committees meet in the mornings, generally for two-and-a-half-hour sessions. The Government may be defeated in committee because its majority is comparatively small, and because much committee work is concerned with details which cut across party lines, rather than with principles. Also the fate of the Government is not threatened by defeat in a Standing Committee. The Opposition can delay the Government's legislative programme at the committee stage, but to speed committee work the Closure, the Guillotine, and the Kangaroo can all be applied.

The committee stage of all Bills relating exclusively to Scotland is taken in Standing Committees made up of thirty

MPs for Scottish seats and twenty others chosen for their interest in the particular Bill, or in order to achieve on the committee a reflection of the party balance of power in the House.[1] Also for Scottish affairs there is the Scottish Grand Committee, made up of all seventy-one MPs for Scottish constituencies, plus an additional ten to fifteen other MPs to maintain the balance of the parties. The Scottish Grand Committee deals with the Second Reading of Scottish Bills (unless the House votes to keep them on the floor of the House), and it spends six days per session considering the Scottish Estimates, and two days on general Scottish debates. A similar Grand Committee exists for Welsh affairs, made up of all MPs for Welsh constituencies, plus five others. Also for legislation may be noted the Opposed and Unopposed Private Bill Committees, which deal with the committee stage of private legislation, and the joint committees of Lords and Commons for the committee stage of some non-contentious legislation. Joint committees may also be used as committees of enquiry.

As well as the Standing Committees for legislation, there are a number of Select Committees appointed to enquire into some aspect of executive activity. These may be *ad hoc* Select Committees, set up from time to time for some enquiry that is specific and limited in its extent, or they may be sessional Select Committees, like the Public Accounts Committee or the Statutory Instruments Committee, which are set up at the beginning of each session, and which are in effect permanent features of the House of Commons' committee system. *Ad hoc* Select Committees, which are limited in their membership to fifteen MPs, are used less today than in the nineteenth century, when much legislation resulted from their enquiries. Between 1867 and 1900 there were, on average, thirty-three Select Committees appointed each year, but between 1945 and 1961 the average was only fifteen a year.[2] They have been replaced in the main by Royal Commissions, departmental

[1] See P. Myers, 'The Select Committee on Scottish Affairs', *Parl. Aff.* 1973–4, pp. 359–70; G. E. Edwards, 'The Scottish Grand Committee 1958–70', *Parl. Aff.* 1971–2, pp. 303–25.

[2] Crick, *The Reform of Parliament*, p. 94.

committees of enquiry, and judicial enquiries. Where they are appointed, Select Committees are most useful for enquiries into subjects where there are no clear party alignments.

The sessional Select Committees, however, are of growing significance in the work of the House. The PAC, the Statutory Instruments Committee, and the Select Committees on European Legislation, Members' Interests and the Parliamentary Commissioner are committees of enquiry which supplement the Commons' general examination of some aspect of executive activity. There are other sessional Select Committees which contribute to the administration of business in the House. The Procedure Committee examines proposals for the reform of Parliamentary procedure,[1] the Selection Committee arranges the composition of the various committees, and the Committee of Privileges, made up of seventeen of the most experienced members of the house, examines cases of alleged breach of Parliamentary privilege. In the day-to-day running of the House, the Speaker is assisted by the Services Committee and its five sub-committees.

In addition to these various official committees of the House, there are a number of committees within each party in the House. Chief of these are the 1922 Committee of backbench Conservative MPs and the PLP, although each of the two main parties has a range of backbench subject committees.[2] Also in this context may be noted the vast range of informal groups, from the Temperance Group and Sports Committee to the Anti-Pollution Group and the Coordinating Committee on Factory Farming.[3]

* * *

In the post-war period considerable criticism has been levelled at the House of Commons Select Committee system.[4]

[1] See H. V. Wiseman, 'Procedure: the House of Commons and the Select Committee', *Parl. Aff.* 1959–60, pp. 236–47; C. J. Boulton, 'Recent Developments in House of Commons Procedure', *Parl. Aff.* 1969–70, pp. 61–71.

[2] See P. Norton, 'Party Committees in the House of Commons', *Parl. Aff.* 1983, pp. 7–27. See also R. Body, 'Unofficial Committees in the House of Commons', *Parl. Aff.* 1957–8, pp. 295–302.

[3] See J. J. Richardson and R. Kimber, 'The Role of All-Party Committees in the House of Commons', *Parl. Aff.* 1971–2, pp. 339–49.

[4] See B. Crick, *The Reform of Parliament*.

While the long-established Public Accounts Committee and Estimates Committee, together with the Statutory Instruments Committee and the Nationalised Industries Committee (formed in 1944 and 1956 respectively), were widely regarded as reasonably effective bodies, it was argued that there were too few such committees and that as a consequence the House had inadequate means of scrutinising the departments of state. The Commons was compared unfavourably with the United States Congress and its extensive specialised Committee system. It was proposed that the Commons committee system be overhauled, either by giving the existing Standing Committees the power to debate general policy as well as examine legislation, or by leaving the Standing Committees as they were and creating new Select Committees.

In 1964 Labour came to power with a commitment to Parliamentary reform and in the 1964–70 period new Select Committees were established for Science and Technology, Race Relations, Agriculture, Education, the Parliamentary Commissioner for Administration, Overseas Development and Scottish Affairs. The reform process was taken a stage further by the Heath Conservative Government in 1971 when, following a recommendation of the Procedure Committee, a new Expenditure Committee was created together with one general sub-committee and five specialist sub-committees (for Defence and External Affairs; Environment; Trade and Industry; Social Services and Employment; Education, Arts and Home Affairs). The Education and Scottish Affairs Committees that had been created by the Labour Government were abolished, but the other committees created in the 1964–70 period operated alongside the special sub-committees of the Expenditure Committee. A Select Committee on European Legislation was also created following Britain's entry to the European Community.

Thus by the mid-1970s the House of Commons Select Committee system had been considerably expanded. The changes, however, did not satisfy the more radical reformers. The range of committees was not yet comprehensive, falling short of the demand for one committee for each department of state. The committees had limited resources and, unlike the Public Accounts Committee, were able to appoint only part-time specialist advisers. The Select-Committees' reports attracted only limited Parliamentary and public attention, and had little impact on Government policy. Demands for further reforms were made, and in 1976 the House of Commons' Committee on Procedure advocated the creation of a Select Committee for each department of state 'to provide the House with the means of scrutinising the activities of the public service on a continuing and systematic basis'.[1] It proposed that there should be twelve committees with the power to command Ministers to attend and provide such information as the committees required, and that committee functions should extend to the examination of departmental policy, administration and finance. The Procedure Committee also proposed that the committees be given more staff and research facilities, and that an additional salary be paid to committee chairmen.

The Labour Government prevaricated over the implementation of these proposals, but the new Conservative Government implemented them soon after taking office in 1979. It abolished the Expenditure Committee and its sub-committees, and the committees created by the Labour Government in the 1964–70 period. In their place it created the twelve committees advocated by the Procedure Committee, together with two further committees on Scottish Affairs and Welsh Affairs.[2] Each committee has about a dozen members, chosen by the Committee of Selection. They are essentially backbench committees and contain few ex-Ministers and no Opposition front-bench spokesmen. The Committees are appointed for a full Parliament. Those that operated in the 1979–83 Parliament were reappointed after the 1983 election with only slight changes of structure and organisation. Each Select Committee is free to choose its own topics of enquiry. While a committee can send for 'persons, papers and records', it does not have the power (recommended by the Procedure Committee) to compel Ministers to attend. Nevertheless, during enquiries into the leak of confidential documents to the press about the Westland affair in 1986, the Defence Commit-

[1] First Report of the Select Committee on Procedure 1977–8.

[2] See G. Drewry (ed.), *The New Select Committees*, London 1985; D. Englefield (ed.), *The Commons' Select Committees – Catalysts for Progress?*, London 1984; M. Rush, 'Parliamentary Committees and Parliamentary Government', *JCCP* 1982, pp. 138–54.

tee questioned the Cabinet Secretary, the Permanent Secretary and other senior civil servants at the Department of Trade and Industry, and the former Minister (Leon Brittan). The Home Affairs Committee and Treasury and Civil Service Committee appoint sub-committees (as did the Foreign Affairs Committee in the 1979–83 Parliament). The chairmen of the committees constitute a Liaison Committee whose function it is to oversee and coordinate the committees' activities.

The expansion of the Select Committee system since the 1960s has been criticised from three principal standpoints. In the first place, civil servants and Ministers (of both parties) have been reluctant to subject their departments to scrutiny by House of Commons committees. MPs who were advocates of a strong Select Committee system when they were on the backbenches, often became less enthusiastic when they achieved office. Thus despite Labour's enthusiasm for Parliamentary reform before coming to office in 1964, the Select Committee on Agriculture was wound-up within two years of being formed after producing reports that were particularly critical of the Foreign Office and Ministry of Agriculture. Second, an influential attitude within Parliament is that it is the chamber of the House of Commons that is the most appropriate and effective arena in which to scrutinise the Government. The House of Commons' function of concentrating the nation's attention on major issues (it is argued) is undermined by the Select Committees, which divert attention and energy away from the Chamber. Third, it is claimed that the effectiveness of Select Committees is undermined by the essentially partisan nature of the House of Commons. Select Committees are most convincing when they achieve an all-party consensus in their reports. When, however, a Committee tackles a controversial issue that is potentially embarrassing for the Government, the adversarial confrontation of the House as a whole is likely to be reproduced on the Committee. Only on relatively non-controversial issues will a bi-partisan approach be possible, and such issues are likely to arouse only limited interest outside Parliament.[1]

[1]See S. Himmelfarb, 'Consensus in Committee', *Parl. Aff.* 1980, pp. 54–66.

TABLE XXXI

Departmental Select Committees 1986–7

Committee	Members	Chairman
Agriculture	11	Con.
Defence	11	Con.
Education, Science and Arts	11	Con.
Employment	11	Lab.
Energy	11	Con.
Environment	11	Con.
Foreign Affairs	11	Con.
Home Affairs*	11	Con.
Trade and Industry	11	Con.
Scottish Affairs	13	Lab.
Social Services	11	Lab.
Transport	11	Lab.
Treasury and Civil Service*	11	Con.
Welsh Affairs	11	Lab.

* Each of these committees has a sub-committee of five members.

These three points of view, in combination, helped to delay the emergence of a comprehensive Select Committee system. Since 1979, however, the departmental Select Committees have established themselves as a key feature of the Commons. While their role remains purely advisory, and only a small proportion of their reports are debated on the floor of the House, the Commons is much better equipped now than in the 1970s and earlier to examine and publicise the activities of Ministers and civil servants. Compared with their predecessors the existing Select Committees are more active (as measured by the number of their meetings and reports), are better served by specialist advisers, attract greater media attention and almost certainly have a greater impact on Government policies. Expert views can be developed through continued service on a committee dealing with one subject. As well as developing the knowledge and critical abilities of MPs, the departmental Select Committees can be a training ground for Ministers and can strengthen the executive by helping to keep the civil service alert.

The Individual Roles of MPs

In addition to the functions of the House of Commons as a collective body, individual MPs perform different roles within the House.[1] Some MPs are Ministers, and others are official front-bench Opposition spokesmen, while among Government and Opposition MPs alike, some are regarded (or regard themselves) as potential Ministers, and their activities and attitudes in the House are likely to be vastly different from those MPs who accept a role as permanent backbenchers. Among backbenchers there are those who are loyal supporters of the party leadership, while others are regularly in rebellion against their leaders. Rebellion by a normally loyal party man is likely to be much more telling than a rebellion by a number of permanent rebels. Also, on both sides of the House it is possible to note various House of Commons 'types'. Some MPs, for example, specialise in a knowledge of Parliamentary procedure, and some devote the bulk of their time to the service of the House by joining the Speaker's Panel, the Services Committee and its sub-committees (which supervise the House of Commons Library, accommodation and catering), or other similar bodies. Other MPs concentrate their activities on furthering unlikely and obscure causes, while others fill the role of Parliamentary characters. Some use the House of Commons to further their own business interests, or to pursue a knighthood or similar honour, while yet others act conspicuously as spokesmen for some pressure group or ideological cause.

One function that is common to all MPs, however, is their responsibility to their constituents.[2] In this capacity the MP deals with problems and grievances raised by individual

[1] See D. Judge, *Backbench Specialisation in the House of Commons*, London 1981; D. Judge, 'British Representative Theory and Backbench Specialisation', *Parl. Aff.* 1980, pp. 40–53.

[2] B. E. Cain (*et al.*), 'The Constituency Component', *CPS* 1983–4, pp. 67–91; D. D. Searing, 'The Role of the Good Constituency Member and the Practice of Representation in Great Britain', *J of P* 1985, pp. 348–81. See also J. E. Schwartz, 'The Impact of Constituency on the Behaviour of British Conservative MPs', *CPS* 1975–6, pp. 75–89; D. G. Crocket, 'The MP and His Constituents', *Parl. Aff.* 1966–7, pp. 281–4; R. Munroe, 'The MP as Representative', *PS* 1977, pp. 577–87.

constituents, and here the MP's role is rather like that of a general welfare officer. The MP may pursue a constituent's cause publicly through questions or debates in the House, or the matter may be dealt with informally and inconspicuously behind the scenes. For some MPs this form of activity occupies the bulk of their time, and a number of backbenchers spend practically the whole of their Parliamentary careers doing conscientious and efficient work on behalf of their constituents, without ever hitting the Parliamentary headlines. This is one aspect of an MP's activity that is often overlooked, and yet it is an aspect that is of increasing importance in face of the extension of state activity into more and more fields.

In the relationship between MPs and their constituents the question arises of whether MPs are representatives, free to speak and act according to their own conscience, subject only to the need to behave in such a way as to secure re-election to office, or whether they are delegates who act according to the instructions of their constituents. It is widely accepted that MPs are indeed representatives who decide issues according to their own judgement, who speak and vote in Parliament as they wish, who cannot be forced to resign, and who are protected by the doctrine that it is a breach of Parliamentary privilege for a group of constituents, or any other body, to seek to limit an MP's freedom of speech. MPs are, of course, limited in their freedom by their ties with their Parliamentary party, and have to bear the consequences of any actions that offend this body. These, however, are ties that exist within Parliament and within the principle that MPs, individually or as members of a Parliamentary party or group, are representatives who are free to make such rules as they think fit to govern their Parliamentary activities.

Nevertheless, assuming that an MP wishes to be returned to office at the next election, the MP has to bear in mind the consequences of any actions that may offend constituents, and this is the essential basis of the democratic principle of representation. In addition to this general electoral control, however, the MP's constituency party association, and the executive committee and officers in particular, have the power to influence the conduct of MPs to an extent that often leads MPs to complain of dictation from the constituency. A local party association sometimes censures an MP for an action that has been taken, or remarks that an MP has made, and MPs are sometimes called upon to attend an association meeting to explain their conduct. Most important of all, however, the constituency party can refuse to readopt the sitting member as the official party candidate for the next election. Since 1979 Labour MPs have had to submit themselves for reselection once in each Parliament, and this has increased the opportunities for constituency activists to exert pressure upon them (although the constituency can produce a 'short-list of one' if it is satisfied with the MP's performance).

Tensions between the MP and his constituency are not new.[1] In the seventeenth and eighteenth centuries in some constituencies a number of Political Associations were formed that sought to impose instructions on MPs, and in their turn many MPs freely pledged themselves to pursue particular policies in Parliament on behalf of their constituents. There was a reaction against this, however, epitomised by Edmund Burke's declaration to the voters of Bristol in 1774 that he represented the whole nation as well as his own constituents. Burke argued that '. . . You choose a member, indeed; but when you have chosen him, he is not a member of Bristol, but he is a member of Parliament.'[2] Burke's theme has often been echoed in more recent conflicts between MPs and their constituents. Nigel Nicolson, elected Conservative member for Bournemouth East and Christchurch in 1955, offended his constituency party by voting in favour of the abolition of capital punishment in February 1956, and by abstaining in a vote of confidence on the Conservative Government's Suez policy in November 1956.[3] A meeting of the local Conservative Association criticised these actions and demanded his

[1] C. Leys, 'Petitioning in the Nineteenth and Twentieth Centuries', *PS* 1955, pp. 45–64.

[2] Speech to the electors of Bristol, 3.11.1774.

[3] See Nigel Nicolson, *People and Parliament*, London 1958; L. W. Martin, 'The Bournemouth Affair: Britain's First Primary Election', *J of P* 1960, pp. 654–81; L. Epstein, 'British MPs and their Local Parties: the Suez Cases', *APSR* 1960, pp. 374–91; A. D. R. Dickson, 'MPs Readoption Conflicts', *PS* 1975, pp. 62–70; R. C. Frasure, 'Constituency Racial Composition and Attitudes of British MPs', *Comp. Pol.* 1970–1, pp. 201–10.

resignation, but Nicolson refused to resign, arguing that he was a *representative* who was free to decide on issues as he thought fit. The Association chose a new prospective candidate, but he resigned after a year, and the Conservative Central Office intervened and arranged a ballot of the Association to choose between Nicolson and some unnamed alternative. Nicolson was narrowly beaten in the ballot and he agreed not to stand at the next election.

S. O. Davies was more successful in his struggles with his local party. He had represented Merthyr Tydfil since 1934, and in 1970 at the age of eighty-three he resisted pressure from the constituency association to give up the seat. Although the association selected another official candidate, Davies opposed him in the 1970 general election and triumphed with a majority of almost 25%. Similarly, in February 1974 Eddie Milne won Blyth as an Independent Labour candidate after Blyth Labour Party had refused to readopt him because of his criticism of the conduct of party affairs in the area. Subsequently, he was defeated by the official Labour candidate at the October 1974 election, although only by seventy-eight votes.

Even more remarkable, perhaps, was the case of Dick Taverne. He quarrelled with the Lincoln Labour Party in 1972 over his pro-Common Market views, and gave up his seat in mid-Parliament. He contested the consequent by-election in 1973 as a Democratic Labour candidate, and easily defeated the Labour nominee. In 1974 Taverne held the seat at the February election, but was narrowly defeated by the Labour candidate in October.

As a general rule it is MPs of 'moderate' opinions in both the main parties who seem most likely to antagonise their local party, perhaps because the local party activists may tend to be more extreme in their views than their MPs, or perhaps because moderate opinions held by an MP can be taken as indicating sympathy with the opposing party. In recent years there have been a number of examples of 'moderate' Labour MPs coming into conflict with 'militant' constituency parties. The most remarkable example was provided by Reginald Prentice, who began the 1974–9 Parliament as a Labour Cabinet Minister. In 1975, however, his Newham North-East constituency association demanded that he submit himself for reselection as Labour candidate for the constituency and after a long struggle with the association (during which time he resigned from the Government), Prentice failed to have this decision reversed. He subsequently joined the Conservative Party, and was adopted as Conservative candidate for Daventry. He won the seat at the 1979 election and became a junior Minister in Mrs Thatcher's Government.[1]

An MP may win his fight with his constituency party if the national party supports him. On occasions, however, the MP comes into conflict with the local party precisely because he has rebelled against the Parliamentary Party Whip, and at times the national party uses the local party to censure a rebel MP. On these occasions there is a clear overlap between pressure on MPs by the party Whips, and pressure on MPs at a constituency level, although on many other occasions the national party often declines to interfere at all in a local dispute, thereby acknowledging local party autonomy.

[1] See P. McCormick, 'Prentice and Newham North-East Constituency', *PS* 1981, pp. 79–90.

9

Parliament: II. The Monarchy and the House of Lords

THE MONARCHY

IN BRITAIN the Monarch personifies the state. Government is carried on in the name of the Monarch, and Ministers, civil servants, members of the judiciary and the armed forces are servants of the Crown. The origins of the Monarchy in Britain can be traced back to the ninth century, with the unification of England under one King. The authority of the Crown was extended to Wales and Ireland by conquest, and in 1603 the thrones of England and Scotland were united in the one person of James I of England and VI of Scotland. The royal succession goes back to the Saxon King Egbert, and its continuity has been broken only once, by the republican period in the mid-seventeenth century. Today the Monarch is also Head of the Commonwealth, though the title and status of the Monarch varies in different parts of the Commonwealth.

Value of the Monarchy

The essential feature of the development of the Monarchy over the centuries has been its adaptability to changing patterns of political power, and in particular in the last three hundred years, its evolution into a Constitutional Monarchy.[1] While Britain is not unique as a Constitutional state with a Monarch as head of state, a number of alternatives exist regarding the nature of the head of state within a Constitutional system of government. In the first place, a clear choice presents itself between a largely ceremonial figurehead, and a head of state who is also the political head of government. The United States, and France under the Fifth Republic, dispense with a purely ceremonial figurehead, and combine the ceremonial role with that of political head of the government, whereas Britain has the Monarch as a non-political figurehead and 'steering-wheel' within the Constitution. Even with a non-political head of state, however, there is a republican alternative, in that in the Fourth French Republic, Presidents Auriol and Coty played a largely ceremonial role, while the Premier was the political head of the government. Similarly, in the West German Federal Republic today the President is head of state while the Chancellor is the political head of the government.

There was a republican movement in Britain in the middle of the last century, when the cost and practical value of the Monarchy were questioned, but the movement failed, and Queen Victoria's reign ended in a blaze of Monarchical fervour. In a 1969 survey of public attitudes to the Monarchy, 13% felt that it should be ended, 30% felt that it should continue as it is, and 55% felt it should continue 'but change with the times'. In a 1973 survey, 80% indicated a preference for a Monarch over a President while in 1983 93% said that the Queen 'did a good job'.[2] Britain remains as one of the few surviving Monarchies in Europe. It is possible to make a distinction, however, between the Monarchies of Scandinavia, and the distinctly more aloof and 'splendid' Monarchy in Britain (with the 1953 Coronation epitomising the British

[1] For general works on the Monarchy today see Kingsley Martin, *The Crown and the Establishment*, London 1963; Sir C. Petrie, *The Modern British Monarchy*, London 1961. See also Sir H. Nicolson, *George V*, London 1952; Sir J. Wheeler-Bennett, *George VI*, London 1958; F. Hardie, *The Political Influence of the British Monarchy 1868–1952*, London 1970; J. Murray-Brown (ed.), *The Monarchy and Its Future*, London 1969.

[2] *Sunday Times*, March 23rd 1969; *The Sun*, April 24th 1983.

Monarchy as the 'Rolls Royce' of Monarchies). Had Edward VIII not abdicated in 1936, there might have been an evolution of the Monarchy into a form more akin to the Scandinavian model, but George VI and Elizabeth II have sought to preserve much of the Monarchy's remoteness and mystique.[1]

Thus as head of state Britain has a Monarch, fulfilling a largely ceremonial role as a constitutional figurehead, but distinctly more aloof and 'royal' than the other surviving Monarchies of Europe. There are undoubtedly a number of merits in this arrangement. In numerous ways it is desirable to separate the political and ceremonial aspects of public life. With a separate ceremonial head of state the political leader is freed from the need to perform formal roles, and thus has more time to devote to political responsibilities. In this respect the British Prime Minister has an advantage over the United States' President. Also, without a separate figurehead, the political President, despite the fact that he is a party political figure, inevitably appears as the centre of national loyalty and acquires a certain aura as a result. This gives him an electoral advantage over his opponents, which can perhaps be seen as undesirable in a democratic system. In Britain on the other hand, although the Prime Minister appears to a certain extent as a national figure as well as a party figure, the Crown remains as the centre of national loyalty. Thus it is possible to 'damn the Government but cheer the Queen', perhaps with greater national cohesion as a result, and certainly with less electoral advantage for the Prime Minister.

The Monarch is a more personalised and attractive symbol of national unity than the vague concept of the State, the flag, or even a President, and the hereditary system at least solves the problem of succession. The selection of a truly independent national figure as a republican figurehead can be difficult. In Britain there can even be disputes over the choice of a Speaker of the House of Commons – perhaps the closest we get to an independent, non-Monarchical figure within the Constitutional machinery. Once chosen, a republican head of

[1] F. I. Greenstein (*et al.*), 'The Child's Conception of the Queen and Prime Minister', *BJPS* 1974, pp. 257–87; J. G. Blumler (*et al.*), 'Attitudes to the Monarchy', *PS* 1971, pp. 149–71; R. Rose and D. Kavanagh, 'The Monarchy in Contemporary Culture', *CP* 1976–7, pp. 548–73.

state is always more open than a Monarch to accusations of party political bias, as was revealed with Presidents Auriol and Coty in the French Fourth Republic. Also, given average ability, the continuity in office that comes from the hereditary system can produce experience, and Prime Ministers have spoken of the value of the political advice given by some Monarchs. The ceremonial that surrounds the Monarchy is largely harmless, and at best has the positive merit of emphasising national traditions and historical values, while the glitter of the Monarchy is a feature of British national life that is often envied abroad.

These various arguments can also be used to defend the Monarchy in its present form, with the emphasis on mystique and ceremonial, which makes it different from the other European Monarchies. The Monarchy is also one of the factors that helps to strengthen Commonwealth ties, and in so far as it is desirable to preserve the Commonwealth, it is necessary to emphasise the role of the Monarchy as a symbol of unity. In a sense, this is an echo of Disraeli's successful attempt to promote British nationalism and Imperial unity through Queen Victoria's role as Empress of India, and the evolution of the British Monarchy from being Head of the Empire to being Head of the Commonwealth has been achieved remarkably smoothly, and with considerable ingenuity.

The Monarchy has many critics, however, who argue that it is a definite liability within the political system. They criticise the hereditary system from the practical point of view of being no real guarantee of merit, while from a general standpoint they condemn the hereditary principle as being undesirable in a democratic system. Critics also see the Monarchy as the centre of the class system in Britain, and claim (with some justification) that the continued existence of the Monarchy helps to promote deference, snobbery, and an acceptance of outdated traditions and values. The cost of the Monarchy is often criticised, though it is extremely difficult to arrive at a clear conclusion as to the actual cost to the state. In 1761 George III surrendered the Crown Lands to the nation in return for an annual income from Parliament, and this arrangement has been renewed at the beginning of each reign.

Today the Crown Lands of some 292,000 acres are administered by the Crown Commissioners, and the annual profit goes to the state. The Queen's annual Civil List amounts to about £5,000,000, but there are a number of additional items of royal expenditure, the precise cost of which is not clear. Allowances are paid to the Queen Mother, the Duke of Edinburgh, and other members of the Royal Family. Revenue from the Duchy of Cornwall goes to Prince Charles, but he surrenders half of this to the Exchequer. Departments of state cover many aspects of royal expenditure, the Department of the Environment being responsible for the maintenance of the royal castles, and the Defence Department for the Queen's Flight and the royal yacht.

The royal family has a large personal fortune which is not diminished by death duties. Queen Victoria handed down more than £2,000,000, and in addition there are valuable royal collections of jewellery, stamps, and pictures. Estimates as to the total value of the royal family's personal wealth vary from £10,000,000 to £60,000,000. One informed estimate[1] is that the total cost of the Monarchy is about £20,000,000 per year, so that on this estimate the Monarchy is a costly institution, and critics argue that a republic would be much cheaper. On the other hand, this is in many ways an artificial estimation, in that the Monarchy has a value, even as a tourist attraction, that offsets much of its cost, so that in some respects the Monarchy is a good national investment.

Constitutional Role of the Monarch

The Crown is the personification of the state, and is the supreme legal authority in Britain. The doctrine of Ministerial Responsibility means that the Monarch acts on the advice of Ministers, but the precise extent of the independent powers of the Monarch is one of the aspects of the unwritten British Constitution that still provides scope for argument among Constitutional lawyers. In external affairs the Royal Prerogative includes the power to declare war, make treaties, and cede

[1] Anthony Sampson, *The Changing Anatomy of Britain*, London 1982, p. 10. See also Martin, *The Crown and the Establishment*, p. 134.

territory, these powers being exercised by the Prime Minister and the Defence and Foreign Ministers. As the head of the judiciary and the source of judicial authority, the Monarch appoints judges and dispenses mercy, but only on the recommendation of the Prime Minister, the Home Secretary, or the Scottish Secretary. As 'the fountain of honour' the Monarch appoints diplomats and senior ranks in the forces, and confers titles, again on the advice of the Prime Minister. In the past, the Monarch's power to create Peerages was the ultimate means of securing a majority in the House of Lords for the Monarch's Ministers, but such action has not been threatened since 1911 and seems inconceivable today. As an integral part of Parliament, the Assent of the Monarch is required as the final stage of the legislative process, but not since Queen Anne refused to accept the Scotch Militia Bill in 1703 has the Royal Assent been denied. In 1913 it was argued in some quarters that the Monarch could and should refuse to accept the highly controversial Irish Home Rule Bill, and theoretically the Monarch could still refuse to grant the Royal Assent, but this would hardly seem to be practical politics today.[1]

In two spheres, the granting of a dissolution and the appointment of a Prime Minister, there have been this century a number of Constitutional controversies involving the role of the Monarch. Parliament is dissolved by the Monarch on the request of the Prime Minister, but it has been argued that in practical as well as theoretical terms the Monarch retains the right to refuse the Prime Minister's request, and also that the Monarch has the right to dissolve Parliament without receiving a request from the Prime Minister.[2] George V was involved in a major controversy over the power of dissolution in 1913, at the height of the controversy over Irish home rule. The Liberal Government's Bill to grant home rule to Ireland had been twice rejected in the Lords, but was presented to

[1]See G. C. Moodie, 'The Crown and Parliament', *Parl. Aff.* 1956–7, pp. 256–64.

[2]See D. E. Butler, *Governing Without a Majority*, London 1983, pp. 122–34; D. J. Heasman, 'The Monarch, the Prime Minister and the Dissolution of Parliament', *Parl. Aff.* 1960–1, pp. 94–107; K. Sainsbury, 'The Constitution – Some Disputed Points', *Parl. Aff.* 1961–2, pp. 213–43; G. C. Moodie, 'The Monarch and the Selection of the Prime Minister', *PS* 1957, pp. 1–20.

Parliament for the third time (under the terms of the Parliament Act 1911) in 1913. The Unionist Opposition, supported by Sir William Anson, A. V. Dicey and other prominent Constitutional lawyers, argued that the Monarch should dissolve Parliament in order that the electorate might 'pronounce' on this controversial Bill, even though the Prime Minister (Asquith) did not want a dissolution.[1] They claimed that a dissolution was politically desirable and constitutionally justified, in that the Monarch retained the right to dissolve Parliament at his discretion, especially at a time when civil rebellion was threatened as a result of Government actions. Other Constitutional experts, however, denied the Monarch's right to dissolve Parliament in these circumstances, against the wishes of the Prime Minister. They argued that the right of dissolution on the Monarch's own initiative had been killed by non-use, and that practical politics made it impossible. Parliament was not dissolved in 1913, and the home rule issue was swamped by the outbreak of war in 1914, but the episode illustrates the problems that can be raised for the Monarch in cases of Constitutional interpretation.

George V was also involved in difficult decisions over the dissolution in 1918 and 1924. With the end of the war in November 1918, Lloyd George requested a dissolution in order that his Coalition Government could be extended into peacetime, with electoral approval for the making of the peace. George V was opposed to a dissolution at the end of 1918 because he felt it to be inopportune. He claimed that the Government was pledged to make the peace treaty before holding an election, and that problems would be involved with soldiers serving abroad, and with the service voters and newly enfranchised women voters making the election result unpredictable. Lloyd George's view prevailed, however, and the election was held in December 1918, producing a big win for the Government.

In 1924 Ramsay MacDonald sought a dissolution after the defeat of his minority Labour Government in the Commons on an issue of confidence. The Parliament was less than a year

[1] For the detailed arguments used in this controversy see Jennings, *Cabinet Government*, Appendix III. See also Nicolson, *George V*, Chs 14 and 15.

old and although a minority Conservative Government had been defeated in the House at the beginning of the year, and could hardly be revived, there was still the theoretical possibility that Asquith might be able to form a minority Liberal Government with Conservative support. MacDonald, however, had earlier warned the King that he would seek a dissolution in the event of his Government's defeat in the House, and the King's Private Secretary had been able to discover that an agreement between the Liberals and the Conservatives would not in fact be attainable. Thus MacDonald was granted a dissolution at once, and a possible constitutional controversy was avoided.

George VI and Elizabeth II seem to have escaped involvement in controversial dissolutions – although the Queen might have been involved in party wrangling in March 1974 if, as seemed possible at the time, the new Labour Government had been defeated at the end of the Queen's Speech debate and had then sought a dissolution. Given the recent developments in the party system, and the increased possibility of hung Parliaments in the future, the question may re-emerge of whether the Monarch is obliged to agree to a request for a dissolution from a Prime Minister at the head of a minority government, even though the Opposition parties may be in a position to sustain an alternative minority government. Again, theoretically the position of the Monarch could still be important if a Government refused to resign after losing the confidence of the Commons on a major issue. There is no precedent as a guide as to what would happen in these circumstances, although it is venturing into the realms of Constitutional fiction to see the Monarch achieving today what could not otherwise be achieved by the pressure of public opinion or the threat of civil revolt.

* * *

The Constitutional principle with regard to the appointment of the Prime Minister is that the choice is made by the Monarch, but again acting on the advice of the retiring Prime Minister or other authoritative figures. The last occasion when the Prime Minister was appointed on the Monarch's own initiative was in 1894, when Queen Victoria chose Lord

Rosebery rather than Spencer or Harcourt. Today there is no difficulty in the selection of the Prime Minister if the reigning Government is successful at a general election, as the Prime Minister then remains in office, as happened in October 1974 and 1983. Similarly, no problem arises if the Government is beaten at a general election and the main Opposition party emerges with a clear majority, as happened in 1964, 1970 and 1979. When a Prime Minister dies or retires between general elections both the Labour and Conservative Parties now have machinery for electing a new party leader who then becomes the Monarch's choice as the new Prime Minister. Labour's machinery operated for the first time in office in 1976, but the Conservative machinery, adopted only in 1965, has not yet been used in office. In the past the retirement of a Conservative Prime Minister between elections meant that the Monarch was sometimes associated with controversies over the choice of Conservative Prime Ministers, and this was particularly the case in 1923, 1957, and 1963.

In the spring of 1923 Bonar Law was forced by ill-health to retire as Prime Minister, and Baldwin and Lord Curzon emerged as rivals to succeed him.[1] Lord Curzon appeared to have a better claim than Baldwin, but in the event the King sent for Baldwin. It is not clear why Curzon was overlooked. One factor that complicated the issue was that Bonar Law declined to advise the King as to his successor. It seems that he expected Curzon to be chosen, but he would not speak in his favour and advised the King to consult Lord Salisbury. The Monarch did seek the advice of Lord Salisbury and Lord Balfour, while L. S. Amery and W. C. Bridgeman, two prominent members of the Government, gave their advice to Lord Stamfordham, the King's Private Secretary. There were suggestions that the Monarch was misled into believing that Bonar Law favoured Baldwin. Lord Stamfordham informed Curzon that the reason for his exclusion was the fact that he was a Peer, but it is possible that the Peerage issue was used merely as an excuse, and that Curzon was passed over because

[1]For details see R. Blake, *The Unknown Prime Minister*, London 1955, pp. 513–34; Amery, *Thoughts on the Constitution*, pp. 21–2; Nicolson, *George V*, pp. 375–9.

of personal factors. Whatever the reason, however, the Monarch was caught up in unsavoury party machinations.

Again in 1957 the Monarch was involved in a certain amount of controversy over the succession to the Premiership. In January 1957 Eden resigned as Prime Minister on the grounds of ill-health. It was widely assumed that R. A. Butler would succeed him, as he had presided over Cabinet meetings in Eden's absence and was the most experienced member of Eden's Government, but Harold Macmillan was in fact appointed. It is not clear what advice, if any, was given to the Queen by Eden, but Churchill and Lord Salisbury were consulted and spoke for Macmillan. Cabinet Ministers were consulted individually by Lord Salisbury and Lord Kilmuir, while backbenchers were sounded by the Chief Whip (Edward Heath). Some backbenchers, however, have denied ever being consulted, and have claimed that Macmillan's selection was a conspiracy. It has also been suggested by Sir Ivor Jennings[1] that the party was prepared to follow either Macmillan or Butler, and that the Queen made a genuine personal choice between them. This seems difficult to support, however, and it appears clear that Churchill and Lord Salisbury stressed that Macmillan was to be preferred. As in 1923, the episode caused speculation over the role of the Monarch, and involved the Crown in what appeared to be doubtful proceedings.

In 1963 the selection of Home as Prime Minister proved to be even more controversial than that of Macmillan in 1957. On October 10th 1963 Macmillan unexpectedly announced that owing to ill-health he intended to resign. The contenders to succeed him were R. A. Butler, Lord Hailsham, Lord Home, Reginald Maudling, Edward Heath, and Iain Macleod, with Butler and Hailsham seeming to have the best chance. The emergence of Home thus came as a surprise to most observers, and again brought attention to bear on the whole process of selection, including the role of the Monarch. It has been claimed that after soundings had been taken among Ministers, backbenchers, Peers, and constituency workers, Home was selected, not necessarily because he was most people's first choice, but because he was overwhelmingly

[1]Jennings, *Cabinet Government*, p. 28.

the least objectionable.[1] Macmillan is said to have acted as a single funnel of opinion for the Queen, and to have recommended Home to her as the clear choice of the party. Critics have said, however, that the soundings conducted within the party were not fairly conducted, and were designed primarily to exclude Butler. It was even suggested in some quarters that the Queen and Macmillan 'conspired' to secure Home's selection against the wishes of the majority of the Cabinet and the party as a whole.[2]

No matter how ill-informed these accusations may have been, and however fair the process of consultation might have been in fact, the process *seemed* to be dubious in 1963, as it did in 1923 and 1957. This inevitably involved speculation as to the role and impartiality of the Monarch in the selection process, and helped to persuade the Conservative Party to change its method of choosing a leader.[3] The existence today of the Labour and Conservative Parties' procedures for electing their leaders does not in itself affect the Constitutional prerogative of the Monarch, in that the Monarch remains free to choose whoever may be regarded as suitable. Nevertheless, in practice it seems inconceivable that the Monarch would now choose as Prime Minister anyone who had not first been elected party leader, provided that in a crisis time was allowed for the election to take place.

It is possible, however, that the Monarch could still play more than a merely formal role in the selection of a Prime Minister in a Parliamentary situation where it was not clear which party could form a Government. In 1931 George V was drawn into the constitutional and political crisis involving the fall of the MacDonald Labour Government and the formation of the National Government.[4] In August 1931 the Labour Government could not agree over the measures to be taken to deal with the economic crisis, and MacDonald took the Government's resignation to the King. No party had an overall

[1] See R. Churchill, *The Fight for the Tory Leadership*, London 1964; Sampson, *Anatomy of Britain Today*, p. 34.

[2] See Paul Johnson, *New Statesman*, 24.1.64.

[3] See above, p. 87.

[4] R. Bassett, *1931 Political Crisis*, London 1958; S. Webb, 'What Happened in 1931', *PQ* 1932, pp. 1–17; H. Dalton, '1931', *PQ* 1958, pp. 356–65; Nicolson, *George V*, p. 465.

majority in the Commons, and there was no clear alternative Government. A dissolution seemed to be impossible because of the immediacy of the economic crisis. A meeting was held on August 24th between the King and the party leaders (MacDonald, Baldwin, and Lord Samuel), and from this meeting MacDonald emerged with the task of forming a National Government. The Conservatives and some Liberals supported MacDonald, but only three former Labour Ministers and a handful of Labour MPs followed him, and he was deprived of his leadership of the Labour Party. George V was criticised for his role in the formation of the National Government, and it was said that either the King realised that the Labour Party would not follow MacDonald, in which case he was wrong to accept him as Prime Minister, or alternatively, the King was used by Baldwin and Lord Samuel in order to escape from their responsibilities. Either way the Monarch does not emerge with credit, and the episode illustrates how the Monarch can be involved in bitter party conflict when the normal Parliamentary situation breaks down.

After the close result of the February 1974 election it seemed possible for a while that the Monarch would be drawn into the controversy over whether the Conservative Government should resign at once, or should attempt to retain office by making an agreement with the Liberals. In the event a crisis did not develop, but the episode served as a reminder that in such ambiguous Parliamentary situations the Monarch's role could still have political significance. The choice of Prime Minister could be far from obvious in a future House of Commons in which Labour, the Conservatives and the Alliance were fairly evenly represented, and it was not immediately clear whether any two parties could cooperate to sustain a minority Government or form a coalition. Certainly, in such a situation the Prime Minister does not necessarily have to come from the largest party in the Commons, still less from the party with the greatest number of votes. As there is in Britain no constitutional court, the choice of Prime Minister in such a situation would have to be determined by informal processes of consultation between the Monarch, her advisers, the party leaders and other prominent political figures. Having acknowledged this, however, it must be stressed that too great an emphasis on historical precedent and Constitutional theorising can produce an exaggerated picture of the Monarch's role. Today the real justification for the retention of the Monarchy has to be sought outside the field of the Monarch's theoretical function as a Constitutional steering-wheel.

THE HOUSE OF LORDS

As with the Monarchy, and as with so many aspects of the British Constitution, the problem with regard to the House of Lords is that of adapting it to a modern political system.[1] Its abolition has long been advocated, but this century Conservative, Liberal and Labour Governments have all preferred to reform its powers or composition. They have recognised that a second chamber can fulfil a number of roles within a modern Constitutional system of government. It can represent territorial interests within the community, as does the Senate in the United States federal system. In a situation where the lower house is largely controlled by the Government, a second chamber can act as a check on the power of the Government, operating either as a popular check, obstructing the Government's work when it feels that it is acting contrary to the wishes of public opinion, or alternatively as a conservative check, obstructing the Government if it is proposing ill-conceived and purely popularity-seeking measures. Yet again, the second chamber can be seen not as an obstructive force, but as a body designed merely to ease the legislative and deliberative burden of the lower house. The House of Lords has never filled the Senatorial role of representing territorial interests, but at different times in its history the Lords has been seen as performing these other functions.

Composition of the House of Lords

The two main aspects of the problem of the House of Lords have been its composition and its functions, the two aspects

[1] See P. Bromhead, *The House of Lords and Contemporary Politics*, London 1958; S. D. Bailey (ed.), *The Future of the House of Lords*, London 1954; Crick, *The Reform of Parliament*, pp. 100–46; J. P. Morgan, *The House of Lords and the Labour Government, 1964–70*, London 1975.

being inevitably closely bound together. Basically the problem has been that of composition, in that the House of Lords is a large and unwieldy body, based on the hereditary principle, with a preponderant number of Conservative Party supporters. Today, there are approximately 1,200 Peers eligible to sit in the Lords (though its quorum is just three members). Of these, about 800 are hereditary Peers, and some 350 are Life Peers created since the Life Peerages Act 1958. Until 1963 the Scottish Peers elected for each Parliament sixteen representative Peers to sit in the Lords, but the Peerage Act 1963 opened membership of the Lords to all Scottish Peers. In addition, there are twenty-one Law Lords and twenty-six Spiritual Peers of the Church of England – the archbishops of York and Canterbury, the Bishops of London, Durham, and Winchester, and the twenty-one senior Bishops in order of appointment to their Sees.[1] The number of hereditary Peers is declining, as under Wilson, Heath and Callaghan only Life Peerages were created. In 1983, however, Mrs Thatcher recommended hereditary Peerages for her deputy Prime Minister, William Whitelaw, and the former Speaker, George Thomas (though neither had a male heir).

Although the total membership makes the House of Lords second in size only to the Chinese People's Congress among the world's legislatures, actual attendance is relatively low. Almost a third of Peers never attend, and only about a quarter attend regularly (that is, attend a third or more sittings). At the beginning of each Parliament, Peers receive a Writ of Summons to attend the Lords, and those who do not reply are excluded from attending the House for the rest of the Parliament. Even among whose who do reply to the Writ of Summons, however, the majority attend only infrequently or not at all. The daily attendance on average is about 300, so that in practice the Lords is a small and intimate body. Attendance can be much greater, however, when controversial issues are being dealt with.

In the early years of the nineteenth century the numbers of Whigs and Tories were fairly evenly balanced in the Lords.

[1] See G. Drewry and J. Brock, 'Prelates in Parliament', *Parl. Aff.* 1970–1, pp. 222–50.

Tory strength declined after the divisions in the party in 1846, but with the split in the Liberal Party in the 1880s, the Conservatives secured a clear dominance in the Lords, and in this century neither the Liberal Party nor the Labour Party has been able to match Conservative numbers in the Lords. Currently about 45% of the 1,200 Peers support the Conservative Party, up to a third support Labour or the Alliance while about a quarter have no pronounced party ties.[1] Among those who attend regularly, the Conservative proportion is not so great. The vast number of infrequent attenders ('the backwoodsmen') remain, however, as a reservoir of potential support for the Conservatives. The House of Lords at present does contain one Communist Peer (Lord Milford) and there are more women active in the Commons than in the Lords.

Conservative dominance in the House of Lords created obvious difficulties in the past for Labour and Liberal Governments. Until 1911 the two Houses of Parliament had virtual legislative equality, except that the most important Bills tended to be introduced in the Commons, and the power of the Lords was limited with regard to financial legislation. It had been recognised as early as the seventeenth century that the Lords could not *initiate* or *amend* financial legislation, and it was claimed in House of Commons resolutions in 1860 that the Lords could not *reject* financial legislation, although the validity of this last claim was questioned. Non-financial legislation was not protected by privilege, however, and in the event of conflict between the Government and the Lords, the ultimate remedy lay in the creation by the Monarch of enough new Peers sympathetic to the Government to swamp the hostile majority in the Lords. This had been done in 1713 in order to secure approval in the Lords for the Treaty of Utrecht. It was threatened in 1832 in order to secure the passage of the Reform Bill through the Lords, and was threatened again in 1911 in order to secure acceptance for the Parliament Bill. This remedy, however, was a somewhat cumbersome means of dealing with obstruction in the Lords,

[1] For details of the composition of the House of Lords, and of the party political affiliations of Peers, see *Dod's Parliamentary Companion* (published annually). See also Vincent, *Parl. Aff.* 1965–6; A. Wedgwood Benn, *The Privy Council as a Second Chamber* (Fabian Tract 305), London 1957.

and in this century Liberal and then Labour Governments have been faced with the task of devising some more workable method of solving the problem presented by Conservative dominance in the Lords.

The most obvious way for Liberal or Labour Governments to deal with the problem would have been to reform the composition of the Lords so as to remove the permanent Conservative majority. A major reform of composition was not attempted, however, largely it would seem because of the fear that as long as the Lords retained the power to obstruct legislation, a reformed and thereby strengthened House of Lords would emerge as a serious rival to the House of Commons. Thus to date, the only changes in composition that have been made are the Life Peerages Act 1958 and the Peerage Act 1963 (both passed by a Conservative Government) which made only minor adjustments of composition. The main way in which the problem of the House of Lords has been tackled has been by the reduction of the obstructive powers of the Lords through the Parliament Acts 1911 and 1949, so as to make the anomalies of composition of less consequence. Even in 1967, when the Labour Government did produce proposals for a major reform of composition, these were accompanied by proposals for a further reduction in the powers of the second chamber.

Over the years there have been numerous proposals for a full-scale reform of composition. The Preamble to the Parliament Act 1911 declared that it was merely a temporary measure until a full-scale reform of composition could be undertaken, and in 1917 a Conference was held under the chairmanship of Lord Bryce to examine the possibilities of a full-scale reform of the Lords. The Conference produced a detailed report in which it was advocated that the second chamber be completely reconstructed, with the new membership based primarily on election by the House of Commons of prominent members of the community, whether they were Peers or not.[1] The Bryce Conference also advocated the creation of a permanent Conference Committee, drawn from both Houses, to settle disputes between the Commons and the

[1]Report from the Second Chamber Conference, Cd. 9038 (1918).

second chamber, but nothing was done to implement these proposals. Similarly in 1948, during the controversy over the second Parliament Bill, another all-party Conference examined the role of the second chamber and reached agreement on certain principles for a reform of composition.[1] The Conference Statement declared that no party should have a permanent majority in the Lords, and that heredity should in itself be no qualification for membership. It was proposed that Lords of Parliament be appointed to serve in a newly constituted second chamber, and that Peers who were not Lords of Parliament should be eligible for the Commons. It was proposed also that women be eligible for membership of the second chamber, and that there should be payment for attendance and disqualification for non-attendance.

Action on these proposals did not result, however, as the Conference could not agree on the precise powers that the second chamber should possess. Nevertheless, some of these proposals were incorporated in the Life Peerages Act 1958, which created a new category of Life Peers and Life Peeresses, whose titles were not hereditary.[2] The 1958 Act also established the payment of an attendance allowance (now £16.50 plus certain expenses). The Act was designed as a means of infusing new life into the House of Lords, though the Labour Opposition criticised the measure as an attempt by the Conservative Government to give new authority to the Lords, while avoiding the basic problem of the hereditary element. Currently the 350 Life Peers and Peeresses are disproportionately prominent among the active members of the Lords.

While the 1958 Act introduced a new element into the Lords, the Peerage Act 1963 allowed hereditary Peers to disclaim their titles (and thus become eligible for membership of the House of Commons).[3] The Act was largely the result of the publicity given to the plight of unwilling heirs to titles by the activities of Anthony Wedgwood Benn, who in 1960 inherited the title of Lord Stansgate and consequently was

[1] Agreed Statement of the Conference of Party Leaders on the Parliament Bill, Cmd. 7380 (1948).

[2] See B. Crick, 'The Life Peerages Act', *Parl. Aff.* 1957–8, pp. 455–65.

[3] See P. Bromhead, 'The Peerage Act and the New Prime Minister', *Parl. Aff.* 1963–4, pp. 57–64.

forced to give up his seat in the Commons. The Peerage Act 1963 allowed existing hereditary Peers twelve months in which to disclaim their titles, and allowed future heirs to titles twelve months in which to disclaim (or one month if they were members of the Commons when they inherited their titles). The hereditary principle remained intact, however, as the Act specified that the title could pass, on the Peer's death, to his heir, unless he also chose to disclaim. In all about a dozen Peers have chosen to disclaim. Among these are Lord Home and Lord Hailsham who were able to disclaim at the time of the Conservative Party leadership contest in 1963, and Lord Stansgate. Lord Home and Lord Hailsham subsequently returned to the Lords as Life Peers. Thus the Act has not led to a great exodus from the Lords, and the general effect of the 1958 and 1963 Acts was to leave almost untouched the original basic problem of composition.

Power of the House of Lords

While the composition of the House of Lords has been changed only slightly, its power and functions have altered considerably this century. The Asquith Liberal Government in 1911 introduced the first legislation to limit the power of the Lords, against a background of great political and Constitutional controversy.[1] The House of Lords had rejected the 1909 Finance Bill, thereby raising the question of the Lords' power with regard to financial legislation. Asquith dissolved Parliament, and when the Liberals won the consequent election in January 1910 (though with a greatly reduced majority) the Lords accepted the Finance Bill. Nevertheless, the Government decided to proceed with a full-scale reform of the powers of the second chamber. A second election was held in December 1910, and again the Liberals retained office. The Government introduced the Parliament Bill and secured its passage through both Houses, though only as a result of the threat to create sufficient Peers to give the Government a majority in the Lords.

The Parliament Act 1911 contained three main provisions

[1]See R. Jenkins, *Mr Balfour's Poodle*, London 1954.

dealing with the maximum length of Parliaments, the power of the Lords with regard to financial legislation, and the power of the Lords with regard to ordinary legislation. The Septennial Act 1716 was amended to make five years rather than seven years the maximum length of a Parliament. A Money Bill (defined in the 1911 Act as a Bill certified by the Speaker as a Bill containing *only* financial clauses) was to become law, with or without the approval of the Lords, one month after being sent to the Lords. Any other Bill (except a Bill to extend the life of a Parliament) that passed the House of Commons in three successive sessions (whether in the same Parliament or not) was to become law without the assent of the Lords, provided a period of two years elapsed between the Second Reading of the Bill in the Commons in the first session, and the Second Reading in the Commons in the third session.

The reduction in the length of Parliaments to a maximum of five years, has to be seen in relation to the other terms of the Act. As the general effect of the Parliament Act was to tilt the Parliamentary balance of power in favour of the Government-dominated House of Commons, at the expense of the Lords, more frequent elections would bring greater electoral pressure to bear on the Commons. Also, a delay power of two years was of more value to the Lords in a five-year Parliament than in a seven-year Parliament, so that the reduction in the length of Parliaments was a form of 'self-denying ordinance' by the Liberal Government. The definition of a Money Bill in the Parliament Act is a very narrow one, and much 'financial' legislation fails to qualify for the Speaker's certificate because it contains administrative as well as financial clauses. Only about half of the annual Finance Bills introduced since 1911 have received the certificate,[1] but since 1911 the Lords have treated certified and non-certified financial legislation with equal respect.

The main terms of the 1911 Act, relating to non-financial legislation, did not remove the Lords' power of veto, but merely provided a means of overcoming the veto after a delay of two years. The machinery was soon tested when the Lords opposed the Irish Home Rule Bill and the Welsh Church

[1]Jennings, *Parliament*, p. 417, for more details.

Disestablishment Bill in 1912. The Bills were reintroduced in the next two sessions, but the outbreak of war in 1914 led to the postponement of their enactment until after the war. The Education Bill of the 1929–31 Labour Government was rejected by the Lords, and the Government's Representation of the People Bill was severely amended, and these Bills would possibly have been reintroduced and passed by the Parliament Act procedure if the Government had survived.

The only Bill to have an uncomplicated passage by the Parliament Act procedure was the second Parliament Bill, introduced in 1947 and passed finally in 1949. This measure came as a result of the fear of the Attlee Labour Government that the Lords would obstruct the Bill to nationalise the iron and steel industry, which the Government was not in a position to introduce until 1948. Thus in 1947 the Government introduced the Parliament Bill which sought to amend the 1911 Act so that a Bill which passed the Commons in two successive sessions (instead of three) was to become law without the assent of the Lords, provided that a period of one year (instead of two) elapsed between the Second Reading in the Commons in the first session and the Second Reading in the Commons in the second session. The House of Lords was naturally opposed to the Bill, and it did not receive the Royal Assent until 1949, under the terms of the original Parliament Act.

Thus the 1949 Act enables a Government to overcome obstruction in the Lords after a delay of one year from the date of a Bill's Second Reading in the Commons (though the Lords retains the power to apply an absolute veto to a Bill that seeks to extend the life of Parliament beyond five years). In fact, the delay amounts to only nine months, as generally some two or three months elapse between the Second Reading of a Bill in the Commons and its First Reading in the Lords. The procedures of the 1949 Act have been used only once. In the 1975–6 session, deadlock was reached over the Labour Government's Bill to nationalise the aircraft and shipbuilding industries, when the Lords insisted on some amendments that the Government would not accept. The Bill was reintroduced in the next session, and duly became law, but only after further opposition in the Commons and the Lords obliged the Government to make major changes in its proposals. The main significance of the Parliament Acts, however, has not been the actual use of the machinery for overcoming obstruction in the Lords, but rather the existence of the machinery as a deterrent to obstruction by the Lords. As was illustrated in the first years of the 1945–50 and 1966–70 Parliaments, there is little point in the Lords rejecting a Labour Government's measures that are bound to become law after the delay period has elapsed. Since 1945, however, obstruction by the Lords has also been deterred by the knowledge that it could be abolished if it sought to obstruct major Government legislation.

It may be questioned whether there is any merit in allowing the second chamber to have even a nominal delaying power. In its defence, and thus in defence of the role of the second chamber as an obstructive body, it is sometimes argued that when (as has usually been the case) a Government dominates the Commons through a secure party majority, the Lords remains as the only real Parliamentary limitation on the Government's power. It is claimed that there should be some such Parliamentary check upon Governments, additional to that imposed by the House of Commons. It is perhaps conceivable that a Government might risk electoral unpopularity in order to force through a particularly controversial piece of legislation, and the delaying power of the Lords could be a deterrent to such an action. Thus to a large extent the question of the delaying power of the Lords is bound up with the concept of the mandate, with the Lords' delaying power being seen as a means of opposing legislation for which the Government has no mandate.

The main objection in the past to the retention of the delaying power has been that the Lords only perform their obstructive function against non-Conservative Governments. While a year or nine months is not a long period of delay, some legislation could be destroyed by a delay of even a few months. Certainly, in the last year of a Parliament, or at any time in a hung Parliament, a non-Conservative Government cannot be sure of being able to pass a Bill through the Commons for a second time, or even of being able to reverse House of Lords amendments to a Bill. Even Conservative Governments, however, have to be wary of the Lords to some extent. It may be noted that the Lords defeated the Heath Government twenty-six times in the 1970–4 Parliament and the Thatcher Government forty-five times in the 1979–83 Parliament, sometimes on major issues.[1] In 1980 the Lords prevented the Thatcher Government from imposing cuts in rural school transport and in the external services of the BBC. In 1984 the Lords made major amendments, against the Government's wishes, to the Local Government (Interim Provisions) Bill after the Bill had only narrowly escaped defeat at Second Reading. The Lords also obliged the Government in 1984 to make significant amendments to its Housing Bill, Trade Union Bill, Telecommunications Bill and Local Government Bill. Unusually, one rebellious Conservative Peer, Lord Alport, was deprived of the whip. In these cases the Lords acted as a supplement to Conservative backbench rebellions in the Commons.

The Future of the Second Chamber

Although there is this clear disagreement over the value of the delaying power, there is less disagreement regarding the other functions of the House of Lords, and in recent years it has undoubtedly fulfilled a useful function in easing the legislative burden of the House of Commons.[2] In every session a number of non-partisan measures are introduced in the Lords and the detailed work done before they are passed to the Commons. The Lords also deals initially with the majority of Private Bills that are introduced each session. Bills that have been passed too quickly through the Commons can be re-examined in the Lords, and amendments made along lines acceptable to the Government. Thus in the 1979–83 Parliament well over two thousand amendments were made to Government Bills in the Lords, and all but a handful were accepted by the Commons. In the 1977–8 session the Gov-

[1] See D. R. Shell, 'The House of Lords and the Thatcher Government', *Parl. Aff.* 1985, pp. 16–32.

[2] See R. L. Borthwick, 'An Early Experiment with Standing Committees in the House of Lords', *Parl. Aff.* 1971–2, pp. 80–6; R. L. Borthwick, 'Public Bill Committees in the House of Lords', *Parl. Aff.* 1972–3, pp. 440–53.

ernment itself proposed ninety-six amendments to the Scotland Bill, and over a hundred amendments to the Wales Bill, during their passage through the Lords.[1]

Further, the Commons timetable often does not allow adequate time for general debate, and although debates in the Lords do not normally attract as much publicity as those in the Commons, it is preferable to have matters raised in the Lords than not raised at all. Debates in the Lords are often of a high standard, with contributions from elder statesmen, and the introduction of television coverage of Lords debates has increased public awareness of this. The House of Lords now makes greater use of Select Committees than in the past, and its European Communities Committee (with seven subject sub-committees) is generally regarded as a more effective scrutineer of European secondary legislation than the equivalent committee in the Commons.

The timetable of the House of Lords is divided almost equally between legislation and general debates, though in recent sessions rather more time has been devoted to legislation.[2] In the consideration of legislation, the Lords spend roughly twice as much time on Bills sent from the Commons as on Bills initiated in the Lords. In this respect, however, a major problem is that most Bills from the Commons reach the Lords late in the session, and often have to be given a rushed hearing. In all, the Lords generally sit for about 150 days per session, some twenty days less than the Commons. Daily sittings, on average, last about six and a half hours, again shorter than in the Commons (although since 1945 the length of the sittings in the Lords has tended to increase). The main difference between the timetable of the Lords and the Commons, however, is that the Commons spend almost one-third of their time on financial legislation and debates, while the Lords spend only one or two days per session on financial matters.

Thus in the functions of initiating and revising legislation, and in general debate, the Lords can supplement the work of the Commons and thereby disprove the argument that if a

[1] See also Lord Morrison, *Government and Parliament*, Ch. 9.

[2] See above, p. 254. See also R. M. Punnett, 'The House of Lords and Conservative Governments', *PS* 1965, pp. 85–8.

second chamber agrees with the lower house it is thereby superfluous. The Lords also has a role to play as a seat for some Government Ministers, and in every Government there are a number of posts filled by Peers.[1] Lord Salisbury was the last Prime Minister (1895–1902) to come from the House of Lords, but Lord Carrington was Foreign Secretary as recently as 1979–82. The desirability of limiting the number of Ministers in the House of Commons is one reason for allocating some Government posts to members of the Lords, but membership of the Lords does confer a number of practical advantages on Ministers. A Peer has no constituency duties, and his attendance at debates and votes is not essential, so that he has more time to devote to Ministerial duties than does a member of the Commons. This is a factor that is perhaps most significant for a Government that has only a small majority in the Commons. In spite of the 'escape route' provided by the Peerage Act 1963, the Peerage has not been stripped of all talent, and the Lords contains hereditary Peers of Ministerial calibre. At the same time, the Lords is also useful as a seat for Ministers, in that any figure who is called upon to serve in the Government, but who does not wish to enter the party political fray of the House of Commons, can be raised to a Peerage and thereby made eligible for Ministerial office. Thus Irwin Bellwin in 1979 and David Young in 1984 were given Life Peerages to enable them to take up posts in Mrs Thatcher's Government, while Lords Bowden, Caradon, Chalfont, and Gardiner in 1963 and 1964, and Lord Harris in 1974, were given Life Peerages and thereby made eligible for Ministerial office in the Wilson Governments. On the whole, however, only limited use has been made of this means of recruiting non-party men into the Government, despite the fact that Life Peerages have made elevation to the Lords more acceptable to those who might otherwise be unwilling to inflict an hereditary title on their heirs.

The general attitude of Conservative Governments towards the House of Lords in this century has been to defend its obstructive powers, and advocate minor reforms of composi-

[1] See R. M. Punnett, 'Ministerial Representation in the House of Lords', *Table* 1961, pp. 67–71, *and* 1964, pp. 69–80.

tion in order to make it more respectable and thus more justifiable in the use of its existing powers. In this tradition a Conservative Party policy committee chaired by Lord Home, proposed in 1978 that the membership of the Lords be reduced to about 400, with one-third nominated and two-thirds directly elected. Liberal and Labour Governments, on the other hand, while gradually removing the obstructive powers of the Lords, have failed to deal with the question of a major reform of composition, and in the main have opposed mild reforms of composition as being irrelevant to the real problem. Abolition of the Lords has not been attempted by any Labour Government, partly it would seem because the second chamber is recognised as being capable of performing useful legislative and deliberative functions, especially for Labour Governments which tend to have heavier legislative programmes than Conservative Governments. Thus it is when a Labour Government is in power that the second chamber is most useful as a constructive legislative body, but in the past it has been precisely then that the Lords, with its permanent Conservative majority, has been most likely to be in conflict with the Government.

The future of the House of Lords seems uncertain. It could be abolished, leaving Parliament as a single-chamber legislature. The value of the Lords as a revising body would seem to militate against this, although Labour's 1983 election manifesto contained a commitment to abolition. It seems unlikely that a Conservative Government would attempt to increase the obstructive powers of the Lords. The abortive attempt at reform made by the Labour Government in 1967–9 could have achieved a lasting settlement.[1] The Government proposed that the reformed second chamber be composed of 230 voting Peers, appointed by the Government of the day, together with a larger number of Peers who could attend the House and speak in its deliberations but could not vote. Composition would be reviewed regularly by a committee to ensure that among the voting Peers the Government had a majority over the main Opposition party, but not an overall majority. Existing hereditary Peers who were not selected to

[1] See Morgan, *The House of Lords and the Labour Government 1964–70*.

be among the 230 voting Peers could remain as non-voting Peers, but their heirs would not have this automatic right. This reformed body would have a delaying power of six months. These proposals, although agreed by Government and Opposition leaders, were resisted by a number of back-benchers on both sides of the House, and consequently were withdrawn.

Thus the need for a 'once-and-for-all' settlement remains clear. Already in this century there have been four Acts of Parliament relating to aspects of the powers and composition of the Lords, and the House of Lords is thus a good example of an element within the Constitution that has unwritten origins, but which has frequently been amended by written statutes. In this respect it can be argued that the House of Lords has received in the past, and continues to receive today, a degree of attention that is out of proportion to its current significance.

Parliament and Government Today

From the examination of the House of Commons and the House of Lords in the last two chapters, and from the discussion in earlier chapters of the relationship between Government and Parliament, it is clear that Parliament performs a variety of functions within the political system. Parliament is a representative and legislative body. It is constitutionally wedded to the Government in that it is the sole source of Ministers. It scrutinises and publicises Ministers' activities and it imposes certain constraints upon them. In the execution of these functions Parliament is strengthened by its great prestige. It is one of the oldest legislatures in the world (though the Isle of Man's Tynwald is older), it has more members and spends more time in session than most, and the procedures and ceremonial of the 'Mother of Parliaments' have been widely copied. In comparison with legislatures in many countries, Parliament (or more specifically the House of Commons) is held in considerable esteem in Britain.

There are, however, clear limits to Parliament's effectiveness. Parliament is certainly a representative assembly in the sense that the House of Commons is composed of the elected representatives of the people. What is more, both Lords and

Commons are channels for the functional representation of particular groups and interests within the community. The House of Commons, however, certainly does not represent the parties strictly in proportion to their electoral strength (even as measured on one specific election day every four years or so), and is very far from being a reflection of the socio-economic structure of the country. While the Commons may be broadly representative of public attitudes, it does not necessarily reflect a national consensus, or even majority opinion, on a particular issue. Indeed MPs reserve the right to act according to their own judgement rather than as constituency delegates.

It is true to say that Parliament legislates in the sense that legislation must be approved by Parliament, Government Bills are amended and publicised as they pass through Parliament and each year a number of Private Members Bills become law. That said, the shape of a Government Bill is determined in detail before it reaches the floor of the House. The bulk of amendments that are made during a Bill's passage are proposed by Ministers themselves or with their approval, and once it has been introduced it is unusual for a Government Bill to fail to reach the Statute Book.

The Commons, and Lords to a lesser extent, are reservoirs of talent from which Ministers are drawn, and in which some Ministerial skills can be acquired (particularly the arts of public persuasion). Parliamentary life, however, does not prepare future Ministers for the administrative and managerial tasks they will be required to perform. More fundamentally, the distinctively British Constitutional requirement that Ministers must be drawn from Parliament imposes a major limitation on the Prime Minister's ability to select talented Ministers.

Parliament constrains the Government in a variety of ways. The Government collectively, and Ministers individually, are answerable to Parliament, and the Government has to be able to achieve a majority in the Commons for its legislative and financial proposals. Ultimately, the House of Commons can destroy a Government by passing a vote of no confidence. When the Government has a clear overall majority in the House, however, the real constraint is imposed by the Government's own backbenchers, who alone are in a position to deny it a majority. The party meeting, and the lines of communication between Ministers and their backbench supporters, are the real processes through which the Government's fate is decided.

There is a variety of procedures through which Parliament can examine and draw attention to the activities of the Government. Parliament, however, sits for less than half the days of the year, the public does not attend in any great numbers, and proceedings of the Commons are not televised. Today the function of drawing attention to the Government's failures, successes and intentions is performed not only by Parliament but by political commentators and by individual MPs in contributions on television and radio and in the press. Nevertheless, Parliament's procedures confer legitimacy upon a number of aspects of the political system, including rule by party, some of the activities of pressure groups and the actions of Ministers (with many Ministerial functions being performed 'in the name of Parliament'). It is also an illegitimising institution, in the sense that the activities of Opposition MPs (and some Government backbenchers) are designed to discredit those in office. Despite their many limitations, therefore, the two Houses of Parliament remain as major arenas in which Constitutional and party conflicts are conducted within the British political system.

part four

The Workings of Government

10

The Treasury and National Finance

THE CONTROL of national finances involves, first of all, control over the proposals for Government expenditure, and secondly, control over the raising of revenue to pay for this expenditure. These processes are theoretically quite distinct, and separate procedures exist for the supervision and control of the two processes by Parliament, the Treasury, and the Government as a whole. In fact, however, control of expenditure and of revenue are inextricably bound up together, in that (as with personal spending) Government spending is inevitably limited by the extent of the potential income.

The Principles of National Finance[1]

A basic principle of national finances is that all taxation is paid into a common fund, the Consolidated Fund (or Exchequer Account), and all expenditure is met from this fund. Before 1787 taxes were levied for specific purposes, and Parliamentary control was more complete through the appropria-

[1]See D. Heald, *Public Expenditure*, London 1983; L. Pliatzky, *Getting and Spending*, London 1982; H. Heclo and A. Wildavsky, *The Private Government of Public Money*, London 1981; A. T. Peacock and D. J. Robertson, *Public Expenditure: Appraisal and Control*, London 1963; A. T. Peacock and J. Wiseman, *The Growth of Public Expenditure in the United Kingdom*, London 1961. See also T. H. Caulcott, 'The Control of Public Expenditure', *Pub. Admin.* 1962, pp. 267–88; M. Wright, 'Public Expenditure in Britain: the Crisis of Control', *Pub. Admin.* 1977, pp. 143–70.

tion of taxes for particular purposes. In 1780, however, the Commissioners of Public Accounts were set up to review the receipt and spending of public monies, and they recommended that there should be one fund into which all revenue should flow, and from which all supply should be drawn. This was duly achieved through the Customs and Excise Act 1787, and in 1866 the Consolidated Fund Act merged the English and Irish Funds into one. Departments with some form of revenue can use some of this as an 'appropriation in aid' to set against their expenditure, but this has to be specified in the estimates, and any excess beyond the specified amount has to go to the Consolidated Fund.

National finances are administered on an annual basis. Surpluses and deficits are accounted for annually, rather than being carried over into the next financial year. Thus deficits are met by borrowings, and surpluses are used to help to reduce the National Debt. Income Tax has to be renewed each year, at the latest one month after the end of the financial year on April 5th, thereby ensuring that there is annual Parliamentary consideration of taxation. Similarly, most expenditure is approved on an annual basis. After 1688 money for the army was granted on an annual basis, but civil expenditure was met from the Civil List which was granted for the whole of the Monarch's reign. This system broke down during the eighteenth century, when Parliament was frequently called upon to meet deficiencies in the Civil List. By 1832 the various civil departments had been removed from the Civil List, leaving this purely as an item of royal expenditure.

Exceptions to the annual basis of expenditure are provided by the Consolidated Fund Services, which are voted once and for all and do not require annual renewal. These items include the interest and management costs of the National Debt, subsidies to Northern Ireland, the Civil List, payments to the EEC, the salaries of the Speaker, Leader of the Opposition, the Judges, the Comptroller and Auditor-General, the Parliamentary Commissioner, and other miscellaneous matters. The Consolidated Fund Services generally account for about 10% of annual expenditure.

A further practical breach in the principle of annual supply is that the Government can, and increasingly does, incur financial liabilities for future years on long-term projects. Not all such projected spending does stem from legislation, however, and in these cases Treasury control and general Ministerial responsibility remain as the only safeguards. Nevertheless, since 1970 the principle of annual financing has been modified to some extent in that an annual White Paper is published which outlines the Government's proposed expenditure over a five year period. These estimates of future expenditure are open to debate in Parliament. There is a Contingencies Fund which can be used for emergency expenditure in anticipation of Parliamentary approval of the estimates. Any department that draws upon the Fund has later to replenish it through its own estimates.

Revenue from taxation is regulated annually by the Government's 'Budget' proposals. The Budget is primarily concerned with raising enough revenue to balance the national finances on an annual basis, but in addition, the Budget is an economic and political weapon. The raising of revenue is only one purpose of taxation. Customs Duties, for example, may be designed to protect home industry from foreign competition, while direct taxes may be used as a means of redistributing wealth. Particularly since 1940, the Budget has been used as a means of influencing the national economic situation through Government financial policy. There can be conflict between the desire to influence the national economy by means of a particular taxation policy, and the wish to balance the Budget on an annual basis. Thus the Public Sector Borrowing Requirement (the difference between government income and expenditure in any one year) is used as one of the regulators of the Government's economic strategy.

The classic principle behind the annual control of finances is that all proposals for expenditure and taxation are initiated only by Ministers of the Crown (a principle established in the eighteenth century), while Parliament, and more particularly the House of Commons, has to approve these proposals. As has been noted elsewhere,[1] finance was fundamental to Parliament's development, and it was the inability of the Norman Kings to live off their own finances that led to the original

[1]See above, Ch. 6. See also P. Einzig, *The Control of the Purse*, London 1959.

summoning of Parliament to consent to taxation proposals. From this, Parliamentary authority developed with the principle that Parliament would not consent to taxation proposals until its grievances were redressed. Thus the British Parliament emerged and developed as a result of practical financial considerations, rather than for the more idealistic principles that are sometimes thought of as underlying Parliament's development. Today the House of Commons retains the traditional financial powers of, firstly, the right to consider and approve the Government's proposals for expenditure, including the detailed appropriation of the money to its specific purposes; secondly, the right to check the Government's spending through the accounting process; and thirdly, the right to grant taxation to meet the cost of the Government's expenditures.

The degree of control that Governments exert over the Commons today, however, means that in practice the House does not 'control' the Government's financial policies any more than it 'controls' the Government in any other aspects of its activities. Today the main control over a Government's financial policy lies with the Government itself, and particularly with the Treasury. Ministers are as anxious as other MPs to keep down taxation levels. Indeed MPs today tend to encourage rather than discourage spending (and therefore higher taxation) to a greater extent than in earlier years. Thus the role of the Commons as the guardian of the public purse has to a large extent been superseded, ultimately by the electorate, and immediately by the Government's own desire to keep public expenditure within acceptable limits.

The commitment of the Thatcher Conservative Government to reduce public expenditure has to be seen in the context of a general growth in public spending over the last century. Gladstone attempted to follow a retrenchment policy in an attempt to ease the burden on the taxpayer, and he was defeated in the Cabinet in 1874 and 1894 because he wished to make cuts in Government expenditure. Lord Randolph Churchill fought a similar battle within the Conservative Party at about the same time, and his son took up the cause for a short while in the early years of this century. The heavy military and social service expenditure of the 1905–14 Liberal Governments, however, and then the 1914–18 war with further massive military spending, destroyed any success that Gladstone might have had in limiting public expenditure. After the war, attempts were made to cut back on Government spending, and the 1922 Geddes Committee on National Expenditure[1] advocated wholesale cuts in departmental spending. In 1931 the crisis within the Labour Government arose primarily over the question of how to make cuts in national expenditure. All this was reversed, however, by the need to re-arm in the late-1930s, followed by the further wartime increase in Government spending. In the immediate post-1945 period there was not the same reaction against massive public expenditure as there had been after 1918, apart from attempts to reduce defence expenditure, which were successful for only a while.

In modern conditions the Government's expenditure commitments are vast, amounting in 1985–6 to some £110 billion. This figure represents well over 40% of Gross Domestic Product, compared with just a third in 1959. The Conservatives came to power in 1979 with an ideological commitment to cut expenditure, but they have not been able to do so: public expenditure increased (even allowing for inflation) in each year between 1976 and 1986. Clearly, any modern government that wishes to reduce public expenditure faces a very difficult political task. It can seek to alter established policies, cutting back or eliminating certain programmes (as with the reduction in subsidies on council-house rents in recent years). The political difficulties involved in this, however, are considerable and the extent of public expenditure is such that only major changes of policy can have any real impact on the overall sum. The Government also has to come to terms with demands for spending in new spheres (such as expenditure on job-creation schemes in face of the increase in unemployment). It might be able to capitalise on a fall in demand (as with the decline in the school-age population in the 1980s), but even if spending per-capita is maintained in such a situation there can be political consequences in being seen to reduce the overall sums allocated to what are regarded as worthy services.

[1] Reports of the Committee on National Expenditure, Cmd. 1581, 1582, 1589 (1922).

A Government can, however, seek to achieve economies in the administration of its policies, and in this it can expect to be supported by Parliament and the Treasury. The purpose behind the annual process of preparation by the departments of detailed expenditure proposals, and the presentation of these proposals to the Treasury and Parliament for scrutiny, is partly to allow an examination of the Government's policies and priorities. The object is also, however, to give Parliament a chance to aid the Treasury and the departments themselves in their task of discovering wastage and inefficiency in the policies of the Government, and in the structure of the government machine.

The Role of the Treasury

The Treasury has a key place, not only in the control of national finances, but in the machinery of government as a whole. The Treasury has evolved over the years from the medieval post of Lord Treasurer.[1] The first stage in the emergence of the Treasury as a department of state came when Burghley, Lord Treasurer from 1572 to 1598, appointed a Secretary to assist him, and this was followed in the reign of James I by the appointment of six Privy Councillors to assist the Lord Treasurer. After this, the post of Lord Treasurer lost its significance and eventually disappeared, and in 1667 Charles II appointed a Commission to perform the Lord Treasurer's work. Only one member of this body was a Privy Councillor, and he became known as the Chancellor of the Exchequer. During the eighteenth century the First Lord of the Treasury Commission acquired responsibilities additional to the Treasury (and with Walpole became recognised as the chief Ministerial office), and the Chancellor of the Exchequer emerged as the senior financial Minister.

[1] For works on the Treasury see Lord Bridges, *The Treasury*, London 1964; H. Roseveare, *The Treasury*, London 1969; S. H. Beer, *Treasury Control*, London 1957; S. Brittan, *Steering The Economy*, London 1969; Sir H. Brittain, 'The Treasury's Responsibilities', *Pub. Admin.* 1961, pp. 1–15; C. Thain, 'The Treasury and Britain's Decline', *PS* 1984, pp. 581–95; G. C. Peden, 'The Treasury as the Central Department of Government 1919–39', *Pub. Admin.* 1983, pp. 371–85.

Because the Treasury's origins are so distant, there is no statute governing its structure and powers, and in this it is unlike most of the other newer departments. Nominally, the Treasury is still managed by the Board of Commissioners of the Treasury, made up of the Prime Minister, Chancellor of the Exchequer, and the five Lord Commissioners, but this body last met in 1921, and then only for ceremonial purposes. In practice, the First Lord of the Treasury is always Prime Minister today, and the Chancellor of the Exchequer remains the senior Treasury Minister. He is assisted by the Chief Secretary to the Treasury (who is normally a member of the Cabinet), a Financial Secretary, an Economic Secretary and a Minister of State. In addition, the Parliamentary Secretary, and the five Lord Commissioners of the Treasury, act as Government Whips. The Treasury is a small department with an establishment of about 2,500. It generally receives a higher standard of recruit than most other departments, as it tends to be the most popular department among recruits to the Principal Grade, about one-third of them naming it as their first choice. The Permanent Secretary to the Treasury, and other senior Treasury officials, receive higher salaries than do officials of equivalent rank in other departments. Promotion is generally slow within the Treasury. There is, however, a big movement of staff from the Treasury to the other departments, and generally about a quarter of the Higher Civil Service (that is, Permanent Secretaries, Deputy Secretaries and Under Secretaries) have had Treasury experience.[1]

The basis of the Treasury's organisation is 'functional', in the sense that it is organised in sections that cover functions common to several departments, rather than in sections that deal with the work of individual departments. Very broadly, its functions today are the raising of revenue, the control of expenditure and the management of the Civil Service. It shares this latter task, however, with the Management and Personnel section of the Cabinet Office, which is responsible for recruitment and promotion in the Civil Service. Treasury Ministers are also responsible for the Board of Inland Revenue, the Customs and Excise Department, the Stationery

[1] P. Sheriff, *Career Patterns in the Higher Civil Service*, London 1976, p. 23.

Office, the Central Office of Information, and a number of other associated matters. The Office of the Parliamentary Counsel, who are responsible for the preparation of Government Bills, is also attached to the Treasury.

Before 1919 there were sometimes two, and even three, Permanent Secretaries to the Treasury, but from 1919 to 1956 there was only one. In 1956 two Permanent Secretaries were appointed, one as Secretary to the Cabinet and also in charge of the management of the Civil Service, and the other in charge of the Treasury's financial and economic responsibilities.[1] In 1962, following the report of the Plowden Committee on the control of public expenditure,[2] the post of Secretary to the Cabinet was detached from the Treasury, and one Permanent Secretary was put in charge of the sections of the Treasury that dealt with the pay and management of the Civil Service, while the other was in charge of the two sections (Finance and Public Sector) that dealt with the Treasury's financial functions of controlling Government expenditure and raising revenue. Until 1964 this second Permanent Secretary was also responsible for the work of the National Economy Section of the Treasury, in supervising national economic policy, but in 1964 this passed temporarily to the Department of Economic Affairs. In 1968 the Civil Service Department was created to take over the Treasury's task of managing the Civil Service. With the abolition of the Civil Service Department in 1981, however, the Treasury regained control of most aspects of Civil Service management. The Treasury's role in managing the Civil Service will be considered in the next chapter: under consideration here are the Treasury's financial responsibilities within the broader context of Parliamentary and Ministerial control of national finances.

[1] For details of Treasury development in this period see S. Brittan, *The Treasury Under the Tories 1951–64*, London 1964; D. N. Chester, 'The Treasury 1956', *Pub. Admin.* 1957, pp. 15–23.

[2] Report of the Committee on the Control of Public Expenditure, Cmd. 1432 (1961). See also D. N. Chester, 'The Treasury 1962', *Pub. Admin.* 1962, pp. 419–26; 'Plowden Report on the Treasury', *Pub. Admin.* 1963, pp. 1–50; U. K. Hicks, 'Plowden, Planning and Management in the Public Services', *Pub. Admin.* 1961, pp. 299–312.

Treasury and Parliamentary Control of Finance: I. The Estimates

The Government's plans for future expenditure are reviewed annually and are announced in an annual White Paper, usually in January each year.[1] The White Paper contains firm expenditure proposals for the next financial year, and more tentative proposals for the subsequent three years. The figures on which the White Paper is based are produced initially by the Public Expenditure Survey Committee (PESC), which is an inter-departmental committee of senior officials headed by the Treasury. PESC gathers together existing departmental plans for expenditure over the next five years, and in June produces a review of them all. During the summer and autumn Ministers then make the final decisions about the nature of the proposals to be included in the January White Paper. This is invariably a time of conflict between the Chancellor and other Ministers. The Treasury's task is to see that policy is being achieved economically, but also to decide on policy issues by declaring what can be afforded. The Chancellor has therefore to support one policy rather than another. Disagreements between the Chancellor and other Ministers are settled ultimately at Cabinet level, with a Cabinet committee (the 'Star Chamber') playing a leading role in recent years.[2]

The Government's expenditure plans for the coming financial year, as outlined in the White Paper, are submitted to Parliament in the form of Estimates. The Defence Estimates differ from the Civil Estimates in form and procedure. With the Civil Estimates each item is examined to see if it can be afforded, but with the Defence Estimates a total figure is fixed and the Secretary of State for Defence then apportions this between the services according to priorities. This procedure is adopted with defence spending because the needs and policies of the armed services are so closely integrated, but the principle perhaps could be usefully extended to other civil depart-

[1]See M. Wright (ed.), *Public Spending Decisions*, London 1980; A. Walker (ed.), *Public Expenditure and Social Policy*, London 1982; P. K. Else and G. P. Marshall, 'The Unplanning of Public Expenditure', *Pub. Admin.* 1981, pp. 253–78.

[2]See S. Jenkins, 'The "Star Chamber", PESC and the Cabinet', *PQ* 1985, pp. 113–21.

ments whose work is closely integrated. The Civil Estimates are divided into Classes, the Classes into Votes, and the Votes into Subheads. Once the estimates are approved, transfers from Subhead to Subhead can be made only with Treasury approval. With the Defence Estimates, however, transfers can be made from one Vote to another (a practice known as virement), but again only with Treasury agreement.

The autumn review of the estimates has lost some of its significance, in that throughout the year the departments have to secure prior Treasury approval for any major policies they may propose, and this prior approval is a major aspect of Treasury financial control. There is no clear rule as to what has to be submitted and what has not, and defence projects differ slightly, in that the Treasury merely looks for value for money within a given sum. Nevertheless, the prior approval of projects involves a more detailed check than the autumn review, though the one form of control does not rule out the other, or make it unnecessary.

The estimates are received by Parliament in February, when the Financial Secretary to the Treasury presents the Civil Estimates, and the Defence Minister the Defence Estimates.[1] Supply is granted by Parliament in two Consolidated Fund Bills, one in March and one in July. The Bill structure dates from the reign of Henry VII, and was designed to prevent the House being rushed into consent. The March Consolidated Fund Bill contains four main items covering three financial years. First of all, it contains Votes on Account for the financial year that is about to begin (that is, 1987–8 in the case of the March 1987 Bill) to enable the departments to keep going until the main estimates have been approved by Parliament in July. The March Bill also contains some Defence Estimates for the financial year about to begin, to allow the service departments to continue to function. The first item in the Defence Estimates is always 'pay etc. of the Officers and Men', and this is approved in the March Bill, and

[1] For a brief but good guide to Parliamentary financial procedure see Taylor, *The House of Commons at Work*, Ch. 6. See also G. Reid, *The Politics of Financial Control*, London 1967; Sir S. Goldman, 'The Presentation of Public Expenditure Proposals to Parliament', *Pub. Admin.* 1970, pp. 247–63; Sir R. Clarke, 'Parliament and Public Expenditure', *PQ* 1973, pp. 137–53.

is then used for general purposes by the Defence Departments. The third item in the March Bill is the Supplementary Estimates needed to cover any deficits incurred in the financial year that is about to end (1986–7 in the case of the March 1987 Bill). Supplementary Estimates can involve big sums if a change of policy or a major miscalculation is involved, and the Treasury will only agree to Supplementary Estimates if the matter cannot wait until the next financial year. If deficits are not discovered until the end of the financial year, they are met by Excess Votes in the next March Bill, so that Excess Votes for 1985–6 were the fourth item contained in the March 1987 Bill.

The July Consolidated Fund Bill contains the remainder of the estimates for the current session. This involves the main Civil Estimates, the bulk of the Defence Estimates, and any Supplementary Estimates for the current session that may already be found to be necessary. The Bill also 'appropriates' all the estimates (including those contained in the March Bill) to their specific purposes, and thus it is also known as the Appropriation Bill. The July Bill is usually the last piece of financial legislation of the session, but a Bill may be necessary in the autumn or early in the next session, in order to deal with some major change of policy. The debates on the March and July Bills are not specifically financial in content, and are mainly an opportunity for backbenchers to raise topics. The consideration of the estimates in the House is done partly by the Treasury and Civil Service Committee and partly by the Whole House, much of the work being done before the Bills are introduced.[1]

Until its abolition in 1967, the Committee of Supply (a Committee of the Whole House) was the traditional means through which the House of Commons exercised financial control, its task being to consider the Government policy that lay behind the estimates. The Committee of Supply originated in the seventeenth century, when the House of Commons chose to sit as a Committee in order to avoid the surveillance of the King's agent, the Speaker. In later years, a more important factor was that the rules of debate and general

[1]See B. Chubb, *The Control of Public Expenditure*, London 1952.

procedure were much less rigid when the House sat as a Committee. In the nineteenth century there was no limit on the number of days the House could devote to the Committee of Supply, but in this century the practice developed of allocating twenty-six 'Supply Days', spread throughout a session.[1] After 1918, it also became the practice for the Opposition to choose the topics to be debated on Supply Days. Usually, supply time was used for general debates on the Government policies that lay behind the estimates, rather than for the consideration of the details of the estimates themselves. There were frequent demands that there should be an end to the pretence that the Committee of Supply was still fulfilling financial functions. Eventually, in 1967, it was abolished, though the Supply Days remained as vehicles for general debates on policy. In 1982 the Supply Days were replaced by nineteen Opposition Days, when the opposition parties determine the topics to be debated, and three Estimates Days, when specific details of the Estimates are examined. While this provides the House as a whole with an opportunity to delve into the details of the Government's spending proposals, three days for this purpose is clearly of limited value.

A Select Committee of the House of Commons (the Treasury and Civil Service Committee) considers the Estimates from the point of view of whether policy is being achieved economically. As well as the consideration of general policy, this also involves scrutiny of the workings and administrative efficiency of the departments. A Select Committee to supplement the work of the Committee of Supply first appeared in 1912, and from time to time since then various committees of different forms and powers have been set up, the present committee dating from 1979. An Estimates Committee was established in 1912, partly because of the big increase in Government spending in the early years of this century, and partly because of the success of the earlier established PAC. At the same time, there was a desire to make economies when the money was being asked for in the estimates, rather than wait

[1]See A. Barker, '"The Most Important and Venerable Function": A Study of Commons Supply Procedure', *PS* 1965, pp. 45–64.

for the accounting process to discover wastage. It was also felt that if less time was spent on the details of the estimates in the Committee of Supply, more time could be devoted to general debates on Government policy.

During the two world wars the Estimates Committee was replaced by a National Expenditure Committee, which operated through sub-committees and was concerned with reviewing the organisation and efficiency of the departments rather than their detailed estimates. In peacetime, however, the Estimates Committee was revived and operated until replaced by the Expenditure Committee in 1971. Unlike its predecessors, the Expenditure Committee considered not just the annual estimates but any papers on public spending that might be put before the House. It had the power to examine witnesses, call for documents from the departments, and appoint advisers to assist it in its deliberations. It had forty-nine members and appointed specialist sub-committees which were designed to be an alternative to some of the Select Committees that had emerged in the Parliamentary reforms of the 1960s.[1]

In 1979 the Expenditure Committee was replaced by the Treasury and Civil Service Committee as part of the overall reform of the Select Committee System.[2] The Treasury and Civil Service Committee has eleven members, most of them experienced in financial and economic affairs. A sub-committee deals with taxation and civil service matters while the main committee is more concerned with broader policy questions. The committee appoints specialist advisers and is probably better equipped than its predecessors to examine the details of departmental spending. At the same time, like its predecessors, its value as a watchdog is still limited by the fact that it is concerned more with broad policy and departmental organisation and methods than with close scrutiny of particular estimates. There is no means of ensuring that the Govern-

[1]See P. Byrne, 'The Expenditure Committee: A Preliminary Assessment', *Parl. Aff.* 1973–4, pp. 273–86; A. Silkin, 'The Expenditure Committee: A New Development', *Pub. Admin.* 1975, pp. 45–66; A. Kennan, 'Recent Work of the General Sub-Committee of the Expenditure Committee', *Parl. Aff.* 1980, pp. 159–65.

[2]See above, p. 276.

ment will take heed of its proposals, and more could perhaps be done to follow up its reports on the floor of the Commons. What is more, as the Treasury and Civil Service Committee is dealing with current spending proposals, it can only really warn for the future. No doubt with the assistance of an 'Examiner of Estimates', with a relationship to the committee similar to that of the C and AG to the PAC, the Treasury and Civil Service Committee could function more effectively.

Once the estimates have been approved by Parliament, departmental spending is supervised by the Treasury and the C and AG. When the departments require the finance that has been estimated for them, they approach the Treasury, which determines whether the money is needed at that time. The C and AG (in his role as Comptroller) then ensures that the money has been approved by Parliament, and the money is then transferred from the Consolidated Fund to the Paymaster-General's account for the departments.

II. The Accounts

The final level of control over expenditure is through the accounting process. Appropriation accounts are prepared by each department, the Permanent Secretary usually being the departmental Accounting Officer. The form of the accounts is based on the estimates, and they show and explain any differences between the estimates and the actual spending. The accounts are examined initially by the C and AG, who receives the accounts of the Civil Departments by September 30th, and those of the Defence Department by December 31st (that is, September 30th or December 31st 1987 for the accounts of the financial year 1986–87. The accounts and the C and AG's reports are sent to Parliament, where they are examined by the PAC.

The PAC dates from 1861, and the post of C and AG from the Exchequer and Audit Act 1866, both inspired by Gladstone's search for financial economies. The task of the C and AG and the PAC is to examine the accounts to see if the money has been spent as Parliament authorised, but also to see if due economy has been observed throughout, and to censure doubtful practices. Thus the work of the PAC is essentially different from the accounting process in the commercial world. The PAC is composed of fifteen members in proportion to party strength in the House, with the chairman being a senior Opposition MP.[1] Members are chosen for their financial knowledge, and are generally reappointed to the committee each session, so that the PAC is essentially specialist. The PAC meets from February to July, after it has received the accounts and report from the C and AG. It has the power to summon civil servants, and question them about the work of their departments. It reports to Parliament in July, and though Parliament may not take account of the committee's detailed findings, the Treasury always does.

The key figure behind the work of the PAC is the C and AG, who, as well as preparing the accounts for the committee, gives a report to the committee of his own opinions and recommendations. The C and AG is a Parliamentary officer, and his salary is one of the Consolidated Fund Services. He is not necessarily a trained accountant himself, but he has a staff of several hundred in the National Audit Office who are trained in audit work. The National Audit Act 1983 made the C and AG an officer of Parliament rather than of the Crown, and created a Public Accounts Commission to take over from the Treasury the financing of the Audit Office. These changes increased the C and AG's independance from Whitehall, allowed an increase in his staff and made possible an extension of 'value-for-money' studies by the enlarged staff.

As well as the work of the C and AG, the fact that the PAC is a specialised committee, both in composition and in the advice that it gets, and the fact that it acts and votes largely along non-party lines, means that it has considerable prestige and authority. The value of the committee is that it acts as a deterrent to inefficiency and extravagance by the departments, but it has the essential weakness of all accounting processes of dealing with past expenditure. Thus if wastage does occur, it can only be revealed and prevented in the future. To some extent the very success of the PAC takes some

[1]See V. Flegman, *Called to Account*, London 1980; V. Flegman, 'The Public Accounts Committee: A Successful Select Committee', *Parl. Aff.* 1980, pp. 166–72; E. L. Normanton, 'Reform in the Field of Public Accountability and Audit', *PQ* 1980, pp. 175–99.

of the responsibility for finance away from the House of Commons as a whole, and this is one of the factors that has prevented control over the estimating process from being more effective. In 1946, it was recommended to the Select Committee on Procedure that the PAC should be combined with the wartime Committee on Expenditure to form a National Expenditure Committee of thirty or so members, and with six or so sub-committees.[1] This proposal has been revived from time to time since then. It is argued that the PAC and the various Estimates and Expenditure Committees have been inadequate in themselves, and have not co-operated with each other to a sufficient degree, and that one powerful committee dealing with both estimates and accounts would be a more adequate check upon expenditure than is the established system. This proposal has been resisted, however, largely on the grounds that the two committees cannot readily be combined. The extra work involved for the C and AG could make him less effective overall, and a better reform might be to give the Treasury and Civil Service Committee an official of its own. The proposal has also been resisted by successive Governments on the grounds that the existing committees are in fact adequate, and that a too-powerful committee would interfere too much with Ministerial responsibility.

III. Economies and Efficiency

The role of Parliament and the Treasury in the control of expenditure may now be summarised. Parliamentary control is exercised primarily through Select Committees of the House of Commons. The Treasury and Civil Service Committee considers the estimates from the point of view of departmental organisation and efficiency, and the PAC, aided by the C and AG, examines the annual accounts. In addition, Parliamentary control is exercised by the passage through Parliament of the Consolidated Fund Bills and the Appropriation Bill, and by the approval of the Financial Resolution that accompanies all Bills involving expenditure. In a much less specific way, Parliamentary control is also exercised through such influence

[1] Report of the Select Committee on Procedure, H.C. 189 of 1945–6.

as Parliament is able to exert over Government legislation and policies in general.

Despite the long-established traditions of Parliament's financial rights, despite the complicated nature of Parliamentary procedure in financial matters, and despite the financial committees in the Commons, the very real limitations of Parliamentary control over expenditure have to be emphasised. Ultimately, of course, with finances as with other matters, Parliamentary power is limited by the degree of control that the Government is able to exert over Parliament. Nevertheless, given that Parliament cannot 'control' Government expenditure to any greater extent than it can 'control' Government policy in general, Parliament's ability to consider and comment upon Government expenditure is still very limited.

In addition to the specific weaknesses of the individual House of Commons committees, the chief general limitation on Parliamentary consideration of expenditure lies in the sheer size of the sum involved, and the limited time available in which to consider it. In 1985–6 expenditure on the Supply Services was almost £100 billion and on the Consolidated Fund Services just over £12 billion. Despite Government attempts at retrenchment, this problem would seem inevitably to be a growing one, while the greater emphasis on long-term projects and long-term planning commitments adds to the difficulty of trying to relate expenditure to an annual procedure. Thus today, Parliament's role with regard to expenditure is primarily to ensure through the accounting process that money is spent as it was appropriated, to publicise Government policies (particularly those that are financially extravagant) and to uncover and publicise any departmental inefficiency that results in financial wastage.

Treasury control of expenditure is achieved most effectively by the examination of the estimates that culminates in the annual autumn review, and by the requirement of prior Treasury approval for all major projects. It is also achieved through the control of virement, through control over actual withdrawals from the Consolidated Fund, and through the examination of the reports of the C and AG. As a more general form of control, Treasury Ministers must approve the

Financial Resolution that accompanies all Bills that involve expenditure, and Treasury Ministers examine all Cabinet memoranda (as do the Law Officers) before they go to the rest of the Cabinet, to ensure that the attention of Cabinet Ministers will be drawn to the financial implications of any proposed policy.

Thus the Treasury's influence is felt at all stages in the financial process. Also, as a result of the policy of Warren Fisher, Permanent Secretary to the Treasury 1919–38, each department has its own Permanent Secretary as Accounting Officer, and the effect is to provide a strong force for economy within each department. To avoid possible censure for departmental extravagance, a Permanent Secretary must officially record any disagreements that he has with his Minister over policies which he feels to be financially unwise.

The specific and detailed control over expenditure that is exercised by the Treasury, is supplemented by departmental controls, and by the general control that exists through the collective responsibility of all members of the Government for all policies, financial and otherwise.[1] It has to be assumed that Ministers are anxious to avoid 'waste', and that they seek to achieve policy objectives by the most economic means. In face of increased public expenditure over the last twenty years Governments have made various attempts to reduce administrative costs by improving managerial efficiency in Whitehall. In order to achieve a rational distribution of resources between departments (and within departments) as early as possible in the planning process, the Conservative and Labour Governments between 1970 and 1979 operated a system of Programme Analysis and Review (PAR).[2] Departmental policy proposals were examined, before the stage of allocating financial resources was reached, by teams of civil servants and outside analysts under the direction of the Chief Secretary to the Treasury. Policy objectives, and the means of achieving the objectives, were assessed and departmental priorities were

[1] See A. S. Moore, 'Departmental Financial Control', *Pub. Admin.* 1957, pp. 169–78.

[2] See A. Gray and B. Jenkins, 'Policy Analysis in British Central Government', *Pub. Admin.* 1982, pp. 429–50; J. J. Richardson, 'Programme Evaluation in Britain and Sweden, *Pub. Admin.* 1981, pp. 253–78.

established. There is clear merit in such an exercise, and PAR did achieve some rationalisation of procedures for distributing financial resources. In 1979, however, the system was abandoned, partly (ironically) as an economy measure because departments were using the exercise as a vehicle to inflate their claims for funds.

In 1979 the new Conservative Government established an Efficiency Unit to examine the administrative procedures of the departments of state with a view to achieving better value for money.[1] The Unit has a staff of half-a-dozen civil servants and former businessmen. It is attached to the Cabinet Office, with its head (originally Sir Derek Rayner) answerable directly to the Prime Minister. The efficiency studies are undertaken by the Departments themselves, under the direction of members of the Unit. Among the enquiries undertaken have been those into the methods of making Social Security payments, the activities of diplomats and the effectiveness of spending on the inner cities.[2] Economically sensible changes proposed by the Unit have not always been politically acceptable, however, and the Unit has been critical of the departments for being slow to react to its recommendations. Nevertheless in its first six years of operation the Efficiency Unit did inspire administrative economies worth about £750 million.

The Conservatives also introduced in 1980 a Management Information System for Ministers (MINIS).[3] This involves the preparation of a detailed description of a department's work patterns so that the Minister and his senior officials can achieve a better understanding of the distribution of tasks within the department. It was hoped that the managerial efficiency of the department would be improved and that a more economical use of resources would result. The system was introduced initially into the Department of the Environ-

[1] See D. Howells, 'Marks and Spencer and the Civil Service', *Pub. Admin.* 1981, pp. 337–78; L. Metcalfe and S. Richards, 'The Impact of the Efficiency Strategy', *Pub. Admin.* 1984, pp. 440–54; N. Warner, 'Raynerism in Practice', *Pub. Admin.* 1984, pp. 7–22.

[2] See above, p. 171.

[3] See Royal Institute of Public Administration, *Management Information and Control in Whitehall*, London 1983.

ment and was later adopted by some other departments after the Select Committee on the Treasury and Civil Service had recommended its expansion.

A more comprehensive system of Financial Management Initiative was introduced in 1982. Under this system a management unit within each department defines the specific tasks of the various sections of the department and assesses their effectiveness in performing these tasks. The system is designed to improve each department's cost-effectiveness by achieving the most efficient use of manpower and resources. The Efficiency Unit supervises the several departmental units.

IV. National Revenue

The national revenue to meet expenditure consists of Ordinary Revenue from the Crown Lands, Extraordinary Revenue from taxation, and revenue from borrowing. Since 1761 annual revenue from the Crown Lands has accrued to the Exchequer in exchange for an annual Civil List payment to the Monarch. Of the Extraordinary Revenue, direct taxes, such as Income Tax, Capital Gains Tax, and Death Duties, are administered by the Inland Revenue, while indirect taxes on goods and commodities, in the form of Customs Duties on foreign goods and Excise Duties on home goods, are administered by the Customs and Excise Departments. In 1985–6 revenue from taxation came to about £90 billion with direct taxes accounting for just over half, indirect taxes about 35%, and miscellaneous receipts about 12%. The precise distribution of the burden between direct and indirect taxation in any one year is, however, a matter partly of economic and partly of political considerations.[1]

The Government's annual Budget proposals for regulating taxation are presented by the Chancellor of the Exchequer to the House of Commons, and are debated before being incorporated in the Finance Bill.[2] The main Budget comes in the spring, though in some years there is an additional Budget

[1] See J. P. Mackintosh, 'The House of Commons and Taxation', *PQ* 1975, pp. 75–86.

[2] See Sir H. Brittain, *The British Budgetary System*, London 1959; A. Williams, *Public Finance and Budgetary Policy*, London 1963.

TABLE XXXII

UK Revenue and Expenditure 1985–6

		Year ending March 31, 1986 (April estimate)
Revenue		£ millions
Inland Revenue		55,300
Customs and Excise		37,300
Other receipts		
Vehicle Excise Duty	2,400	13,250
National Insurance Surcharge	30	
Gas Levy	520	
Broadcasting Receiving Licences	990	
Interest and Dividends	910	
Others	8,400	
Total Revenue		105,850
Expenditure		
Supply Services		98,100
Consolidated Fund Services		
National Debt Interest and Management	7,700	12,160
Northern Ireland	1,800	
European Community	2,600	
Other Services	60	
Total Expenditure		110,260
Deficit		4,410

dealing with interim measures. In the 1974–9 Parliament there was an average of three Budgets a year.

In preparing the Budget, the Chancellor of the Exchequer is advised by the Budget Committee of the Treasury.[1] This committee, which meets regularly from July until the Budget is presented at the start of the financial year, includes the Permanent Secretary in charge of the Treasury's financial section, the heads of the Public Sector and Finance Groups of the Treasury, and senior figures from the Inland Revenue and the Customs and Excise Departments. It meets as early as

[1] See Lord Amory, 'Preparing the Budget', *Parl. Aff.* 1960–1, pp. 451–9.

July to consider the effect of the previous Budget, and to see if interim measures are needed. The Chancellor of the Exchequer is most directly involved in the committee's work from November onwards, when Budget preparations proceed concurrently with the examination of the estimates of departmental expenditure. The utmost secrecy surrounds the preparation of the Budget, and though the Chancellor of the Exchequer consults with the Prime Minister, and perhaps senior colleagues, over taxation proposals, Ministers sometimes complain of being ignored in these matters. Before the Budget proposals are revealed, reviews of the economic situation and the statistical background to the proposals are provided by the publication of economic and statistical data, including the White Paper on the Preliminary Estimates of National Income and Expenditure, and the Economic Survey.

The Budget itself is presented by the Chancellor of the Exchequer to the House of Commons before May 4th, the last day for the annual renewal of Income Tax. Immediately after the Chancellor's Budget speech, the Budget Resolutions are approved by the House in order to legalise the collection of any taxes that are to be operative immediately. There then follows four or five days of debate on the Budget proposals on the floor of the House, after which the Finance Bill, incorporating the Budget proposals, is introduced. The Finance Bill passes through the House during the next three months on a strict timetable, with the various stages taken on different days. In a normal session of about 170 sittings, a dozen or so days are generally devoted to the Finance Bill in the Commons. The Bill must be given a second reading within twenty days of the completion of the Budget debates.

Until 1968 the committee stage of the Bill was always taken on the floor of the House, but since 1968 detailed and technical clauses have been dealt with in a Standing Committee of fifty members. This avoids spending time on the floor of the House on points of technical detail. Changes in the detailed proposals frequently occur during the Bill's passage through the House, and the influence of industrial and commercial pressure groups is felt particularly at the committee stage, when debates tend to be highly technical. The Government is loath to use the guillotine procedure too vigorously, and sometimes gives way to criticism in order to save time. Amendments are often made on the Government's own initiative (though fewer changes would be necessary if the Chancellor revealed more to his colleagues during the preparation of the Budget). After passing the Commons, the Bill goes to the Lords where it receives formal approval, generally after only one day or half a day of debate on general financial policy.

Very often, some provisions of the Finance Bill relate purely to administrative changes, and there is perhaps a case for a separate Tax Management Bill to deal with detailed administrative changes. On the whole, the problem of tax reform has been neglected over the years, partly because of the antiquity of the tax system, and the administrative and political problems involved in making fundamental changes, but also because the Treasury's prime concern is with how much money is to be raised rather than with the equity of the method. The sub-committee of the Treasury and Civil Service Committee, however, may include a review of taxation methods in its enquiries.

For maximum efficiency it is necessary for some taxes to become operative as soon as they are announced, long before the Finance Bill is finally passed. This is achieved today through the terms of the Provisional Collection of Taxes Act 1913, which was passed following a legal battle fought by Gibson Bowles, a Conservative backbench MP. In 1912 he refused to pay certain taxes on the grounds that although the House of Commons had passed resolutions approving the tax proposals, the collection of the taxes was not legal until the Finance Bill had received the Royal Assent. He argued that the practice of collecting some taxes as soon as they were announced, was a circumvention of Parliamentary control of finance, and an imposition on individual rights. The Court upheld Bowles' objection, and ruled that taxes could not become operative until Parliament (and not merely the Commons) had approved them. The Court pointed out that a mere resolution of the House of Commons did not make law.[1]

Thus there followed in 1913 the Provisional Collection of Taxes Act, which permits the collection of taxes up to August

[1] *Bowles* v. *the Bank of England* (1913) 82 L.J. Ch. 124.

5th on the strength of what is proposed in the Budget Resolution, although the Finance Bill must then receive the Royal Assent by August 5th. This applies only to variations in existing taxes and not to new taxes. At first it applied only to Income Tax and Customs and Excise Duties, but it has since been extended to other taxes. Also, the Import Duties Act 1932 established the principle that the level of import duties could be varied without further legislative approval, and this principle has been extended to other taxes until today most indirect taxes can be varied by up to 10%. This provides the Chancellor of the Exchequer with a flexible means of influencing the economy between Budgets.

Because there are definite economic and political limitations on the amount of money that can be raised by taxation at any one time, some revenue has to be obtained by long-term and short-term borrowing. The amount of money that the Government owes as a result of this borrowing makes up the National Debt. There has been a huge increase in the National Debt this century, partly as a result of the borrowing that was necessary to pay for the vast expenditure during the two world wars. On March 31st 1913 the National Debt stood at just over £650 million, but by 1919 it had risen to over £7.4 billion. This figure was slightly reduced by 1923, but by 1945 it had almost trebled to more than £21.3 billion. It has increased greatly since 1945, largely as a result of financing investment in schools, roads, the nationalised industries, and other tangible projects, and today it stands at about £100 billion. Nominally, control over the Debt is in the hands of the National Debt Commissioners, who were first appointed in 1786, and who include the Chancellor of the Exchequer, the Speaker of the House of Commons, and the Master of the Rolls. In fact, however, their responsibilities are performed by the Director of the National Investment and Loans Office, which was formed in 1980 through the merger of the National Debt Office and the Public Works Loan Board.

Since 1945 there has been little attempt to reduce the size of the Debt, largely because peacetime borrowing, more than wartime borrowing, is used to finance progressive investment in the public services. As early as 1716, however, the principle was established that any excess of revenue at the end of the financial year should go to a Sinking Fund to pay off the Debt, and this principle was reinforced in the Exchequer and Audit Act 1866. Also, attempts were made in the past to set aside specific repayment sums each year, and for this purpose a New Sinking Fund was established in 1875. This project failed, however, with the vast increase in the Debt after 1914, though the management costs and interest on the Debt are now a permanent charge on the Consolidated Fund.

In addition to the various long-term borrowings, short-term borrowing is necessary to help to manage the day-to-day finances of the departments. Income and expenditure is not spread evenly over the year, and income from taxation accrues mainly in the last quarter of the financial year, so that daily deficits in the first three-quarters of the year have to be met by borrowing. The Bank of England cooperates with the Treasury in this matter, and the Treasury tries to reduce outside borrowing to a minimum by making full use of the public money within the Government's control, like the National Insurance Fund. Ultimately, day-to-day borrowing can be made from the Bank of England, while in the last quarter of the financial year any daily surplus of revenue is absorbed by the Bank.[1]

Thus, with income as with expenditure, real control lies with the Treasury. Nevertheless, despite the obvious limitations that exist on the Commons' ability to influence revenue policy, the Commons' power to amend the details of the Government's taxation proposals is greater than its ability to alter Government expenditure proposals. Budget debates in the Commons, and the debates at the various stages of the Finance Bill, are more 'financial' in content than are the debates on the Consolidated Fund and Appropriation Bills. Such control as the House of Commons is able to achieve over national finances today is exerted primarily over the details of the Finance Bill.

The Coordination of Economic Policy[2]

Until 1964 the Treasury had the direct responsibility for the coordination of national economic planning. In October 1964,

[1] For the general role of the Bank in national finances see A. C. L. Day, 'The Bank of England in the Modern State', *Pub. Admin.* 1961, pp. 15–26; R. A. Chapman, 'The Bank of England', *Parl. Aff.* 1970–1, pp. 208–21.

[2] See J. Mitchell, *Groundwork to Economic Planning*, London 1966.

however, when the Wilson Labour Government came to power, the Department of Economic Affairs was created, with the Deputy Prime Minister, George Brown, as Minister for Economic Affairs. The DEA's life was short, as it was abolished in 1969, but it represents the most direct and ambitious of the many attempts that have been made to remove from the Treasury the direct responsibility for the control of long term economic policy. Before 1914, economic policy as such was the preserve primarily of the Treasury, but with other departments, like the Board of Trade, also involved in economic policy to some extent. In 1925 a Cabinet Committee on economic research was created, and was succeeded in 1930 by the Economic Advisory Council. The Prime Minister was chairman of this body, but as with all such advisory committees, its authority was limited, in that it did not have the backing of a department of state. In 1939 the Central Economic Information Service was set up within the Cabinet Secretariat, and in 1941 this was divided into the Central Statistical Office and the Economic Section. During the war, however, the real control of economic policy lay with the Lord President of the Council, and the Treasury's influence was limited by the emphasis in the wartime economy on physical controls rather than controls through Treasury financial policy. This arrangement was continued by the Labour Government after 1945, but in 1947 Sir Stafford Cripps was made Minister for Economic Affairs, and when later in 1947 he was appointed Chancellor of the Exchequer, he took his responsibility for economic policy to the Treasury with him. This marked a reaction against physical controls as a means of economic planning, and was the beginning of a period of more direct Treasury control through monetary and fiscal means.

Churchill, in his Government formed in 1951, tried to limit the Treasury's responsibility for economic planning by means of a committee to supervise the work of R. A. Butler, the Chancellor of the Exchequer, although the Treasury retained ultimate authority. Towards the end of the long Conservative period of office, the 1962 changes in Treasury organisation, the creation of the National Economic Development Council and the National Incomes Commission, the appointment in 1963 of Edward Heath as President of the Board of Trade and

Secretary of State for Industry, can all be seen as attempts to establish economic planning machinery, and reduce the Treasury's absolute control of economic planning.[1] Nevertheless, throughout the Conservative period of office from 1951 to 1964, the Treasury retained final responsibility for the control of economic planning. Treasury control was achieved first of all through the Central Statistical Office in the Cabinet Secretariat (responsible for providing factual information about economic growth), secondly through the Economic Section of the Treasury (responsible for the study of economic problems), and thirdly through the two National Economy Groups of the Treasury (responsible for economic forecasting and the development of policies for economic growth). Economic planning was aided by the Treasury's direct responsibility for the Budget, and for the supervision of Government expenditure.

Thus before 1964, various attempts to control economic policy had been made – through advisory committees before 1940; through physical controls under non-departmental Ministers from 1940 to 1947; and through Treasury control after 1947. Various other methods were also canvassed from time to time. It was proposed, for example, that there should be a coordinating committee for economic policy, made up of Ministers and officials and presided over by the Prime Minister. It was suggested that there should be an extension of the power and status of NEDC to give it the authority of a full department of state, with more access to the centres of power. It was also suggested that the Treasury should lose its functions with regard to the management of the Civil Service and the control of Government expenditure, leaving it purely as a department for raising revenue and controlling economic policy.

In 1964, however, these proposals were all rejected in favour of the creation of a special department for economic planning. The Government maintained that the DEA was desirable because the Treasury was essentially economy-

[1] See J. Mitchell, 'The Functions of NEDC', *PQ* 1963, pp. 354–65; H. Phelps Brown, 'The National Economic Development Organisation', *Pub. Admin.* 1963, pp. 239–46.

minded, and lacked the necessary approach for an economic planning department.[1] The Government argued that the Treasury approach was too negative, merely telling the departments what they could do rather than what they must do. Attempts to control the economy by fiscal and monetary means were seen as inadequate, and a more positive approach towards economic planning was sought from an entirely new department. It was further argued that the Treasury was overworked, and lacked the staff necessary for long-term planning, while Chancellors of the Exchequer had too many responsibilities and tended to leave too much influence over economic planning in the hands of Treasury officials. The big differences in economic prosperity from one region of Britain to another, were also presented as a factor that produced a need for a new department which could include among its functions the development of economic policy from a regional as well as a national standpoint.

The creation of the DEA, and its subsequent activities, were criticised by those who saw Treasury control as the best means of regulating economic policy. They argued that as the Treasury's main concern is with financial policy, and as the Budget is a major economic weapon, the Treasury should have responsibility for economic policy in general. They claimed also that the Treasury's special place in the machinery of government, with its direct influence over all departments, could not be matched by the DEA, even under a dynamic and high-ranking Cabinet Minister.

The DEA's critics were proved correct. It failed to achieve the ends for which it was created, partly, perhaps, because it had to operate against a background of almost continuous economic restraint. With the balance of payments and sterling crises of the 1964–8 period, the 1967 devaluation, and the cuts in public expenditure which accompanied it, the Treasury regained its role as the main department controlling economic policy. The DEA's original powers were gradually reduced, and it was finally abolished in 1969.

Since 1969 the traditional means of economic control have

[1] See, for example, 701 H.C. Deb. 5s. 214–48, *and* 720 H.C. Deb. 5s. 1155–78, for Government and Opposition attitudes.

prevailed and the Treasury has been the dominant department in the formulation of short-term and long-term economic policy. Over the last ten years the Treasury has had two Ministers in the Cabinet (the Chancellor of the Exchequer and the Chief Secretary to the Treasury). These two Ministers are also invariably members of the key Cabinet committee that determines economic strategy. On questions of economic management such as the levels of taxes and interest rates, control of the money supply and the determination of public sector pay scales, the central role is played by the Treasury. Other departments, particularly Trade and Industry, Employment, Energy and Agriculture, are inevitably closely involved in economic policy, but no single department rivals the Treasury in the determination of economic policy.

With successful relations at an individual level, the Treasury, the planning of national economic policy, and the Government machine as a whole, no doubt would benefit from a division of power between the Treasury and a separate economic Ministry on the lines of the short-lived DEA. At present, however, the Treasury remains as the centre of the Government machine, with its authority enhanced by the failure over the last twenty years of the DEA and the Civil Service Department to make lasting inroads into Treasury financial and managerial responsibilities. The fundamental nature of finance in the process of government, together with the influence that goes with the management of the Civil Service, means that the Chancellor of the Exchequer and the other Treasury Ministers have a special place in the Ministerial hierarchy, and Treasury officials are regarded as the core of the Civil Service. This goes some way towards achieving a central directing force within British government.[1]

[1] See S. Brittan, *Steering the Economy: The Role of the Treasury*, London 1969; A. H. Hanson, *Planning and the Politicians*, London 1969; Political and Economic Planning, *Economic Planning and Policies in Britain, France and Germany*, London 1969.

11

The Central Administration

A CIVIL SERVANT may be formally defined as a servant of the Crown employed in a civil capacity who is paid wholly and directly from money voted by Parliament.[1] This excludes the political and judicial servants of the Crown, and also the armed forces, who are employed in a military and not a civil capacity. It also excludes public servants in local government, the health service and the public corporations, who are not 'servants of the Crown', and are not paid directly from money voted by Parliament. In all, there are about 600,000 civil servants in Britain – some 3% of the working population. About 100,000 are industrial civil servants, such as employees in naval dockyards and Royal Ordnance factories, and some 500,000 are non-industrial civil servants (who are the main concern of this examination). The non-industrial civil servants are distributed unevenly among the various departments. The Treasury has about 2,500, while the Ministry of Defence has over 100,000, the Department of Health and Social Security just under 100,000 and the Board of Inland Revenue about 75,000. These last three departments between them account for over half the non-industrial Civil Service. The Civil Service has expanded appreciably this century, and in the 1970s alone the number of non-industrial civil servants rose by about 15%. Under the Thatcher Government, however, the trend

[1] Based on a definition by the Royal Commission on the Civil Service 1929–31 (The Tomlin Commission), Cmd. 3909 (1931).

has been reversed and the number of non-industrial civil servants is now about 8% less than in 1979.[1]

Development of the Civil Service

As with so many aspects of British government, the modern structure of the Civil Service is a result of various *ad hoc* developments over the past two centuries.[2] In the eighteenth century, and for much of the nineteenth century, Civil Service organisation was chaotic. Recruitment was largely by patronage, or by the purchase of sinecure posts, with the heads of the various departments having almost complete independence in the question of recruitment. There was little suggestion of appointments being made according to ability, and there was no system of examinations to test the ability of potential recruits. Civil Service pay consisted partly of regular salaries paid out of departmental receipts, and partly of additional bonuses and perquisites, the extent of which varied from department to department. The only overall supervision was provided by the Auditors of Imprest, who exercised a very general and limited control over departmental accounts.

Some attempts at reform were made in the early years of the nineteenth century, in the interests of economy, but it was not until the appearance in 1854 of the Report on the Organisation of the Permanent Civil Service[3] by Sir Stafford Northcote (Secretary at the Board of Trade) and Sir Charles Trevelyan (an Assistant Secretary at the Treasury), that fundamental changes were made in Civil Service organisation. The report was inspired largely by the earlier introduction of competitive examinations as a basis for recruitment to the Indian Civil Service, and by reforms in the organisation of Oxford and Cambridge Universities, with the emphasis on examinations

[1] See G. K. Fry, 'The Development of the Thatcher Government's "Grand Strategy" for the Civil Service', *Pub. Admin.* 1984, pp. 322–35; C. Painter, 'The Thatcher Government and the Civil Service', *PQ* 1983, pp. 292–7.

[2] For a general history of the Civil Service see E. Cohen, *The Growth of the British Civil Service*, London 1965; H. Parris, *Constitutional Bureaucracy*, London 1969.

[3] H.C.P. 27 (1854).

as a test of ability. In 1848, a House of Commons Select Committee enquiry into the costs of the Civil Service, before which Sir Charles Trevelyan gave evidence, led to the appointment of Northcote and Trevelyan to enquire into the whole structure and organisation of the Civil Service – just as in 1966 a House of Commons Estimates Committee enquiry into the Civil Service[1] led to the appointment of the Fulton Commission for a full-scale enquiry into the service. The Northcote–Trevelyan Report attacked the existing system of patronage, and recommended that recruitment should be by open-examinations as with the Indian Civil Service. They advocated the creation of a Civil Service Commission as an independent body to organise recruitment, and they proposed that there should be two classes throughout the service, junior posts recruited between the ages of 17 and 21, and senior posts recruited from University graduates. They further proposed that within each class there should be a system of promotion by merit in order to stimulate talent and ambition.

These recommendations were naturally criticised by those who benefited from the existing system of patronage and departmental independence, but more significantly the report was attacked by those who argued that academic ability was not the best criterion on which to base recruitment. It was also argued that a Civil Service based on academic talent would become *too* efficient and *too* powerful, and would consequently be a threat to the authority of Ministers. Thus opposition to the proposals was strong, but they were implemented after the Crimean War had revealed inefficiencies in army organisation which also reflected on the home Civil Service. In 1855, three Commissioners were appointed and were given the task of organising (for those departments that requested it) a system of examinations for Civil Service recruits. They were to devise qualifying examinations to test the ability of potential recruits, and also competitive examinations of a limited type, whereby two or three candidates competed for one post.

A system of open competition examinations, however, did not emerge until 1870, when Gladstone introduced a system of

[1] *Recruitment to the Civil Service*, Sixth Report of the Estimates Committee Session 1964–5, H.C. 308 (1965). See also E. N. Gladden, 'The Estimates Committee Looks at the Civil Service', *Parl. Aff.* 1965–6, pp. 233–40.

open competition for all departments except the Home Office and the Foreign Office (who were particularly opposed to the principle of open competition). All the departments were unified into one 'Civil Service', and certain general rates of pay and pensions were laid down, so that today civil servants belong to an integrated service, with common conditions of employment, standards, and traditions.

Since 1870 the Civil Service has been subjected to a number of enquiries, including, in particular, the 1890 Ridley Commission,[1] the 1914 Macdonnell Commission,[2] the 1918 Gladstone Committee,[3] the 1931 Tomlin Commission,[4] and the 1968 Fulton Commission,[5] (although none of these enquiries had the significance of the Northcote–Trevelyan enquiry).[6] The Civil Service that has emerged from these several enquiries is characterised above all by its permanence, impartiality and anonymity. It is 'permanent' in the sense that it is comprised of career civil servants who, for the most part, remain within the service throughout their working lives. It is 'impartial' in the sense that a civil servant is required to be loyal to successive Governments (and to successive Ministers within the same Government). It is 'anonymous' in that it is Ministers, and not the civil servants, who are answerable to Parliament and the public for the work of their departments.

There are clear limits to each of these principles. There are some temporary civil servants, and a number of permanent civil servants spend sabbatical years in Universities or industry. In 1985 over 200 senior civil servants were seconded to the private sector. As an election approaches a civil servant's impartiality is tested as he combines service to the current Minister with preparations for policies that are likely to be introduced if there is a change of government. The names of civil servants are reported by the media more often than in the

[1] Report of the Commission on Civil Establishments.

[2] Report of the Commission on the Civil Service, Cmd. 7338 (1914).

[3] Report of the Committee on Problems of Recruitment to the Civil Service.

[4] Report of the Commission on the Civil Service, Cmd. 3909 (1931).

[5] Report of the Committee on the Civil Service, Cmd. 3638 (1968).

[6] See E. Hughes, 'Postscript to the Civil Service Reforms of 1855', *Pub. Admin.* 1955, pp. 299–306; G. K. Fry, *Statesmen in Disguise*, London 1969.

past, and civil servants appear before Parliamentary committees and are discussed in debates. Despite these qualifications, however, the central characteristics of Civil Service permanence, impartiality and anonymity remain.

Modern Structure of the Civil Service

The non-industrial Civil Service can be divided into three main groups.[1] Firstly, there are the departmental classes, like the Diplomatic Service, the Inland Revenue Officers, and the Ministry of Education Inspectorate, who are restricted to one department, and whose conditions of service are largely controlled by their own department. Secondly, there are the members of the Administration Group, who are common to most departments, and whose conditions of service are controlled by the Treasury. Thirdly, there are the specialist groups of lawyers, scientists, and medical advisers, who are recruited for their specialist qualifications, but who (unlike the departmental classes) are common to several departments.

The Administration group was formed in 1971 by the merger of the old Administrative, Executive and Clerical classes, in implementation of one of the major recommendations of the Fulton Commission. Within the Administration Group, the top six grades (the old Administrative Class) are Permanent Secretary, Deputy Secretary, Under Secretary, Assistant Secretary, Senior Principal and Principal. The holders of these posts, who number about 2,500 in all, are concerned with the formulation and administration of policy. Permanent Secretaries, Deputy Secretaries and Under Secretaries are in regular personal contact with Ministers, and the 700 or so holders of these posts make up the 'Higher Civil Service'.[2] In most years about half of the recruits to the grade of Principal and above are promoted or transferred from other

[1] For general works on the Civil Service see G. K. Fry, *The Changing Civil Service*, London 1985; Lord Crowther-Hunt and P. Kellner, *The Civil Servants*, London 1980; G. Drewry, *The Civil Service Today*, London 1984.

[2] R. A. Chapman, *The Higher Civil Service in Britain*, London 1970. See also P. Sheriff, *Career Patterns in the Higher Civil Service*, London 1976; J. S. Harris and T. V. Garcia, 'The Permanent Secretaries: Britain's Top Administrators', *PAR* 1966, pp. 31–44.

parts of the service, and the other half are recruited from University graduates with good honours degrees. In the past the bulk of graduate recruits were drawn from Oxford and Cambridge Universities, but attempts have been made to broaden the intake.

The recruitment of graduates to the Administration Group is based on a combination of written examinations and interviews, organised by the Civil Service Commission. There is an initial two days of written tests, followed (for those who qualify) by a further two days of oral and written exercises with the Civil Service Selection Board.[1] A Final Selection Board involves a further general series of interviews. The most talented of the recruits that emerge from this process are placed in a 'fast stream' of administrative trainees who are given the chance of accelerated promotion. The selection process is designed to assess the candidates' academic ability, their general intelligence and their personal qualities. The emphasis that is put on interviews is often criticised, however, as giving an advantage to recruits who have the 'correct' social background of public school and Oxbridge.

The second category of posts within the Administration Group consists of Executive Officers and the grades of Senior and Higher Executive Officers. The 70,000 or so who fill these posts are responsible for the execution of policy under the supervision of the senior grades. They are recruited partly from those who leave school at 18 with good leaving qualifications, partly (and increasingly) from graduates, and partly (about 75% in recent years) by promotion from clerical posts. There are about 200,000 clerical staff, recruited mainly from 16-year-old school leavers.

The Diplomatic Service has a separate structure and organisation from that of the Home Civil Service. It was formed in 1965 through the amalgamation of the Foreign Service, the Commonwealth Service, and the Trade Commissioner Service. This followed the 1964 report of the Plowden Committee on the overseas services, which advocated the merger of the Commonwealth and Colonial Offices, and the formation of a common Diplomatic Service for the Foreign and Common-

[1] See R. A. Chapman, *Leadership in the British Civil Service*, London 1984.

wealth Offices.[1] Members of the Diplomatic Service are employed in various types of diplomatic, consular or information work in Britain or abroad, and their numbers are supplemented by various advisers who are seconded to the Service from other departments and the armed forces.

The holders of the top posts in the Home Civil Service (Principal and above) fall very broadly into two groups – those who were recruited into the class directly from University, and those who were promoted or transferred from other grades within the Civil Service. The former group tend to have more exclusive middle-class and upper-middle-class backgrounds than the latter, and tend to be drawn disproportionately from the public schools and Oxbridge, while the promotees,[2] in the main, have an educational background of state school and provincial University.[3] The social and educational exclusiveness of the direct entrants has frequently been criticised, and with this in mind the House of Commons Expenditure Committee in 1977 called for a thorough review of the recruitment procedures.[4]

The presence of a large proportion of promotees reduces somewhat the exclusiveness of the top levels of the Service, and means that the 'Higher Civil Service' is composed of more diverse social elements, and is less academic and 'amateur', than is often imagined. It has been claimed, for example, that the social background of Assistant Secretaries and above is more akin to that of Labour Ministers than of Conservative Ministers.[5] It remains true, however, that in the very highest posts of the Home Civil Service the direct entrants are more numerous. In his historical survey of the social structure of the Higher Civil Service, R. K. Kelsall revealed that its social

[1] Report of the Committee on the Overseas Services, Cmd. 2276 (1964).

[2] Here and throughout, 'promotees' refers to those who were promoted or transferred from other classes in the service.

[3] R. K. Kelsall, *Higher Civil Servants in Britain*, London 1955. See also K. Robinson, 'Selection and the Social Background of the Administrative Class', *Pub. Admin.* 1955, pp. 383–8; and a rejoinder by R. K. Kelsall, *Pub. Admin.* 1956, pp. 169–74; P. E. Sheriff, 'Unrepresentative Bureaucracy', *Soc.* 1974, pp. 447–62.

[4] H.C. 535 (1977).

[5] Blondel, *Voters, Parties and Leaders*, p. 201.

exclusiveness declined between 1929 and 1950.[1] The percentage of Oxbridge graduates fell from 66% to 60% while the percentage who had attended local authority schools increased from 17% to 21%. A 1976 survey showed that the percentage from local authority schools had increased further to 38% but that the percentage of Oxbridge graduates had returned to the 1929 figure.[2] In 1965, the Estimates Committee enquiry into the structure of the Administrative Class also revealed that between 1957 and 1963 there was an *increase* in Administrative Class entrants drawn from boarding schools, from Oxbridge, and from families in Class I of the Registrar General's social groupings.[3] In an analysis of applicants for appointment as Administration Trainees in the 1971–5 period, the Expenditure Committee found that two-thirds of all applicants, but three-quarters of successful applicants, were from middle-class homes (that is, Classes I and II of social groupings), while a fifth of all applicants, but half of successful applicants, had Oxbridge degrees.[4] In 1985 also, Oxbridge graduates accounted for just 15% of applicants, but 64% of successful applicants, for posts as Administrative Trainees.

The Diplomatic Service has always been more socially exclusive than the Home Civil Service. In 1964 the Plowden Committee revealed that 78% of the successful applicants to the senior branch of the Foreign Service came from public schools or direct grant schools, while 95% were from Oxbridge.[5] The Plowden Committee pointed out that there was a need for entrants to the proposed Diplomatic Service to be drawn from state schools and from provincial Universities – although the Plowden Committee also advocated the payment of additional educational allowances to enable members of the Diplomatic Service to send their children to boarding schools.

[1] *Higher Civil Servants in Britain*, p. 16.
[2] P. Sheriff, *Career Patterns in the Higher Civil Service*, London 1976, p. 12.
[3] H.C. 308 (1965).
[4] H.C. 535 (1977).
[5] Cmd. 2276 (1964).

The Continuing Problems of Reform

The creation of the Administration Group in 1971 was generally welcomed.[1] The change was designed to break down some of the formal barriers within the Home Civil Service, and to permit the development of more flexible recruitment and promotion policies. It was designed also to end the tendency for the higher grades of the Executive Class and the lower grades of the Administrative Class to be involved in overlapping work. The Fulton Commission argued that the professional and scientific classes within the service should have a much better chance than they have at present of reaching the top levels of the service. At present the technical experts are to be found alongside the general administrators, but the distinction between 'administrators' and 'experts' is clearly preserved throughout the service.[2]

The 'amateur tradition' of the British Civil Service is based on the notion that administration is an art which is best learnt by experience, which needs no specifically technical qualifications, and which requires little formal post-entry training. The main requirement is that recruits should have a broad general education, a 'good mind', and the ability to examine all issues, technical or not, from the standpoint of the intelligent amateur. Thus the Permanent Secretary and other leading figures in the Departments of Trade and Industry do

[1] Report on the Fulton Commission, Cmd. 3638 (1968). See also G. K. Fry, 'Some Weaknesses in the Fulton Report on the British Home Civil Service', *PS* 1969, pp. 484–94; M. J. Fores and J. B. Heath, 'The Fulton Report: Job Evaluation and the Pay Structure', *Pub. Admin.* 1970, pp. 15–22; R. G. S. Brown, 'Fulton and Morale', *Pub. Admin.* 1971, pp. 185–96; Sir J. Dunnett, 'The Civil Service: Seven Years After Fulton', *Pub. Admin.* 1976, pp. 371–8; C. Painter, 'The Civil Service: Post-Fulton Malaise', *Pub. Admin.* 1975, pp. 427–41. See also G. K. Fry, *The Administrative Revolution in Whitehall*, London 1981; R. A. Chapman and J. R. Greenaway, *The Dynamics of Administrative Reform*, London 1980.

[2] See V. Subramaniam, 'Specialists in British and Australian Government Services: A Study in Contrast', *Pub. Admin.* 1963, pp. 357–74; Sir James Dunnett, 'The Civil Service Administrator and the Expert', *Pub. Admin.* 1961, pp. 223–38; Z. M. T. Tarkowski and A. V. Turnbull, 'Scientists versus Administrators', *Pub. Admin.* 1959, pp. 213–56; K. Gillender and R. Mair, 'Generalist Administrators and Professional Engineers', *Pub. Admin.* 1980, pp. 333–56.

not need to have training in business management; officials of the Ministry of Defence do not need to have military backgrounds; officials of the Ministry of Agriculture do not need to have experience in agriculture; the officials of the Ministry of Health do not need to have medical degrees. The theory is that specifically technical information can be supplied by the experts from outside the Civil Service who serve on advisory committees, or by the specialist classes within the Civil Service, who nevertheless remain distinct from the general administrators who occupy the highest posts in the service.

The amateur basis of the Civil Service means, however, that civil servants are often at a disadvantage in their dealings with industry at a technical level. This was perhaps illustrated by some of the early negotiations that took place between civil servants and representatives of the oil firms over the question of the taxation of profits from the development of North Sea oil fields. Thus it is often argued that the amateur tradition is out of date in face of the technical needs of the modern state. It is claimed that there should be more recruitment for specific technical qualifications rather than for general ability; that there should be more post-entry training for all civil servants; and that (as the Fulton Commission proposed) there should be greater opportunities for members of the specialist classes to reach the top administrative posts. It is also argued that there should be an increase in the number of specialists who are brought into the Civil Service on a temporary basis from the Universities, industry, and the public corporations, and that there should be more secondment of civil servants to industry.[1]

As there is no equivalent in Britain to the French École Nationale d'Administration, which gives a broad pre-entry training to recruits to the French Civil Service,[2] it is perhaps all the more necessary to recruit more graduates for their

[1]See P. Sheriff, 'Outsiders in a Closed Career: the Example of the British Civil Service', *Pub. Admin.* 1972, pp. 397–418.

[2]See A. Stevens, 'The Role of the Ecole Nationale d'Administration', *Pub. Admin.* 1978, pp. 283–96. See also W. A. Robson, *The Civil Service in Britain and France*, London 1956; E. Strauss, *The Ruling Servants: Bureaucracy in Russia, France and Britain*, London 1961; C. H. Sisson, *The Spirit of Public Administration and some European Comparisons*, London 1966.

specific qualifications rather than for their general abilities as revealed in academic achievements in Arts subjects. In 1964 the Plowden Committee emphasised the importance of the commercial work of the overseas departments.[1] The committee urged the recruitment of more people competent in languages and technical subjects, and called for the recruitment of more science graduates. In 1977 the Expenditure Committee pointed out (and deplored the fact) that between 1971 and 1975, of those applying for posts as Administration Trainees, 43% of all applicants and 57% of successful applicants had Arts degrees.[2]

Various forms of post-entry training exist within the service. Members of the Inland Revenue Department, for example, have to learn taxation principles after entry, while all entrants to the Civil Service undergo a short post-entry induction course. A system of day-release classes exists for the clerical grades. On the recommendations of the Assheton Committee[3] in 1944 a Director of Training and Education was appointed at the Treasury, and Training Officers were set up in some departments. Only in the last twenty years, however, has a comprehensive programme of post-entry training been developed. In 1963 the Treasury Centre for Administrative Studies was set up to provide courses for entrants to the Administrative Class. Although the Plowden Committee rejected the idea of a Diplomatic Service Staff College, it recommended that there should be more training in languages for members of the Diplomatic Service.[4] Then, in 1968, Fulton advocated the creation of a Civil Service College to develop a wide range of post-entry training schemes, and this was implemented in 1970. The College absorbed the functions of the Centre for Administrative Studies and initiated a variety of other training courses in administration, management, and vocational subjects at various levels.

With regard to the problems of recruitment policy and of

[1] Cmd. 2276 (1964).

[2] H.C. 535 (1977).

[3] Report of the Committee on the Training of Civil Servants, Cmd. 6525 (1944). See also D. Hubback, 'The Treasury's Role in Civil Service Training', *Pub. Admin.* 1957, pp. 99–110.

[4] Cmd. 2276 (1964).

post-entry training of new recruits, however, it must be emphasised that just as the majority of the present Permanent Secretaries, Deputy Secretaries, and Under Secretaries were recruited just after the last war, any immediate changes that are made in recruiting policy and post-entry training will not affect the composition of the top ranks of the Civil Service until today's recruits reach these levels in twenty or more years' time.

Management of the Service

Each department is responsible for its own internal organisation, and the departmental Minister is the 'primary' employer for each department, performing this function on behalf of the Crown. There are Establishment and Finance Officers in each department, and they and the Training Officers, who are attached to most departments, help to achieve uniformity throughout the service. Before the creation of the Civil Service Department in 1968, general control of the Civil Service was exercised by the Treasury.[1] The Joint Permanent Secretary to the Treasury was head of the Civil Service, and was chief adviser to the Prime Minister on Civil Service matters. Technically, the Treasury's authority was based on an Order in Council of 1956 (which replaced an Order in Council of 1920), but in practical terms the Treasury's power was based on its financial role within the machinery of government. The Treasury's role was thus somewhat delicate, forming the employer's side of the National Whitley Council negotiating machinery for conditions of service. As well as this, the Treasury controlled the size and structure of the service, determining the total numbers to be employed, and their distribution throughout the departments. In recruitment matters, however, responsibility lay with six Civil Service Commissioners who controlled the arrangements for the recruitment to all grades, and who allocated new entrants to the departments.[2]

[1] See J. Garnett, *Managing the Civil Service*, London 1981; Lord Bridges, *The Treasury*, London 1964.

[2] Sir George Mallaby, 'The Civil Service Commission: Its Place in the Machinery of Government', *Pub. Admin.* 1964, pp. 1–10.

In 1968, the Fulton Commission proposed that a special Civil Service Department be created to take over the management and recruitment functions from the Treasury and the Civil Service Commissioners. The Government accepted the recommendation, and the new department was created with the Prime Minister as its head.[1] The initial task of the department was to create the Civil Service College, and review and implement the other recommendations of the Fulton Commission.

In the 1970s, however, there were renewed calls for tighter financial control over the Civil Service and for a return to Treasury control to achieve this. The House of Commons Expenditure Committee in 1978 criticised the Fulton Commission's findings and argued for the re-establishment of Treasury control over manpower. The new Conservative Government in 1979 was anxious to reduce public expenditure and saw Treasury control as a means to this end. It was difficult, it was argued, for the Treasury to control public expenditure as a whole while the Civil Service Department was responsible for Civil Service manpower and expenditure. Accordingly, in 1981 the Civil Service Department was abolished and its functions were divided between the Treasury, the Cabinet Office and a new Management and Personnel Office attached to the Cabinet Office. The Treasury acquired responsibility for Civil Service numbers, pay and conditions of service; the Cabinet Office assumed control over the machinery of government; the Management and Personnel Office was given responsibility for Civil Service recruitment and training and for general management of the service. The Cabinet Secretary became Head of the Civil Service.

For clerical and executive officers, departmental promotion procedure is based on interview boards and on annual reports that are made about each member of the service. For the posts of Principal and Assistant Secretary, promotions are made by the departmental Minister on the advice of his Permanent Secretary. Promotion to the rank of Permanent Secretary is made by the Prime Minister, advised by the Senior Appoint-

[1]See R. A. Chapman, 'The Rise and Fall of the CSD', *PP* 1983, pp. 41–62; C. Pollitt, 'The CSD: A Normal Death?', *Pub. Admin.* 1982, pp. 73–6.

ments Selection Committee. This body is composed of a small group of Permanent Secretaries, chaired by the Cabinet Secretary. The power to appoint Permanent Secretaries can be a vital aspect of Prime Ministerial influence over the Civil Service. In Mrs Thatcher's first few years in office, an unusually large number of Permanent Secretaries reached retirement age, so that by 1986 she had appointed the vast majority of Permanent Secretaries then in post.

Pay and conditions of service are determined by National and Departmental Whitley Councils, which consist of representatives of the Treasury and the Permanent Secretary of the departments on the official side, and representatives of the various Civil Service unions on the Trade Union side.[1] About 80% of civil servants belong to Trade Unions. The Association of First Division Civil Servants is the main body for senior grades, while the Society of Civil and Public Servants and the Civil and Public Services Association represent most of the executive and clerical grades. Other more specialised bodies are the Inland Revenue Staff Federation and the Institute of Professional Civil Servants. Union activity is coordinated by the Council of Civil Service Unions. Pay negotiations can be assisted by the Civil Service Arbitration Tribunal. Following the recommendations of the Priestly Commission on Civil Service salaries, the Civil Service Pay Research Unit was created to examine the salary situation in similar occupations outside the service, so as to achieve the principle of comparability. In 1980, however, the principle of comparability was abandoned, and the Pay Research Unit abolished, on the grounds that comparison between the public and private sectors was inappropriate.

With regard to the pay and conditions within the Civil Service, the general impression remains of lower salaries than in private industry, but of regular increments, assured promotion to certain levels, security of tenure, good pension schemes, and (at least in the lower grades) fairly good hours of work and generous holidays. The hours of work, however, is one sphere in which Civil Service conditions have deterior-

[1] See J. Gretton and A. Harrison, *How Much Are Public Servants Worth?*, London 1982.

ated, in that for most of the nineteenth century a five- or six-hour day was normal, and even up to 1939, most lower-grade civil servants enjoyed a short working day.

The political activities of civil servants are formally restricted. The Trade Disputes Act 1927 forbade strike action by Civil Service Unions, and although this Act was repealed in 1946, the tradition persisted.[1] Civil Service Union militancy increased in the 1970s, however, and in 1973 the first Civil Service strike action occurred in the form of a one-day stoppage by clerical and executive officers. This was followed by a series of strikes between 1979 and 1982 (including a prolonged strike in 1981), and one consequence was that membership of trade unions was banned at the Government's communications headquarters at Cheltenham. The 1949 Masterman Committee of enquiry into the political activities of civil servants produced certain guiding principles, which were accepted in modified form. The principles that apply today are, firstly, that there are no restrictions on industrial civil servants, or non-industrial civil servants in the minor grades; secondly, the clerical grades are free to indulge in political activity short of Parliamentary candidature; and thirdly, the executive officers and above are free to belong to a political party, but should not indulge in any activity beyond this. These principles form part of the Civil Service 'code of behaviour', and civil servants have thus to resign their posts if they wish to pursue a Parliamentary career.

* * *

The 'image' of the Civil Service is often presented as one of slowness and caution, contrasted with the enterprise and slickness of private industry.[2] The popular picture of the Higher Civil Servant is that of an aloof and reticent, but extremely authoritative and influential figure at the centre of power, while of the lower levels of the service the impression is

[1] See M. P. Kelly, *White Collar Proletariat*, London 1980; G. Drewry, 'The GCHQ Case – A Failure of Government Communications', *Parl. Aff.* 1985, pp. 371–86.

[2] N. Nagler, 'The Image of the Civil Service in Britain', *Pub. Admin.* 1979, pp. 127–42.

often that of slow and uninspired handling of routine tasks. At the same time, it is probably true to say that in Britain the public attitude towards the Civil Service is more favourable than in most countries. Civil servants in Britain are generally regarded as honest and conscientious, and the British Civil Service is not equated with corruption and the misuse of power in the way that are many bureaucrats elsewhere. To a considerable extent, caution and formalism do characterise Civil Service activities, largely because the principle of public accountability means that minor Civil Service actions can be the subject of Parliamentary scrutiny.[1] Undoubtedly the Civil Service as a whole tends to be slow in changing its methods of work. The popular concept of the Civil Service contains basic inconsistencies, however, in that the picture of Civil Service caution is hardly compatible with the equally common notion of civil servants 'running the country' while Ministers merely look on.

Changes introduced by the Conservative Government since 1979 have sought to increase the overall efficiency of the Civil Service. The Civil Service Department and the Central Policy Review Staff were abolished and Treasury control over Civil Service manpower increased. The Efficiency Unit and the system of Management Information for Ministers were introduced in an effort to make the departments more cost-effective. Civil Service numbers have been reduced by about a fifth since 1979 and the principle of comparability between Civil Service and private sector pay scales has been attacked. The reformed Select Committee system has provided the House of Commons with a more effective means of scrutinising individual departments.

These developments have had a significant impact on the Civil Service. The question remains, however, of how much power civil servants wield, and where the 'balance of influence' lies between civil servants and their Ministers. This can be looked at from the point of view of the general

[1] W. Hampton, 'Parliament and the Civil Service', *Parl. Aff.* 1963–4, pp. 430–8; E. N. Gladden, 'Parliament and the Civil Service', *Parl. Aff.* 1956–7, pp. 165–79; S. E. Finer, 'Princes, Parliaments and the Public Service', *Parl. Aff.* 1980, pp. 353–72.

relationship between Ministers and civil servants in the policy-making process, and also in relation to the question of the powers of the executive through delegated legislation and administrative adjudication.

The Balance of Influence

The permanent officials who are in touch with the details of their departments' work must be closely involved in the formulation of policy, but the principles of public accountability demand that the responsibility should lie with the Ministers.[1] One solution to the problem is to have a popularly elected or a politically nominated Civil Service. Thus in Britain in the pre-Northcote and Trevelyan era, most civil servants were appointed through a system of patronage, and in the USA today most of the top national and local administrators are political appointees, with a Republican President tending to surround himself with Republican civil servants who vacate their posts if a Democratic President is elected.

The British Civil Service is permanent, in the sense that civil servants remain in power despite changes of Government. The electoral defeat of a Government, and the emergence of a new set of Ministers, does not lead to wholesale changes in the Civil Service. The principle behind a permanent and neutral Civil Service is that it is possible for independent and impartial (in the sense of non-partisan) administrators to serve Governments of differing political complexions. It is claimed that the British experience proves this, and that this system allows the development of continuity in policy, and prevents the nepotism that is often associated with a politically nominated administration. It is often argued, however, that today the role of top civil servants is so

[1] See B. Sedgemore, *The Secret Constitution*, London 1980; L. Blair, 'The Civil Servant: Political Reality and Legal Myth', *PL* 1958, pp. 32–49; Sir Charles Cunningham, 'Policy and Practice', *Pub. Admin.* 1963, pp. 229–38; M. R. Gordon, 'Civil Servants, Politicians and Parties', *Comp. Pol.* 1971–2, pp. 29–58; D. Allen, 'Ministers and Their Mandarins', *G and O* 1977, pp. 135–49; M. Wright, 'Ministers and Civil Servants: Relations and Responsibilities', *Parl. Aff.* 1976–7, pp. 293–313; Lord Crowther-Hunt, 'Mandarins and Ministers', *PQ* 1980, pp. 373–99.

significant, and their involvement in the policy-making process is so great, that the tradition of a truly independent and non-partisan Civil Service (at least at the very top of the administrative structure) is almost impossible to achieve. Between the wars, many Socialists argued that the Civil Service was essentially conservative (if not Conservative with a capital 'C'), and that a 'Socialist' Government would meet with obstruction from the Civil Service.[1] Today many who argue that the Labour Governments have not been truly 'Socialist' Governments still claim that a Government with a red-blooded Socialist programme would need to have a different Civil Service to carry through this programme.

The theoretical 'distribution of power' between Ministers and their civil servants is that the Ministers make the policy decisions, and these decisions are then executed by the Civil Service, but undoubtedly the reality of the situation is very far from this theoretical concept. Inevitably, civil servants are bound up to a considerable extent in the policy-making process. Because of the very extent of Governmental activities today as compared with the pre-1914 period, and because of the technical nature of much of the work of modern government, it is clear that considerable initiative in policy making now rests with civil servants, particularly the Permanent Secretaries, and the Deputy and Under Secretaries.

Ministers are frequently moved from department to department, and they cannot hope to obtain a detailed knowledge of the workings of their departments. Each department has an on-going 'point of view' on matters within its sphere, and this persists regardless of the Minister or the party in power. Most Ministers are also members of the Commons, and they have Parliamentary and constituency duties as well as Ministerial responsibilities. In this respect Ministers who are drawn from the House of Lords have an advantage. Although a Permanent Secretary may try to keep a Minister informed of the most important aspects of the department's activities, there must inevitably be many matters that escape him, and many decisions that are made in the lower levels of

[1]See in particular Harold Laski, *Parliamentary Government in England*, London 1938.

the departmental structure can be much more significant than is at first realised. Much legislation is described as 'Civil Service legislation', in that it is concerned with minor technical and administrative matters, or, as with Consolidation Bills, is concerned with gathering existing legislation into one composite statute. Perhaps as much as three-quarters of all Bills emerge from Whitehall rather than from the party manifesto. Civil Service initiative with such legislation is considerable, while (as is revealed below) civil servants have considerable initiative with regard to delegated legislation.

At a more significant level, civil servants are sometimes accused of misusing their wide discretionary powers. In a submission to the Fulton Committee in 1966, the NEC of the Labour Party attacked the Civil Service for excessive secrecy in its activities, and for withholding information from Ministers in efforts to persuade them to adopt particular policies.[1] In 1977 the Expenditure Committee argued that civil servants frequently sought to undermine their Minister's intentions by tactics of delay and obstruction, by seeking support from civil servants and Ministers in other departments, and by persistently advocating alternatives that the Minister had rejected.[2]

Despite all of these considerations, however, it is necessary to avoid the conclusion that civil servants make all the important decisions, and that Ministers are thereby merely observers. It has often been pointed out that politicians struggle long and hard to attain Ministerial rank, and that they are thus unlikely to be prepared to surrender initiative to the Civil Service when they do gain office. Similarly, a stock-in-trade of politicians has to be the ability to influence people, and this will be a considerable advantage to a Minister in his dealings with the Civil Service. Most Ministerial contact with his department is through the Permanent Secretary. Some Ministers even choose to deal solely with the Permanent Secretary (using him as a funnel for all departmental attitudes), and a

[1] *The Times*, 2.1.67. See J. B. Christoph, 'Administrative Secrecy in Britain', *PAR* 1975, pp. 23–31. See also R. Pyner, 'Sarah Tisdall, Ian Willmore and the Civil Servant's "Right to Leak"', *PQ* 1985, pp. 72–81.

[2] See H.C. 535 (1977). See also Brian Chapman, *British Government Observed*, London 1963. For a defence of the Civil Service see D. N. Chester's review of Chapman's book in *Pub. Admin.* 1963, p. 375.

strong Minister can presumably impose his will on the Permanent Secretary to a considerable degree. The fact that policy decisions have to be acceptable to the Cabinet, the Treasury, the Party, and Parliament, means that the Minister, through his contact with these bodies, retains the last word on all policy decisions. It can be argued that the real limitation on a Minister's power is not the Civil Service, but is the pressure groups, advisory committees, and technical experts outside the Government machine, on whom Ministers and civil servants rely for technical information.[1]

It is extremely difficult, however, to come to any clear conclusion as to how much influence lies with the Civil Service, and where the precise division is to be found between the power of Ministers and that of civil servants.[2] To a considerable extent it must vary from situation to situation. There must be variations from department to department, and from one Minister to another, with some Ministers clearly being stronger than others, and more capable of dominating their departments. It has been said that a Minister will be able to get his way in the department if he is clear in his own mind precisely what he wishes to achieve. A Government that newly comes to power generally has a number of predetermined policies that it wishes to implement, while a Government that has been in power for a long time is probably more inclined to be conditioned into accepting 'the departmental point of view'. At the same time, there is a clear distinction between major policies which are often incorporated in the party programme, and which will be the concern of the Minister, and lesser issues which can be handled by an Under Secretary or Assistant Secretary, and which will only be referred to the Minister if they acquire sudden significance, perhaps through a Parliamentary question. All of these considerations are clearly variables, and make difficult the application of any final and definite rule on this question.

One proposal that has been made for increasing the power of the Minister within his department is that the Minister should have his own private team of advisers drawn from

[1] For details see Political and Economic Planning, *Advisory Committees in British Government*, London 1960.

[2] See *Pub. Admin.* 1965, pp. 251–87, for further discussions on this theme.

outside the Civil Service. Normally, each Minister has his Private Office, consisting of a Private Secretary (generally a Principal or Assistant Secretary) and a few personal assistants within the department. In 1970 Edward Heath extended this principle by introducing businessmen into the Civil Service Department. In the Wilson and Callaghan Governments of 1974–9 more extensive use was made of temporary special advisers, with roughly half of the departments having one or two of them at one time or another. Recruited largely from Transport House and the Universities, their role was to act as a link between the Minister and the party, provide a specifically partisan comment on departmental policies, alert the Minister to important developments in other departments, and generally act as the Minister's confidant within the department. In 1979 Mrs Thatcher announced that the Conservative government would use special advisers, but that they would be paid for by the party rather than out of public funds as had been the case in the 1974–9 period.[1] Conservative Ministers have made use of a smaller number of special advisers than their Labour predecessors. In 1986 there were about twenty advisers, on five-year contracts, distributed among the departments. Mrs Thatcher's own Policy Unit at 10 Downing Street is rather smaller than was James Callaghan's, but has probably been more influential. It has been suggested that each Minister should have a team of ten to twenty special advisers, filling posts even up to the rank of Permanent Secretary, but no Labour or Conservative Prime Minister has yet seen fit to implement this.

The Problem of Delegated Legislation

Another and more specific aspect of the authority of the Civil Service is involved in the question of the delegation by Parliament of direct legislative authority to the executive. Many Acts of Parliament merely lay down the broad outline of

[1] G. Chowdharay-Best, 'A Note on the Temporary Civil Servant', *Pub. Admin.* 1976, pp. 333–40; R. Klein and J. Lewis, 'Advice and Dissent', *PP* 1977–8, pp. 1–26; J. E. Mitchell, 'Special Advisers: a Personal View', *Pub. Admin.* 1978, pp. 87–98; P. Neville-Jones, 'The Continental Cabinet System', *PQ* 1983, pp. 232–42.

proposed changes, and include a clause which delegates to the Minister the power to work out the details of the provisions – a process which has been well defined as 'the statutory practice whereby the Parliament empowers the executive (generally a Minister or the Queen in Council) to make rules and regulations'.[1] The main purposes for which powers are delegated by Parliament in this way are to allow the amendment of existing legislation in order to bring it up to date; to create machinery to administer the Act; or, most generally, to allow the departments to decide details within the framework of legislation that consists only of broad principles. Often quite wide powers are delegated. The Transport Act 1985 allows parts of the Act to be repealed by delegated legislation, while the Education (Scotland) Act 1980 allows the Minister to make such 'incidental, supplementary and consequential provisions' as he feels to be necessary. Delegation often also involves subdelegation, whereby the Minister is empowered to delegate powers to his departmental officials, subject to his confirmation, and two or three tiers of delegation can be involved in the granting of delegated powers.

The justification of the practice is three-fold. In the first place, it is a speedy process which avoids the delay that is frequently involved in the consideration of legislative proposals in Parliament. Secondly, it is a flexible process which allows regular revision of legislation without involving constant Parliamentary approval of this revision. Thirdly, in many instances Parliament is not competent to deal with aspects of highly technical legislation, and the detail of such legislation is best worked out by the Ministers and the departments, once Parliament has approved the principles. The delegation of legislative authority to the executive is a means of combating the limitations of the Parliamentary legislative process.

The growth of the practice of delegated legislation is largely a twentieth-century phenomenon.[2] It has developed in the main from the increase in the scope of government activities

[1] J. A. G. Griffith and H. Street, *Principles of Administrative Law*, London 1967, p. 4.

[2] See J. Eaves, *Parliament and the Executive in Great Britain*, London 1957, for a survey of this development.

with the development of the Welfare State after 1906, and more particularly since 1945, with the extension of government activities into more and more social, economic, and industrial spheres. These developments have meant that Parliament has not had the time, and has not been technically competent, to deal with many of the details of the consequent legislation. This was particularly the case during and immediately after the two world wars, and the Defence of the Realm Act 1914, and the Emergency Powers Acts of 1939 and 1940, empowered the Government to make such regulations as were necessary to meet the wartime emergencies. Many of the regulations introduced during the second world war were retained for a while after 1945, and wide powers were granted to the Government by the Emergency Laws Act and the Supplies and Services Act of 1945. The extension of state activity through the nationalisation and social welfare schemes of post-war Governments involved further big increases in delegated legislation. More recent extensions of government responsibilities in the social and economic spheres, together with British membership of the European Community, have led to further increases in delegated legislation.

Criticisms of the whole principle of delegated legislation are sometimes made, and it is condemned as a practice that offends the principle that legislation should be made in Parliament. It is argued (perhaps somewhat unrealistically) that Parliamentary procedure should be reformed so as to make unnecessary the delegation of legislative powers. More generally, however, critics acknowledge that delegated legislation is necessary, but claim that the methods of Parliamentary supervision of the process are inadequate. Concern over the problem was most acute during the 1920s and 1930s. In 1929 in *The New Despotism*[1] Lord Hewart claimed that the Old Despotism of *Royal* domination of Parliament had been replaced by the New Despotism of *executive* domination of Parliament, which was proving to be just as big a threat to Parliament's authority and to public liberties, with Parliament being used as a cloak for executive despotism. Similarly,

[1] London 1929.

W. A. Robson in *Justice and Administrative Law*,[1] stressed the Constitutional problems involved in these developments. Much of the concern was not over the question of the delegation of powers to the Minister, but was over the sub-delegation of these powers to civil servants. The disquiet that was aroused led to the appointment of the Donoughmore Committee to enquire into the question of delegated legislation. The Committee reported in 1932,[2] and declared that the growth of delegated powers was necessary and was not getting out of hand. This assuaged public disquiet somewhat, and during the wartime emergency the public was prepared to accept the delegation of wide legislative powers to the executive.

In 1946, however, the Select Committee on Procedure,[3] which had been set up as part of the post-war enquiry into the machinery of government, criticised the existing machinery for Parliamentary scrutiny (which was based on the Rules Publication Act 1893), and in 1952 the Select Committee on Delegated Legislation made a more detailed analysis of the problem. The main criticisms that emerged from these post-war enquiries were that the executive was assuming the legislative role of Parliament to an unacceptable extent, and that many of the powers that were delegated to Ministers were too loosely defined. It was widely argued that there should be closer Parliamentary scrutiny of delegated powers; that there should be more consultation with affected parties; that there should be definite limits on the powers that were delegated; and that fuller publicity should be given to the power that was delegated to the executive.[4]

While recently concern over the question of delegated legislation has been less marked (partly because the system of Parliamentary supervision of delegated powers has worked more smoothly than in the 1950s) membership of the Euro-

[1] London 1930. See also Sir C. K. Allen, *Bureaucracy Triumphant*, London 1931; Sir C. Carr, *Delegated Legislation*, London 1921.

[2] Cmd. 4060 (1932). A. B. Keith, *The Constitution Under Strain*, London 1942; D. G. T. Williams, 'The Donoughmore Report in Retrospect', *Pub. Admin.* 1982, pp. 273–92.

[3] Report of the Select Committee on Procedure, H.C. 181 of 1945–6.

[4] See C. Hollis, *Can Parliament Survive?*, London 1949; G. W. Keeton, *The Passing of Parliament*, London 1952.

pean Community has meant that the amount of delegated legislation has increased considerably. The European Communities Act 1972 allows the executive to implement any of Britain's European Community obligations by means of Statutory Instruments. A vast number of directives and regulations emerge from the European Commission and Council of Ministers each year, and while some are implemented by Act of Parliament, or simply by administrative action, most are implemented by Statutory Instruments. The House of Commons Procedure Committee in 1978 recognised the necessity for a balance between the Government's need to exercise legislative authority and the desirability of Parliamentary scrutiny. The Committee was critical, however, of the established process of Parliamentary examination.

The Control of Delegated Powers[1]

Safeguards against the dangers inherent in delegated legislation are to be found in various forms. Some safeguards are provided by the process of consultation that takes place with affected parties before a Bill is introduced into Parliament.[2] Thus some of those who are to be affected by delegated powers are able to comment upon, and perhaps influence the contents of, the parent statute. At the other end of the process, once the powers are in operation, judicial safeguards exist to ensure that any powers that have been delegated have not been exceeded. The Courts can be used to question whether executive actions have a legal authority, based either on prerogative powers, or on legislative or delegated legislative authority. In the case of delegated powers, the Courts can check that executive actions have not exceeded the powers granted by the parent statute, and that the correct procedures of consultation and adequate publicity have been observed. Within this judi-

[1] For general surveys see Griffith and Street, *Principles of Administrative Law*; J. F. Garner and B. L. Jones, *Administrative Law*, London 1985; H. W. R. Wade, *Administrative Law*, London 1961; P. P. Craig, *Administrative Law*, London 1983; N. Hawke, *An Introduction to Administrative Law*, London 1984. See also F. A. R. Berrion, *Statutory Interpretation*, London 1984.

[2] J. F. Garner, 'Consultation in Subordinate Legislation', *PL* 1964, pp. 105–24.

cial control, however, a great limitation has always been that some delegated powers are so wide as to justify almost any action by the executive.

Thus Parliamentary scrutiny of the actual granting of delegated powers remains as the most important safeguard. The existing means of Parliamentary scrutiny are based primarily on the Statutory Instruments Act 1946.[1] The Act clarified and modified the existing methods of control rather than introduced new principles. The term 'Statutory Instrument' was used to describe the documents that grant delegated powers (replacing the multiplicity of Rules and Orders that had existed before), and the Select Committee that had been set up in 1944 to scrutinise the process of delegated legislation, was put on a permanent basis as the Statutory Instruments Committee. Today the methods of Parliamentary supervision rest partly on the activities of Select and Standing Committees, and partly on the initiative of individual MPs, who are often prompted in this by pressure groups.[2]

All Statutory Instruments are published by HMSO and are placed on general sale to the public. They are formally presented to Parliament, with copies being sent to the Speaker of the Commons and the Lord Chancellor, and to all MPs who ask for them. The MP can then take action under the procedures allowed (with the parent statute determining which procedure will be used). One procedure which allows for little more than the publicising of the process, is that the Statutory Instrument comes into effect after being laid before Parliament. The two most frequently used procedures, however, require that while the Instrument comes into operation as soon as it is presented to Parliament, it has then to be approved by an affirmative resolution within a specified period, or can be annulled by a resolution of either House

[1] J. T. Craig, 'The Working of the Statutory Instruments Act 1946', *Pub. Admin.* 1961, pp. 181–92.

[2] See A. Beith, 'Prayers Un-answered', *Parl. Aff.* 1981, pp. 165–73; J. E. Kersell, 'Parliamentary Ventilation of Grievances Arising out of Delegated Legislation', *PL* 1959, pp. 152–68; E. H. Beet, 'Parliament and Delegated Legislation, 1945–53'; *'Pub. Admin.* 1955, pp. 325–32; P. Byrne, 'Parliamentary Control of Delegated Legislation', *Parl. Aff.* 1975–6, pp. 366–77; J. E. Kersell, *Parliamentary Supervision of Delegated Legislation*, London 1960.

within forty days. Under these procedures the Instrument has to be approved or annulled as a whole, and cannot be amended.

Prayers for Annulment can be taken on any day at the close of normal business. Although the Prayers are invariably defeated by the imposition of the Government Whip, the procedure provides a means of publicising the Statutory Instrument. While the procedures of the Parliament Acts 1911 and 1949, for overcoming the veto of the House of Lords, do not apply to Statutory Instruments, only rarely does the Lords reject Instruments.[1] In 1968, however, it did reject a controversial order dealing with the economic sanctions against Rhodesia.

In addition to this form of scrutiny by individual MPs, supervision of delegated legislation is achieved through Select and Standing Committees. A Select Committee was established in 1944 to examine the form and legality of all Statutory Instruments. It was replaced in 1973 by a Joint Committee of Lords and Commons to overcome the duplication of work by the two Houses. The Committee has seven members from each House and is chaired by an Opposition MP. The seven members from the Commons also meet separately to scrutinise such Instruments as are laid only before the Commons. The Joint Committee has the services of Parliamentary counsel and can require Ministers and civil servants to attend its hearings. It considers about half of the two thousand Instruments that are introduced in most sessions. A limitation on its effectiveness is that it deals with the form of the Instruments rather than the policy behind them. Also, it brings its findings to the attention of the House but cannot enforce them. Statutory Instruments that are subject to the affirmative and negative procedures referred to above can be passed for special examination to one of six Standing Committees on Statutory Instruments. The Standing Committee enquiries are made into the merits as well as the form of the Instruments, but generally only about 5% of Instruments are examined in this way.

A Statutory Instrument can be brought to the attention of

[1] J. E. Kersell, 'Upper Chamber Scrutiny of Delegated Legislation', *PL* 1959, pp. 46–60.

Parliament on any nine counts – including if it imposes a charge; if it cannot be challenged in the Courts; if it has a retrospective effect; if it involves an unjustifiable delay in its publication; or if it contains obscurities in form. While Parliament's ability to scrutinise Statutory Instruments in the Select and Standing Committees has increased in recent years, the sheer volume of delegated legislation, the inability of Parliament to amend (as opposed to approve or reject) an Instrument and the lack of time on the floor of the House to follow-up scrutiny by the Committees, mean that Parliamentary control over delegated legislation remains limited.

The Problem of Administrative Adjudication

Linked with the question of delegated legislation is that of administrative adjudication, whereby machinery is created, generally in the form of a tribunal, to determine cases of alleged misuse or non-use of executive powers.[1] Disputes between an individual and the state sometimes can be settled by political action through an MP, by judicial action through the Courts, or (where the machinery exists) by action through a tribunal that has been specially created. This last practice has been defined as 'the statutory power of the Administration to decide issues arising between individuals and the Administration, or occasionally, between two parts of the Administration itself',[2] The main feature of the process is that the department itself, or, more particularly, the machinery that it creates, is the judge of its own case in instances of alleged maladministration.[3]

Very often the factors that make it desirable to delegate legislative authority from Parliament (the need for speed, and the technical nature of the issue) also make it necessary to create administrative adjudication machinery to consider

[1]See F. F. Ridley, 'The Citizen Against Authority', *Parl. Aff.* 1984, pp. 1–32.

[2]Griffith and Street, *Principles of Administrative Law*, p. 4.

[3]For general surveys, see H. W. R. Wade, *Towards Administrative Justice*, Ann Arbor, 1963; H. J. Elcock, *Administrative Justice*, London 1969; K. Wheare, *Maladministration and its Remedies*, London 1973; P. Birkinshaw, *Grievances, Remedies and the State*, London 1985.

aspects of the administration (or maladministration) of the matter concerned. Public concern over the question of administrative law has thus been closely linked with concern over delegated legislation, and between the wars the writings of Lord Hewart and W. A. Robson, and the enquiry by the Donoughmore Committee, were concerned with administrative law as well as delegated legislation. Similarly, since 1945 the problem has been emphasised by the increase in governmental activity, with the consequent need for speedy means of assessing claims for social benefits, or for judging appeals for compensation in cases of compulsory purchase.

One justification of the use of administrative tribunals as a means of redress is that without tribunals the Law Courts would be grossly overworked, but tribunals have advantages over the Courts for citizen and state alike. Tribunals are cheap, speedy, less hidebound by formalised legal rules, accessible to the public, and are composed of experts in the matter to be dealt with. Also, any constitutional theory of the rigid separation of judicial and executive powers is irrelevant to the British system, in that there is nothing novel in the notion of the executive assuming judicial powers. Even without the tribunal system, the overlap between the executive and judiciary in Britain is quite considerable: judges are appointed on the advice of the Lord Chancellor and the Prime Minister, while the Lord Chancellor, the Attorney-General, and the other law officers are members of the Government as well as being judicial figures. It is also argued (rather idealistically) that ultimately the best control over Ministers, departments, and tribunals, is a political and Parliamentary one, and that within this general safeguard the departments can be trusted not to abuse the tribunal system.

The objections in principle to the system of administrative tribunals, however, are based partly on opposition to the increase in executive authority and the range of executive influence, and partly on the argument that no matter how fair the system may be, it *seems* to be unjust, in that it offends the general principle that no party should judge a case in which it is itself involved. Tribunals are thus objected to on the grounds that justice must not only be done, but must be seen to be done. Nevertheless, even when the need for administrative tribunals is accepted in principle, the practical operation of the existing system is often criticised as not fully achieving the three principles of 'openness, fairness, and impartiality', which are seen as being essential to the satisfactory operation of the system. Proposals to introduce more uniformity and informality into the rules of operation of the various tribunals are often resisted, however, as being likely to destroy many of their basic advantages of speed, cheapness, and informality. Thus the difficulty is that of balancing administrative effectiveness with judicial fairness, it being impossible to achieve maximum effectiveness and maximum fairness at the same time.

* * *

Concern over the problem of administrative tribunals reached a head in the mid-1950s, following the Crichel Down episode.[1] Crichel Down was an area of land in Dorset that had been requisitioned by the Air Ministry in 1940 as a bombing range. It was agreed when the land was acquired that the previous owner was to have the chance of taking over the land when the Air Ministry released it. After the war, however, when the Air Ministry no longer had use for the land, it was offered to various other departments, and the Ministry of Agriculture decided to take it over and develop it for agricultural purposes. The original owner claimed the land, but the Ministry of Agriculture ignored the original undertaking and would not relinquish its claim. The Minister of Agriculture, Sir Thomas Dugdale, eventually agreed to a public enquiry, and when the report of the enquiry was published in 1954,[2] the Minister resigned. The incident aroused much concern, because it was revealed by the report that there had been a lack of contact between the Minister and his department. It was not clear to what extent the Minister had been informed on the matter, and it was thus quoted as an example of the

[1] See K. C. Wheare, 'Crichel Down Revisited', *PS* 1975, pp. 268–86. See also H. W. R. Wade, 'Are Public Inquiries a Farce?', *Pub. Admin.* 1955, pp. 389–94; R. M. Jackson, 'Tribunals and Inquiries', *Pub. Admin.* 1955, pp. 115–24; G. Marshall, 'The Courts, Ministers and the Parliamentary Process', *Pub. Admin.* 1956, pp. 51–60.

[2] Cmd. 9176 (1954).

increased powers of the executive. It was only because of the eventual initiative of the Minister that an enquiry had been held, and the incident revealed the lack of safeguards that there were for the citizen against the administrative machine.

As a result of the public concern, a committee was set up in 1955, under the chairmanship of Sir Oliver Franks, to look into the question of administrative adjudication. The Committee reported in 1957,[1] and most of its proposals were implemented in the Tribunals and Inquiries Act 1958 (subsequently consolidated in the Tribunals and Inquiries Act 1971). The bulk of the Committee's proposals were accepted in full by the Government, and most of the others were accepted in a modified form. It was thus praised as a useful report that led to practical achievement, though its critics maintained that it did not tackle the heart of the problem.[2]

It is debatable to what extent the existing system of tribunals (which is based partly on gradual developments over several years, and partly on machinery created by the 1958 and 1971 Acts) achieves a satisfactory balance between the two factors of administrative efficiency and judicial fairness. There are a multiplicity of tribunals, most of them products of social welfare and state planning legislation. The list includes Industrial Tribunals, the Lands Tribunal, Local Valuation Courts, Rent Tribunals, Mental Health Review Tribunals, National Health Service and Social Security Tribunals. In all, some sixty different kinds of tribunals deal with more than a quarter of a million cases each year.

Some degree of uniformity of structure and procedure for these various tribunals resulted from the findings of the Franks Committee. The members of Tribunals are appointed and dismissed by the Lord Chancellor, or by the Minister of the department concerned.[3] Appeals on points of law are

[1] Cmd. 218 (1957).

[2] See W. A. Robson, 'Administrative Justice and Injustice: A Commentary on the Franks Report', *PL* 1958, pp. 12–31; G. Marshall, 'The Franks Report on Administrative Tribunals and Enquiries', *Pub. Admin.* 1957, pp. 347–58.

[3] S. McCorquodale, 'The Composition of Administrative Tribunals', *PL* 1962, pp. 298–326; W. E. Cavanegh and G. N. Hawker, 'Laymen on Administrative Tribunals', *Pub. Admin.* 1974, pp. 207–22; W. E. Cavanegh and D. Newton, 'Administrative Tribunals: How People Become Members', *Pub. Admin.* 1971, pp. 197–218.

allowed to the Court of Appeal. Most significantly of all, perhaps, the 1958 Act created a Council of Tribunals to supervise the working of the whole system. The Council consists of fifteen members appointed by the Lord Chancellor, with the Parliamentary Commissioner serving as an ex officio member.[1] A separate Scottish Committee is appointed by the Lord Advocate. The Council advises departments on the creation, organisation and procedure of tribunals, and reports on aspects of their activities as requested by the Lord Chancellor. It is, however, a purely advisory body. Its members are part-timers, it operates on a small budget and it lacks the means to undertake detailed and continuous supervision of the tribunals. What is more it is concerned with the procedure of the tribunals, rather than with the substance of the issues they handle, and the scope of the Council's activities has been criticised as being too narrow.[2] Nevertheless, it generally deals with fifty to a hundred complaints each year.

Considerable secrecy still surrounds the activities of some tribunals, and great variations still exist between the procedures of the different tribunals. Some tribunals allow legal representation at the hearings and keep detailed records of the proceedings. Thus the Lands Tribunal (which deals with disputes over the valuation of property) is appointed by the Lord Chancellor and has a legally qualified chairman. It sits in public, travels in circuit around the country, and gives a written report explaining the reasons for the decision. Some other tribunals, however, have less formalised and open procedures.

The Parliamentary Commissioner

Continued dissatisfaction with the existing structure of the tribunals system has produced various proposals for a wholesale reorganisation.[3] A proposal for an amalgamation of

[1] D. G. T. Williams, 'The Council on Tribunals', *PL* 1984, pp. 73–88.

[2] See H. W. R. Wade, 'The Council on Tribunals', *PL* 1960, pp. 351–66; J. A. G. Griffith, 'The Council and the Chalkpit', *Pub. Admin.* 1961, pp. 369–74; J. F. Garner, 'The Council on Tribunals', *PL* 1965, pp. 321–47; S. A. de Smith, 'The Council on Tribunals', *Parl. Aff.* 1958–9, pp. 320–8.

[3] See, for example, Sir John Whyatt, *The Citizen and the Administration*, London 1962. See also G. Marshall, 'Tribunals and Enquiries: Developments Since the Franks Report', *Pub. Admin.* 1958, pp. 261–70; K. C. Wheare, 'The Redress of Grievances', *Pub. Admin.* 1962, pp. 125–8.

the existing multiplicity of tribunals into three broad groups was rejected by the Franks Committee because of the lack of any marked overlapping of functions between the tribunals. The Committee also rejected proposals for the creation of a single tribunal in each region to deal with all complaints in that region. It was claimed that such a body would lack specialist knowledge of the many matters with which it would have to deal. For a similar reason the Franks Committee rejected a proposal for an overall Administrative Appeals Tribunal to hear appeals from all tribunals on questions of fact or law. Other proposals that have been made are that there should be set up Inspectors of Tribunals, and that legal aid should be available for hearings before tribunals.

Most drastically of all, it has been suggested that there should be created a distinct Administrative Law Division within the legal system. In France, the structure of the Courts is divided into three branches, Criminal, Civil, and Administrative. Within the Administrative Law Branch, a Council of State supervises the various specialist courts for military, financial, or social service administration, and also supervises prefectorial councils in each of a number of regions.[1] In Germany the courts structure is divided into distinct branches for Civil Law, Criminal Law, Administrative Law, social security questions, labour relations, and financial questions. Each of the branches has its own Appeals Court.[2] In the USA the Supreme Court has functions of general supervision over the executive, including administrative law questions. Any attempt to model any of these structures would clearly involve a fundamental reorganisation of the administrative law system, and of the whole legal structure in Britain, and these proposals have been resisted partly because of the difficulties involved in transplanting foreign institutions.

One change that has been made, based on foreign example, has been the introduction of an Ombudsman, or Parliamentary Commissioner for Administration, to examine complaints of maladministration. Such an official has existed in Sweden

[1]See C. E. Freedeman, *The Conseil D'Etat in Modern France*, New York, 1961.

[2]See A. J. Heidenheimer, *The Governments of Germany*, New York 1966, Ch. 7.

since 1915. A Parliamentary Commissioner was established in Britain in 1967 after more than a decade of arguments as to the desirability of such a creation.[1] One of the arguments used to support the creation was that the existing tribunals system was an inadequate means of dealing with public grievances, and that there were many complaints that were not covered by the tribunals system. At the same time, redress through Parliament was becoming increasingly difficult as government activities continued to expand, and thus it was claimed that there was a need for some supplementary means of dealing with grievances. It was argued that the Ombudsman worked satisfactorily in Scandinavia and New Zealand, and that a similar official could usefully be introduced in Britain.

The proposal met with considerable opposition, however, particularly among MPs who felt that it would lead to a diminution of their authority. It was argued that what worked well in a country like Sweden, with only 7 million population, would not necessarily work in Britain with a population of 55 million, and that much of the Parliamentary Commissioner's activities would be inevitably superficial. The form in which the Parliamentary Commissioner finally appeared in 1967 also aroused much criticism. He is an officer of Parliament and can only act on complaints he receives through an MP. He deals only with maladministration and cannot question matters of policy. He has no executive authority. When he upholds a complaint, he invites the department in question to remedy its error. If the department does not comply, he reports the case to Parliament where the Select Committee for the Parliamen-

[1] See F. Stacey, *The British Ombudsman*, London 1971; T. E. Utley, *Occasion for Ombudsman*, London 1961; J. D. B. Mitchell, 'The Ombudsman Fallacy', *PL* 1962, pp. 24–33; S. A. de Smith, 'Anglo-Saxon Ombudsman?', *PQ* 1962, pp. 9–19; W. B. Gwyn, 'The British PCA: "Ombudsman or Ombudsmouse"?', *J of P* 1973, pp. 45–69; R. Gregory and A. Alexander, 'Our Parliamentary Ombudsman', *Pub. Admin.* 1972, pp. 313–32 *and* 1973, pp. 41–60; K. A. Friedmann, 'The Public and the Ombudsman: Perception and Attitudes in Britain and in Alberta', *CJPS* 1977, pp. 497–526; G. Marshall, 'Reforming the Parliamentary Commissioner', *Pub. Admin.* 1977, pp. 465–8; W. B. Gwyn, 'The Ombudsman in Britain', *Pub. Admin.* 1982, pp. 177–96; D. Clark, 'The Ombudsman in Britain and France', *WEP* 1984 (III), pp. 64–90.

tary Commissioner examines it.[1] Thereafter Parliamentary pressure determines whether the Commissioner's recommendations are enforced.

Many of the several hundred complaints that the Commissioner receives each year have to be rejected because they are outside his competence. It is clear that in order to be seen to be active on his constituents' behalf an MP will often pass on a complaint that he knows to be outside the Commissioner's sphere.[2] In about a quarter of the two hundred or so cases that he does examine each year the Commissioner does find some degree of maladministration, with 'unreasonable delay' being the most frequent error. Perhaps inevitably, most complaints are stimulated by the Inland Revenue and the Department of Health and Social Security. The Commissioner's most celebrated case, however, was in 1967 when twelve survivors of the Sachsenhausen concentration camp were eventually awarded compensation by the Government after the Commissioner had criticised the Foreign Office's handling of their claims. He was less successful in 1975 when he criticised the Department of Industry for failing to anticipate the collapse of the Court Line holiday firm. He argued that compensation should be paid to those who lost money because of the collapse, but the Government refused to do so. In such a situation the Commissioner has no means of enforcing his recommendation.

The Parliamentary Commissioner's sphere of competence does not extend to the nationalised industries, the armed forces or the police. Initially, many of the complaints that he received related to the health service and local government, which were also outside his terms of reference. In view of this, separate health service and local government Commissioners were established. There are now three Health Service Commissioners (one each for England, Scotland and Wales), three local Government Commissioners for England and one each for Scotland and Wales, and a Parliamentary Commissioner

[1] See R. Gregory, 'The Select Committee on the Parliamentary Commissioner for Administration 1967–1980', *PL* 1982, pp. 49–88.

[2] L. H. Cohen, 'The Parliamentary Commissioner and the MP Filter', *PL* 1972, pp. 204–14.

for Northern Ireland.[1] Despite these developments the activities of the Parliamentary Commissioner have not satisfied those reformers who sought an institution with sweeping powers to investigate alleged maladministration. The most frequently heard criticism is that while the public has direct access to the Health Service and Northern Ireland Commissioners (and to the Local Commissioners if a councillor declines to pass on a complaint), an approach to the Parliamentary Commissioner must be channelled through an MP. The MPs remain reluctant to surrender this aspect of their role: as with other aspects of the reform of government in Britain, the original proposals have been diluted, not so much as a result of the conservatism of Ministers, but because of the conservatism of Parliament.

[1] H. J. Elcock, 'Opportunity for Ombudsman: the Northern Ireland Commissioner for Complaints', *Pub. Admin.* 1972, pp. 87–93.

12

Nationalisation and Privatisation

THE RELATIONSHIP between the state and industry has long been a major issue in British politics. In the post-war period especially, the respective merits of public and private enterprise have been debated at length by the parties, and the nationalisation issue has been prominent in some general election campaigns. The Labour Government of 1945–51, and to a lesser extent those of 1964–70 and 1974–9, brought a number of basic industries into public ownership. Since 1979 the Conservative Government has sought to reduce the size of the public sector through a policy of denationalisation (or 'privatisation'). In addition to party political considerations, however, the question of the nationalised industries is significant because of their important role in the economy, and because of the particular relationship that exists between Parliament, Ministers and the public corporations that manage the nationalised concerns.

State Participation in Industry

Over the last century and a half there has been in Britain a gradual increase in state intervention in industry. In the early nineteenth century the functions of government were seen as being little more than to maintain internal order, guard against external attack and regulate currency, while in the economic sphere it was assumed that maximum prosperity would be best achieved by the free play of market forces – a principle epitomized by the nineteenth-century free-trade movement. This principle was discredited to some extent during the nineteenth century, however, by many of the social consequences of the industrial revolution. It came to be accepted that state activity in the form of Factory Acts, Mines Acts, and Public Health Acts, was necessary in order to counter some of the worst effects of industrialisation. It was also recognised that state intervention in industry was necessary at times for the good of industry itself, as for example through trade union legislation to achieve a balance of power between employer and employee, so that 'healthy competition' could develop between these opposing forces.

State intervention in the economic life of the nation increased during the two world wars. It was further boosted by the wide popularity of the Keynesian concept of general economic planning, and then by the early post-war attempts to achieve planned economic progress. In the post-war period there has been a broad acceptance of the concept of the mixed economy, though the question of just how much state intervention in industry is desirable has remained a controversial issue between (and within) the parties. In the last ten years the state's role in industry has been examined more critically than at any time since the 1940s as laissez faire attitudes have revived.

State intervention in industry can take various forms.[1] At one level the state intervenes in the free market in an attempt to make it operate more effectively. Thus the Government provides statistical information on which industry can base its future plans, it provides Job Centres to help the redeployment of labour, it creates arbitration machinery to help settle industrial disputes. The Government also intervenes to protect one party in the free market process against another. Protection for workers through Employment Acts and Wages Councils, protection for shareholders through Company Acts,

[1]See Royal Institute of Public Administration, *Allies or Adversaries?*, London 1981; J. W. Grove, *Government and Industry in Britain*, London 1962; M. Stewart, 'Planning and Persuasion in a Mixed Economy', *PQ* 1964, pp. 148–60; J. Hills, 'Government Relations With Industry: Japan and Britain', *Polity* 1981–2, pp. 222–48; D. R. Steel, 'Government and Industry in Britain', *BJPS* 1982, pp. 449–503.

protection for consumers through Fair Trading Acts, all represent aspects of state activity that are designed to reform and regulate the system of free competition between economic forces.

A rather different form of state activity is represented by attempts to establish an overall economic plan for industry, where it is felt that the free play of market forces will not fully satisfy national needs (as opposed to purely private needs). This form of state activity is exemplified by Government attempts to encourage production in certain industries in order to stimulate exports and curb imports, or to encourage industry to move to particular parts of the country. Overall economic planning by the Government can be implemented by fiscal controls and incentives, as with financial burdens on industry through taxation, or by financial aid to industry as with grants, tax concessions, and protective tariffs. Alternatively, direct physical controls can be used, perhaps by placing statutory limits on incomes, prices, production, or investment. These different methods of seeking to control industry have all been used with varying degrees of success by British Governments since 1945.

Most directly of all, however, state intervention in industry can take the form of direct industrial participation by the state, either by the acquisition of private industries, or by the creation of new state enterprises where previously there was no activity. Thus rather than attempting to modify and improve the private sector of the economy, private enterprise is replaced by public enterprise. This can involve state ownership of the whole of industry, or, as in Britain, it can involve state ownership of only sections of industry in a mixed economy. The justification of this form of state activity, the details of how it can be achieved, and the problems that it involves, are considered in the rest of this chapter.[1]

[1]See W. A. Robson, *Nationalized Industry and Public Ownership*, London 1962; A. H. Hanson, *Nationalization: a Book of Readings*, London 1963; R. Kelf-Cohen, *British Nationalization 1945–73*, London 1973; M. Shanks, *The Lessons of Public Enterprise*, London 1963; G. L. Reid and K. Allen, *Nationalized Industries*, London 1970; W. Thornhill, *The Nationalized Industries*, London, 1968; L. Tivey (ed.), *The Nationalized Industries Since 1960*, London 1973; R. Pryke, *The Nationalized Industries*, London 1981; P. Curwen, *Public Enterprise*, London 1986.

The Public Enterprise Debate

The arguments advanced over the years to justify the public ownership of industry in Britain have been based partly on ideological principles, and partly on pragmatic considerations.[1] Socialists have long advocated public ownership as a means of achieving basic Socialist ideals. They have seen public ownership as a means towards a fairer distribution of wealth throughout the community, by eradicating unearned private income from profits and dividends, and as a means of achieving production for use rather than for profit. Socialists have also argued that it is in the public interest that the essential industries (or 'the commanding heights of the economy') should be publicly owned, with this being particularly true for the public utilities.

As well as ideological arguments such as these, there are other arguments of principle that can be advanced in support of public ownership. It can be argued, for example, that where a monopoly situation exists it is best controlled by the state, as a public monopoly is ultimately answerable to democratic controls through the political process. Large-scale organisations have certain advantages, such as large-scale planning, rationalisation, and economies of scale, which can apply just as well to large publicly owned organisations as to large private enterprise concerns. Also, in some situations only the state is in a position to act, perhaps because vast capital sums are required for development, without there being any immediately apparent commercial returns. Similarly, the state may take over and run at a financial loss some sector of industry where private enterprise can no longer produce profits. This may be done because the industry is seen as vital to the national economy, or because a particularly large number of jobs is at stake. Public ownership of large sections of industry can also be a vital means of influencing national economic policy, as through policies of wage or price restraint. Alternatively, public ownership of highly profitable concerns can be used as a means of raising national revenue.

[1] For pre-1945 works on public ownership see H. Morrison, *Socialization and Transport*, London 1933; P. Snowden, *If Labour Rules*, London 1923; W. A. Robson, *Public Enterprise*, 1937; T. E. O'Brien, *British Experiments in Public Ownership and Control*, London 1937.

These various arguments, of course, are not universally accepted. The opponents of public ownership claim that there are a number of illogicalities in the theory and the practice, and that many of the supposed advantages of public ownership apply only when the whole of industry is publicly owned. The champions of private enterprise claim that individual freedom is reduced by state ownership, and that supply and demand, and the free play of market forces, form a better basis for economic progress than state control through public ownership. They further claim that public bodies are not fitted to run commercial concerns, and that the economic performance of the nationalised industries in Britain demonstrates this.

Although ideological and theoretical arguments form the background to the public enterprise debate, in practice nationalised concerns have been established in Britain for largely pragmatic reasons. In 1908 the Liberal Government created the Port of London Authority in order to establish unified public control over the vast complex of London docks. In 1926 the Conservative Government established the Central Electricity Generating Board to bring standardisation and overall national control to electricity generation. Also in 1926, the British Broadcasting Corporation was set up as a public body (though free from direct Ministerial control) because of the fundamental importance of broadcasting as a means of communication.[1] In 1933 the National Government set up the London Passenger Transport Board to achieve the integration of road and rail passenger transport within the London area. In 1939 the Chamberlain Government established the British Overseas Airways Corporation as a publicly owned body, partly because of the importance of the airlines for international prestige, and partly because of the vast subsidies that were required for the effective development of the airlines.

Thus before 1945 there was already established by non-Socialist Governments some tradition of public ownership based on pragmatic motives. In the vast extension of public ownership that was undertaken by the 1945–51 Labour Governments, largely pragmatic arguments were used to justify

[1]M. Kinchin Smith, 'The BBC: a Pioneer Public Corporation', *Pub. Admin.* 1978, pp. 25–34.

the various measures.[1] The nationalisation of the Bank of England in 1946 was accepted with little dissent because it was generally recognised that the Bank had a special place in the finances of the nation, and because there had long been a close link between the Bank and the Treasury. The Coal Nationalisation Act embodied the oldest of the Labour Movement's public ownership proposals, but in fact the main justifications for the Act in 1946 lay in the findings of the Technical Advisory Committee on Coal Mining (the Reid Committee) which reported in 1945.[2] The Committee claimed that the British mines were in need of large-scale modernisation, and public ownership was widely seen as the best practical means of implementing the Committee's recommendations. Also in 1946, the Civil Aviation Act created British European Airways and British South American Airways (later merged with BOAC) as public corporations, for much the same reasons as the creation of BOAC in 1939.

In the case of road and rail transport, the Report of the Royal Commission on Transport in 1930[3] had advocated the modernisation (though not the nationalisation) of the railways in order to allow them to meet road competition. The Commission had argued for the coordination of road and rail transport, and in 1947 there was already a big overlap in the ownership of private enterprise road and rail concerns. After the war, there was a big need for capital investment in the railways, and public ownership was seen by the Labour Government as an essential part of transport reconstruction and integration. The inclusion of road transport in the public ownership proposals, however, led to strong opposition from the industry and from the Conservative Party.[4]

The public utilities of gas and electricity were brought under full public ownership in 1947 and 1948. The Central Electricity Generating Board had been created in 1926 to standardise electricity generation, and in 1936 the McGowan

[1] See D. N. Chester, *The Nationalisation of British Industry, 1945–51*, London 1975.

[2] Cmd. 6610 (1945).

[3] Cmd. 3751 (1930).

[4] J. J. Richardson, 'The Administration of De-nationalization: the Case of Road Haulage', *Pub. Admin.* 1971, pp. 385–402.

Committee[1] reported on the need for changes in the organisation of electricity (about two-thirds of which was municipally owned). The McGowan Committee had favoured privately owned regional organisations to work with the local authorities, but in 1947 electricity distribution was brought under national control. It was argued that national control of electricity generation, and the operation of the grid system, logically called for national control of distribution, and that national control was the best means of achieving a big capital expansion in the electricity industry. In the case of the gas industry (about one-third of which was municipally owned), the Heyworth Committee[2] of enquiry in 1945 found that the industry was reasonably efficient, but was in need of much larger units to make the best use of its resources, and the Government used the report to justify complete public ownership of the industry.

In the case of iron and steel, however, the background to the Government's proposals was very different from the background to the earlier public ownership measures.[3] No impartial technical committee had enquired into the industry, and although the industry had been in difficulty during the depression years, its profitability was re-established in the 1940s. Despite opposition in and out of Parliament, the Attlee Government proceeded with the Iron and Steel Bill, which duly became law, and was brought into operation after the 1950 general election. After the Conservatives' victory at the 1951 general election, however, the bulk of the iron and steel industry was returned to private hands. Thus the controversy over the desirability of public ownership of iron and steel continued, and to a considerable extent the whole public ownership debate in the 1950s centred on the steel industry issue. With the return of a Labour Government to power in 1964, fresh public ownership proposals were introduced, and in 1967 the thirteen major steel firms were brought under

[1] Report of the Committee on Electricity Distribution.

[2] Report of the Committee of Inquiry into the Gas Industry, Cmd. 6699 (1945).

[3] See G. W. Ross, *The Nationalization of Steel*, London 1965; D. McEachern, *A Class Against Itself*, London 1980.

public ownership, accounting for 90% of the basic steel production in Britain.

As well as renationalising the steel industry, the 1964–70 Labour Government created the National Freight Corporation and the National Bus Company to manage publicly owned sectors of the road haulage and road passenger transport industries. In the 1974–9 period the Labour Government nationalised the aircraft and shipbuilding industries, and the National Enterprise Board was set up with powers to purchase a public stake in private concerns.

While nationalisation is associated primarily with the Labour Governments of the post-war period (and with the 1945–51 Government in particular), Conservative Governments before 1979 were not altogether opposed to the *principle* of public ownership. In its rhetoric the Conservative Party was highly critical of the performance of nationalised industries, and the Conservative Governments of 1951–64 and 1970–74 did return some parts of the public sector to private hands: steel and road haulage were denationalised by the Churchill Government, and Thomas Cook and the state-owned parts of the licenced trade by the Heath Government. For the most part, however, Conservative Governments accepted the mixed economy, came to terms with the expansion of the public sector and even contributed to that expansion. Conservative (or Conservative-dominated) Governments before 1945 established public corporations to manage the BBC, BOAC and London Transport; in 1954 the Churchill Government created the Atomic Energy Authority;[1] the Heath Government brought Rolls Royce and Upper Clyde Shipbuilders into public ownership when they encountered financial difficulties.

The Conservative Government elected in 1979, however, rejected the post-war consensus on public ownership and has pursued an active policy of returning parts of the public sector to private hands. This policy of denationalisation has taken

[1]See R. Darcy Best, 'The United Kingdom Atomic Energy Authority', *Pub. Admin.* 1956, pp. 1–16. See also D. Abel, 'British Conservatives and State Ownership', *J of P* 1957, pp. 227–39; N. Harris, *Competition and the Corporate Society*, London 1973.

various forms.[1] In the first place, some public corporations have been converted into limited companies and their shares sold to the public (with preference given to employees and small investors). British Aerospace and British Telecom were disposed of in this way, while the National Freight Corporation was sold to a consortium of employees and managers. Britoil was formed as a new private concern to take-over the exploration and production activities of the British National Oil Corporation. Most dramatically of all, in 1986 the Gas Act provided for the sale of the British Gas Corporation, and plans were announced for the sale of the Regional Water Authorities in England and Wales.

The Government also disposed of some or all of the shares that the state had acquired in certain concerns. The National Enterprise Board's holdings in Ferranti and ICL were sold, as were some or all of the state's shares in Cable and Wireless, British Petroleum, Amersham International, the British Sugar Corporation and Associated British Ports. Profitable parts of some other publicly-owned concerns were disposed of. Through the Transport Act 1981 some British Rail hotels, some office buildings and Sealink Ferries were sold. In 1984 the profitable Jaguar section of British Leyland was sold. The Government also pursued a 'liberalisation' policy, breaking the monopoly of some nationalised industries and encouraging more competitive practices. The Oil and Gas (Enterprise) Act 1982 allowed oil companies to sell gas to industry, while the Energy Act 1983 permitted the private generation of electricity.

The motives behind this policy of denationalisation were partly pragmatic and partly ideological. The sale of state assets produced a large amount of revenue for the exchequer (with the sale of British Telecom alone raising some £4 billion). The contraction of the public sector also reduces

[1] See D. Steel and D. Heald (eds), *Privatising Public Enterprise*, London 1984; J. Le Grand and R. Robinson, *Privatisation and the Welfare State*, London 1984; K. Ascher, *The Politics of Privatisation*, London 1986; S. Young, 'The Nature of Privatisation in Britain 1979–85', *WEP* 1986 (II), pp. 235–52; D. Heald, 'Will the Privatisation of Public Enterprises Solve the Problem of Control?' *Pub. Admin.* 1985, pp. 7–22; P. Dunleavy, 'Explaining the Privatisation Boom', *Pub. Admin.* 1986, pp. 13–34.

direct Ministerial responsibility (not least in the sphere of public sector pay), and frees the Treasury from demands for funds for capital investment. In addition to these practical considerations, however, the denationalisation measures reflected the Thatcher Government's ideological commitment to the view that commercial concerns are run more effectively by private enterprise than by the state (not least because of the inconsistencies of Ministerial intervention), that share ownership should be extended to as many individuals as possible, and that both personal freedom and economic efficiency demanded that the public sector be reduced in size.

Opponents of the denationalisation policy, as well as rejecting the unfavourable comparisons between public and private enterprise, have condemned the disposal of valuable public assets (or 'the family silver'). They have pointed out that with the sale of its profitable concerns the state would be left with only loss-making concerns that required public subsidies to remain in operation, and that while the exchequer might make a large initial capital gain from the sale of assets, over the longer term it would lose the revenue that came from them. They have also argued that the creation of a private monopoly for an essential service (as in the case of gas, telecommunications and water) is particularly undesirable, and have predicted that the government's machinery for regulating the prices charged by these private utilities is likely to prove both bureaucratic and ineffective.

For the most part, however, the denationalisation policies have not met the same strength of resistance, and have not inspired the same level of public debate, as the nationalisation measures of post-war Labour Governments. The Labour Opposition in Parliament, the Chairmen and Boards of the nationalised industries, and the employees in the specific industries concerned, have been relatively restrained in their reaction to the Government's policies. Thus the Thatcher Government has demonstrated that in at least two respects denationalisation is easier to achieve than nationalisation – because the sale of state assets (at least initially) adds to, rather than absorbs, public funds, and because the public sector is less vocal in its own defence than is private enterprise (partly, no doubt, because some Board chairmen have been appointed specifically because of their sympathy for denationalisation).

Forms of Public Enterprise

Public enterprise can take many forms, and various means can be used to administer publicly owned or publicly controlled concerns. Municipal control of commercial concerns was widely advocated by the early Socialists, and even in the nineteenth century 'Gas and Water Socialism' envisaged local authorities as the best means of managing public utilities. Before 1939 more than two-thirds of electricity distribution, and about one-third of the gas industry was under municipal control. Today a high proportion of municipal authorities provide their own passenger transport services. The post-war extension of nationalisation was to some extent at the expense of municipal undertakings, and within the party politics of local government, private enterprise interests have been quick to condemn local authority enterprise as 'gambling with the rates'. There are, however, many instances of joint trading by groups of local authorities, as with joint ownership of airports.

Some public enterprises are operated by the departments of state. This generally means that the Minister is directly responsible for all aspects of policy and administration, and that the employees of the concern are civil servants (industrial or non-industrial as the case may be). It also generally means that the Treasury has direct control over the finances of the concern, all income and expenditure being paid into and out of the Exchequer. Until their denationalisation in 1971, the State Management Schemes for the control of the licensed trade in parts of Cumberland and parts of Scotland were run directly by the Home Office and the Scottish Office.[1] Until 1969 the Post Office was run by a department of state, although between 1956 and 1984 a series of steps were taken towards greater financial and administrative autonomy. Until 1956 all Post Office financial surpluses were paid into the Exchequer, and thus represented a form of national revenue.

[1] See R. M. Punnett, 'State Management of the Liquor Trade', *Pub. Admin.* 1966, pp. 193–212.

In 1956 a requirement was introduced whereby the Post Office paid £5 million per year to the Treasury, but retained any additional surplus for its own uses. A system of completely self-contained Post Office finances was introduced by the Post Office Act 1961, and in 1969 the Post Office's freedom from day-to-day Ministerial control was taken a stage further, when the Post Office Act created a public corporation to administer its affairs. In 1981 British Telecom was formed as a separate public corporation to manage the Post Office's telecommunications and data processing services, and was then sold to the public in 1984.

A public corporation is characterised by the fact that it is run by an administrative Board rather than directly by the Minister, with the Minister being responsible to Parliament for overall policy, but not for day-to-day administration. The employees of a public corporation are not civil servants, and thus can be recruited on terms of employment determined by the corporation itself. A public corporation also has a self-contained financial structure, in that annual surpluses are used for the corporation's own purposes, and are not transferred to the Exchequer as national revenue.

The theory is that the public corporation combines the commercial freedom that is enjoyed by a private concern, with the public accountability that is desired for a publicly owned concern – the basic assumption being that commercial freedom is restricted by an excessive degree of detailed Ministerial control. The question of precisely where the line is to be drawn between Ministerial control of policy, but not of administration, is, however, a matter of considerable and continuing controversy. This and some of the other problems involved in the public corporation form of structure are considered later in this chapter.

There are other forms of public enterprise which provide even more commercial freedom, and less Ministerial control, than is the case with the public corporation. Government purchase of shares in private concerns can achieve public control, or even full public ownership, without altering the basic administrative structure by which the concern is operated, and thus without destroying the private enterprise facade of the concern. Share purchase as a method of public enterprise can involve the purchase of all the shares by the Government, and the creation of a holding company to manage the Government's interests. Alternatively, state holdings can take the form of only part ownership, with Government control of a concern being secured by the ownership of 51% of the stock. The Suez Finance Co. (in which the Government secured a controlling interest during the nineteenth century) and British Petroleum were early examples of this type of mixed enterprise, and over the years, the state acquired interests in various assorted concerns. In general, such Government share purchase has been motivated by a desire to protect essential national interest, or save an industry from financial difficulties, or provide an injection of public capital. In 1975 the National Enterprise Board was set up as a vehicle through which this policy could be pursued more coherently. The NEB invested in some profitable concerns and provided capital for a number of ailing industries, most notably British Leyland in 1975. In 1979 the NEB had funds of almost £1.5 billion at its disposal. The Conservative Government, however, reduced its role considerably. It brought the NEB's investment programme under direct Ministerial control, prohibited it from investing in profitable concerns and restricted it to providing aid to small businesses and to economically depressed regions.

Share purchases enable the Government to partake of the profits of a concern in a way that is not always the case with other forms of public enterprise, and also enable the state to influence policy without having sole and direct responsibility (although the Government may not choose to use its power in this direction).[1] As a form of public enterprise, however, share purchase is condemned by sections of the Labour Party who argue that it merely links the state with the sins of private enterprise. They also claim that there is no adequate Parliamentary supervision of industries in which the Government acquires shares, and that even with acceptance of the mixed

[1]See in particular Hugh Gaitskell, *Socialism and Nationalization* (Fabian Tract 300), London 1956. See also J. Dugdale, 'The Labour Party and Nationalization', *PQ* 1957, pp. 254–9; H. E. Weiner, *British Labour and Public Ownership*, London 1960; E. Eldon Barry, *Nationalization in British Politics*, London 1966.

economy, there is still room for more direct public ownership of whole firms and industries. At the same time, share purchase by the state is condemned by private enterprise as representing a subversive and hidden form of Government interference in the private sector, giving the Government power without responsibility.

In this context the role of quasi-autonomous non-governmental organisations ('quangos') should be noted.[1] There are several hundred such bodies, including the Arts Council, the University Grants Committee, the Manpower Services Commission and the Advisory, Conciliation and Arbitration Service. Some are purely advisory bodies (the Advisory Committee on Pesticides) while others execute policy on behalf of the Government and distribute public funds (the University Grants Committee). They are like public corporations in that they are devices through which Ministers and civil servants can distance themselves from direct involvement in some social, cultural or economic service, while retaining ultimate control. Like public corporations they are not staffed by civil servants and are not subject to day-to-day Ministerial control, but they differ from public corporations in that they are financed largely or entirely from the exchequer.

Their numbers increased considerably in the 1960s and 1970s as Labour and Conservative Governments saw them as convenient means of relieving Ministers and departments of some of their functions. In 1980 the Pliatzky report on non-departmental public bodies identified almost 500 with executive functions and about 1500 with advisory functions. The extent and growth in the number of quangos was criticised because it increased Ministerial patronage and confused even further the question of Ministerial responsibility. Because of this, and as part of the Conservative Government's drive to reduce the scope of the public sector, a number of quangos have been abolished since 1979 and some others have been brought under closer Ministerial control.[2] Several hundred

[1] See A. Barker (ed.), *Quangos in Britain*, London 1982; P. Holland, *The Governance of Quangos*, London 1981; D. N. Chester, 'Fringe Bodies, Quangos and All That', *Pub. Admin.* 1979, pp. 51–4.

[2] See R. Presthus, 'Mrs Thatcher Stalks the Quango', *PAR* 1981, pp. 312–7; C. Hood, 'The Politics of Quangocide', *PP* 1980, pp. 247–66.

still remain, however, covering a considerable range of activities.

* * *

From the above discussion it can be seen that many of the assumptions about public enterprise are not necessarily valid. In the first place, despite the party rhetoric, public ownership is not entirely a partisan issue. Labour, Conservative, Liberal, and Coalition Governments have all been responsible for extending public ownership in Britain, while the nationalisation measures of the Labour Governments were introduced for pragmatic as much as doctrinal reasons. Secondly, public enterprise can be furthered by means other than by full-scale nationalisation, in that municipal or regional enterprises represent alternatives to nationalisation, while share purchase represents a means of achieving public control of private industry that does not involve direct management through a public corporation or department of state. Also, full public ownership of a firm or an industry is not essential in order to achieve public control, and ownership of part of a firm or part of an industry, through mixed enterprise, can be enough to give the state a large measure of control. Finally, public enterprise is not necessarily to be equated with unprofitability, in that there is a strong case to be made out for the public ownership of highly profitable concerns as a form of public investment. In recent years, however, this issue has proved to be particularly controversial, with Labour Governments of the 1960s and 1970s seeking to extend public participation in profitable enterprises, while the Conservative Government since 1979 has sought to confine public ownership to concerns that could not be viable in the private sector.

Problems of the Public Corporations: I. Ministerial Control[1]

While public enterprise takes many forms in Britain today, the public corporation is the principal means through which the nationalised industries are managed. Public corporations

[1] W. A. Robson, 'Ministerial Control of the Nationalised Industries', *PQ* 1969, pp. 103–12 and 494–6.

are run by Boards of ten or so members appointed by the Minister. They are drawn from industry or the public service, and in the main they are appointed for their general business qualifications. They are not recruited as direct representatives of interests, and the principle of workers' control does not form the basis of Board membership. It has often proved difficult to recruit suitable members for the Boards, partly because many of the industries involved have unattractive images, but also because salaries and terms of appointment have been less attractive than those applying in private industry. For these reasons there is a fairly regular turnover of Board chairmen. The role of the chairman of the Board is vital, with the relationship between the chairman and the Minister being in many ways the key to the question of the degree of commercial freedom that is allowed to the public corporations. The several Board chairmen meet together in the Nationalised Industries' Chairmen's Group, and consult regularly with Ministers and the Treasury.

The Ministers chiefly involved with the affairs of the nationalised industries are the Secretaries of State for the Environment, Energy, Trade and Industry and Transport. The creation of a special post of Minister for the Nationalised Industries has been advocated from time to time, but no such post has yet been created. As part of his Overlords scheme in 1951, Churchill experimented with a Minister for the Coordination of Transport, Fuel and Power, but with little success. In the case of the public corporations created before 1945, there was a tenuous level of Ministerial control. The corporations were in the main financially self-supporting, and this was reflected in their degree of administrative independence. In general, the post-1945 Acts gave greater statutory powers to the Ministers than did the pre-1945 legislation. The statutory powers given to the Minister are generally the power to appoint and dismiss the members of the Board, the power to give general directives on policy matters, particularly on matters affecting the national interest, and specific powers with regard to accounts, training, and research policy, which vary from one corporation to another. The Minister and the Treasury also have control over the needs of the corporations for capital investment. Much Ministerial intervention in the affairs of a public corporation is by means of informal 'backstairs' pressure at a personal level between Ministers and Board members. This can be seen as perhaps the least desirable form of control, in that it enables the Minister to wield power without being seen to have direct responsibility.

Resistance to excessive Ministerial control of public corporations is based on the view that the industries will prosper commercially only when they are given something approaching the degree of freedom of activity that is enjoyed by a private enterprise concern, and this view greatly influenced the attitude of Labour Ministers (particularly Herbert Morrison) in the creation of the public corporations after 1945. As well as this consideration, however, close Ministerial supervision subjects the nationalised industries to the political inconsistencies that accompany changes of Government, or changes of Minister within the same Government, or changes of policy by the same Minister. The consequent overloading of Ministers and their departments with responsibility for the detailed administration of the nationalised industries inevitably contributes to the problems of an overworked central government machine.

The case for independence from Ministerial control, however, is not universally accepted. A greater degree of Ministerial control than exists at present is often demanded because of the vital economic nature and monopolistic position of the industries, and because of the extent of the public interest bound up in them. It is also claimed that coordination and rationalisation (often quoted as major justifications for public ownership) are only possible through strict Ministerial control. The fuel and power industries, for example, have been quoted recently as exemplifying the need for more Ministerial control in order to achieve a coordinated policy in face of the energy crisis, while it is argued that the role of the nationalised industries in economic planning demands more direct Ministerial control.[1] Thus it has been suggested that the Minister should in fact be Chairman of the Board of a public corpor-

[1] See W. G. Shepherd, *Economic Performance under Public Ownership*, London 1965. See also W. A. Robson, 'Ministerial Control of the Nationalized Industries', *PQ* 1969, pp. 103–12 *and* 494–6.

ation, thereby reviving the proposal of some of the earliest advocates of public corporations.[1]

Despite these numerous arguments in favour of tight Ministerial control, however, the experiences of the nationalised industries in the post-war period provide a powerful case for less rather than more Ministerial involvement. Inconsistencies in the attitudes of successive Ministers towards the nationalised industries have been evident in numerous areas, not least in that of pricing policy. Under the same Government, and sometimes under the same Minister, the industries have been called upon at one time, to aim for financial self-sufficiency by increasing prices if necessary, but at another to postpone price increases as a contribution to a Government attack upon inflation. In this respect the Morrisonian dictum of commercial freedom for public-owned concerns has proved to be an attractive but elusive goal.

II. Parliamentary Supervision

Whatever the merits or demerits of close Parliamentary scrutiny of the affairs of the public corporations, there are several factors that limit the effectiveness of Parliament for this purpose.[2] The overcrowded Parliamentary timetable, the technical nature of many of the issues, and the limitations that exist today on Parliamentary control of any Minister, all restrict Parliament's ability to scrutinise the nationalised industries. The problem is increased by the difficulty of distinguishing between policy and day-to-day administration in the affairs of the nationalised industries, and thus of identifying those matters for which the Minister is directly responsible to Parliament. This is reflected, for example, in the case of Parliamentary questions to Ministers. Early in the 1945–50

[1] See in particular A. H. Hanson, *Parliament and Public Ownership*, London 1962.

[2] See Hanson, *Parliament and Public Ownership*; E. P. Pritchard, 'The Responsibility of the Nationalized Industries to Parliament', *Parl. Aff.* 1963–4, pp. 439–49; A. H. Hanson, 'Parliamentary Control of Nationalized Industries', *Parl. Aff.* 1957–8, pp. 328–40; G. H. Daniel, 'Public Accountability of the Nationalized Industries', *Pub. Admin.* 1960, pp. 27–34; L. Tivey, 'Structure and Politics in the Nationalised Industries', *Parl. Aff.* 1978–9, pp. 159–75.

Parliament the principle was established, and has been adhered to ever since, that questions on policy matters were permissible while questions on day-to-day administration were not, but the problem remains of determining where the dividing line is to be drawn between 'policy' and 'administration'. Ultimately, responsibility for determining what questions are permissible rests with the Speaker, but even when the Speaker permits a question the Minister can deny responsibility. Thus in the immediate post-war years, and to a lesser extent since then, Ministers often refused to answer questions because they regarded the matter as one of day-to-day administration, or else answered the question for information while denying actual responsibility. Successive Governments have chosen not to allow any relaxation in the rules governing the admissibility of questions, despite frequent demands that there should be a change in the practice. In some ways it is ironic that the most persistent questioners are often those critics of the nationalised industries who wish to see them being more commercially successful, and yet any increase in MPs' powers to question Ministers would presumably lead to more Ministerial control over the industries, and thus to a lessening of their commercial freedom.

MPs can also raise matters connected with the nationalised industries during debates in the normal Parliamentary timetable. The Government allocates a number of days each session to the discussion of the Annual Reports of the various industries, although debates on the Annual Reports are often devoted to minor constituency grievances rather than big general issues. All the public corporations, except the BBC, were created by statute (the BBC being created by Royal Charter), and any legislation amending these original statutes, or any legislation creating further public corporations, provides additional opportunities for debating the principles and general issues involved in public enterprise. Further, the normal methods of Parliamentary control over delegated legislation can give an opportunity for comment on any Statutory Instruments that apply to the corporations.

Parliamentary control over the financial affairs of the public corporations is limited basically by the principle that the aim of a public corporation is to have a self-contained financial structure, free from Treasury control, and thus free from direct Parliamentary supervision. It has frequently been proposed that the Comptroller and Auditor General should examine the accounts of the nationalised industries, but successive governments have resisted this. Nevertheless, in so far as a nationalised industry depends on the Treasury for capital for investment, the Treasury, Parliament, and the C and AG do have direct control over corporation finances.

The most useful medium for Parliamentary supervision of the public corporations was probably the Select Committee on Nationalised Industries, which was set-up in 1956 but abolished in 1979 when the Select Committee system was reformed.[1] This committee examined the reports and accounts of the nationalised industries, generally dealing with one industry each year, although it sometimes looked at broad issues such as pricing policy or Ministerial control. It increased Parliamentary and public knowledge about the nationalised industries and probably helped towards a reduction of partisanship in Parliament about the nationalisation issue. With its abolition in 1979, and the introduction of the new committee system, Select Committee scrutiny of the nationalised industries became fragmented. Particular industries are examined by the Select Committees on Transport, Energy and Trade and Industry, but their activities lack the coordinated approach of the Nationalised Industries Committee.

Various proposals have been made to increase the efficiency and extent of Ministerial control and Parliamentary supervision. As has been noted above, it has been proposed that the Minister should be chairman of the Board of a public corporation, and that there should be a special Minister of (or for) the Nationalised Industries. It has been proposed that a special Commission should be appointed to examine the efficiency of

[1]See D. Coombes, *The MP and the Administration*, London 1966; Sir Toby Low, 'The Select Committee on Nationalized Industries', *Pub. Admin.* 1962, pp. 1–16; E. Davies, 'The Select Committee on Nationalized Industries', *PQ* 1958, pp. 378–88; D. Coombes, 'The Scrutiny of Ministers' Powers by the Select Committee on Nationalized Industries', *PL* 1965, pp. 9–29; D. N. Chester, 'The Select Committee on the Nationalized Industries', *Pub. Admin.* 1956, pp. 93–5.

the nationalised industries, although the proposals vary as to the form that this body should take. To secure greater consideration of the annual capital investment plans of the industries, it has been suggested that a Nationalised Industries Investment Bill should be introduced each year. It has been suggested that each nationalised industry should have a Policy Council, made up of civil servants from the relevant departments, representatives of the Board, trade unions and consumers, and some independent members. The Council would provide a buffer between the Board and the Minister and thereby reduce the Minister's direct role in the affairs of the industry. These various proposals have been resisted in the interests of the commercial freedom of the industries, although one of the functions of the National Enterprise Board is to scrutinise the industries' capital expenditure plans and requirements.

It is very difficult to compare the accountability of a public corporation with that of a private firm. On the one hand, Parliament is much more in touch with the affairs of the public corporations than are the shareholders of a private concern, but on the other hand the size, importance, and monopoly basis of the public corporations means that they are much more powerful than private concerns, and there is much greater need for detailed control.

As a supplement to public accountability through Parliament the Monopolies and Mergers Commission has a continuing supervisory function, enquiring into a group of nationalised industries each year. Consumer Councils also exist for each industry. They act as advisory bodies as well as complaints bodies, and can have an impact on policy. Critics of the Consumer Councils say that they lack staff and resources, are too closely linked with the Boards and are not sufficiently well-known to the public. In 1982 the Post Office Users National Council did win a notable victory when its protests persuaded the Post Office to postpone a planned increase in telephone charges. On the whole, however, the consumer is not noticeably more satisfied with the service from nationalised concerns than with the service from private enterprise.[1]

[1]See M. Howe, 'The Transport Act 1962 and the Consumers Con-

III. Financial Structure[1]

A basic requirement that follows from the principle of a self-contained financial structure for public corporations is that a corporation should pay its way, taking an average of good and bad years. There has been much confusion as to precisely what is meant by 'taking an average of good and bad years', although the 1961 White Paper on the Financial and Economic Obligations of the Nationalised Industries defined this as being over a five-year period.[2] More recently (following the recommendations of a 1978 White Paper) Governments have sought to set specific financial targets for each nationalised industry, and have demanded that these targets should determine pricing policy. A second basic requirement is that any financial surplus that a corporation produces should be used for its own purposes (that is, to form a reserve, finance capital investment, repay loans, or reduce future prices), thus benefiting consumers and employees, rather than being transferred to the Exchequer as a form of national revenue. This vision of a public corporation as a self-contained financial unit was largely achieved in the case of the public corporations created before 1945, but the financial difficulties of the post-1945 public corporations have meant that it has not been achieved in their case. The vast sums needed initially for compensation payments and for capital investment programmes, combined with the subsequent inability of some of the corporations to avoid trading losses, have meant that the actual financial arrangements for these corporations have been very different from the theoretical ideal of financial self-sufficiency.

The payment of compensation to shareholders in the event of nationalisation is necessary on the grounds of equity and political expediency, but compensation payments load the nationalised industries with a large initial debt. Various methods can be used to determine the level of compensation

[1] See C. D. Foster, *Politics, Finance and the Role of Economics*, London 1971.
[2] Cmd. 1337 (1961).

---

sultative Committees', *Pub. Admin.* 1964, pp. 45–56; G. Mills and M. Howe, 'Consumer Representation and the Withdrawal of Railway Services', *Pub. Admin.* 1960, pp. 253–62.

that is to be paid. One method is to base the figure on Stock Exchange share prices on given dates, as was done with transport, private gas and electricity holdings, and iron and steel in 1951. Alternatively, the average price over a given period can be taken, as with aircraft and shipbuilding in 1977. Again, compensation can be based on assessments made by an arbitration tribunal, as with coal, or it can take the form of a token sum determined by the Government, as with payments to local authorities for their gas and electricity undertakings. It is generally accepted that in most cases the awards were more than generous, and railway and coal shareholders in particular benefited as a result of nationalisation.

Financial needs for capital investment present a particularly acute problem when an industry is greatly in need of modernisation, as was the case with the railways and the coal industry, or when there is a rapidly expanding consumer demand, as with electricity, atomic energy, the airlines, and gas[1] (at least with the development of North Sea gas). All the major nationalised industries were faced early in their lives with the problem of how money for capital investment was to be raised.[2] To meet the needs out of trading surpluses was not practical because of the large sums required, and because of the commercial instability of most of the industries. The compensation payments and capital needs of the NCB came solely from the sale of Government stock backed by the Treasury, but the other nationalised industries raised the bulk of their compensation and investment finance through the sale of their own stock. In 1956, however, the Government placed a restriction on the market borrowing of these industries, and since then all the nationalised industries have been dependent on the Treasury for their capital projects. In their turn, Treasury loans to the nationalised industries are raised primarily by Treasury borrowing rather than by taxation.

The financing of capital investment by loans from the

[1] W. D. Targett, 'Financial Objectives: the Record of British Gas', *Pub. Admin.* 1977, pp. 171–80.

[2] See S. Please, 'Government Control of the Capital Expenditure of the Nationalized Industries', *Pub. Admin.* 1955, pp. 31–42; R. J. S. Baker, *The Management of Capital Projects*, London 1962; M. Howe, 'Financing State Steel', *Pub. Admin.* 1971, pp. 309–20.

Treasury has been criticised as providing the nationalised industries with too ready a source of finance. Certainly, the Treasury often has no adequate economic yardstick by which to measure the capital needs of the nationalised industries, and an impression emerges of technical experts asking for vast sums for modernisation projects, the true necessity and economic desirability of which the Treasury has no satisfactory means of judging. The commercial instability of the railways, and perhaps of the NCB, limits their ability to raise capital on the open market, but the other nationalised industries, and particularly the Electricity Boards, could conveniently raise capital on the open market.

The 1961 White Paper on the Financial and Economic Obligations of the Nationalised Industries[1] (as well as recommending five years as the period over which a balance should be achieved between losses and surpluses), recommended that in future a much bigger share of a nationalised industry's capital investment should come from its own reserves. The 1961 White Paper recommended that the industries should produce sufficient surpluses to cover costs, build up reserves, and also redeem their capital. In 1967 a further White Paper proposed that Treasury loans for investment should only be forthcoming if there was a guaranteed rate of return.

It has been difficult for many of the nationalised industries to generate surpluses, or produce fixed rates of return on capital, because of uneconomic services they have been required to maintain 'in the public interest'. If an uneconomic service has to be maintained, attempts can be made to reduce the loss by normal commercial methods of increasing prices or reducing costs through greater efficiency. Alternatively, the principle of cross-subsidisation can be applied, with the losses of one service being compensated by the surplus from another service. It is debatable, however, to what extent the principle of cross-subsidisation is economically or morally justified, and how far it can be logically extended (with, perhaps, rail losses being subsidised by road profits in an overall transport scheme). As yet another alternative, the loss on a service can

[1]Cmd. 1337 (1961).

be officially accepted and a subsidy paid by the Treasury to cover the cost of uneconomic but socially necessary services, as with some rail or air services to remote areas.[1]

The distinction between a 'nationalised' and a 'socialised' concern can be said to be that a nationalised concern seeks to clear its losses like any private concern, whereas a socialised concern is one which, if necessary, provides services at a financial loss to itself, as a form of social service, relying on subsidies to clear any such losses. By this definition, the public corporations were not designed to operate as socialised concerns, in that they are statutorily required to cover their losses, and the 1961 White Paper emphasised this. In fact, however, the majority of the public corporations, and the railways in particular, have continued to provide services that were not commercially viable, as a matter of social responsibility. Only relatively recently have Governments recognised the need to subsidise the public corporations for the maintenance of uneconomical services. The 1967 White Paper emphasised this principle and the Transport Act 1968 allowed for the provision of specific grants to cover losses incurred in the maintenance of services which are economically non-viable, but which the Government feels to be socially desirable. Nevertheless it may be questioned whether the public corporation, with its requirement to be economically viable, is the best medium through which to run concerns that have social as well as commercial obligations.[2]

Public Ownership in Britain: an Assessment

The denationalisation policy implemented by the Thatcher Government reflects the dissatisfaction that has been felt about the record of the nationalised industries in the post-war period.[3] The nationalised industries are often criticised as being unwieldy, impersonal and bureaucratic, and as being commercially inefficient as a consequence. It is claimed that there is little employee loyalty, and little desire to please the

[1] See M. R. Garner, 'The Financing of the Nationalized Industries', *Pub. Admin.* 1981, pp. 466–73.

[2] See D. Coombes, *State Enterprise: Business or Politics*, London 1971.

[3] See, for example, Kelf-Cohen, *British Nationalization 1945–73.*

consumer, partly because of the impersonal nature of the concerns, and partly because of the lack of the 'incentives' that exist in private enterprise. It is argued that the nationalised industries are protected from competition by their monopolistic position, but despite this (or because of it) they have not achieved markedly better consumer services, and have not achieved the 'new millennium' in industrial relations that was expected in many quarters. As far as their financial record is concerned, it is argued that because the industries are so big there can be no adequate Ministerial or Treasury assessment of the economic viability of capital investment projects. Because of this, and because of a blind faith in large-scale investment as the answer to the industries' problems, it is claimed that there has been much wastage of capital which was acquired too easily. Critics thus advance proposals for wholesale denationalisation, for more decentralisation, for the introduction of greater incentives within the industries, and for greater competition between the industries themselves, and between the industries and private enterprise.

In defence of the record of the nationalised industries, however, it must be pointed out that they have suffered because successive governments have failed to produce sufficiently detailed and long-term plans for the industries. The Labour Governments have had only *ad hoc* plans for nationalisation, with no overall strategy, and certainly no 'twenty-year plan', while the post-war Conservative Governments have been very largely unsympathetic towards the public corporations. The main industries nationalised in the 1945–50 period were financially derelict before nationalisation, and were greatly in need of capital development. The financial difficulties of the nationalised industries were accentuated by the more than generous compensation paid on nationalisation; by the requirement that the public corporations should redeem their capital; and by the lack of any clear definition as to whether they were to provide commercial or social services. They have been expected to produce cheap and sometimes unprofitable services, and yet clear their losses, and they have incurred losses as a result of being used by the Government as a means of subsidising the private sector. Their financial problems have been increased when profitable aspects of their operations have been sold to the private sector. Many of the criticisms of the nationalised industries become irrelevant when it is realised that the purpose and policies of a public concern are basically different from those of a private enterprise concern, so that the criteria that are used to judge the success of a private firm cannot necessarily be applied to a public corporation. The fundamental differences that exist between a private firm, a department of state, and a public corporation in matters such as financial policy, management structure, accountability, and general objectives, are not always appreciated, and this leads to much confusion over the evaluation of the success of public corporations.

With regard to their trading position, they have not always benefited from their monopolistic position because social and political pressure has been applied to prevent this, and in many respects they have less freedom to operate than private concerns. Far from the nationalised industries being protected from competition, there has been intense competition in the fuel and power field, with gas, electricity and coal facing competition from oil,[1] while the airlines are subject to considerable competition at an international level, and to some competition within the United Kingdom. Examples can be quoted of the industries being encouraged to 'buy British', even when this was not economic; of them 'selling cheap and buying dear' in their dealings with private enterprise; and of limits being placed on their manufacturing and export policies in order to prevent damage to private enterprise interests.[2] Thus the nationalised industries have been used to give general help to private industry and to the community at large, which may be a legitimate use of the public sector of industry, but which should be acknowledged as being incompatible with the maintenance of economic services.

Any attempt to draw up a final 'balance sheet' as to the overall failure or success of the nationalised industries is, of course, hindered by the close party political involvement in the public enterprise issue. What is clear, however, is that

[1] See G. L. McVey, 'Policy for Fuel', *PQ* 1964, pp. 46–57.

[2] See, for example, M. Shanks (ed.), *The Lessons of Public Enterprise*, London 1963.

opponents of nationalisation have presented such a case against the post-1945 nationalised industries, and against the public corporation as a means of administering publicly owned concerns, that it will be difficult for a future Labour Government to reverse the denationalisation policy that has been followed since 1979.

13

Local Government

A SYSTEM of local government such as operates in Britain can be regarded as valuable in a number of respects.[1] It can serve to protect local interests within the broader framework of a national system of government. Local authorities can concern themselves with the details of the particular problems of a locality in a way that is difficult for the central government. This can produce a more effective handling of local affairs, while at the same time, a system of local government can relieve the work burden of the central government. In this respect, some services can be administered more efficiently at a local level than at a national level. Local government can be a political and administrative training ground for central government, and although in Britain there is little movement of officials between central and local government, many MPs serve a political apprenticeship on local councils. The number of MPs with local government experience has increased from about a third in 1945 to over two-thirds today (while among MPs elected for the first time in 1983, over half were former councillors).[2] Local government can also bring the citizen into

[1] For general descriptions of local government in Britain see T. Byrne, *Local Government in Britain*, London 1986; W. Thornhill (ed.), *The Growth and Reform of English Local Government*, London 1971; P. G. Richards, *The Local Government System*, London 1983; Lord Redcliffe-Maud and B. Wood, *English Local Government Reformed*, London 1974; J. Stanyer, *Understanding Local Government*, London 1976; A. Alexander, *Local Government in Britain Since Reorganisation*, London 1982; J. Stewart, *Local Government*, London 1983; G. Jones and J. Stewart, *The Case for Local Government*, London 1985.

[2] M. Burch and M. Moran, 'The Changing British Political Elite 1945–1983', *Parl. Aff.* 1985, p. 15.

closer contact with the details of government, and this can perhaps increase the political consciousness of the public. Local government can thus play a valuable role in a political system, although fundamental to its role is the relationship between the local and central governments.[1]

Local and Central Government

While the local government seeks to preserve local interests, the central government safeguards national interests, and brings standardisation to the whole system. Although both of these functions are important, they are often irreconcilable, so that a balance has to be sought between the two. To some extent, attitudes towards this balance reflect partisan considerations. Thus the importance of the independence of local authorities from central control was championed in the 1970s by Conservative opponents of the Labour Government's policy of extending comprehensive education, and in the 1980s by Labour opponents of the Conservative Government's policy of selling council houses to their tenants.

In Britain, local government is legally subordinate to the central government. The local authorities can only engage in activities for which they have statutory authority, and they must perform the tasks that are demanded of them. Their powers are conferred by statute – either general Acts which apply to all local authorities, or private Acts which are promoted by local authorities themselves, and which apply only to individual authorities or groups of authorities. Some statutes demand that local authorities provide and administer certain services, while others merely permit the local authorities to provide certain services if they so desire. Legis-

[1]See M. Goldsmith (ed.), *New Research In Central–Local Government Relations*, London 1985; S. Ranson (*et al.*), *Between Centre and Locality*, London 1985; R. A. W. Rhodes, *Control and Power in Central–Local Government Relations*, London 1981; E. Page, 'The Measurement of Central Control', *PS* 1980, pp. 117–20; A. Dunsire, 'Central Control Over Local Authorities', *Pub. Admin.* 1981, pp. 173–88; J. G. Gibson (*et al.*), 'The Measurement of Central Control in England and Wales', *PS* 1982, pp. 432–6; R. A. W. Rhodes, 'Continuity and Change in British Central–Local Relations', *BJPS* 1984, pp. 261–84.

lative control is thus the most fundamental form of central control over local government, in that the whole basis of the system can be altered by Act of Parliament. In addition, however, central control is exerted by administrative, financial and judicial means.

In Great Britain, the Secretaries of State for the Environment, Wales, and Scotland are the Ministers primarily responsible for local government, although the Secretaries of State for Education, Health and Social Security, and Home Affairs are also involved. As is revealed in more detail below,[1] the central government is able to exert influence over local government through the control of grants and loans to local authorities, and through the examination of local authorities' accounts. In addition, Ministerial consent is required for certain actions by local authorities, including the making of by-laws, and the appointment of some officials. Building plans require Ministerial approval, and the administration of some services, particularly the police, fire brigade, and education, is subject to examination by Ministry inspectors.[2] Some legislation that gives powers to local authorities, particularly with regard to planning and land development, allows for appeals to the appropriate Minister. Ultimately, the central government can remove a local authority's powers if it has neglected its duties.

Judicial control can be exerted over local authorities, in that like any citizen, they are subject to the jurisdiction of the law courts. Local authorities must not be guilty of non-feasance (neglecting their duties) or misfeasance (improper use of powers).[3] The judicial remedy for non-feasance lies in the application to the High Court for a writ of Mandamus, ordering the authority to do its duty, or in an Indictment for the neglect of duty. Ordinary civil action against a local

[1] See p. 434.

[2] J. S. Harris, 'Central Government Inspection of Local Services in Britain', *PAR* 1955, pp. 26–34; Sir James Dunnett, 'The Relationship Between Central and Local Government in the Planning of Road Schemes', *Pub. Admin.* 1962, pp. 253–66.

[3] See W. O. Hart, *Introduction to the Law of Local Government and Administration*, London 1957; Sir I. Jennings, *Principles of Local Government Law*, London 1960.

authority is also allowed for in some legislation. In the case of misfeasance, a remedy lies in the application for a writ of Certiorari if the local authority is abusing its powers, or for a writ of Prohibition if it is about to abuse its powers. Local authorities can also be restrained by an injunction.

Although central government has final legal control, local authorities retain considerable practical initiative. They are ultimately responsible for the efficient administration of a vast range of public services. They account for 25% of public expenditure and 40% of public sector employees. In negotiations or confrontations with central government they can speak with a special knowledge of local circumstances, and can claim to have a local electoral mandate. They will be able to gather support from the Opposition parties at Westminster, and particular local authorities may well have allies on the Government side of the House. Central control over local government is to be welcomed if it maintains the efficiency of the local government system, achieves the standardisation of local government services throughout the country, protects the citizen from the abuse of power by the local authorities, reduces the chances of corruption in the system, and helps towards the attainment of national financial, economic, and general planning policies. It is clearly undesirable, however, if it reduces efficiency through needless controls, destroys local initiative, and leads to over-centralisation and remoteness.

The History and Structure of Local Government

In England the origins of local government can be traced back to the Saxon period, when local administrative independence was enjoyed by the shires (similar in size to the modern counties), and by the hundreds (combinations of townships), both of which were under the authority of members of the nobility.[1] In addition, there were some townships or boroughs which had some independence from noble domination. After

[1]See J. J. Clarke, *A History of Local Government in the United Kingdom*, London 1955; K. B. Smellie, *A History of Local Government*, London 1957; B. Keith Lucas, *The History of Local Government in England: Josef Redlich and Francis W. Hirst*, London 1970; B. Keith-Lucas and P. G. Richards, *A History of Local Government in the Twentieth Century*, London 1978.

1066 some towns were granted royal charters, and were allowed to administer their own affairs, while in the counties powerful nobles were given the title of Justice of the Peace, with the power to administer affairs in parts of the county. These developments formed the basis of the distinction between counties and boroughs in the modern local government structure. By the sixteenth century, parishes had emerged as the main local administrative units in the counties outside the independent boroughs. In the middle ages the functions of the local administrators were primarily the upkeep of roads, bridges, and jails, but in 1601 the Poor Relief Act called upon parishes to provide for the poor and destitute, for which purpose they were given the power to levy rates.

The modern shape of local government dates only from the nineteenth century, however, and is largely a product of the need to deal with conditions created by the industrial and agrarian revolutions.[1] The social and economic distress at the beginning of the nineteenth century led to the Poor Law Amendment Act 1834, which provided for poor relief to be administered at a local level, supervised by the Poor Law Commissioners in London. The Police Act 1829 created the Metropolitan police force, and the Municipal Corporations Act 1835 reformed the local government system in a number of boroughs, extending the franchise, introducing a borough audit, and ending a number of corrupt practices. The responsibilities of local authorities in the spheres of public health and housing were developed during the nineteenth century, particularly by the Public Health Acts of 1848 and 1878, while in 1870 the Education Act allowed for the creation of School Boards with the power to levy rates to build schools. Towards the end of the century there emerged a new structure to allow for the more effective management of these local services. The Local Government Act 1888 established the structure and powers of county and county borough councils, and that of 1894 established urban districts, rural districts, and parishes. The Local Government Act 1933 gathered various existing

[1] See V. D. Lipman, *Local Government Areas, 1834–1945*, London 1949; C. J. Pearce, *The Machinery of Change in Local Government 1888–1974*, London 1980.

statutes into one comprehensive measure. This structure survived until replaced by the present structure in 1974.

Very broadly, the services that local authorities provide today can be classed either as environmental, protective, or personal services. The environmental services are those that are concerned with the citizens' immediate physical surroundings, and they include road construction and maintenance, the provision of street lighting, water supplies, recreation grounds, street cleansing, and refuse disposal. The protective services are concerned with the safety of the citizen, and are primarily the provision of police and fire services. The personal services, concerned with the individual well-being of citizens, include the provision of housing, education (including school meals, further education grants, libraries and museums, as well as schools), and health services (including child welfare clinics, day nurseries, and health visitors). Local authorities also provide trading services, such as passenger transport services in some areas, but local authority trading is today much less widespread than before 1945.

In the first forty years of this century, there was an expansion of the public health and sanitation services provided by local authorities, and since 1945 they have acquired new responsibilities for town and country planning, child care, welfare services, and health services. In recent years local authorities have provided more artistic, recreational and sporting services. On the other hand, since 1945 the local authorities have lost their responsibility for hospitals, school health services, gas, electricity, and water services, and at present there is much pressure for the nationalisation of other services (especially aspects of education). Recently some services, such as school meals and refuse collection, have been transferred to private contractors in some areas. Water and sewage services, which until 1974 were provided by local authorities, are now the responsibility of Regional Water Boards in England and Wales. In 1986, however, the Government announced plans for the privatisation of these bodies.

* * *

The merits of a two-tier system of authorities, as opposed to a system of 'all-purpose' or 'most purpose' authorities, have been debated at length. When a single authority provides all the services in one area, its responsibility is clear (and is apparent to the consumer), and policy can be readily coordinated. A two-tier system, on the other hand, makes possible a rational distribution of functions so that each type of authority can perform the tasks for which it is best fitted: common services can be provided at a county or regional level, while more local services can be dealt with by district bodies. Under the old system of local government, the county boroughs were all-purpose authorities. Under the current system (established by the London Government Act 1963, the Local Government Acts 1972 and 1985, and the Local Government [Scotland] Act 1973) a two-tier system operates in Scotland and most of England and Wales, while in London and the main English conurbations there is a single-tier system.

In England there are thirty-nine top-tier County authorities, ranging in size from Kent with almost 1,500,000 inhabitants, to the Isle of Wight with just over 100,000 inhabitants. The counties are divided into 296 second-tier districts, mostly with populations of 60,000 to 100,000. The counties provide services for which uniformity of action throughout the area is particularly desirable (such as education, strategic planning, police, fire and refuse disposal), while the districts are responsible for more specifically local services (such as housing, refuse collection, building regulations and environmental health). In all, the services provided by the counties account for over 80% of expenditure.

Greater London is divided into thirty-two boroughs (plus the City of London Corporation), and the other metropolitan areas into a total of thirty-six districts. These districts and London boroughs are responsible for the bulk of the services in their area, but there are also joint boards that manage some common services such as transport, civil defence, fire and (outside London) police. The joint boards are financed by the districts or boroughs and are composed of councillors drawn from them. Police services in London are controlled by the Home Office, and bus and underground services by the London Regional Transport Authority. In the twelve inner-London boroughs education is administered by the Inner London Education Authority, which (unlike other joint boards) is directly elected on the basis of two members per-Parliamentary constituency.

Between 1974 and 1986 London and the six metropolitan areas were like the rest of England in having a two-tier structure.[1] The Local Government Act 1985, however, abolished the top tier (the Greater London Council and the Metropolitan Counties) and transferred their functions to the second-tier authorities or to joint boards. For much of the time the Greater London Council and the Metropolitan County Councils had been under Labour control, and had pursued high-spending policies in face of the social problems of the inner-cities. The Conservative Government saw their abolition as one means of attacking local government expenditure. Opponents of the change, however, rejected the Government's claim that the new system would save £100 million per year, and criticised the transfer of vital services to indirectly elected joint boards.

In Wales, dating from 1974, there are eight counties with populations ranging from 100,000 to 500,000, and thirty-seven districts with populations of 20,000 to 300,000. The division of functions between the counties and districts in Wales is broadly similar to that in England, although the Welsh districts have some of the functions (refuse disposal, provision of libraries) that in England are performed by the counties.

Throughout England and Wales, links with the pre-1974 local government structure have been retained wherever practical. Many of the district boundaries correspond exactly to those of the old county boroughs or county districts, and many other districts were formed by the merger of two or more of the old units. Some of the districts adopted the title of 'borough', and retained a Mayor as first citizen and chairman of the council. The old system of parish councils was retained and the powers of the councils extended. Some 300 former urban districts and small boroughs became parishes. For the basic grass roots level the Government has encouraged the creation of neighbourhood councils for communities of up to 10,000

[1] See N. Flynn (*et al.*), *Abolition or Reform?* London 1985; T. Clegg (*et al.*), *The Future of London Government*, London 1985; K. Young and P. L. Garside, *Metropolitan London: Politics and Urban Change 1837–1981*, London 1982; K. Young, 'Metropolis R.I.P.?', *PQ* 1986, pp. 36–46.

TABLE XXXIII

Distribution of Principal Local Government Services

	England and Wales				Greater London		Scotland[a]	
	Counties		Metropolitan Areas					
Principal Services	Counties	County Districts	Joint Boards	Metro Districts	Joint Boards	Boroughs	Regions	Districts
Overall planning	✓			✓		✓	✓	
Transport	✓		✓		✓		✓	
Police[b]	✓		✓				✓	
Fire	✓		✓		✓		✓	
Education[c]	✓			✓	✓	✓	✓	
Social services	✓			✓		✓	✓	
Housing		✓		✓		✓		✓
Environment		✓		✓		✓		✓
Leisure		✓		✓		✓		✓
Roads	✓			✓		✓	✓	
Local planning		✓		✓		✓		✓
Water[d]							✓	

[a] In addition three island authorities (Orkney, Shetland and Western Isles) responsible for all services except police, fire and education.
[b] In London a Home Office function.
[c] Inner London Education Authority for inner London; Boroughs outside inner London.
[d] Regional Water Authorities in England and Wales.

FIGURE I

The Structure of English Local Government, Before and After the London Government Act 1963 and the Local Government Acts 1972 and 1985

Pre-1963 Structure

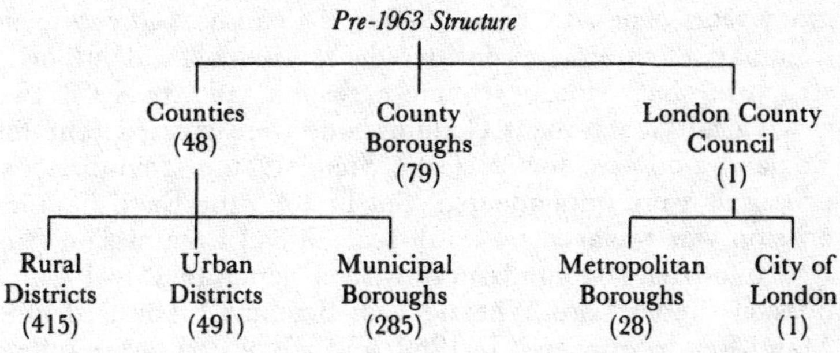

1974 Structure

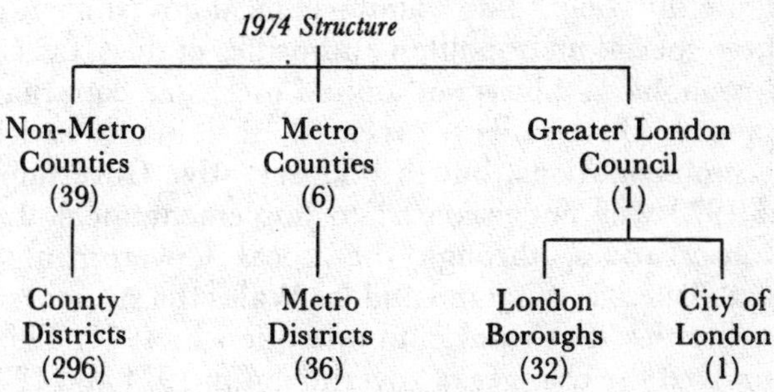

1986 Structure

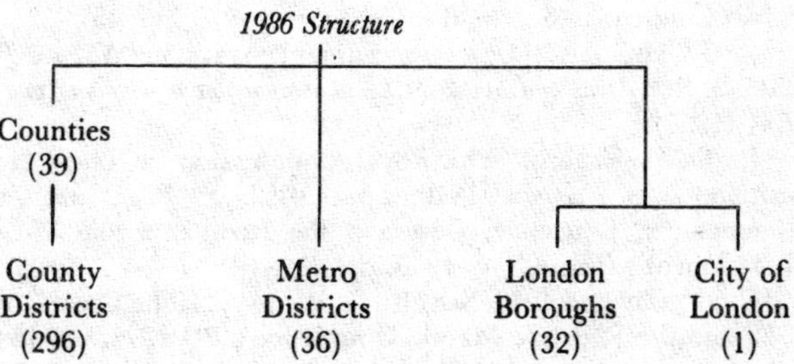

population.[1] These are designed to encourage citizen participation in community affairs, provide a channel of communication between councillors and electors, and even provide some local services such as pre-school playgroups.

The present local government structure is a product of many years of debate. From 1945 to 1949 a Local Government Boundary Commission considered a revision of local authority structure, but without concrete results, and in 1958 two new Local Government Commissions were created (one for England and one for Wales).[2] Some of the Commissions' proposals were implemented, but in 1965 the English Commission was replaced by a full-scale Royal Commission (the Redcliffe-Maud Commission) with a separate Royal Commission (under Lord Wheatley) for Scotland.[3] The Redcliffe-Maud Report appeared in 1969, and advocated the complete overhaul of local government boundaries and functions.[4] It proposed the division of England into eight 'provinces'. Within these broad regional divisions it proposed the formation of fifty-eight large 'unitary' local government areas, plus three special metropolitan authorities of the GLC type, for the Birmingham, Liverpool and Manchester conurbations. The Labour Government accepted the main Redcliffe-Maud recommendations, but the Conservative Government elected in 1970 was not prepared to implement them. Instead, the Conservatives, through the Local Government Act 1972, established for England and for Wales the structure of two-tier authorities that came into operation in 1974. This structure survived the changes of government in 1974 and 1979. In their 1983 election manifesto, however, the Conservatives indicated

[1] See W. Hampton and J. J. Chapman, 'Towards Neighbourhood Councils', *PQ* 1971, pp. 247–54 *and* 414–22. See also J. Prophet, 'The Case for Parish Councils in Scotland', *Pub. Admin.* 1971, pp. 457–62.

[2] J. G. Thomas, 'Local Government Areas in Wales', *PL* 1962, pp. 160–74. See *Areas and Status of Local Authorities in England and Wales*, Cmd. 9831 (1956).

[3] J. P. Mackintosh, 'The Royal Commission on Local Government in Scotland', *Pub. Admin.* 1970, pp. 49–56; E. Page and A. Midwinter, 'Remoteness, Efficiency, Cost and the Reorganisation of Scottish Local Government', *Pub. Admin.* 1980, pp. 439–64.

[4] Cmd. 4039 and 4040. See also G. W. Jones, 'The Local Government Act 1972 and the Redcliffe-Maud Commission', *PQ* 1973, pp. 154–66.

that they would modify the system by abolishing the top-tier metropolitan authorities, and this was achieved through the Local Government Act 1985.

In Scotland the local government system evolved in a different pattern from England and Wales, and it remains a distinct system today. The Wheatley Commission, reporting in 1969, advocated the replacement of the four hundred or so counties, counties of cities, burghs and districts that had operated since 1929, by fewer and larger authorities. Unlike the Redcliffe-Maud Report these recommendations were acceptable to the Heath Conservative Government, and were implemented through the Local Government (Scotland) Act 1973. The new structure, which came into operation in 1975, is of seven top-tier regional authorities and thirty-seven second-tier district authorities. The regions range in population from Strathclyde, with over 2,500,000 (almost half the total population of Scotland), to the Borders, with just under 100,000.[1] Scotland's only large conurbation, Clydeside, does not have a metropolitan council of its own, but forms part of the larger Strathclyde region. The division of functions between the regions and districts is similar to that between the English counties and districts, with education and social services being the responsibility of the top tier.

The Personnel of Local Government

The Council. County Councils have sixty to a hundred members and district and borough councils fifty to eighty. In all, there are now about 26,000 councillors (or closer to 100,000 if parish and community councillors are included). County, district and parish councillors all serve for four-year terms. Local government elections in England and Wales are normally held on the first Thursday in May. For electoral purposes the counties are divided into single-member divisions, whereas the districts are divided into wards, each represented by three councillors (or multiples of three). The county councils are elected *en bloc*, all councillors retiring

[1]See A. H. Dawson, 'The Idea of the Region and the 1975 Reorganisation of Scottish Local Government', *Pub. Admin.* 1981, pp. 279–94.

together every four years. Elections for the metro district councils, however, are held in each of the three years that fall between county council elections, with a third of the council retiring each time. On this pattern an election is held annually in each ward of the district. The county districts are free to follow the county council pattern of *en bloc* elections every four years, or the metro district pattern of annual elections, and most have opted for the *en bloc* pattern. In Scotland regional and district councillors are elected *en bloc* in single-member divisions for four-year terms, with the district council elections coming in the middle year between regional elections.

The system of annual elections in the metro districts means that changes in party composition on the councils come more gradually than in the counties. Annual elections involve greater expense and administrative upheaval, however, and it can be argued that the more infrequent the elections, the more stable is the system. Also, annual elections are hardly practical for county councils, as only one councillor serves each division of the county.

A chairman of the council is elected annually by the councillors from among their own number. In boroughs the chairman often carries the title of Mayor. In the pre-1974 local government system aldermen formed part of the council. They were elected for six-year terms by the councillors, usually from their own ranks. While the aldermen added a degree of continuity and stability to the council they were frequently criticised as being an undemocratic and self-perpetuating aspect of council composition, and they were not incorporated in the new local government pattern. Outsiders can (and in Scotland must) be coopted onto particular committees, though they do not thereby become members of the council. The Education Act 1944, for example, requires that education committees must contain educational experts, and this will necessitate cooption if the expertise is not to be found among the councillors. As well as providing expertise, cooption permits non-partisan figures to participate in local government.

To be eligible to serve as a councillor, a person must live or work in the local authority area in which he seeks to serve. Anyone who holds a paid office with the local authority is disqualified, as are undischarged bankrupts, and anyone who has been sentenced to more than three months' imprisonment (without the option of a fine) over the previous five years. Councillors can be removed from office if they have failed to attend council meetings over the previous six months, or if they have been surcharged by the Audit Commission within the previous five years, for sums of more than £500. Unlike Parliamentary elections, no financial deposit is required from candidates, although there are restrictions on the amount of money that can be spent by each candidate on his election campaign.[1] To qualify for the vote in local elections, a person must be a British subject, aged 18 or over, and resident in the area. Until 1969 non-residents were also eligible to vote in an area if they held property there. In this way some people could vote in more than one local authority, through a residential qualification in one and a property qualification in another. This property qualification was ended, however, by the Representation of the People Act 1969.

* * *

The 'quality' of council members is often criticised. Some people become councillors out of a desire to serve the local community, and out of a genuine interest in local government affairs. Others regard council service as a means of gaining local prestige, or as a stage in a party political career, perhaps as a preliminary to a Parliamentary candidature.[2] Many people are deterred from local council service, however, by financial considerations. Councillors have long received loss of earnings allowances, but until recently these were far from generous. The Maud Committee on the Management of Local Government recommended in 1967 that councillors be paid an honorarium, the Wheatley Commission in 1969 advocated the

[1] For details of the law of local government elections see A. N. Schofield, *Local Government Elections*, London 1954. See also B. Keith-Lucas, *The English Local Government Franchise*, London 1952.

[2] See J. Brand, 'Party Organization and the Recruitment of Councillors', *BJPS* 1973, pp. 473–86; K. Newton, 'Role Orientations and Their Sources Among Elected Representatives in English Local Politics', *J of P* 1974, pp. 615–36; I. Gordon, 'The Recruitment of Local Politicians', *PP* 1979, pp. 1–38; I. Gordon and P. Whiteley, 'Social Class and Political Attitudes: the Case of Labour Councillors', *PS* 1979, pp. 99–113.

payment of a substantial salary, and the Robinson Committee on the remuneration of councillors advocated in 1977 special responsibility payments for committee chairmen. Although salaries have not been introduced, the allowances have been much improved. Councillors can now claim a daily attendance allowance, and travel and subsistence allowances, while some authorities have adopted the Robinson Committee's proposal on additional responsibility payments. Apart from financial considerations, however, many people are prevented from serving as council members because the nature of their employment would prevent them from attending council and committee meetings, while many others are deterred by the amount of time and work involved in being a council member. The Robinson Committee in 1977 found that councillors spend an average of sixty-nine hours per week on council business (though there are undoubtedly considerable variations around this average figure).

It is dangerous to make generalisations about the social background of the several thousand citizens who serve as local government councillors in England, Wales, and Scotland, as information is limited. A national survey of 4,000 councillors undertaken for the Maud Committee in 1964 indicated that the vast majority of councillors were businessmen, farmers, professional men, or other non-manual workers: only 19% were classed as 'blue-collar' workers. More than half were aged over 55, and almost 90% were male. These broad patterns were confirmed in a survey for the Robinson Committee in 1977, though this enquiry did find that 17% of councillors were women (a much bigger proportion than in the House of Commons). The national pattern, of course, will not be reflected on every council. A comparison of the composition of four county and nine borough councils in the Greater London area in 1959[1] revealed that the upper and middle classes formed two-thirds of council members in the counties, but just half in the boroughs, while there were many more retired people on the county councils than on the borough

[1] L. J. Sharpe, 'The Politics of Local Government in Greater London', *Pub. Admin.* 1960, pp. 157–72.

councils. Similarly, an analysis of the social background of the Newcastle-under-Lyme borough council between 1932 and 1962 revealed that nearly two-thirds of council members in this period were non-manual workers, even though this group formed less than a third of the total population of the borough in 1962.[1] In an historical analysis of the social composition of three local authorities in the south-east of England (Kent county, Croydon county borough, and Lewisham metropolitan borough), it was found that the proportion of middle-class members of the councils declined between 1930 and 1958, as did the proportion of retired people on the council.[2] The proportion of working-class members of the council increased from 4% to 11% in Kent, from 8% to 30% in Croydon, and from 6% to 50% in Lewisham. This trend is probably typical of most councils.

The Officials. The policy decisions that are made by the council are administered by the various local government officials and employees, who range from the Chief Executive and the staff in the council offices, to the school teachers, transport staff, managers of municipal enterprises, and manual workers employed in the local government service. Local authorities are statutorily obliged to appoint some officers, such as the heads of some specified departments, but this requirement varies with the type of authority.

In general, local government officers are appointed and dismissed at the discretion of the council, and although the Secretary of State for the Environment (or the Secretary of State for Scotland) retains the power of veto over some appointments, this is only rarely applied. Those who fill the senior posts in local government administration, and the heads of departments in particular, normally have professional qualifications. In 1968, the Mallaby Committee on the staffing of Local Government emphasised the problems encountered by many local authorities (and especially the

[1] Bealey, Blondel, and McCann, *Constituency Politics*, p. 304.
[2] Sharpe, *BJS* 1962.

smaller ones) in recruiting suitably qualified officers.[1] The career prospects of local government officers, however, were improved considerably by the formation of larger local government units and the consequent creation of more attractive top level posts. In salary terms senior local government posts now compare favourably with those in the civil service and other professions.

The 'trade union' of local government officers is the National and Local Government Officers Association, catering for all grades. NALGO has a record of cooperation rather than conflict with the local authorities. Rates of pay and conditions of service are governed by recommendations made by Whitley Councils, composed of representatives from NALGO and other unions, and representatives of the local authorities. Chief of these Councils is the National Joint Council for Local Authorities' Administrative, Professional, Technical, and Clerical Servants.[2]

Officials cannot stand as candidates at elections of the council which employs them, and members of the council (and ex-councillors for a period of at least twelve months after their retirement) cannot become council employees. The officials are expected to be politically non-partisan in their attitudes, in the same tradition as the permanent and neutral Civil Service. As with the Civil Service, however, the activities of the senior officials are inevitably bound up with political issues to a considerable extent. The Chief Executive, treasurer, education officer and other heads of departments attend council and committee meetings in an advisory capacity, but Chief Constables are further removed from involvement with the council. The heads of departments are concerned primarily with managerial and administrative matters, but the distinction between administrative and policy issues can be as blurred in

[1] See B. Wood, 'Staffing Problems in the Re-organization of Local Government', *Pub. Admin.* 1971, pp. 279–90; G. A. Boyne, 'Socio-economic Conditions, Central Policies and Local Authority Staffing Levels', *Pub. Admin.* 1986, pp. 69–82.

[2] L. Kramer, 'Reflections on Whitleyism in English Local Government', *Pub. Admin.* 1958, pp. 47–70; M. McIntosh, 'The Negotiation of Wages and Conditions of Service for Local Authority Employees in England and Wales', *Pub. Admin.* 1955, pp. 149–62, *and* 307–24 *and* 401–18.

local government as it is in central government. There is much informal contact between heads of departments and members of the council, particularly the chairmen of the various committees of the council, and the question of where the power of councillors ends (or should end), and that of officers begins (or should begin) remains one of the issues of local government.[1]

Under the old local government structure the clerk of the council was the principal officer.[2] His main responsibilities were to ensure that the council operated within its legal powers, and to guide and coordinate the overall activities of the council. His considerable legal and administrative responsibilities, however, generally prevented him from giving a positive overall lead in policy matters.[3] The Mallaby and Maud Committees in 1967 both recommended that the role of the clerk of the council should be expanded. The Bains Committee, set up in 1971 to frame recommendations on questions of management for the new local government units, echoed this. It advocated that the new authorities should appoint chief officers who were free from specific departmental duties, with the legal and secretarial responsibilities of the old-style clerks being handled by a subordinate officer. The majority of the larger new counties and districts have followed this recommendation, and have appointed a 'Chief Executive' as principal officer in charge of the overall management of the authority.[4]

Local Government in Operation

To a considerable extent, local authorities are free to make their own internal arrangements for the conduct of their

[1] See J. Stanyer, 'Elected Representatives and Management in Local Government', *Pub. Admin.* 1971, pp. 73–97 and 269–89.

[2] See C. Barratt, 'The Town Clerk in British Local Government', *Pub. Admin.* 1963, pp. 157–72.

[3] See J. Elliott, 'The Harris Experiment in Newcastle-upon-Tyne', *Pub. Admin.* 1971, pp. 149–62; G. H. Chipperfield, 'The City Manager and Chief Administrative Officer', *Pub. Admin.* 1964, pp. 123–32.

[4] See J. Boynton, *Job at the Top*, London 1986; M. Laffin and K. Young, 'The Changing Roles and Responsibilities of Local Authority Chief Officers', *Pub. Admin.* 1985, pp. 41–60; B. Wilson, 'Who Would Be a Chief Executive?', *Pub. Admin.* 1975, pp. 231–40.

affairs, although in practice, basic procedures vary little between authorities of similar types. All local councils must meet at least four times a year. The county councils generally meet more frequently than this minimum, and district councils usually meet once per month. The public and the press are admitted to council meetings, although the council can go into private session if it is felt that this is in the public interest. The chairman of the council is in charge of council meetings. He is expected to be neutral, although he can exercise a casting vote. Council meetings take the form of an examination of proposals made by the committees of the council. Questions of principle are decided by the council, but the committees work out the details of policies. At meetings of the full council, the chairmen of the committees introduce their proposals, which are debated and then accepted, rejected, or referred back to the committee. In most local authorities, however, and certainly in the largest authorities, the work of the council (and its committees) is dominated by party political organisations, with council decisions really being controlled by party group meetings.

The standing committees of local government are functional, in that each committee deals with a particular service, or group of services, provided by the council. The most important and busiest committees are divided into subcommittees. In most authorities an overall management committee, usually called a Policy and Resources Committee, is appointed, composed of committee chairmen, or of the senior members of the majority party on the council.[1] It acts as a 'Cabinet', supervising and co-ordinating the work of the various committees. On other councils, this supervising and coordinating function is performed by the leader of the majority party, acting with his colleagues in group meetings, and on other small councils it is performed by the whole council. Some committees are required by statute, but the majority are created at the discretion of the council. The vast majority of the committees are advisory, and merely make proposals

[1] R. Greenwood (*et al.*), 'The Policy Committee in English Local Government', *Pub. Admin.* 1972, pp. 157–66; R. James, 'Is there a Case for Local Authority Policy Planning?', *Pub. Admin.* 1973, pp. 147–64.

which the whole council accepts or rejects, but the council vests its authority in some committees, and gives them executive powers. In addition to the standing committees there may be various specialist committees appointed to deal with particular problems. There are also joint committees or boards which are made up of representatives from more than one authority, and which deal with services, such as an airport or area planning, in which more than one authority is involved. In the larger authorities, committee membership is generally in proportion to party strength on the council, with the majority party taking all or most of the committee chairmanships. Sometimes an attempt is made to put a councillor from each ward on the most important committees, but this is not really practical in the very large councils.

As well as the general principle that the smaller the decision-making body the more effective it will be, a principal merit of the committee system is that it brings individual members of the council into closer contact with the details of administration than would otherwise be possible. The committee system enables councillors to become specialised in particular subjects, and allows the council's responsibilities to be shared out among groups of councillors, with the full council meeting only occasionally to consider committee recommendations. This is perhaps especially important in the case of the county councils, where geographical considerations can mean that council meetings are held less frequently than in the boroughs. The committee system is often criticised, however, as taking authority away from the council as a whole, and placing it in the hands of small groups of councillors. Local government officials often criticise the committee system as giving councillors too much power over the details of administration. Also, specialisation in itself need not be a virtue, and can merely produce narrowness in outlook.

Following recommendations of the Maud Committee in 1967, a number of councils reduced the number of their committees and sub-committees. The Bains Committee, set up in 1971 to produce recommendations on questions of management for the new local government units, echoed the Maud Committee in advocating a streamlined committee structure for the new local authorities. The new authorities have accepted this general principle and the broad pattern in the reformed local government system has been the creation of fewer but more powerful committees than under the old system. In general, however, it can be said that the value of the committee system depends to a large degree on the type of council involved, with the larger the council, and the greater its responsibilities, the greater the need for committees to deal with detailed matters.

The control of local authority expenditure is partly an internal responsibility of the council and its officials, and partly an external matter in the hands of the Audit Commission. The internal control is exercised by the whole council, and all expenditure requires council authorisation. More specifically, control is exercised by the Finance Committee and the treasurer. General financial policy is determined by the full council and the Finance Committee, and is applied throughout the year through the approval or rejection of all plans that involve expenditure.[1] In addition to this general control, there is the annual process of preparing and securing approval for the council's 'Budget' of proposed expenditure, and planned income for meeting the expenditure. This begins with the preparation of departmental estimates by the officials of the departments. This process usually takes place in the autumn, to fit in with the financial year beginning in April, and the chairmen of the committees generally work in close cooperation with the heads of the departments in this matter.

The estimating process can be very precise, as the sums dealt with are not as big as those dealt with in national finance, nor are the annual variations as great. All the estimates are examined in detail by the Finance Committee. It is usually made up of the senior or most important members of the council, or of the chairmen of all the committees. After the

[1] J. Alt, 'Some Social and Political Correlates of County Borough Expenditures', *BJPS* 1971, pp. 49–62; R. Greenwood (*et al.*), 'The Politics of the Budgetary Process in English Local Government', *PS* 1977, pp. 25–47, *and* 1978, pp. 109–18; J. N. Danzigar, 'Assessing Incrementalism in British Municipal Budgeting', *BJPS* 1976, pp. 335–50; D. E. Ashford (*et al.*), 'The Expenditure-Financing Decision in British Local Government', *PP* 1976–7, pp. 5–24.

Finance Committee's scrutiny, the approval of the full council is generally a formality, although disputes between the Finance Committee and a particular committee may have to be settled by the full council.

At the end of the financial year the examination of the accounts is undertaken by the Audit Commission. This body was established in 1982, replacing the District Audit Service. The Controller and his staff are appointed by the Secretary of State and are drawn from the commercial world to a greater extent than was the case with the old District Audit Service. As with the examination of central government accounts by the Comptroller and Auditor General, the Audit Commission is concerned not only with assessing the general financial state of the authority, and pointing out irregularities, but also with ensuring that all expenditure has been authorised. The Audit Commission also acts as a local government 'efficiency unit', assessing whether local authorities are operating in the most economic and cost-effective way.

If the Audit Commission uncovers any wastage of public money caused by neglect or malpractice, it must surcharge the councillors or officials who are responsible. If the sum involved is greater than £2,000, the councillors concerned can be excluded from council service for five years. When Clay Cross Council refused to implement the Housing Finance Act 1971 (which allowed the central government to set the level of local authority rents), the councillors were disqualified from future service and required to meet the costs of their action.[1] In 1985 eighty-one councillors from Liverpool and Lambeth were surcharged for sums of around £200,000 and disqualified from office for defying the 1984 rate capping legislation and failing to levy rates that were within central government guidelines.

Finally in this context it may be noted that as well as the Audit Commission's financial check on local mis-government, there now exist five Commissioners for Local Administration (one each for Scotland and Wales and three for England), created by the Local Government Act 1974. Each Commissioner examines complaints of maladministration made

[1] R. Minns, 'The Significance of Clay Cross: Another Look at District Audit', *PP* 1973–4, pp. 309–30; A. Mitchell, 'Clay Cross', *PQ* 1974, pp. 165–78.

against local authorities in the particular region for which he is responsible.[1] The complaints can be made through a councillor, or (in contrast to the situation with the Parliamentary Commissioner) can come directly from a member of the public. As with the Parliamentary Commissioner, however, the Local Commissioner's terms of reference are confined to administrative matters (such as delay, incompetence or bias on the part of officials), and do not extend to policy considerations. He issues a public report but has no power to compel a local authority to redress a grievance.

Local Government Income[2]

Local authorities spend some £35 billion each year (about a quarter of all public expenditure). Education accounts for about 40% of this, and housing another 10%. The main sources of income to meet this expenditure are the rates, government grants, and loans. Authorities also gain revenue from trading enterprises, although a distinction has to be made between those services (like transport) which may produce a trading profit, and others for which a charge is made (as with library fines) but which are not run on commercial lines. Since 1977 local authorities have also been able to raise revenue by promoting lotteries.

Loans. Local authorities borrow money mainly in order to pay for capital investments that cannot readily be financed from current income from rates or grants, but also on the principle that the cost of investments with long-term benefits should be met by loans which can be repaid gradually over the life of the asset, as the benefits of the investment materialise. As with private concerns, local authorities can raise loans by issuing stock on the Stock Exchange, by internal borrowing from the authorities' own funds, by private mortgages, or by a

[1] D. Foulkes, 'The Work of the Local Commissioner For Wales', *PL* 1978, pp. 264–89; C. M. Chinkin and R. J. Bailey, 'The Local Ombudsman', *Pub. Admin.* 1976, pp. 267–82.

[2] See N. P. Hepworth, *Finance of Local Government*, London 1984; C. D. Foster (*et al.*), *Local Government Finance in a Unitary State*, London 1980; A. Midwinter, *The Politics of Local Spending*, London 1983; K. Newton and T. Karran, *The Politics of Local Expenditure*, London 1985.

bank overdraft in the case of small sums. Some large authorities also borrow abroad. In addition, local authorities can borrow from the central government through the Public Works Loan Board, while a small authority can borrow from a larger one. Loans from the Public Works Loan Board are repaid in instalments, with the rates of interest fixed by the Treasury. The larger authorities tend to rely mainly on the open market, while the smaller authorities rely more on the Loan Board. Whichever source is used, however, the vast majority of loans require Ministerial consent. This is designed to ensure that the authorities only borrow what they can afford to repay, and thereby maintain the reputation of local authorities as good financial investments. Control over local authority borrowing is also a valuable form of government influence over the economy.

Rates. Just over a third of local government income comes from the rates. The basic principle behind the rates is that of the taxation of property in proportion to the benefit that accrues to the occupier, and it represents the main form of local authority income from local sources. A property, be it a house, factory, business premises, or an area of land, is assessed in terms of a gross annual rental value. Until 1950, local authorities were themselves responsible for making the assessments, but the Local Government Act 1948 transferred this task to the Board of Inland Revenue as from 1950, in an attempt to achieve a national standard of assessments. A reassessment of values is normally made every five years. Deductions are made from the gross annual rental value of the property, to cover the cost of repairs and maintenance, and this produces a net annual rental value, which represents the rateable value of the property. This rateable value is then used as the basis for calculating the annual rates to be paid by the property owner. The council fixes a rate poundage according to its financial needs for that year. If the rate poundage is fixed at 50p in the £, someone who owns property with a rateable value of £900 will pay 900 × 50p, or £450. If the rate poundage is 80p in the £, he will pay 900 × 80p, or £720.[1]

[1] D. N. King, 'Why Do Local Authority Rate Poundages Differ?', *Pub. Admin.* 1973, pp. 165–74.

In England and Wales the district councils are the rating authorities. They receive notice from the counties, the parishes and the various joint boards of the rates that they require, and collect these sums on their behalf. In the counties, where education (by far the most costly service) is a county rather than district responsibility, the bulk of the rate revenue has to be passed on to the county council. In Scotland the top tier regional councils are the rating authorities. Over £11 billion is raised in rates each year, about 45% of it coming from domestic property. Before 1963, commercial premises were given a 20% concession on their rateable value, and industrial premises had a 50% concession (compared with a 75% concession between 1925 and 1958). These concessions were removed in 1963, but agricultural land remains exempt from rates. The Layfield Committee, set up in 1974 to examine the rating system, argued that the agricultural concession should end, but the Government rejected the proposal.[1] In rented property the landlord often pays the rates, and allows for this in the rent that he charges to his tenants. In so far as the payment of rates stimulates interest in local government, this distinction between paying rates directly, and paying them through a rent, can be significant.

In an attempt to curb rate increases the Conservative Government acquired new controls over local authorities through the Local Government Acts 1982 and 1984. The 1982 Act obliged local authorities that were faced with unforeseen expenditure to seek Ministerial approval before levying a supplementary rate. The 1984 Act gave the Minister the power to prevent a local authority increasing its rates beyond a certain figure if he felt that the authority's expenditure was excessive. In the first year of the operation of this 'rate-capping' Act, eighteen local authorities were required either to reduce their proposed rate increases or, in some cases, to levy a rate that was lower than in the previous year. The Government's justification for this limitation on the traditional freedom of local authorities to determine the level of their own rates was that in a number of big-spending authorities large rate increases were placing unacceptable burdens on some ratepayers.

[1] J. V. Miller (*et al.*), 'The Layfield Report', *Pub. Admin.* 1977, pp. 1–58.

The rating system is a convenient form of taxation, in that it is cheap and easy to administer. In some ways land and buildings form a good basis for taxation, as unlike some forms of income they cannot be concealed from the assessors. The rating system, however, has many weaknesses. In the first place size of house is not necessarily a good indication of wealth, or of the ability to pay, and extremely profitable commercial or industrial concerns can be housed in small premises. The rating system also tends to discourage improvements to property, in that the better the property the higher the rates. The bigger the family, and thus the bigger the house that is required, the higher the rates are likely to be, although since 1965 there has been in operation a system of rate rebates for low income groups. The rates tend to be more unpopular than most other forms of taxation, to some extent because rates involve an actual cash payment, while most other forms of taxation are deducted at source. All local authorities are now required to allow for the payment of rates in monthly instalments, and this has removed objections to the payment of rates in a lump sum. Opposition to the rates, however, is also based partly on the tarnished image of local government, with local authorities often being thought of by the public as being guilty of much wasteful expenditure.

Numerous proposals have been made over the years for alternative forms of local revenue to supplement or even replace the rates. The Layfield Committee proposed a local income tax, and over the years sales tax, entertainments tax and betting levy have all been advocated.[1] It has also been suggested that part of National Insurance contributions could go to local authorities. Levies on restaurant meals, hotel accommodation, and advertising displays have also been proposed.[2] In opposition in 1974 the Conservatives declared that they intended to 'abolish' the rating system, but in their 1979 and 1983 election manifestos they pledged only to

[1]See R. J. Bennett, 'The Local Income Tax in Britain', *Pub. Admin.* 1981, pp. 295–310.

[2]See K. J. Davey, 'Local Autonomy and Independent Revenues', *Pub. Admin.* 1971, pp. 45–50; D. E. Ashford, 'The Effects of Central Finance on the British Local Government System', *BJPS* 1974, pp. 305–22; A. Crispin, 'Local Government Finance: Assessing the Central Government's Contribution', *Pub. Admin.* 1976, pp. 45–62.

'reform' it. In face of discontent over rate increases, however, the Government in 1986 announced plans to phase-out domestic rates in England by the early 1990s (and in Wales and Scotland before that). As a replacement the Government rejected local income tax and sales tax and proposed a flat-rate community charge payable by all adults. A community register would be compiled on similar lines to the electoral register. Business premises would continue to pay rates, but the rate poundage would be set nationally and the revenue distributed to local authorities on a population basis. The initial level of the business rate would be determined by the Government of the day, but subsequently would be adjusted only in line with inflation. In support of the replacement of domestic rates by a community charge, the Government argued that it would increase the proportion of the population who made a direct contribution to the income of local authorities and would thereby produce a closer relationship between those who benefit from local services and those who paid for them.

Grants. A small proportion (about 10%) of the grants that are paid by the central government to local authorities are in the form of particular service grants, towards the cost of specific services. Some of these, like the police grant, are calculated on a percentage basis, and the size of the grant is in direct proportion to the local authority's expenditure on that service. Other specific service grants are calculated on a unit basis, with payments being made for each unit of a particular service, as in the case of housing. The main central government grants to local authorities, however, are the rate support grants which are not tied to specific services but are distributed as a general form of revenue.[1] The present system of rate support grants was established by the Local Government Planning and Land Act 1980, and is the latest of various systems that have been used over the last thirty years to

[1] See R. J. Bennett, *Central Grants to Local Governments*, London 1982; D. Heald, 'The Scottish Rate Support Grant', *Pub. Admin.* 1980, pp. 25–46; G. Bramley and A. Evans, 'Block Grant – Some Unresolved Issues', *PP* 1981, pp. 173–204; T. Rhodes and S. J. Bailey, 'Equity, Statistics and Distribution of the Rate Support Grant', *PP* 1979, pp. 83–98.

provide local authorities with general revenue. The Secretary of State makes an annual estimate of the sum each local authority needs to spend in the next financial year in order to maintain common national standards in its various services. On the basis of this assessment, and after negotiations between the local authorities and the central government departments concerned, the Secretary of State sets the level of grant for the year. The negotiations between central and local government are conducted in the Consultative Council on Local Government Finance.[1] In the 1974–9 period of Labour Government this body played a major part in bringing the two levels of government into consultation. After 1979, however, its role became more nominal as Ministers adopted a more confrontational approach to the local authorities. In negotiations over finance the local authorities are represented by their 'peak' organisations – the Association of Metropolitan Authorities, the Association of County Councils, the Association of District Councils and the Convention of Scottish Local Authorities.

The various grants that are paid to local authorities serve to ease the rate burden, and enable the local authorities to undertake services that they could not afford if they were dependent solely on local revenue. They enable the central government to exert control over local government, although the degree of control varies with the type of grant. Unit and percentage grants allow the central government to encourage the development of certain services. Before 1958 there were a greater number of specific grants paid for education, health and welfare services, fire services, town planning and various other services. The Local Government Act 1958 reduced the number of particular services grants and replaced them by the general grant, thereby giving the local authorities greater freedom over the way in which they decided priorities for expenditure among the different services. This principle has been maintained since 1958, even though the method of calculating the size of the grant has changed on various occasions. Nevertheless, even though the rate support grant is

[1] See R. A. W. Rhodes, 'Corporate Bias in Central–Local Relations', *PP* 1986, pp. 221–46.

a general contribution to each local authority's revenue (rather than a series of grants for specific purposes), the system allows central government to control the overall level of local authority spending. Any authority that exceeds the estimated expenditure on which the grant is based is liable to be penalised by having the size of its grant reduced.

Over the years there has been an increase in local authority revenue from both rates and government grants. Until the second world war, on the national average, income from rates exceeded that from grants, but since 1945 the reverse has been the case. The 1966 Act sought to achieve a regular annual increase of 1% in the proportion of grant revenue as opposed to rate revenue, and the Act also established machinery to ensure that the effect of transferring more of the financial burden from rates to grants would be to ease particularly the rate burden of householders, as opposed to industrial and commercial property owners. In 1976 central government grants accounted for about two-thirds of local government revenue. Since then the trend has been reversed, as the Conservative Government has sought to reduce local government's dependence on national funds, and currently about half of local government revenue is from central grants.

In general it may be said that the greater the dependence of local authorities on central government grants, the greater will be the degree of central government control over local government (for good or ill). As central control tends to produce uniformity, the greater the dependence on government grants, the greater will be the degree of uniformity of standards and practices throughout the local government system. The more the local authorities depend upon local sources of income, the more aware the public is likely to be of the financial implications of local government activities, and as a result, the more interest they are likely to take in local government affairs. Because of the particular unpopularity of the rates as a form of taxation, however, the more dependent local authorities are on the rates, the more cautious they are likely to have to be in their policies. Thus the balance that is achieved between local authority revenue from rates and from government grants is of fundamental importance for the nature of the local government system.

Party Politics and Public Attitudes

Throughout this chapter passing references have been made to the role of political parties on councils. Not all councils are run on party lines, and as with so many other aspects of local government, the nature and extent of party political activity varies considerably between the different types of local authority, and even between authorities of the same type.[1] At one extreme, 'party' organisation can merely involve a group of council members organising themselves for the purpose of handling council affairs, while at the other extreme it can involve all the facets of political party organisation. On some councils one party has a monopoly of all the seats. On others an opposition party exists, but it may be small and destined to be permanently in opposition.[2] Party control of the council can involve one party monopolising the council chairmanship, the committee chairmanships, and perhaps even all the committee places.

Party politics in local government is not a new development, and although party labels have appeared on ballot papers only since 1969, there were parties and groups in local politics even in the nineteenth century. Local councils, however, now reflect the national party conflict more closely than they did under the pre-1974 structure. Public dissatisfaction with successive Labour and Conservative Governments in the 1970s and 1980s has been reflected in local government elections, and there has been a clear tendency for the party that is in power at Westminster to lose control of the local authorities. Since 1979 Labour-controlled councils (not least the Greater London Council and the Metropolitan Councils before their abolition) have been in conflict with the Conservative Government over its policies of encouraging council

[1] J. Gyford and M. James, *National Parties and Local Politics*, London 1983; J. Gyford, *Local Politics in Britain*, London 1983; J. G. Bulpitt, *Party Politics in English Local Government*, London 1967; K. Young, *Local Politics and the Rise of Party*, London 1975; W. Grant, *Independent Local Politics in England and Wales*, London 1977; J. Stanyer, 'Electoral Behaviour in Local Government', *PS* 1970, pp. 187–204; W. P. Grant, '"Local" Parties in British Local Politics', *PS* 1971, pp. 201–12; G. Green, 'National, City and Ward Components of Local Voting', *PP* 1972–3, pp. 45–54.

[2] See D. G. Green, *Power and Party in an English City*, London 1980.

house sales, raising council house rents and reducing public expenditure.

The attitudes of the main political parties vary over the question of party politics in local government, with the Labour Party being much more conscious of its value. In a survey in Newcastle-under-Lyme in 1958,[1] Conservative voters were found to be two to one in favour of leaving party politics out of local government, compared with only a small minority of Labour voters, and these tendencies were supported by survey findings in Glasgow in 1964.[2] The Labour Party usually retains its name in local government politics, and studies of voting behaviour at local government elections suggest that it draws its support from much the same social and demographic groups as in national politics. The main opposition to the Labour Party, however, may be provided by Anti-Socialists, Progressives, Municipal Party or Independents, although these generally correspond more or less to the national Conservative Party in their policies and attitudes, and in the sources of their electoral support.

The extent of party politics on local councils is still widely criticised today. It is argued that doctrinal party attitudes are irrelevant in many of the issues dealt with in local government, and that party domination of local council elections can exclude non-party men from council service. While the party that is in power in national politics changes every few years, some local councils have permanent majorities for one party, producing permanent single-party government. In such cases, council meetings and council elections tend to be mere formalities, and there is less public interest in local government as a result. It was found, for example, in an analysis of London borough elections between 1945 and 1958, that there was a direct correlation between voting turnout and the strength of party control on the council, with the turnout declining from one borough to another as the strength of the opposition party declined.[3]

[1] F. Bealey and J. D. Bartholomew, 'The Local Elections in Newcastle-under-Lyme, May 1958', *BJS* 1962, pp. 273–85 and 350–68.

[2] I. Budge, 'Electors' Attitudes towards Local Government: A Survey in a Glasgow Constituency', *PS* 1965, pp. 386–92.

[3] Sharpe, *Pub. Admin.* 1960.

The value of party politics in local government, however, is that opinion has to be organised if it is to be effective, and party organisation helps to provide the stability and consistency that is essential in any form of government. The alternative to control by parties is government by personalities, which is perhaps an undesirable alternative. On the larger councils, party politics is in many ways inevitable, in that some local government issues are matters which reflect national political party issues. Similarly, on every council a broad distinction tends to emerge between those who wish to develop services, and those who wish to keep expenditure (and thus the rates) at the lowest possible level, and this distinction corresponds very roughly to the respective attitudes of Labour and Conservative politicians.

* * *

It is generally assumed that there is a great deal of public apathy towards local government, and there is much evidence to support this assumption. Voting turnout tends to be much lower at local elections than at general elections,[1] and surveys have suggested that few people attend council meetings, or can even name their councillors. In Newcastle-under-Lyme in 1958, a quarter of those interviewed had not heard of the impending local elections one week before polling day, and few could name a candidate.[2] In one survey conducted in Glasgow soon after the municipal elections of 1964, only about a third of those interviewed could name the newly elected councillor for their ward.[3] In another survey in Glasgow, conducted two months before the 1965 municipal elections, 80% of those interviewed were unable to name any of the three councillors for their ward, while 14% could name one only.[4] Surveys conducted for the Maud Committee and the Redcliffe-Maud Commission revealed that a quarter of respondents could not spontaneously name a single service

[1] See K. Newton, 'Turnout and Marginality in Local Elections', *BJPS* 1972, pp. 251–5; P. Davies and K. Newton, 'An Aggregate Data Analysis of Turnout and Party Voting in Local Elections', *Soc.* 1974, pp. 213–32.

[2] Bealey, *BJS* 1962.

[3] Budge, *PS* 1965.

[4] J. Brand, *Glasgow Herald*, 3. and 4.6.65.

provided by their borough or district council, and half could not name any service provided by the county council. A 1981 survey found that two-thirds of respondents did not know which tier of local government was responsible for particular services, while half could not name their own local authority.[1] In NALGO's nationwide survey of public attitudes to local government, 81% of those interviewed claimed to have read about council affairs in the press, and 17% said that they belonged to ratepayers' associations, but only 6% said that they attended council meetings.[2]

The general lack of public interest in local government is often attributed to the supposedly poor quality of local councillors, or to the prevalence of party political attitudes in local government, which are often regarded as being irrelevant in local issues. Most people also see local government as being concerned primarily with minor questions which do not arouse a great deal of interest, despite the fact that they affect people's daily lives. The fact that local government is subordinate to the central government also contributes to the general image of local government as being of relatively little importance. For most people, such interest as they do have is bound up with the payment of rates, and in this context the ratepayer's prime concern tends to be with the limiting of local government expenditure in order to keep rate payments low. Here, however, there is often an inconsistency in public attitudes. The survey in Newcastle-under-Lyme in 1958, for example, revealed that the majority of people felt that the rates were too high, but at the same time the majority wished to see more local government services provided, and also wanted local government to be subject to less central control. To satisfy all of these demands, increased services would presumably have to be financed by increased central government grants, with the central government at the same time seeking less control over the spending of its grants – an approach to local government that no Labour or Conservative Government is likely to adopt.

[1] See Byrne, *Local Government in Britain*, p. 264.

[2] NALGO Survey, *Pub. Admin.* 1957. See also K. Newton, 'Links Between Leaders and Citizens in a Local Political System', *PP* 1972–3, pp. 287–306.

14

Regional Government and the European Community

THE BRITISH system of government, in which sovereignty resides solely at the centre, is often contrasted with the American federal system. In a federal system there are two levels of government (additional to local government), each with responsibility for particular policies; each level of government is entrenched, in the sense that neither one can abolish the other; the functions performed by each level of government are also entrenched, in that while the two governments may cooperate with each other over policy, neither can unilaterally assume the functions assigned to the other.[1] Two variations of the federal principle are devolution within a unitary system and confederalism. In a system of devolution regional units exist but they are subordinate to the centre: the units and their functions are conferred, and can be terminated, by the centre. In a confederation a number of independent states establish a central organisation, with particular functions, but retain the ability to abolish it or remove its functions. Although Britain is neither a federation nor a state within a federation, various forms of devolution operate within the unitary Constitution, and Britain participates in a confederal relationship with other states in the European Commun-

[1] For studies of federalism see W. H. Riker, *Federalism: Origin, Operation, Significance*, Boston 1964; C. J. Friedrich, *Trends of Federalism in Theory and Practice*, New York 1968; G. Sawer, *Modern Federalism*, London 1969; K. C. Wheare, *Federal Government*, London 1953.

ity. There are those who argue that a fully entrenched federal system is logical for multi-national Britain, and that it would be desirable for the European Community to evolve into a Federal States of Europe. Whether or not Britain does become a 'federation within a federation' at some time in the future, the two issues of regional government within the United Kingdom and Britain's involvement with the European Community are of current significance.

Regionalism and Devolution

There are various examples of devolution within the United Kingdom.[1] As was noted in Chapter 6,[2] the Channel Islands and the Isle of Man have their own Parliaments and are largely self-governing. In 1922 Northern Ireland was given administrative and legislative independence in most areas of policy. Although Northern Ireland became largely self-governing, the relationship between London and Belfast was not a federal one, as Westminster retained the power to withdraw the functions that it had devolved to the Northern Ireland Parliament, and did so in 1972. Even under direct-rule from London, however, the Northern Ireland Office in Belfast is the centre for the administration of the province. The Scottish Departments of Education, Industry, Home, Health and Agriculture and Fisheries are based in Edinburgh rather than Whitehall. This reflects the fact that Scotland has its own legal system, and that in many important areas of government (including the education and local government systems) Scottish practice differs significantly from that of England and Wales. There is a Welsh Office in Cardiff,

[1] For studies of the territorial structure of the UK see A. H. Birch, *Political Integration and Disintegration in the British Isles*, London 1977; V. Bogdanor, *Devolution*, London 1979; B. Burrows and G. Denton, *Devolution or Federalism?* London 1980; H. M. Drucker and G. Brown, *The Politics of Nationalism and Devolution*, London 1980; D. Heald, *Financing Devolution Within the United Kingdom*, Canberra 1980; P. Madgwick and R. Rose (eds), *The Territorial Dimension in United Kingdom Politics*, London 1982; R. Rose, *Understanding the United Kingdom*, London 1982; J. G. Bulpitt, *Territory and Power in the United Kingdom*, London 1983.

[2] See especially pp. 179–82.

though with a more limited role than that of the Scottish Office. Within England the departments of state use a range of regional units for the administration of services,[1] while the nationalised industries and other public bodies have a variety of regional structures.

It has often been proposed that the process of decentralisation should be taken much further, and over the last hundred years various schemes of legislative, executive and administrative devolution have been advocated. In the 1880s, as a result of Gladstone's attempts to settle the Irish question, 'home-rule-all-round' was advocated. The Irish Nationalists were devolutionalists rather than separatists, and sought a large degree of self-government for Ireland within the United Kingdom. This approach inspired Scottish and Welsh Home Rule Bills to match the Irish Bills of 1886 and 1892, but they were unsuccessful. When the Irish issue revived after 1910 (with the minority Liberal Government's dependence on the support of the Irish Nationalists) home-rule-all-round was again advocated. A number of schemes were advanced for devolution, or for the adoption of a federal Constitution, inspired in part by the apparent success of the federal systems adopted in Canada in 1867 and Australia in 1901. These proposals revived when the Irish question was re-opened after the 1914–18 war. The refusal of the south of Ireland to settle for anything less than independence, however, removed any chance there might have been that a limited form of Irish home rule would have been followed by similar schemes for Scotland and Wales.

Centralist sentiments predominated during and after the second world war, but interest in regional government revived in the 1960s in face of growing concern about regional economic disparities.[2] When the Labour Party came to power in 1964 it announced plans for the creation of regional bodies

[1] See B. W. Hogwood and M. Keating, *Regional Government in England*, London 1982.

[2] See W. Thornhill (ed.), *The Case for Regional Reform*, London 1972; H. V. Wiseman, 'Regional Government in the United Kingdom', *Parl. Aff.* 1965–6, pp. 56–82; Sir Keith Joseph, 'Local Authorities and Regions', *Pub. Admin.* 1964, pp. 215–26; P. Self, 'Regional Planning and the Machinery of Government', *Pub. Admin.* 1964, pp. 227–40; D. Donnison, 'The Economics and Politics of the Regions', *PQ* 1974, pp. 179–89.

to work alongside the local authorities and deal with transport, housing and economic policy on a regional basis. In England eight Economic Planning Boards (originally called Regional Planning Boards) were set up, with separate Boards for Scotland and Wales. The Boards were composed of members of the central government departments concerned with regional problems, and they were accompanied by Economic Planning Councils made up of members drawn from the local authorities, industry, trade unions and other bodies in the regions.

This structure, however, did not satisfy the advocates of regional government: the Boards were concerned almost entirely with economic affairs, the members of the Councils were nominated rather than being directly elected, and in no real sense did the Boards become a third tier of government. One of the proposals of the Redcliffe-Maud Commission in 1969 was that England should be divided into eight 'Provinces' for the administration of some local government services. The actual local government structure that was established in 1973, with its emphasis on the creation of larger units, removed much of the urgency from the regional government issue in England. In Scotland and Wales, however, the question of regionalism is linked closely with that of nationalism, and the SNP and Plaid Cymru favour the complete independence of Scotland and Wales.[1] In face of the electoral challenge of the SNP and Plaid Cymru in the 1970s,

[1] See H. J. Hanham, *Scottish Nationalism*, London 1969; N. McCormick (ed.), *The Scottish Debate*, London 1970; G. McCrone, *Scotland's Future: the Economics of Nationalism*, London 1969; J. N. Wolfe (ed.), *Government and Nationalism in Scotland*, London 1969; A. Butt-Philip, *The Welsh Question*, London 1975. See also J. P. Mackintosh, 'Devolution, Regionalism and the Reform of Local Government: The Scottish Case', *PL* 1964, pp. 19–32; J. P. Mackintosh, 'Scottish Nationalism', *PQ* 1967, pp. 389–402; L. Gunn, 'Devolution: a Scottish View', *PQ* 1977, pp. 129–39; S. White and J. W. Dickson, 'The Politics of Scottish Self-Government', *SJS* 1977–8, pp. 1–10; G. Daniel, 'Devolution to Wales', *PQ* 1977, pp. 140–8; P. Luke and D. Johnson, 'Devolution, By Referendum? A Look at the Welsh Situation', *Parl. Aff.* 1975–6, pp. 332–39; L. J. Sharpe, 'Devolution and Celtic Nationalism in the UK', *WEP* 1985 (3), pp. 82–100; I. McAllister and A. Mughan, 'Values, Protest and Minority Nationalism in Wales', *BJPS* 1984, pp. 230–42.

both the main parties came to accept the principle of some form of devolution for Scotland and Wales, though there remained strong groups of anti-devolutionists in both main parties.

Following the success of the nationalist parties in by-elections and local government elections in 1967 and 1968, the then Conservative Government set up a Royal Commission on the Constitution to examine in detail the implications of various devolution proposals. The Commission reported in 1973 and rejected the principle of Scottish and Welsh separatism, but made detailed recommendations for the devolution of some powers from Westminster to Scotland and Wales. It proposed the creation of Scottish and Welsh Assemblies, with Ministers drawn from, and responsible to, the Assemblies. For the English regions it proposed the creation of Councils to advise on regional policy. The Commission proposed that the Scottish and Welsh Assemblies be responsible for those matters which were in the hands of the Scottish and Welsh Secretaries of State and the Local Advocate, although the Westminster Parliament would retain ultimate legislative authority. The Assemblies were to be financed by a block grant from Westminster.

In face of the renewed success of the SNP and Plaid Cymru at the 1974 general elections, the new Labour Government announced its acceptance of the broad principles of the Royal Commission's report, and set up a 'devolution unit' in the Cabinet Office, under the direction of the Lord President of the Council, to frame detailed plans. Proposals for Scotland and Wales were duly published in a White Paper in 1975 and a Scotland and Wales Bill was introduced in 1976. The Bill followed broadly the recommendations of the Royal Commission, creating Scottish and Welsh Assemblies and executives with limited powers, financed by a block grant from central government. The measure encountered strong Parliamentary opposition from anti-devolutionists in both main parties, however, and the Government (lacking an overall majority) was forced to abandon it.

The proposals were revived in the next session, but on this occasion they were presented as separate Bills for Scotland and Wales. The two Bills passed through all their stages on a very carefully controlled timetable, though the Government was obliged to accept an amendment which required that the Acts should come into operation only if they received the support, in referendums in Scotland and Wales, of at least 40% of the *electorate* (and not just of those voting).[1] The Scottish and Welsh referendums were duly held in March 1979.[2] The Wales Act was rejected decisively with only 20% of those voting (and 12% of the total Welsh electorate) supporting it. In Scotland 52% of those voting supported the Scotland Act, but as they amounted to only a third of the total Scottish electorate, the Act failed to meet the 40% requirement. With this blow to its proposals the Government postponed further consideration of the matter until after the general election. With Labour's defeat at the 1979 election the Acts were repealed, public interest waned and the Thatcher Government largely ignored the issue.

The Regional Issue Today

The stimulus behind the demands for regional government has varied over the years, but certain common themes do emerge. Advocates of devolution have argued that the multinational and highly regionalised nature of the United Kingdom ought to be reflected more fully in the structure of government. The allocation of some functions of government to regions, they also argue, would ease the problem of the overloading of central government and would combat feelings of territorial remoteness (real or imagined). Further, it is claimed that regional assemblies can improve the quality of democracy in various ways – by providing opportunities for local experimentation in policies and institutions; by recognising the existence of regional majorities within a national minority; by creating additional centres of opposition and

[1] See V. Bogdanor, 'The 40 Per Cent Rule', *Parl. Aff.* 1980, pp. 249–63; D. Balsom and I. McAllister, 'Whose Vote Counts', *PQ* 1980, pp. 218–22.

[2] See J. Bochel (*et al.*) (eds), *The Referendum Experience: Scotland 1979*, London 1981; D. Foulkes (*et al.*), *The Welsh Veto: The Wales Act 1978 and the Referendum*, London 1983; B. Jones and S. Wilford, 'Further Considerations on the Referendum', *PS* 1982, pp. 16–27.

thereby providing parties and politicians with further opportunities for office.

For their part, opponents of the various devolution proposals have questioned whether there is any substantial demand for a regional tier of government, especially in face of the existence of a healthy local government system. They have argued that while an additional level of government might relieve the central government's burden, it would add to the overall scale of government within the United Kingdom. It would thus increase costs and would create problems of inter-governmental relations. Many have also claimed that Scottish and Welsh Assemblies would serve as staging-posts on the 'slippery slope' to the disintegration of Britain, stimulating rather than undermining separatist tendencies.

Whatever the demand for Scottish and Welsh Assemblies might be, the case for an English Assembly, or for regional Assemblies within England, is less clear. Indeed, the very size of England (with some four-fifths of the population of the United Kingdom) has always caused problems for those seeking to devise a regional structure.[1] The existence of Assemblies only for Scotland, Wales and Northern Ireland would leave England disadvantaged. On the other hand, the inclusion of an English Assembly in a comprehensive scheme of devolution would produce a grossly unbalanced four-nation structure, while the sub-division of England would involve the formation of somewhat arbitrary regions that would inevitably cut across the range of administrative units that are used by the departments of state.

Over the years centralist sentiment has triumphed over the demands for regional Assemblies. It would be a mistake, however, to dismiss the question of regional government as a dead issue.[2] Northern Ireland is a constant reminder of the regionalised nature of the United Kingdom. Despite the failure of attempts over the last ten years to re-establish a Northern Ireland Assembly, and regardless of any long-term

[1] See A. V. Dicey, *England's Case Against Home Rule*, London 1973 (original edition 1886). See also C. B. Fawcett, *Provinces of England*, London 1961; B. C. Smith, *Regionalism in England*, London 1965.

[2] See M. Keating, 'Whatever Happened to Regional Government', *LGS* 1985 (6), pp. 111–33.

commitment to the principle of a united Ireland, all the Great Britain parties favour the re-creation of a devolved structure for Northern Ireland. Within Great Britain a feature of the 1979 and 1983 elections was the distinctly regional character of voting behaviour, with different regions responding to the prospects of a Conservative Government with varying degrees of enthusiasm. Since 1983 economic disparities between north and south have been reflected in the considerable regional variations in the level of unemployment.

Thus there exist social, economic and behavioural bases for a regionalised political structure. Currently, any general election result other than the re-election of a majority Conservative Government would be likely to lead to the re-emergence of the issue, as all the parties except the Conservatives favour the creation of some form of devolution within Great Britain. Labour favours the creation of a Scottish Assembly and executive, with wider powers than those proposed in the 1974–9 period.[1] While the Scottish and Welsh nationalists seek independence rather than devolution, they might be expected (as in the 1974–9 Parliament) to support devolution proposals as a first step towards independence. A major feature of the Alliance is the strong commitment of both the Liberals and the SDP to decentralisation. The Liberals had long advocated a federal structure for Britain, and one of the first and clearest commitments made by the SDP on its formation was to a Scottish Assembly (to be elected by a system of proportional representation) that would be responsible for all areas of policy except trade, defence and foreign affairs. The agreed Alliance policy for the 1983 general election reflected the SDP's commitment to devolution, rather than the Liberal's federal preference, but the proposed Scottish Assembly was to have a wide range of powers, including economic development and taxation. The Alliance proposed that devolution should be extended to Wales and the English regions as the demand developed, though economic development agencies should be established at once in each English region.

[1] See M. Keating and D. Bleiman, *Labour and Scottish Nationalism*, London 1980; J. B. Jones and M. Keating, 'The Labour Party's Devolution Policy', *G and O* 1982, pp. 279–92.

Thus the impetus for regional self-government remains, and a devolution package might be expected to emerge from a majority or minority Labour or Alliance government, from a coalition that contained the Alliance or Labour, or even from a minority Conservative Government that required the support of the Alliance or the Nationalists. Any such development, however, is likely to be in the form of further devolution within the unitary Constitution, rather than the formation of a Federal Kingdom. Although Britain has been responsible for creating a vast number of federations throughout the world, there remains a powerful anti-federalist sentiment within Britain that is based partly on attachment to the doctrine of the ultimate supremacy of Parliament, partly on suspicion of the 'legalism' that is associated with federal constitutions and partly on the assumption that conflicts between entrenched states and a federal government would be harder to resolve than conflicts within a devolved system.

Britain and the European Community[1]

A Federal States of Europe has long been the vision of some European statesmen, but the immediate origins of the European Community lie in the post-war attempts to achieve closer cooperation among European countries. The stimulus for this was provided by the desire to solve the long-standing Franco-German conflict, by concern at the emergence of the superpowers of the USA and USSR, and by Europe's immediate post-war economic privations. A free-trade area was seen as a means of providing protection against the expanding economies of countries outside Europe, while the efficient use of American economic aid required the creation of cooperative machinery. To these ends various European cooperative organisations emerged in the 1940s and 1950s, including the Organisation for European Economic Cooperation in 1948, the Council of Europe in 1949 and the Western European Union in 1954.

The most significant development, however, was the forma-

[1]See F. E. C. Gregory, *Dilemmas of Government*, London 1983; W. Wallace (ed.), *Britain in Europe*, London 1980.

tion in 1951 of the European Coal and Steel Community. In 1946, through the Benelux Treaty, Belgium, the Netherlands and Luxembourg had formed a free-trade bloc, and had agreed to pursue certain common economic policies. In the 1951 Treaty of Paris the Benelux countries, together with France, West Germany, and Italy, agreed to operate a common pricing policy for coal and steel and to remove internal tariff barriers. The success of the ECSC in integrating the iron and steel industries stimulated moves for further economic integration, and following the 1955 Messina Conference the six ECSC countries established the European Economic Community and Eurotom through the 1957 Treaty of Rome. 'The six' agreed to remove all internal tariffs, establish a common external tariff, allow the free movement of labour and capital, pursue common welfare and agriculture policies and cooperate in the development of nuclear energy.

Britain had been invited to participate in the formation of the ECSC but the Labour Government indicated that it was not prepared to involve the newly-nationalised British coal and steel industries in a supranational organisation. The Conservatives were no more enthusiastic when they came to office in 1951. At the Messina Conference Britain expressed interest in some reduction in tariff barriers, but not in the broader developments. In general the British attitude in the 1940s and 1950s was that political, military, economic and cultural 'cooperation' with continental countries (on the lines of OEEC, the Council of Europe and the Western European Union) was highly desirable, but moves towards 'integration' were not, especially if they hinted at the eventual development of a European federal structure.[1]

As well as a reluctance to surrender a degree of sovereignty to a European authority, Britain's attitude to the emerging Community was influenced by the incompatibility between European free trade and Commonwealth preference (which provided Britain with relatively cheap food and a market for manufactured goods). The assumed 'special relationship' with the USA was also seen as more important to Britain than the European connection. What is more, in the 1950s, the six had

[1]See P. Einzig, *The Case Against Joining the Common Market*, London 1971.

TABLE XXXIV

Stages in the Development of the Community

1946	Benelux free trade area created
1951	European Coal and Steel Community formed (Treaty of Paris)
1955	Messina Conference
1957	European Economic Community and Euratom formed (Treaty of Rome)
1961	Initial British application (rejected 1963)
1967	Second British application (rejected 1968)
1969	Third British application (accepted 1972)
1973	Britain, Denmark and Ireland admitted
1975	British membership confirmed by referendum
1981	Greece admitted
1985	Greenland withdrew
1986	Spain and Portugal admitted

not demonstrated the economic success that they were to achieve later, while Britain was still relatively self-confident. Neither of the two main parties was particularly European in its outlook: the Conservatives had an imperial tradition, and Labour claimed to be internationalist, but neither was particularly committed to the European dimension.

In the early 1960s, however, the economic success of the Community (in contrast to Britain's increasing difficulties), a decline in enthusiasm for the Commonwealth connection and Britain's search for a new world role all helped to increase the appeal of the Community. What is more, the USA (far from providing an alternative to the European connection) encouraged Britain to seek entry.[1] Negotiations conducted by the Macmillan Government in 1961–3, and a further application by the Wilson Government in 1967–8, were both terminated when President de Gaulle (exercising the power of a member state to veto the admission of a new member) indicated that

[1]See J. Moon, *European Integration in British Politics 1950–63*, London 1985; N. Beloff, *The General Says No*, London 1963; U. Kitzinger, *The Second Try*, London 1968; U. Kitzinger, *Diplomacy and Persuasion*, London 1973; W. Pickles, *Britain and Europe*, London 1967; C. W. Frey, 'Meaning Business', *JCMS* 1967–8, pp. 225–30; U. Kitzinger, 'Britain's Crisis of Identity', *JCMS* 1967–8, pp. 334–58.

British membership was unacceptable to France.[1] Following de Gaulle's retirement in 1969, the Wilson Government initiated further negotiations, and these were subsequently brought to fruition by the Heath Government in 1972. The European Communities Act 1972 gave effect to British membership on January 1st, 1973.[2]

Labour, in opposition, criticised the terms of entry negotiated by the Heath Government, and condemned the Government for failing to consult the electorate about their acceptability. Largely in an attempt to avoid immediate conflict between Labour's pro-Community and anti-Community groups, the party undertook when next in office to re-open the issue and submit it to a referendum. Accordingly, the Wilson Government elected in February 1974 renegotiated Britain's terms of membership, claimed to have achieved major concessions over agriculture policy and financial arrangements, and in the referendum that was duly held in June 1975 advocated a vote for continued membership on the new terms. Two-thirds of the electorate voted in the referendum and gave a two-to-one vote in favour of membership.[3]

In 1967 the institutions of the ECSC, the EEC and Eurotom were merged (so that it is legitimate to refer to a single 'European Community'). With the entry of Greece in 1981, and Spain and Portugal in 1986, the Community now embraces twelve countries and over 300 million people.[4] In

[1] See D. Evans, *While Britain Slept*, London 1975; S. Z. Young, *Terms of Entry*, London 1973.

[2] See E. M. Wall, *European Communities Act 1972*, London 1972; J. Forman, 'The European Communities Act', *CMLR* 1973, pp. 39–55.

[3] See D. E. Butler and U. Kitzinger, *The 1975 Referendum*, London 1976; A. King, *Britain Says Yes*, Washington 1977; R. Pierce (*et al.*), 'Referendum Voting Behaviour', *AJPS* 1983, pp. 43–63; K. R. Simonds, 'The British Referendum', *CMLR* 1975, pp. 258–60; R. E. M. Irving, 'The United Kingdom Referendum June 1975', *ELR* 1975–6, pp. 3–12; A. P. Brier and A. P. Hill, 'The Estimation of Constituency and Party Voting in the British Referendum of June 1975', *PS* 1977, pp. 93–102; S. L. Bristow, 'Partisanship, Participation and Legitimacy in Britain's EEC Referendum', *JCMS* 1975–6, pp. 297–310.

[4] See F. Nicholson and R. East, *From the Six to the Twelve*, London 1986; P. Dagtoglou, 'The Southern Enlargement of the European Community', *CMLR* 1984, pp. 149–62.

addition to the acceptance of a common external tariff and the removal of internal tariffs, membership involves participation in the Common Agricultural Policy and in regional aid policies. It requires the acceptance of VAT as a common tax (though not at a common rate); the free movement of capital, labour and social benefits; common pricing policies in the coal and steel industries; and cooperation in the development of nuclear power. Increasingly it involves cooperation in foreign policy in efforts to produce a European stance on major issues. Ministers, civil servants, parties and pressure groups participate in the Community procedures that produce and administer its policies.[1]

Community Institutions

In marked contrast to the situation with the British Constitution, the bulk of the Community's Constitutional rules are codified.[2] The principal Constitutional documents are the 1951 Treaty of Paris and the 1957 Treaty of Rome, which laid down the institutional framework of the three Communities and established their rules of operation. These basic documents have been supplemented by subsequent Community laws, and by legislation passed by national Parliaments (such as Britain's European Communities Act 1972). In addition, various conventions have evolved to supplement the written rules.

The relationship between the various institutions of the Community (and in particular between the Commission and the Council of Ministers) reflects the attempt by the member states to further their interests by mutual cooperation while ultimately preserving their national independence. The

[1] See P. Taylor, 'The European Communities and the Obligations of Membership', *Inter. Aff.* 1981, pp. 236–53.

[2] See D. Lasok and J. W. Bridge, *Law and Institutions of the European Communities*, London 1982; C. Sasse, *Decision Making in the European Communities*, New York 1977; H. and W. Wallace (eds), *Policy Making in the European Communities*, London 1977; H. Arbuthnot and G. Edwards (ed.), *A Common Man's Guide to the Common Market*, London 1979; C. D. Ehlermann, 'Legal Status, Functioning and Probable Evolution of the Institutions of the European Communities', *CMLR* 1973, pp. 195–207.

Commission's role is to prepare legislation, initiate legal action against those who infringe Community laws, administer Community funds and prepare the annual budget. It is composed of seventeen Commissioners, two from each of Britain, France, Germany, Italy and Spain and one from each of the other members. The Commissioners are appointed by the national Governments to serve for four-year terms, which can be renewed. Britain's Commissioners have traditionally come from the ranks of the two main parties, though Commissioners are not representatives of parties or their national governments: they are essentially servants of the Community, their appointment has to be acceptable to the other members and they are required to pursue the interests of the Community as a whole. They cannot be removed from office individually, but the European Parliament has the power (as yet unused) to dismiss the Commission en bloc.

The Commission is chaired by the President who emerges from the ranks of the Commission by mutual consent and serves for a two-year term. Each Commissioner deals with a particular policy area, though the Commission as a whole remains collegially responsible for all aspects of its affairs. There is a staff of some 12,000 civil servants, distributed among twenty departments (or Directorates-General). The British members of this civil service have come partly from Whitehall and partly from outside government. The Commission was designed to be a truly 'European' institution that would rise above the immediate national interests. It is frequently attacked, however, as a remote bureaucracy (or 'technocracy') that is free from political control by the national governments or the European Parliament.

The Council of Ministers is the voice of the national governments within the institutions of the Community. The Council has various guises, in that at its meetings each country is represented by the departmental Minister most appropriate for the matter under consideration. The Council of Ministers considers, and then accepts, rejects or amends, the legislative and budgetary proposals that are submitted by the Commission. In effect, the Council takes the major policy decisions, adjusting the collective view of the Commission to the separate national interests. Its meetings are thus essentially forums for international bargaining. Each country in turn holds the Presidency of the Council of Ministers for six months and is responsible for organising its business in that period.[1] There are separate meetings of the heads of state (the European Council) and of Foreign Ministers, at which major political issues are dealt with.

On the least significant issues decisions are taken in the Council on the basis of a majority vote, and on middle-range issues a system of weighted voting is used. For this purpose Britain, France, West Germany and Italy each have ten votes, Spain eight, Belgium, Greece, the Netherlands and Portugal five, Denmark and Ireland three and Luxembourg two (with a proposal requiring fifty-four of the seventy-six votes for approval). On the most significant issues, however, unanimity is required, so that in effect each country can exercise a veto on major matters (including the admission of new members, treaty changes and major policy items). Attitudes to the unanimity rule inevitably are ambivalent. British Ministers welcome the veto when its use prevents the implementation of a policy that threatens an important British interest, but deplore its use when it prevents agreement on a policy from which Britain stands to gain. Over the years there have been attempts to abolish it, or to reduce the range of matters on which it could be applied. The 1966 Luxembourg Accord, however, retained the veto, on French insistence, and each member has been prepared to make use of it as the final means of preserving a vital national interest.[2] Nevertheless, its acceptance is a matter of convention, and in May 1982 a British veto on agricultural policy was simply 'ignored' and the majority view implemented.

The Committee of Permanent Representatives (Coreper) is the civil service parallel to the Council of Ministers. It consists of the ambassador and other civil servants from each country and it deals initially with all the proposals that come from the Commission. It meets more regularly than the Council of

[1]See C. O'Nuallain, *The Presidency of the European Council of Ministers*, London 1985.

[2]See W. Nicoll, 'The Luxembourg Compromise', *JCMS* 1984–5, pp. 35–44; J. Lambert, 'The Constitutional Crisis 1965–66', *JCMS* 1965–6, pp. 195–228.

Ministers, and even though it operates on the unanimity rule it is able to reach decisions on most of the matters that come before it. These are sent to the Council of Ministers for formal approval, together with those matters on which agreement has not been reached and a Ministerial decision is required. Coreper works closely with the Commission's civil servants, and tends to identify rather more closely with the Community-wide approach than does the Council of Ministers.

The Court of Justice is the Community's Supreme Court.[1] It is composed of thirteen judges (one from each member country plus one), who can be removed only by the unanimous verdict of the other judges. It is thus even further removed from the control of the national governments than is the Commission. It examines alleged breaches of Community laws that are brought to its attention by the Commission, the national governments or private bodies. In 1979 Britain was brought before the Court for failing to apply the Community law on the tachograph (the 'spy in the cab' of commercial road vehicles), and in 1982 the Court held that British practice breached the Community's equal pay requirements. In each case the British Government was obliged to take action to comply with the Court's ruling. The Court does not deal with matters of domestic law, but it does give guidance to national courts on how to reconcile domestic laws with Community laws. The judges reach their decisions by majority vote but deliver a single verdict, so that national views cannot be identified.

Functional and territorial representation is provided through the Economic and Social Committee and the European Parliament. The 189 members of the Economic and Social Committee are appointed by the Council of Ministers to provide advice on social and economic policy. They are drawn largely from trade unions and employers' organisations and serve for four years. All proposals on social and economic matters go before the Committee and it provides a forum for European-wide interest groups such as the European Union

[1] See A. M. Donner, 'The Constitutional Powers of the Court of Justice of the European Communities', *CMLR* 1974, pp. 127–40.

of Industries, the European Committee of Farmers Organisations and the European Federation of Trade Unions.[1]

The European Parliament has 518 members, directly elected for five-year terms, representing the member-countries broadly in proportion to their population.[2] Until 1962 it was known as the Assembly, and until the introduction of direct elections in 1979 it was composed of delegates from the member-countries' Parliaments. The European Parliament participates in the Community's law-making process by commenting on the Commission's proposals, and it can attempt to initiate legislation by making requests to the Commission for action. It scrutinises the work of the Commission through its dozen or so specialist subject committees and has a limited influence over expenditure.

The budgetary process begins in June, when each of the Community institutions submits estimates of its expenditure for the coming year.[3] The Commission prepares the draft budget and passes it to the Council of Ministers, which normally reduces the sums involved. In the autumn the amended budget goes to the Parliament, which can vary the size of a limited number of items and can reject the budget in its entirety (which it did for the first time in 1979). Parliament, however, does not have direct control over the Community's income. Some two-fifths of revenue comes from the common external tariff, another two-fifths from sources such as levies on food imports and taxes on the salaries of the Community's

[1] See J. A. Sargent, 'Pressure Group Development in the EC', *JCMS* 1981–2, pp. 269–86; A. B. Philip, 'Pressure Group and Policy Formation in the European Communities', *PP* 1982, pp. 459–76; W. Grant, 'Industrialists and Farmers: British Interests and the European Community', *WEP* 1978, pp. 89–107.

[2] See M. Palmer, *The European Parliament*, London 1981; P. Scalinga, *The European Parliament*, London 1980; D. Marquand, *Parliament For Europe*, London 1979; J. Fitzmaurice, *The European Parliament*, London 1978; V. Herman, 'The Powers and Functions of the Directly Elected European Parliament', *Parl. Aff.* 1980, pp. 79–91; R. Bieber, 'Achievements of the European Parliament 1979–84', *CMLR* 1985, pp. 283–304; R. Bourguignon-Wittke (*et al.*), 'Five Years of the Directly Elected European Parliament', *JCMS* 1985–6, pp. 39–60.

[3] See P. J. G. Kapteyn, 'The European Parliament, the Budget and Legislation in the Community', *CMLR* 1972, pp. 386–410.

TABLE XXXV

Composition of the European Parliament, 1986

Group Members		UK Members	
Socialist Group	172	Lab. 32/SDLP (N.I.) 1	
European Peoples Party	118		
European Democratic Group	63	Con. 45/OUP (N.I.) 1	
Communists and Allies	46		
Liberal and Democratic Group	42		
European Democratic Alliance	34	SNP 1	
Rainbow Group	20		
European Group	16		
Non-attached	7	DUP (N.I.) 1	
	518		81

employees. None of these sources is under the direct control of Parliament.

Other basic weaknesses of the Parliament are that it does not itself make legislation, and neither the Council nor the Commission is directly responsible to it. The Parliament does have the power to dismiss the Commission as a whole, through a motion approved by a two-thirds majority, but has no power to dismiss individual Commissioners.

The Parliament operates on party lines, with the various national parties organised into Groups (see Table XXXV).[1] In the semi-circular chamber the Members of the European Parliament sit in party Groups rather than in national blocs. Each Group is served by a secretariat and strives to achieve cohesion and discipline. For the 1984 election the Groups sought, with some success, to produce agreed manifestos. Parliamentary business is organised through the Groups and Group spokesmen have precedence in debate.

The introduction of direct elections for the European Parlia-

[1]See G. and P. Pridham, *Transnational Party Cooperation and European Integration*, London 1981; S. Henig, *Political Parties in the European Community*, London 1979; J. P. Sweeney, 'The Left in Europe's Parliament', *CP* 1983–4, pp. 171–90; L. L. Fowler (*et al.*), 'Changing Patterns of Voting Strength in the European Parliament', *CP* 1982–3, pp. 159–76; G. Pridham, 'Transnational Party Groups in the European Parliament', *JCMS* 1975, pp. 266–79.

ment (envisaged in the Treaty of Rome but not implemented until 1979), was seen as a means of raising Parliament's status and visibility, and thereby altering the balance among the Community institutions. Direct elections, however, were not universally welcomed. Some feared that a directly-elected Parliament would threaten the status of the national Parliaments, while others questioned whether the election of a Parliament that did not at the same time involve the election of a Government would arouse public interest in countries that had Parliamentary-Cabinet systems (and certainly in Britain in the 1979 and 1984 European elections only a third of the electorate voted). Prior to 1979 those members of the national Parliaments who served in the European Parliament provided a direct domestic involvement in Community affairs. While dual-membership is still permissible, and while of the British parties only Labour prevented its MPs from standing in the 1984 European elections, the workload involved is generally regarded as unacceptable.[1]

Britain resisted attempts to apply a uniform electoral system for the European Parliament. In 1984 the first-past-the-post system was used in Great Britain, and the Single Transferable Vote in Northern Ireland, while other countries used the Regional List system. The Conservatives, Labour and the Alliance contested all seventy-eight seats in Great Britain, and the Nationalists all the seats in Scotland and Wales.[2] In Great Britain the turnout of a third of the electorate was lower than in any other country. In Northern Ireland, however, where there was a single three-member constituency, turnout was almost two-thirds. As is shown in Table XXXVI, the Conservatives 'won' the election, but compared with 1979 they lost fifteen seats to Labour. In Northern Ireland the Official Unionists, Democratic Unionists and SDLP each won one of the three seats. The outcome in Great Britain was just as disproportional as that of the 1983 general election: the Alliance received a fifth of the votes but did not win a single

[1] See V. Herman and R. Van Schendelen (eds), *The European Parliament and National Parliaments*, London 1979.

[2] See M. Holland, *Candidates For Europe*, London 1986; M. Holland, 'The Selection of Parliamentary Candidates', *Parl. Aff.* 1981, pp. 28–46.

TABLE XXXVI

1984 Elections for the European Parliament (Great Britain)

	Votes		Seats	
	N	%	N	%
Cons.	5,426;796	40.8	45	57.7
Lab.	4,865,220	36.5	32	41.0
Alln.	2,591,657	19.5	—	—
SNP	230,590	1.7	1	1.3
Plaid Cymru	103,031	0.8	—	—
Others	95,524	0.7	—	—

seat, while the Conservatives won almost three-fifths of the seats with just two-fifths of the votes.[1]

The Impact of Membership

British Sovereignty. Many opponents of British membership of the Community have argued that it has involved a major loss of sovereignty. There is much confusion, however, between the Constitutional and practical senses of the term 'sovereignty'. As far as practical sovereignty (in the sense of a nation's freedom of action) is concerned, it is clearly the case that membership of any international organisation involves the loss of a certain amount of freedom of action. Membership of NATO restricts Britain's freedom to deploy its defence forces, membership of the United Nations involves commitments in a range of matters and participation in GATT limits

[1] See D. Butler and P. Jowett, *Party Strategies in Britain*, London 1985; D. Butler and D. Marquand, *European Elections in British Politics*, London 1981; J. Lodge and V. Herman, *Direct Elections to the European Parliament*, London 1982; V. Herman and M. Hagger, *The Legislation of Direct Elections to the European Parliament*, London 1980; C. Cook and M. Francis, *The First European Elections*, London 1979; H. Berrington, 'European Elections Mandate For Change', *WEP* 1980, pp. 242–6; J. G. Blumler and A. D. Fox, 'The Involvement of Voters in the European Elections of 1979', *EJPR* 1980, pp. 359–86; K. Reif (*et al.*), 'The First European Elections', *EJPR* 1980, pp. 1–158; J. Lodge, 'Euro-Elections and the European Parliament', *Parl. Aff.* 1985, pp. 40–55.

the tariff policies that Britain can pursue. Membership of the European Community can be seen as simply adding to an already long list of international commitments that impose constraints on British independence. What is more, supporters of the Community argue that, far from limiting Britain's independence, membership of the Community has strengthened Britain economically, and accordingly has enhanced Britain's political position in the world. While such an argument begs a number of questions (not least about the economic benefits of membership), it is certainly the case that an isolated but weak nation does not necessarily enjoy freedom of action.

Membership of the Community, however, involves more extensive commitments than any other international body to which Britain belongs. The European Community is far from being simply a free-trade organisation, but requires the acceptance of common policies and standards in a range of social and economic matters. Community institutions are better developed, and more formidable, than those of the other international organisations with which Britain is involved. What is more, the Community has considerable potential for development and there are constant pressures to strengthen the decision-making institutions and extend the range of obligations that membership involves.

On joining the Community Britain was obliged to accept the twin principles that Community law applies to all members, and that in any conflict it is Community law that takes precedence.[1] The principles apply to Community laws that were in existence when Britain joined the Community, as well as to laws that have been framed since 1973. These Community laws take various forms. A vast number of laws emerge each year from the institutions of the Community in the form

[1] See J. Usher, *European Community Law and National Law*, London 1981; P. S. R. F. Mathijsen, *A Guide to European Community Law*, London 1972; J. W. Bridge, 'National Legal Tradition and Community Law', *JCMS* 1981, pp. 351–76; L. P. Suetens, 'The Relationship Between Community Law and Domestic Law', *CMLR* 1964–5, pp. 433–40; J. Forman, 'The Attitude of British Courts to Community Law', *CMLR* 1976, pp. 388–415; J. W. Bridge, 'Community Law and English Courts and Tribunals', *ELJ* 1975–6, pp. 13–21.

of regulations, directives and decisions. A 'regulation' is binding on all members and specifies both the policy objective and the means of achieving the objective. A 'directive' specifies a policy objective that is binding on members, but allows each member to determine the means of achieving the objective. A 'decision' applies only to a particular country, organisation or individual. The Treaties of Paris and Rome laid down the basic conditions of membership, and subsequent treaties admitting new members, or establishing trade agreements with non-members, also specify commitments that are universally binding. Decisions of the Court of Justice constitute a growing body of case-law.

Clearly, Community laws must be binding, and must take precedence over domestic laws, if the Community is to operate as an effective unit. The precedence of Community law, however, has important implications for the British constitutional doctrine of Parliamentary Sovereignty. As noted in Chapter 6,[1] the four strands of this doctrine are that there is no higher legislative authority than Parliament (in the sense of the Monarch, Lands and Commons acting in concert); no court can declare Acts of Parliament to be invalid; there is no legal limit to Parliament's sphere of legislation; and no Parliament can bind a successor or be bound by a predecessor. There is a clear conflict between the concept of a perpetually supreme national Parliament and the subordination of that Parliament's laws to laws that are made by an external body.

When Britain joined the Community the consequent legal obligations were reconciled with the doctrine of Parliamentary Sovereignty by the terms of the European Communities Act 1972. That Act specified that Community laws would apply in Britain and would take precedence over existing laws that had been made by Parliament. As the European Communities Act was an Act of the British Parliament, and as it could be repealed or amended by a future Act of the British Parliament, the legal supremacy of Parliament was maintained.

No legal difficulty arises with laws that were in existence when Britain joined the European Community. The 1972 Act unambiguously subordinated existing British laws to existing

[1]See above p. 187.

Community laws. A potential difficulty exists, however, with British and Community laws that have emerged since 1972. The European Communities Act sought to extend into the future the supreme and binding nature of Community law. It would be constitutionally possible, however, for a future British Parliament to declare one of its Acts to be exempt from the terms of the European Communities Act, and to be superior to any Community laws. The British courts would be obliged to recognise the supremacy of the new Act of Parliament over all existing British and Community laws, on the basis that the Parliament that passed the 1972 Act cannot bind its successors, and in any conflict between two Acts of Parliament it is the later Act that takes precedence. While such a development would (in British terms) be legally valid, it would be incompatible with the conditions of membership of the Community, and no doubt the Court of Justice would find Britain to be in breach of its obligations as a Community member.

Ultimately the predominance of Community law over domestic law depends on the willingness of the British courts to accept that principle. The supremacy of Community law could be reinforced by one of a variety of procedures. Each Act of Parliament could contain a clause that acknowledged its subordination to Community law. Alternatively, an annual European Communities Act could assert the supremacy of Community law over all the domestic laws passed in that session. Yet again, each Community law could be enshrined subsequently in an Act of Parliament, thereby fusing Community and domestic laws. The legislative burden involved in this process, however, would be truly enormous.

The legal consequences of membership should not be overstated. The bulk of English and Scottish law remains unaffected by membership. Most Community laws relate to matters on which there were no existing British legal requirements, so that Community laws have tended to supplement, rather than replace, British laws. Also, the application of Community laws rests with the member states themselves. The Court of Justice can declare a member's action (or inaction) to be a breach of the law, and the Community can impose economic penalties on recalcitrant members, but there is no Community police force. It is also the case that in major matters, and within the practical constraints imposed by the need to come to terms with its partners, a member can use its veto in the Council of Ministers to prevent the enactment of major developments to which it objects. Ultimately, both the enactment and the application of Community laws depends upon the willingness of the governments of the member states to live within the law.

Whitehall. The Ministerial and departmental workload has increased considerably as a result of membership of the Community.[1] Ministers and civil servants participate directly in the Community's decision-making processes, and the departments of state are required to implement the policies that emerge from these procedures and to process the vast number of documents that the Community generates each year. The Council of Ministers meets about sixty times each year, with the Council of Agriculture Ministers accounting for about twenty meetings and the Economic and Foreign Affairs Councils about a dozen each.[2] Ministers also attend meetings of fringe bodies, such as the Standing Committee on Employment, while the Prime Minister participates in regular heads-of-state meetings. Ministers will also be involved in ad hoc meetings with Commissioners and Ministers of other member states.[3] The nature of the tasks performed by Ministers and civil servants have also changed in that departments that previously had an almost exclusively domestic role are now involved regularly and directly in international contacts. Many civil servants spend most of their time in Brussels, where the skills they require are those of international negotiators.

These consequences of membership have been much greater for some departments than for others. The Ministry of Agriculture has experienced the greatest increase in its work-

[1] See H. and W. Wallace, 'The Impact of Community Membership on the British Machinery of Government', *JCMS* 1972–3, pp. 243–62; Sir C. Soames, 'Whitehall Into Europe', *Pub. Admin.* 1972, pp. 271–9; H. Wallace, 'The Impact of the European Communities on National Policy-Making', *G and O* 1971, pp. 520–38.

[2] See Gregory, *Dilemmas of Government*, p. 140.

[3] See K. J. Mortelmans, 'The Extramural Meetings of the Ministers of the Member States of the Community', *CMLR* 1974, pp. 62–91.

load and in its status within the departmental and Ministerial hierarchy. The Treasury and the departments of Trade, Transport and Energy have also been affected appreciably, while the Foreign Office has acquired an enhanced role. Some other departments, however, including Education and the Home Office, have been affected only marginally.

Within the Minister–Civil Servant relationship, membership has increased the influence of the civil service. While the Ministerial workload has increased, there has been no comparable increase in the number of Ministers to cope with it. The number of civil servants, on the other hand, has grown in the most directly involved departments. As much of the business of the Community involves negotiation over detailed matters, much discretion has to be delegated to the civil service negotiators based in Brussels. The increase in civil service initiative, particularly through participation in Coreper, has placed the concept of Ministerial responsibility under greater strain than ever.

In contrast to former practice, when the India Office, Colonial Office and Commonwealth Office were established to manage Britain's overseas responsibilities, there has been no attempt to create a Ministry of European (or Community) Affairs, and Community business has been managed on a functional rather than a geographical basis. Initially, Britain's attempts to enter the Community were handled by the Foreign Office, though with civil service negotiators drawn from the most directly involved departments. Since 1973 the Foreign Office has retained something of a coordinating role, dealing initially with Community documents, briefing departments about matters that are to be covered at forthcoming meetings of the Council of Ministers, and advising the departments about the implications of Council decisions. The Cabinet Office has also had a coordinating role, through a small European Secretariat. Each department, however, remains directly responsible for its own sphere of policy. What is more, within each department Community business is distributed through the several functional divisions, rather than being concentrated into an exclusive European division.

The diffusion of Community affairs throughout the established Whitehall machine has meant that departments which previously were predominantly domestic in their orientation have had to develop a European perspective. This has emphasised the range of policy areas affected by membership and has demonstrated the links between the European and domestic dimensions of policies. These links are such that had a special European Ministry been created, it would almost inevitably have been accused of impinging upon the domestic departments' responsibilities. As it is, even the Foreign Office in its limited coordinating role has been attacked for encroaching on the domestic arena. Nevertheless, there has been no single departmental or Ministerial champion of the European cause, nor a single target for anti-Community sentiment. The coordination of European business has to be achieved through inter-departmental procedures, and the collective responsibility of the whole government for Community policies has been emphasised.

In the Heath Government a degree of coordination was achieved through the Chancellor of the Duchy of Lancaster acting as a non-departmental 'Minister for Europe'. This arrangement was abandoned by Wilson in 1974, however, and was not revived in the Callaghan or Thatcher Governments. At Cabinet level, coordination is achieved principally through a Cabinet committee, chaired by the Foreign Secretary. Various ad hoc committees are also used to reconcile departmental points of view. These Ministerial committees are shadowed by meetings of officials and there are regular meetings of the departmental Permanent Secretaries and the Permanent Representative to the Community. As, however, meetings of the Council of Ministers and of Coreper are essentially forums for negotiations, the departments of state and Parliament are unable to bind the negotiating Ministers and civil servants too closely.

Westminster. Parliament uses various procedures to supervise Ministers in their European roles. All documents that are published by the Community are presented to Parliament and are made available to MPs and Peers. Proposed changes in Community laws are accompanied by explanatory memoranda, prepared by the Whitehall department concerned. The Government produces a White Paper every six months, outlining recent and forthcoming Community developments, and each session six days in the Commons timetable are allocated to debates on the White Papers and Community affairs in general. After each meeting of the Council of Ministers a Ministerial statement is read to the House, and Community business has a specific place in the Question Time rota.

The domestic Parliaments have no specified role in the Community's law-making process.[1] Community legislation originates in the departments of the Commission, where civil servants produce a draft proposal. After consultations between civil servants and interested parties the proposal is submitted to the Commission and (when approved) to the Council of Ministers. The Council will seek the views of the European Parliament, and there will be discussion between the Council, Coreper and the Commission in the search for an agreed formula. If this is forthcoming, the Council of Ministers will give its final approval and the measure will become part of the body of Community law.

While the domestic Parliaments do not participate directly in this process, procedures have been established to allow the Commons and the Lords to examine and comment upon all proposals before they receive final approval in the Council of Ministers. The principal vehicles for this are the House of Commons' Select Committee on European Legislation and the House of Lords' Select Committee on the European Community, both established in 1974.[2] The task of the House of Commons Committee is to examine the 700 or so proposals that are made each year to changes in Community laws, and draw the attention of the House to the most significant of them. It is then up to the House as a whole to find time to debate the matter and make Ministers aware of MPs' views. The Committee's function is thus to act as a filter: it does not concern itself with the merits of the proposals but simply identifies those that 'raise questions of legal or political importance'. The Committee has sixteen members and has the

[1] See M. Niblock, *The EEC: National Parliaments in Community Decision Making*, London 1971; A. C. Evans, 'Participation of National Parliaments in the European Community Legislative Process', *PL* 1981, pp. 388–98. See also, above p. 453.

[2] See above p. 368.

services of legal and documentation officers. It usually contains a balance of Community supporters and critics, and in order to maintain its unity it tends to tread warily in politically sensitive areas. It takes evidence from British Ministers and civil servants, but not from the European Commissioners, who are prohibited from giving evidence before domestic Parliaments.

Unlike the Commons Committee, the House of Lords Committee does concern itself with the merits of the proposals it examines and makes highly political judgements about their desirability. It differs from the House of Commons Committee also in that it functions through half-a-dozen subcommittees, each specialising in a subject area. One of the subcommittees considers the legal implications of each proposal. The chairman of the main committee identifies the controversial items (usually about a quarter of the whole) and they are passed to the appropriate subcommittee for consideration. The subcommittee delivers its findings to the main committee and a report is presented to the House. The main committee has twenty-four members, selected in such a way that no party has an overall majority. The subcommittees, however, are open to any Peers who care to attend, and thus draw upon the wide range of expertise that is available in the Lords.

While there is a clear division of labour between the committees of the two Houses, the House of Lords Committee is widely regarded as being the more effective. The Lords committee has more time at its disposal, the Peers are anxious to demonstrate that this is an area in which they have a distinct contribution to make and the political climate in the Lords is somewhat less hostile to the Community. As a consequence, civil servants and other witnesses are prepared to be more forthcoming than when facing the Commons committee. Above all, while the Commons' committee is clearly subordinate to the House as a whole (simply drawing proposals to the attention of the House), the findings and opinions of the Lords' Committee are judged in their own right. Some of the reports of the House of Lords Committee are debated subsequently on the floor of the House, but for the most part the Committee is itself regarded as speaking for the House as a whole.

The scrutiny procedures in the Commons and the Lords publicise the proposed Community laws, highlight particularly significant proposals and allow an informed Parliamentary view to emerge. The essential fact, however, is that Parliamentary approval is not required for Community laws, and in their role as European law-makers Ministers are not obliged to act according to the expressed wishes of Parliament. Indeed, a Minister may not approve of the particular policies to which he has been obliged to accede in the Council of Ministers as part of a compromise package. In Parliament and in public the Minister may express his reservations about a certain policy, but present it as an inevitable consequence of participation in the decision-making processes of the Community.

Successive Governments have agreed that Ministers will not give their approval in the Council of Ministers to any proposals that have not yet passed through the scrutiny procedures of Parliament. Nevertheless, while Ministers will note the opinions of Parliament, they still retain the right to ignore the Parliamentary point of view. Ultimately, of course, the Commons could pass a vote of no confidence in a Government that ignored the Parliamentary view on a succession of Community issues. In this, however, as in other aspects of the relationship between Government and Parliament, the constraints upon the use of this ultimate Parliamentary power are vast. The scrutiny procedures also suffer from the usual limitations that are imposed by the Parliamentary timetable. The House of Commons does not always find time to debate matters referred to it by the Select Committee. Many items are considered in the relative obscurity of Standing Committees, while debates that do take place on the floor of the House tend to be late at night. Community laws, for the most part, deal with technical matters, rather than with broad issues of principle, and thus only rarely provoke Parliamentary and public interest. Relatively few MPs specialise in Community affairs, their general approach tends to be unsympathetic to the Community and its policies, and the Labour and Conservative backbench groups on European affairs are not particularly influential within their parties.

TABLE XXXVII

House of Commons Votes on the Principle of Membership of the Community

	Oct. 1971		April 1975	
	Pro-membership	Anti-membership	Pro-membership	Anti-membership
Con.	282	39	249	8
Lab.	69	198	137	145
Lib.	5	1	12	—
Other	—	6	—	19
	356	244	398	172

Source: H. Lazar, 'British Populism', *PSQ* 1976–7, pp. 259–77.

Europe and the Party System

The issue of British membership of the Community has been difficult to accommodate within the British adversarial pattern of confrontation between Government and Opposition.[1] The Westminster system assumes a high degree of intra-party cohesion on major issues, but for a quarter of a century the European issue has cut across the normal party divide. Before 1960 there was no issue at all, in that the parties and the public showed only marginal interest in the formation and development of the Community, but when the issue of British membership did come to the fore in the 1960s distinct pro-European and anti-European groups emerged in each party. As is shown in Table XXXVII, in the two major votes in the House of Commons on the principle of British membership (in October 1971 on the question of entry and in April 1975 on the acceptability of the re-negotiated terms), the majority in favour of membership was made up of a mix of Labour, Conservative and Liberal MPs. In each case most Conservatives and Liberals voted in favour of membership, while the majority of Labour MPs (together with the Nationalists and others) voted against. Nevertheless, a sizeable minority of Labour MPs voted in favour of membership, while a smaller minority of Conservatives voted against.

[1] See R. J. Lieber, *British Politics and European Unity*, Berkeley 1970.

The intra-party divisions were highlighted during the 1975 referendum campaign, when all-party groups were formed to present the case for and against Britain's continued membership. The anti-membership National Referendum Campaign included 'Conservatives Against the Treaty of Rome', 'Liberals Say No to the Common Market', the cross-party 'Common Market Safeguards Campaign' and the non-party 'Get Britain out'. Equally, the Britain in Europe organisation included the 'Conservative Group for Europe', 'Labour Campaign for Britain in Europe', 'Liberal European Action Group' and the 'Trade Union Alliance'. Most Labour Cabinet Ministers advocated continued membership, but the NEC and a majority of Labour MPs and activists campaigned against. Leading figures from all parties shared platforms and campaigned together.

Given the importance of the issue, the strength of feeling it aroused and the persistence of the intra-party divisions, it might have been expected that it would have had a marked and lasting effect upon the party system. Certainly, the tariff issue produced major realignments in the party system on two occasions in the nineteenth century – in the 1840s when the repeal of the duty on imported corn split the Tory Party, and in the 1880s when the free-trade issue helped to drive the Liberal Imperialists into the Conservative ranks. In fact, party ranks closed quickly after the 1975 Referendum and the adversarial confrontation between the two main parties was renewed.

To some extent, however, the seeds of the Alliance were sown through the cooperation between the Liberals and the leading figures of the 'Labour Campaign for Britain in Europe' who subsequently formed the SDP. The split in the Labour Party that produced the SDP did not occur until some seven years after the referendum, and was precipitated by more than just the European issue. The strongly anti-Community stance taken by the Labour Party in the 1979–83 Parliament, however, contributed significantly to dissatisfaction within the party, and some have seen a strong commitment to the Community as the prime characteristics of the Alliance.

It is the smaller parties that have shown the greatest

conviction and consistency in their attitude to the European Community. The Communist Party, Scottish and Welsh nationalists and the National Front have consistently opposed British membership, while the Alliance has been strongly in favour. It is true that the Liberals' enthusiasm dates only from the 1960s, and that the party contains an anti-Community minority. Majority Liberal opinion, however, has been firmly in favour of membership since 1962. In the 1984 elections for the European Parliament the Alliance produced much the most integrationist manifesto of all the British parties, advocating British participation in the European Monetary System, the adoption of a common electoral system for European elections, increased authority for the Commission and restrictions on the use of the veto in the Council of Ministers.

The European issue was a potentially dangerous one for the Conservatives, given the party's imperial and protectionist traditions. Certainly, when the possibility of British membership of the Community first emerged in the 1950s, Conservative patriots were concerned about the potential loss of national sovereignty, the farming interests expressed major reservations about the Common Agricultural Policy and the policy of Commonwealth trading preference was seen as a barrier to the acceptance of European free trade. The 'Imperial' Conservative Party of the 1950s evolved relatively painlessly into a broadly 'European' party, which initiated Britain's first application in 1960, eventually completed the process in 1972 and currently supports continued British membership. The party's generally pragmatic approach to policy, and its traditional loyalty to the views of the established leader, helped to avoid a major division on the European issue. In this respect Edward Heath's long-standing commitment to membership was significant. Neither Heath nor Macmillan sought to instigate a great intra-party debate over the issue. In the 1959–64 Parliament Macmillan approached the question of Britain's possible membership one stage at a time, avoiding a single 'point of decision'. In the 1970–4 Parliament Heath was able to benefit from the momentum that had been established by the Wilson Government's applications. No Minister resigned from the Macmillan or Heath Cabinets over the issue, so that there was no prestigious focus for Conservative resistance to the Government's policies. Enoch Powell did emerge as a fierce critic of membership, but he isolated himself from the bulk of the party over other issues.

In the 1960s Labour might well have developed a pro-Community stance, seeking links with the increasingly powerful Social Democratic parties of the continent. After much hesitation, however, Labour opposed Macmillan's attempt to secure entry to the Community.[1] In a major speech at the 1962 Labour Party Conference Hugh Gaitskell declared that Britain would be turning its back on 'a thousand years of history' if it weakened its links with the Commonwealth in favour of Europe. Subsequently party policy followed a tortuous path. The 1964–70 Labour Government twice initiated negotiations for membership, but Labour in opposition opposed entry on the terms achieved by the Heath Government. In the 1975 referendum the Labour Cabinet (but not the NEC) advocated acceptance of the revised terms it had negotiated, but with the return to opposition in 1979, hostility towards the Community intensified. Whereas in the 1960s and 1970s the predominant view in the party was that membership was desirable 'provided the terms were acceptable', in the 1980s Labour has been more critical of the very principle of membership. The 1980 and 1981 Labour Conferences advocated British withdrawal, and the manifesto for the 1983 election declared that a Labour Government would achieve this within the lifetime of a Parliament. Since 1983 Labour policy statements have placed rather less emphasis on the importance of withdrawal. Nevertheless, in its manifesto for the 1984 election for the European Parliament Labour rejected British participation in the European Monetary System, opposed any increase in the power of the Parliament and reserved Britain's right to withdraw from the Community.

To some extent the gyrations over the years in Labour policy towards the Community reflect the difference between

[1]See L. J. Robins, *The Reluctant Party*, London 1980; K. Featherstone, 'Socialists and European Integration', *EJPR* 1981, pp. 407–19; P. Byrd, 'The Labour Party and the European Community 1970–75', *JCMS* 1975, pp. 469–83; H. Lazar, 'British Populism: the Labour Party and the Common Market Parliamentary Debate', *PSQ* 1976–7, pp. 259–77.

being in office and being in opposition. As well as any Constitutional obligation there may be on Her Majesty's Opposition to oppose the Government in order to stimulate a public debate, it is tempting in opposition to attack a Government that is pursuing a major initiative that appears to have only limited public support.[1] More than that, however, changes in Labour's stance reflect differences in the distribution of power within the party between opposition and office. Anti-Community sentiment has been stronger on the NEC, among constituency activists and at the party Conference than in the PLP, while within the PLP it has been stronger on the backbenches than among front-benchers. In the 1975 House of Commons vote on the renegotiated terms, for example, two-thirds of Cabinet Ministers voted in favour of the terms while 54% of backbenchers voted against. Given the particular distribution of its strength within the party, the influence of the anti-Community group has been greatest in opposition, when the NEC and the Conference increase their influence within the decision-making procedures.

Conclusion

The mechanics of Labour's commitment to withdraw from the Community would be the amendment of the European Communities Act to end the supremacy of Community law, the repeal of any established Community laws that were unacceptable, and the negotiation of a new trading arrangement with the Community. This strategy, however, would not be easy to implement.[2] A minority Labour Government would have difficulty in persuading the Alliance (or the Conservatives) to sustain it in office in face of such a policy. Even if agreement was forthcoming, a minority Government might be brought down on another issue before the policy could be implemented. Equally, a coalition government of which Labour was a member would be unlikely to be able to include

[1] See R. Jowell and G. Hainville (eds), *Britain into Europe: Public Opinion and the EEC 1961–75*, London 1975; D. E. Butler, 'Public Opinion and Community Membership', *PQ* 1979, pp. 151–6.

[2] See J. Palmer, 'Britain and the EEC: the Withdrawal Option', *Inter. Aff.* 1982, pp. 638–47.

the policy in an agreed programme. At the very least, the pro-Community parties would demand that the issue be submitted to a further referendum, which could not be guaranteed to produce a majority for withdrawal. A majority Labour Government, with the prospects of remaining in office for at least a full Parliament, would be able to secure the necessary legislation. Labour's most devoted pro-Community MPs have joined the SDP, so that the party would be more united on the issue than was the case in the 1970s. A majority Government could ignore demands for a referendum, and even if the House of Lords rejected a withdrawal Bill it could become law after a year under the terms of the Parliament Act.

In practical terms, however, it would be difficult to negotiate a satisfactory post-withdrawal arrangement with the Community. Some 40% of British trade is with the eleven other countries that now comprise the Community. They would be unlikely to wish to make any particular concessions to British interests, and even if a satisfactory arrangement was forthcoming it would have to be ratified by the Parliament of each member as well as by the Community as a whole. Although Greenland (as a Danish dependency) negotiated a tidy withdrawal in 1985, this is not a precedent for the withdrawal of a core-member.[1]

Assuming that Britain does remain a member, British Governments in the immediate future are likely to be asked to work towards increased integration of the Community.[2] In December 1985 agreement was reached in the Council of Ministers on a package of reforms designed to strengthen the Community. It was agreed that in the Council of Ministers in the spheres of social and tariff policy there should be increased

[1]See F. Harhoff, 'Greenland's Withdrawal From the European Communities', *CMLR* 1983, pp. 13–33.

[2]See P. Taylor, *The Limits of European Integration*, London 1985; M. Burgess (ed.), *Federalism and Federation in Western Europe*, London 1986; K. Kaiser (*et al.*), *The European Community: Progress or Decline?*, London 1983; M. Rutherford, *Can We Save the Common Market?*, London 1981; V. Bogdanor, 'The Future of the European Community', *G and O* 1986, pp. 161–76; G. Ionescu and J. Pinder, 'A British Lead to a Federal Europe?', *G and O* 1984, pp. 279–86; U. Everling, 'Possibilities and Limits of European Integration', *JCMS* 1979–80, pp. 217–28.

use of qualified majority voting (at the expense of the unanimity rule), and that there should be a reform of the powers of the Parliament in order to increase its ability to influence the Commission and the Council. It was also agreed that there should be greater cooperation on foreign policy, that the Community's role should be extended in the spheres of monetary, health and environmental policy, and that economic policies should seek to reduce the disparities between the north and south of Europe. As the institutional reforms involve amendments to the Treaty of Rome, each member is required to give its approval. Accordingly, the European Communities (Amendment) Bill was introduced in 1986 to give effect to the changes.[1]

Critics have seen the proposals as a major step towards greater integration and thus as a threat to the independence of each member state. Even with these developments, however, the European Community is still very far from constituting a federal organisation. With twelve members rather than the original six, cooperation is all the harder to achieve. The Council of Ministers remains essentially a forum for international negotiations and the unanimity rule still applies on major matters. The Commission lacks the authority of a popularly elected body and the ability of the Parliament to inspire a 'European' perspective is limited. The Community has no police or military forces and thus lacks the final ability to enforce decisions. Ultimately, British withdrawal is Constitutionally feasible, though practically difficult. Thus just as any changes in the internal structure of the United Kingdom are likely to be in the form of devolution within a unitary Constitution, rather than the adoption of a federal Constitution, so in its involvement with the European Community Britain is likely to remain part of a confederal structure rather than of the Federal States of Europe that was envisaged by some of the founding fathers of the Community.

[1] See J. Lodge, 'The Single European Act', *JCMS* 1985–6, pp. 203–24; J. P. Jacqué, 'The Draft Treaty Establishing the European Union, *CMLR* 1985, pp. 19–42.

part five

Conclusion

15

The Nature of the British Political System

Democracy in Britain

Modern concepts of western democracy are based largely on the principles of free and regular elections, a broad suffrage, and the existence of a party (or coalition of parties) capable of forming an alternative government. Also implied is the view that all sections of society should participate in the political process, at least to the extent of voting at elections. Many would also claim that, for a true democracy, it is necessary that the political leaders, as well as being representative of the views of the electorate, should be drawn from all social, economic, religious, and ethnic groups within the community, and should not be drawn merely from an exclusive section of society. It is further implied that in a democracy, between elections, pressure groups and the mass media should give expression to public opinions, although attitudes vary as to the extent to which the Government should, or in practical terms could, be expected to respond to public opinions between elections.

In Britain the nature of the party system means that there exists an alternative government, and the electorate is given the opportunity, at regular intervals, to elect this alternative government to power. Her Majesty's Loyal Opposition is formally recognised within Parliament, and the official post of Leader of the Opposition carries with it a salary paid as one of the Consolidated Fund Services. The Government and

Opposition parties present themselves to the electorate at least every five years (other than in wartime emergencies), and in practice general elections are held every three to four years. The voters are then able to examine the record and proposals of the Government and of the Opposition, and also the general images of the parties and their leaders, and vote for the party that they find most acceptable, or least objectionable. The party favoured by the majority becomes the Government, and (apart from exceptional circumstances) remains in power for four or so years, conscious that at the end of that period it will have to submit itself to the electorate once again. All adults, with a few exceptions, are eligible to vote, and although voting is not compulsory, some 70% to 80% of the electorate normally do vote at general elections. The parties pay for the cost of their candidates' election campaigns, and salaries are paid to MPs and Ministers of the Crown, so that in this respect financial considerations need not form a barrier to political participation. For those people who do not choose to be active through the political parties, a multiplicity of pressure groups exist that provide an opportunity for political influence. The system of local government (although subordinate to the central government in the British unitary system) provides another means of political participation that is available to all members of the community.

These various considerations represent the main institutional features of British democracy. While accepting the undoubtedly democratic basis of the system, it is necessary to realise that many of these features operate in a manner that is very different from the way that is suggested by idealised democratic theory. The electoral system, for example, has a number of deficiencies when looked at from the point of view of achieving in the House of Commons a true reflection of the views of the electorate. A candidate can be elected without receiving an absolute majority of the votes, as happened in over half of the constituencies in 1983. The proportion of seats that the respective parties win can be very different from the proportion of votes that they get, and in 1983 the Conservatives won 61% of the seats on the basis of just 42% of the votes. A party can gain a majority of seats without getting even a *simple* majority of votes, as happened in the 1929, 1951 and February 1974 elections. These aspects of the electoral system were considered in more detail in Chapter 2, but as well as these criticisms of the detailed working of the electoral system, other and more fundamental criticisms are often levelled at British democracy. In order to examine the chief of these criticisms it is necessary to consider, first of all, the extent to which the people of Britain actually do participate in the political process; secondly, the credibility of the notion of an alternative government; and thirdly, the extent to which, between elections, Governments take note of, and respond to, public wishes.

Government of the People?

To what extent do the British people participate in the political processes? In general the vast majority of people in Britain play little or no direct part in the activities of the political parties. Most people's involvement extends no further than voting at elections, and some people do not participate even to this extent. While the membership of the British political parties is high in comparison with parties in other countries, active party members form only a very small proportion of the total membership. Further, at this level, but more particularly at a Parliamentary and Ministerial level, some social groups are over-represented in proportion to their numbers in the community as a whole. There exists in Britain an undoubted social elite, based in particular on the exclusive educational background of a limited section of the community, and this social elite holds a degree of political influence that is out of all proportion to its numerical strength. In the case of the Conservative Party in Parliament, and especially in Conservative Governments, a dominant position is occupied by the upper- and upper-middle-class element, whose educational background is that of public school, Oxbridge, and the law or big business. In the long periods this century when the Conservative Party has been in power (thirty-nine years alone, and a further sixteen years in Coalition), this exclusive social element has thus enjoyed a preponderant share of Ministerial power. Even when the Labour Party (or earlier the Liberal Party) has been in office, this exclusive social element has not been excluded entirely from Ministerial power, in that Liberal and Labour Governments have also included a number of Ministers with that type of social background. Also, this social elite is conspicuous among the top levels of the civil service, so that whichever political party is in power, the social elite retains considerable influence throughout the executive machine.

The existence of a small group who at any given time have a dominant share of political and economic power, is to be found in any political system, be it democratic or totalitarian, but in Britain this group is characterised by its *social* exclusiveness, and by its ability to perpetuate itself through the educational and social system. Marxists claim that this group constitutes a distinct Ruling Class, which has pronounced boundaries, which enjoys almost exclusive power, and which is dedicated to the maintenance of the existing social and capitalist system. Non-Marxists, however, would reject the notion that there is in Britain today a 'conspiracy' by a completely dominant and totally exclusive Ruling Class, and a more widely held view is that of a predominant (although not exclusive) share of political power being held by the upper-middle-class–public school–Oxbridge-based elite. This section of society does not have rigid boundaries, and in many ways its very strength is that it is flexible and fluid, and does accept newcomers into its ranks, thereby placating and encompassing potential opposition. It does not have an exclusive share of power. Not all Conservative Ministers and MPs, and not all top civil servants, have an exclusive social background, while within the Labour Party the social elite, though influential, is very far from dominant. Indeed, the powerful position of the working-class trade union element within the Labour Party represents a very major limitation on any notion that the upper-middle class has an exclusive share of political influence in Britain. In the Labour Party, political activity through a trade union leading to Parliament has represented an alternative means to Ministerial power for those members of society whose schooling was restricted to an elementary or secondary school, who attended no University, and who were manual workers or 'white collar' union officials before entering Parliament. The part played by the trade unions in the affairs of the Labour Party, not least in their role in the selection of the party's Parliamentary candidates, means that in many respects the trade unionists form an elite within the Labour Party. The place of the trade unionists within the Labour Party, however, is not as dominant as that of the upper-middle-class element within the Conservative Party, and the trade unionists have nothing like a monopoly of Ministerial power when the Labour Party is in office. Indeed, to a great extent the trade unions have been content to use their power and influence within the Labour Party to support party leaders who were drawn from the ranks of the party's intelligentsia.

Nevertheless, both the main parties have their respective elites, which in the case of the Conservative Party overlaps with the social elements that dominate the Civil Service, the business world, and other centres of power. Although the basis of recruitment to the Civil Service is by open competition, and although membership of the political parties, and thus ultimately Parliamentary candidature, is open to all, access to these centres of power is dominated by limited sections of society. Political activity through a pressure group is open to most people, and the leaders of the various pressure groups in Britain are drawn from various sections of society, and not merely from the trade union and social elites. Some of the most powerful groups, however, are those that represent trade union and business interests, so that in this respect also, the influence of the elites that dominate the two main parties extends to the most powerful pressure groups.

An Alternative Government

The existence of an opposition party is a safeguard for democracy only if it is a real and genuine alternative, and is not merely a pale shadow of the existing Government party, and also if it has a real chance of gaining power. For much of the nineteenth century there was a regular swing of the electoral pendulum from Government to Opposition, with the parties alternating in office at regular intervals. In part this seemed to be because a Government acquired a certain amount of unpopularity merely because it was the Government, and was thereby defeated after it had been in power, perhaps, for only one Parliament. This regular swing of the pendulum was particularly marked in the period from 1868 to 1895, when Conservative (or Unionist) and Liberal Governments alternated in power. From 1895 to 1905 there was a continuous period of Unionist rule, followed by a decade of Liberal rule which was interrupted by the first world war and the split in the Liberal Party during the war. Between the wars the upheavals in the party system produced by the decline of the Liberal Party and the rise of the Labour Party, followed by the emergence of the National Government out of the traumatic events of 1931, meant that Conservative Governments, or Conservative-dominated Coalitions, held office for practically the whole of the inter-war period. The Labour election victory of 1945, and then the Conservative win in 1951, suggested that there had been a return to a regular alternation in office by two main parties, but at both the 1955 and 1959 elections the Conservative Government secured an increase in its majority in the Commons.

Thus in the early 1960s the question often asked was 'Must Labour lose?'[1] It was thought by many political commentators and activists that the Conservatives, having come to terms in the 1950s with the Welfare State and the mixed economy, had succeeded in capturing the middle ground of British politics and had become an electorally dominant party of the centre and right. It was felt that Labour's links with the trade unions, and its continuing commitment to nationalisation, were major electoral disadvantages. Further, some political sociologists argued that with the increased affluence of the 1950s, and the consequent 'embourgeoisement' of the working class, the Labour Party was losing its appeal among large sections of its traditional support.[2] What is more, after the 1959 election it was widely argued that in the post-war period an incumbent Government had acquired two major advantages over the Opposition (additional to its traditional advantage of being able to hold the election at a time of its own

[1] See M. Abrams and R. Rose, *Must Labour Lose?*, London 1960.

[2] W. G. Runciman, '"Embourgeoisement", Self-Rated Class and Party Preferences', *SR* 1964, pp. 137–54.

choosing within the five-year limit). Firstly, given the post-war extent of Government intervention in the economy, the Government had the means to lull the electorate into a sense of economic well-being through the creation of a short-term, pre-election economic boom. Secondly, the greater attention that was being paid to the opinion polls provided the Government with a guide (additional to by-elections and local government elections) to the extent of its popularity among the electorate, and thus to the wisdom of holding a general election. Labour had failed to capitalise on these advantages in 1951, but the Conservatives did so in 1955 and 1959, and perhaps could continue to do so indefinitely into the future.[1]

This widely held view, in combination with the other assumptions about the electoral decline of the Labour Party, seemed to suggest in the early 1960s that the electoral pendulum had ceased to swing and that Britain's party system had evolved into a pattern of one-party dominance, with the Conservatives as the preponderant party of government, and Labour doomed to opposition. In fact, under the leadership of Harold Wilson, Labour went on to win four of the five elections of the 1960s and early 1970s. Thus by the mid-1970s the question being posed was not 'Must Labour lose?' but 'Must the Tories lose?' With its electoral victories in 1964, 1966, and February and October 1974, Labour was widely thought to have captured the middle ground from the Conservatives, and thereby to have become the natural party of government, joining the Canadian Liberals, American Democrats and Swedish and German Social Democrats as an electorally dominant party of the centre-left. Support for such a view came from some of the studies of British electoral behaviour that appeared in the 1960s and early 1970s.[2] They suggested, firstly, that Labour had an appreciably higher level of support than the Conservatives among younger voters, and, secondly, that once party loyalties were acquired by the politically impressionable 18–25 age group, they were gener-

[1] See J. P. Mackintosh, *The British Cabinet*, London 1963, pp. 573–8. See also G. N. Sanderson, 'The "Swing of the Pendulum" in British General Elections', *PS* 1966, pp. 349–60.

[2] See D. E. Butler and D. Stokes, *Political Change in Britain*, London (first edition 1969).

ally retained throughout adult life. The clear implication was that time was on Labour's side. Provided that Labour could continue to appeal more successfully than the Conservatives to younger voters, it would build up a core of Labour identifiers that would give it a distinct and growing electoral advantage in the 1980s and beyond.

Labour's decisive defeats at the 1979 and 1983 elections clearly have destroyed these assumptions. Indeed, taking the post-war period as a whole a major feature of electoral competition has been its evenness. Of the twelve elections between 1945 and 1983, Labour has won six (1945, 1950, 1964, 1966, February and October 1974), and the Conservatives six (1951, 1955, 1959, 1970, 1979 and 1983). If the 1950s belonged to the Conservatives, and the 1960s to Labour, honours were even in the 1970s. It should be noted, however, that the six Conservative successes have all produced Governments with clear working majorities (the smallest being Churchill's seventeen in 1951), while only in 1945 and 1966 were Labour's wins truly decisive. Indeed, since the 1920s when Labour replaced the Liberals as the main alternative to the Conservatives, the 1945 and 1966 elections are the only ones that Labour has won with double-figure majorities. The elections of 1950, 1964 and October 1974 produced only very small overall Labour majorities, while minority Labour Governments were formed after the 1923, 1929 and February 1974 elections. Labour was defeated in the other ten elections between 1922 and 1983, suffering particularly heavy defeats in 1924, 1931, 1935, 1959 and 1983.

Contrary to the view, popular after the 1959 election, that the pendulum had ceased to swing, it is clearly the case that it has continued to swing throughout the post-war period, though at an uneven rate.[1] The Government of the day has won six of the post-war elections (1950, 1955, 1959, 1966, October 1974 and 1983), but has been turned out as a result of the other six (1945, 1951, 1964, 1970, February 1974 and 1979). The pertinent question, perhaps, is not 'Must Labour

[1]See R. M. Punnett, 'Must Governments Lose?', *Parl. Aff.* 1981, pp. 392–408; R. Aron, 'Alternation in Government in the Industrialised Countries', *G and O* 1982, pp. 3–21; T. Yantek, 'Government Popularity in Great Britain Under Conditions of Economic Decline', *PS* 1985, pp. 467–83.

lose?' or 'Must the Tories lose?', but 'Must Governments lose?' The precarious nature of a Government's position, as suggested by these electoral facts, is reinforced by the pattern of by-election results and opinion poll findings, which suggest that during every Parliament since 1945 the Government of the day has passed through at least one period of acute unpopularity (see Table XXXVIII).[1] The extent of a Government's mid-term unpopularity, of course, can be easily exaggerated. At by-elections the electors are well aware that they are not choosing a Government, and are thus more likely than at a general election to record a 'protest' vote, while opinion pollsters are posing a hypothetical question when, in the middle of a Parliament, they ask people how they would vote *if* there were to be a general election the next day. Nevertheless, even allowing for distortions that may occur because of these factors, it is normally the case that there is a distinct mid-term movement of opinion against the Government. In half of the post-war Parliaments the Government has not been able to recover from this, and has been turned out at the subsequent general election.

In comparison with other countries in which single-party governments are the norm, this is a very high proportion of Government defeats. In countries that are governed by Coalitions (such as the Netherlands or Italy), changes in the party composition of the Government occur regularly. In countries with single-party governments, however, the usual pattern is one of single-party dominance over a period of time. Thus, for example, the Canadian Liberals have won eleven of the sixteen elections since 1935, while in Ireland Fianna Fail has been the leading party at all elections since 1932. In South Africa the National Party has been in office continuously since 1948, in India the Congress Party was in power from 1948 to 1977, and in Sweden the Social Democrats ruled from 1936 to 1976 (though at times in a Coalition). In Northern Ireland the Unionists won all the elections to Stormont over fifty years. The United Kingdom is unusual in the regularity with which

[1] See S. Stray and M. Silver, 'Do By-elections Demonstrate a Government's Unpopularity?', *Parl. Aff.* 1980, pp. 264–70; S. Stray and M. Silver, 'Government Popularity, By-Elections and Cycles', *Parl. Aff.* 1983, pp. 49–55.

TABLE XXXVIII

Gallup Poll: Size of Government Party Lead over Main Opposition Party

Parliament	Govt % Lead	Parliament	Govt % Lead	Parliament	Govt % Lead
1945–50		1959–64		1974	
(Lab. Govt)		(Con. Govt)		(Lab. Govt)	
1946 Jan.	19	1960 Jan.	4	1974 May	13½
May	3	May	2	Sept.	3
1947 Jan.	3	Sept.	6		
June	0	1961 Jan.	3	1974–9	
Sept.	−4	May	3	(Lab. Govt)	
1948 Jan.	−1	Sept.	−2	1975 Jan.	14½
May	−3	1962 Jan.	0	May	−6
Sept.	−5	May	−4	Sept.	3
1949 Jan.	−3	Sept.	−7	1976 Jan.	−5
May	−4	1963 Jan.	−11	May	−3
Sept.	−6	May	−9	Sept.	−½
1950 Jan.	0	Sept.	−13	1977 Jan.	−13
		1964 Jan.	−9	May	−15½
1950–1		May	−17	Sept.	−4½
(Lab. Govt)		Sept.	−2	1978 Jan.	0
1950 May	2			May	0
Sept.	3	1964–6		Sept.	−7
1951 Jan.	−11	(Lab. Govt)		1979 Jan.	−7½
May	−8	1965 Jan.	7		
Sept.	−11	May	−2	1979–83	
		Sept.	6	(Con. Govt)	
1951–5		1966 Jan.	6	1979 May	−1½
(Con. Govt)				Sept.	−4½
1952 Jan.	−3	1966–70		1980 Jan.	−9
May	−4	(Lab. Govt)		May	−4½
Sept.	−7	1966 May	18	Sept.	−9½
1953 Jan.	−3	Sept.	3	1981 Jan.	−13½
May	2	1967 Jan.	3	May	−3½
Sept.	−3	May	−7	Sept.	−4½
1954 Jan.	−1	Sept.	−4	1982 Jan.	−2
May	−1	1968 Jan.	−6	May	13½
Sept.	−5	May	−28	Sept.	13½
1955 Jan.	1	Sept.	−10	1983 Jan.	12½
May	3	1969 Jan.	−22	May	17½
		May	−22		
1955–9		Sept.	−10	1983–	
(Con. Govt)		1970 Jan.	−8	(Con. Govt)	
1955 Sept.	3	May	8	1983 Sept.	21
1956 Jan.	−1			1984 Jan.	3½
May	−3	1970–4		May	2
Sept.	−2	(Con. Govt)		Sept.	1
1957 Jan.	−5	1970 Sept.	3½	1985 Jan.	6
May	−7	1971 Jan.	−4½	May	−3½
Sept.	−13	May	−12	Sept.	−½
1958 Jan.	−6	Sept.	−19	1986 Jan.	−4½
May	−10	1972 Jan.	−7½	May	−9½
Sept.	2	May	−6	Sept.	−5
1959 Jan.	0	Sept.	−11		
May	1	1973 Jan.	−5½		
Sept.	5	May	−5½		
		Sept.	−9		
		1974 Jan.	2		

Source: Figures for 1945–60 are taken from Butler and Freeman, *British Political Facts*, pp. 133–5; figures for 1960–79 are taken from *Gallup Political Index*, issued monthly by Social Surveys (Gallup Poll) Ltd.

in the post-war period, the two main parties have chased each other into and out of office.

Some commentators have seen this adversarial system, with the regular alternation of single party governments, as a major weakness of the British political system, and as a cause of many of Britain's post-war political and economic problems.[1] It has been seen as producing instability and lack of continuity in policy, with each new Government undoing many of the policies of its predecessors, and in turn having its policies revised by its successor. Frequently cited examples of such discontinuities are the nationalisation, denationalisation and renationalisation of the iron and steel industry in the 1948–67 period; Labour's pledges to reverse the 'privatisation' measures of the Thatcher Government; changes by the Labour and Conservative Governments since 1970 in the laws governing trade union rights and obligations; the changes of policy over the extension of comprehensive schooling in the 1960s and 1970s; and the creation, abolition and re-creation of bodies to monitor pay and price increases. It is argued that faced with the distinct possibility of a change of Government, those opposed to current Government policies (such as the steel owners in the 1950s, or the local authorities seeking to preserve grammar schools in the 1970s) tend to withhold their cooperation until they can be saved by the (inevitable) arrival of a new and more friendly Government. This complicates the process of government and encourages the politics of confrontation.

This interpretation of the consequences of alternating single-party governments, however, has been challenged on two particular grounds. In the first place, it is pointed out that changes of policy occur not only when there is a change of government, but also during the lifetime of a government – as, for example, with the 'U turns' on incomes policy that have been made by Labour and Conservative Governments alike. Each party when in office has demonstrated that it is perfectly capable of generating its own inconsistencies and reversals of

[1]See S. E. Finer, *Adversary Politics and Electoral Reform*, London 1975. See also A. Cox, *Adversary Politics and Land*, London 1984; A. M. Gamble and S. A. Walkland, *The British Party System and Economic Policy 1945–1983*, London 1984; N. Johnson, *In Search of the Constitution*, London 1977.

policy. Second, it has been argued that the adversarial interpretation of British party competition is fundamentally wrong because it confuses words with deeds: while the style and rhetoric of successive Governments may be very different, their output is remarkably similar.

The far left and far right have long seen the succession of Labour and Conservative Governments in these terms. Their view is that Tweedledum and Tweedledee change places but have less impact on policy than do civil servants, pressure groups and other powerful forces within and beyond Britain. This view is not confined to the ideological extremes, and many commentators have seen all British Governments as being constrained by 'the realities of office'. Commenting particularly on the Governments in the 1960s and 1970s, Richard Rose maintained that the changes that occur in policies over time owe more to the variety of pressures to which all British Governments are subjected than to differences of ideology. He maintains that: 'The differences in office from one party to another are less likely to arise from contrasting intentions than from the exigencies of government.'[1]

The nature of the Thatcher Government has meant that it has been more difficult in the 1980s than earlier in the post-war period to discount the impact of ideology on government output. As was discussed in Chapters 1 and 2, one of the major themes of the Conservative campaigns in 1979 and 1983 was that it was essential for Britain to break-out from the debilitating post-war consensus. In office the Thatcher Government has sought to make a particular virtue out of ideological distinctiveness and consistency of deed as well as of word. Nevertheless, despite the implementation of distinctive policies in some areas (most notably privatisation and trade union rights and obligations) the Conservative Government's performance has lagged behind its declared intentions in the key areas of taxation policy and public expenditure. The tax burden has been shifted between categories of taxpayer, and between direct and indirect taxation, while the priorities of public expenditure have altered. The overall level of public

[1] *Do Parties Make a Difference?*, p. 141. See also L. J. Sharpe and K. Newton, *Does Politics Matter?*, London 1984.

expenditure, however, and the share of personal wealth that is consumed by the Government in taxation, have remained much higher than was implied by the Conservative policy statements of 1979 and 1983. Even the Thatcher Government, therefore, has found itself under attack on the one hand for being divisive and extreme, but on the other for failing to be as ideologically consistent in practice as it has been in rhetoric.

Minorities and Coalitions

In face of dissatisfaction with the post-war pattern of alternating Labour and Conservative Governments (either because it is seen as producing undesirable inconsistencies of policy, or because it is regarded as essentially sham warfare), some observers have argued that Britain would be better served by minority or coalition governments. It was noted in Chapter 2 that a change to hung (or 'balanced') Parliaments, in which no party had an overall majority, could be made more likely by a reform of the electoral system. On the basis of past British voting patterns, a reformed electoral system that rewarded the parties with seats in proportion to the votes they received would be likely to produce a succession of hung Parliaments. Normally, the operation of the first-past-the-post electoral system has converted the winning party's minority of votes into a majority of seats. Even without a change in the electoral system, the recent developments in the party system that were discussed in Chapter 3 mean that hung Parliaments are more likely in the immediate future than at any time since the 1930s.

Clearly, it is easy to overstate the likelihood of Britain experiencing hung Parliaments, and thus minority or coalition governments, in the near future. It may be that the fractionalisation of the party system will be short-lived, and that a two-party pattern will soon re-establish itself (as was the case between the wars and in the nineteenth century). The 1983 election demonstrated that, under the present system, in a multi-party battle in which the winning party achieves little more than two-fifths of the vote, it can still emerge with a huge majority of seats. What is more, even if a more proportional electoral system is introduced, the electorate might adjust its behaviour and give one party an overall majority of both votes and seats. Nevertheless, David Butler's judgement remains valid: 'Britain in the 1980s is the scene of developments which make the un-interrupted continuance of the decisive majorities of the 1950s and 1960s more and more unlikely'.[1]

In a Parliament in which no party has an overall majority, a single-party minority government may be formed, sustained by the Parliamentary votes of one or more other parties.[2] Alternatively a coalition may be formed, with two or more parties combining to share Ministerial posts between them. The two types of government are very different, but are often confused. A coalition government may not necessarily have a majority of the seats in Parliament. Had a Conservative–Liberal Coalition emerged after the February 1974 election (as was considered briefly) it would have been just short of an overall majority. Minority coalitions emerge from time to time in European countries. Usually, however, a coalition is formed precisely in order to secure a Parliamentary majority, and the term 'minority government' is normally used as shorthand for a 'single-party minority government'.

Table XXXIX shows that while the 'normal' pattern of single-party majority governments has prevailed for almost two-thirds of the time this century, Britain has had some experience of both coalitions and single party minority governments. Indeed, between 1910 and 1945 there were far more years of minority or coalition governments than of single party majority governments. In addition, 'quasi-coalitions' were in office 1895–1905 and 1935–40, when parties that were subsequently to merge held office together (Conservatives and some Liberal Unionists in 1895 and Conservatives and some National Liberals in 1935). All the minority Governments have been Labour or Liberal, and this reflects the difficulty that these parties have had in achieving commanding election victories.

A minority government can be 'supported' or 'unsupported', depending on whether it has made a formal agree-

[1] D. E. Butler, *Governing Without a Majority*, London 1983, p. 9.

[2] See J. S. Rasmussen, 'Who Gets Hung In a Hung Parliament?', *BJPS* 1986, pp. 135–54.

TABLE XXXIX

British Minority and Coalition Governments 1900–86

Single Party Minority			Coalition	
1910–15	Asquith	Liberal	1915–16	Asquith
1924	MacDonald	Labour	1916–22	Lloyd George
1929–31	MacDonald	Labour	1931–5*	MacDonald
1974	Wilson	Labour	1940–5	Churchill
1976–9	Wilson/Callaghan	Labour		

*The coalition formed in 1931 'withered away' in stages between 1932 and 1940, but 1935 is a reasonable terminal date.

ment with another party. The 1974–9 Labour Government lacked an overall majority for much of the time, but it was only during 1977 and 1978 that it was formally supported by the Liberals through the 'Lib-Lab Pact'. This agreement did not constitute a coalition, as the Liberals were not part of the Government, but in return for their assured support in Parliament the Liberals were consulted on aspects of the Government's policy and strategy.[1] For most of the 1974–9 period, however, the Labour Government (like earlier minority Labour Governments) was 'unsupported' and relied for its Parliamentary majority on the ad hoc support of Liberals, Nationalists and others. The 1910–15 Liberal Government was also 'unsupported', although it was sustained by the Irish Nationalists who were dependent upon the Liberal Government for the introduction of a Home Rule Bill.

Minority government places some qualification upon the two-party adversarial system by making the governing party dependent upon others for a Parliamentary majority.[2] If a formal pact is forged, a fringe party is involved in an acknowledged supportive role that stops short of actual participation in office. It thus has influence without direct responsibility,

[1] See D. Steel, *A House Divided*, London 1980; A. Michie and S. Haggart, *The Pact*, London 1978.

[2] See K. Strom, 'Minority Governments in Western Democracies', *CPS* 1984–5, pp. 199–228; V. Herman and J. Pope, 'Minority Governments in Western Democracies', *BJPS* 1973, pp. 191–212.

while the government has responsibility without full control of events. At the same time, the Government has some excuse for inactivity or failure.

A minority government is often thought to lack the legitimacy of a government that has an overall Parliamentary majority (though it should be remembered that few of the British governments that have had a Parliamentary majority have also had an electoral majority). A minority government is also widely regarded as 'unstable'. The 1910–15 and 1974–9 periods demonstrate that minority governments can survive, though they have to pay a price for third party support. In order to attract fringe party support a minority government can make policy concessions, try to avoid measures that will stimulate inter-party conflict and use its vast patronage powers to advantage. If the Parliamentary balance is held by two or three parties, the government may be able to play off one against another. The government's position will be strengthened by the fact that the fringe parties have to appear to be using their influence responsibly. The only possible alternative government may be unacceptable to the fringe party, and in any case it is unlikely to be eager to precipitate an election that could produce a majority Parliament. Nevertheless, as well as making concessions to the fringe parties, the government has to placate its own backbenchers, and it is the difficulties involved in combining these two tasks that makes minority government seem precarious.

Various Constitutional issues can arise with a minority government, and the Monarch as the Constitutional arbiter may be drawn into controversy.[1] It may not be clear just which party is best able to form the government. A minority government need not necessarily be formed by the party with the largest number of seats in the House. While the largest party in Parliament may have the biggest moral claim to office, the ultimate factor is the ability of a particular party to secure a Parliamentary majority through the support of other parties. Thus in 1924, after the fall of the Conservative Government, a minority Labour Government was formed

[1] See D. E. Butler, *Governing Without a Majority*, London 1983; V. Bogdanor, *Multi-party Politics and the Constitution*, London 1983.

with tacit Liberal backing even though Labour had sixty-seven fewer seats than the Conservatives.

The Monarch might also be involved in controversy over the question of whether a Prime Minister in a minority government must be granted a dissolution, even though an alternative minority government could be formed in that Parliament. The issue was discussed, in theoretical terms, during the 1974 Parliament, when there was the remote possibility that the Conservatives, Liberals and Nationalists might be able to sustain an alternative to the minority Labour Government. The weight of opinion was that while the Monarch would certainly not be obliged constitutionally to grant the Prime Minister's request, there would be considerable political dangers in not doing so. Clearly, in a specific case much would depend on the political strength of the Prime Minister, the credibility of the alternative government, its chances of survival and the stage reached in the Parliament.

Post-war European experience suggests that where hung Parliaments are the norm, rather than being just an occasional interlude in the prevailing pattern of majority Parliaments, coalition governments are more likely to emerge than minority governments. In post-war European hung Parliaments, coalitions have been in office for about two-thirds of the time and minority governments for about one-third. A minority government, rather than a coalition, is likely to emerge, however, when a party is only just short of an overall majority, when single-party governments are regarded as the norm or when particular ideological considerations prevent parties coming together. The first-past-the-post electoral system also encourages a minority government rather than a coalition because the coalition partners cannot compete with each other without splitting the vote, whereas under an electoral system in which the voter lists the candidates in order of preference (such as the Alternative Vote or the Single Transferable Vote) coalition partners can run in tandem and agree to exchange second preferences. Further, the first past the post system discourages a coalition because an election is always capable of producing a major change in the parties' seats, with a relatively small change in their shares of votes. A minority government can always live in the hope that the next election result will be very different from the last. It may be noted, however, that in 1910 and 1974 minority governments were unsuccessful in attempts to secure a clear overall majority through an early dissolution. The December 1910 election produced a result very similar to that of January, while in October 1974 Labour secured an overall majority of just three seats (and this was soon eaten away in by-elections).

A coalition government may be an all-party (or 'grand') coalition, in which each party that has seats in the legislature is represented in the government (as is invariably the case in Switzerland). Alternatively, it may be a coalition in which two or three parties share office, but others remain outside the government and constitute an opposition (as has usually been the pattern in post-war Germany). The 1940–5 and 1915–16 British governments were virtually all-party coalitions, in that Ministers were drawn from all the main parties and only a few independent groups and individuals remained in opposition. The 1916–22 and 1931–2 coalitions, on the other hand, were limited in their composition and encountered strong opposition from the excluded parties.[1]

A coalition government is not simply a device to deal with the 'problem' of a hung Parliament, but can be formed as an end in itself even though one party has enough seats to govern on its own. In 1940 the Churchill coalition was formed to meet the particular need for unity in face of a wartime crisis, even though the Conservatives had a clear majority in the Commons. Similarly, the coalition that had been formed during the first world war remained in office after 1918 even though the Conservatives had enough seats to govern alone. All of the British coalitions were formed in face of a major military or economic crisis, and each sought to be a government of national unity. The 1915 and 1940 coalitions were fairly successful in achieving this aim, but the 1916 and 1931 coalitions probably fostered disunity through the creation of a particularly embittered opposition. The 1918 and 1931 general elections, with their landslide victories for the

[1]See D. E. Butler (ed.), *Coalitions in British Politics*, London 1978; A. J. Beattie, 'The Two Party Legend', *PQ* 1974, pp. 288–99; M. Laver, 'Coalitions in Britain', *Parl. Aff.* 1977, pp. 107–11.

government, suggest that the appeal of a coalition can be electorally rewarding.

The debate about the merits and defects of coalition governments is often obscured by the lack of distinction between all-party and two-party coalitions. Advocates of coalitions argue that they would end the 'party games' of each government revising much of its predecessor's work; that they would encourage moderation by obliging the Coalition partners to abandon their more ideological policies; that they would remove the pressures for 'opposition for its own sake'; and that they would make possible a 'Ministry of all the talents'. For their part, the advocates of single party governments question at least some of these claims and point to a number of supposed deficiencies of coalition governments. Coalitions, they argue, are essentially fragile because they require close inter-party cooperation, and must inevitably produce fudged and expedient policies. They also argue that coalitions cloak responsibility by spreading it among a number of parties, remove from the electorate the 'straight choice' between a government and an opposition, and are essentially undemocratic because they are made and unmade by party managers rather than the electorate. Clearly, however, many of these claims and counter claims apply only to all-party coalitions: when a two (or three) party coalition is faced by a sizeable opposition party, many of the features of the two-party battle will persist.

As with minority governments, coalitions can involve a variety of political and constitutional problems that do not arise with single party majority governments. Clearly, the most basic question is which parties should be included in the coalition.[1] Here, the search for an all-party 'government of

[1]See W. H. Riker, *The Theory of Political Coalitions*, London 1962; L. C. Dodd, *Coalitions in Parliamentary Government*, New York 1976; E. C. Browne and J. Dreijmanis (eds), *Government Coalitions in Western Democracies*, London 1982. See also A. Lijphart (*et al.*), 'New Approaches to the Study of Cabinet Coalitions', *CPS* 1984–5, pp. 155–279; M. N. Franklin and T. T. Mackie, 'Familiarity and Inertia in the Formation of Governing Coalitions in Parliamentary Democracies', *BJPS* 1983, pp. 275–98; M. N. Franklin and T. T. Mackie, 'Reassessing the Importance of Size and Ideology for the Formation of Governing Coalitions in Parliamentary Democracies', *AJPS* 1984, pp. 671–92.

national unity' clashes with the concept of the 'minimum winning coalition' – the notion that the coalition most likely to persist is one that has just enough partners to achieve a Parliamentary majority and no more. The allocation of posts between the partners involves clear difficulties. A practical principle is that the parties should receive posts in proportion to their Parliamentary strength, with perhaps some slight over-representation of the smallest partner. This ignores individual merit, however, and still leaves the question of which particular posts should go to each party. Disagreements over the policies to be implemented are likely to be even more difficult to reconcile than questions of personnel. As bargaining over the legislative programme is likely to be particularly difficult once a party has fought an election on its policy commitments, potential coalition partners need to anticipate difficulties when framing their manifestos.

Many of the normal rules of the game that apply to single-party majority governments do not convert readily to coalitions. The leader of the largest party is not necessarily the most acceptable Prime Minister, and a less controversial compromise candidate may well make the best choice. Although the Conservatives were the numerically dominant partner in each coalition except 1915–16 (and even in 1915 had virtually the same number of MPs as the Liberals), non-Conservative Prime Ministers were at the head of the coalitions of 1915 (Asquith), 1916 (Lloyd George) and 1931 (MacDonald). Even Churchill in 1940 was only on the fringes of the Conservative hierarchy, and was acceptable as coalition Prime Minister partly because of this.

The Prime Minister's power to appoint and dismiss Ministers, and seek a dissolution of Parliament, are affected by the need to consider what is acceptable to the coalition partners. The principle of collective responsibility may have to be stretched, as in the 1931 coalition when a Ministerial 'agreement to differ' was necessary to accommodate Liberal and Conservative views on tariff policy. The collective view of the Cabinet may matter less than the agreements that are reached by the leaders of the parties. Party discipline has to be strong if the party leaders are to be able to come to binding agreements (and it was noted in Chapter 6 that in the last fifteen years

Labour and Conservative backbenchers have shown a greater tendency to rebel than previously).

Each spell of coalition government this century was followed by major changes in the party system. The 1915–22 spell of coalition ended the dominance of the Liberals, restored the Conservatives to office and helped to precipitate the three-party politics of the 1920s. The formation of the 1931 coalition again restored the Conservatives to office, allowed them subsequently to absorb the National Liberals and crippled Labour for a decade. Participation in the 1940–5 coalition helped to revive Labour's credibility and contributed to the party's victory in 1945. Thus British coalitions have been interludes in the 'normal' pattern of single-party governments, and they have been too intermittent to give a clear indication of the style of politics that might emerge if coalitions became the norm rather than the exception. It may be, however, that the true function of coalitions in Britain is precisely to provide a brief stimulus to the realignment of the party system.

Governments and Public Opinion

Apart from the ultimate possibility of unpopularity leading to electoral defeat, what are the other considerations that cause Governments to take note of public wishes between general elections? The doctrine of the mandate is sometimes advanced as one such consideration. This doctrine states that a Government is only constitutionally justified in introducing policies for which it has an electoral mandate. The doctrine implies that a Government can only introduce measures that have previously been submitted for approval to the electorate at a general election, and any policies that have been so presented and approved by the electorate must be carried to fruition. The Government has, of course, to deal with unexpected events and crises that develop between elections, but such crises apart, Government policies must have electoral approval. Thus in the past there have been instances of Parliament being dissolved in order that the Government might secure an electoral mandate for a specific issue. In the two elections of 1910, the Liberal Government sought electoral approval for the specific issues of the 1909 Finance Bill and the reform of the powers of the House of Lords. In 1923 Baldwin secured an early dissolution of Parliament and sought a mandate for specific proposals for tariff reform. In February 1974, in the midst of an industrial confrontation with the National Union of Miners, Heath dissolved Parliament in an effort to strengthen the Government's position by securing electoral support for its incomes policy. One of the arguments quoted to justify the retention of a delaying power by the House of Lords is that the Lords should be able to delay legislation until such time as the electorate has had time to consider and pronounce upon it.

In general, however, theoretical support for the mandate doctrine has come primarily from the Labour and Liberal Parties. Their view of the Constitution sees Constitutional authority as stemming from the people, with the electorate having the right to pronounce on specific policies as well as choose the Government. Thus the proud boast of the Labour Government at the 1950 general election (though not in 1979) was that it had achieved all the manifesto commitments for which it had received a mandate in 1945. Again in the 1966 election campaign, the Labour Party claimed that given a full Parliament the Government would fulfil all the pledges made in 1964, and renewed and extended in 1966. To a considerable extent the 1970 general election was fought over the question of whether Labour had 'kept its promises'. The 'Tory view of the Constitution', on the other hand, is that Constitutional authority stems from the Crown, and the role of the electorate is to choose the Government but not Government policies. Thus at an election the Government is seen as securing a general mandate to rule as it thinks fit, without necessarily being committed to specific policies. Reflecting this principle, the Conservatives in 1983 (as in most elections) produced a manifesto that was much less specific than Labour's.

Despite this theoretical distinction between the parties' Constitutional attitudes over the mandate, in practice the clearest distinction in attitudes towards the doctrine tends to be between the Government and the Opposition. Opposition parties tend to support the doctrine, criticising the Government for introducing measures for which it has no mandate, while Governments tend to ignore the doctrine, regarding it as an undesirable limitation on their ability to deal with issues in a pragmatic fashion. Certainly the practicality of the doctrine can be questioned, in that while the parties may submit detailed policy proposals to the electorate in their election manifestos, election campaigns tend to be fought on general issues rather than on detailed policy items, and electoral loyalties are determined in the main by party images and personalities rather than by individual policy items. The elections of 1910 and 1923, when specific mandates were sought, illustrated the difficulty, in an election campaign, of isolating specific items of policy for electoral approval. Although a Government may strive to complete in one Parliament all the measures proposed in its election programme (whether or not the electorate had been aware of the details), in practice the mandate doctrine does not prevent a Government from adapting its policies to changing circumstances, nor does it prevent a Government from introducing entirely new measures to deal with particular situations, without submitting these measures for electoral approval. In practice, therefore, the mandate doctrine does not greatly hamper a Government's freedom of action between elections, and does not represent a major electoral limitation on a Government's activities.

In the early and middle years of a Parliament a Government is in a position to ignore to a large extent public attitudes as expressed in the press, on TV and radio, through opinion polls or by-elections, or through pressure groups or constituency contacts with MPs. It can pursue its policies in the knowledge that it has three or four years in which to build up its popularity before the next general election is due. A Government's position is helped by the fact that the strength of party loyalties in Britain is such that no matter how unpopular the Government might be with the majority of the electorate (made up of the Opposition parties' supporters, and all or most of the normally uncommitted voters), there is always a substantial minority among the electorate (consisting of the Government party's die-hard supporters) on whose support the Government can rely in virtually all circumstances. The Government's position is further strengthened by the widespread lack of political enthusiasm among the electorate, which manifests itself particularly in a willingness to 'leave it to the Government'. Thus the Labour Government's decision to hold a referendum in June 1975, on the question of whether Britain should remain a member of the EEC, was criticised by many as being an abdication by the Government of its own responsibility to decide such policy matters.[1] Political demonstrations and rallies, and other such forcible expressions of political attitudes, involve in the main only a small percentage of the population, and for the vast majority of the people in Britain political activity extends only to voting at general elections (and perhaps not even to that). At times of major political crisis, there is increased public interest and participation in pressure group activities connected with the crisis, but even at such times there remains an underlying willingness to leave matters to the Government's initiative, or at least to the Government and Opposition leaders and MPs to fight out among themselves. The vast majority of people in Britain, though perhaps firm in their views, remain reticent about giving expression to these views.

Nevertheless, there are limits to the extent to which the electorate is happy to 'leave it to the Government', and there are limits to the extent to which the Government can ignore public attitudes. Just as the majority of people are prepared to trust the Government, so Governments are anxious not to betray this trust. Governments rely greatly on the goodwill of the various interests with which they deal, and prefer discussion, agreement and compromise to the imposition of Government wishes on unwilling interests. Thus Governments are loath to adopt statutory powers of coercion until informal persuasion and goodwill have failed to achieve the desired ends. The desire to maintain government by mutual consent is something that affects all British Governments, and tends to produce considerable modifications in Government intentions in the process of translating party ideals and policies into legislative and executive realities.

[1] See R. Shepherd, 'Leadership, Public Opinion and the Referendum', *PQ* 1975, pp. 25–35; J. P. Mackintosh, 'The Case Against a Referendum', *PQ* 1975, pp. 73–82 and 153–60.

The Art of the Possible

So far in this chapter the emphasis has been placed on the limitations of British democracy. The cataloguing of deficiencies, however, should not be allowed to distract attention from the basic qualities of the system. The overriding feature of the British system is that of government by mutual consent, and this alone justifies the claim that the system is fundamentally democratic. Indeed, in many ways the British system is democratic to a fault, in that too often Governments resist desirable changes that are not acceptable to the overwhelming majority of the people of Britain, thereby producing a tendency towards stagnation. The need to preserve a high degree of trust between rulers and ruled is, however, only one of numerous factors that limits what Governments can achieve. The formal concentration of authority in the hands of the Cabinet, and particularly in the hands of the Prime Minister, suggests that Governments in Britain have virtually unlimited powers. This formal concentration of authority is based on a number of constitutional and political considerations which were discussed in Chapters 6 and 7. In practical terms, however, there is a marked distinction between what the formal concentration of authority permits a Government to do, and what practical considerations allow it to do. The dependence of Governments upon pressure groups for information and administrative cooperation has been examined in earlier chapters, as has the complexity of the administrative machine, and the dependence of Ministers upon civil servants. As well as this, a Government's power is diffused among several elements within the community. In addition to the importance of the Civil Service in the formulation and administration of Government policies, the cooperation of affected parties is also crucial. For the development of an energy policy the Government depends upon the cooperation of the nationalised industries, British and foreign oil companies, and a wide range of trade unions. For the administration of education policy the Government depends upon the local authorities, and the cooperation of the various teachers' organisations, while for the achievement of national economic plans the Government relies particularly upon the trade unions and business interests. Thus Governments frequently declare that the extension of national prosperity depends upon a partnership between the Government and the various elements and interests within the state, thereby acknowledging the extent to which all Governments need the voluntary cooperation of the community as a whole.

A Government's annual legislative programme gives ample evidence of the amount of legislation that stems from Civil Service and pressure group sources. Governments are faced each year with legislation that must be enacted annually (as with the annual financial legislation); with numerous routine but essential administrative measures; with legislation that unexpectedly has been made necessary by previous measures; with legislation to deal with sudden crises. Also, the complexity of the process of preparing and passing through Parliament a major piece of legislation limits the number of measures that a Government can produce in any one session, and this is particularly true of major and controversial measures. Thus a Government that comes to power with a big legislative programme, as did Labour in 1945, 1964, and 1974, often finds that legislative priorities have to be established, with inevitable disagreements as to the order of the priorities. In this respect the Government is also limited in what it can achieve by the numerous different elements that exist within the British parties, and by the consequent difficulty of producing policies that will be acceptable to 'moderate' and 'extremist' elements alike.

All Government activities that have international effects are inevitably limited by Britain's standing in the world, and by Britain's international obligations. Thus MPs who call upon Governments to pursue an independent foreign policy underestimate Britain's dependence upon her allies in economic as well as political terms. All Governments since 1945 have faced recurring economic crises over the strength of sterling and Britain's trading position, and inevitably this has limited what Governments can achieve in terms of foreign and domestic affairs. Ambitious social welfare schemes, public building plans, and other forms of public enterprise, cannot be financed unless a healthy and expanding economy can provide the Government with adequate revenue, and at the same time maintain a healthy balance of trade. Consequently, all post-war Governments have emphasised the need for a healthy economy, and particularly increased exports, as an essential basis for their policies. Demands for greater governmental control over the economy are in large part stimulated by the desire to achieve sure and steady economic prosperity, and end the recurrent economic crises that limit what a Government can achieve in its domestic and foreign policies.

One of the major developments in British politics in this century, and particularly since 1945, has been the extension of Governments' social and economic activities. As well as this (and to some extent because of it), other vital developments have been the growth in the size of the administrative machine (with consequent problems in Minister–Civil Service relationships), and the increased Government contact with, and dependence upon, pressure groups for information, policy formulation and administrative cooperation. These factors, combined with the increased limitations on Britain's ability to 'go it alone' in international affairs, have greatly restricted the ability of British Governments to act decisively and independently in domestic and external matters. Over the years, the British political system has been characterised by its durability, evolving as it has over several centuries without the dramatic political upheavals that have occurred in most other nations of the world. In the 1980s and 1990s the durability of the system is likely to be severely tested, as means are sought of dealing with the problem of maintaining the democratic bases of the system, while at the same time overcoming the practical factors that limit the ability of British Governments to take the speedy and decisive actions that are required in the modern world.

Bibliography

THIS BIBLIOGRAPHY contains books and articles on British government and politics that have appeared in the 1980s. For a pre-1980 bibliography see the fourth edition (and earlier editions) of the book.

The bibliography is divided into three sections.

Section 1 contains a selection of general books that have been written about British government and politics, and which contain sections dealing with some or most of the themes covered in this book.

Section 2 contains more detailed texts and articles that relate to topics dealt with in specific chapters, arranged according to chapter topics. Studies of particular post-war governments are included among readings for Chapter 7. Studies of specific policy areas are included under Chapter 5.

Section 3 contains a selection of political biographies, autobiographies and memoirs. It also contains leading politicians' statements of personal and party philosophy.

The abbreviations used for the titles of the journals referred to in the bibliography (and in the footnotes in the text) are as follows:

AAA	*Annals of the American Academy of Political and Social Science*
AJPH	*Australian Journal of Politics and History*
APSR	*American Political Science Review*
ASR	*American Sociological Review*
BJPS	*British Journal of Political Science*
BJS	*British Journal of Sociology*
CMLR	*Common Market Law Review*
CP	*Comparative Politics*
CPS	*Comparative Political Studies*
EJPR	*European Journal of Political Research*
EJS	*European Journal of Sociology*
ELJ	*European Law Journal*
ELR	*European Law Review*
G and O	*Government and Opposition*
Inter. Aff.	*International Affairs*

ISSJ	*International Social Science Journal*
JAS	*Journal of American Studies*
JBS	*Journal of British Studies*
JCCP	*Journal of Commonwealth and Comparative Politics*
JCMS	*Journal of Common Market Studies*
JDS	*Journal of Development Studies*
J of P	*Journal of Politics*
JRSS	*Journal of the Royal Statistical Society*
LGS	*Local Government Studies*
LQR	*Law Quarterly Review*
LSQ	*Legislative Studies Quarterly*
Man. Sch.	*Manchester School of Economic and Social Studies*
MJPS	*Midwest Journal of Political Science*
MLR	*Modern Law Review*
PAR	*Public Administration Review*
Parl.	*The Parliamentarian*
Parl. Aff.	*Parliamentary Affairs*
PL	*Public Law*
Pol.	*Politics*
Pol. & Soc.	*Politics and Society*
Poli. Sci.	*Political Science*
Polity	*Polity*
POQ	*Public Opinion Quarterly*
PP	*Policy and Politics*
PQ	*Political Quarterly*
PS	*Political Studies*
PSQ	*Political Science Quarterly*
Pub. Admin.	*Public Administration*
R of P	*Review of Politics*
SJS	*Scottish Journal of Sociology*
Soc.	*Sociology*
SR	*Sociological Review*
Table	*The Table*
UTLJ	*University of Toronto Law Journal*
WP	*World Politics*
WPQ	*Western Political Quarterly*
YB	*Yorkshire Bulletin of Economic and Social Research*

SECTION 1: GENERAL BOOKS

A. J. Baker, *Examining British Politics*, London 1984.
A. R. Ball, *Modern Politics and Government*, London 1983.

S. H. Beer, *Modern British Politics*, London 1982.

S. H. Beer, *Britain Against Itself*, London 1982.

M. Beloff & G. Peele, *The Government of the United Kingdom: Political Authority in a Changing Society*, London 1985.

H. Berrington (ed.), *Change in British Politics*, London 1984.

A. H. Birch, *The British System of Government*, London 1986.

R. L. Borthwick & J. E. Spence, *British Politics in Perspective*, London 1984.

I. Budge & D. McKay (*et al.*), *The New British Political System*, London 1985.

M. Burch & B. Wood, *Public Policy in Britain*, London 1983.

D. Butler & G. Butler, *British Political Facts 1900–1985*, London 1985.

J. Dearlove & P. Saunders, *Introduction to British Politics*, London 1984.

H. Drucker (*et al.*), *Developments in British Politics*, London 1986.

P. Dunleavy & C. Husbands, *British Democracy at the Crossroads*, London 1985.

F. N. Forman, *Mastering British Politics*, London 1984.

W. H. Greenleaf, *The British Political Tradition (vols I and II)*, London 1983.

J. Greenwood & D. Wilson, *Public Administration in Britain*, London 1984.

W. B. Gwyn & R. Rose (eds), *Britain: Progress & Decline*, London 1980.

A. H. Hanson & M. Walles, *Governing Britain*, London 1984.

B. Harrison, *Peaceable Kingdom: Stability and Change in Modern Britain*, London 1982.

J. Harvey & L. Bather, *The British Constitution and Politics*, London 1982.

L. Heron, *Alas, Alas for England: What Went Wrong with Britain?*, London 1981.

HMSO, *Britain: An Official Handbook*, London (annually).

N. Johnson, *In Search of the Constitution: Reflections on State and Society in Britain*, London 1980.

B. Jones & D. Kavanagh, *British Politics Today*, London 1983.

D. Kavanagh, *British Politics: Continuities and Change*, London 1985.

C. Leys, *Politics in Britain*, London 1983.

L. J. Macfarlane, *Issues in British Politics Since 1945*, London 1982.

P. J. Madgwick, *Introduction to British Politics*, London 1984.

K. Middlemas, *Politics in Industrial Society: The Experience of the British System Since 1911*, London 1980.

R. Miliband, *Capitalist Democracy in Britain*, London 1984.

M. Moran, *Politics and Society in Britain*, London 1985.

P. Norton, *The British Polity*, London 1984.

F. Randall, *British Government and Politics*, London 1984.
P. G. Richards, *Mackintosh's The Government and Politics of Britain*, London 1984.
S. G. Richards, *Introduction to British Government*, London 1984.
R. Rose, *Politics in England: Persistence and Change*, London 1985.
R. Rose & I. McAllister, *United Kingdom Facts*, London 1982.
A. Sampson, *The Changing Anatomy of Britain*, London 1982.
G. Smith & N. W. Polsby, *British Government and Its Discontents*, London 1981.
A. Stewart (ed.), *Contemporary Britain*, London 1983.
D. T. Studlar & J. L. Waltman, *Dilemmas of Change in British Politics*, London 1984.
C. Turpin, *British Government & the Constitution: Text, Cases & Materials*, London 1985.

SECTION 2: SPECIALISED BOOKS AND ARTICLES

Chapter 1

G. Alderman, *The Jewish Community in British Politics*, London 1983.
G. A. Almond & S. Verba, *The Civic Culture Revisited*, Boston 1980.
J. Alt, *The Politics of Economic Decline*, London 1980.
D. Ashford, *Policy and Politics in Britain: the Limits of Consensus*, London 1981.
I. Bradley, *The English Middle Classes are Alive and Kicking*, London 1982.
D. Coates, *The Context of British Politics*, London 1984.
D. Coates & J. Hillard, *The Economic Decline of Modern Britain*, London 1986.
S. Cohen & J. Young (eds), *The Manufacture of News*, London 1981.
J. Curran & J. Seaton, *Power Without Responsibility: the Press and Broadcasting in Britain*, London 1985.
J. Ermisch, *The Political Economy of Demographic Change*, London 1983.
F. Field, *Inequality in Britain: Freedom, Welfare and the State*, London 1981.
D. Fraser, *The Evolution of the British Welfare State*, London 1984.
A. Gamble, *Britain in Decline*, London 1985.
J. Goldthorpe, *Social Mobility and Class Structure in Britain*, London 1980.
R. Harris, *Gotcha! The Media, the Government and the Falklands Crisis*, London 1982.

M. Harrison, *TV News: Whose Bias?*,London 1985.
G. Heald (*et al.*), *The Gallup Survey of Britain*, London 1986.
A. Hetherington, *News, Newspapers & Television*, London 1985.
R. W. Johnson, *The Politics of Recession*, London 1985.
R. Jowell & S. Witherspoon, *British Social Attitudes: The 1985 Report*, London 1985.
R. Jowell & C. Airey, *British Social Attitudes: The 1984 Report*, London 1984.
W. Kennet (ed.), *The Rebirth of Britain*, London 1982.
Z. Layton-Henry, *The Politics of Race in Britain*, London 1984.
P. J. Madgwick (*et al.*), *Britain Since 1945*, London 1982.
A. Marwick, *British Society Since 1945*, London 1982.
A. May & K. Rowan (eds), *Inside Information: British Government & the Media*, London 1982.
R. Miles & A. Phizachlea, *White Mary's Country: Realism in British Politics*, London 1984.
D. G. Pearson, *Race, Clan & Political Activism: A Study of West Indians in Britain*, London 1981.
A. Phizachlea & R. Miles, *Labour and Racism*, London 1981.
F. Reeves, *British Racial Discourse*, London 1983.
B. Sendall, *Independent Television in Britain*, London 1982.
A. Sked and C. Cook, *Post-War Britain: A Political History*, London 1984.
P. Taylor-Gooby, *Public Opinion, Ideology & State Welfare*, London 1985.
J. Tunstall, *The Media in Britain*, London 1983.
HMSO, *Social Trends*, London (annually).

G. Alderman, 'Anglo-Jewry: the Politics of an Image', *Parl. Aff.* 1984, pp. 160–82.
M. Banton, 'The Influence of Colonial Status upon Black–White Relations in England 1948–58', *Soc.* 1983, pp. 546–59.
J. Benyon, 'Going Through the Motions: The Political Agenda, the 1981 Riots and the Scarman Inquiry', *Parl. Aff.* 1985, pp. 409–22.
A. Gamble, 'The Future of British Politics', *Parl. Aff.* 1982, pp. 396–407.
R. J. Johnston & P. J. Taylor, 'Political Geography: A Politics of Places Within Places', *Parl. Aff.* 1986, pp. 135–49.
D. Kavanagh, 'Whatever Happened to Consensus Politics?', *PS* 1985, pp. 529–46.
S. McBride, 'Mrs Thatcher & the Post-War Consensus: The Case of Trade Union Policy', *Parl. Aff.* 1986, pp. 330–40.

W. L. M. Messina, 'Race and Party Competition in Britain: Policy Formation in the Post-Consensus Period', *Parl. Aff.* 1985, pp. 423–36.

W. L. Miller, J. Brand & M. Jordan, 'On the Power or Vulnerability of the British Press: A Dynamic Analysis', *BJPS* 1982, pp. 357–74.

K. Morgan, 'Regional Regeneration in Britain: the 'Territorial Imperative' and the Conservative State', *PS* 1985, pp. 560–77.

N. H. Schwartz, 'Race & the Allocation of Public Housing in Great Britain: The Autonomy of the Local State', *CP* 1983–4, pp. 205–22.

D. D. Searing, 'A Theory of Socialization: Institutional Support & Deradicalization in Britain', *BJPS* 1986, pp. 341–76.

J. Seaton, 'Politics, Parties and the Media in Britain', *WEP* 1985, pp. 9–26.

M. Stanks, 'Paying For Broadcasting: Public Funds For a Public Service', *PQ* 1985, pp. 374–85.

J. Tunstall, 'Media Policy Dilemmas and Indecisions', *Parl. Aff.* 1984, pp. 310–26.

B. Walden, 'Broadcasting and Politics', *Parl. Aff.* 1982, pp. 356–66.

S. Welch and D. T. Studler, 'The Impact of Race on Political Behaviour in Britain', *BJPS* 1985, pp. 528–40.

A. Wright, 'Local Broadcasting and the Local Authority', *Pub. Admin.* 1982, pp. 307–19.

Chapter 2

V. Bogdanor, *What is Proportional Representation?*, London 1984.

V. Bogdanor & D. Butler, *Democracy and Elections: Electoral Systems and Their Consequences*, London 1983.

D. Butler & D. Kavanagh, *The British General Election of 1979*, London 1980.

D. Butler & D. Kavanagh, *The British General Election of 1983*, London 1984.

I. Crewe & M. Harrop, *Political Communications: The General Election Campaign of 1983*, London 1986.

B. Gunter (*et al.*), *Television Coverage of the 1983 General Election*, London 1986.

R. J. Johnson, *The Geography of English Politics: the 1983 General Election*, London 1985.

E. Lakeman, *Power to Elect: the Case For Proportional Representation*, London 1982.

I. McAllister & R. Rose, *The Nationwide Competition for Votes: the 1983 British Election*, London 1984.

I. McLean, *Elections*, London 1980.

H. R. Penniman (ed.), *Britain At the Polls 1979*, Washington 1981.

A. Ranney (ed.), *Britain at the Polls 1983*, Durham (North Carolina) 1985.

R. Worcester & M. Harrop (eds), *Political Communications: the General Election Campaign of 1979*, London 1982.

R. Aron, 'Alternation in Government in the Industrialised Countries', *G and O* 1982, pp. 3–21.

J. Bochel & D. Denver, 'Candidate Selection in the Labour Party: What the Selectors Seek, *BJPS* 1983, pp. 45–70.

I. Budge, 'Strategies, Issues and Votes: British General Elections 1950–1979', *CPS* 1982–3, pp. 171–96.

J. A. Chandler, 'The Plurality Vote: a Reappraisal', *PS* 1982, pp. 87–94.

J. Curtice & M. Steed, 'Turning Dreams Into Reality: The Division of Constituencies Between the Liberals and the Social Democrats', *Parl. Aff.* 1983, pp. 166–82.

J. Curtice & M. Steed, 'Electoral Choice and the Production of Government: The Changing Operation of the Electoral System in the United Kingdom Since 1955', *BJPS* 1982, pp. 249–98.

D. Glencross, 'Television and the General Election of 1983: Could We Have Used More Freedom?', *Parl. Aff.* 1984, pp. 267–70.

G. Gudgen & P. J. Taylor, 'The Decomposition of Electoral Bias in a Plurality Election', *BJPS* 1980, pp. 515–20.

B. Gunter (*et al.*), 'Viewers' Experiences of Television Coverage of the 1983 General Election', *Parl. Aff.* 1984, pp. 271–82.

W. Harvey Cox, 'The 1983 General Election in Northern Ireland: Anatomy and Consequences', *Parl. Aff.* 1984, pp. 40–58.

J. Hills, 'Candidates: the Impact of Gender', *Parl. Aff.* 1981, pp. 221–8.

M. Holland, 'The Selection of Parliamentary Candidates: Contemporary Developments and the Impact of the European Elections', *Parl. Aff.* 1981, pp. 28–46.

D. Kavanagh, 'Election Campaigns and Opinion Polls: British Political Parties and the Use of Private Polls', *Parl. Aff*, 1982, pp. 267–81.

D. Kavanagh, 'The Politics of Manifestos', *Parl. Aff.* 1981, pp. 17–27.

M. Laver, 'On Party Policy, Polarisation and the Breaking of Moulds: the 1983 British Party Manifestos in Context', *Parl. Aff.* 1984, pp. 33–39.

I. McAllister, 'Campaign Activities and Electoral Outcomes in Britain 1979 and 1983', *POQ* 1985, pp. 489–503.

P. McCormick, 'Prentice and Newham North-East Constituency: the Making of Historical Myths', *PS* 1981, pp. 73–90.

D. Oliver, 'Reform Of The Electoral System', *PL* 1983, pp. 108–26.

M. Pugh, 'Political Parties and the Campaign For Proportional Representation 1905–14', *Parl. Aff.* 1980, pp. 294–307.

R. M. Punnett, 'Must Governments Lose? British Inter-Party Competition in Comparative Perspective', *Parl. Aff.* 1981, pp. 392–408.

J. S. Rasmussen, 'How Remarkable Was 1983? An American Perspective on the British General Election', *Parl. Aff.* 1983, pp. 371–88.

J. S. Rasmussen, 'Women's Role In Contemporary British Politics: Impediments to Parliamentary Candidature', *Parl. Aff.* 1983, pp. 300–15.

W. H. Riker, 'The Two-Party System and Duverger's Law: An Essay on the History of Political Science', *APSR* 1982, pp. 753–66.

C. Smith, 'How Complete Is The Electoral Register?', *PS* 1981, pp. 275–8.

S. Stray & M. Silver, 'Government Popularity, By-Elections and Cycles', *Parl. Aff.* 1983, pp. 49–55.

S. Stray & M. Silver, 'Do By-Elections Demonstrate a Government's Unpopularity?', *Parl. Aff.* 1980, pp. 264–70.

E. Vallance, 'Women Candidates in the 1983 General Election', *Parl. Aff.* 1984, pp. 301–9.

T. Yantek, 'Government Popularity in Great Britain Under Conditions of Economic Decline', *PS* 1985, pp. 467–83.

Chapter 3

B. Baker, *The Far Left: An Expose of the Extreme Left in Britain*, London 1981.

A. Ball, *British Political Parties: The Emergence of a Modern Party System*, London 1981.

R. Behrens, *The Conservative Party From Heath to Thatcher*, London 1980.

A. Beith, *The Case for the Liberal Party and the Alliance*, London 1983.

R. Blake, *The Conservative Party from Peel to Thatcher*, London 1985.

V. Bogdanor (ed.), *Liberal Party Politics*, London 1983.

V. Bogdanor, *The People and the Party System*, London 1982.

I. Bradley, *Breaking the Mould? The Birth and Prospects of the SDP*, London 1981.

K. D. Brown (ed.), *The First Labour Party 1906–14*, London 1985.

D. Coates and G. Johnston (eds), *Socialist Strategies*, London 1983.

D. Coates (*et al.*) (eds), *A Socialist Anatomy of Britain*, London 1985.

C. Cook, *A Short History of the Liberal Party 1900–1984*, London 1984.

C. Cook & I. Taylor (eds), *The Labour Party*, London 1980.

A. Cox, *Adversary Politics and Land*, London 1984.

M. Crick, *Militant*, London 1984.

J. Curran (ed.), *The Future of the Left*, London 1984.

D. H. Davies, *The Welsh Nationalist Party 1925–45*, London 1983.

K. D. Ewing, *Trade Unions, the Labour Party and the Law*, Edinburgh 1982.

N. Fielding, *The National Front*, London 1981.

S. E. Finer, *The Changing British Party System 1945–79*, Washington 1980.

G. Foote, *The Labour Party's Political Thought: A History*, London 1986.

A. M. Gamble & S. A. Walkland, *The British Party System and Economic Policy 1945–1983*, London 1984.

S. Haseler, *The Tragedy of Labour*, London 1980.

B. Hindess, *Parliamentary Decmocracy and Socialist Politics*, London 1982.

D. Howell, *British Social Democracy: A Study In Development and Decay*, London 1980.

D. Howell, *British Workers and the Independent Labour Party*, London 1983.

S. Ingle, *British Political Parties*, London 1986.

R. Jenkins, *Partnership or Principle: Writings and Speeches on the Making of the Alliance*, London 1985.

B. Jones & M. Keating, *Labour and the British State*, London 1985.

J. Jupp, *The Radical Left in Britain 1931–1941*, London 1982.

D. Kavanagh (ed.), *The Politics of the Labour Party*, London 1982.

D. Kogan & M. Kogan, *The Battle For the Labour Party*, London 1982.

Z. Layton-Henry (ed.), *Conservative Party Politics*, London 1980.

D. Lipsey & D. Leonard (eds), *The Socialist Agenda: Crosland's Legacy*, London 1981.

L. Minkin, *The Labour Party Conference*, London 1980.

A. Mitchell, *Four Years in the Death of the Labour Party*, London 1983.

A. Mitchell, *The Case for Labour*, London 1983.

R. Morgan and S. Silvestri (eds), *Conservatives and Moderates in Western Europe*, London 1983.

P. Norton & A. Aughey, *Conservatives and Conservatism*, London 1981.

F. O'Gorman, *British Conservatism*, London 1986.

F. O'Gorman, *The Emergence of the British Two-Party System*, London 1982.

C. Patten, *The Tory Case*, London 1983.

H. Pelling, *A Short History of the Labour Party*, London 1985.

M. Pinto-Duschinsky, *British Political Finance 1830–1980*, Washington 1982.

M. Pugh, *The Tories and the People 1880–1935*, London 1985.

J. Ramsden, *The Making of Conservative Party Policy: the Conservative Research Department Since 1929*, London 1980.

R. Rose, *Do Parties Make A Difference?*, London 1984.

R. Scruton, *The Meaning of Conservatism*, London 1980.

L. J. Sharpe & K. Newton, *Does Politics Matter? The Determinants of Public Policies*, London 1984.

D. Steel, *A House Divided: the Lib-Lab Pact and the Future of British Politics*, London 1980.

H. Stephenson, *Claret and Chips: the Rise of the SDP*, London 1982.

A. Taylor, *The Trade Unions and the Labour Party*, London 1986.

S. Taylor, *The National Front in English Politics*, London 1982.

N. Tracey, *The Origins of the Social Democratic Party*, London 1983.

A. Warde, *Consensus and Beyond: the Development of Labour Party Strategy Since the Second World War*, London 1982.

P. Whiteley, *The Labour Party in Crisis*, London 1983.

P. Zentner, *Social Democracy in Britain*, London 1983.

A. Young, *The Reselection of MPs*, London 1983.

J. M. Bochel & D. T. Denver, 'The SDP and the Left-Right Dimension', *BJPS*, 1984, pp. 386–92.

V. Bogdanor, 'The Social Democrats and the Constitution', *PQ* 1981, pp. 285–94.

V. Bogdanor, 'Reflections on British Political Finance', *Parl. Aff.* 1982, pp. 367–80.

J. Brand (*et al.*), 'The Birth and Death of a Three-Party System: Scotland in the Seventies', *BJPS* 1983, pp. 463–88.

J. Bulpitt, 'The Discipline of the New Democracy: Mrs Thatcher's Domestic Statecraft', *PS* 1986, pp. 19–39.

H. M. Drucker, 'Changes in the Labour Party Leadership', *Parl. Aff.* 1981, pp. 369–91.

H. M. Drucker, 'Intra-Party Democracy in Action: the Election of the Leader and Deputy Leader By the Labour Party in 1983', *Parl. Aff.* 1984, pp. 283–300.

L. D. Epstein, 'What Happened to the British Party Model?', *APSR* 1980, pp. 9–22.

B. J. Evans & A. J. Taylor, 'The Rise and Fall of Two-Party Electoral Cooperation', *PS* 1984, pp. 257–72.

Lord Houghton, 'The Party We Love', *PQ* 1981, pp. 149–59.

C. T. Husbands, 'When the Bubble Burst: Transient and Persistent National Front Supporters 1974–79', *BJPS* 1984, pp. 249–60.

R. J. Johnston, 'A Further Look at British Political Finance', *PS* 1986, pp. 466–73.

D. Kavanagh, 'Power in British Political Parties: Iron Law or Special Pleading?', *WEP* 1985 (3) pp. 5–22.

A. King, 'Whatever is Happening to the British Party System?', *Parl. Aff.* 1982, pp. 241–51.

R. Levy, 'The Search for a Rational Strategy: the SNP and Devolution 1974–79', *PS* 1986, pp. 236–48.

J. M. Luty, 'The Spread of the Plaid Cymru: the Spatial Impress', *WPQ* 1981, pp. 310–36.

I. McAllister & A. Mughan, 'Attitudes, Issues and the Labour Party Decline in England, 1974–1979', *CPS* 1985–6, pp. 37–57.

S. M. McBride, 'Corporatism, Public Policy and the Labour Movement: A Comparative Study, *PS* 1985, pp. 439–56.

P. McCormick, 'The Labour Party: Three Unnoticed Changes', *BJPS* 1980, pp. 381–7.

P. Mair & I. McAllister, 'A Territorial versus a Class Appeal? The Labour Parties of the British Isles' Periphery', *EJPR* 1982, pp. 17–34.

D. Marquand, 'Club Government – the Crisis of the Labour Party in the National Perspective', *G and O* 1981, pp. 19–36.

P. Norton, 'Britain: Still a Two-Party System?', *WEP* 1984 (4), pp. 27–45.

M. Pinto-Duschinsky, 'Trends in British Political Funding 1979–1983', *Parl. Aff.* 1985, pp. 328–47.

G. Pridham, 'Not So Much a Programme – More a Way of Life: European Perspectives on the British SDP-Liberal Alliance', *Parl. Aff.* 1983, pp. 183–217.

R. Rose, 'Still the Era of Party Government', *Parl. Aff.* 1983, pp. 282–99.

W. Rudig & P. D. Lowe, 'The "Withered" Greening of British Politics: a Study of the Ecology Party', *PS* 1986, pp. 262–84.

C. Seymour-Ure, 'The SDP and the Media', *PQ* 1982, pp. 433–42.

Chapter 4

M. Anwar, *Votes and Policies: Ethnic Minorities and the General Election, 1979*, London 1984.

I. Budge & D. Fairlie, *Explaining and Predicting Elections*, London 1983.

J. Clemens, *Polls, Politics and Populism*, London 1983.

I. Crewe (ed.), *Electoral Change in Western Democracies: Patterns and Sources of Electoral Volatility*, London 1985.

P. Dunleavy, *Urban Political Analysis*, London 1980.

M. N. Franklin, *The Decline of Class Voting in Britain*, London 1985.

M. Harrop & W. Miller, *Electoral Behaviour*, London 1986.

A. Heath (*et al.*), *How Britain Votes*, London 1985.

H. Himmelweit (*et al.*), *How Voters Decide*, London 1981.

C. T. Husbands, *Radical Exclusionism and the City: the Urban Support of the National Front*, London 1983.

M. Kinnear, *The British Voter: An Atlas and Survey Since 1885*, London 1981.

J. Lovenduski & J. Hills (eds), *The Politics of the Second Electorate: Women and Public Participation*, London 1981.

I. McLean, *Dealing In Votes*, London 1982.

W. L. Miller, *The End of British Politics? Scots and English Political Behaviour in the Seventies*, London 1981.

A. Mughan, *The Politics of Turnout in British Parliamentary Elections*, London 1986.

V. Randall, *Women and Politics*, London 1982.

D. R. Robertson, *Class and the British Electorate*, London 1984.

R. Rose & I. McAllister, *Voters Begin to Choose: From Closed-Class to Open Elections in Britain*, London 1986.

B. Sarlvik & I. Crewe, *Decade of Dealignment*, London 1983.

E. Scarborough, *Political Ideology and Voting*, London 1984.

K. D. Wald, *Crosses on the Ballot: Patterns of British Voter Alignment Since 1885*, New York 1983.

R. Waller, *Almanac of British Politics*, London 1983.

R. Waller, *The Atlas of British Politics*, London 1985.

D. Balsam (*et al.*), 'The Red and the Green: Patterns of Partisan Choice in Wales', *BJPS* 1983, pp. 299–326.

T. Barton & H. Doning, 'The Social and Attitudinal Profile of Social Democratic Party Activists', *PS* 1986, pp. 296–305.

A. R. Bodman, 'The Neighbourhood Effect: a Test of the Butler–Stokes Model', *BJPS* 1983, pp. 243–9.

V. Borooah & R. Van Der Ploeg, 'The Changing Criteria of Economic Success: Performance and Popularity in British Politics', *Manch. Sch.* 1982, pp. 61–78.

M. Burch & M. Moran, 'The Changing British Political Elite 1945–1983: MPs and Cabinet Ministers', *Parl. Aff*, 1985, pp. 1–15.

B. E. Cain & J. Ferejohn, 'Party Identification in the United States and Great Britain', *CPS* 1981–2, pp. 31–48.

B. E. Cain, 'Blessed Be The Tie That Unbinds: Constituency Work and the Vote Swing in Great Britain', *PS* 1983, pp. 103–11.

J. Chapman, 'Marital Status, Sex, the Formation of Political Attitudes in Adult Life', *PS* 1985, pp. 592–609.

H. D. Clarke & M. C. Stewart, 'Dealignment of Degree: Partisan Change in Britain 1974–8, *J of P* 1984, pp. 689–718.

G. W. Cox, 'The Development of a Party-Oriented Electorate in England, 1832–1918', *BJPS* 1986, pp. 187–216.

D. Denver & G. Hands, 'Marginality and Turnout in General Elections in the 1970s', *BJPS* 1985, pp. 381–7.

L. le Duc, 'Partisan Change and Dealignment in Canada, Great Britain and the United States', *CP* 1984–5, pp. 379–98.

L. le Duc, 'The Dynamic Properties of Party Identification: A Four-Nation Comparison', *EJPR* 1981, pp. 257–68.

M. N. Franklin, 'How The Decline of Class Voting Opened the Way to Radical Change in British Politics', *BJPS* 1984, pp. 483–508.

M. N. Franklin & E. C. Page, 'A Critique of the Consumption Cleavage Approach in British Voting Studies', *PS* 1984, pp. 521–36.

M. Harrop, 'The Changing British Electorate', *PQ* 1982, pp. 385–402.

M. Harrop (*et al.*), 'The Bases of National Front Support', *PS* 1980, pp. 271–83.

A. Heath (*et al.*), 'Understanding Electoral Change in Britain', *Parl. Aff.* 1986, pp. 150–64.

D. A. Hibbs, 'Economic Outcomes and Political Support for British Governments Among Occupational Classes: a Dynamic Analysis', *APSR* 1982, pp. 259–84.

J. Hudson, 'The Relationship Between Government Popularity and Approval for the Government's Record in the United Kingdom', *BJPS* 1985, pp. 165–86.

C. Husbands, 'Government Popularity and the Unemployment Issue 1966–1983', *Soc.* 1985, pp. 1–18.

R. J. Johnson, 'Testing the Butler–Stokes Model of a Polarization Effect Around the National Swing in Partisan Preferences, England 1979', *BJPS* 1981, pp. 113–17.

J. Kelley & I. McAllister, 'Ballot Paper Cues and the Vote in Australia and Britain: Alphabetic Voting, Sex and Title', *POQ* 1984, pp. 452–66.

A. King, 'The Rise of the Career Politician in Britain – and its Consequences', *BJPS* 1981, pp. 249–85.

W. W. Lammers & J. L. Nyomarkay, 'Socialist Elites and Technological Societies: Cabinet Member Career Patterns in

Austria, France, Germany and Great Britain', *Polity* 1984–5, pp. 40–65.

M. Laver, 'Are the Liverpool Liberals Really Different? A Path Analytic Interpretation of Local Voting in Liverpool 1973–82', *BJPS* 1984, pp. 243–8.

Z. Layton-Henry & D. T. Studlar, 'The Electoral Participation of Black and Asian Britons: Integration or Alienation', *Parl. Aff.* 1985, pp. 307–18.

A. Lewis & D. Jackson, 'Voting Preferences and Attitudes to Public Expenditure', *PS* 1985, pp. 457–66.

A. Lewis, 'Attitudes to Public Expenditure and their Relationship to Voting Preferences', *PS* 1980, pp. 284–92.

I. McAllister & J. Kelley, 'Party Identification and Political Socialization: A Note on Australia and Britain', *EJPR* 1985, pp. 111–18.

I. McAllister, 'Having Tenure and Party Choice in Australia, Britain and the United States', *BJPS* 1984, pp. 509–21.

C. Marsh, 'Predictions of Voting Behaviour from a Pre-Election Survey', *PS* 1985, pp. 642–8.

W. L. Miller, 'What Was the Profit in Following the Crowd? The Effectiveness of Party Strategies on Immigration and Devolution', *BJPS* 1980, pp. 15–38.

P. Norris, 'The Gender Gap in Britain and America', *Parl. Aff.* 1985, pp. 192–201.

P. Norris, 'Conservative Attitudes in Recent British Elections: an Emerging Gender Gap', *PS* 1986, pp. 120–8.

T. Park (*et al.*), 'Trade Unions and the Labour Party: Changes in the Group of Trade Union Sponsored MPs', *PS* 1986, pp. 306–12.

R. Pinkey, 'Dealignment, Realignment or Just Alignment: a Mid-Term Report', *Parl. Aff.* 1986, pp. 47–62.

R. M. Punnett, 'Regional Partisanship and the Legitimacy of British Governments', *Parl. Aff.* 1984, pp. 141–59.

J. Rasmussen, 'Female Political Career Patterns and Leadership Disabilities in Britain: the Crucial Role of Gatekeepers in Regulating Entry to the Political Elite', *Polity* 1980–1, pp. 600–20.

J. Rasmussen, 'The Electoral Costs of Being a Woman in the 1979 British General Election', *CP* 1982–3, pp. 461–75.

J. Rasmussen, 'Women Candidates in British By-Elections: A Rational Choice Interpretation of Electoral Behaviour', *PS* 1981, pp. 265–74.

R. Rose, 'From Simple Determinism to Interactive Models of Voting: Britain as an Example, *CPS* 1982–3, pp. 145–70.

D. T. Studlar & S. Welch, 'Mass Attitudes on Political Issues in Britain', *CPS* 1981–2, pp. 327–56.

K. D. Wald, 'Institutional Obstacles to Partisan Mobilization? Another Look at the "Franchise Factor" in British Party Development', *EJPR* 1984, pp. 1–23.

R. Waller, 'The 1979 Local and General Elections in England and Wales: is there a Local National Differential?', *PS* 1980, pp. 443–50.

M. P. Wattenberg, 'Party Identification and Party Images: a Comparison of Britain, Canada, Australia and the United States', *CP* 1982–3, pp. 23–40.

S. Welch & D. T. Studlar, 'The Policy Options of British Political Activists', *PS* 1983, pp. 604–19.

E. S. Wellhofer, 'To "Educate Their Volition to Dance In Their Chains": Enfranchisement and Realignment in Britain 1885–1950', *CPS* 1984–5, pp. 3–34 and pp. 351–72.

P. Whiteley, 'Predicting the Labour Vote in 1983: Social Background versus Subjective Evaluations, *PS* 1986, pp. 82–98.

P. Whiteley, 'Who Are the Labour Activists?', *PQ* 1981, pp. 160–70.

P. Williams, 'Party Realignment in the United States and Britain', *BJPS* 1985, pp. 97–116.

Chapter 5

a) General

G. Alderman, *Pressure Groups and Government in Great Britain*, London 1984.

A. R. Ball, *Pressure and Politics in Industrial Societies*, London 1986.

D. Barnes & E. Reid, *Governments and Trade Unions: the British Experience 1964–79*, London 1980.

W. N. Coxall, *Parties and Pressure Groups*, London 1981.

F. Field, *Poverty and Politics*, London 1982.

P. R. Jones, *Doctors and the BMA: a Case Study of Collective Action*, London 1981.

M. Lilly, *The National Council for Civil Liberties: the First Fifty Years*, London 1984.

P. Lowe & J. Goyder, *Environmental Groups in Politics*, London 1983.

D. Marsh (ed.), *Pressure Politics: Interest Groups in Britain*, London 1983.

R. M. Martin, *TUC: the Growth of a Pressure Group 1868–1976*, London 1980.

K. Middlemas, *Industry, Unions and Government*, London 1983.

B. Pimlott & C. Cook (eds), *Trade Unions in British Politics*, London 1982.

J. Porritt, *Seeing Green: the Politics of Ecology Explained*, London 1984.

R. Taylor & C. Pritchard, *The Protest Makers: the British Nuclear Disarmament Movement of 1958–1965, Twenty Years On*, London 1982.

S. Ward, *Organising Things: a Guide to Successful Political Action*, London 1984.

D. Wilson, *Pressure: the A to Z of Campaigning in Britain*, London 1984.

D. Balsom & J. Baylis, 'Public Opinion and the Parties' Defence Policies', *PQ* 1986, pp. 187–94.

T. Chafer, 'Politics and the Perception of Risk: a Study of the Anti-Nuclear Movement in Britain and France', *WEP* 1985 (1), pp. 5–23.

J. Chapman, 'The Political Implications of Attitudes to Abortion in Britain', *WEP* 1986 (1), pp. 7–31.

W. Grant, 'Business Interests and the British Conservative Party', *G and O*, 1980, pp. 143–61.

G. Jordan, 'Parliament Under Pressure', *PQ* 1985, pp. 174–82.

D. Marsh & G. Locksley, 'Trade Union Power: the Recent Debate', *WEP* 1981, pp. 19–37.

D. Marsh & G. Locksley, 'Capital in Britain: its Structure, Power and Influences Over Policy', *WEP* 1983 (2), pp. 36–60.

M. Moran, 'Finance Capital and Pressure-Group Politics in Britain', *BJPS* 1981, pp. 381–404.

D. Sanders & E. Tanenbaum, 'Direct Action and Political Culture: the Changing Political Consciousness of the British Public', *EJPR* 1983, pp. 45–62.

J. A. Sargent, 'British Finance and Industrial Capital and the European Communities', *WEP* 1983 (2), pp. 14–35.

A. J. Taylor, 'The Modern Boroughmongers? The Yorkshire Area (NUM) and Grassroots Politics', *PS* 1984, pp. 385–400.

R. H. Thomas, 'Hunting as a Political Issue', *Parl. Aff.* 1986, pp. 19–30.

b) Policy Studies

E. Ashby & M. Anderson, *The Politics of Clean Air*, London 1982.

I. F. W. Baher & J. Gooch (eds), *Politicians and Defence: Studies in the Formulation of British Defence Policy*, London 1981.

A. Blower, *The Limits of Power: the Politics of Planning Policy*, London 1980.

S. Cooper, *Public Housing and Private Property 1970–84*, London 1985.

C. Crouch, *The Politics of Industrial Relations*, London 1982.
T. Dalyell, *A Science Policy For Britain*, London 1983.
D. Donnison, *The Politics of Poverty*, London 1982.
P. Dunleavy, *The Politics of Mass Housing in Britain 1945–75*, London 1981.
W. H. Fishbein, *Wage Restraint by Consensus: Britain's Search for an Incomes Policy Agreement 1965–79*, London 1984.
W. Grant, *The Political Economy of Industrial Policy*, London 1982.
W. Grant & S. Nath, *The Politics of Economic Policymaking*, London 1984.
A. Gray & B. Jenkins, *Policy Analysis and Evaluation in British Government*, London 1983.
J. A. G. Griffith, *The Politics of the Judiciary*, London 1985.
C. Ham, *Health Policy in Britain*, London 1985.
J. Higgins (*et al.*), *Government and Urban Poverty: Inside the Policy Making Process*, London 1983.
B. W. Hogwood & L. A. Gunn, *Policy Analysis for the Real World*, London 1984.
B. W. Hogwood & B. G. Peters, *Policy Dynamics*, London 1982.
R. Klein, *The Politics of the National Health Service*, London 1983.
S. MacGregor, *The Politics of Poverty*, London 1981.
P. Malpass & A. Murie, *Housing Policy and Practice*, London 1982.
D. Marsh & J. Chambers, *Abortion Politics*, London 1981.
J. Michaels, *The Politics of Secrecy*, London 1982.
J. Moon & J. J. Richardson, *Unemployment in the UK: Politics and Policies*, London 1985.
M. Moran, *The Politics of Banking*, London 1984.
P. Mosley, *The Making of Economic Policy*, London 1984.
P. Norton (ed.), *Law and Order and British Politics*, London 1984.
D. W. Parsons, *The Political Economy of British Regional Policy*, London 1986.
R. Reiner, *The Politics of the Police*, London 1985.
A. Robertson & C. Sandford, *Tax Policy-Making in the United Kingdom*, London 1983.
M. Ryan, *The Politics of Penal Reform*, London 1983.
P. Taylor, *Smoke Ring: the Politics of Tobacco*, London 1984.
R. H. Thomas, *The Politics of Hunting*, London 1983.
R. Williams, *The Nuclear Power Decisions*, London 1980.
E. Wistrich, *The Politics of Transport*, London 1983.

Chapter 6

S. H. Bailey (*et al.*), *Civil Liberties: Cases and Materials*, London 1985.
C. Campbell (ed.), *Do We Need a Bill of Rights?*, London 1980.

I. Harden & N. Lewis, *The Noble Lie: the British Constitution and the Rule of Law*, London 1986.

J. Jaconelli, *Enacting a Bill of Rights: the Legal Problem*, London 1980.

J. Jowell & D. Oliver (eds), *The Changing Constitution*, London 1985.

P. McAuslan & J. McEldowney (eds), *Law, Legitimacy and the Constitution*, London 1985.

G. Marshall, *Constitutional Conventions: the Rules and Forms of Political Accountability*, London 1984.

P. Norton, *The Constitution in Flux*, London 1982.

P. O'Higgins, *Cases and Materials of Civil Liberties*, London 1980.

C. Turpin, *British Government and the Constitution: Text, Cases and Material*, London 1985.

H. W. R. Wade, *Constitutional Fundamentals*, London 1980.

J. Walker, *The Queen Has Been Pleased: the British Honours System*, London 1985.

M. Zander, *A Bill of Rights?*, London 1985.

M. Zander, *The Law-Making Process*, London 1985.

T. R. S. Allan, 'The Limits of Parliamentary Sovereignty', *PL* 1985, pp. 614–36.

V. Bogdanor, 'Dicey and the Reform of the Constitution', *PL* 1985, pp. 652–78.

D. L. Ellis, 'Collective Ministerial Responsibility and Collective Solidarity', *PL* 1980, pp. 367–96.

G. Marshall, 'What are Constitutional Conventions?', *Parl. Aff.* 1985, pp. 33–9.

W. L. Miller, J. A. Brand & M. Jordan, 'Governing Without a Mandate: its Causes and Consequences for the Conservative Party in Scotland', *PQ* 1981, pp. 203–13.

C. Munro, 'Dicey on Constitutional Conventions', *PL* 1985, pp. 637–51.

R. Rose, 'Law as a Resource of Public Policies', *Parl. Aff.* 1986, pp. 297–314.

D. B. Searing, 'Rules of the Game in Britain: Can the Politicians Be Trusted?', *APSR* 1982, pp. 239–58.

Chapter 7

S. Barrett & C. Fudge (eds), *Policy and Action: Essays on the Implementation of Public Policy*, London 1981.

D. S. Bell (ed.), *The Conservative Government 1979–84: an Interim Report*, London 1985.

J. Blondel, *Government Ministers in the Contemporary World*, London 1985.

V. Bogdanor, *Multi-party Politics and the Constitution*, London 1983.
D. Bonner, *Emergency Powers in Peacetime*, London 1985.
N. Bosanquet & P. Townsend (eds), *Labour and Equality: a Fabian Study of Labour in Power 1974–79*, London 1980.
J. Bruce-Gardyne, *Mrs Thatcher's First Administration: the Prophets Confounded*, London 1984.
D. E. Butler, *Governing Without a Majority*, London 1983.
D. Coates, *Labour in Power? A Study of the Labour Government 1974–1979*, London 1980.
M. Cockerell (*et al.*), *Sources Close to the Prime Minister*, London 1984.
P. Cosgrave, *Thatcher: the First Term*, London 1985.
R. Eatwell, *The 1945–51 Labour Governments*, London 1980.
D. Englefield, *Whitehall and Westminster: Government Informs Parliament*, London 1985.
J. D. Fair, *British Interparty Conferences: a Study of the Procedure of Conciliation in British Politics 1867–1921*, London 1980.
S. Hall and M. Jacques, *The Politics of Thatcherism*, London 1983.
N. Henderson, *The Private Office*, London 1984.
P. Hennessy, *Cabinet*, London 1986.
M. Holmes, *The First Thatcher Government 1979–1983*, London 1985.
M. Holmes, *The Labour Government 1974–79*, London 1985.
M. Holmes, *Political Pressure and Economic Policy – British Government 1970–1974*, London 1982.
P. Jackson (ed.), *Implementing Government Policy Initiatives: the Thatcher Administration 1979–83*, London 1985.
K. Jeffery & P. Hennessy, *States of Emergency*, London 1983.
G. Kaufman, *How to be a Minister*, London 1980.
W. Keegan, *Mrs Thatcher's Economic Experiment*, London 1984.
A. King (ed.), *The British Prime Minister*, London 1985.
J. M. Lee, *The Churchill Coalition 1940–45*, London 1980.
D. Lewis & H. Wallace (eds), *Policies into Practice*, London 1984.
T. T. Mackie & B. W. Hogwood, *Unlocking the Cabinet*, London 1985.
K. O. Morgan, *Labour in Power 1945–51*, London 1984.
J. F. Naylor, *A Man and an Institution: Sir Maurice Hankey, the Cabinet Secretariat and the Custody of Cabinet Secrecy*, London 1984.
R. Ovendale (ed.), *The Foreign Policy of the British Labour Governments 1945–51*, London 1984.
H. Pelling, *The Labour Governments 1945–51*, London 1984.
D. C. Pitt and B. C. Smith, *Government Departments: an Organizational Perspective*, London 1981.
C. Pollitt, *Manipulating the Machine: Changing the Pattern of Ministerial Departments 1960–83*, London 1984.
P. Riddell, *The Thatcher Government*, London 1985.
R. Rose and E. Suleiman (eds), *Presidents and Prime Ministers*, Washington 1980.

Royal Institute of Public Administration, *Policy and Practice: the Experience of Government*, London 1980.

Royal Institute of Public Administration, *The Home Office: Perspectives on Policy and Administration*, London 1983.

M. Rush, *The Cabinet and Policy Formation*, London 1984.

A. Seldon, *Churchill's Indian Summer: The Conservative Government 1951–55*, London 1981.

J. Turner, *Lloyd George's Secretariat*, London 1980.

D. Wass, *Government and the Governed*, London 1984.

P. Weller, *First Among Equals: Prime Ministers in Westminster Systems*, Sydney 1985.

R. K. Alderman & J. A. Cross, 'The Reluctant Knife: Reflections on the Prime Minister's Power of Dismissal', *Parl. Aff.* 1985, pp. 387–408.

R. K. Alderman & J. A. Cross, 'Patterns of Ministerial Turnover in Two Labour Cabinets', *PS* 1981, pp. 425–30.

Lord Boyle, 'Ministers and the Administrative Process', *Pub. Admin.* 1980, pp. 1–13.

Tony Benn, 'The Case For a Constitutional Premiership', *Parl. Aff.* 1980, pp. 7–22.

R. Brazier, 'Choosing A Prime Minister, *PL* 1982, pp. 395–417.

E. Browne (*et al.*), 'The Process of Cabinet Dissolution', *AJPS* 1986, pp. 628–50.

M. Burch, 'Mrs Thatcher's Approach to Leadership in Government: 1979–June 1983', *Parl. Aff.* 1983, pp. 399–416.

M. Dougan (*et al.*), 'The Selection of Cabinet Ministers in Contrasting Political Systems', *IPSR* 1981, pp. 125–234.

G. Drewry, 'Lord Haldane's Ministry of Justice', *Pub. Admin.* 1983, pp. 396–414.

I. G. Eagles, 'Cabinet Secrets as Evidence', *PL* 1980, pp. 263–87.

M. N. Franklin & T. T. Mackie, 'Reassessing the Importance of Size and Ideology for the Formation of Governing Coalitions in Parliamentary Democracies', *AJPS* 1984, pp. 671–92.

M. N. Franklin & T. T. Mackie, 'Familiarity and Inertia in the Formation of Governing Coalitions in Parliamentary Democracies', *BJPS* 1983, pp. 275–98.

P. Hennessy, 'Michael Heseltine, Mottram's Law and the Efficiency of Cabinet Government', *PQ* 1986, pp. 137–43.

C. Hood (*et al.*), 'Scale Economies and Iron Laws: Mergers and Demergers in Whitehall 1971–84', *Pub. Admin.* 1985, pp. 61–78.

J. Hudson, 'Prime Ministerial Popularity in the UK: 1960–81', *PS* 1984, pp. 86–97.

S. James, 'The Central Policy Review Staff 1970–83', *PS* 1986, pp. 423–40.

J. M. Lee, 'The Machinery of Government: the Prospect of Redefining the Issues Under Mrs Thatcher's Administration', *Parl. Aff.* 1980, pp. 434–47.

A. Lijphart (*et al.*), 'New Approaches to the Study of Cabinet Coalitions', *CPS* 1984–5, pp. 155–279.

T. T. Mackie & B. W. Hogwood, 'Decision Arenas in Executive Decision Making: Cabinet Committees in Comparative Perspective', *BJPS* 1984, pp. 285–312.

Sir Patrick Nairne, 'Managing the Elephant: Reflections on a Giant Department', *PQ* 1983, pp. 243–56.

M. J. Painter, 'Policy Coordination in the Department of the Environment 1970–1976', *Pub. Admin.* 1980, pp. 135–54.

C. Pollitt, 'Rationalizing the Machinery of Government: the Conservatives 1970–4', *PS* 1980, pp. 84–98.

J. Radcliffe, 'The Role of Politicians and Administrators in Departmental Reorganization: the Case of the Department of the Environment', *Pub. Admin.* 1985, pp. 201–18.

J. S. Rasmussen, 'Who Gets Hung in a Hung Parliament? A Game Theory Analysis of the 1987–88 British General Election', *BJPS* 1986, pp. 135–54.

C. Seymour-Ure, 'British "War Cabinets" in Limited Wars: Korea, Suez and the Falklands', *Pub. Admin.* 1984, pp. 181–200.

L. J. Sharpe, 'Central Coordination and the Policy Network', *PS* 1985, pp. 361–81.

M. Steed, 'The Formation of Governments in the United Kingdom', *PQ* 1983, pp. 54–65.

K. Strom, 'Minority Governments in Parliamentary Democracies', *CPS* 1984–5, pp. 199–228.

K. Theakston, 'The Use and Abuse of Junior Ministers: Increasing Political Influence in Whitehall', *PQ* 1986, pp. 18–35.

P. Weller, 'Do Prime Ministers' Departments Really Create Problems?', *Pub. Admin.* 1983, pp. 59–78 (and G. W. Jones, pp. 79–84).

P. Weller, 'The Vulnerability of Prime Ministers: a Comparative Perspective', *Parl. Aff.* 1983, pp. 96–117.

Chapters 8 and 9

K. Bradshaw & D. Pring, *Parliament and Congress*, London 1981.

I. Burton & G. Drewry, *Legislation and Public Policy*, London 1981.

G. Drewry (ed.), *The New Select Committees: a Study of the 1979 Reforms*, London 1985.

D. Englefield, *Parliament and Information*, London 1981.

D. Englefield (ed.), *The Commons' Select Committees – Catalysts for Progress?*, London 1984.

V. Flegmann, *Public Expenditure and the Select Committees of the Commons*, London 1986.

S. Ingle & P. Tether, *Parliament and Health Policy: the Role of MPs 1970–75*, London 1981.

D. Judge, *Backbench Specialisation in the House of Commons*, London 1981.

D. Judge (ed.), *The Politics of Parliamentary Reform*, London 1983.

P. Laundy, *The Office of Speaker in the Parliaments of the Commonwealth*, London 1984.

D. Marquand (ed.), *John P. Mackintosh on Parliament and Social Democracy*, London 1982.

E. Marshall, *Parliament and the Public*, London 1982.

D. A. Miers & A. C. Page, *Legislation*, London 1982.

A. Mitchell, *Westminster Man*, London 1982.

R. K. Mosley, *Westminster Workshop: a Students Guide to British Government*, London 1985.

R. Needham, *Honourable Member: an Inside Look at the House of Commons*, London 1983.

P. Norton (ed.), *Parliament in the 1980s*, Oxford 1985.

P. Norton, *The Commons in Perspective*, London 1981.

P. Norton, *Dissension in the House of Commons 1974–1979*, London 1980.

A. Paterson, *The Law Lords*, London 1983.

M. Phillips, *The House Divided: Women In Westminster*, London 1980.

C. Powell & A. Butler, *The Parliamentary and Scientific Committee: the First Forty Years 1939–1979*, London 1980.

M. Rush, *Parliament and the Public*, London 1980.

M. Rush, *Parliamentary Government in Britain*, London 1981.

M. Rush (ed.), *The House Of Commons: Services and Facilities 1972–1982*, London 1983.

S. A. Walkland & M. Ryle (eds), *The Commons Today*, London 1981.

J. G. Blumler, 'The Sound of Parliament', *Parl. Aff.* 1984, pp. 250–66.

I. Burton & G. Drewry, 'Public Legislation: a Survey of the Sessions 1981–82 and 1982–83', *Parl. Aff.* 1985, pp. 219–52.

B. E. Cain (*et al.*), 'The Constituency Component: a Comparison of Service in Great Britain and the United States', *CPS* 1983–4, pp. 67–91.

E. W. Crowe, 'Cross-Voting in the British House of Commons: 1945–74', *J of P* 1980, pp. 487–510.

E. W. Crowe, 'Consensus and Structure in Legislative Norms: Party Discipline in the House of Commons', *J of P* 1983, pp. 907–31.

K. Featherstone, 'Socialists and European Integration: the Attitudes of British Members of Parliament', *EJPR* 1981, pp. 407–20.

B. Franklin, 'A Leap in the Dark: MP's Objections to Televising Parliament', *Parl. Aff.* 1986, pp. 284–96.

B. Gould, 'Televise Parliament to Revise the Chamber', *Parl. Aff.* 1984, pp. 243–9.

R. Gregory, 'Executive Power and Constituency Representation in United Kingdom Politics', *PS* 1980, pp. 63–84.

Sir John Hoskyns, 'Whitehall and Westminster: an Outsider's View', *Parl. Aff.* 1983, pp. 137–47.

S. Himelfarb, 'Consensus in Committee: the Case of the Select Committee On Race Relations and Immigration', *Parl. Aff.* 1980, pp. 54–66.

D. Judge, 'British Representative Theory and Parliamentary Specialisation', *Parl. Aff.* 1980, pp. 40–53.

D. Judge, 'The Politics of MPs Pay', *Parl. Aff.* 1984, pp. 59–75.

P. M. Leopold, 'Freedom of Speech in Parliament – its Misuse and Proposals for Reform', *PL* 1981, pp. 30–51.

M. A. McCarthy & R. A. Moodie, 'Parliament and Pornography: the 1978 Child Protection Act', *Parl. Aff.* 1981, pp. 47–62.

P. M. McCormick, 'The Triumph of Caucus', *AJPH* 1982, pp. 32–43.

P. M. McCormick, 'Prentice and Newham North-East Constituency: the Making of Historical Myths', *PS* 1981, pp. 73–90.

D. Marsh (*et al.*), 'Private Members' Bills and Moral Panic: The Case of the Video Recording Bill (1984)', *Parl. Aff.* 1986, pp. 179–96.

W. Mishler, 'Scotching Nationalism in the British Parliament: Crosscutting Cleavages Among MPs', *LSQ* 1983, pp. 5–28.

A. Mitchell, 'A House Buyer's Bill: How Not to Pass a Private Members' Bill', *Parl. Aff.* 1986, pp. 1–18.

M. Moran, 'Parliamentary Control of the Bank of England', *Parl. Aff.* 1980, pp. 67–78.

P. Norton, 'Party Committees in the House of Commons', *Parl. Aff.* 1983, pp. 7–27.

P. Norton, '"Dear Minister" – the Importance of MP-To-Minister Correspondence', *Parl. Aff.* 1982, pp. 59–72.

P. Norton, 'The House of Commons and the Constitution: the Challenges of the 1970s', *Parl. Aff.* 1981, pp. 253–71.

P. Norton, 'The Changing Face of the British House of Commons in the 1970s', *LSQ* 1980, pp. 333–58.

D. Pannick, 'The Law Lords and the Needs of Contemporary Society', *PQ* 1982, pp. 318–28.

J. S. Rasmussen & J. M. McCormick, 'The Influence of Ideology on

British Labour MPs in Voting on EEC Issues', *LSQ* 1985, pp. 203–22.

P. G. Richards, 'The SDP In Parliament', *Parl. Aff.* 1982, pp. 136–42.

P. G. Richards (*et al.*) (The Study of Parliament Group), 'Private Bill Procedure: a Case For Reform', *PL* 1981, pp. 206–27.

D. Robertson, 'Judicial Ideology in the House of Lords: a Jurimetric Analysis', *BJPS* 1982, pp. 1–26.

M. Rush, 'Parliamentary Committees and Parliamentary Government: the British and Canadian Experience', *JCCP* 1982, pp. 138–54.

M. T. Ryle, 'The Legislative Staff at the British House of Commons', *LSQ* 1981, pp. 497–520.

J. E. Schwartz, 'Exploring a New Role in Policy Making: the British House of Commons in the 1970s', *APSR* 1980, pp. 23–37.

D. D. Searing, 'The Role of the Good Constituency Member and the Practice of Representation in Great Britain', *J of P* 1985, pp. 348–81.

D. R. Shell, 'The House of Lords and the Thatcher Government', *Parl. Aff.* 1985, pp. 16–32.

E. Vallance, 'Women In the House of Commons', *PS* 1981, pp. 407–14.

D. M. Wood, 'Comparing Parliamentary Voting on European Issues in France and Britain', *LSQ* 1982, pp. 101–18.

Chapter 10

C. Carter, *The Purpose of Government Expenditure*, London 1984.

V. Flegmann, *Called to Account: The Public Accounts Committee of the House of Commons 1965–6/1977–8*, London 1980.

D. Heald, *Public Expenditure*, Oxford 1983.

H. Heclo & A. Wildavsky, *The Private Government of Public Money*, London 1981.

C. Hood & M. Wright, *Big Government in Hard Times*, London 1981.

L. Pliatzky, *Getting and Spending*, London 1982.

L. Pliatzky, *Paying and Choosing: the Intelligent Person's Guide to the Mixed Economy*, London 1985.

Royal Institute of Public Administration, *Management Information and Control in Whitehall*, London 1983.

A. Walker (ed.), *Public Expenditure and Social Policy: an Examination of Social Spending and Social Priorities*, London 1982.

M. Wright (ed.), *Public Spending Decisions: Growth and Restraint in the 1970s*, London 1980.

P. K. Else & G. P. Marshall, 'The Unplanning of Public Expenditure: Recent Problems in Expenditure Planning and the Consequences of Cash Limits', *Pub. Admin.* 1981, pp. 253–78.

V. Flegmann, 'The Public Accounts Committee: a Successful Select Committee?', *Parl. Aff.* 1980, pp. 166–72.

A. Gray and B. Jenkins, 'Policy Analysis in British Central Government: the Experience of PAR', *Pub. Admin.* 1982, pp. 429–50.

S. Jenkins, 'The "Star Chamber", PESC and the Cabinet', *PQ* 1985, pp. 113–21.

G. W. Jones and M. Stewart, 'The Treasury and Local Government', *PQ* 1983, pp. 5–15.

A. Kennan, 'Recent Work of the General Sub-Committee of the Expenditure Committee', *Parl. Aff.* 1980, pp. 159–65.

M. Moran, 'Monetary Policy and the Machinery of Government', *Pub. Admin.* 1981, pp. 47–62.

E. L. Normanton, 'Reform in the Field of Public Accountability and Audit: A Progress Report', *PQ* 1980, pp. 175–99.

G. C. Pedan, 'The Treasury as the Central Department of Government 1919–1939', *Pub. Admin.* 1983, pp. 371–85.

J. J. Richardson, 'Programme Evaluation in Britain and Sweden', *Parl. Aff.* 1982, pp. 160–80.

C. Thain, 'The Treasury and Britain's Decline', *PS* 1984, pp. 581–95.

C. Thain, 'The Education of the Treasury: the Medium-term Financial Strategy 1980–84', *Pub. Admin.* 1985, pp. 260–86.

Chapter 11

a) Civil Service

R. A. Chapman, *Leadership in the British Civil Service*, London 1984.

R. A. Chapman & J. R. Greenaway, *The Dynamics of Administrative Reform*, London 1980.

Lord Crowther-Hunt & P. Kellner, *The Civil Servants: an Enquiry into Britain's Ruling Class*, London 1980.

G. Drewry, *The Civil Service Today*, London 1984.

D. Englefield (ed.), *Today's Civil Service: a Guide to its Work With Parliament and Industry*, London 1986.

G. K. Fry, *The Changing Civil Service*, London 1985.

G. K. Fry, *The Administrative 'Revolution' in Whitehall: a Study of the Politics of Administrative Change in British Central Government Since the 1950s*, London 1981.

J. Garrett, *Managing the Civil Service*, London 1981.

A. Gray & W. I. Jenkins, *Administrative Politics in British Government*, London 1985.

J. Gretton & A. Harrison, *How Much Are Public Servants Worth?*, London 1982.

A. Hardcastle (*et al.*), *Management Information and Control in Whitehall*, London 1983.

M. P. Kelly, *White Collar Proletariat: the Industrial Behaviour of British Civil Servants*, London 1980.

K. G. Robertson, *Public Secrets: a Study in the Development of Government Secrecy*, London 1982.

B. Sedgemore, *The Secret Constitution*, London 1980.

J. Stanyer, *The Mangement of Modern Britain*, London 1986.

H. Young & A. Sloman, *No Minister*, London 1982.

E. Brimelow, 'Women In the Civil Service', *Pub. Admin.* 1981, pp. 313–36.

R. A. Chapman, 'The Rise and Fall of the CSD', *PP* 1983, pp. 41–62.

W. P. Collins, 'Public Participation in Bureaucratic Decision-Making', *Pub. Admin.* 1980, pp. 465–78.

F. Cooper, 'Changing the Establishment', *PQ* 1986, pp. 267–77.

A. Doig, 'A Question of Balance: Business Appointments of Former Civil Servants', *Parl. Aff.* 1986, pp. 63–78.

G. Drewry, 'Lawyers in the UK Civil Service', *Pub. Admin.* 1981, pp. 15–46.

G. Drewry, 'The GCHQ Case – a Failure of Government Communications', *Parl. Aff.* 1985, pp. 371–86.

K. Ennals, 'The Management Information System for Ministers in the Department of the Environment', *LGS* 1981 (1), pp. 39–46.

S. E. Finer, 'Princes, Parliaments and the Public Services', *Parl. Aff.* 1980, pp. 353–72.

G. K. Fry, 'Government and the Civil Service: a View of Recent Developments', *Parl. Aff.* 1986, pp. 267–83.

G. K. Fry, 'The Development of the Thatcher Government's "Grand Strategy" for the Civil Service', *Pub. Admin.* 1984, pp. 322–35.

K. Gillender and R. Mair, 'Generalist Administrators and Professional Engineers: Some Developments Since the Fulton Report', *Pub. Admin.* 1980, pp. 333–56.

R. E. Goodin, 'Rational Politicians and Rational Bureaucrats in Washington and Whitehall', *Pub. Admin.* 1982, pp. 23–41.

P. A. Hall, 'Policy Innovation and the Structure of the State: the Politics-Administration Nexus in France and Britain', *AAA* 1983 (466), pp. 43–60.

D. Howells, 'Marks and Spencer and the Civil Service: a Comparison of Culture and Method, *Pub. Admin.* 1981, pp. 337–78.

Lord Crowther-Hunt, 'Mandarins and Ministers', *Parl. Aff.* 1980, pp. 373–99.

N. Johnson, 'Change in the Civil Service: Retrospect and Prospect', *Pub. Admin.* 1985, pp. 415–34.

P. Neville-Jones, 'The Continental Cabinet System: the Effects of Transferring it to the United Kingdom', *PQ* 1983, pp. 232–42.

D. Judge, 'Specialists and Generalists in British Central Government: a Political Debate, *Pub. Admin.* 1981, pp. 1–14.

D. Lewis, 'The Quality of Future Civil Servants', *Parl. Aff.* 1980, pp. 422–33.

R. Lowe, 'Bureaucracy Triumphant or Denied? The Expansion of the British Civil Service, 1919–1939', *Pub. Admin.* 1984, pp. 291–310.

L. Metcalfe & S. Richards, 'The Impact of the Efficiency Strategy: Political Clout or Cultural Change?', *Pub. Admin.* 1984, pp. 440–54.

C. Painter, 'The Thatcher Government and the Civil Service: Economy, Reform and Conflict, *PQ* 1983, pp. 292–7.

B. G. Peters, 'Burning the Village: the Civil Service Under Reagan and Thatcher', *Parl. Aff.* 1986, pp. 79–97.

W. Plowden, 'What Prospects For the Civil Service?', *Pub. Admin.* 1985, pp. 393–414.

C. Pollitt, 'The CSD: a Normal Death?', *Pub. Admin.* 1982, pp. 73–6.

C. Pollitt, 'Performance Measurement in the Public Services: some Political Implications, *Parl. Aff.* 1986, pp. 315–29.

R. Pyper, 'Sarah Tisdall, Ian Willmore and the Civil Servants' Right to Leak', *PQ* 1985, pp. 72–81.

F. F. Ridley, 'The British Civil Service and Politics: Principles in Question and Tradition in Flux', *Parl. Aff.* 1983, pp. 28–48.

N. Summerton, 'A Mandarin's Duty', *Parl. Aff.* 1980, pp. 400–21.

N. Warner, 'Raynerism in Practice: Anatomy of a Rayner Scrutiny', *Pub. Admin.* 1984, pp. 7–22.

D. Wass, 'The Civil Service at the Crossroads', *PQ* 1985, pp. 227–41.

b) Administrative Law

P. Birkinshaw, *Grievances, Remedies and the State*, London 1985.

R. Brazier & H. Street (eds), *DeSmith's Constitutional and Administrative Law*, London 1984.

P. P. Craig, *Administrative Law*, London 1983.

J. M. Evans, *DeSmith's Judicial Review of Administrative Action*, London 1980.

J. L. Garner & B. L. Jones, *Administrative Law*, London 1985.
T. J. Grout, *Public Law*, London 1984.
C. Harlow & R. Rawlings, *Law and Administration*, London 1984.
N. Hawke, *An Introduction to Administrative Law*, London 1984.
I. N. Stevens & D. C. M. Yardley, *The Protection of Liberty*, London 1982.
H. Street, *Freedom: the Individual and the Law*, London 1982.
E. C. S. Wade & A. W. Bradley, *Constitutional and Administrative Law*, London 1985.

A. Beith, 'Prayers Unanswered: a Jaundiced View of the Parliamentary Scrutiny of Statutory Instruments', *Parl. Aff.* 1981, pp. 165–73.
D. Clark, 'The Ombudsman in Britain and France: a Comparative Evaluation', *WEP* 1984 (3), pp. 64–90.
R. Gregory, 'The Select Committee of the Parliamentary Commissioner for Administration 1967–1980', *PL* 1982, pp. 49–88.
W. B. Gwyn, 'The Ombudsman in Britain: a Qualified Success in Government Reform', *Pub. Admin.* 1982, pp. 171–96.
P. McAuslan, 'Administrative Law, Collective Consumption and Judicial Policy', *MLR* 1983, pp. 1–20.
Judge McKee, 'A Personal View of the Work of Industrial Tribunals', *MLR* 1986, pp. 314–23.
F. F. Ridley, 'The Citizen Against Authority: British Approaches to the Redress of Grievances', *Parl. Aff.* 1984, pp. 1–32.
Lord Scarman (*et al.*), 'Judicial Review', *Pub. Admin.* 1986, pp. 133–96.
D. G. T. Williams, 'The Council of Tribunals: The First Twenty-Five Years', *PL* 1984, pp. 73–88.
D. G. T. Williams,' The Donoughmore Report in Retrospect', *Pub. Admin.* 1982, pp. 237–92.

Chapter 12

K. Ascher, *The Politics of Privatisation*, London 1986.
R. Baldwin, *Regulating the Airlines: Administrative Justice and Agency Discretion*, London 1985.
A. Barker (ed.), *Quangos in Britain: Government and the Networks of Public Policy-Making*, London 1982.
P. Curwen, *Public Enterprise: a Modern Approach*, London 1986.
L. Hannah, *Engineers, Managers and Politicians: the First Fifteen Years of Nationalised Electricity Supply in Britain*, London 1982.

P. Holland, *The Governance of Quangos*, London 1981.

C. Hood & A. Dunsire, *Bureaumetrics: the Quantitative Comparison of British Central Government Agencies*, London 1981.

J. Le Grand & R. Robinson, *Privatisation and the Welfare State*, London 1984.

D. McEachern, *A Class Against Itself: Powers in the Nationalisation of the British Steel Industry*, London 1980.

R. Pryke, *The Nationalised Industries*, London 1981.

Royal Institute of Public Administration, *Allies or Adversaries? Perspectives on Government and Industry in Britain*, London 1981.

J. G. Smith (ed.), *Strategic Planning in Nationalised Industries*, London 1984.

D. Steel & D. Heald (eds), *Privatising Public Enterprise*, London 1984.

D. Chambers, 'Plans as Promises: What Does "Corporate Planning" Mean in a Publicly-Owned Corporation?', *Pub. Admin.* 1984, pp. 35–49.

P. Dunleavy, 'Explaining the Privatization Boom: Public Choice versus Radical Approaches, *Pub. Admin.* 1986, pp. 13–34.

M. R. Garner, 'Auditing the Efficiency of Nationalised Industries: Enter the Monopolies and Mergers Commission', *Pub. Admin.* 1982, pp. 409–28.

M. R. Garner, 'British Airways and British Aerospace: Limbo For Two Enterprises', *Pub. Admin.* 1980, pp. 13–24.

M. R. Garner, 'The Financing of the Nationalised Industries: Note on the Report of the Treasury and Civil Service Committee', *Pub. Admin.* 1981, pp. 466–73.

D. Heald, 'Will the Privatisation of Public Enterprises Solve the Problem of Control?', *Pub. Admin.* 1985, pp. 7–22.

J. Hills, 'Government Relations With Industry: Japan and Britain – a Review of Two Political Arguments', *Polity* 1981–2, pp. 222–48.

C. Hood, 'The Politics of Quangocide', *PP* 1980, pp. 247–66.

Sir Arthur Knight, 'The Control of the Nationalised Industries', *PQ* 1982, pp. 24–35.

R. Presthus, 'Mrs Thatcher Stalks the Quango: a Note on Patronage and Justice in Britain', *PAR* 1981, pp. 312–7.

D. R. Steel, 'Government and Industry in Britain', *BJPS* 1982, pp. 449–503.

L. Tivey, 'Nationalized Industry as Organised Interests', *Pub. Admin.* 1982, pp. 42–55.

S. Young, 'The Nature of Privatization in Britain 1979–85', *WEP* 1986 (2), pp. 235–52.

Chapter 13

A. Alexander, *Local Government in Britain Since Reorganisation*, London 1982.

A. Alexander, *The Politics of Local Government in the UK*, London 1982.

L. G. Bayley, *Local Government: is it Manageable?*, London 1980.

R. J. Bennett, *Central Grants to Local Governments: the Political and Economic Impact of the Rate Support Grant in England and Wales*, London 1982.

N. Boaden (*et al.*), *Public Participation in Local Services*, London 1982.

M. Boddy & C. Fudge (eds), *Local Socialism*, London 1984.

Sir J. Boynton, *Job at the Top*, London 1986.

T. Burgess & T. Travers, *Ten Billion Pounds: Whitehall's Takeover of the Town Halls*, London 1980.

T. Bush & M. Kogan, *Directors of Education*, London 1982.

H. Butcher (*et al.*), *Community Groups in Action*, London 1980.

T. Byrne, *Local Government in Britain*, London 1986.

G. E. Cherry, *The Politics of Town Planning*, London 1982.

T. Clegg (*et al.*), *The Future of London Government*, London 1985.

M. Cross & D. Mallen, *Local Government and Politics*, London 1982.

S. S. Duncan & M. Goodwin, *Local Government in Crisis: Centralization versus Autonomy in Britain*, London 1986.

H. Elcock, *Local Government: Politicians, Professionals and Public in Local Authorities*, London 1982.

B. Elliott & D. McCrane, *The City: Patterns of Domination and Conflict*, London 1982.

R. Farnell, *Local Planning in Four English Cities*, London 1983.

K. Fenwick & P. McBride, *The Government of Education*, London 1981.

M. Floyd, *Policy Making and Planning in Local Government*, London 1984.

C. D. Foster (*et al.*), *Local Government Finance in a Unitary State*, London 1980.

N. Flynn (*et al.*), *Abolition or Reform? The GLC and the Metropolitan County Councils*, London 1985.

M. Goldsmith, *Politics, Planning and the City*, London 1980.

M. Goldsmith (ed.), *New Research in Central–Local Government Relations*, London 1985.

D. G. Green, *Power and Party in an English City: an Account of Single-Party Rule*, London 1980.

R. Greenwood (*et al.*), *Patterns of Management in Local Government*, London 1980.

J. Gyford & M. James, *National Parties and Local Politics*, London 1983.

J. Gyford, *Local Politics in Britain*, London 1983.
J. Gyford, *The Politics of Local Socialism*, London 1985.
W. Hampton, *Local Government and Urban Politics*, London 1986.
R. J. Haynes, *Organisation Theory and Local Government*, London 1980.
A. Henney, *Inside Local Government: a Case For Radical Reform*, London 1984.
N. P. Hepworth, *The Finance of Local Government*, London 1984.
R. Jeffries, *Tackling the Town Hall: a Local Authority Handbook*, London 1982.
G. W. Jones (ed.), *New Approaches to the Study of Central–Local Government Relationships*, London 1980.
G. Jones & J. Stewart, *The Case for Local Government*, London 1985.
M. Keating & A. Midwinter, *Urban Policy in Scotland*, London 1985.
M. Laffin, *Professionalism and Policy: the Role of the Professions in the Central–Local Government Relationship*, London 1986.
G. Lees & J. Lambert, *Cities in Crisis*, London 1985.
M. Loughlin (*et al.*), *Half Century of Municipal Decline 1935–1985*, London 1985.
A. Midwinter, *The Politics of Local Spending*, London 1983.
K. Newton (ed.), *Urban Political Economy*, London 1981.
K. Newton & T. Karran, *The Politics of Local Expenditure*, London 1985.
H. Page, *Local Authority Borrowing: Past Present and Future*, London 1986.
C. J. Pearce, *The Machinery of Change in Local Government 1888–1974*, London 1980.
S. Ranson (*et al.*), *Between Centre and Locality*, London 1985.
G. Rhodes, *Inspectorates in British Government*, London 1981.
R. A. W. Rhodes, *The National World of Local Government*, London 1986.
R. A. W. Rhodes, *Control and Power in Central–Local Government Relations*, London 1981.
P. G. Richards, *The Local Government System*, London 1983.
A. Seldon (ed.), *Town Hall Power or Whitehall Power?*, London 1981.
J. Stanyer, *Assessing Local Government*, London 1984.
J. Stewart, *Local Government: the Conditions of Local Choice*, London 1983.
K. Young (ed.), *National Interest and Local Government*, London 1983.
K. Young & P. L. Garside, *Metropolitan London: Politics and Urban Change 1837–1981*, London 1982.

A. Alexander, 'Officers and Members in the New Local Government System – Parallel Structures and Interactive Processes', *LGS* 1981 (6), pp. 33–44.

S. Bailey, 'Rates Reform – Lessons From the Scottish Experience', *LGS* 1986, pp. 21–36.

G. A. Bayne, 'Changes in Labour Power on District and County Councils – Regional Patterns and Policy Consequences', *LGS* 1985 (4), pp. 91–106.

G. A. Bayne, 'Socio-economic Conditions, Central Policies and Local Authority Staffing Levels', *Pub. Admin.* 1986, pp. 69–82.

B. J. A. Binder, 'Relations Between Central and Local Government Since 1975 – Are the Associations Failing?', *LGS* 1982 (1), pp. 35–44.

R. J. Bennett, 'The Local Income Tax in Britain: a Critique of Recent Arguments Against Its Use', *Pub. Admin.* 1981, pp. 295–310.

P. Birkinshaw, 'Freedom of Information, the Elected Member and Local Government', *PL* 1981, pp. 545–58.

G. Bramley, 'Incrementalism Run Amok? Local Government Finance in Britain', *Pub. Admin.* 1985, pp. 100–107.

G. Bramley and A. Evans, 'Block Grant – Some Unresolved Issues', *PP* 1981, pp. 173–204.

S. L. Bristow, 'Women Councillors – An Explanation of the Under-representation of Women in Local Government', *LGS* 1980 (3), pp. 73–80.

A. Bruce and G. Lee, 'Local Election Campaigns', *PS* 1982, pp. 247–61.

A. Crispin, 'The New Block Grant and Education – Central Control or National Direction', *LGS* 1980 (6), pp. 25–38.

A. H. Dawson, 'The Idea of the Region and the 1975 Reorganization of Scottish Local Government', *Pub. Admin.* 1981, pp. 279–94.

V. Duke & S. Edgell, 'Local Authority Spending Cuts and Local Political Control', *BJPS* 1986, pp. 253–68.

A. Dunsire, 'Central Control Over Local Authorities: a Cybernetic Approach', *Pub. Admin.* 1981, pp. 173–88.

H. Elcock, 'Tradition and Change in Labour Party Politics: the Decline and Fall of the City Boss', *PS* 1981, pp. 439–47.

C. Evans, 'Privatization of Local Services', *LGS* 1985 (6), pp. 97–110.

J. G. Gibson (*et al.*), 'Central–Local Financial Relations, *LGS* 1982 (3), pp. 1–104.

J. G. Gibson (*et al.*), 'The Measurement of Central Control in England and Wales', *PS* 1982, pp. 432–6.

D. G. Green, 'Inside Local Government – A Study of a Ruling Labour Group', *LGS* 1980 (1), pp. 33–50.

R. Greenwood, The Politics of Central–Local Relations in England and Wales 1974–81', *WEP* 1982, pp. 253–69.

R. Greenwood, 'Changing Patterns of Budgeting in English Local Government', *Pub. Admin.* 1983, pp. 149–68.

J. Gyford & M. James, 'The Development of Party Politics on the Local Authority Associations', *LGS* 1982 (2), pp. 23–46.

D. Heald, 'The Scottish Rate Support Grant: How Different From the English and Welsh?', *Pub. Admin.* 1980, pp. 25–46.

K. Isaac-Henry, 'Taking Stock of the Local Authority Associations', *Pub. Admin.* 1984, pp. 129–46.

B. Jacobs, 'Labour Against the Centre – the Clay Cross Syndrome', *LGS* 1984 (2), pp. 75–88.

R. E. Jennings, 'The Changing Representational Role of Local Councillors in England', *LGS* 1982 (5), pp. 67–86.

G. W. Jones & J. D. Stewart, 'Policy-Making in Central and Local Government Compared', *LGS* 1982 (1), pp. 73–80.

P. P. Kantor & D. G. Lawrence, 'Constitutuency Focus and Urban Policy Making: Local Politics in London', *PS*1981, pp. 51–72.

M. Kogan, 'The Central–Local Government Relationship – A Comparison Between the Education and Health Services', *LGS* 1983 (1), pp. 65–86.

M. Laffin & K. Young, 'The Changing Roles and Responsibilities of Local Authority Chief Officers', *Pub. Admin.* 1985, pp. 41–60.

M. Laughlin, 'The Restructuring of Central–Local Government Legal Relations', *LGS* 1985 (6), pp. 59–74.

B. Loveday, 'Central Coordination, Police Authorities and the Miners' Strike', *PQ* 1986, pp. 60–73.

B. Loveday, 'The Role of the Police Committee', *LGS* 1983 (1), pp. 39–52 (and 1984 (5) pp. 27–50).

C. Martlew (*et al.*), 'Women and Local Government in Scotland', *LGS* 1985 (2), pp. 47–66.

A. Midwinter (*et al.*), 'Current Expenditure Guidelines in Scotland – A Failure of Indicative Planning', *LGS* 1984 (2), pp. 21–32.

A. Midwinter (*et al.*), '"Excessive and Unreasonable": the Politics of the Scottish Hit List', *PS* 1983, pp. 394–417.

M. Minogue & J. O'Grady, 'Contracting Out Local Authority Services in Britain', *LGS* 1985, pp. 35–50.

K. Newton, 'Is Small Really So Beautiful? Is Big Really So Ugly? Size, Effectiveness, and Democracy in Local Government', *PS* 1982, pp. 190–206.

E. Page, 'The Measurement of Central Control', *PS* 1980, pp. 117–20.

E. Page, 'The Value of Local Autonomy', *LGS* 1982 (4), pp. 21–42.

E. Page, & A. Midwinter, 'Remoteness, Efficiency, Cost and the Reorganization of Scottish Local Government', *Pub. Admin.* 1980, pp. 439–64.

R. Pinkney, 'An Alternative Political Strategy? Liberals in Power in English Local Government', *LGS* 1984 (3), pp. 69–84.

C. Rallings & M. Thrasher, 'Assessing the Electoral Performance of the Alliance', *LGS* 1986 (2), pp. 31–36.

R. A. W. Rhodes, 'Intergovernmental Relations in the Post-War Period', *LGS* 1985 (6), pp. 35–58.

R. A. W. Rhodes, 'Analysing Intergovernmental Relations', *EJPR* 1980, pp. 289–322.

R. A. W. Rhodes, 'Continuity and Change in British Central–Local Relations: "the Conservative Threat", 1979–83', *BJPS* 1984, pp. 261–84.

R. A. W. Rhodes, 'Corporatism, Pay Negotiations and Local Government', *Pub. Admin.* 1985, pp. 287–308.

R. A. W. Rhodes, 'Corporate Bias in Central–Local Relations: a Case Study of the Consultative Council on Local Government Finance', *PP* 1986, pp. 221–46.

D. Rosenberg, 'The Languages of Role: Treasurers in UK Local Governments', *PP* 1985, pp. 155–74.

B. Roweth, 'Statistics For Policy: Needs Assessment in the Rate Support Grant', *Pub. Admin.* 1980, pp. 173–86.

A. Sbragia, 'Capital Markets and Central–Local Politics in Britain', *BJPS* 1986, pp. 311–40.

P. Self, 'Rescuing Local Government', *PQ* 1982, pp. 292–303.

C. Skelcher, 'From Programme Budgeting to Policy Analysis: Corporate Approaches in Local Government', *Pub. Admin.* 1980, pp. 155–72.

P. Smith & J. Stewart, 'Local Authority Expenditure Targets', *LGS* 1985 (4), pp. 21–42.

M. Thrasher, 'The Concept of a Central–Local Government Partnership: Issues Obscured By Ideas', *PP* 1981, pp. 455–70.

J. B. Woodham, 'Local Government – Central Control and Local Stewardship', *LGS* 1980 (5), pp. 3–17.

K. Young, 'Metropolis, R.I.P?', *PQ* 1986, pp. 36–46.

Chapter 14

a) Devolution

P. Arthur, *Government and Politics of Northern Ireland*, London 1984.

D. Balsam & M. Burch, *A Political and Electoral Handbook for Wales*, London 1980.

F. Bealey and J. Sewel, *Politics of Independence: a Study of a Scottish Town*, London 1981.
P. Bew (*et al.*), *The State in Northern Ireland 1921–72*, London 1980.
P. Bew & H. Patterson, *The British State and the Ulster Crisis*, London 1985.
D. Birrell & A. Murie, *Policy and Government in Northern Ireland*, London 1980.
J. Bochel (*et al.*) (eds), *The Referendum Experience: Scotland 1979*, London 1981.
B. W. Bogwood & M. Keating, *Regional Government in England*, London 1982.
K. Boyle (*et al.*), *Ten Years On in Northern Ireland*, London 1980.
K. Boyle, & T. Hadden, *Ireland: a Positive Proposal*, London 1985.
J. Bulpitt, *Territory and Power in the United Kingdom*, London 1983.
B. Burrows & D. Denton, *Devolution or Federalism? Options for a United Kingdom*, London 1980.
J. Darley (ed.), *Northern Ireland: the Background to Conflict*, London 1984.
H. M. Drucker, (ed.), *John P. Mackintosh on Scotland*, London 1982.
H. M. Drucker & G. Brown, *The Politics of Nationalism and Devolution*, London 1980.
M. Farrell, *Northern Ireland: the Orange State*, London 1981.
D. Foulkes (*et al.*), *The Welsh Veto: the Wales Act 1978 and the Referendum*, London 1983.
J. F. Gallagher & J. L. DeGregory, *Violence in Northern Ireland*, London 1985.
D. Heald, *Financing Devolution Within the United Kingdom: a Study of the Lessons From Failure*, Canberra, 1980.
M. Keating & D. Bleiman, *Labour and Scottish Nationalism*, London 1980.
M. Keating & A. Midwinter, *The Government of Scotland*, Edinburgh 1983.
J. G. Kellas, *Modern Scotland*, London 1980.
J. G. Kellas, *The Scottish Political System*, London 1984.
D. McCrone (ed.), *The Scottish Government Yearbook 1986*, Edinburgh 1986.
M. MacDonald, *Children of Wrath: the Tragedy of Northern Ireland*, London 1986.
P. Madgwick & R. Rose (eds), *The Territorial Dimension in United Kingdom Politics*, London 1982.
E. Moxon-Browne, *Nation, Class and Creed in Northern Ireland*, London 1983.
T. Nairn, *The Break-Up of Britain*, London 1982.
S. Nelson, *Ulster's Uncertain Defenders*, London 1984.

P. O'Malley, *The Uncivil Wars: Ireland Today*, Dublin 1984.
D. W. Parsons, *The Political Economy of British Regional Policy*, London 1985.
D. G. Pringle, *One Island, Two Nations*, London 1985.
M. Rees, *Northern Ireland: a Personal Perspective*, London 1985.
R. Rose, *Understanding the United Kingdom*, London 1982.
D. Watt (ed.), *The Constitution of Northern Ireland: Problems and Prospects*, London 1981.

P. Arthur, 'Policing and Crisis Politics: Northern Ireland as a Case Study', *Parl. Aff.* 1986, pp. 341–53.
D. Balsam and I. McAllister, 'Whose Vote Counts: Electoral Registration and the "40 Per Cent" Rule', *PQ* 1980, pp. 218–22.
V. Bogdanor, 'The 40 Per Cent Rule', *Parl. Aff.* 1980, pp. 249–63.
T. G. Carroll, 'Disobedience and Violence in Northern Ireland, *CPS* 1981–2, pp. 3–30.
S. Grasmuck, 'Ideology of Ethnoregionalism: the Case of Scotland', *Pol. & Soc.* 1980, pp. 471–94.
D. Heald & M. Keating, 'The Impact of the Devolution Commitment on the Scottish Body Politic', *AJPH* 1980, pp. 386–402.
B. Jones & R. Wilford, 'Further Considerations of the Referendum', *PS* 1982, pp. 16–27.
J. Barry Jones & M. Keating, 'The Labour Party's Devolution Policy', *G and O* 1982, pp. 279–92.
M. Keating, 'Whatever Happened to Regional Government?', *LGS* 1985 (6), pp. 111–33.
I. McAllister & A. Mughan, 'Values, Protest and Minority Nationalism in Wales', *BJPS* 1984, pp. 230–42.
R. Morris, 'The Politics of Nationalism: Reflections on the Economics of the SDP', *PQ* 1983, pp. 16–31.
L. J. Sharpe, 'Devolution and Celtic Nationalism in the UK', *WEP* 1985 (3), pp. 82–100.

b) Britain and Europe

M. Burgess (ed.), *Federalism and Federation in Western Europe*, London 1986.
D. Butler & P. Jowett, *Party Strategies in Britain: a Study of the 1984 European Elections*, London 1985.
D. Butler & D. Marquand, *European Elections and British Politics*, London 1981.
M. Charlton, *The Price of Victory*, London 1983.
A. Daltrop, *Politics and the European Communities*, London 1982.
F. E. C. Gregory, *Dilemmas of Government: Britain and the European Community*, London 1983.

S. Henig, *Power and Decision in Europe*, London 1980.

V. Herman & M. Hagger, *The Legislation of Direct Elections to the European Parliament*, London 1980.

M. Holland, *Candidates For Europe*, London 1986.

K. Kaiser (*et al.*), *The European Community: Progress or Decline?*, London 1983.

D. Lasok & J. W. Bridge, *Law and Institutions of the European Communities*, London 1982.

J. Lodge & V. Herman, *Direct Elections to the European Parliament*, London 1982.

J. Moon, *European Integration in British Politics 1950–1963: a Study of Issue Change*, London 1985.

F. Nicholson and R. East, *From the Six to the Twelve: the Enlargement of the European Communities*, London 1986.

C. O'Nuallain, *The Presidency of the European Council of Ministers*, London 1985.

M. Palmer, *The European Parliament*, London 1981.

G. and P. Pridham, *Transnational Party Cooperation and European Integration*, London 1981.

L. J. Robins, *The Reluctant Party: Labour and the EEC 1961–75*, London 1980.

M. Rutherford, *Can We Save the Common Market*, London 1981.

P. Scalinga, *The European Parliament*, London 1980.

P. Taylor, *The Limits of European Integration*, London 1985.

J. Usher, *European Community Law and National Law: the Irreversible Transfer*, London 1981.

W. Wallace (ed.), *Britain in Europe*, London 1980.

M. L. Balinski & H. P. Young, 'Fair Representation in the European Parliament', *JCMS* 1981 (2), pp. 361–73.

H. Berrington, 'European Elections: Mandate For Change', *WEP* 1980, pp. 242–6.

R. Bieber, 'Achievements of the European Parliament 1979–1984', *CMLR* 1985, pp. 283–304.

J. G. Blumler & A. D. Fox, 'The Involvement of Voters in the European Elections of 1979: its Extent and Sources', *EJPR* 1980, pp. 359–86.

V. Bogdanor, 'The Future of the European Community: Two Models of Democracy, *G and O* 1986, pp. 161–76.

R. Bourguignon-Wittke (*et al.*), 'Five Years of the Directly Elected European Parliament', *JCMS* 1985–6, pp. 39–60.

J. W. Bridge, 'National Legal Tradition and Community Law: Legislative Drafting and Judicial Interpretation in England and the European Community', *JCMS* 1981, pp. 351–76.

P. Dagtoglou, 'The Southern Englargement of the European Community', *CMLR* 1984, pp. 149–62.

R. J. Dalton & R. Duval, 'The Political Environment and Foreign Office Opinions: British Attitudes Toward European Integration 1972–1979', *BJPS* 1986, pp. 113–34.

A. C. Evans, 'Participation of National Parliaments in the European Community Legislative Process', *PL* 1981, pp. 388–98.

K. Featherstone, 'Socialists and European Integration: the Attitudes of British Labour Members of Parliament', *EJPR* 1981, pp. 407–19.

J. Fitzmaurice, 'Reflections on the European Elections', *WEP* 1980, pp. 233–41.

L. L. Fowler (*et al.*), 'Changing Patterns of Voting Strength in the European Parliament', *CP* 1982–3, pp. 159–76.

S. George, 'The European Parliament and the Requirements of Democratic Government', *WEP* 1981, pp. 134–9.

I. Gordon & P. Whiteley, 'Swings and Roundabouts: an Ecological Analysis of the European and General Election Results in Great Britain', *PS* 1981, pp. 586–603.

M. Hagger, 'Legislating For Direct Elections – the Passage of a Constitutional Bill', *Parl. Aff.* 1980, pp. 271–93.

N. Haigh, 'Devolved Responsibility and Centralization: Effects of EEC Environmental Policy', *Pub. Admin.* 1986, pp. 197–208.

F. Harhoff, 'Greenland's Withdrawal From the European Communities', *CMLR* 1983, pp. 13–33.

V. Herman, 'The Powers and Functions of the Directly Elected European Parliament', *Parl. Aff.* 1980, pp. 79–91.

M. Holland, 'The Selection of Parliamentary Candidates: Contemporary Developments and the Impact of the European Elections', *Parl. Aff.* 1981, pp. 28–46.

G. Ionescu & J. Pinder, 'A British Lead to Federal Europe?', *G and O* 1984, pp. 279–86.

J. P. Jacqué, 'The Draft Treaty Establishing the European Union', *CMLR* 1985, pp. 19–42.

M. Jenkins, 'Britain and the Community Budget', *CMLR* 1980, pp. 493–507.

J. Lodge, 'Euro-Elections and the European Parliament', *Parl. Aff.* 1985, pp. 40–55.

J. Lodge, 'The Single European Act: Towards a New Europe Dynamism?', *JCMS* 1985–6, pp. 203–24.

J. Lodge, 'European Union and the First Elected European Parliament: the Spinelli Initiative', *JCMS* 1983–4, pp. 377–402.

I. McAllister, 'Party Organisation and Minority Nationalism: a Comparative Study in the United Kingdom', *EJPR* 1981, pp. 237–56.

D. Marquand, 'Parliamentary Accountability and the European Community', *JCMS* 1980–1, pp. 221–37.

W. Nicoll, 'The Luxembourg Compromise', *JCMS* 1984–5, pp. 35–44.

W. Nicoll, 'Paths to European Unity', *JCMS* 1984–5, pp. 199–206.

A. Norton (*et al.*), 'Europe, Local Government and Regional Development', *LGS* 1980 (4), pp. 3–80.

J. Palmer, 'Britain and the EEC: the Withdrawal Option', *Inter. Aff.* 1982, pp. 638–47.

C. Payne & P. J. Brown, 'Forecasting the British Election to the European Parliament', *BJPS* 1981, pp. 235–44.

A. B. Philip, 'Pressure Groups and Policy Formation in the European Communities', *PP* 1982, pp. 459–76.

R. Pierce (*et al.*), 'Referendum Voting Behaviour: the Norwegian and British Referenda on Membership in the European Community', *AJPS* 1983, pp. 43–63.

J. Plaskitt, 'The House of Lords and Legislative Harmonization in the European Community, *Pub. Admin.* 1981, pp. 203–14.

R. Pryce, 'Relaunching the European Community', *G and O* 1984, pp. 486–500.

K. Reif (*et al.*), 'The First European Election', *EJPR* 1980, pp. 1–158.

J. A. Sargent, 'Pressure Group Development in the EC: the Role of the British Bankers Association', *JCMS* 1981–2, pp. 269–86.

N. Sonntag & K. Featherstone, 'Looking Towards the 1984 European Elections: Problems of Political Integration', *JCMS* 1983–4, pp. 269–82.

M. Svennevig & B. Gunter, 'Television Coverage of the 1984 European Parliamentary Election', *Parl. Aff.* 1986, pp. 165–78.

Jane P. Sweeney, 'The Left in Europe's Parliament: the Problematic Effects of Integration Theory', *CP* 1983–4, pp. 171–90.

P. Taylor, 'The European Communities and the Obligations of Membership: Claims and Counter Claims', *Inter. Aff.* 1981, pp. 236–53.

H. Wallace, 'Negotiations and Coalition Formation in the European Community', *G and O* 1985, pp. 453–72.

W. Wallace, 'Europe as a Confederation: the Community and the Nation State', *JCMS* 1982–3, pp. 57–68.

D. M. Wood, 'Comparing Parliamentary Voting on European Issues in France and Britain', *LSQ* 1982, pp. 101–17.

SECTION THREE: POLITICAL BIOGRAPHIES, AUTOBIOGRAPHIES AND MEMOIRS

B. Arnold, *Margaret Thatcher: a Study in Power*, London 1984.

J. Barnes & D. Nicholson (eds), *The Leo Amery Diaries, Vol I, 1896–1926*, London 1980.

J. Barnett, *Inside the Treasury*, London 1982.

D. Bence & C. Branson, *Roy Jenkins*, London 1982.

A. W. Benn, *Arguments for Democracy*, London 1981.

J. Boyd Carpenter, *A Way of Life: the Memoirs of John Boyd Carpenter*, London 1980.

M. & E. Brock (eds), *H. H. Asquith: Letters to Venetia Stanley*, London 1982.

T. Burridge, *Clement Attlee: a Political Biography*, London 1986.

Lord Butler, *The Art of Memory*, London 1982.

J. Campbell, *Roy Jenkins*, London 1983.

D. Carlton, *Anthony Eden: a Biography*, London 1981.

B. Castle, *The Castle Diaries 1964–70*, London 1984.

B. Castle, *The Castle Diaries 1974–76*, London 1980.

M. Colquhoun, *A Woman in the House*, London 1980.

P. Cosgrave, *R. A. Butler: an English Life*, London 1983.

P. Cosgrave, *Carrington: a Life and a Policy*, London 1985.

J. Critchley, *Westminster Blues*, London 1985.

S. Crosland, *Tony Crosland*, London 1982.

J. A. Cross, *Lord Swinton*, London 1982.

Lord Denning, *The Closing Chapter*, London 1983.

D. Dilks, *Neville Chamberlain, Vol I, 1869–1929*, London 1984.

D. Dutton, *Austen Chamberlain: Gentleman in Politics*, London 1985.

M. Egremont, *Balfour*, London 1980.

H. Evans, *Downing Street Diary: the Macmillan Years 1957–63*, London 1981.

M. Falkender, *Downing Street in Perspective*, London 1983.

N. Fisher, *Harold Macmillan: a Biography*, London 1982.

M. Foot, *Another Heart and Other Pulses*, London 1984.

L. W. Fuchser, *Neville Chamberlain and Appeasement*, New York 1983.

I. Gilmour, *Britain Can Work*, London 1983.

G. Goodman, *The Awkward Warrior, Frank Cousins: His Life And Times*, London 1984.

R. Griffiths, *S. O. Davies: a Socialist Faith*, London 1983.

J. Grigg, *Lloyd George – From Peace to War*, London 1985.

J. Grimond, *A Personal Manifesto*, London 1983.

K. Harris, *Attlee*, London 1984.

S. Haggart & D. Leigh, *Michael Foot: a Portrait*, London 1981.
G. Hutchinson, *The Last Edwardian at No. 10: an Impression of Harold Macmillan*, London 1983.
D. Jay, *Change and Fortune: a Political Record*, London 1980.
R. Jay, *Joseph Chamberlain*, London 1981.
H. Jenkins, *Rank and File*, London 1980.
D. Judd, *King George VI*, London 1982.
J. Lee, *My Life With Nye*, London 1980.
R. Lewis, *Margaret Thatcher: a Personal and Political Biography*, London 1984.
R. F. Mackay, *Balfour: Intellectual Statesman*, London 1985.
J. Morgan (ed.), *The Backbench Diaries of Richard Crossman*, London 1981.
K. O. Morgan & J. Morgan, *Portrait of a Progressive: the Political Career of Christopher Viscount Addison*, London 1980.
D. Owen, *A Future That Will Work*, London 1984.
D. Owen, *Face The Future*, London 1981.
J. Parker, *Father of the House*, London 1982.
B. Pimlott, *Hugh Dalton*, London 1985.
F. Pym, *The Politics of Consent*, London 1984.
L. Radice, *Beatrice and Sidney Webb*, London 1984.
Lord Redcliffe-Maud, *Experiences of an Optimist*, London 1981.
W. Rogers, *The Politics of Change*, London 1982.
K. Rose, *Curzon: a Most Superior Person*, London 1985.
P. Rose, *Backbencher's Dilemma*, London 1981.
E. Shinwell, *Lead With the Left: My First Ninety-Six Years*, London 1981.
D. Steel (ed.), *Partners in One Nation: a New View of Britain 2000*, London 1985.
M. Stewart, *Life and Labour: an Autobiography*, London 1980.
N. St John-Stevas, *The Two Cities*, London 1984.
G. Thomas, *Mr Speaker*, London 1985.
B. Vernon, *Ellen Wilkinson*, London 1982.
N. Wapshott & G. Brock, *Thatcher*, London 1983.
P. M. Williams (ed.), *The Diary of Hugh Gaitskell 1945–1956*, London 1983.
P. M. Williams, *Hugh Gaitskell*, London 1982.
S. Williams, *Politics is for People*, London 1980.
W. Wyatt, *Confessions of an Optimist*, London 1985.

Index